The Concept of Permanent Establishment in the Insurance Business

The Concept of Permanent Establishment in the Insurance Business

Daniele Frescurato

Wolters Kluwer

Published by:
Kluwer Law International B.V.
PO Box 316
2400 AH Alphen aan den Rijn
The Netherlands
E-mail: international-sales@wolterskluwer.com
Website: lrus.wolterskluwer.com

Sold and distributed by:
Wolters Kluwer Legal & Regulatory U.S.
7201 McKinney Circle
Frederick, MD 21704
United States of America
Email: customer.service@wolterskluwer.com

ISBN 978-94-035-3283-7

e-Book: ISBN 978-94-035-3284-4
web-PDF: ISBN 978-94-035-3285-1

About the Author

Daniele Frescurato is an international tax professional born in Vicenza (Italy). He graduated in International Economics at the University of Verona (Italy) with full marks in 2007 and obtained an LL.M. in International Tax Law at Vienna University of Economics and Business Administration (Austria) in 2015. He is also an Italian Chartered Accountant and Certified Auditor registered with the local association of Vicenza (Italy) since 2013.

Daniele regularly participates and speaks in conferences, seminars and other events in the areas of domestic, European and international tax law. He is also an author of some publications in the same areas.

After having worked as a tax consultant for five years in tax and legal firms, first in Luxembourg and then in Italy, he has been working as an international tax manager in the International Tax Affairs department at Assicurazioni Generali SpA in Trieste (Italy) since 2012. His main areas of expertise are M&A, business restructurings and other financial transactions.

Table of Contents

Preface

This book is aimed at investigating the concept of permanent establishment in the insurance business based on its specific features, value chain and business models. More precisely, this book is focused on the specific circumstances under which insurance companies can give rise to a dependent agent permanent establishment when marketing, promoting and distributing their products in foreign jurisdictions without establishing a fixed place of business therein.

To this end, the author follows a systematic approach, thereby outlining the general framework in which insurance companies operate, the regulatory landscape, and the functional analysis of the insurance business with a specific focus on the KERT functions.

Against this background, the author explains the main elements that may give rise to the existence of a dependent agent permanent establishment in the context of the insurance business and subsequently scrutinizes the most common business models adopted by insurance companies to assess whether the peculiar features of such models may give rise to the existence of a dependent agent permanent establishment in a foreign country.

Following this examination, this book also provides a comparative analysis regarding the definition of dependent agent permanent establishment adopted in Swiss double tax treaties with the practice of other countries to assess different approaches adopted when dealing with this topic.

Based on the findings presented throughout this book, the author argues that a specific provision concerning insurance should be considered in the permanent establishment article. For this reason, the author proposes a (partial) redefinition of the concept of dependent agent permanent establishment contained in the main model treaties through the introduction of a new paragraph intended to make it correlated to the definition of establishment adopted for regulatory purposes.

This book is an edited version of the doctoral dissertation that has been approved by the Faculty of Law of the University of Zurich under the title "*The concept of permanent establishment in the insurance business*" on May 27, 2020.

The doctoral dissertation has been carried out under the supervision of Prof. Dr. Madeleine Simonek and Prof. Dr. Helmut Heiss.

This doctoral dissertation was finalized on September 18, 2019. Developments occurred thereafter (among others, developments concerning topics within the scope of the analysis addressed in Chapter 5) have not been taken into consideration.

List of Abbreviations

1963 OECD Draft	OECD Draft double taxation convention on income and capital as of July 30, 1963
1963 OECD Draft Commentary	Commentaries on the articles of the draft convention as of July 30, 1963
1976 US Model	Convention between the United States of America and the Government of ••• for the avoidance of double taxation and the prevention of fiscal evasion with respect to taxes on income and capital published on May 18, 1976
1977 OECD Model	OECD Model Convention with Respect to Taxes on Income and on Capital as of April 11, 1977
1977 US Model	Convention between the United States of America and the Government of ••• for the avoidance of double taxation and the prevention of fiscal evasion with respect to taxes on income and capital published on May 17, 1977
1979 UN Manual	Manual for the Negotiation of Bilateral Tax Treaties between Developed and Developing Countries published as of January 1, 1979
1980 UN Model	United Nations Model Double Taxation Convention between Developed and Developing Countries as of January 1, 1980
1980 UN Model Commentary	Commentaries on the Articles of the United Nations Model Double Taxation Convention between Developed and Developing Countries as of January 1, 1980
1981 US Model	Convention between the United States of America and the Government of ••• for the avoidance of double taxation and the prevention of fiscal evasion with respect to taxes on income and capital published on June 16, 1981

1992 OECD Model	OECD Model Convention with Respect to Taxes on Income and on Capital as of July 23, 1992
1992 OECD Model Commentary	Commentaries on the Articles of the Model Tax Convention as of July 23, 1992
1994 OECD Model	OECD Model Convention with Respect to Taxes on Income and on Capital as of March 31, 1994
1994 OECD Model Commentary	Commentaries on the Articles of the Model Tax Convention as of March 31, 1994
1996 US Model	Convention between the United States of America and the Government of ••• for the avoidance of double taxation and the prevention of fiscal evasion with respect to taxes on income and capital published on September 20, 1996
1996 Technical Explanation	United States Model Income Tax Convention of September 20, 1996 Technical Explanation
2000 OECD Model	OECD Model Convention with Respect to Taxes on Income and on Capital as of April 29, 2000
2000 OECD Model Commentary	Commentaries on the Articles of the Model Tax Convention as of April 29, 2000
2001 UN Model	United Nations Model Double Taxation Convention between Developed and Developing Countries as of January 1, 2001
2001 UN Model Commentary	Commentaries on the Articles of the United Nations Model Double Taxation Convention between Developed and Developing Countries as of January 1, 2001
2003 Discussion Draft on Part II	Discussion Draft on the Attribution of Profits to Permanent Establishments (Pes): Part II (Banks) as of March 4, 2003
2003 Discussion Draft on Part III	Discussion Draft on the Attribution of Profits to Permanent Establishments (Pes: Part III (Enterprises Carrying on Global Trading of Financial Instruments) as of March 4, 2003
2003 OECD Model	OECD Model Convention with Respect to Taxes on Income and on Capital as of January 28, 2003
2003 OECD Model Commentary	Commentaries on the Articles of the Model Tax Convention as of January 28, 2003
2003 UN Manual	Manual for the Negotiation of Bilateral Tax Treaties between Developed and Developing Countries as of January 1, 2003
2004 Discussion Draft on Part I	Discussion Draft on the Attribution of Profits to Permanent Establishment—Part I (General Considerations) as of August 2, 2004

2005 Discussion Draft on Part IV	Discussion Draft of the Report on the Attribution of Profits to a Permanent Establishment Part IV (Insurance) as of June 27, 2005
2005 OECD Model	OECD Model Convention with Respect to Taxes on Income and on Capital as of July 15, 2005
2005 OECD Model Commentary	Commentaries on the Articles of the Model Tax Convention as of July 15, 2005
2006 Draft Report	Report on the Attribution of Profits to Permanent Establishments—Parts I (General Considerations), II (Banks) And III (Global Trading) as of December 2006
2006 US Model	Convention between the United States of America and the Government of ••• for the avoidance of double taxation and the prevention of fiscal evasion with respect to taxes on income and capital published on November 15, 2006
2006 Technical Explanation	United States Model Technical Explanation accompanying the United States Model Income Tax Convention of November 15, 2006
2007 Discussion Draft on Part IV	Report on the Attribution of Profits to Permanent Establishments Part IV (Insurance) as of August 22, 2007
2008 OECD Model	OECD Model Convention with Respect to Taxes on Income and on Capital as of July 17, 2008
2008 OECD Model Commentary	Commentaries on the Articles of the Model Tax Convention as of July 17, 2008
2008 OECD Report	Report on the Attribution of Profits to Permanent Establishments as of July 17, 2008
2010 OECD Model	OECD Model Convention with Respect to Taxes on Income and on Capital as of July 22, 2010
2010 OECD Model Commentary	Commentaries on the Articles of the Model Tax Convention as of July 22, 2010
2010 OECD Report	2010 Report on the Attribution of Profits to Permanent Establishments as of July 22, 2010
2010 OECD TP Guidelines	OECD Transfer Pricing Guidelines for Multinational Enterprises and Tax Administrations as of July 22, 2010
2011 UN Model	United Nations Model Double Taxation Convention between Developed and Developing Countries as of January 1, 2011
2011 UN Model Commentary	Commentaries on the Articles of the United Nations Model Double Taxation Convention between Developed and Developing Countries as of January 1, 2011
2014 OECD Model	OECD Model Convention with Respect to Taxes on Income and on Capital as of July 15, 2014

2014 OECD Model Commentary	Commentaries on the Articles of the Model Tax Convention as of July 15, 2014
2016 UN Manual	Manual for the Negotiation of Bilateral Tax Treaties between Developed and Developing Countries as of January 1, 2016
ABI	Association of British Insurers
AOA	Authorized OECD Approach
Art. or Arts.	Article or Articles
ALM	Asset Liability Management
B2B	Business to Business
B2C	Business to Customer
BEPS Project	OECD/G20 Base Erosion and Profit Shifting Project
ch. or chs.	chapter or chapters
CRM	Customer Relationship Management
DTA	Double Tax Agreement
ECJ	European Court of Justice
EEA	European Economic Area
EEA Agreement	Agreement on the European Economic Area of May 2, 1992
EEC	European Economic Community
EEC Treaty	Treaty Establishing the European Economic Community of May 25, 1957
EFTA	European Free Trade Association
EIOPA	European Insurance and Occupational Pensions Authority
et al.	*et alia* (and others)
et seq.	*et sequentes* (and the following)
ed. or eds.	editor or editors
EU	European Union
FINMA	Swiss Financial Market Supervisory Authority
G20	Group of Twenty
GDP	Gross Domestic Product
GWPs	Gross Written Premiums
HR	Human Resources
HTTP	HyperText Transfer Protocol
ICC	International Chamber of Commerce
IFA	International Fiscal Association
IP	Internet Protocol
ISL	Insurance Supervision Law

ISO	Insurance Supervision Ordinance
ISP	Internet Service Provider
IT	Information Technology
IVASS	Istituto per la Vigilanza sulle Assicurazioni
KERT function	Key Entrepreneurial Risk-Taking function
let.	Letter
MLI	Multilateral Convention to Implement Tax Treaty Related Measures to Prevent Base Erosion and Profit Shifting as of November 24, 2016
No. or no.	Number
OECD	Organisation for the Economic Cooperation and Development
OECD CFA	OECD Committee on Fiscal Affairs
OECD Model	OECD Model Convention with Respect to Taxes on Income and on Capital as of November 21, 2017, except if preceded by specific year, in which case, the then-current version
OECD Model Commentary	Commentaries on the Articles of the Model Tax Convention as of November 21, 2017, except if preceded by specific year, in which case, the then-current version
OECD TP Guidelines	OECD Transfer Pricing Guidelines for Multinational Enterprises and Tax Administrations as of May 19, 2017, except if preceded by specific year, in which case, the then-current version
OEEC	Organisation for the European Economic Cooperation
ORSA	Own Risk Solvency Assessment
p. or pp.	page or pages
para. or paras.	paragraph or paragraphs
RITC	Reinsurance To Close
SME	Small and medium-sized enterprise
sub-para. or sub-paras.	Sub-paragraph or sub-paragraphs
TCP	Transmission Control Protocol
TFEU	Treaty on the Functioning of the European Union of December 13, 2007
TRAF	Tax Reform and AHV Financing
TOBA	Terms of Business Agreement
UN	United Nations
UN Committee of Experts	UN Committee of Experts on International Cooperation in Tax Matters

UN ECOSOC	UN Economic and Social Council
UN Model	United Nations Model Double Taxation Convention between Developed and Developing Countries as of January 1, 2017, except if preceded by specific year, in which case, the then-current version
UN Model Commentary	Commentaries on the Articles of the United Nations Model Double Taxation Convention between Developed and Developing Countries as of January 1, 2017
UK	United Kingdom
US	United States
US Model	Convention between the United States of America and the Government of ••• for the avoidance of double taxation and the prevention of fiscal evasion with respect to taxes on income and capital published on February 17, 2016, except if preceded by specific year, in which case, the then-current version
Vienna Convention	Vienna Convention on the Law of Treaties of May 23, 1969

CHAPTER 1

Preliminary Remarks

Chapter 1 is intended to set the scene for the present book. To this end, before turning to the description of the research, this introductory chapter briefly illustrates the notion of insurance, along with its historical development from ancient times to its current state of play and potential future developments. Following this premise, Chapter 1 sets out the background in which this research is framed, the purposes of the research, along with the research questions that are later addressed in Chapter 6, the outline and the methodology of the study.

1.1 HISTORICAL BACKGROUND

The unpredictability rooted in the human condition has generated an inner physiological need for security ever since ancient times.[1] In general, such a need for security may be twofold. On the one hand, it may be intended as a need for security against something (e.g., security against hunger or security against inability to work). On the other hand, it may also be regarded as a need for security of doing something (e.g., a business activity) without hindrance and without bearing any related risk.[2]

In ancient times, both forms of the very same need for security have been fulfilled by spreading the risk related to a harmful event among multiple people in such a way that each of them bore only a small part of it. The basis for this practice is the idea of mutual assistance, according to which the burden stemming from a harmful event that occurred to one of the group members is spread among all members.[3]

Arrangements by which one or more individuals assume a risk to which others are exposed—that is, an arrangement for aiding the unfortunate—are as old as human society itself. As a matter of fact, societies organized for the purposes of—among others—extending aid to their unfortunate members by means of a common fund

1. *See* Marco Rossetti, *Il diritto delle assicurazioni—Volume 1* (Milano: Cedam, 2011) pp. 9-10.
2. *See* Marco Rossetti, *Il diritto delle assicurazioni—Volume 1*, p. 10.
3. *See* Marco Rossetti, *Il diritto delle assicurazioni—Volume 1*, p. 10.

established with contributions from all members are as old as recorded history.[4] In archaic societies, for example, evidence of mutual arrangements have been found among caravaneers in Egypt, or among fishermen in Phoenicia, whereby in the event of a loss of the animal or the boat of one of the members, due to unforeseeable circumstances, such a loss was replaced at a cost shared between all other members.[5]

In Greece and its colonies, there are evidence of mutual societies—known as *Eranoi* (stemming from *èranos*, which means contribution or share)—in the fifth century BC. As a matter of fact, among their main functions, such societies—although largely religious and ritualistic—also provided for the economic support of their poorest members.[6]

Similar societies—called, among others, *Collegia, Sodalitates, Corpora, Universitates, Societates*—started to flourish in Rome ahead of the sixth century before Christ with mutual assistance and charity purposes. Such societies also carried on many of the functions of insurance societies, providing, for instance, support for their sick and aged members and burial for those deceased. In certain instances, each member was required to contribute to the establishment of a common fund to be subsequently used for mutual assistance purposes. In other circumstances, such a contribution was required only upon occurrence of the harmful event to spread the related burden among all members.[7]

In addition, it is unquestioned that Roman law also provided for some legal institutes (e.g., the *fenus nauticum*)[8] which enshrined elements of risk, transfer of risk and a very basic concept of premium (*periculi pretium*). However, such arrangements were generally conceived as ancillary clauses to a main contract. In fact, Roman law did not envisage legal arrangements for the assumption of risk (the *susceptio periculi*) by a person not involved in the deal (i.e., a third party) under a separate contract autonomous and distinct from the underlying trade or business. In other words, Roman law did not provide for legal arrangements entailing a coordination of the above elements in an organic vision to create an independent legal institute with its own structure and function. Hence, it may be argued that—on the one hand—Romans knew the practice of insurance, but—on the other hand—Romans did not know insurers.[9]

4. *See* William Reynolds Vance, "The Early History of Insurance Law," *Columbia Law Review* (1908) p. 3.
5. *See* Georges Hamon, *Histoire générale de l'assurance en France et à l'étranger* (Paris, L'Assurance moderne, 1897) p. 17, Charles Farley Trenerry, *The Origin and Early History of Insurance: Including the Contract of Bottomry* (London, The Lawbook Exchange, Ltd., 1926) p. 45 and Joseph Hémard, *Théorie et pratique des assurances terrestres* (Paris, Contant-Laguerre, 1924), p. 146.
6. *See—inter alia—*Antonio La Torre, *Cinquant'anni col diritto—Diritto delle assicurazioni—Volume 2* (Milano: Giuffrè, 2008) p. 9 and Marco Rossetti, *Il diritto delle assicurazioni—Volume 1*, p. 11.
7. *See—inter alia—*Antonio La Torre, *Cinquant'anni col diritto—Diritto delle assicurazioni—Volume 2*, p. 9 and Marco Rossetti, *Il diritto delle assicurazioni—Volume 1*, p. 11.
8. *See* Marco Rossetti, *Il diritto delle assicurazioni—Volume 1*, pp. 16 et seq. for an overview of the most relevant institutes.
9. *See* Marco Rossetti, *Il diritto delle assicurazioni—Volume 1*, p. 19.

Subsequently, the collapse of the Roman Empire caused the end of a political and economic stability that was preserved for centuries. The emergence of Roman-barbarian kingdoms and the end of a strong central power led—among others—to a significant stagnation of the economy.

Nonetheless, as from the tenth century, at the time when commercial trade began to flourish again, the issue of managing economic risks by means of legal arrangements came up again. Interestingly, as in ancient times, this issue was addressed by spreading such risks among many people organized in communities. On the one hand, there is evidence of communities in which the association was established for charitable, solidarity, or general care purposes. In such communities, similar to the Roman *Collegia*, the goal was to alleviate the condition of the poorest people.[10] By contrast, we also have evidence of other communities in which the association was not established to alleviate the suffering of its poorest members, but rather to preserve the assets of its members. To put it differently, the main purpose of the association was to protect its members against a common risk of impoverishment.[11,12] Such practices undoubtedly upheld the idea that the risk of a harmful event for a single individual may be better dealt with in communities to the extent that such risk is spread among their members. However, none of them contemplated the idea of transferring the risk to a third party in consideration for the payment of a premium.

Furthermore, we have evidence that—in the Middle Ages—merchants have sought methods to transfer risks by means of other contractual arrangements (such as maritime loans, loans entered into for insurance purposes, Commandries and *Securitates*).[13] Still, none of such contractual arrangements may be considered as a primary form of insurance to the extent that the transfer of risk was taking place between parties of an underlying trade or business. In other words, no one had thought that the assumption of risk as such could be regarded as a commercial activity itself.[14]

The idea of combining: (*i*) a risk—intended as a negative factor affecting a trade or business in terms of economic cost—borne by one of the parties to such a trade or business and (*ii*) a guarantee—construed as a protection provided, at certain conditions, by a third party came up at the beginning of the fourteenth century in commercial cities of Northern Italy.[15]

10. *See* Antonio La Torre, *Cinquant'anni col diritto—Diritto delle assicurazioni—Volume 2*, pp. 13 et seq. and Marco Rossetti, *Il diritto delle assicurazioni—Volume 1*, pp. 21 et seq. for a few examples of such communities.
11. *See* Antonio La Torre, *Cinquant'anni col diritto—Diritto delle assicurazioni—Volume 2*, pp. 18 et seq. and Marco Rossetti, *Il diritto delle assicurazioni—Volume 1*, pp. 22 et seq. for a few examples of such communities.
12. La Torre is of the opinion that the mutual maritime may be considered as a separate form of mutuality. To this effect, *see* Antonio La Torre, *Cinquant'anni col diritto—Diritto delle assicurazioni—Volume 2*, pp. 21 et seq. This distinction is instead disregarded by other authors. To this effect, *see—inter alia*—Antigono Donati, *Trattato del diritto delle assicurazioni private—Volume 1* (Milano: Giuffrè, 1952) p. 59.
13. *See* Antonio La Torre, *Cinquant'anni col diritto—Diritto delle assicurazioni—Volume 2* pp. 40 et seq. and Marco Rossetti, *Il diritto delle assicurazioni—Volume 1*, pp. 24 et seq. for an overview of such arrangements.
14. *See* Marco Rossetti, *Il diritto delle assicurazioni—Volume 1*, p. 26.
15. *See* Antonio La Torre, *Cinquant'anni col diritto—Diritto delle assicurazioni—Volume 2*, p. 53.

We may then argue that commercial insurance, as practiced so extensively in modern times, has its origin at the beginning of the fourteenth century, when the assumption of risk became the object of a separate business activity.[16] In such a way, risks underlying a trade or business are no longer transferred to another party to the trade or business, rather to a third party, which—in consideration for the payment of a premium—takes up such risks and bears the consequences thereof.[17] This practice came into life essentially because—in such a period—the needs of merchants concerned about the fate of goods shipped by sea met the needs of financiers, who were constantly looking for good business opportunities.[18] And the assumption of risk in consideration for the payment of a premium soon became a good business opportunity.

In the following centuries, the fast development of commercial insurance persuaded legal experts[19] and States to delve into and regulate this new contract properly. Most notably, following some pieces of legislation issued in Genoa and in other Italian cities,[20] the earliest evidence of a comprehensive set of regulations on the insurance business may be found in a series of ordinances in the City of Barcelona, published in 1435, which contained extensive provisions for the regulation of marine insurance.[21] Two centuries after, in 1681, the Marine Ordinances of Louis XIV were published in France. Such ordinances, supposed to be largely the work of Jean-Baptiste Colbert, the Minister of Finance, provided for the regulation of the insurance business with a completeness of detail that paved the way for the subsequent *Code de Commerce.*[22]

The eighteenth century then saw the gradual differentiation of the marine insurance into a number of new and different lines of business (such as the fire protection insurance, the trade credit insurance and other forms of non-life insurance),[23] and the development of the insurance business carried on in the form of joint-stock companies.[24]

16. Research established that the first insurance transaction entered into was dated February 20, 1343, whereby the counselor of an Italian merchant based in Palermo insured ten packages of fabric worth 680 florins shipped by sea from Pisa to Sicily. To this effect, *see* Federigo Melis, *Origini e sviluppi delle assicurazioni in Italia (secoli XIV-XVI)* (Roma: Istituto Nazionale delle Assicurazioni, 1975) pp. 7 and 184.
17. *See* Antonio La Torre, *Cinquant'anni col diritto—Diritto delle assicurazioni—Volume 2*, pp. 53 et seq.
18. Marco Rossetti, *Il diritto delle assicurazioni—Volume 1*, p. 27.
19. The first comprehensive treatise on insurance is the *Tractatus de assecurationibus et sponsionibus*, which was written by the Portuguese Petrus Santerna and published in Venice in 1552.
20. *See* Marco Rossetti, *Il diritto delle assicurazioni—Volume 1*, p. 45.
21. *See* William Reynolds Vance, *Columbia Law Review*, (1908) p. 8, Antonio La Torre, *Cinquant'anni col diritto—Diritto delle assicurazioni—Volume 2*, pp. 79 et seq. and Marco Rossetti, *Il diritto delle assicurazioni—Volume 1*, p. 45.
22. *See* William Reynolds Vance, *Columbia Law Review*, (1908) p. 10, Antonio La Torre, *Cinquant'anni col diritto—Diritto delle assicurazioni—Volume 2*, p. 81 and Marco Rossetti, *Il diritto delle assicurazioni—Volume 1*, p. 46.
23. *See* Antonio La Torre, *Cinquant'anni col diritto—Diritto delle assicurazioni—Volume 2*, p. 94 for an overview of such new lines of non-life insurance.
24. Such companies were first established in England. In particular, we have evidence that the very first insurance company was the *Fire Office*, which was established in London by Nicholas Barbon in 1680 and was engaged in the business of fire protection insurance. To this effect, *see* Marco Rossetti, *Il diritto delle assicurazioni—Volume 1*, p. 56.

Such latter development completed the full picture of the modern insurance business with the idea that an insurance contract must necessarily be connected and integrated into an insurance activity. Indeed, each insurance contract was previously seen as an independent transaction and—thus—an insurer could not prevent the risk of an unexpected collapse in the case of a harmful event. The growth of insurance companies made it clear that the cost of a single insurance act was to be assessed together with all similar acts entered into by the very same insurance company and—as such—the conclusion of many insurance contracts allowed to spread the cost of claims to premiums paid by policyholders who did not suffer from any damage.[25]

In the nineteenth century, the range of insurance widened further with the appearance of life and health insurance.[26] Also, in the same period, a number of countries introduced systematic regulations on the insurance business in their legislation.[27] However, it should be recalled that such regulations have been designed in a liberal period and therefore were intended to limit as much as possible the public intervention in the insurance industry to the ultimate detriment of the policyholders.[28]

A better balance between insurance companies and policyholders has been achieved in more recent years—at the time when the insurance business has reached its utmost expansion with additional lines of business reflecting the new social and economic structure brought about by the scientific and technological progress—to the extent that the insurance business underwent significant regulatory intervention (both at domestic and international level) setting forth the monitoring and supervision needed to establish discipline in the integrated market we all know today.

1.2 THE CURRENT STATE OF PLAY

The Oxford English Dictionary defines insurance as "an arrangement by which a company or the state undertakes to provide a guarantee of compensation for specified loss, damage, illness, or death in return for payment of a specified premium."[29]

Based on this definition, leaving aside public insurance (which is out of the scope of this research), we may then contend that insurance replaces the possibility that a given policyholder will have to bear an occasional and uncertain loss as a consequence of a harmful event with the certainty that such a policyholder will have to pay a known amount (i.e., the premium, which may be much less than the potential loss) to an insurance company. It goes without saying that this reduces uncertainty and may enable policyholders to prevent severe losses which could be worrying or even

25. *See* Marco Rossetti, *Il diritto delle assicurazioni—Volume 1*, p. 59.
26. *See* Antonio La Torre, *Cinquant'anni col diritto—Diritto delle assicurazioni—Volume 2*, pp. 94 et seq.
27. *See*, for example, the *Code de Commerce* issued in France in 1807 and similar regulations in other civil law countries.
28. *See* Marco Rossetti, *Il diritto delle assicurazioni—Volume 1*, pp. 60-61.
29. To this effect, *see* the Oxford English Dictionary, available online at https://en.oxforddictionaries.com/definition/insurance.

catastrophic. Essentially, by purchasing an insurance cover, such a policyholder transfers the economic risk of a harmful event to an insurance company.[30]

The insurance company will then pool all the premiums received by the policyholders and will make use of such premiums to settle the claims of policyholders that actually suffered damages. In such a way, the policyholders will eventually contribute to bearing the losses of the few policyholders that—in the absence of insurance—would have been in the difficult situation of bearing the loss themselves.[31]

Keeping this in mind, it is fair to say that—in almost seven hundred years of history—the traits of insurance and the insurance companies themselves have changed significantly.[32] As of today, insurance is a huge and rather complex business, both in terms of the relevant number and the variety of activities carried on. In fact, insurance has achieved an increasingly important role in the social and economic framework of the modern world.[33] Insurance is indeed a truly global industry that boasts some of the world's largest companies operating on a large scale across different markets and jurisdictions.

In the light of this preeminent role, it is therefore no surprise that the operations of insurance companies and insurance intermediaries are now subject to a wide variety of supervisory laws and regulations generally intended to ensure financial stability of insurance companies, as well as fair and adequate service and treatment for policyholders.

Currently, the global insurance industry is undergoing turbulent times with the continuing low interest rate environment, a challenging equity market, and tighter regulatory regimes. At a global level, the insurance industry experienced strong premium growth in 2015, at 5.6%, whereas growth in 2016 has been slower, at 4.4%. In 2016, the total premiums reached EUR 4.6 trillion, up from EUR 4.4 trillion in 2015. This strong performance primarily stems from growth in the health business, which experienced 6.0% growth in 2016 (reaching EUR 1 trillion in GWPs), still down from 9.0% in 2015. The life business experienced a 3.8% growth in 2016 (reaching EUR 2.2 trillion in GWPs), compared to 4.8% in 2015, whereas the growth in the non-life business remained more stable at 4.2%, reaching EUR 1.4 trillion in GWPs.[34]

More in detail, in life insurance, Africa, Asia-Pacific, and Latin America have driven most of the growth in 2016, while the Middle East has benefited from stable growth. To the contrary, Europe and North America have experienced a decline, partly

30. *See* Robert Merkin, *Insurance Law: An Introduction* (London: Informa Law from Routledge, 2007) p. 1.
31. *See* Robert Merkin, *Insurance Law: An Introduction*, p. 1.
32. In this respect, La Torre takes the view that the fundamental features of insurance (i.e., the mutuality principle, the transfer of risk and the payment of a premium) which determined the emergence of the insurance business in the past may still be found in the modern insurance business. To this effect, *see* Antonio La Torre, *L' assicurazione nella storia delle idee. La risposta giuridica al bisogno di sicurezza economica: ieri e oggi* (Roma: Giuffrè, 1995), pp. 171-172.
33. *See* Marco Rossetti, *Il diritto delle assicurazioni—Volume 1*, pp. 68-69.
34. *See* McKinsey&Company, "*Global Insurance Industry Insights: An in-depth perspective—McKinsey Global Insurance Pools—seventh edition, 2018,*" available online at www.mckinsey.com, p. 10.

due to the sluggish economic growth combined with weak capital market performance.[35] In the non-life business, at the regional level, although the Asia-Pacific region accounts for only 23 % of the global market, it has been the major driver of growth. In contrast, Americas and Europe are growing much slower.[36] In the health business, while North America remains the biggest contributor to the absolute growth globally, the fastest-growing regional market overall is Asia-Pacific, mainly fueled by the efforts of companies in China and India to increase health insurance penetration, with China focusing on its aging population and India on its rural population.[37]

Looking ahead, economic growth can lead to a higher demand for insurance products.[38] In fact, improved economic activity will raise the demand for non-life insurance, improve income and spending, which will increase investment appetite and create greater demand for protection and saving needs, which in turn will boost the sale of life insurance. On the other hand, among the key challenges to be faced in the future, specific attention should be paid to trade wars and growing protectionism, which may hit trade volumes and demand for insurance products.[39]

The adoption of disruptive digital technologies (most importantly, blockchain, artificial intelligence and big data analytics) will be combining systems, businesses and services to create new value propositions for customers, which will have insurance as a key service. Therefore, cross-sector convergence is becoming increasingly important, and this is leading to a fundamental redesign of traditional value chains as well as the need to enter into long-term collaborative relationships with IT partners that can help creating an integrated digital experience for customers.[40]

In the life business, the increasing demand coming from empowered customers in emerging markets, the rising life expectancy and the corresponding reduced role of the public sector will probably generate opportunities for insurance companies in terms of life products (most notably, private insurance and wealth solutions from one side and retirement, long-term care and longevity products from the other side). On the other hand, the continued regulatory pressure, the harsh competition from alternative products and the structural decline in developed markets mainly due to falling populations and stagnant income might hinder growth.[41]

In the non-life business, insurance companies will need to adapt their products to emerging customer needs. For instance, cyber insurance will represent one of the fastest-growing lines in an increasingly connected world. Also, self-driving cars might generate growth opportunities in future years. Specific attention should be also paid to climate change risks. In fact, while the changing environment could create additional

35. *See* McKinsey&Company, "*Global Insurance Industry Insights: An in-depth perspective—McKinsey Global Insurance Pools—seventh edition, 2018*," pp. 16 et seq.
36. *See* McKinsey&Company, "*Global Insurance Industry Insights: An in-depth perspective—McKinsey Global Insurance Pools—seventh edition, 2018*," pp. 22 et seq.
37. *See* McKinsey&Company, "*Global Insurance Industry Insights: An in-depth perspective—McKinsey Global Insurance Pools—seventh edition, 2018*," pp. 27 et seq.
38. *See* OECD, "*Global Insurance Market Trends 2017*," available online at www.oecd.org, p. 8.
39. *See* EY, "*Global insurance trends analysis 2018*," available online at www.ey.com.
40. *See* EY, "*Global insurance trends analysis 2018.*"
41. *See* EY, "*Global insurance trends analysis 2018.*"

opportunities, the absence of reliable precedents related to covering evolving climate risks could be a major challenge for insurance companies.[42]

1.3 RESEARCH FRAMEWORK

As a general rule, the legal justification for the right to tax and—thus—the assignment of the jurisdiction to tax among States is considered to be the principle of sovereignty.[43,44] Based on the exercise of this supreme authority of sovereignty, the jurisdiction to tax grants each and every State the right to impose its own taxes. In other words, the jurisdiction to tax may be regarded as the right of a State to levy its own taxes over either a person or a source of income. It follows that a State may determine its taxing rights by shaping its own tax system and by identifying taxable persons and sources. Hence, in principle, any State may subject any entity or any item of income to tax, even though such entities or income are not located in its territory.

Nevertheless, in the broader context of international relationships, it may be argued that the jurisdiction to tax of a country is restricted by international law,[45] its limited ability to enforce its jurisdiction, and its economic and political relations with the other countries.[46]

Most importantly, current international law permits taxation of foreign economic transactions only to the extent that there is a sufficient or reasonable connection between the taxpayer and the taxing State.[47] In other words, for a State to justify the

42. *See* EY, "*Global insurance trends analysis 2018.*"
43. To this effect, *see*—among others—Eric C.C.M. Kemmeren, "Legal and Economic Principles Support an Origin and Import Neutrality-Based over a Residence and Export Neutrality-Based Tax" in: Michael Lang/Pasquale Pistone/Josef Schuch/Claus Staringer/Alfred Storck/Martin Zagler (eds.) *Tax Treaties: Building Bridges between Law and Economics* (Amsterdam: IBFD, 2010) pp. 244 et seq., António Carlos dos Santos/Cidália Mota Lopes, "Tax Sovereignty, Tax Competition and the Base Erosion and Profit Shifting Concept of Permanent Establishment," *EC Tax Review* (2016) pp. 296 et seq. and Stjepan Gadžo, *Nexus Requirements for Taxation of Non-Residents' Business Income: A Normative Evaluation in the Context of the Global Economy* (Amsterdam: IBFD, 2018) para. 2.1.
44. Sovereignty was defined by Jean Bodin in the *Six Books of the Commonwealth* (1576) as "*the most high, absolute, and perpetual power of a State,*" namely the supremacy of a State over the public administration bodies and over the laws themselves, which are eventually an expression of such a power.
45. In this regard, it is fair to say that some scholars take a different view by arguing that a practice of limiting the jurisdiction to tax does not constitute a restriction set forth under international law to the extent that it is not coupled with the conviction that such practice is mandatory (*opinio juris sive necessitatis*). To this effect, *see* Giuseppe Corasaniti/Paolo De' Capitani di Vimercate/Victor Uckmar/Caterina Corrado Oliva, *Diritto tributario internazionale—Manuale—Seconda Edizione* (Padova: CEDAM, 2012) pp. 49-50 and Loredana Carpentieri/Raffaello Lupi/Dario Stevanato, *Il diritto tributario nei rapporti internationali* (Milano: Il Sole 24 Ore, 2003) pp. 20-21 and 100 et seq.
46. *See* Michael Kobetsky, *International Taxation of Permanent Establishments: Principles and Policy* (Cambridge: Cambridge University Press, 2011) pp. 23-24 and Eric C.C.M. Kemmeren in: Michael Lang/Pasquale Pistone/Josef Schuch/Claus Staringer/Alfred Storck/Martin Zagler (eds.) *Tax Treaties: Building Bridges between Law and Economics*, pp. 244 et seq. and footnotes cited therein.
47. *See—inter alia*—Reuven S. Avi-Yonah, *International Tax as International Law: An Analysis of the International Tax Regime* (Cambridge: Cambridge University Press, 2007) p. 5 and Klaus Vogel/Alexander Rust, "Introduction" in: Ekkehart Reimer/Alexander Rust (eds.) *Klaus Vogel*

imposition of taxes, there must be a relevant link between such a State and the taxable person. In fact, the imposition of taxes—which may be regarded as a contribution to public expenses for the use of production factors availed of in the production of income—may be justified only to the extent that there is a sufficient or reasonable relationship with the State concerned and its territory.[48]

In general, a sufficient or reasonable connection is considered to exist based on certain criteria (such as citizenship, incorporation of a company under national law, domicile, residence, statutory seat of a company, place of effective management of an enterprise, permanent establishment, situation of land, place of labor and so forth).[49] In their domestic tax rules, countries may however adopt different criteria (or a combination of different criteria) to establish the existence of such a sufficient connection and determine the imposition of taxes. Hence, in the current global economy, it is rather common that taxpayers engaging in cross-border transactions are taxed more than once on the very same item of income (phenomenon of double taxation).[50]

This phenomenon has of course a detrimental effect on the movement of goods, services, capital, technology and individuals.[51] As a result, the removal of double taxation is of paramount importance for the development of economic relations between different countries, an optimal allocation of resources and greater welfare for the two countries concerned.[52]

Although most countries have unilaterally implemented regulations for the avoidance of double taxation in their domestic legislation, such unilateral measures are usually insufficient to prevent double taxation to the extent that they are neither comprehensive nor mutually consistent.[53] For this reason, in order to solve common

on Double Taxation Convention—4th edition (Alphen aan den Rijn: Kluwer Law International, 2015) p. 14 and footnotes cited therein.

48. *See* Eric C.C.M. Kemmeren in: Michael Lang/Pasquale Pistone/Josef Schuch/Claus Staringer/Alfred Storck/Martin Zagler (eds.) *Tax Treaties: Building Bridges between Law and Economics*, pp. 244 et seq.
49. *See* Eric C.C.M. Kemmeren in: Michael Lang/Pasquale Pistone/Josef Schuch/Claus Staringer/Alfred Storck/Martin Zagler (eds.) *Tax Treaties: Building Bridges between Law and Economics*, pp. 244 et seq. and footnotes cited therein.
50. In this regard, it is worth noting that customary international law does not forbid double taxation. Most notably, double taxation will be consistent with international law as long as each individual legislation is consistent with international law. To this effect, *see* Klaus Vogel/Alexander Rust in: Ekkehart Reimer/Alexander Rust (eds.) *Klaus Vogel on Double Taxation Convention—4th edition*, p. 14.
51. To this effect, *see—inter alia*—OECD Model Commentary on the Introduction, para. 1.
52. *See* Kevin Holmes, *International Tax Policy and Double Tax Treaties—Second Revised Edition* (Amsterdam: IBFD, 2014) ch. 2.
53. *See—inter alia*—Klaus Vogel/Alexander Rust in: Ekkehart Reimer/Alexander Rust (eds.) *Klaus Vogel on Double Taxation Convention—4th edition*, p. 19 and Giuseppe Corasaniti/Paolo De' Capitani di Vimercate/Victor Uckmar/Caterina Corrado Oliva, *Diritto tributario internazionale—Manuale—Seconda Edizione*, p. 4.

issues in the field of juridical international double taxation,[54,55] most countries have now entered into bilateral agreements to mutually agree on the (partial or complete) relinquishment of their taxing rights for the avoidance of double taxation.[56]

In a nutshell, a DTA[57] may be generally defined as a "*term generally used to denote an agreement between two (or more) countries for the avoidance of double taxation.*"[58] In terms of legal effects, DTAs are international agreements subject to the rules of public international law and governed by the provisions contained in the Vienna Convention,[59] which—to a large extent—codifies the rules of customary international law.[60,61] Therefore, after the negotiation rounds, DTAs—for the purposes of international law—come into existence upon the declaration of consent to contract by both contracting States.[62] As a matter of fact, upon the conclusion of a DTA, the two contracting States accept an international law obligation.[63]

The binding force under international law must however be distinguished from the internal applicability,[64] which is instead a matter of domestic law of the contracting States.[65] Particularly, the process of domestic implementation mainly depends on

54. International juridical double taxation may be generally defined as "*the imposition of comparable taxes in two (or more) States on the same taxpayer in respect of the same subject matter and for identical periods.*" To this effect, *see* Introduction to the OECD Model, para. 1.
55. By contrast, such bilateral agreements are not intended to prevent economic double taxation, which is generally used to describe "*the situation that arises when the same economic transaction, item of income or capital is taxed in two or more States during the same period, but in the hands of different taxpayers.*" For this definition, *see* Klaus Vogel/Alexander Rust in: Ekkehart Reimer/Alexander Rust (eds.) *Klaus Vogel on Double Taxation Convention—4th edition*, p. 12.
56. Although there is no legal basis to argue that bilateral tax agreements cannot generate tax liability, in practice, they only serve as a limitation on tax liabilities. To this effect, *see—inter alia*—Michael Lang, *Introduction to the Law of Double Taxation Conventions—2nd edition* (Vienna: Linde, 2013) ch. 3 and Giuseppe Corasaniti/Paolo De' Capitani di Vimercate/Victor Uckmar/Caterina Corrado Oliva, *Diritto tributario internazionale—Manuale—Seconda Edizione*, p. 11.
57. A DTA is also referred to as a "*double tax convention,*" a "*double tax treaty*" or simply a "*tax treaty.*"
58. *See* Julie Rogers-Glabush, *International Tax Glossary—7th edition* (Amsterdam: IBFD, 2015).
59. The full text of the Vienna Convention is accessible online at http://legal.un.org/ilc/texts/instruments/english/conventions/1_1_1969.pdf.
60. *See* Klaus Vogel/Alexander Rust in: Ekkehart Reimer/Alexander Rust (eds.) *Klaus Vogel on Double Taxation Convention—4th edition*, p. 24, Kevin Holmes, *International Tax Policy and Double Tax Treaties—Second Revised Edition*, ch. 3 and Giuseppe Corasaniti/Paolo De' Capitani di Vimercate/Victor Uckmar/Caterina Corrado Oliva, *Diritto tributario internazionale—Manuale—Seconda Edizione*, p. 5.
61. Customary international law has been defined as law that "*results from a general and consistent practice of states followed by them from a sense of legal obligation.*" For this definition, *see* Reuven S. Avi-Yonah, *International Tax as International Law—An Analysis of the International Tax Regime*, p. 5 and footnote cited therein.
62. *See* Klaus Vogel/Alexander Rust in: Ekkehart Reimer/Alexander Rust (eds.) *Klaus Vogel on Double Taxation Convention—4th edition*, p. 26 and Kevin Holmes, *International Tax Policy and Double Tax Treaties—Second Revised Edition*, ch. 4.
63. *See* Michael Lang, *Introduction to the Law of Double Taxation Conventions—2nd edition*, ch. 2.
64. *See* Klaus Vogel/Alexander Rust in: Ekkehart Reimer/Alexander Rust (eds.) *Klaus Vogel on Double Taxation Convention—4th edition*, p. 27.
65. The binding force under international law and domestic law must also be distinguished from the effective date, which is usually explicitly provided by the treaty wording. *See* Klaus

whether the country is a monist or dualist country. In a monist country, upon ratification, a DTA enters into force both at the international and the domestic level simultaneously and takes effect per se with no need for any further domestic implementation. Conversely, under a dualist system, a DTA has no internal recognition until it is transposed into domestic law by means of a legislative enactment.[66]

It follows that, in monist countries, international law prevails over national law and—therefore—DTAs are ranked above domestic tax statutes. As a result, even though a monist country may in practice enact a law overriding a DTA, domestic courts that become aware of the issue would generally hold and declare the legislation to be ineffective.[67] In dualist countries, following their internal application pursuant to the relevant domestic procedure, DTAs become part of the legal order of the States and—thus—they receive the force of domestic law. Typically, DTAs have the status of special legislation (*leges speciales*) in relation to the general rules of domestic legislation (*leges generalis*) and thus have priority over national laws. Hence, while DTAs override domestic tax law that is effective at the time of their domestic implementation, changes in domestic law normally will not affect existing DTAs.[68,69]

That being said, it is also worth noting that—as opposed to "*conflict rules*"[70] in private international law—DTAs do not deal with the issue of choosing between applicable domestic and foreign provisions. In fact, as Vogel stated, DTAs "*establish an independent mechanism to avoid double taxation through restriction of tax claims in areas where overlapping tax claims are expected, or are at least theoretically possible.*"[71] Consequently, DTAs are usually regarded as "*rules of limitation of law*"[72] or "*distributive rules.*"[73]

Vogel/Alexander Rust in: Ekkehart Reimer/Alexander Rust (eds.) *Klaus Vogel on Double Taxation Convention—4th edition*, p. 24.

66. *See—inter alia*—Jacques Sasseville, "A Tax Treaty Perspective: Special Issues" in: Guglielmo Maisto (ed.) *Tax Treaties and Domestic Law* (Amsterdam: IBFD, 2006) pp. 38 et seq. and Sachin Sachdeva, "Overriding Tax Treaty Overrides: Proposing a Solution," *European Taxation* (2013) pp. 468 et seq.
67. This is the practice in pure monist countries. *See* Sachin Sachdeva, *European Taxation*, (2013) p. 470. Other countries instead apply a temperate monism.
68. *See* Klaus Vogel "The Domestic Law Perspective" in: Guglielmo Maisto (ed.) *Tax Treaties and Domestic Law* (Amsterdam: IBFD, 2006) pp. 3 et seq.
69. This rule however does not apply if the legislator—when changing the general domestic legislation—explicitly or implicitly intends to repeal the special (domestic) legislation. To this effect, *see* Klaus Vogel in: Guglielmo Maisto (ed.) *Tax Treaties and Domestic Law*, pp. 3 et seq. This may be clearly regarded as a violation of international law, whereas the question as to whether this may be admitted at the level of the domestic general legislation is beyond the scope of this research.
70. In German, "*Kollisionsnormen.*" For this definition, *see* Klaus Vogel/Alexander Rust in: Ekkehart Reimer/Alexander Rust (eds.) *Klaus Vogel on Double Taxation Convention—4th edition*, p. 23.
71. *See* Ekkehart Reimer/Alexander Rust, *Klaus Vogel on Double Taxation Convention—Volume I*, p. 29 and Giuseppe Corasaniti/Paolo De' Capitani di Vimercate/Victor Uckmar/Caterina Corrado Oliva, *Diritto tributario internazionale—Manuale—Seconda Edizione*, pp. 10-11.
72. In German, "*Grenznormen.*" For this definition, *see* Klaus Vogel/Alexander Rust in: Ekkehart Reimer/Alexander Rust (eds.) *Klaus Vogel on Double Taxation Convention—4th edition*, p. 23.
73. In German, "*Verteiligungsnormen.*" For this definition, *see* Klaus Vogel/Alexander Rust in: Ekkehart Reimer/Alexander Rust (eds.) *Klaus Vogel on Double Taxation Convention—4th edition*, p. 29.

To this end, the most important model agreements which lay the basis for the conclusion of the vast majority of DTAs—namely, the OECD Model and the UN Model—are now organized into seven chapters as follows:[74]

- Chapter I (Arts. 1 and 2) regulates the requirements for application of the DTA.
- Chapter II (Arts. 3-5) provides essential definitions.
- Chapter III (Arts. 6-21) contains the distributive rules regarding income taxes.
- Chapter IV (Art. 22) contains the distributive rules for capital taxes.
- Chapter V (Art. 23) provides additional legal consequences supplementing the rules of Chapters III and IV, as far as such rules do not imply a definitive legal consequence in and of themselves.
- Chapter VI (Arts. 24-28) contains additional provisions regarding nondiscrimination, a mutual agreement procedure for resolving uncertainties, differences of opinion and any remaining cases of double taxation, an exchange of information, a reservation for the tax privileges of diplomats and consular officials, and a rule for extending the DTA to dependent territories.
- Chapter VII (Arts. 29 and 30) regulates the entry into force and the termination of the DTA.[75]

With specific regard to income from business activities realized by international enterprises operating on a global level, Art. 7 of such model treaties provides that a contracting State may tax the business profits derived by an enterprise of the other contracting State only to the extent that the entrepreneurial activity exercised by such an enterprise in the first-mentioned State reaches a certain degree of intensity. This is measured based on the concept of permanent establishment enshrined in Art. 5 of such model treaties. Hence, under all such model treaties, the existence of a permanent establishment is the decisive criterion for the taxation of income from business activities.

This rule is intended to ensure that income from business activities realized by an enterprise will be taxed by a foreign country only in the event that such business activities have created significant economic connections between the enterprise and that State (i.e., the State of source).[76] By contrast, should the economic connections with a foreign country be only loose, taxation on such business activities is reserved for the State of which the enterprise is a resident (i.e., the State of residence) only.[77]

In general, domestic tax law governing cross-border transactions is inclined to establish rather broad requirements for taxing income from business activities with a

74. The US Model is not formally organized into chapters, but follows a similar pattern, save for Art. 22, which is an anti-treaty-shopping provision.
75. *See—inter alia*—Klaus Vogel/Alexander Rust in: Ekkehart Reimer/Alexander Rust (eds.) *Klaus Vogel on Double Taxation Convention—4th edition*, pp. 29-30 and Loredana Carpentieri/Raffaello Lupi/Dario Stevanato, *Il diritto tributario nei rapporti internationali*, pp. 73 et seq.
76. In such a case, the State of residence is then required to provide relief against double taxation by means of Art. 23 of the model treaties.
77. *See* Klaus Vogel, *Klaus Vogel on Double Taxation Conventions* (London: Kluwer Law International, 1997) p. 280.

view to extending as much as possible domestic taxation. Conversely, the concept of permanent establishment adopted in the context of DTAs is usually narrower to simplify taxation and encourage liberalization of international trade.[78] Consequently, taxation by the State of source is—in a way—restricted in favor of taxation by the State of residence. However, this tendency may result in a satisfactory division of the tax revenue only to the extent that exports and imports are relatively balanced between the contracting States. On the contrary, in a situation where the flows of capital investments and trade are not balanced, this tendency will unilaterally favor the State of residence to the detriment of the State of source.[79] To prevent such fallouts, certain countries (particularly, developing countries) wish to adopt a broader definition of permanent establishment in their DTAs to restore taxation in State of source. This is precisely the reason why—among others—a special provision for agents in the insurance business (who do not usually conclude contracts and thus—in principle—are not regarded as dependent agents of the foreign insurance company) may now be found in the UN Model[80] and is also contemplated in the OECD Model Commentary[81] for the treaty partners to discuss.

With this in mind, insomuch as the existence of a permanent establishment has been determined, it is then necessary to attribute profits to that permanent establishment. The general tax principles for attributing profits to a permanent establishment are now provided under Art. 7 of the OECD Model.[82] However, it is fair to say that, in past years, the interpretation of such rules in various countries differed considerably and thus gave rise to issues of double taxation and double non-taxation.

To solve such issues, in July 2010, the OECD came up with a new version of Art. 7 in the 2010 OECD Model and the 2010 OECD Model Commentary,[83] along with the

78. *See* Klaus Vogel, *Klaus Vogel on Double Taxation Convention,* p. 280.
79. *See* Klaus Vogel, *Klaus Vogel on Double Taxation Convention,* p. 280.
80. *See* UN Model, Art. 5, para. 6.
81. *See* OECD Model Commentary on Art. 5, para. 114.
82. Such principles are—to a certain extent—also incorporated in Art. 7 of the UN Model and Art. 7 of the US Model. With specific respect to the UN Model, it should be recalled that Art. 7 of the UN Model broadly follows Art. 7 of the 2008 OECD Model. In fact, the new version of Art. 7 that was included in the 2010 OECD Model—which takes into consideration dealings between different parts of an enterprise—has not been adopted in the UN Model. This was because the OECD approach was found to be in direct conflict with Art. 7, para. 3, of the UN Model, which generally disallows deductions for amounts "*paid*" (otherwise than toward reimbursement of actual expenses) by a permanent establishment to its head office. For further comments on such a different treatment in attribution of profits to permanent establishments, *see—inter alia*—Michael Lennard, "The UN Model Tax Convention as Compared with the OECD Model Tax Convention—Current Points of Difference and Recent Developments," *Asia-Pacific Tax Bulletin* (2009) p. 7, Michael Lennard, "Update on the United Nations Tax Work," *Asia-Pacific Tax Bulletin* (2010) p. 11, Michael Lennard, "Update of the United Nations Model Tax Convention," *Asia-Pacific Tax Bulletin* (2012) p. 97 and Raffaele Petruzzi/Viktoria Wöhrer, "Business Profits, Permanent Establishments and Associated Enterprises" in: Michael Lang/Pasquale Pistone/Alexander Rust/Josef Schuch/Claus Staringer (eds.) *The UN Model Convention and Its Relevance for the Global Tax Treaty Network* (Amsterdam: IBFD, 2017) para. 2.3.2.2.
83. For further comments, *see* Alexandra Wintsch, "Attribution of Profits to Permanent Establishments: The 2008 Article 7 versus the 2010 Article 7 of the OECD Model Tax Convention," *International Transfer Pricing Journal* (2017) pp. 343 et seq. and Josine S.A. van Wanrooij, "Comments on the Proposed Article 7 of the OECD Model Convention," *Intertax* (2009) pp. 299 et seq.

new 2010 OECD Report.[84] In this update, the OECD developed the AOA, which introduced a "*functionally separate entity approach.*"[85] More to the point, under this approach, the profits of the different parts of an enterprise are to be allocated on the basis of a fiction that the permanent establishment must be considered as a separate and independent enterprise. In general, the AOA—which was introduced by the OECD to align the rules for business profits provided under Art. 7 of the 2010 OECD Model with those of the arm's length principle enshrined in Art. 9 of the 2010 OECD Model and in the 2010 OECD TP Guidelines[86]—consists of a two-step analysis aimed at determining the profits attributable to a permanent establishment.

The first step requires assuming the permanent establishment as a separate entity by carrying out a functional and factual analysis for the purposes of ascertaining the functions performed by the permanent establishment and their related risks, the assets needed to perform those activities, the rights and obligations attributable to the permanent establishment, the free capital to be allocated to the permanent establishment and the nature of its "*internal dealings*" with the rest of the enterprise of which it is a part.[87] In doing so, in the financial industry, in light of the special relationship between risk and financial assets, the specific focus falls on establishing where the KERT functions are undertaken. In particular, the main KERT function of insurance companies is generally the assumption and management of insurance risk/business (i.e., the underwriting).[88] Under the second step, the internal dealings between the permanent establishment and the other parts of the enterprise identified in the first step must be priced by means of an analogical application of the comparability analysis and the transfer pricing methods provided for under the OECD TP Guidelines.[89] This analysis will eventually provide for a calculation of the profits or losses of the permanent establishment deriving from all its activities, including transactions with other unrelated enterprises, transactions with related enterprises and dealings with other parts of the enterprise.[90]

84. The 2010 OECD Report consists of four different parts (Part I: general considerations; Part II: special considerations for banks; Part III: special considerations for enterprises carrying on global trading of financial instruments; Part IV: special considerations for insurance companies).
85. For an overview of this approach, *see—inter alia—*Roberto Bernales, "The Authorized OECD Approach: An Overview" in: Carlos Gutiérrez/Andreas Perdelwitz (eds.) *Taxation of Business Profits in the 21st Century—Selected Issues under Tax Treaties* (Amsterdam: IBFD, 2013) ch. 6.
86. *See* 2010 OECD Report, Part I, para. 53.
87. For general guidance on the first step of the analysis, *see* 2010 OECD Report, Part I, paras. 57-182.
88. *See* 2010 OECD Report, Part IV, paras. 69 and 94.
89. For general guidance on the second step of the analysis, *see* 2010 OECD Report, Part I, paras. 183-223.
90. For a recent update on the implementation of the AOA, *see* Steef Huibregtse/Louan Verdoner/Igne Valutyte/René Offermanns "Status of Implementation of the Authorized OECD Approach into Domestic Tax Law and Tax Treaties," *European Taxation* (2015) pp. 363 et seq. and 402 et seq.

1.4 RESEARCH AIMS AND QUESTIONS

Against the background depicted in the previous sections, the topic of this research concerns the concept of permanent establishment in the insurance business. Needless to say, in the context of international taxation, the existence of a permanent establishment is probably one of the most frequent issues that tax directors, tax advisors, government officials and tax courts have to deal with in their daily activities.[91] As of today, in an increasingly globalized economy, this issue is—to some extent—even more relevant than ever before in light of the fact that taxation is a crucial element of the competitiveness of countries and economic systems.

Considering the magnitude of the issue, the large number of implications and the studies already conducted thereon, this research is not intended to provide a general overview of the permanent establishment concept in the context of international tax law. Rather, this research is aimed at investigating the concept of permanent establishment in the insurance business in light of its specific features, value chain and business models. As a matter of fact, in addressing the concept of permanent establishment, the importance of the specific business is essential in understanding the boundaries of what in law and practice may be regarded as conditions for the existence of a permanent establishment. Most notably, given that an insurance company may carry on its insurance business in a foreign jurisdiction without necessarily establishing a fixed place of business therein, this research is focused on circumstances under which the conduct of insurance business can in such a way fulfill the requirements to constitute a dependent agent permanent establishment.

In essence, the purpose of this research is to describe and explain the main elements that may give rise to the existence of a dependent agent permanent establishment in the context of the insurance business by devising an analytical framework for the purposes of subsequently assessing the (most common) business models adopted by insurance companies in order to market, promote and distribute their products in foreign jurisdictions without establishing a fixed place of business therein.

This systematic approach presupposes a thorough analysis of the insurance industry with a specific focus on the regulatory landscape and its latest developments, which significantly affect the way insurance companies conduct their business in foreign jurisdictions (for instance, by influencing the decision of whether setting up a subsidiary, establishing a branch or operating through an insurance agent). Indeed, as most entities operating in the financial markets, insurance companies carry on their business in a highly regulated environment that constrains both operational and capital structures. This is particularly the case in the EU, where the Member States have agreed upon a legal and regulatory framework stipulating a separate definition of establishment for regulatory purposes.

Leveraging on such an analysis, this book will examine the correlation between the definition of dependent agent permanent establishment for tax purposes enshrined

91. *See* Jacques Sasseville/Arvid A. Skaar, "General Report" in: IFA (ed.) *Is there a permanent establishment?*, Cahiers de droit fiscal international, Vol. 94a (The Hague: Sdu Uitgevers, 2009) p. 21.

in Art. 5 of the model treaties and the definition of establishment adopted for regulatory and supervisory purposes—along with their respective areas of overlapping and divergence—in view of addressing the question of whether such concepts should be eventually aligned.

In addition to this, such a systematic approach requires having a clear picture of the value chain in the insurance industry with a view to determining where the value is being created, to which entity and/or part of an enterprise such value should be attributed and—thus—where such value should be subject to tax. To reach the purpose of the research, this book will then provide a functional and factual overview of the insurance business with a specific focus on the KERT functions.

In examining the functions performed, the value chain analysis can provide useful guidance in respect of the elements that may give rise to the existence of a dependent agent permanent establishment. Hence, the outcome of such an analysis will be particularly useful to answer another key research question, namely the question as to whether the identification of KERT functions within the framework of a functional and factual analysis performed in the context of the AOA for the purposes of attributing profits to a permanent establishment under Art. 7 of the OECD Model may potentially affect the currently existing standards for determining the existence of a dependent agent permanent establishment under Art. 5 of the model treaties.

To this end, it is important to note that—for the purposes of answering this second research question—the focus of this research will be limited to the first step of the AOA. Although closely connected with the topic of the present research, the pricing of the relevant transactions under the second step of the AOA remains outside the scope of this research and will be referred to only where necessary. In fact, the application of the second step of the AOA in the context of the insurance business might be the subject matter of more specific future research in that field.

Furthermore, with a view to providing a comprehensive assessment regarding the existence of an agency permanent establishment in the insurance business, this research will analytically scrutinize the specific measures concerning insurance agents. Such measures have been recently under the spotlight in the context of the work undertaken by the OECD on the BEPS Project, in which Action 7 specifically dealt with proposed changes to Art. 5 of the OECD Model and the OECD Model Commentary to prevent the artificial avoidance of the permanent establishment status. Even though the outcome of the discussion in the context of Action 7 of the BEPS Project was that no specific rule for insurance enterprises should be added to Art. 5 of the OECD Model and—thus—existing concerns related to cases where a large network of exclusive agents are used to sell insurance for a foreign insurer should be addressed through more general changes to Art. 5, paras. 5 and 6, of the OECD Model,[92] a specific provision may still be found in the UN Model and is also contemplated in the OECD Model Commentary for the contracting parties to discuss.

Most notably, this research will examine their underlying rationale and fundamental elements, along with their concrete application in business models and country

92. *See* OECD, "*Preventing the Artificial Avoidance of Permanent Establishment Status—Action 7: 2015 Final Report*" (Paris: OECD, 2015).

practices. This examination will serve as a basis to address the question as to whether a specific provision for agents in the insurance business should be considered when discussing the scope of Art. 5 of a DTA. Moving from this, the research will also elaborate on a few alternative approaches specifically tailored to the way in which insurance companies market, promote and distribute their products in foreign jurisdictions.

In such a way, the author hopes that this book may lay the foundations for future academic research and nurture debate on the opportunity to develop changes to the definition of dependent agent permanent establishment currently enshrined in the model treaties, their respective commentaries and the attribution of profits thereto.

1.5 RESEARCH OUTLINE AND METHODOLOGY

As it appears from the preceding sections, this research will delve into the concept of dependent agent permanent establishment in the insurance business by developing an analytical framework for the purposes of assessing the business models adopted by insurance companies and answering the specific research questions briefly outlined above.

Within this structure, the starting point for such a systematic approach is an overview of the specialties of the insurance business before going into the specific tax issues in depth. In more concrete terms, this book is divided into seven chapters with a research design articulated in such a way so as to follow a general-to-specific pattern.

After this introductory chapter, Chapter 2 approaches the broad subject matter in a general manner by providing an overview of the insurance business and its specific features. More specifically, the first section describes the regulatory landscape in which the insurance companies conduct their business with a specific focus on the EU and Switzerland touching upon the definition of establishment adopted for such regulatory purposes. The second section continues this general outline of the insurance business by providing an overview of the value chain in the insurance business from the development of the insurance product to the administration of claims stemming from the insurance contracts and the management of assets covering insurance liabilities. Among others, this overview is intended to specifically determine which functions within a particular insurance enterprise may be regarded as the KERT functions in the context of the first step of the AOA.

Thereafter, Chapter 3 develops an analytical framework by discussing the agency permanent establishment concept enshrined in the main model treaties and the specific insurance provision which may be found in the UN Model and is also contemplated in the OECD Model Commentary. More specifically, Chapter 3 will specifically deal with the historical development of such a concept in the model treaties—highlighting the main differences and similarities in the definitions enshrined in the different model treaties—and the reasoning behind measures dealing with insurance agents.

Within this analytical framework, Chapter 4 aims at describing the (most common) business models adopted by global insurance companies with a particular focus on the specific features of such models that may give rise to the existence of a dependent agent permanent establishment in a foreign country. It is important to note that, by distinguishing various categories of insurance business models, this research is not intended to design an irrefutable classification system of cases whereby an insurance company may be deemed to have a dependent agent permanent establishment in a foreign country. As a matter of fact, in practice, the number of business models and deviations therefrom may be indefinite and thus any attempt to scientifically categorize each and every case may be inadequate and beyond the scope of a work in the field of international tax law. Rather, this book is limited at devising consistent methods of analysis to provide a comprehensive scrutiny of material elements and circumstances that may be found in the main business models to critically assess the existence of a dependent agent permanent establishment.

Subsequently, after an examination of the main business models, Chapter 5 aims at examining the Swiss policy and the definition of dependent agent permanent establishment adopted in DTAs concluded by Switzerland with a specific focus on the insurance business. When doing so, this research will also compare the definition adopted in Swiss DTAs with the practice of other countries (particularly, Italy and other major EU and OECD Member States) to assess different approaches adopted when dealing with this specific issue. Again, it should be noted that such a critical assessment does not pretend to cover all countries in the world but it is instead limited to selected countries that contemplate specific measures for the insurance business and—thus—may serve as a significant comparable for the purposes of the present research.

As a final step of the research, Chapter 6 is aimed at providing answers to the research questions and to some normative claims in respect of the topics depicted in the previous chapters. More specifically, the research questions are addressed in the following order: (*i*) whether a specific provision for agents in the insurance business should be considered when discussing the scope of Art. 5 of a DTA, (*ii*) whether the identification of KERT functions within the framework of a functional and factual analysis performed in the context of the AOA for the purposes of attributing profits to a permanent establishment under Art. 7 of the OECD Model may potentially affect the currently existing standards for determining the existence of a dependent agent permanent establishment under Art. 5 of the model treaties, and (*iii*) whether the definition of dependent agent permanent establishment enshrined in Art. 5 of the model treaties and the definition of establishment adopted for regulatory purposes should be aligned. Next, based on the answers to the research questions, the final sections of this chapter also take a normative stand by assessing a few alternative approaches to the currently existing measures dealing with insurance agents.

The various elements of the research are finally tied together in Chapter 7 in a general conclusion. More to the point, the purpose of this concluding chapter is to deliver a final wrap-up of the research findings, revisit the overall research aims and provide some remarks on what the answers to the research questions may entail for future academic research and future developments of the concept of permanent establishment.

CHAPTER 2

Overview of the Insurance Business

Chapter 2 approaches the broad subject matter in a general manner by providing an overview of the insurance business and its specific features. To begin with, this chapter describes the regulatory landscape, along with its major requirements, which significantly affect the way insurance companies conduct their business in foreign jurisdictions, with a specific focus on the EU single insurance market and Switzerland. In doing so, this chapter delves into the definition of establishment adopted for regulatory purposes in such jurisdictions, with a thorough analysis of their critical elements. Second, this chapter complements the general outline of the insurance business with an overview of its value chain from the development of the insurance product to the administration of claims stemming from the insurance contracts and the management of assets covering insurance liabilities. For such purposes, this analysis scrutinizes the essential functions of an insurance company—with a specific focus on the KERT functions—with a view to identifying where the added value is being created, to which entity and/or part of an enterprise such value should be attributed, and where such value should be subject to tax.

2.1 OVERVIEW OF THE REGULATORY FRAMEWORK

2.1.1 The Rationale for Insurance Regulation

The predominant economic foundation for regulation is generally based on the presence of market failures.[93] According to this theory, the role of regulation is to restrict the actions of entrepreneurs in a certain industry to maximize the social welfare conditions as near as possible to those that would occur in a perfect competitive market.[94]

93. *See* Robert W. Klein, "The Insurance Industry and Its Regulation: An Overview" in: Martin F. Grace/Robert W. Klein (eds.) *The Future of Insurance Regulation in the United States* (Washington: The Brookings Institution, 2009) p. 25 and footnotes cited therein.
94. It is worth noting that two alternative views on regulation have emerged more recently, namely the capture theory of regulation and the public choice theory of regulation. For an overview of

The regulation in the insurance sector differs from that of other industries to the extent that the potential market failures are also different.[95] As a matter of fact, the nature of insurance, as a service, shows distinctive features which may give rise to specific issues. Remarkably, the major characteristic which differentiates insurance from other industries is the inversion of the production cycle. In fact, traditionally an insurance company receives the payment of a premium prior to the payment of a claim.[96] It follows that the service, namely the payment of a claim, is provided after it is bought by the policyholder by means of the payment of a premium.[97]

Therefore, it is of paramount importance to secure that the management of an insurance company will be of sufficient competence at managing risks for the insurance company not to become insolvent in the interval between the payment of the premium and the date of the claim as well as of sufficient integrity not to misappropriate the funds that should properly remain available to meet such claims.[98] Furthermore, insomuch as a financial distress of an insurance company may also result from a market shock (such as an interest rate decrease or a real estate crisis) or the externality brought about by the failure of other players on the market, it is essential that the focus of solvency regulation is not on the individual company, but on the industry as a whole so as to prevent systemic issues that may disrupt the financial system.[99]

Besides the solvency issues, regulation should also ensure fair treatment of the policyholders by guaranteeing that the services offered by the insurance companies are fair and fairly priced. Arguably, the fiduciary nature of insurer operations and the extensive influence of insurance on members of the society require regulation on the entry into the market, the investment practice and the level of service. In addition, the complexity of insurance products requires scrutiny of insurance contracts and their pricing as well as the licensing of insurance intermediaries to ensure their competence.[100]

At last, although the need for solvency and fairness dominate the regulatory philosophy, another reason for the regulation of insurance may arise from the uncertainties inherent in the insurance pricing process. According to this view, which is however not generally accepted, competition in some fields of insurance might

---

such theories, *see* Emmett J. Vaughan/Therese M. Vaughan, *Fundamentals of Risk and Insurance, Tenth Edition* (Hoboken: John Wiley & Sons Inc., 2008) pp. 100-101.

95. *See* Emmett J. Vaughan/Therese M. Vaughan, *Fundamentals of Risk and Insurance, Tenth Edition*, p. 101.
96. In recent years, the payment of the premium by instalment has become more common. However, it is to be expected that at least a part of the premium will have been paid before any claim arises.
97. The timespan between such two events may range from a few days in non-life contracts to a significant number of years in life contracts.
98. *See* Andrew McGee, *The Single Market in Insurance: Breaking Down the Barriers* (Dartmouth: Ashgate, 1998) p. 3.
99. For a general overview of the contagion and systemic risk in the insurance sector, *see* Benjamin Lorent, "Risks and Regulation of Insurance Companies. Is Solvency II the Right Answer?," *Centre Emile Bernheim—CEB Working Paper No. 08/007* (2008) pp. 12 et seq.
100. *See* Emmett J. Vaughan/Therese M. Vaughan, *Fundamentals of Risk and Insurance, Tenth Edition*, p. 101.

become excessive and thus should be kept under regulatory control to the extent that, when struggling for business, insurance companies may underestimate future losses and thus fail.[101]

2.1.2 The EU Single Insurance Market

In Europe, EU law has had a significant effect on the regulation of insurance business.[102] Indeed, the EU law changed the rules for financial services companies operating across borders within Europe by establishing a single market for insurance as well as for other financial industries.[103]

Historically, Europe had separate regulatory frameworks in every country. In fact, the insurance industry was subject to some state control even before the EU harmonization process started.[104] Nevertheless, the scope of the state control and the extent to which such control was exercised varied significantly among countries. Such differences in how state supervision was exercised mainly derived from different regulatory interests of States. This resulted in different regulatory attitudes ranging from very liberal approaches to other forms of substantive regulation.[105]

Such a fragmented system started to come under pressure with the creation of the EU and the establishment of a single market envisaged by the Treaty of Rome signed on March 25, 1957, which formed the EEC (now the EU). More to the point, the realization of a single market in the insurance business was closely associated with two major principles enshrined in the EEC Treaty (now the TFEU), namely the freedom of establishment and the freedom to provide services,[106] and was mentioned for the first time in the two General Programmes issued by the European Commission on such two

101. *See* Emmett J. Vaughan/Therese M. Vaughan, *Fundamentals of Risk and Insurance, Tenth Edition*, pp. 101-102.
102. This section is not intended to provide a comprehensive overview of the EU insurance legislation. Rather, the main focus is on EU measures designed to realize a single insurance market in order to delve into the concept of permanent establishment for regulatory purposes.
103. By contrast, in the United States, insurance continues to be regulated by the states despite several attempts to establish some form of federal insurance regulation. To this effect, *see* Robert W. Klein in: Martin F. Grace/Robert W. Klein (eds.) *The Future of Insurance Regulation in the United States*, pp. 1 et seq.
104. In Italy, for instance, following some pieces of legislation concerning life insurance, the first comprehensive set of insurance regulation was introduced in 1923 and later reorganized in a Consolidated Act in 1959. For an overview of the Italian regulatory background, *see—inter alia*—Marco Rossetti, *Il diritto delle assicurazioni—Volume 1*, p. 61 et seq., Ernesto Pucci, "L'accesso all'attività assicurativa e riassicurativa" in: Marco Prosperetti/Alessandro Colavolpe (eds.) *Le Assicurazioni* (Milano: Ipsoa, 2012) pp. 19 et seq., Antigono Donati/Giovanna Volpe Putzolu, *Manuale di Diritto delle Assicurazioni—Ottava Edizione Aggiornata* (Milano: Giuffrè, 2006) pp. 9 et seq. and Luigi Farenga, *Diritto delle Assicurazioni Private* (Torino: Giappichelli, 2001) pp. 16 et seq.
105. *See* Kristin Nemeth, "European Insurance Law: A Single Insurance Market," *European University Institute—EUI Working Paper LAW No. 2001/4* (2001) pp. 13 et seq.
106. The free movement of capital, which comes into play with cross-border investments of large insurance companies, is beyond the scope of this thesis.

freedoms in 1961.[107] In a nutshell, in the insurance context, the right of establishment—which is now laid down in Arts. 49-55 of the TFEU—confers the right for EU insurance companies to establish themselves in any other EU Member State by setting up agencies, branches or subsidiaries to sell insurance products within that EU Member State. Conversely, the freedom to provide services—which is now set forth under Arts. 56-62 of the TFEU—provides the right for EU insurance companies to sell insurance products to policyholders located in any EU Member State from an establishment elsewhere in the EU.[108]

As opposed to the previous fragmented system, the move toward a single market in the insurance business was intended to provide the EU citizens with access to a wider range of insurance products and enable insurance companies authorized in an EU Member State to freely operate in other EU Member States.[109] Nevertheless, at that point in time, in order to achieve the objective of establishing such a single insurance market, it was necessary to dismantle a number of barriers impeding inter-state trade within the EU.[110] Among others, the establishment of a single market required the breaking down of regulatory barriers, which inhibited free access to markets. However, at the same time, it was also essential to have in place certain minimum standards to prevent a race to the bottom in which EU Member States could offer weak regulation and—as a result—poorly regulated insurance companies could operate throughout the EU single market.[111]

With such objectives in mind, over the subsequent decades, the creation of such a single market in the insurance business with the establishment of a common regulatory framework has been achieved through the intervention of the EU legislator by means of three generations of EU Directives,[112] each containing one EU Directive on the life insurance business and one EU Directive on the non-life insurance business in order to properly address the different issues raised in each business.[113]

The first wave of EU Insurance Directives gave European insurance companies the right to establish their own branches, offices or agencies in other EU Member

107. *See* the General Programme for the abolition of restrictions on freedom of establishment, OJ 1962, No. 2/36, and the General Programme for the abolition of restrictions on freedom to provide services, OJ 1962, No. 2/32.
108. *See* Robert Merkin/Angus Rodger, *EC Insurance Law* (London: Longman, 1997) p. 1.
109. *See* John Lowry/Philip Rawlings/Robert Merkin, *Insurance Law: Doctrines and Principles—Third Edition* (Oxford: Hart Publishing, 2011) p. 18.
110. *See* Andrew McGee, *The Single Market in Insurance: Breaking Down the Barriers*, p. 6.
111. *See* John Lowry, Philip Rawlings/Robert Merkin, *Insurance Law: Doctrines and Principles—Third Edition*, p. 18.
112. The use of EU Directives rather than EU Regulations may be justified by the principles of mutual recognition and minimum harmonization of national provisions laid down by the ECJ in the *Cassis de Dijon* case. To this effect, *see* Francesco Seatzu, *Insurance in Private International Law: A European Perspective* (Oxford: Hart Publishing, 2003) p. 4.
113. Council Directive 64/225/EEC of 25 February 1964 on the abolition of restrictions on freedom of establishment and freedom to provide services in respect of reinsurance and retrocession has been first introduced to abolish all restrictions on the establishment and the provision of services in the field of reinsurance.

States. More to the point, the First Non-Life Directive[114]—which was issued in 1973—laid down a common regulatory structure for non-life insurance companies, thereby facilitating the abolition of national restrictions on the right of an insurance company established in an EU Member State to become established in another EU Member State.[115] Next to this harmonization measure, a separate EU Directive was adopted on the very same date in order to abolish any restrictions on freedom of establishment by requiring EU Member States to allow insurance companies to become established without discriminations on grounds of nationality.[116] The result was a structure under which an insurance company established in any EU Member State could become established in any other EU Member State, provided that such insurance company complied with regulatory rules of the host country, such rules to a large extent being harmonized within the EU, so that an insurance company satisfying the requirements of its home country would most probably satisfy the requirements for becoming established in other EU Member States.[117]

The corresponding EU Directive harmonizing the regulatory provisions regarding the life business only followed in 1979.[118] The First Life Insurance Directive mainly echoed the principles already set out in the First Non-Life Insurance Directive in terms of classification, authorization and freedom of establishment in the life insurance business.

Having set up the principle of freedom of establishment within the EU, the next significant challenge for the EU Commission was the introduction of the freedom to provide insurance services within the EU by allowing an insurance company authorized and established in any EU Member State to sell its insurance products in any other EU Member State without the need for further authorization or establishment.[119]

In this respect, it is remarkable that the first step toward the freedom to provide services was already taken in 1978, at the time when the Co-Insurance Directive was enacted.[120] Such EU Directive required EU Member States to lift restrictions on the participation in co-insurance within the EU by insurance companies established therein. More precisely, a participating co-insurer was not required to seek authorization in the country in which the leading insurer had its head office and the regulation concerning the technical reserves was left to the regulatory authorities of the EU Member State in which each participating co-insurer was established.[121]

114. First Council Directive 73/239/EEC of 24 July 1973 on the coordination of laws, regulations and administrative provisions relating to the taking-up and pursuit of the business of direct insurance other than life assurance.
115. *See* Robert Merkin/Angus Rodger, *EC Insurance Law*, p. 5.
116. Council Directive 73/240/EEC of 24 July 1973 abolishing restrictions on freedom of establishment in the business of direct insurance other than life assurance.
117. *See* Robert Merkin/Angus Rodger, *EC Insurance Law*, p. 5.
118. First Council Directive 79/267/EEC of 5 March 1979 on the coordination of laws, regulations and administrative provisions relating to the taking up and pursuit of the business of direct life assurance.
119. *See* Robert Merkin/Angus Rodger, *EC Insurance Law*, p. 7.
120. Council Directive 78/473/EEC of 30 May 1978 on the coordination of laws, regulations and administrative provisions relating to Community co-insurance.
121. *See* Robert Merkin/Angus Rodger, *EC Insurance Law*, p. 8.

However, the move toward the freedom to provide services was subsequently hindered by four cases—collectively known as the insurance cases—which were brought before the ECJ by the EU Commission against some EU Member States for their failure to implement the Co-Insurance Directive.[122] In such cases, the ECJ specifically addressed the scope of freedom permitted to an insurance company authorized and established in an EU Member State to insure risks located within another EU Member State. Most importantly, the ECJ ruled that where an insurance company established in an EU Member State wished to sell its insurance products in another EU Member State by setting up a branch or agency therein, such a branch or agency could be required to comply with the regulatory requirements of the host country. Conversely, if such an insurance company wished to sell its insurance products in another EU Member State other than through a branch or agency, the regulatory authorities of the host country could not insist upon the insurance company setting up a branch or agency, it being sufficient for such an insurance company to have some form of permanent representation. In addition, by arguing that the freedom to provide services could be restricted by provisions which are justified by the general good, the ECJ maintained that such an insurance company could be subjected to the requirement of authorization by the regulatory authorities of the host country to the extent that this was necessary in the wider public interests to protect the policyholders in the interests of the general good.[123]

As a consequence of such cases, the EU Commission could not move directly to the application of the freedom to provide services in the EU insurance industry. Most notably, in answer to such public interest constraints, the EU Commission developed a compromise position whereby an insurance company established and authorized in an EU Member State could sell insurance products directly into another EU Member State without authorization provided by the regulator of such other EU Member State to the extent that the policyholders were not in the need of the protection conferred by such authorization. In doing so, the EU Commission adopted different methods for the life insurance business and the non-life insurance business.[124]

The Second Non-Life Directive[125]—which was issued in 1988—moved toward the realization of the freedom to provide services by regulating instances where an insurance company established and authorized in an EU Member State was permitted to sell its insurance products directly to policyholders in another EU Member State without any establishment in such other EU Member State. In doing so, a distinction

122. ECJ, December 4, 1986, C-252/83, *Commission of the European Communities v. Kingdom of Denmark* [1986] ECR 3713, ECJ, December 4, 1986, C-205/84, *Commission of the European Communities v. Federal Republic of Germany* [1986] ECR 3755, ECJ, December 4, 1986, C-206/84, *Commission of the European Communities v. Ireland* [1986] ECR 3817 and ECJ, December 4, 1986, C-220/83, *Commission of the European Communities v. French Republic* [1986] ECR 3663.
123. *See* Robert Merkin/Angus Rodger, *EC Insurance Law*, p. 9.
124. *See* Robert Merkin/Angus Rodger, *EC Insurance Law*, p. 9.
125. Second Council Directive 88/357/EEC of 22 June 1988 on the coordination of laws, regulations and administrative provisions relating to direct insurance other than life assurance and laying down provisions to facilitate the effective exercise of freedom to provide services and amending Directive 73/239/EEC.

was drawn between large risks and mass risks.[126] In the case of large risks of a commercial character, an EU insurance company was free to sell its insurance products in another EU Member State, provided only that such an insurance company informed the regulatory authorities of the latter State of its intentions and of the nature of the risks to be covered. By contrast, in the case of mass risks of a consumer nature, EU Member States remained free to impose an authorization requirement on an EU insurance company wishing to sell its insurance products into is territory by way of provision of services, i.e., without any establishment therein.[127]

In addition, following a position taken by the ECJ in the context of the insurance cases,[128] the Second Non-life Directive extended the freedom of establishment by explicitly providing that "*any permanent presence of an undertaking in the territory of a Member State shall be treated in the same way as an agency or branch, even if that presence does not take the form of a branch or agency, but consists merely of an office managed by the undertaking's own staff or by a person who is independent but has permanent authority to act for the undertaking as an agency would.*"[129]

The Second Life Directive[130]—which was enacted in 1990—introduced new measures toward achieving the freedom to provide services in the life insurance business. Nevertheless, in order to do so, it was again necessary to devise a pattern aimed at distinguishing between policyholders who needed protection and those who did not. Hence, the Second Life Directive distinguished between policyholders who had taken the initiative in seeking the commitment and ordinary policyholders.[131] More precisely, in the former case, the policyholder was deemed not to be in need of protection and—therefore—an EU insurance company was not required to be authorized by the regulatory authorities of the host country, provided only that such authorities were informed about the activities of the insurance company. On the contrary, in the case of ordinary policyholders, an EU insurance company was still required to be authorized by the regulatory authorities of the host country.[132]

Furthermore, the Second Life Directive also brought life insurance into line with non-life insurance with respect to the scope of the freedom of establishment by explicitly providing that an EU insurance company could operate in another EU Member State through a permanent presence as opposed to a full-fledged branch or agency.[133]

126. *See* Art. 5 of the Second Non-Life Directive for a definition of large risks.
127. *See* Robert Merkin/Angus Rodger, *EC Insurance Law*, p. 10.
128. ECJ, December 4, 1986, C-205/84, *Commission of the European Communities v. Federal Republic of Germany* [1986] ECR 3755, para. 21.
129. *See* Art. 3 of the Second Non-Life Directive.
130. Council Directive 90/619/EEC of 8 November 1990 on the coordination of laws, regulations and administrative provisions relating to direct life assurance, laying down provisions to facilitate the effective exercise of freedom to provide services and amending Directive 79/267/EEC.
131. *See* Art. 13 of the Second Life Directive for the list of circumstances in which a policyholder was considered to have taken the initiative.
132. *See* Robert Merkin/Angus Rodger, *EC Insurance Law*, p. 12 and Francesco Seatzu, *Insurance in Private International Law: A European Perspective*, p. 14.
133. *See* Art. 3 of the Second Life Directive.

Two years later, the Third Non-Life Directive[134] and the Third Life Directive[135] completed the (slow) progress toward the EU single insurance market by creating a single EU license system based on the principle of the home country control.[136] In light of this principle, which is still applicable as of today, EU insurance companies are required to be authorized by the regulatory authorities of the EU Member State in which they have their principal place of business, but that single authorization gives them a passport to carry on insurance business throughout the EU relying either on the freedom of establishment or on the freedom to provide services, subject only to notifying authorities of any other EU Member State into which they wish to expand their activities.[137] It follows that, for the purposes of the provision of insurance by way of services, the distinction drawn in the second generation of EU Insurance Directives between large and mass risks (in the non-life insurance business) and between policyholders who sought the commitment and those who did not (in the life insurance business) has been abolished.[138] Pursuant to such measures, EU Member States only retain limited residual powers to protect their policyholders: (*i*) in the event that the home country authorities fail to act to prevent the insurance company from infringing the domestic law of the host country or (*ii*) by imposing restrictions on contracts on the basis of the concept of the general good.[139]

Finally, a few years ago, in the interest of clarity and simplification, the EU legislator eventually tied up the regulatory environment by consolidating all relevant measures in the field of insurance and reinsurance regulation in a single measure with the enactment of the Solvency II Directive,[140] which now forms the basis of a comprehensive system for the regulation and supervision of insurance and reinsurance undertakings of the EU.[141]

At last, in terms of territorial application, a word needs to be said about the fact that, under the EEA Agreement, which came into effect on January 1, 1994, this comprehensive system of insurance regulation and supervision established in the EU is also applicable to three of the EFTA countries (namely, Iceland, Norway and Liechtenstein).[142] On the other hand, insurance companies established in third countries

134. Council Directive 92/49/EEC of 18 June 1992 on the coordination of laws, regulations and administrative provisions relating to direct insurance other than life assurance and amending Directives 73/239/EEC and 88/357/EEC.
135. Council Directive 92/96/EEC of 10 November 1992 on the coordination of laws, regulations and administrative provisions relating to direct life assurance and amending Directives 79/267/EEC and 90/619/EEC.
136. The three life insurance Directives have been subsequently consolidated by Directive 2002/83/EC of the European Parliament and of the Council of 5 November 2002 concerning life assurance.
137. *See* Andrew McGee, *The Single Market in Insurance: Breaking Down the Barriers*, pp. 10-11.
138. *See* Robert Merkin/Angus Rodger, *EC Insurance Law*, p. 13.
139. *See* Robert Merkin/Angus Rodger, *EC Insurance Law*, p. 14.
140. Directive 2009/138/EC of the European Parliament and of the Council of 25 November 2009 on the taking-up and pursuit of the business of Insurance and Reinsurance (as subsequently amended).
141. It is fair to say that this piece of legislation did not introduce significant amendments to the previous set of legislation for the purposes of the right of establishment and the freedom to provide services.
142. Special arrangements between the EU and Switzerland will be dealt with under para. 2.1.4.

cannot rely upon the freedom of establishment and the freedom to provide services within the EEA. Hence, third-country insurance companies wishing to carry on business within the EEA are required to set up a subsidiary or a branch in an EEA Member State by obtaining a prior authorization of the regulatory authorities of such a State.[143] If a non-EEA insurance company creates a subsidiary in the EEA, such a subsidiary may then invoke the freedom of establishment and the freedom to provide services. On the contrary, a branch of a third-country insurance company requires a full authorization in each EEA Member State in which it operates.[144]

2.1.3 Demarcation Between the Right of Establishment and the Freedom to Provide Services

In the context of the EU single insurance market,[145] the demarcation between the right of establishment and the freedom to provide services is not clear-cut and thus has raised some uncertainty as to what provisions should apply in specific circumstances. True, the establishment of an insurance company in countries other than that of incorporation—and, as a consequence, the application of the right of establishment as opposed to the freedom to provides services—may be revealed by formal indicators if any such establishment is referred to in the articles of association, public registries or any other official document. Nevertheless, this is not always the case insomuch as the presence of an insurance company in the territory of another EU Member State may also be generated by factual circumstances.[146]

Against this background, it should be noted that the Solvency II Directive now stipulates that the term "*'establishment' of an undertaking means its head office or any of its branches.*"[147]

In the light of this definition, reference should be first made to the "*head office*" of an insurance company. This is a formal notion—which cannot be susceptible to misunderstanding—referring to the place indicated in the articles of association as the official statutory seat of the insurance company, irrespective of whether this place corresponds to the place where the business operations are actually carried on.[148]

On the contrary, the scope of the wording "*any of its branches*" appears to be less straightforward. In this regard, the Solvency II Directive provides that the term "*'branch' means an agency or a branch of an insurance or reinsurance undertaking which is located in the territory of a Member State other than the home Member State.*"[149] In this context, it has been contended that a branch *stricto sensu* may be regarded as a

143. As an alternative solution, non-EEA insurance companies may also make the decision of reinsuring EEA risks without a presence or authorization within the EEA.
144. *See* Marco Rossetti, *Il diritto delle assicurazioni—Volume 1*, pp. 163 et seq.
145. This section is not intended to delve into the company law of each and every EU Member State. Rather, the focus is on EU measures designed to realize a single insurance market.
146. *See* Giulio Partesotti/Marco Ricolfi, *La nuova disciplina dell'impresa di assicurazione sulla vita in attuazione della Terza Direttiva* (Padova: CEDAM, 2000) p. 38 and footnotes cited therein.
147. *See* Art. 13 of the Solvency II Directive, no. 12.
148. *See* Giulio Partesotti/Marco Ricolfi, *La nuova disciplina dell'impresa di assicurazione sulla vita in attuazione della Terza Direttiva*, p. 37 and footnotes cited therein.
149. *See* Art. 13 of the Solvency II Directive, no. 11.

fixed place of business established by an insurance company which—on the one hand—lacks a separate legal personality from that of its head office but—on the other hand—may avail of an endowment fund as well as some sort of administrative independence. On the other hand, as to the concept of an agency, some authors have defined it as a branch of a smaller size, whereas other scholars took the view that it may be regarded as a place of business lacking any administrative independence from the head office.[150] In spite of such attempts to define the above expressions, however, the Solvency II Directive does not eventually take a final stand on them.[151]

On the top of this, in line with the insurance cases and the previous EU Insurance Directives, the Solvency II Directive provides that "*any permanent presence of an undertaking in the territory of a Member State shall be treated in the same way as a branch, even where that presence does not take the form of a branch, but consists merely of an office managed by the own staff of the undertaking or by a person who is independent but has permanent authority to act for the undertaking as an agency would.*"[152]

In view of addressing the uncertainty arising out of such a regulatory framework, some years ago, the EU Commission issued an Interpretative Communication so as to clarify the principles governing the right of establishment and the freedom to provide services, as interpreted by the ECJ.[153,154] At a first glance, one may argue that—in this Interpretative Communication—the EU Commission simply followed the ECJ case law by identifying the relevant criteria for drawing a line between the right of establishment and the freedom to provide services. However, at a closer look, two main elements should be considered. At first, the criteria identified by the EU Commission are of a rather pragmatic nature. Second, the interpretations provided by the EU Commission were aimed at integrating the principles enshrined in the ECJ case law in the context of the single insurance market. In doing so, it appears as if the EU Commission was intended to extend the concept of the freedom to provide services as a consequence of the process of legislative harmonization.[155]

To begin with, the EU Commission tried to make clear the demarcation between the right of establishment and the freedom to provide services based on a conceptual

150. *See* Giulio Partesotti/Marco Ricolfi, *La nuova disciplina dell'impresa di assicurazione sulla vita in attuazione della Terza Direttiva*, pp. 708-709 and footnotes cited therein.
151. Interestingly, Art. 4, para. 1. (17), of the Regulation (EU) No. 575/2013 of the European Parliament and of the Council of 26 June 2013 on prudential requirements for credit institutions and investment firms and amending Regulation (EU) No. 648/2012 stipulates that "*branch*" means a place of business which forms a legally dependent part of an institution and which carries out directly all or some of the transactions inherent in the business of institutions.
152. *See* Art. 145, para. 1, of the Solvency II Directive.
153. Commission Interpretative Communication on the freedom to provide services and the general good in the insurance sector (2000/C 43/03).
154. Such a document, which was delivered after a wide-ranging consultation process involving all interested parties, was aimed at clarifying the scope of the freedom of establishment vis-à-vis the freedom to provide services. However, it has no legally binding effect. Therefore, it can neither anticipate the interpretation of the ECJ nor does it impose any new obligations on EU Member States.
155. *See* Diana Cerini, "Note in tema di esercizio dell'attività assicurativa in regime di libertà di prestazione di servizi e in regime di stabilimento," *Diritto ed Economia dell'Assicurazione* (1999) pp. 155-179.

analysis. More specifically, the Interpretative Communication clarified that the concept of the provision of services should be distinguished from that of establishment by its temporary nature.[156] In this respect, in *Gebhard*, the ECJ maintained that the temporary nature of the provision of services must be determined in the light of its duration, regularity, periodicity and continuity. Nonetheless, the fact that the provision of services is temporary does not mean that the provider of services may not equip himself with some form of infrastructure in the host country (including an office, chambers or consulting rooms) insofar as such infrastructure is necessary for the purposes of performing the services in question.[157] Interestingly enough, some authors brought this line of reasoning even further by arguing that—in order to remain in the scope of the freedom to provide services—specific attention should be paid not only to the temporary nature but also to the recurrence to the extent that such a recurrence may eventually fulfill the criteria of continuity and permanence. To put it in different terms, according to such a view, provisions of services which are in principle of a temporary character may fall within the scope of the right of establishment rather than the freedom to provide services in the case that they turn out to be recurrent.[158]

Besides the temporary nature of the provision of services, the Interpretative Communication also clarified that a host country is entitled to take steps to prevent a service provider whose activity is entirely or mainly directed toward its territory from improperly exercising the freedom to provide services in order to circumvent the rules of professional conduct which would be applicable to him if he were established in the territory of that country.[159] This clarification stems from the ECJ jurisprudence which—in such situations—excluded the application of the provisions on the freedom to provide services in favor of the rules concerning the right of establishment. Most notably, although this goes beyond the provisions of the TFEU, the ECJ developed such a consolidated case law in the field of circumvention that may be found in the context of the freedom to provide services.[160] In this regard, it has been argued that, under the extreme assumption that the insurance activity is "*entirely*" carried on in a certain country, it is beyond doubt that there is an attempt to circumvent the rules on the right of establishment in such host country. Conversely, it may be more complex to determine objective parameters to ascertain whether the insurance activity is "*mainly*" carried on in a certain country. For instance, one may consider the turnover, the number of insurance contracts, the assets deployed, the staff employed in such a host country and so forth.[161] In this context, the EU Commission could have looked at such situations more closely and have attempted to think about and provide additional guidance to that end. However, the EU Commission only took the view that a situation

156. *See* para. I.A.1.(a) of the Interpretative Communication.
157. ECJ, November 30, 1995, C-55/94, *Reinhard Gebhard v. Consiglio dell'Ordine degli Avvocati e Procuratori di Milano* [2000] ECR I-04165, para. 27.
158. *See* Ernesto Pucci in: Marco Prosperetti/Alessandro Colavolpe (eds.) *Le Assicurazioni*, pp. 65 et seq. and footnotes cited therein.
159. *See* para. I.A.1.(b) of the Interpretative Communication.
160. *See—inter alia*—ECJ, December 4, 1986, C-205/84, *Commission of the European Communities v. Federal Republic of Germany* [1986] ECR 3755, para. 22.
161. *See* Marco Frigessi di Rattalma, "La libertà di prestazione assicurativa nel diritto comunitario derivato," *Diritto e Pratica dell'Assicurazione* (1989) p. 393.

where an insurance company is frequently being approached within its own territory by customers residing in other EU Member States could not be regarded as a circumvention, unless it were demonstrated that there was an intention on the part of the insurance company to circumvent the national rules of such other countries.[162]

In this respect, it is also worth noting that some authors identified another scheme to carry on insurance business under the freedom to provide services, sometimes referred to as "*self-procurement.*" This is for instance the situation where an Italian resident individual goes to France and concludes an insurance policy with a French insurance company to cover a commitment or risk situated in Italy. In such a case, the question arises as to whether the insurance company should be preliminary authorized to carry on insurance business by way of provision of services in an EU Member State other than that of incorporation. Under such circumstances, based on a systematic interpretation of the EU provisions, there are good grounds to argue that the answer to this question should be positive. In fact, the provision of services comes into play in the case that a commitment or risk is covered by an insurance company established in another EU Member State. More to the point, the Solvency II Directive—when providing the specific definition of "*host Member State*"—stipulates that "*for life and non-life insurance, the Member State of the provisions of services means, respectively, the Member State of the commitment or the Member State in which the risk is situated, where that commitment or risk is covered by an insurance undertaking or a branch situated in another Member State.*"[163] Having regard to this provision, read in conjunction with the definitions of "*Member State in which the risk is situated*"[164] and "*Member State of the commitment,*"[165] it may be argued that this situation falls within the scope of the rules governing the provision of services in all respects and—thus—the insurance company should be preliminary authorized to conclude any such contract.[166]

As opposed to the temporary nature of the services, the Interpretative Communication clarified that—in principle—a business carried on "*for an indefinite period via a permanent presence*" should be instead covered by the provisions of the TFEU on the right of establishment.[167] This clarification stemmed from previous ECJ jurisprudence which excluded the application of the freedom to provide services in the case of a "*permanent presence*" in another EU Member State. In particular, in *Gebhard*, the ECJ maintained that "*a national of a Member State who pursues a professional activity on a stable and continuous basis in another Member State where he holds himself out from an established professional base to, amongst others, nationals of that State comes under*

162. *See* para. I.A.1.(b) of the Interpretative Communication.
163. *See* Art. 13 of the Solvency II Directive, no. 9.
164. *See* Art. 13 of the Solvency II Directive, no. 13.
165. *See* Art. 13 of the Solvency II Directive, no. 14.
166. *See* Ernesto Pucci in: Marco Prosperetti/Alessandro Colavolpe (eds.) *Le Assicurazioni*, pp. 68 et seq. and Maurizio Hazan/Stefano Taurini, "Assicurazioni Private," *Itinera—Guide Giuridiche Ipsoa* (2015) pp. 110 et seq.
167. *See* para. I.A.2. of the Interpretative Communication.

the provisions of the chapter relating to the right of establishment and not those of the chapter relating to services."[168,169]

In addition, the Interpretative Communication made reference to *Commission v. Germany* (one of the four insurance cases already touched upon above),[170] whereby the ECJ also held that "*an insurance undertaking of another member state which maintains a permanent presence in the member state in question comes within the scope of the provisions of the treaty on the right of establishment, even if that presence does not take the form of a branch or agency, but consists merely of an office managed by the undertaking's own staff or by a person who is independent but authorized to act on a permanent basis for the undertaking, as would be the case with an agency.*"[171,172]

Considering such case law, on the one hand, it may be concluded that an office set up on a permanent basis by a foreign insurance company in another country which is engaged in the business of insurance and directly managed by the staff of a foreign insurance company falls within the scope of the right of establishment. Conversely, if such an office is engaged in activities other than insurance activities (such as activities aimed at reconnoitering the local market in view of a subsequent development of the business therein), it does not qualify as a branch for regulatory purposes.[173]

In this respect, it should additionally be recalled that the ECJ maintained that the definition of "*establishment*" cannot be extended with a view to encompassing a subsidiary of an insurance company established in another EU Member State. Most importantly, in *Kvaerner*, the ECJ was specifically confronted with an analysis of the definition of "*establishment*" laid down in Arts. 2(c), 2(d) and 3 of the Second Non-Life Directive (which has been reproduced with a few amendments in the text of the Solvency II Directive). In doing so, the ECJ acknowledged that the concept of "*establishment*" should be interpreted in the broadest sense, whatever the formal term used. Nevertheless, the ECJ then held that "*it cannot (...) be inferred that a subsidiary constitutes a form of permanent presence which must be treated in the same way as an agency or branch and therefore be regarded as an establishment within the meaning of Article 2(c) of the Directive.*"[174] In addition, the ECJ went further by arguing that such

168. ECJ, November 30, 1995, C-55/94, *Reinhard Gebhard v. Consiglio dell'Ordine degli Avvocati e Procuratori di Milano* [2000] ECR I-04165, para. 39.
169. Likewise, in other cases, the ECJ stated that a permanent presence may also be found if the economic activity in another country is carried on "*for an indefinite period*" or "*without a foreseeable limit to its duration.*" *See* ECJ, July 25, 1991, C-221/89, *The Queen v. Secretary of State for Transport, ex parte Factortame Ltd and others* [1991] ECR I-3905, para. 20 and ECJ, October 5, 1988, C-196/87, *Udo Steymann v. Staatssecretaris van Justitie* [1988] ECR 6159, para. 16, respectively.
170. As already outlined above, the position taken by the ECJ therein has been reflected in the second wave of EU Insurance Directives and subsequently restated in the Solvency II Directive.
171. *See* para. I.A.2. of the Interpretative Communication.
172. ECJ, December 4, 1986, C-205/84, *Commission of the European Communities v. Federal Republic of Germany* [1986] ECR 3755, para. 21.
173. This conclusion was reported in the Draft Commission Interpretative Communication on the freedom to provide services and the general good in the insurance sector (97/C 365/04). However, it has been eventually deleted from the final version of the Interpretative Communication.
174. *See* ECJ, June 14, 2001, C-191/99, *Kvaerner plc v. Staatssecretaris van Financiën* [2001] ECR I-04447, para. 39.

an extension would create a problem for an interpretation of the definition of "*subsidiary*" which was enshrined in Art. 1(i) of the Second Non-Life Directive. Consequently, the ECJ concluded that "*in the light of the preceding considerations, the definition of 'establishment' in Article 2(c) of the Directive does not include subsidiaries.*"[175]

On the other hand, an insurance company may be regarded as carrying on an insurance activity in another country under the rules of the right of establishment in the event that such an insurance company has recourse to an independent person in the other country.[176] Nonetheless, in such a case, it appears that, in order to fulfill the condition of a permanent presence, the independent person should not only act on behalf of the foreign undertaking,[177] but he also should do so on a stable and continuous basis.

In such a latter case, in order to assess the elements indicating a permanent presence in another country, according to the EU Commission, some valuable suggestions may be obtained from ECJ case law concerning the interpretation of the concept of a branch in accordance with the Brussels Convention on civil and commercial matters.[178]

In particular, the Interpretative Communication recalled *De Bloos*, whereby the ECJ held that "*one of the essential characteristics of the concepts of branch or agency is the fact of being subject to the direction and control of the parent body.*"[179,180] Furthermore, in *Somafer*, the ECJ—when assessing whether a sole commissionaire could be regarded as a branch, agency or other establishment—also maintained that "*the concept of branch, agency or other establishment implies a place of business which has the appearance of permanency, such as the extension of a parent body, has a management and is materially equipped to negotiate business with third parties so that the latter, although knowing that there will if necessary be a legal link with the parent body, the head office of which is abroad, do not have to deal directly with such parent body but may transact business at the place of business constituting the extension.*"[181,182]

175. *See* ECJ, June 14, 2001, C-191/99, *Kvaerner plc v. Staatssecretaris van Financiën* [2001] ECR I-04447, para. 41.
176. In the Interpretative Communication, the notion of independent person refers to structures that are legally separate from the insurance company they call on, irrespective of their form or designation. To this effect, *see* para. I.A.3.(a) of the Interpretative Communication (footnote 26).
177. The fact that such an independent person acts in its own name or in the name of the foreign undertaking does not appear to be relevant. To this effect, *see* Marco Frigessi di Rattalma, *Diritto e Pratica dell'Assicurazione*, (1989) p. 392 and Giulio Partesotti/Marco Ricolfi, *La nuova disciplina dell'impresa di assicurazione sulla vita in attuazione della Terza Direttiva*, p. 40 and footnotes cited therein.
178. 1968 Brussels Convention on jurisdiction and the enforcement of judgments in civil and commercial matters.
179. *See* para. I.A.3.(a) of the Interpretative Communication.
180. ECJ, October 6, 1976, C-14/76, *A. De Bloos, SPRL v. Société en commandite par actions Bouyer* [1976] ECR 1497, para. 20.
181. ECJ, November 22, 1978, C/33/78, *Somafer SA v. Saar-Ferngas AG* [1978] ECR 2183, para. 12.
182. This line of reasoning has been confirmed in ECJ, April 6, 1995, C-439/93, *Lloyd's Register of Shipping v. Société Campenon Bernard* [1995] ECR I-961, para. 18. Similarly, in case *SAR*

Moreover, in *Blanckaert & Willems*, which concerned a Belgian furniture manufacturer carrying on business in Germany through a local furniture agency, the ECJ held that "*an independent commercial agent who merely negotiates business (...), inasmuch as his legal status leaves him basically free to arrange his own work and decide what proportion of his time to devote to the interests of the undertaking which he agrees to represent and whom that undertaking may not prevent from representing at the same time several firms competing in the same manufacturing or marketing sector, and who, moreover, merely transmits orders to the parent undertaking without being involved in either their terms or their execution, does not have the character of a branch, agency or other establishment.*"[183]

At last, in addition to such case law, the Interpretative Communication also referred to the Opinion of Advocate-General Darmon in *Shearson Lehman Hutton*[184] and to the report on the Brussels Convention on civil and commercial matters prepared by Mr. Jenard[185] to corroborate the reasoning that there is a branch, agency or other establishment in the event the foreign company is represented by an intermediary having the power to enter into binding contracts with third parties.[186]

In the light of all the foregoing, irrespective of whether the intermediary is a natural person or a legal person, the EU Commission clarified that—in order to fall within the scope of the right of establishment—such an independent person must meet the following three cumulative conditions:[187]

(1) He must be subject to the direction and control of the insurance company he represents.
(2) He must be able to commit the insurance company.
(3) He must have received a permanent brief.

As a result, according to the EU Commission, it is only where the independent person cumulatively fulfils all such requirements—and therefore acts as a genuine extension of the insurance company in the host country—that the operations of such an insurance company fall within the scope of the rules governing the right of establishment.[188] To put it in other words, it clearly emerged that—in line with ECJ case

Schotte, the ECJ held that the jurisdiction with respect to a branch, agency or other establishment under Art. 5, para. 5, of the Brussels Convention on civil and commercial matters may be extended to the case of a company which "*maintains no dependent branch, agency or other establishment in another contracting state but nevertheless pursues its activities there through an independent company with the same name and identical management which negotiates and conducts business in its name and which it uses as an extension of itself.*" *See* ECJ, December 9, 1987, C-218/86, *SAR Schotte GmbH v. Parfums Rothschild SARL* [1987] ECR 4905, para. 17.

183. ECJ, March 18, 1981, C-139/80, *Blanckaert & Willems PVBA v. Luise Trost* [1981] ECR 819, para. 13.
184. *See* Opinion of Advocate-General Darmon on ECJ, January 19, 1993, C-89/91, *Shearson Lehmann Hutton Inc. v. TVB Treuhandgesellschaft für Vermögensverwaltung und Beteiligungen mbH* [1993] ECR-I 139, delivered on October 27, 1992, point 45.
185. *See* Official Journal of the European Communities, C 59, Volume 22, March 5, 1979, p. 31.
186. *See* para. I.A.3.(a) of the Interpretative Communication.
187. *See* para. I.A.3.(a) of the Interpretative Communication.
188. *See* para. I.A.3.(a) of the Interpretative Communication.

law—any such criterion cannot be considered in isolation for the purposes of determining the right of establishment. Rather, it is essential for the independent person in the host country to be subject to the direction and control of the insurance company, empowered to act as a representative on a permanent basis and able to commit the foreign insurance company when concluding insurance contracts.[189]

Starting with the condition (1), the Interpretative Communication clarified that it should be ascertained whether—in the light of the links established between the insurance company and the independent person—the latter has sufficient freedom to organize his activities, to decide how much time he will devote to the insurance company and, particularly, to represent competitors at the very same time.[190]

In this regard, the EU Commission argued that an exclusive brief granted to an independent person may be construed as an indication that such an intermediary is subject to the direction and control of the foreign insurance company.[191,192] However, the principle of exclusiveness does not appear to be a decisive criterion insomuch as the ECJ excluded the application of the rules on the right of establishment "*when the grantee of an exclusive sales concession is subject neither to the control nor to the direction of the grantor.*"[193] What is more, a full reliance on the principle of exclusiveness would also exclude independent persons from falling within the scope of the right of establishment simply to the extent that they work for more than one company. As a result, the existence of an exclusive mandate may indicate that an independent person is under the direction and the control of a foreign insurance company, but this must always be assessed in accordance to the nature and the extent of the functions assigned to such an intermediary.[194]

Furthermore, where an independent person represents a number of different insurance companies (typically, with regard to different classes of insurance products), the Interpretative Communication clarified that the first condition concerning an intermediary to be subject to the direction and control of the insurance company he represents may be fulfilled in respect of the insurance company which has given him an exclusive mandate. As a result, insomuch as the remaining two conditions are also satisfied, such an insurance company would need to be authorized in the host country

189. To this effect, *see* the Opinion of the Economic and Social Committee on the Draft Interpretative Communication on the freedom to provide services and the general good in the insurance sector (98/C 407/08).
190. *See* para. I.A.3.(a)(i) of the Interpretative Communication.
191. *See* para. I.A.3.(a)(i) of the Interpretative Communication.
192. In a similar vein, *see also* Marco Frigessi di Rattalma, *Diritto e Pratica dell'Assicurazione*, (1989) p. 392.
193. *See* ECJ, October 6, 1976, C-14/76, *A. De Bloos, SPRL v. Société en commandite par actions Bouyer* [1976] ECR 1497, para. 23. This line of reasoning appears to be confirmed in ECJ, March 18, 1981, C-139/80, *Blanckaert & Willems PVBA v. Luise Trost* [1981] ECR 819 and in ECJ, January 19, 1993, C-89/91, *Shearson Lehmann Hutton Inc. v. TVB Treuhandgesellschaft für Vermögensverwaltung und Beteiligungen mbH* [1993] ECR-I 139.
194. To this effect, *see* the Opinion of the Economic and Social Committee on the Draft Interpretative Communication on the freedom to provide services and the general good in the insurance sector (98/C 407/08) and Ernesto Pucci in: Marco Prosperetti/Alessandro Colavolpe (eds.) *Le Assicurazioni*, pp. 66-67.

under the rules of the right of establishment. By contrast, the remaining insurance companies would be subject to the rules governing the freedom to provide services.[195]

With respect to the condition (2), the Interpretative Communication made clear that—in order to assess whether this condition is satisfied—it should be ascertained whether the acts and decisions of the independent person can commit the insurance company vis-à-vis third parties in such a way that the latter may conclude business with such an independent person with no need to contact the insurance company itself.[196]

This commitment stems primarily from the brief given to the independent person to conclude insurance contracts on behalf and for the account of the foreign insurance company.[197] As a result, specific attention should be paid to the main elements of the brief given by the insurance company to the independent person. For instance, in a situation where the independent person can make an offer containing all the essential features of the prospective insurance contract, but the foreign insurance company can still refuse any such offer submitted by the intermediary and signed by the customer, condition *b*) is not satisfied. As opposed to this, the power granted to the intermediary to accept and settle a claim may show the intention of the insurance company to be directly committed to the relevant policyholder.[198]

Regarding the condition *c*), the Interpretative Communication took the view that the capacity of the independent person to commit an insurance company must be based on a long-term, continuous brief rather than a brief which is limited in time or a one-off instruction.[199]

In this respect, the EU Commission additionally clarified that an insurance company which—for the purposes of carrying on insurance business temporarily and occasionally in another EU Member State—has recourse to independent persons established in that other EU Member State may still be subject to the rules governing the freedom to provide services. Indeed, the Commission took the opinion that any such insurance company must be able to use certain services in the host country to carry on its activities. For example, the EU Commission clarified that an insurance company operating under the freedom to provide services must be able to use:[200]

- a local expert to assess the risks to be covered under the freedom to provide services;
- a local expert to assess damage caused under risks covered by insurance contracts negotiated under the freedom to provide services;

195. *See* para. I.A.3.(a)(i) of the Interpretative Communication.
196. *See* para. I.A.3.(a)(ii) of the Interpretative Communication.
197. Although the EU Commission did not adopt a clear stance on the use of insurance brokers in concluding insurance contracts, it would appear that—in view of their professional activities—insurance brokers can only be considered to come under the freedom to provide services. To this effect, *see* the Opinion of the Economic and Social Committee on the Draft Interpretative Communication on the freedom to provide services and the general good in the insurance sector (98/C 407/08).
198. *See* para. I.A.3.(a)(ii) of the Interpretative Communication.
199. *See* para. I.A.3.(a)(iii) of the Interpretative Communication.
200. *See* para. I.A.3.(a)(iii) of the Interpretative Communication.

- canvassers who do not conclude insurance contracts and whose activity is limited to sending insurance offers received from potential policyholders to the insurance company for acceptance;
- local legal services, medical or actuarial services established in the host country;
- a permanent structure for collecting the premiums for insurance contracts entered into under the freedom to provide services;
- a permanent structure for receiving notices of claims relating to insurance contracts concluded under the freedom to provide services for transmission to the insurance company for a decision to accept or refuse each claim; and
- a permanent structure for managing files relating to claims.

Furthermore, similar to what has already been outlined in respect of an office directly managed by the staff of the insurance company, the Interpretative Communication clearly pointed out that—in order to fall within the scope of the right of establishment—the brief given to the independent person should concern the activities that are part of the insurance company's objects, namely the business of insurance. Hence, a brief given to an independent person to carry on activities other than insurance cannot be taken into consideration when assessing the arrangements for carrying on insurance activities in the host country. For instance, a brief given to an investment company to manage a securities portfolio or a brief given to a real estate company to manage real estate held by the insurance company in the host country do not give rise to a permanent presence in the host country.[201] By the same token, it may be argued that, irrespective of their appointment on a permanent basis, a fiscal representative and a representative for the management of claims required to comply with applicable rules for the purposes of carrying on insurance business in the host country by way of provision of services do not represent an establishment of the foreign insurance company in the host country.[202]

The Interpretative Communication then addressed a few questions raised by the recent technological developments which affected the insurance business. At first, the EU Commission touched upon the case of electronic machines, to be intended as fixed, ATM-type electronic machines capable of performing insurance activities. In doing so, the EU Commission acknowledged that such machines may be covered by the rules governing the right of establishment in the case where they fulfill the three conditions listed above. However, the Interpretative Communication clarified that such machines are unlikely to be the only place of business of an insurance company in a certain country. In fact, it is more likely that such machines are attached to a branch or agency in the same country. In that case, any such machine cannot be regarded as an entity in its own right to the extent that it is covered by the rules governing the establishment to which it is related. Conversely, in a situation where any such machine constitutes the only presence of an insurance company in a certain country, the EU Commission took

201. *See* para. I.A.3.(a)(iii) of the Interpretative Communication.
202. *See* Giulio Partesotti/Marco Ricolfi, *La nuova disciplina dell'impresa di assicurazione sulla vita in attuazione della Terza Direttiva*, p. 39 and footnotes cited therein.

the view that it may be possible to treat it as a provision of services in the host country.[203]

In addition, the EU Commission also tackled the use of remote means of communication (such as a telephone, a fax, the press, and so forth) and particularly via electronic commerce (e.g., via the Internet) to conclude insurance contracts covering a risk or a commitment situated in a country other than that of establishment. In this specific regard, the EU Commission acknowledged that, while the insurance activity is usually carried on by the insurance company in the country of establishment, the initiative for the conclusion of such insurance contracts—in most cases—comes from the prospective policyholder, who makes use of his own equipment to contact and to seek to conclude an insurance contract electronically with an insurance company willing to do so. In this context, as already outlined above in the case of the "*self-procurement,*" the location of the risk or the commitment covered by an insurance contract is the fundamental element for the purposes of determining the rules applicable to any such insurance transaction. Hence, the EU Commission took the view that, in accordance with the existing regulatory framework, insurance activities carried on via electronic commerce (e.g., via the Internet) and covering a risk or a commitment situated in an EU Member State other than that of establishment are subject to the provisions relating to the freedom to provide services.[204]

On the other hand, the EU Commission also took the view that the use of electronic commerce for the sole purposes of advertising, providing commercial information or enhancing awareness of the insurance company cannot be regarded as insurance activities.[205] Nonetheless, it has been contended that this situation should require closer analysis, particularly in cases where the advertisement constitutes commercial canvassing, ranking as an actual invitation, issued at a distance, to enter into a contract or where it precedes a physical journey by the supplier with a view of concluding a contract. For this reason, it has been submitted that the EU Commission could have looked more closely at situations where an advertisement contains the intention to conclude an insurance contract, such as where there is a reference to telephone numbers, postal and e-mail accounts, Internet websites, markets on which the insurance products are available, and so forth.[206]

In the light of all the foregoing, it may be argued that, in the case where an insurance company carries on insurance business in a country other than that of establishment through an actual presence therein, the decisive condition to make a distinction between the right of establishment and the freedom to provide services lies on the (temporary or permanent) nature of such a presence in the host country. On the contrary, when the insurance company carries on insurance business in a country other than that of establishment with no actual movement in the host country, the temporary or permanent character of the activities cannot be regarded in isolation as

203. *See* para. I.A.3.(b) of the Interpretative Communication.
204. *See* para. I.A.6.(a) of the Interpretative Communication.
205. *See* para. I.A.6.(b) of the Interpretative Communication.
206. To this effect, *see* the Opinion of the Economic and Social Committee on the Draft Interpretative Communication on the freedom to provide services and the general good in the insurance sector (98/C 407/08).

the pivotal element to make such a distinction. Rather, reference should be made to the cumulative fulfillment of all requirements outlined above.[207]

This clearly shows that the EU Commission intended to adopt a more flexible approach vis-à-vis the pattern depicted by the ECJ case law. Indeed, it appears as if—in border-line circumstances—the analysis should be focused on the question as to whether the insurance company has the intention to establish a structure in the territory of the host country.[208] However, in doing so, specific attention should be paid not to leave aside a guiding principle established by the ECJ and confirmed by the EU Commission, which requires any recharacterization of the regime applicable to be based on the identification of an attempt by the insurance company to circumvent national rules which would be applicable in the host country.[209]

After all, in the case that there is no actual movement of an insurance company in the host country, any distinction between the right of establishment and the freedom to provide services to be made only on the basis of the temporary or permanent character of the activities does not appear to be neither logical nor in line with juridical principles. As a matter of fact, any such reasoning would eventually lead to the conclusion that an insurance company has an establishment in the country where the services are actually rendered and—as a consequence—would require the insurance company to create a fictitious establishment in such a country.[210]

This also holds true in the case that the insurance activities are carried on in the host country through a local intermediary, also considering that—to some extent—a provision of services cannot be rendered without a number of preparatory or auxiliary activities which do not specifically concern the business of insurance. This reasoning has been acknowledged by the EU Commission to the extent that the Interpretative Communication clarified that an independent person may give rise to an establishment of the insurance company in the host country only in a situation where such an independent person carries on insurance activities. It follows that, in order to ascertain whether the activities entrusted to an independent person may create an establishment in the host country, a qualitative assessment (rather than a quantitative assessment) of such activities should be conducted.[211]

The flexible approach adopted by the EU Commission has been finally reflected in respect of the development in the field of IT to the extent that the Interpretative Communication clarified that the use of remote means of communication (particularly, the electronic commerce) to conclude insurance contracts should be regarded as insurance business carried on under the freedom to provide services with no actual movement on the part of the contracting parties.[212]

207. Diana Cerini, *Diritto ed Economia dell'Assicurazione*, (1999) p. 169.
208. Diana Cerini, *Diritto ed Economia dell'Assicurazione*, (1999) p. 169.
209. *See* para. I.A.1.(b) of the Interpretative Communication and footnotes cited therein.
210. *See* Diana Cerini, *Diritto ed Economia dell'Assicurazione*, (1999) p. 170.
211. *See* Diana Cerini, *Diritto ed Economia dell'Assicurazione*, (1999) pp. 170 et seq.
212. The legal framework for information society services has been set out by the Directive 2000/31/EC of the European Parliament and of the Council of 8 June 2000 on certain legal aspects of information society services, in particular electronic commerce, in the Internal Market (the E-Commerce Directive). However, the E-Commerce Directive provided for a specific carve-out for insurance activities carried on by insurance companies falling under the

2.1.4 The Swiss Insurance Regulation

Switzerland was among the first European countries to introduce a comprehensive public system for the supervision of private insurance business. Such a supervision is mainly rooted in a legislation which has been shaped in the course of the twentieth century. Over time, the ongoing development of the insurance regulation brought into life five legislative acts, 11 ordinances and several unpublished directives at the departmental and office level which ended up with the creation of a rather complicated supervisory system.[213] Therefore, in order to simplify the previously highly fragmented supervision framework, the Swiss Federal Council recently decided to consolidate the previous acts and ordinances into the following measures:

- the Federal Law on the Supervision of Insurance Companies (ISL);[214] and
- the Ordinance on the Supervision of Insurance Companies (ISO).[215]

The ISL has the character of a framework enactment focused on securing the long-term stability of insurance companies, improving the protection of policyholders, and incorporating the most important supervisory developments in the EU. Most importantly, it lays down principles in many areas and leaves the specification of the details in a wide range of matters at the ordinance level. In doing so, the ISL has assigned a whole series of complex and elaborated new areas and responsibilities to the insurance supervision, which necessarily entails a detailed regulation.[216]

The ISO—as lastly revised in 2015 on the themes of solvency models, qualitative risk management, e.g., requirements for directors, the ORSA, disclosure, insurance technical reserves, the supervision of insurance brokers and some additional minor amendments—governs in greater detail the supervision of private insurance companies and insurance activity in Switzerland.[217]

The Swiss supervisory landscape is integrated by the FINMA's Insurance Supervision Ordinance (ISO-FINMA)[218]—as lastly revised in 2015 to introduce a minimum structure of the balance sheet and income statement and a presentation of business activities in the annual financial statements to take better account of the specifics of the insurance business and improve transparency regarding the financial situation of

scope of the EU Insurance Directives (now transposed in the Solvency II Directive). Therefore, with respect to the conditions to carry on cross-border electronic insurance activities under the freedom to provide services in the internal market, an insurance company is subject to the provisions which are now enshrined in the Solvency II Directive.

213. *See* Vincent Brulhart, *Droit des assurances privées* (Bern: Stämpfli Editions SA, 2008) p. 28.
214. In Italian, "*Legge federale sulla sorveglianza delle imprese di assicurazione del 17 dicembre 2004,*" which entered into force on January 1, 2006.
215. In Italian, "*Ordinanza sulla sorveglianza delle imprese di assicurazione private del 9 novembre 2005,*" which entered into force on January 1, 2006.
216. For further details, *see* information available online at www.finma.ch.
217. For further details, *see* information available online at www.finma.ch.
218. In Italian, "*Ordinanza dell'Autorità federale di vigilanza sui mercati finanziari sulla sorveglianza delle imprese di assicurazione private del 9 novembre 2005,*" which entered into force on January 1, 2006.

insurance companies—which is intended to define in more detail certain provisions of the ISL and the ISO.[219]

In addition, the Swiss supervisory authority makes use of circulars to explain how it applies financial market legislation in carrying out its supervisory activities. The main aim of the circulars is to ensure that the supervisory authority applies financial market legislation consistently and appropriately. Such circulars clarify partially defined legal norms and define how FINMA will exercise its available discretion.[220] While FINMA circulars do not require an explicit basis in formal legislation, their content must be linked to an overarching legal provision. FINMA can decide whether or not to use circulars to define its practice. Before issuing a circular, FINMA usually runs a consultation for the relevant stakeholders. On the top of this, FINMA also publishes a collection of key rulings and decisions based on the applicable financial market law and in accordance with the relevant circulars.[221]

In the context of such a supervisory background,[222] a license to engage in the business of insurance is generally required for: (*i*) Swiss insurance companies which write direct insurance or reinsurance and (*ii*) insurance companies established abroad in respect of their insurance activities conducted in Switzerland or conducted from Switzerland, subject to any contrary provisions laid down in international treaties.[223,224] To this effect, an insurance activity is deemed to exist in Switzerland, regardless of the type of contract and where it is concluded, in the event that: (*i*) a natural person or a legal entity domiciled in Switzerland is among the policyholders or insured persons or (*ii*) property located in Switzerland is insured.[225,226]

On the contrary, insurance companies established in a foreign country and Swiss branches of foreign insurance companies which only engage in reinsurance in Switzerland may carry on such reinsurance business in Switzerland without a license.[227] In addition, insurance companies established in a foreign country which do not have a branch in Switzerland are not subject to supervision in Switzerland in the event that they only provide coverage for: (*i*) risks in connection with marine transport, air transport and cross-border transportation, (*ii*) risks located outside Switzerland, or (*iii*) war risks.[228] Furthermore, insomuch as special circumstances justify it, the Swiss

219. For further details, *see* information available online at www.finma.ch.
220. For instance, FINMA has recently published a number of new and revised insurance circulars to adjust its implementing provisions following the revision of the ISO and the ISO-FINMA.
221. For further details, *see* information available online at www.finma.ch.
222. For an overview of the Swiss regulatory provisions, *see* Evan M. Spangler, *Swiss Supervisory Laws and Regulations for the Business of Insurance* (Bern: Stämpfli Editions SA, 2010) pp. 1 et seq.
223. *See* Arts. 2, para. 1, and 3, para. 1, of the ISL.
224. In addition, insurance intermediaries are subject to the supervision under the ISL and, under some circumstances, are required to register with FINMA. Insurance groups and insurance conglomerates may also be subject to supervision by FINMA.
225. *See* Art. 1, para. 1, of the ISO.
226. It is worth noting that this provision prohibits the practice of "*self-procurement*" by impeding a Swiss resident from obtaining an insurance contract from an unlicensed insurance company outside Switzerland.
227. *See* Art. 2, para. 2, of the ISL.
228. *See* Art. 1, para. 2, of the ISO.

supervisory authority may also exempt from supervision insurance companies that transact insurance business which is of a slight economic importance or which affects only a small group of policyholders.[229]

With this in mind, it is worth noting that a license is required for each line of business an insurance company is intended to write. What is more, a license to write a line of direct insurance business also includes a license to write reinsurance for the very same line.[230] However, on the one hand, life insurance companies cannot write non-life insurance business and, on the other hand, non-life insurance companies cannot write life insurance business. In addition, in principle, Swiss insurance or reinsurance companies may only engage in insurance business and activities which are directly related to the insurance business, but FINMA can approve the conduct of other activities to the extent that such latter activities do not jeopardize the interests of the policyholders.[231]

The licensing requirements are essentially the same for Swiss and foreign insurance companies. Specifically, in addition to the requirements prescribed for Swiss insurance companies[232] and subject to any contrary provisions laid down in international treaties, a foreign insurance company wishing to transact insurance business in or from Switzerland must:[233]

- be licensed in its jurisdiction of incorporation;
- establish a branch in Switzerland and appoint a general representative to manage the branch who is authorized to bind the insurance company;[234]
- have in its home country a solvency margin compliant with the requirements of the ISL;
- establish an organizational fund in Switzerland compliant with the requirements of the ISL; and
- provide a security deposit in Switzerland in an amount equal to the share of the solvency margin attributable to the insurance business written in or from Switzerland.

It follows that a foreign insurance organization wishing to transact insurance business in or from Switzerland—and therefore required to obtain an insurance license in Switzerland—must either establish a subsidiary which is organized under the laws of Switzerland or establish a Swiss branch compliant with a number of local requirements.[235]

229. *See* Art. 2, para. 3, of the ISL.
230. *See* Art. 3, para. 5, of the ISO.
231. *See* Art. 11, paras. 1 and 2, of the ISL.
232. *See* Art. 4, para. 2, of the ISL.
233. *See* Art. 15, paras. 1 and 2, of the ISL.
234. For additional specific requirements of the general representative, *see* Arts. 16 et seq. of the ISO.
235. In this respect, it is also worth noting that, under Art. 20, para. 1, of the ISO, foreign insurance companies carrying on their activities from Switzerland exclusively abroad must prove that (*i*) they are authorized to carry on insurance business in their home countries, and (*ii*) the supervisory authorities of their home countries agree with the establishment of a branch in Switzerland.

With specific respect to the establishment of a Swiss branch, it is worth noting that neither Swiss insurance law nor Swiss company law provide for a specific definition of a Swiss branch of a foreign company. On this point, among others, the Federal Law on Private International Law (the Swiss PIL Act)[236] acknowledges a general principle that a foreign company may have a branch in Switzerland.[237] Nonetheless, this provision is only intended to designate the applicable law in certain matters regarding a branch of a foreign company with no specific legal definition as such. Hence, it has been submitted that the notion of "*branch*" to be used for foreign companies may be assimilated to that provided for branches of Swiss companies.[238]

To this effect, even though there is no legal definition for a branch of a Swiss company either, some clarification may be found in the jurisprudence. In particular, the Swiss Supreme Federal Court has maintained that the term "*branch*" may be intended as a business establishment that—while being part, from a legal point of view, of the head office from which it depends—carries on in its premises an activity similar to that of the latter and has in this respect a certain economic and operational independence.[239] It follows that a branch[240] may be regarded as a business establishment which is characterized by the following two essential features:[241]

(1) a certain economic and operational independence vis-à-vis the head office; and
(2) a juridical dependence vis-à-vis the head office.

As to the former, moving from the case law of the Swiss Supreme Federal Court, it has been submitted that the branch must be territorially separated from the head office. It must also have its own permanent management and, in principle, its own staff to carry on its activities on an ongoing basis. In addition, the branch must also have its own independence in terms of external relationships with third parties (a so-called *direct access to the market*) and a certain economic and commercial independence with respect to internal relationships with the head office. At last, the branch must also be engaged in activities of a similar nature to that of the head office to create a single economic structure with the latter.[242] By contrast, from a legal perspective, the branch still forms part of a single legal entity together with the head office. To put it in other

236. In Italian, "*Legge federale sul diritto internazionale privato (LDIP) del 18 dicembre 1987,*" which entered into force on January 1, 1989.
237. *See* Art. 160 of the Swiss PIL Act.
238. *See* Arthur Meier-Hayoz/Peter Forstmoser/Peter Iordanov, *Droit Suisse des sociétés* (Bern: Stämpfli Editions SA, 2015) p. 867.
239. *See* Arthur Meier-Hayoz/Peter Forstmoser/Peter Iordanov, *Droit Suisse des sociétés*, pp. 862-863 and case law cited therein.
240. In German, "*Geschäftsbetriebe.*" *See* Arthur Meier-Hayoz/Peter Forstmoser/Peter Iordanov, *Droit Suisse des sociétés*, p. 863.
241. *See* Arthur Meier-Hayoz/Peter Forstmoser/Peter Iordanov, *Droit Suisse des sociétés*, p. 863.
242. *See* Arthur Meier-Hayoz/Peter Forstmoser/Peter Iordanov, *Droit Suisse des sociétés*, pp. 863-864 and case law cited therein.

terms, as opposed to the case of a subsidiary, the branch does not have a separate legal personality, distinct from that of the head office.[243]

That being said, at international level, it is worth noting that—although Switzerland is not an EU Member State and thus EU measures outlined in the previous sections cannot be applied in its territory—it has concluded a bilateral agreement with the EU regarding non-life insurance services.[244,245] Such an agreement, which entered into force on January 1, 1993, secured freedom of establishment for Swiss insurance companies engaged in the non-life insurance business in all EU Member States and vice versa.[246,247] In order to do so, with respect to the conditions of access, such an agreement provides for the application of the territoriality principle. This means that, for instance, a Swiss insurance company wishing to set up an agency or branch in the territory of an EU Member State requires prior authorization by the relevant supervisory authority of the host EU Member State.[248] Nevertheless, it is fair to say that, in general, the conditions required for the purposes of such an authorization are less burdensome vis-à-vis the requirements to be complied with by insurance companies established in third countries.[249]

In addition, Switzerland concluded an international agreement with the Principality of Liechtenstein on direct insurance.[250] Among others, such an agreement, which entered into force on July 9, 1998, was aimed at establishing the substantive requirements in view of guaranteeing—on a reciprocal basis—insurance companies of one contracting party the freedom of establishment and the freedom to provide direct insurance services in the other country.[251,252] As such, under the conditions of the agreement, Swiss insurance companies may benefit from the freedom of establishment in the Principality of Liechtenstein and the freedom to provide direct insurance services therein. To this end, insurance companies are required to obtain a license issued in their home country, which is valid in both countries.[253] Once authorized, the license

243. *See* Arthur Meier-Hayoz/Peter Forstmoser/Peter Iordanov, *Droit Suisse des sociétés*, p. 864 and case law cited therein.
244. Agreement between the European Economic Community and the Swiss Confederation concerning direct insurance other than the life insurance concluded in Luxembourg on October 10, 1989.
245. In the context of the EU, this international agreement has been approved with the Council Decision 91/370/EEC of 20 June 1991 and implemented by means of the Council Directive 91/371/EEC and Council Regulation 2155/91, both issued on the very same date of approval.
246. The kinds of insurance not covered by this agreement as well as any point or question not specifically governed by the provisions of the agreement remain subject to the applicable domestic law.
247. On January 24, 2019, Switzerland and the UK signed a bilateral agreement on direct insurance other than life assurance to ensure the continuation of the current regulations in these areas even after the UK has left the EU.
248. *See* Art. 7, para. 2, of the agreement.
249. *See* Arts. 10 et seq. of the agreement.
250. In German, "*Abkommen zwischen der Schweizerischen Eidgenossenschaft und dem Fürstentum Liechtenstein betreffend die Direktversicherung sowie die Versicherungsvermittlung,*" concluded in Bern on December 19, 1996.
251. *See* Art. 1.a), of the agreement.
252. According to Art. 2.a), this agreement is applicable to insurance companies only. As a consequence, it is not applicable to reinsurance companies or social insurance schemes.
253. *See* Art. 1 of the annex to the agreement.

holders remain subject to supervision of the regulatory authority in their home country, not only with respect to the domestic insurance activities but also in respect of the activities carried on under the freedom of establishment and the freedom to provide services in the other country.[254]

Lastly, a word needs to be said about the fact that a few years ago Switzerland has hosted the conclusion of the Revised Lugano Convention,[255,256] which governs issues of jurisdiction and enforcement of judgments between the EU Member States and the EFTA countries other than Liechtenstein.[257] In this respect, although the allocation of jurisdiction among different countries is beyond the scope of this research, it should be borne in mind that this international agreement—which serves the purpose of extending the Brussel Regime to EFTA Member States[258]—provides for special jurisdictional rules in respect of matters relating to insurance.[259]

2.2 OVERVIEW OF THE INSURANCE VALUE CHAIN

2.2.1 Background of the Analysis

An analysis of the insurance value chain may provide significant hints in view of ascertaining how much and at which stage value is added by an insurance company to its products. To this end, the present analysis is intended to scrutinize the main functions of an insurance company—with a specific focus on the KERT functions—for the purposes of answering the research question as to whether the identification of such KERT functions in the context of the first step of the AOA may potentially affect the currently existing standards for determining the existence of a dependent agent permanent establishment under Art. 5 of the model treaties in Chapter 6.

Against this background, at the outset, it is worth noting that, in general, a value chain may be regarded as the whole range of internal processes, functions and activities—including design, production, marketing and distribution—companies generally go through in order to bring a product or a service from an initial stage of conception to the final stages of delivery and support to the costumers.[260]

Clearly, the value chain and the underlying functions mainly depend on the specific industry a certain company is involved in. For instance, with respect to

254. *See* Art. 3, para. 1, of the annex to the agreement.
255. Convention on jurisdiction and the recognition and enforcement of judgments in civil and commercial matters concluded in Lugano on October 30, 2007, which replaced the previous Lugano Convention of September 16, 1988.
256. In the context of the EU, this international agreement has been approved with the Council Decision 2009/430/EC of 27 November 2008.
257. The Swiss Federal Council is also the official depository for the Revised Lugano Convention, including information on its ratification.
258. The Brussels Regime is a set of rules regulating which courts have jurisdiction in legal disputes of a civil or commercial nature which has been introduced by the 1968 Brussels Convention on jurisdiction and the enforcement of judgments in civil and commercial matters, replaced by the Council Regulation No. 44/2001 of 22 December 2000 and by the Regulation No. 1215/2012 of the European Parliament and of the Council of 12 December 2012.
259. To this effect, *see* Arts. 8-14 of this agreement.
260. For the purposes of this analysis, which is patterned after the functional analysis contained in the 2010 OECD Report, Part IV, the insurance value chain will be scrutinized in terms of

companies that produce goods, the value chain generally starts with the purchase of raw materials used to make their products, and consists of every activity that is performed in view of selling such goods to the final customers. On the other hand, in the context of a service industry, and particularly in the insurance industry, the value chain will look very different from that of a manufacturing industry to the extent that the creation of the added value for the final customers is also different.[261]

As a matter of fact, insurance companies are complex organizations characterized by a number of peculiarities which exert influence on the organizational structure, as well as on the strategic and the business processes.[262] In particular, the main feature of the insurance industry is the inversion of the expense-revenue cycle to the extent that—as opposed to other industries where the recognition of revenues is usually the final stage of the production cycle—the collection of premiums should be regarded as the starting point of the production cycle. To put it in other terms, the production cycle of an insurance company is inverted insomuch as the collection of premiums precedes the payment of potential claims and benefits.[263]

As such, the inversion of the production cycle significantly affects the economic pattern of an insurance company, along with its financial statements and equity capital. Indeed, the collection of premiums prior to the payment of potential claims and benefits requires the insurance company to account for a number of estimated items in the financial statements, such as technical provisions measured at the best estimate plus a risk margin. On the other hand, this kind of production cycle should—in principle—serve as a source of self-financing for the insurance company, except for unforeseen circumstances that may jeopardize such a mechanism. In such a latter case, the equity capital—which is subject to strict forms of regulation—may come to the rescue of an insurance company to restore an economic and financial balance.[264]

What is more, the inversion of the production cycle also has an influence on the functional structure of insurance companies. Indeed, such an inversion implies that insurance companies have a significant amount of cash available stemming from the upfront collection of premiums, which must be actively and professionally managed to cover future potential claims and benefits, administrative expenses and eventually profits to shareholders. For this reason, besides the activities related to the insurance technical management, insurance companies are also characterized by a significant role of the activities related to the management of the investments covering their

operational functions. The analysis of the internal processes and the integration of such processes with the functions performed in the form of an organizational matrix is beyond the scope of this research.

261. *See* Leonardo Felician, *La catena del valore nelle imprese di assicurazione* (Trieste: Edizioni Goliardiche, 2007) pp. 30 et seq.
262. For an overview of the strategic and business processes of an insurance company, *see*—among others—Luigi Selleri, *Economia delle imprese di assicurazioni* (Milano: Giuffrè, 1965) pp. 67 et seq., Luigi Selleri, *Economia e management delle imprese di assicurazione* (Milano: Etas libri, 1991) ch. 4, Luigi Selleri, *Impresa di assicurazione e strategie di valore* (Milano: Etas libri, 2003) ch. 4, and Andrea Bellucci, *Strategia, gestione del rischio e creazione di valore nelle imprese assicurative* (Torino: Giappichelli, 2014) pp. 17 et seq.
263. *See* Antonello Di Mascio, *Le imprese di assicurazione: il nuovo modello di gestione* (Milano: Egea, 2001) ch. 3.
264. *See* Antonello Di Mascio, *Le imprese di assicurazione: il nuovo modello di gestione*, ch. 3.

reserves and capital, which is gaining more and more importance over the recent years.[265]

It follows that the simultaneous existence of the activities related to the insurance technical management and the activities related to the management of investments covering technical reserves and capital, which are highly interrelated and complementary over the production cycle of the insurance business, characterizes the functional structure of an insurance company and brings about specific functions that may be found when analyzing an insurance company vis-à-vis other industrial, commercial or financial entities.[266]

In addition, the functions performed by an insurance company and the relative importance of those functions to the profitability of any such a company also depend on a number of factors, including the type of insurance business (namely, life, non-life, or reinsurance), the line of business and the insurance products sold on the market.[267] On the top of this, it should be stressed that the relative importance of the functions may also largely vary on the basis of the particular facts and circumstances characterizing the specific insurance company under analysis.[268]

With this in mind, the following analysis—patterned after the functional analysis contained in the 2010 OECD Report, Part IV—is intended to provide an overview of the most important functions that may be found in a traditional insurance business,[269] starting with the development of an insurance product to the management of investments covering insurance technical reserves. Specifically, the functions dealt with in the next sections will be the following:

- product development;
- sales and marketing;
- underwriting;
- risk management;
- contract and claims management;
- asset management; and
- support functions.

It goes without saying that such functions cannot be regarded in isolation to the extent that such functions are interdependent, that is to say (horizontally and vertically) integrated in such a way so as to achieve, maintain and possibly further develop a competitive advantage vis-à-vis the competitors through their coordination and optimization. However, for the purposes of this research, the following sections will

265. *See* Antonello Di Mascio, *Le imprese di assicurazione: il nuovo modello di gestione*, ch. 3.
266. For an overview of the key operational drivers of such technical and investment activities, *see*—among others—Antonello Di Mascio, *Le imprese di assicurazione: il nuovo modello di gestione*, ch. 3, Andrea Bellucci, *Le imprese di assicurazione. Profili gestionali, organizzativi e contabili* (Torino: Giappichelli, 2004) pp. 126 et seq. and Andrea Bellucci, *Strategia, gestione del rischio e creazione di valore nelle imprese assicurative*, pp. 90 et seq.
267. *See* 2010 OECD Report, Part IV, para. 23.
268. *See* 2010 OECD Report, Part IV, para. 25.
269. In this regard, it should be noted that this does not attempt to be a definitive analysis to the extent that other functions might also have a significant role in the context of the insurance business.

provide an overview of each function separately, whereas the final section will delve into the concept of KERT functions in the context of the insurance industry.

2.2.2 The Main Functions of an Insurance Business

2.2.2.1 Product Development

The first stage of the insurance value chain is the technical, legal and mathematical structuring of insurance products,[270] which is preliminary to all remaining activities.[271]

This presupposes *in primis* a thorough analysis of the competition, the market and the underlying trends.[272] Particularly, in the insurance market—which is a mature market—it is rather difficult to develop a brand-new product. Therefore, it is of paramount importance to carry on a benchmark analysis in order to assess the market offer and the positioning of the competitors and—as a consequence—understand their competitive advantages, if any. This benchmark analysis may then pave the way for the purposes of developing a unique selling proposition to stand out from competition to the extent that a me-too-strategy is usually not successful.[273]

An analysis of the market demand is also important to the extent that it sometimes allows an insurance company to discover opportunities (such as market niches) that have been overlooked by the competitors and therefore would not otherwise come up from an extensive analysis of the competition. In doing so, it is also useful to scrutinize foreign markets since ideas successfully introduced in other countries could represent game changers when replicated in other markets. When assessing innovative products, insurance companies should aim at properly understanding customers' needs and developing an original business model. To this end, insurance companies sometimes outsource market studies and focus groups[274] to third parties to better understand what the reaction of potential customers might be.[275]

Similarly, an analysis of the emerging trends—among others, the aging population, the advent of the digital economy and the extensive use of new mobile devices—may be particularly helpful to find out ideas for developing new products and services as well as to get rid of existing lines of business or products that are no longer desirable for customers and thus eventually not profitable for the insurance company.[276]

The development of an insurance product then comprises the structuring of the product in the light of the information gathered through the analysis of the competition,

270. *See* 2010 OECD Report, Part IV, para. 26.
271. *See* Leonardo Felician, *La catena del valore nelle imprese di assicurazione*, p. 37.
272. For instance, a significant trend noticed over the recent years is the progressively aging population.
273. *See* Leonardo Felician, *La catena del valore nelle imprese di assicurazione*, pp. 37-38.
274. Over the recent years, insurance companies have also commissioned hackathons, events—which typically last for several hours or days—in which a large number of people meet to engage in developing new ideas or projects.
275. *See* Leonardo Felician, *La catena del valore nelle imprese di assicurazione*, p. 38.
276. *See* Leonardo Felician, *La catena del valore nelle imprese di assicurazione*, pp. 38-40.

the market, and the underlying trends outlined above. Specifically, this means assessing the quantitative, qualitative, geographical and time-related features of the insurance cover in the context of the insured risk acceptance and savings processes. In addition, it involves determining the scope and features of the advisory and processing services.[277] In more concrete terms, this mainly requires the determination of the pricing of the insurance product, the services related to it, the target in terms of clients, the distribution channels, the purchasing terms and conditions.[278]

In this regard, it is worth noting that the pricing of an insurance product is not limited to the determination of the premium. In fact, the pricing also includes the stipulation of the extent of the cover and all technical details such as the inclusion of a (fixed or proportional) deductible. As a matter of fact, an insurance company does not always aim at enticing potential customers by offering the lowest premium. For instance, it may also offer an insurance product with some additional services at the same premium established by the competitors or even at a higher premium in the event that the brand is perceived as something valuable.[279]

The determination of the most appropriate pricing for an insurance product is rather complex and variable over time. Indeed, the pricing for insured risks to be underwritten for new insurance products requires mathematical skills and thus is generally carried on by actuaries or—in some cases—is outsourced to third parties which provide specialist services to insurance companies. For example, some organizations compile claim statistics and make them available to member institutions. Instead, other companies use proprietary mathematical models and processes to produce data for use by clients.[280]

In general, in the case of standardized products, the determination of the pricing takes into consideration the estimated cost of claims that will be generated on the contracts concerned, applicable loadings for costs and expenses that will be necessary to bear on the contracts concerned (such as commissions, acquisition expenses, administration expenses, expenses for claims handling as well as other overhead costs and expenses), and the gross profit margin expected for the insurance company.[281]

The variables that may be used for the purposes of the pricing are—in principle—plentiful. In a competitive market, a well-defined pricing prepared on the basis of suitable variables may represent a competitive edge. Most importantly, a proper selection of risks—by virtue of a differentiation between good risks and bad risks—is the key driver for leading such a market. Among others, it is essential to reduce as much as possible the underwriting leakage, that is the assumption of bad risks at a loss. It follows that an insurance company which is capable to tailor a specific pricing for each potential customer on the basis of suitable variables will most probably assume good risks at better conditions and thus stand out from competition.[282]

277. *See* 2010 OECD Report, Part IV, para. 26.
278. *See* Leonardo Felician, *La catena del valore nelle imprese di assicurazione*, p. 41.
279. *See* Leonardo Felician, *La catena del valore nelle imprese di assicurazione*, p. 41.
280. *See* 2010 OECD Report, Part IV, para. 28.
281. *See* Leonardo Felician, *La catena del valore nelle imprese di assicurazione*, p. 48.
282. *See* Leonardo Felician, *La catena del valore nelle imprese di assicurazione*, pp. 45-47.

Clearly, besides the determination of a proper pricing, an insurance company should also aim at achieving a competitive market positioning through an innovation of products, processes and distribution channels. In this regard, it is fair to say that insurance companies have generally been keen on making use of new distribution channels (such as the telephone and the Internet) or improving internal processes for the purposes of finalizing an insurance policy. On the contrary, in the insurance market—which is a mature market—the introduction of brand-new products is way more difficult. Among others, over the recent years, insurance companies have developed multi-risk products (which combine different classes of risks), insurance products bundled with other bank products and services,[283] and personalized insurance products intended to establish a regular interaction with the customer.[284]

2.2.2.2 Sales and Marketing

The second stage of the insurance value chain includes acquiring clients, assessing requirements, advising clients and finally providing them with quotes and offers.[285]

To begin with, sales, marketing and acquisition activities presuppose at first an identification, an analysis as well as an understanding of the potential customer needs. Such activities pave the way for a definition of a general marketing strategy, which may be segmented into products, regions, countries and so forth. The marketing strategy also encompasses a definition of marketing and acquisition programs as well as the development and the application of training and educational programs.[286]

In doing so, insurance companies generally consider a number of different brand and advertisement campaigns depending upon the specific products and distribution channels concerned. In addition, insurance companies usually take into consideration new means of marketing and advertisement (such as the call centers, the Internet and social networks),[287] which are becoming more and more popular and—thus—allow insurance companies to spread their advertising messages broadly at lower costs. Therefore, among others, insurance companies generally consider investing in advertising campaigns on the Internet to attain an effective online presence (for instance, by improving their page ranking in the search engines).[288]

Next, at the sales stage, the requirements of the customers are duly assessed, and then a suitable offer is usually made. In doing so, some advisory activities may also come into play. In particular, in certain lines of business (such as life insurance), where risks of losses and financial security issues are increasingly linked to a multitude of legal parameters of a judicial and fiscal nature, the advisory function is increasingly important, and the advisory process only when provided to the customer by or on

283. *See* Leonardo Felician, *La catena del valore nelle imprese di assicurazione*, pp. 49-50.
284. For instance, this is the case of black box insurance contracts in the context of car insurance and behavioral-based life insurance products that encourage and reward customers to improve health and well-being.
285. *See* 2010 OECD Report, Part IV, para. 30.
286. *See* 2010 OECD Report, Part IV, para. 29.
287. For instance, nowadays insurance companies make extensive use of Facebook, LinkedIn and Twitter to advertise their products.
288. *See* Leonardo Felician, *La catena del valore nelle imprese di assicurazione*, pp. 59-74.

behalf of the insurance company should be regarded as a component of the actual market service, regardless of how this added value is organized (in-house or independent sales force, brokers, Internet methods and so forth).[289]

In this regard, it is worth noting that the organization of the sales and marketing function—most importantly, the reliance on internal sales staff or the outsourcing to independent intermediaries—is strictly linked to the specific business models adopted by the insurance companies,[290] and—in turn—to the type of insurance business carried on (namely, life, non-life, or reinsurance). As such, for example, in a life insurance company, which is generally focused on the retail market, the nature of the marketing function will be quite different from a marketing function that may be found in a life reinsurance company, which usually deals with other insurance companies. By contrast, as a general rule, non-life companies engaged in the context of international insurance and reinsurance rely heavily on brokers, which eventually may end up with performing functions going even beyond sales and marketing.[291]

Furthermore, the organization and the relative importance of the sales and marketing functions will also depend on a number of facts and circumstances, such as the profitability of specific lines of business and the underlying economic trends, as well as on the specific features of the country or the geographic region concerned.[292] For example, in the context of the Italian market, non-life insurance products have historically been distributed through a widespread network of insurance agents.[293]

Lastly, it is worth noting that an insurance contract generally covers a contractually agreed period of time. However, it is fair to say that the prospect of entering into a long-term relationship with the customer leads the insurance company to extend the business effort beyond the time of the actual sale of an insurance policy by providing after-sale support services. To this end, insurance companies have therefore developed services of CRM intended to strengthen client relationships over the long run so as to increase the level of client satisfaction and eventually the value for both parties.[294] Among others, this requires an ongoing analysis of the client needs in order to better understand such needs, to properly manage potential complaints and to put into place concrete actions so as to improve the insurance products and services provided in view of preventing termination and lowering marketing costs and efforts to attract new customers.[295]

289. *See* 2010 OECD Report, Part IV, para. 30.
290. The (most common) business models adopted by global insurance companies, along with their related organizational structures, are subsequently discussed in more detail in Chapter 4.
291. *See* 2010 OECD Report, Part IV, paras. 32-33.
292. *See* 2010 OECD Report, Part IV, para. 32.
293. *See* Leonardo Felician, *La catena del valore nelle imprese di assicurazione*, p. 75.
294. *See* 2010 OECD Report, Part IV, para. 31.
295. *See* Leonardo Felician, *La catena del valore nelle imprese di assicurazione*, pp. 74-76.

2.2.2.3 *Underwriting*

In general, underwriting is the process of classifying, selecting and pricing insurance risks which is carried on in view of accepting insurance risks and eventually concluding insurance contracts. To put it in other words, the role of the underwriting function is to determine whether and under which conditions an insurance company is willing to provide insurance products and services to the potential customers.[296]

As acknowledged by the OECD, the objective of the underwriting function is not the selection of risks that will not generate losses but to avoid the misclassification of risks according to the pricing of insurance contracts.[297] As a matter of fact, underwriters should protect the insurance company from acquiring non-profitable business. However, this cannot mean that every risk should be declined. Rather, the decision has to be balanced with the necessity of accepting well-understood risks to grow the insurance business. As such, it may be argued that the ultimate goal of the underwriting function is to develop and maintain profitable books of insurance business in order to eventually support the overall profitability of the insurance company.[298]

The underwriting activities are usually governed by an underwriting policy,[299] which sets (broad or detailed) parameters for determining the amount of risks to assume, determines the nature and size of business of an insurance company and may—depending on the facts and circumstances of the insurance company concerned—be one of the major factors affecting the profitability of the insurance operations.[300] Other factors that may influence the insurance practices are the following:[301]

- the financial capacity of the company, essentially its surplus;
- the regulatory framework concerning the maximum risk capacity;
- the technical skills and abilities of the personnel;
- the availability and cost of reinsurance; and
- the strategic business goals.

For standardized products, underwriting activities may be—to a certain extent—automated. On the contrary, in the case of complex products, the process may be very complex and require strong specialist skills (such as insured risk engineering, explanation of judicial, medical, physical implications and so forth). Such activities may be carried on by underwriters but may require the assistance or approval of other personnel, such as actuaries (e.g., to assist with pricing and assess the likelihood of

296. *See* 2010 OECD Report, Part IV, para. 34.
297. *See* 2010 OECD Report, Part IV, para. 35.
298. *See* Lionel Macedo, "*The Role of Underwriter in Insurance*," Primer series on insurance, Issue 8, September 2, 2009, available online at www.worldbank.org/nbfi, p. 4.
299. The definition of the underwriting policy is part of risk management. To this effect, *see* 2010 OECD Report, Part IV, para. 34.
300. *See* 2010 OECD Report, Part IV, para. 35.
301. *See* 2010 OECD Report, Part IV, para. 35.

claims), legal staff (e.g., for contractual advice) and support staff for administrative matters (e.g., premium and claim processing).[302]

It goes without saying that the exact nature and importance of the relevant activities depends primarily on the type of insurance products concerned and the facts and circumstances of the insurance companies concerned. For instance, risk selection is likely to be less important for certain lines of standardized products (such as low value insurance products) and reinsurance, where product development, sales and marketing and risk management appear to be more important functions.[303]

Nevertheless, it is fair to say that there are a number of standard activities that may be generally identified in the context of the underwriting process of an insurance company, regardless of the specific lines of business and type of products concerned.[304]

Within the framework of the underwriting policy, underwriting presupposes a process of identifying and classifying the degree of risk represented by a proposed insurance contract. Indeed, an insurance company requires knowledge of key pieces of information to properly evaluate the potential customers. In order to do so, insurance companies use relevant information gathered from a number of sources to identify possible risks. Among others, insurance companies use relevant information contained in the application form. For instance, in the context of life insurance, insurance companies look at any factors (such as occupation, dangerous hobbies, and so forth) that could make the applicant more likely to die before his or her natural life expectancy. In addition, insurance companies also make use of databases available to check on the risk exposure, possible past claims, or declined applications in the past.[305]

Upon the completion of identifying the risks, insurance companies analyze and classify the specific risks into the appropriate risk class. Classifying risks into classes allows an insurance company to determine the appropriate premium rate that should be charged. Indeed, not having such differentiation of the risk classes would result in some insured contracts being charged too much premium while others will be cross-subsidized as they would be charged less than the actual cost for insurance. In a competitive market, this cross-subsidy will create a serious competitive disadvantage for the insurance company.[306] The classification of risks is usually made on the basis of selected criteria and the use of relevant statistics.[307] In fact, it is standard for insurance companies to have specific guidelines in order to identify various classes of risks according to the likelihood of a claim, which may also be of help to decline risks that do not meet any of such classes.[308]

After this classification procedure is completed (for instance, by classifying risks in specific categories, such as preferred, standard, or substandard risks), insurance companies then select the risks they are willing to cover, verify capacity limits, and

302. *See* 2010 OECD Report, Part IV, para. 36.
303. *See* 2010 OECD Report, Part IV, para. 34.
304. For a general flow of the underwriting activities, *see* Leonardo Felician, *La catena del valore nelle imprese di assicurazione*, p. 106.
305. *See* Lionel Macedo, "*The Role of Underwriter in Insurance*," p. 9.
306. *See* Lionel Macedo, "*The Role of Underwriter in Insurance*," p. 12.
307. *See* 2010 OECD Report, Part IV, para. 34.
308. *See* Lionel Macedo, "*The Role of Underwriter in Insurance*," p. 12.

determine the insurance coverage and the premiums according to risk, cost and market conditions, or according to the applicable premium rate tables. In this regard, it is worth noting that underwriters may be involved in the pricing or setting of premiums for an insurance contract but, in the event that the insurance product is standardized and premiums are set by reference to applicable premium rate tables, underwriters are generally less involved in the pricing of such contract once the risk has been classified and selected. For instance, in the context of the life insurance business, underwriters are generally only involved in the classification and selection of risks and the pricing of such risks is done by actuaries.[309]

In addition to this, the OECD takes the view that the underwriting function may also include a risk retention analysis.[310] More to the point, according to the OECD, part of the underwriting decision may involve an analysis of how much of the insured risk should be retained by the insurance company and how much of such risk can and should be simultaneously laid off to a reinsurance company and on what terms.[311]

The final step of the underwriting process is the acceptance of insurance risks, that is the conclusion of the insurance contract—which exposes the insurance company to insurance risk—with the finalization of the insurance policy between the insurance company and the policyholder and the payment of the premium by the latter. In most of the cases, this underwriting activity requires the intervention of the relevant salespersons managing the relationships with the final customers. However, it is fair to say that this activity is not characterized by significant differences with respect to the specific lines of business and type of products concerned.[312]

2.2.2.4 Risk Management

The overall risk of an insurance company is comprised of a number of separate elements.[313] In general, insurance companies need to manage the following risks: insurance risks, risks associated with investment activities, risks associated with risk management and reinsurance, operational risks, foreign exchange risks, liquidity risks, reputation risks and other risks related to life and health insurance business lines.[314] Other types of risks may also include strategic risks, contagion and related party risks, balance sheet and market risks, counterparty default risks, legal and regulatory risks.[315]

309. *See* 2010 OECD Report, Part IV, para. 34.
310. This underwriting activity has been introduced in the 2007 Discussion Draft on Part IV. *See* s. 2.2.3 for further details.
311. *See* 2010 OECD Report, Part IV, para. 34.
312. *See* Andrea Bellucci, *Le imprese di assicurazione. Profili gestionali, organizzativi e contabili*, p. 106.
313. *See* 2010 OECD Report, Part IV, para. 38.
314. *See* 2010 OECD Report, Part IV, paras. 56-58.
315. Rodney Lester/Oliver Reichart, "*Insurance Governance and Risk Management*," Primer series on insurance, Issue 11, November 2009, available online at www.worldbank.org/nbfi, pp. 5-7.

Among such risks, insurance risk[316] and investment risks[317] are traditionally dealt with within the overall risk management function of an insurance company. In order to manage such risks, insurance companies generally have a comprehensive range of risk management tools, including claims adjustment policies, portfolio policies, reinsurance policies and investment policies (such as the ALM policies).[318]

In this context, a significant role is played by the actuaries, who are generally responsible for the calculation of premiums, the analysis of the claims experience (probabilities, claims distribution, and so forth),[319] the setting of investment assumptions, as well as setting aside the necessary insurance technical reserves[320] by relying on their mathematical models.[321]

With respect to some insurance business (among others, life insurance business), it is also important to match the maturity of asset portfolios with liabilities for the period of risk. In order to do so, insurance companies usually develop ALM policies establishing investment guidelines for specific lines of business or specific product lines.[322] Such investment guidelines generally define the long-term strategic asset allocation policy (including acceptable classes of securities, credit and other risk parameters, maturities) taking into account the nature and term of the liabilities, product guarantees and options as well as regulatory requirements with the goal of maximizing the risk-adjusted value creation. In general, the ALM policies related to specific lines of business or specific product lines are usually developed and maintained in compliance with an overall ALM policy established by the head office for the insurance company (or, where applicable, for the group) as a whole.[323]

The risk management function also comprises the capital management, which entails establishing and maintaining a capital management process (including the setting of target rates of return on capital and monitoring progress against such targets), performing the capital allocation to the various lines of business and parts of the

316. Insurance risk may be defined as the potential for the amount or timing of actual claims cash flows to differ from expected cash flows. To this effect, *see* 2010 OECD Report, Part IV, para. 56.
317. Investment risks generally include market risk, credit risk and concentration risk. To this effect, *see* 2010 OECD Report, Part IV, para. 56.
318. *See* 2010 OECD Report, Part IV, para. 38.
319. In general, in the context of the experience analysis, the actuaries develop the methods of analysis, identify and prepare the necessary data, and then perform their analyses. Thereafter, they interpret the results, communicate this information to appropriate members of management, and propose actions that might be taken in response to the information. To this effect, *see* Michael Hafeman, "*The Role of the Actuary in Insurance*," Primer series on insurance, Issue 4, May 2009, available online at www.worldbank.org/nbfi, p. 12.
320. *See* 2010 OECD Report, Part IV, para. 38.
321. Some of such actuarial models are rather simple, perhaps consisting of only one mathematical formula. On the contrary, other actuarial models, such as those used to test the capability of an insurance company to withstand a range of adverse scenarios, can instead be extremely complex. To this effect, *see* Michael Hafeman, *The Role of the Actuary in Insurance*, p. 5.
322. The main objective of ALM is to reduce the risk to an insurance company that exists in the case that assets and liabilities are mismatched, for example, if a change in market conditions might cause an increase in the value of liabilities while also causing a decrease in the value of assets. On a more positive note, ALM can help an insurance company to invest its assets more effectively and generate higher profits. To this effect, *see* Michael Hafeman, *The Role of the Actuary in Insurance*, p. 11.
323. *See* 2010 OECD Report, Part IV, para. 38.

organization (considering, among others, the different solvency regulations and capital requirements).[324]

In addition, the OECD recognized the decision to use reinsurance to manage the insurance risk exposure to be of central importance to the risk management process.[325] In a nutshell, reinsurance—which may be defined as "*the insurance of the risk borne by the insurer*"[326]—is generally intended to limit the volatility of claims, by minimizing the probability that such claims must be dealt with by a single insurance company, and to limit the oscillations of such claims.[327] The key components of this process are: the analysis of the insured risk portfolio, the establishment of the reinsurance requirements, the negotiation, structuring and conclusion of agreements with the reinsurance company, the financial execution of the reinsurance transaction, and the ongoing cooperation with the reinsurance company (managing statistics, distributing information, and so forth).[328]

The functions that may be generally found in a reinsurance company relative to an insurance company are broadly similar to those of a primary insurance company relative to the policyholders. In fact, a reinsurance company has a sales function (e.g., through performing marketing activities), performs underwriting activities (e.g., by accepting ceded risks from insurance companies and determining reinsurance premiums), performs pooling activities (e.g., by pooling the risks ceded to it by multiple insurance companies, and undertaking similar risk management activities as described for insurance companies).[329]

A reinsurance company may also decide to (retro) cede risks that it does not want to bear.[330] More precisely, retrocession is reinsurance ceded by a reinsurance company to another insurance or reinsurance company in order to release a part of the risks it has written and, in this way, stabilizing its results and homogenizing its liabilities. To put it in other terms, retrocession may be regarded as reinsurance for a reinsurance company. For instance, retrocession may be of help in the event that an insurance company writes very large risks that exceed the capacity of the national market and which—when ceded to reinsurance—also exceed the risks that any reinsurance company wishes to retain for its own account.[331]

324. *See* 2010 OECD Report, Part IV, para. 39.
325. *See* 2010 OECD Report, Part IV, para. 40.
326. *See* Fundación Mapfre, "*An Introduction to Reinsurance,*" Institute of Insurance Science 2013, available online at www.fundacionmapfre.org, p. 1.
327. *See* Giovanni Cucinotta/Laura Neri, *Le Assicurazioni* (Bologna: Il Mulino, 2005) p. 91. For further comments on the historical development of reinsurance, *see also* Andreas Schwepcke, *Reinsurance: Principles and State of the Art—A Guidebook for Home Learners—2nd Edition*, (Unterföhring: Swiss Re Germany AG, 2004) pp. 1 et seq. and Anna Dokuchayeva/Berwin Cohen, "The History and Taxation of Offshore Reinsurance Companies," *Tax Management International Journal* (2016).
328. *See* 2010 OECD Report, Part IV, para. 40.
329. *See* 2010 OECD Report, Part IV, para. 40.
330. *See* 2010 OECD Report, Part IV, para. 40.
331. *See* Fundación Mapfre, "*An Introduction to Reinsurance,*" p. 17 and Andreas Schwepcke, "*Reinsurance: Principles and State of the Art—A Guidebook for Home Learners—2nd Edition,*" p. 13.

Besides such traditional forms of risk transfer, the OECD also recognized alternative methods of risk management now employed in the context of the insurance business, which are mainly aimed at overcoming the barriers to insurability and second at optimizing the management of the insurance risk from the point of view of both diversification and cost.[332] Among others, financial reinsurance is a form of transaction between an insurance company and financial investors, which mainly focuses on purely financial effects such as capital management, solvency relief, influencing financial and earnings position rather than on the transfer of insurance risk as is the case in traditional reinsurance.[333] Most frequently, such financial reinsurance contracts combine the techniques of the capital markets into insurance through securitization, often through the use of special purpose vehicles to issue securitized financial products in such a way as to access a much wider range of potential investors.[334]

By contrast, it is important to note that the OECD did not specifically recognize co-insurance as a risk management tool. In a nutshell, co-insurance involves the joint assumption of a specific risk—which may be too burdensome for a single insurance company—between several insurance companies to the effect that such a risk is shared based on percentages between such insurance companies. Hence, the insurance premium and the potential claims are shared on the basis of the same percentages. Most frequently, in the context of co-insurance, a leading insurance company will be responsible for administering various aspects of the insurance policy (such as premium, any claims, and the insurance documents) in consideration for a commission.[335]

2.2.2.5 Contract and Claims Management

With regard to the insurance business, the conclusion of an insurance contract cannot be regarded as the final stage of the value chain. Indeed, insurance companies are required to monitor contracts or groups of contracts (also referred to as insurance portfolios) over their lifecycle. As a matter of fact, post-closing activities may be burdensome, both in terms of transactions and operating expenses. Among others, such post-closing activities encompass replying to request of information, maintaining the information on contractual amendments and developments, maintaining accounts on payments, renewal and termination of contracts, management of claims and complaints.[336]

---

332. *See* 2010 OECD Report, Part IV, para. 41.
333. *See* Eugene N. Gurenko/Alexander Itigin/Renate Wiechert, "*Insurance Risk Transfer and Categorization of Reinsurance Contracts*," The World Bank Finance and Private Sector Development Non-Banking Financial Institutions, December 2012, available online at http://documents.worldbank.org/curated/en/2012/12/17124490/insurance-risk-transfer-categorization-reinsurance-contracts, p. 4.
334. For instance, this is the case of motor insurance securitization or catastrophe bonds (CAT bonds) in the context of non-life business or financing tools aimed at monetizing future income, such as value-in-force securitization (VIF securitization) and reserve funding securitization, and other structured transactions for risk transfer in the context of life business.
335. *See* Giovanni Cucinotta/Laura Neri, *Le Assicurazioni*, p. 90 and Andreas Schwepcke, *Reinsurance: Principles and State of the Art—A Guidebook for Home Learners—2nd Edition*, p. 14.
336. *See* Leonardo Felician, *La catena del valore nelle imprese di assicurazione*, p. 117.

In a competitive environment, such post-closing activities—where an insurance company is required to deliver on the promises made at the time of concluding an insurance contract—may represent a competitive edge for an insurance company with the aim of establishing lasting relationships with the customers based on mutual trust. Therefore, this function may be a key driver for an insurance company to differentiate itself from competitors in an attempt to gain market share.[337]

In this context, the monitoring of contracts plays a key role for the purposes of a proper management of insurance portfolios. Among others, this monitoring includes maintaining accounts on payments of insurance premiums, which is usually carried out on a monthly basis through electronic reporting systems. Nevertheless, insofar as salespersons are at times allowed to deviate from standard pricing and payment conditions or grant specific discounts on insurance premiums, an insurance company is also required to monitor and check such deviations for consistency.[338]

The monitoring of insurance contracts may also create opportunities in terms of cross-selling—which is the practice of selling additional insurance products or services to an already existing customer—or up-selling—which is the attempt to persuade existing customers to purchase upgrades or other add-ons to insurance contracts already subscribed—to make a more profitable sale. Such campaigns are usually carried on in cooperation with salespersons, who generally have a direct relationship with existing customers. However, the insurance company may retain a significant role for the purposes of selecting target customers as well as steering and coordinating such campaigns.[339]

A proper monitoring of contracts also includes a clean-up of accounts related to insurance contracts already expired or insurance contracts concluded by customers who are late with the payment of the relevant insurance premiums. Such activities are usually carried on in liaison with the financial reporting function at the closing of accounting periods (particularly, at half year or at year end) to properly draw up financial accounts.[340]

In addition, in the context of management of insurance portfolios, insurance companies usually put high priority to an effective complaint management. Indeed, besides offering insurance companies an opportunity to resolve immediate problems, complaints may also provide constructive ideas for improving products, adapting marketing practices, upgrading services, or modifying promotional material and product information. Such information gathered through complaint handling may additionally be combined with other quantitative data available on insurance portfolios (e.g., premiums and claims of a given insurance portfolio) through data mining applications to obtain useful information in view of improving the retention of existing customers and the profitability of insurance portfolios.[341]

337. *See* 2010 OECD Report, Part IV, para. 43.
338. *See* Leonardo Felician, *La catena del valore nelle imprese di assicurazione*, pp. 125-126.
339. *See* Leonardo Felician, *La catena del valore nelle imprese di assicurazione*, p. 126.
340. *See* Leonardo Felician, *La catena del valore nelle imprese di assicurazione*, p. 126.
341. *See* Leonardo Felician, *La catena del valore nelle imprese di assicurazione*, pp. 123 and 126.

Furthermore, in the context of the insurance industry, which bases its credibility on honoring its underlying pledge to provide assistance at the time of the loss, another strategic area may be identified in the claims management.[342] This involves a number of activities put into place to ascertain, assess and—in the case that all contractual requirements are fulfilled—settle the claims for damages suffered by the policyholders upon occurrence of a damaging event (in the case of non-life insurance) or pay either a lump sum or an annuity if an event occurs involving human life (in the case of life insurance).[343]

In general, both in life insurance and non-life insurance, the claims handling procedure begins with a notification—in writing or other means acceptable under the terms of an insurance contract—to be filed by the policyholder within the deadline provided for under the applicable legislation to apprise the insurance company of the facts pertinent to a claim.[344]

Subsequently, in the context of life insurance, the procedure is generally straightforward. As a matter of fact, after the filing of such a notification, the claim is assessed on the basis of the facts and supporting documents provided and a decision is finally made on the claim, along with the computation of the benefit to be paid to the policyholder and the settlement of a benefit in the form of a lump sum or an annuity.[345]

On the contrary, claims handling in non-life insurance is generally more complicated to the extent that it usually requires additional work in the field of claims assessment, processing and adjusting. Indeed, following the lodging of a notification, the insurance company takes all the reasonable steps—*in primis*, by examining all applicable legal provisions and contractual papers—to assess whether the damaging event is actually covered by the insurance policy and whether all terms and conditions of such an insurance policy are met in order to further process the claim. Following such an investigation, the insurance company will then formally open a claim and process it. When doing so, the insurance company will normally segment and assign the relevant files to claims adjusters or claims examiners based on specific criteria (most frequently, the geographical location of the claims). In general, claims adjusters cooperate with insurance appraisers and investigators in insurance investigations and claims resolution to determine the value of insured items and rule out insurance fraud. To this end, insurance companies may hire independent claims adjusters or create an in-house claims department to assess, evaluate, investigate, and process all insurance claims. After calculating the value of the specific claim, the insurance company will then issue a settlement check and proceed with the payment. Nevertheless, where the claim is denied or the policyholder believes that the amount of the settlement is

342. In this respect, *see also* OECD, "*Guidelines for good practice for insurance claim management*," available online at www.oecd.org.
343. *See* Andrea Bellucci, *Le imprese di assicurazione. Profili gestionali, organizzativi e contabili*, p. 107.
344. *See* Leonardo Felician, *La catena del valore nelle imprese di assicurazione*, p. 127.
345. *See* Andrea Bellucci, *Le imprese di assicurazione. Profili gestionali, organizzativi e contabili*, p. 107.

inadequate, such a policyholder can appeal against the decision made by the insurance company and start a litigation process to be eventually brought in a court of law.[346]

2.2.2.6 Asset Management

As already outlined above,[347] in the context of the insurance business, the inversion of the production cycle significantly affects the economic pattern of an insurance company. Following the upfront collection of premiums, insurance companies are required to put aside sufficient provisions from the premium payments to properly cover future potential claims and benefits, administrative expenses and eventually profits to shareholders. In addition, shareholder capital needs to be held as a buffer to ensure that an insurance company has adequate funds to pay claims or benefits in scenarios where actual liabilities are larger than what has been reserved. Hence, insurance companies must hold sufficient assets to cover both the technical reserves for expected claims and benefits and the shareholder capital that acts as an additional buffer to meet adverse surprises in claims and benefits.[348]

In this context, the role of the asset management function in an insurance company is to manage professionally the funds generated by the technical insurance business, maximizing risk-adjusted returns while meeting regulatory requirements on its assets and other financial constraints. In doing so, insurance asset management must ensure that investment returns preserve the solvency, both regulatory and economic, of the insurance company, earn the return commensurate with the use of its capital and enable the insurance company to continue to underwrite profitable insurance business.[349]

The asset management function in an insurance company has peculiar features vis-à-vis other players in the financial markets. Indeed, income from investments of monetary resources is an important source available for an insurance company to meet its commitments. However, an insurance company is also exposed to the risk that the investment yield is lower than that expected and therefore, at the time of paying out claims and benefits to policyholders, the value of the investments is lower than that originally predicted.[350]

As a result, the main challenge for insurance asset management is to manage the potential mismatch in value of its assets and liabilities to ensure that such a mismatch will not jeopardize the insurance company as a going concern. Insurance investment risk, therefore, is when investments become insufficient to pay the liabilities due to

346. *See* Leonardo Felician, *La catena del valore nelle imprese di assicurazione,* pp. 129-135 and Andrea Bellucci, *Le imprese di assicurazione. Profili gestionali, organizzativi e contabili,* p. 108.
347. *See* s. 2.2.1 above.
348. *See* Andrea Bellucci, *Le imprese di assicurazione. Profili gestionali, organizzativi e contabili,* p. 109.
349. *See* Zurich Financial Services, "*Investment Management: a creator of value in an insurance company,*" March 2009, Second Edition, available online at www.zurich.com, p. 5.
350. *See* Giovanni Cucinotta/Laura Neri, *Le Assicurazioni,* p. 81.

adverse changes in the capital markets. It follows that the analysis and the management of such relative movements in value—the so-called ALM[351]—is a crucial process for the purposes of insurance asset management.[352]

In addition, the asset management relating to the insurance industry needs to comply with particularly stringent, external regulatory constraints, such as the set of rules governing the solvency regime. Indeed, among others, insurance regulators set requirements regarding the types of investments that qualify for solvency calculations. For example, some regulators do not allow certain investments to cover technical reserves. In addition, regulators often disadvantage holding certain asset classes by imposing significant statutory capital requirements to hold them.[353]

Hence, to ensure that the assets are managed in a sound and prudent manner that is consistent with their risk profile and applicable regulatory constraints, insurance companies are required to develop and then follow a well-structured investment process with appropriate steps for implementation, the complexity of which is dependent upon the nature of the business underwritten.[354]

To begin with, the top management of the insurance companies in liaison with the risk management function should develop a clear strategic investment policy on the basis of a proper assessment of the balance between risk and return and their risk appetite.[355] This should pave the way for a consistent asset allocation in terms of the asset mix over the investment categories selected.[356] In particular, depending upon the nature of their liabilities, insurance companies typically hold—either directly or through dedicated investment vehicles (such as investment funds)—equities and other equity-like instruments, corporate bonds and other fixed income instruments, government bonds, debts, deposits and other rights, as well as real estate property. In general, non-life insurance companies—which should mainly cover short-term liabilities—are generally more focused on liquid financial instruments, such as government bonds, corporate bonds, debts and other similar instruments. On the other hand, life insurance companies—which should typically cover long-term liabilities—are generally more prone to invest in equities and real estate property. Nevertheless, it is fair to say that—in the aftermath of the recent financial turmoil, life insurance companies are

351. *See* s. 2.2.2.4 for an overview of ALM policies.
352. *See* Zurich Financial Services, "*Investment Management: a creator of value in an insurance company*," p. 6.
353. *See* Zurich Financial Services, "*Investment Management: a creator of value in an insurance company*," p. 7.
354. For a schematic overview of such steps, *see* Central Bank of Ireland, "*Guidelines for Insurance Undertakings on Asset Management*," available online at www.centralbank.ie, pp. 4-5.
355. In this respect, it is worth noting that—from a regulatory perspective—the assumption of risks results in the absorption of capital for insurance companies. As a consequence, careful consideration should be given to the fact that the assumption of financial risks may lead to the absorption of capital which might be otherwise used to cover insurance risks (which are generally more profitable for insurance companies). To this effect, *see* Alberto Floreani, *Economia delle imprese di assicurazione* (Bologna: Il Mulino, 2011) p. 155.
356. *See* Andrea Bellucci, *Le imprese di assicurazione. Profili gestionali, organizzativi e contabili*, p. 109.

increasingly moving away from equity investments to more stable investments like corporate bonds.[357]

In the light of such investment guidelines, the investment managers—account taken of the relevant economic circumstances and their prospective developments—assess the instruments available on the market to properly select the investments, execute the investments and manage such investments. In doing so, besides a simple administration of the assets under management which entails the receipt of dividend, interest, rental and other forms of income, asset managers also control, measure and ensure proper recording and performance monitoring with a view to accurately examining the investment results achieved and the risks taken.[358]

In addition to this, insofar as an insurance company is required to carefully consider its financial position to maintain a certain amount of cash available to pay out claims and benefits to policyholders, asset managers also regularly monitor the financial and real estate markets for trading opportunities in order to dispose of investments with a view of maximizing the economic value for the insurance company.[359]

When carrying on all the above investment activities, in the context of the non-life business, the investment managers tend to work independently of the underwriters and salespersons and—since they do not have to interact with the customers—they can be located far from them. Conversely, in the life industry, the policyholders may have more control over the investments made, so that the connection between the customers and investment managers is closer and requires closer proximity. In addition, investment managers work with the regulatory compliance personnel to the extent that the risk associated with assets is closely monitored by regulatory agencies.[360]

Lastly, it is worth noting that, depending on the approach adopted by the top management, the above investment activities may carried out by insurance groups internally (most frequently, with the creation of dedicated in-house asset management companies)[361] in order to leverage on internal competences in managing multi-asset portfolios or may be otherwise outsourced (in whole or in part) to independent asset managers[362] in order to avail of specific investment management skills held by leading asset managers.[363]

357. *See* Giovanni Cucinotta/Laura Neri, *Le Assicurazioni*, pp. 81-86.
358. *See* Andrea Bellucci, *Le imprese di assicurazione. Profili gestionali, organizzativi e contabili*, p. 109.
359. *See* Andrea Bellucci, *Le imprese di assicurazione. Profili gestionali, organizzativi e contabili*, p. 110.
360. *See* 2010 OECD Report, Part IV, para. 45.
361. This is for instance the case of the Generali Group.
362. This is for instance the case of the Zurich Group, which engages third-party asset managers to manage large parts of its investment portfolio. To this effect, *see* Zurich Financial Services, *Investment Management: A Creator of Value in an Insurance Company*, p. 16.
363. *See* 2010 OECD Report, Part IV, para. 46.

2.2.2.7 *Support Functions*

In addition to the most significant functions outlined in the previous sections, an insurance company will also have to undertake a number of support functions some of which are particular to the insurance industry, while others are of a more general nature.[364]

Among important support functions recognized by the OECD, the treasury function is generally responsible for the cash management such as borrowing funds on the most advantageous terms possible.[365] In order to do so, it goes without saying that the relationship with the banking system is of paramount importance for a proper cash flow management. Most importantly, such a close relationship is critical to borrow funds both in the long run through bonds and loans and in the short period through credit lines and overdrafts, and to properly manage the payment cycle on a daily basis. In addition to this, the treasury function also needs to work closely with the investment managers to coordinate investments and divestments with liquidity needs relating to takings and disbursements.[366]

Moreover, in the insurance industry, which is a highly regulated environment, the regulatory compliance function plays a significant role in the context of a proper corporate governance.[367] Among others, the compliance function should take care of advising the administrative, management or supervisory body on compliance with the laws, regulations and administrative provisions adopted pursuant to the Solvency II Directive. It should also deal with an assessment of the possible impact of any changes in the legal environment on the operations of the insurance company concerned and the identification and assessment of compliance risk.[368]

Furthermore, another important support function concerns the IT and operations management, which deals with the ongoing business operations and procedures of an insurance company with a view of creating and maintaining an efficient operating platform. Among others, the operations management includes the following activities:

- the management of the IT infrastructure, including coordinating the provisioning, capacity, performance and availability of the computing, networking and application environment;[369]
- the premises and facilities management, which is aimed at ensuring that the workplaces are clean, safe, and secure; and
- the procurement and logistics management, which deals with the sourcing of products and services essential for the ongoing business operations.[370]

364. *See* 2010 OECD Report, Part IV, para. 47.
365. *See* 2010 OECD Report, Part IV, para. 47.
366. *See* Leonardo Felician, *La catena del valore nelle imprese di assicurazione*, pp. 148-149.
367. *See* the (30) whereas of the Solvency II Directive.
368. *See* Art. 46 of the Solvency II Directive.
369. This may also include the development of information technology and systems that can be used to determine pricing and calculate reserves, advertising, claims experience data. To this effect, *see* 2010 OECD Report, Part IV, para. 47.
370. For an overview of such activities, *see* Leonardo Felician, *La catena del valore nelle imprese di assicurazione*, pp. 150-151.

Other back office functions recognized by the OECD are premiums handling, accounting, auditing, legal services and training.[371] Most notably, the accounting function is responsible for providing all stakeholders with reliable and timely financial information through a process of integrated reporting. Among others, the accounting function provides shared services that generally include the following activities:[372]

- insurance technical accounting;[373]
- general accounting;
- financial accounting;
- debt collection;
- compliance with statutory requirements regarding a proper accounting system (such as the maintenance of accounting registers and other relevant documentation); and
- preparation of the yearly financial statements and other interim reporting packages.[374]

Another important back office function is the internal audit function, whose role is to verify that internal controls rules are followed by providing an independent evaluation of the adequacy and effectiveness of the internal control system and highlighting any need for updating, developing a common approach, methodology, methods and organizational standards.[375,376]

The legal function is instead of the utmost importance in supporting the business operations in view of ensuring full compliance with all applicable laws, rules and regulations and ultimately maintain integrity and reputation. Specifically, the legal function is accountable for addressing, supervising and controlling the overall legal

371. *See* 2010 OECD Report, Part IV, para. 47.

372. *See* Leonardo Felician, *La catena del valore nelle imprese di assicurazione*, pp. 142-148.

373. In this regard, it should however be recalled that the responsibility of coordinating the process of calculation, validation and reporting of technical provisions according to the applicable regulatory framework lies with the actuarial function. To this effect, *see* Art. 48 of the Solvency II Directive.

374. In this respect, it is worth noting that—as a reaction to major corporate and accounting scandals—certain countries have introduced specific regulations aimed at improving the corporate governance of companies (particularly, public listed companies) and ensuring that the financial information reported to the market is reliable, complete and timely. Therefore, financial reporting by large insurance companies listed on regulated markets must be supported by an effective internal control system, which should be constantly improved and adapted to normal developments in business activities, and any changes in the underlying regulatory framework. To this end, large insurance companies have introduced specific functions to create an internal control system governing the financial reporting process to support the top management in the definition, implementation and monitoring of the methodological and operating related framework aimed at ensuring the accuracy, reliability and promptness of financial reporting for disclosure to the market.

375. *See* Art. 47 of the Solvency II Directive.

376. For an overview of the internal audit function, *see* Leonardo Felician, *La catena del valore nelle imprese di assicurazione*, pp. 155-159.

framework, also managing the relationships with external legal counsels that may be engaged by the insurance company from time to time to deal with specific matters.[377]

Furthermore, the HR is the function within an insurance company that focuses on the recruitment, the training, and the development of people in line with a consistent people strategy throughout the organization. Over the recent years, in the context of a modern organization, besides standard activities relating to the staff recruitment and administration,[378] the HR function has assumed a strategic role in supporting the top management. Among others, the HR function is now in charge of the following:[379]

- leadership development with a specific focus on the top managers and their successors;
- continuing education and training;
- definition, development and coordination of the organizational model;
- coordination and support of change management initiatives;
- definition and development of a reward and compensation strategy based on performance management and incentive systems (most frequently, through balanced scorecards); and
- professional people management, with competences and entrepreneurial spirit.

Lastly, the OECD recognized the importance of the loss control function, which is aimed at preventing those losses that can be prevented, minimize those that cannot be prevented and verify valid claims or deny claims for uninsured items, and the credit analysis function, which assesses the creditworthiness of the various counterparties (including reinsurance companies, policyholders and partners in investments).[380]

By contrast, it is important to note that the OECD did not specifically recognize the importance of the planning and control function, which oversees the preparation of the budgets for a specific period (most frequently, for a one- to three-year period), monitors and—if need be—adjusts the budgets, compares actual results with expected standards, and takes corrective actions in the case the latter have not been achieved. When doing so, the planning and control function generally defines, measures and systematically evaluates over the period of time concerned a number of key performance indicators (KPIs), which are aimed at measuring the progress against the strategic objectives adopted by the top management.[381] Needless to say, such indicators largely vary between companies depending on the line of business,[382] the top

377. For instance, this may well be the case of insurance companies which outsource legal assistance over the course of legal proceedings and material litigations against policyholders.
378. Standard HR activities like timekeeping, holiday and leave planning, salary and wage management and other related activities are now generally managed through enterprise resource planning (ERP) systems.
379. *See* Leonardo Felician, *La catena del valore nelle imprese di assicurazione*, pp. 141-142.
380. *See* 2010 OECD Report, Part IV, para. 47.
381. *See* Leonardo Felician, *La catena del valore nelle imprese di assicurazione*, pp. 151-155.
382. Among others, in the life business, the annual premium equivalent (APE) is a common indicator used by insurance companies where the sales of a given entity are estimated by taking the value of regular premiums, plus 10% of any new single premiums written for the fiscal year. Conversely, in the non-life business, the loss ratio is calculated by dividing the total

management philosophy in terms of continuous and consistent improvement in quality as well as its integration into the company culture.[383]

2.2.3 KERT Functions in the Insurance Industry

As with any other for-profit organization, the ultimate objective for the top management of a standard insurance company lies on the creation of value for its stakeholders. As a matter of fact, the creation of value is the *raison d'être* of an insurance company to eventually ensure its survival and its future development in the long run.[384]

In pursuing such ultimate target, the top management of an insurance company can make use of a number of different drivers in an attempt to achieve, protect and possibly increase its competitive advantage, which is in turn closely linked to the creation of value. Such drivers for value creation may be found along the insurance value chain in any of the functions outlined in the previous section. For instance, such drivers may range from product innovation in the context of the product development function, to sales and marketing strategies aimed at maximizing sales productivity, optimally configuring distribution channels, or clearly delineating value propositions for final customers to cost leadership or operational excellence strategies in the context of contract and claims management.[385]

However, despite the fact that any of such functions may incorporate some drivers for value creation, when confronted with the issue of determining the profits to be attributed to a permanent establishment, the OECD specifically developed the concept of the KERT functions. More to the point, the concept of KERT functions as a mechanism to allocate risks, assets and capital to a permanent establishment has been first used in the 2003 Discussion Draft on Part II[386] and in the 2003 Discussion Draft on Part III[387] and then further developed in the 2004 Discussion Draft on Part I.[388]

In the latter document, KERT functions have been defined as "*those which require active decision making with regard to the most important profit generators of the business.*"[389] Hence, KERT functions are first of all functions.[390] In addition, such functions require active decision-making.[391] It follows that any function not requiring

incurred losses by earned premiums, whereas the combined ratio is calculated by taking the sum of incurred losses and expenses and then dividing them by earned premiums.

383. For instance, a number of insurance companies carefully monitor the claim processing cycle time in order to improve the customer satisfaction.
384. *See* Luigi Selleri, *Impresa di assicurazione e strategie di valore,* ch. 7.
385. For a broad overview of such drivers for value creation, *see* Luigi Selleri, *Impresa di assicurazione e strategie di valore,* ch. 7 and Andrea Bellucci, *Strategia, gestione del rischio e creazione di valore nelle imprese assicurative*, pp. 90 et seq.
386. Among others, *see* 2003 Discussion Draft on Part II, para. 45.
387. Among others, *see* 2003 Discussion Draft on Part III, para. 203.
388. Among others, *see* 2004 Discussion Draft on Part I, para. 56.
389. *See* 2004 Discussion Draft on Part I, para. 77.
390. The OECD TP Guidelines describe functions as activities and responsibilities. To this effect, *see* OECD TP Guidelines, para. 1.51.
391. Collier and Vella highlighted a lack of additional guidance in respect of what amounts to active decision-making which may give rise to conceptual and practical issues. To this effect, *see* Richard Collier/John Vella, "Five Core Problems in the Attribution of Profits to Permanent Establishments," *World Tax Journal* (2019) para. 2.2.

active decision-making,[392] whether or not involving people,[393] by definition cannot be regarded as a KERT function.[394] On the top of this, such functions must concern the most important profit generators of the business. To put it in more concrete terms, the KERT mechanism requires identifying the key[395] profit-generating functions as part of a functional analysis and then assigning those functions to the part of the enterprise where key decisions relating to such functions are made.[396]

In the context of the attribution of profits to a permanent establishment, the KERT mechanism was purported to consider the business activities of the permanent establishment as different from the activities of the rest of the enterprise.[397] In particular, such a mechanism required the KERT functions of the whole enterprise to be determined at a first stage, and then the extent to which the permanent establishment undertakes one or more of such KERT functions was to be ascertained for the purposes of the attribution of risks and assets. In addition, it was also pointed out that it was important to reward any other function carried out by the permanent establishment in accordance with the arm's length principle.[398]

According to the 2004 Discussion Draft on Part I, the functional analysis should take into consideration the functions performed by the personnel of the enterprise as a whole (including the permanent establishment) and assess the significance of them in generating the profits of the business activities. Such people functions could range from routine functions to KERT functions. This seems to mean that the KERT functions were above any other functions, that is, functions performed by high-level people of the permanent establishment. In addition, the other functions performed by the permanent establishment should also be rewarded under the arm's length principle. The ultimate effect of this is that the profits to be attributed to a permanent establishment were the profits that the permanent establishment would have earned at arm's length as if it were a legally distinct and separate enterprise performing the same or similar functions under the same or similar conditions.[399]

The holistic use of the concept of KERT functions as a way of attributing assets and risks within an enterprise provoked some criticism (particularly, in respect of the

392. In this respect, a question may however arise as to what happens in the case that the most important profit generators do not require active decision-making. To this effect, *see* Roberto Bernales in: Carlos Gutiérrez/Andreas Perdelwitz (eds.) *Taxation of Business Profits in the 21st Century—Selected Issues under Tax Treaties*, para. 6.4.1 and footnotes cited therein.

393. On the contrary, the concept of significant people functions concerns functions performed by personnel acting on behalf of an enterprise. To this effect, *see* 2010 OECD Report, Part I, para. 62.

394. *See* Roberto Bernales in: Carlos Gutiérrez/Andreas Perdelwitz (eds.) *Taxation of Business Profits in the 21st Century—Selected Issues under Tax Treaties*, para. 6.4.1.

395. It is worth noting that the OECD has not defined the term "*key.*"

396. *See* Mitchell J. Tropin, "OECD PE Draft to Replace KERT Concept with 'Significant People Function' Concept," *BNA Tax Management Transfer Pricing Report* (2006).

397. *See* Roberto Bernales in: Carlos Gutiérrez/Andreas Perdelwitz (eds.) *Taxation of Business Profits in the 21st Century—Selected Issues under Tax Treaties*, para. 6.4.1.

398. *See* 2004 Discussion Draft on Part I, para. 56.

399. *See* Roberto Bernales in: Carlos Gutiérrez/Andreas Perdelwitz (eds.) *Taxation of Business Profits in the 21st Century—Selected Issues under Tax Treaties*, para. 6.4.1.

application of such concept outside the financial sector). In answer to such criticism, the 2006 Draft Report introduced the innovative concept of significant people functions to develop a mechanism to carry out a functional and factual analysis that would allow positioning the permanent establishment as if it were a distinct and separate enterprise.[400]

Nevertheless, the 2006 Draft Report retained the concept of KERT functions for the financial industry.[401] In particular, the 2006 Draft Report stated that in the light of the special relationship between risks and financial assets in the financial sector, the AOA uses the KERT function terminology in describing the functions relevant to the attribution of both risks and assets in the financial sector, but that terminology is not used for other sectors.[402] Moreover, the 2006 Draft Report clarified that "*[o]utside the financial enterprise sector, risks may be less intimately linked with assets, so that there may be less overlap between the significant people functions relevant to the assumption of risk and those relevant to the economic ownership of the assets.*"[403]

The KERT language for the financial industry introduced in the 2006 Draft Report has been subsequently confirmed in the 2008 OECD Report[404] and in the 2010 OECD Report.[405] Consequently, the KERT approach is now applicable in relation to financial enterprises, where the same significant people functions will generally be relevant to both the assumptions of risks and the economic ownership of the assets.[406]

With respect to the insurance business, the OECD published the 2005 Discussion Draft on Part IV providing guidance on how insurance companies should attribute profits to permanent establishments, saying traditional transaction-based transfer pricing methods can be applied by insurance companies to head office—permanent establishments situations in an effective manner.[407] A couple of years later, the OECD published the 2007 Discussion Draft on Part IV, substantially revising the section on

400. For a focus on the concept of significant people functions, *see—inter alia*—W. Joseph Murphy/Geoffrey Armstrong, "Transfer Pricing in the context of a PE: the OECD view," *BNA Tax Management Transfer Pricing Report* (2007), Erik Kamphuis, "Significant People Functions and Functional Ownership: The New Motto in Transfer Pricing," *BNA Tax Management Transfer Pricing Report* (2008) and Erik Kamphuis, "Proposed OECD Risk Allocation Examination Process And Its Implications for Transfer Pricing Design," *BNA Tax Management Transfer Pricing Report* (2009).
401. For further comments on such amendments, *see—inter alia*—Mitchell J. Tropin, "KERT Will Apply to Financial Intermediaries, But Not Other Taxpayers, OECD Official Says," *BNA Tax Management Transfer Pricing Report* (2006), Mitchell J. Tropin, *BNA Tax Management Transfer Pricing Report,* (2006) and Tamu N. Wright, "OECD Removes KERT Language From Most of PE Income Allocation Project," *BNA Tax Management Transfer Pricing Report* (2007).
402. *See* 2006 Draft Report, Part I, para. 19.
403. *See* 2006 Draft Report, Part I, para. 19.
404. *See* 2008 OECD Report, Part I, para. 19.
405. *See* 2010 OECD Report, Part I, para. 16.
406. *See* 2010 OECD Report, Part I, para. 16.
407. *See* BNA, "OECD Releases Draft Guidance on Allocating Profits to Insurance Pes, Affiliates," *BNA Tax Management Transfer Pricing Report* (2005).

reinsurance and amending the definition of KERT functions adopted in the previous draft.[408] Such specific guidance on the insurance industry has been subsequently incorporated into the 2008 OECD Report[409] and the 2010 OECD Report.[410]

In the 2005 Discussion Draft on Part IV, the OECD asserted that "*[o]f particular importance will be the determination of the key entrepreneurial risk-taking functions of the enterprise and the extent to which the PE undertakes those functions. These key entrepreneurial risk taking functions are those which require active decision-making with regard to the taking on and day-to-day management of the individual risks and portfolios of risks that have been identified as the most important under the functional and factual analysis. It is these key entrepreneurial risk-taking functions that are likely to impact most directly on the profitability of the insurance enterprise.*"[411]

In this respect, the OECD went further saying that "*a particular insurance business may have one or more key entrepreneurial risk taking functions, each of which has to be taken into account.*"[412] Such KERT functions require two key decisions: "*(1) the decisions as to what insured risks to accept and on what terms; and (2) which of those insured risk to retain and which to reinsure.*"[413]

As a consequence, according to the 2005 Discussion Draft on Part IV, the KERT functions in the insurance industry have been identified in the functions that required active decision-making on a day-to-day basis in relation to the most important risks taken by the insurance business.[414] As the original decision to take on risk may be made in one location and the day-to-day management of the risk in another location, the KERT functions could be split between two locations with regard to a particular set of risks.[415]

Furthermore, the OECD added that "*[o]nce assets and associated investment income have been attributed to the part of the enterprise performing the key entrepreneurial risk taking functions, it will also be important to reward other functions in accordance with the arm's length principle.*"[416] When doing so, according to the OECD, "*there is no presumption that these other functions are by nature of low value. This will be determined by the functional and comparability analyses based on the particular facts and circumstances.*"[417,418]

408. *See* Molly Moses, "OECD Releases New Draft of Part IV On Insurance in Profit Attribution Report," *BNA Tax Management Transfer Pricing Report* (2007).
409. *See* 2008 OECD Report, Part IV.
410. *See* 2010 OECD Report, Part IV.
411. *See* 2005 Discussion Draft on Part IV, para. 75.
412. *See* 2005 Discussion Draft on Part IV, para. 76.
413. *See* 2005 Discussion Draft on Part IV, para. 76.
414. Industry representatives mainly questioned this approach to the extent that the decisions of the functions responsible for such activities are monitored on a quarterly or annual basis, not day-to-day. *See* John Neighbour/Jennifer Coletta, "Attribution of Profits to Insurance Branches," *The Tax Journal* (2006) p. 21.
415. *See* Erica Howard/Robin Saunders, "The future of Part IV (Insurance of the OECD report on attribution of profits to PEs," *BNA Tax Management Transfer Pricing Report* (2007a).
416. *See* 2005 Discussion Draft on Part IV, para. 77.
417. *See* 2005 Discussion Draft on Part IV, para. 77.
418. Such statements have been maintained in the following drafts and reports. To this effect, *see* 2007 Discussion Draft on Part IV, para. 71, 2008 OECD Report, Part IV, para. 71 and 2010 OECD Report, Part IV, para. 71.

In the 2007 Discussion Draft on Part IV, the OECD revised the KERT language arguing that "*a key entrepreneurial risk-taking function is one which requires active decision-making with regard to the assumption and/or management (subsequent to the transfer) of the individual risks and portfolios of risks that have been identified as the most important under the functional and factual analysis.*"[419] With this in mind, the OECD stated that "*an insurance business will have one key entrepreneurial risk-taking function, the assumption of insurance risk by performing the underwriting function.*"[420] Thereafter, the OECD further clarified that "*the key entrepreneurial risk-taking function in the insurance industry is the assumption of insurance risk. It is the assumption of insurance risk that creates the need for an insurance enterprise to hold an amount of assets sufficient to support the reserves and surplus relevant to that risk. Accordingly, the economic ownership of investment assets of an insurance enterprise will be attributed to the part or parts of the enterprise that perform the function of assuming insurance risk, to the extent appropriate to support that risk.*"[421]

Therefore, according to the 2007 Discussion Draft on Part IV, the KERT function in the insurance business has been identified in the assumption of insurance risk, which is carried out by the underwriting function. Interestingly, the underwriting function was however extended to encompass the analysis of how much risk should be retained and how much should be "*simultaneously*" laid off to a reinsurance company, but this was very much presented as part of the decision to accept risk.[422]

On the other hand, the 2007 Discussion Draft on Part IV took the approach that there was no function of ongoing risk management in respect of insurance risk which involves a sufficient degree of active decision-making to merit recognition as a KERT function.[423] In particular, the OECD asserted that "*the management of that risk subsequent to its assumption generally does not involve the kind of active decision-making that justifies treating that management function as a key entrepreneurial risk-taking function.*"[424] In addition, although recognizing that "*[t]he underwriting activity typically include risk management functions related to setting the underwriting policy and the parameters for determining the amount of risk to underwrite,*" the OECD eventually concluded that "*[s]uch parameter-setting, without further involvement in assuming or managing the risk, would not generally be considered a function forming part of the key entrepreneurial risk-taking function of the assumption of insurance risk.*"[425]

Such a new language describing a KERT function adopted in the 2007 Discussion Draft on Part IV has generally pleased industry representatives. Nevertheless, although the long-term nature of much insurance means that such decisions are not made with the same frequency as those of a trader managing a book of securities, it has been

419. *See* 2007 Discussion Draft on Part IV, para. 68.
420. *See* 2007 Discussion Draft on Part IV, para. 69.
421. *See* 2007 Discussion Draft on Part IV, para. 73.
422. *See* Erica Howard/Robin Saunders, "Attribution of profits to permanent establishments: insurance update," *BNA Tax Management Transfer Pricing Report* (2007b).
423. *See* Erica Howard/Robin Saunders, *BNA Tax Management Transfer Pricing Report* (2007b).
424. *See* 2007 Discussion Draft on Part IV, para. 68.
425. *See* 2007 Discussion Draft on Part IV, para. 70.

submitted that the business of insurance is so fundamentally concerned with risk that it appears counterintuitive to conclude that the ongoing management of risk does not involve key decisions. In the light of this, certain commentators have generally expressed a recommendation that the definition of risk assumption was to be expanded to include the ongoing management of insurance risk.[426]

Another issue addressed by some commentators concerned the nature of the risk assumed by an insurance company. Indeed, while in many cases insurance risk is the most significant entrepreneurial risk involved in generating profits for the company, certain types of insurance products in life insurance are primarily investment products. As a result, according to some commentators, there may well be instances where the KERT function should be regarded as the decision leading to the assumption (and ongoing management) of investment risk, where the principal risk borne by the insurance company is linked to the performance of the underlying investments rather than the necessity to pay out claims or benefit to the policyholder.[427]

The failure to recognize internal reinsurance—to be construed as the transfer of risk between the head office and its permanent establishment(s)—as a KERT function was another common complaint. Among others, some commentators argued that the 2007 Discussion Draft on Part IV did not consider that—in many cases—once the insurance risks have been assumed by a permanent establishment, the insurance contract may have no further connection with such a permanent establishment. Rather, the insurance risks may be wholly shifted to (and managed by) another part of the insurance company. In addition to this, according to other commentators, the 2007 Discussion Draft on Part IV appeared to improperly draw a distinction between reinsurance activities carried on as part of the original risk assumption process, which should be regarded as part of the KERT function, and reinsurance taken out at a later stage, which is instead not regarded as such.[428]

In spite of the above comments put forward by industry representatives, the guidance provided by the OECD in the 2007 Discussion Draft on Part IV has been mostly confirmed when incorporating such specific guidance on how insurance companies should attribute profits to a permanent establishment in the 2008 OECD Report and ultimately in the 2010 OECD Report, albeit a number of minor changes has been made to the language. As a result, according to the OECD, in determining profits to be attributed to a permanent establishment, the insurance business will only have one KERT function, which is the assumption of insurance risk.[429,430]

426. To this effect, *see* Erica Howard/Robin Saunders, *BNA Tax Management Transfer Pricing Report* (2007b) and Molly Moses, "OECD Told to Broaden KERT Definition, Recognize Reinsurance in Part IV of Report," *BNA Tax Management Transfer Pricing Report* (2007).

427. *See* Erica Howard/Robin Saunders, *BNA Tax Management Transfer Pricing Report* (2007b).

428. *See* Molly Moses, *BNA Tax Management Transfer Pricing Report*, (2007).

429. *See* 2008 OECD Report, paras. 68-69 and 2010 OECD Report, paras. 68-69.

430. It is worth noting that the reference to the underwriting function carrying on the assumption of insurance risk contained in the 2007 Discussion Draft of Part IV has been deleted in the 2008 OECD Report and in the 2010 OECD Report.

Similarly, the OECD confirmed that the ongoing risk management does not generally constitute a KERT function in the insurance industry.[431,432] In this particular respect, when confirming that the setting of the underwriting policy and the parameters for determining the amount of risk to underwrite, without further involvement in assuming or managing the risk, would not generally be considered a function forming part of the KERT function of the assumption of insurance risk,[433] the OECD went even further clarifying that the "*senior management's setting of overall strategic parameters which are changed infrequently, with little further ongoing, active involvement in the decision-making relating to the assumption of risk, would not generally be considered a key entrepreneurial risk-taking function.*"[434]

Finally, it is important to note that the OECD also provided relatively detailed guidance on the treatment of permanent establishments that are deemed to arise because of the activities of a dependent agent.[435,436] However, after acknowledging that such permanent establishments raise specific issues that need to be addressed, the OECD has concluded that they should be subject to the same profit attribution rules adopted for other types of permanent establishments.[437,438] In particular, the attribution of profits to a dependent agent permanent establishment—as opposed to the dependent agent enterprise itself—would result from functions (including KERT functions) being performed by the dependent agent enterprise on behalf of the foreign

431. *See* 2008 OECD Report, para. 68.

432. This also appears to be consistent with the changes to the OECD TP Guidelines in the aftermath of the BEPS Project, whereby the OECD argues that control over risk does not necessarily involve the day-to-day mitigation to have control of the risks. To this effect, *see* OECD TP Guidelines, para. 1.65.

433. It is worth noting that the guidance on such parameter-setting has been moved from 2007 Discussion Draft on Part IV, para. 70 to 2008 OECD Report, para. 94 and 2010 OECD Report, para. 94.

434. *See* 2008 OECD Report, para. 94 and 2010 OECD Report, para. 94.

435. *See* 2010 OECD Report, paras. 113-121.

436. This specific guidance has been included in the 2005 Discussion Draft on Part IV and subsequently confirmed in the 2007 Discussion Draft on Part IV, the 2008 OECD Report and in the 2010 OECD Report with minor changes.

437. *See* 2010 OECD Report, para. 116.

438. This conclusion has been endorsed in the additional guidance issued in March 2018 by the OECD (which was preceded by two discussion drafts, one issued in July 2016 and the other in June 2017) on how the existing rules of Art. 7 of the OECD Model apply to permanent establishments resulting from the amendments introduced in the context of Action 7 of the BEPS Project. *See* OECD, "*Additional Guidance on the Attribution of Profits to Permanent Establishments—BEPS Action 7*," Paris (March 2018), pp. 13 et seq. For further comments on such additional guidance, *see—inter alia*—Dinis Tracana, "The Effect of the OECD/G20 BEPS Initiative on the Attribution of Profits to Permanent Establishments: The Special Case of Agency Permanent Establishments," *Bulletin for International Taxation* (2017) pp. 214 et seq., Raffaele Petruzzi/Raphael Holzinger, "Profit Attribution to Dependent Agent Permanent Establishments in a Post-BEPS Era," *World Tax Journal* (2017) pp. 263 et seq., Gary D. Sprague, "Additional Guidance on the Attribution of Profits to Permanent Establishments—A Welcome Development," *BNA Tax Management Transfer Pricing Report* (2018), Bob Stack/Jamie Hawes, "OECD Guidance Doesn't Resolve Fundamental Issue for Attribution of Profits to Permanent Establishments," *BNA Tax Management Transfer Pricing Report* (2018), Luca Bonfanti, "L'Additional Guidance dell'OCSE per l'attribuzione del reddito alla stabile organizzazione," *Fiscalità & Commercio Internazionale* (2018) no. 11 pp. 39 et seq. and Richard Collier/John Vella, *World Tax Journal*, (2019) para. 2.4.1.

insurance company. This eventually results in the right for the host country to tax two different legal entities,[439] namely the dependent agent enterprise itself on the profits earned in the host country (including the remuneration for services provided to the foreign insurance company) and the dependent agent permanent establishment on the profits attributed on the basis of the AOA (over and above the remuneration earned by the dependent agent enterprise itself).[440]

439. This is also referred to as the dual taxpayer approach. To this effect, *see* Harald Moshammer/Michael Tumpel, "Attribution of Profits to a Dependent Agent PE" in: Michael Lang/Pasquale Pistone/Josef Schuch/Claus Staringer/Alfred Storck (eds.) *Dependent Agents as Permanent Establishments* (Vienna: Linde, 2014) pp. 235-236.

440. *See* 2010 OECD Report, paras. 114 et seq.

CHAPTER 3
Analysis of the Double Tax Treaty Law

Chapter 3 develops an analytical framework by discussing the concept of dependent agent permanent establishment that is enshrined in the main model treaties, i.e., the OECD Model and the UN Model, along with a side view of the US Model. To this end, Chapter 3 touches upon the historical development of the permanent establishment concept, starting from the early history with the emergence of such a concept in the German Empire in the nineteenth century up to the most recent developments, and the provisions that can be now found in the main model treaties, shedding specific light on the changes introduced in the aftermath of the BEPS Project. This chapter is intended to describe the main elements that may give rise to the existence of a dependent agent permanent establishment in the context of the insurance business, highlighting the main differences and similarities in the definitions contained in the different model treaties. For this reason, this chapter also delves into the specific measures dealing with insurance, i.e., the insurance agent provision which may be found in the UN Model and the special clause for insurance agents that is contemplated in the OECD Model Commentary.

3.1 BACKGROUND OF THE ANALYSIS

As already outlined in Chapter 1,[441] this chapter is aimed at examining the concept of dependent agent permanent establishment enshrined in the main model treaties, i.e., the OECD Model and the UN Model, along with a side view on the US Model.[442,443] In order to do so, this chapter will touch upon the historical development of the permanent establishment concept, starting from the early history with the emergence of such a concept in the German Empire in the nineteenth century up to the most recent developments, and the provisions that can be found in the main model treaties, shedding specific light on the changes introduced in the aftermath of the BEPS Project.

441. *See* s. 1.5 above.
442. This side view is mainly aimed at discussing some interesting case law in the field of insurance. The US Model will not be discussed in Chapter 4.
443. The definition of permanent establishment which may be found in other model treaties is beyond the scope of this research.

This chapter does not pretend to offer a general comprehensive analysis of the permanent establishment concept contained in the model treaties. Rather, the purpose is to provide an analytical framework aimed at describing and explaining the main elements that may give rise to the existence of a dependent agent permanent establishment in the context of the insurance business. Therefore, this chapter will mainly consider the concept and the extent of the agency permanent establishment provision, with a specific focus on the special insurance agent provision which may be found in the UN Model and is also addressed in the OECD Model Commentary.

3.2 THE EVOLUTION OF THE PERMANENT ESTABLISHMENT CONCEPT IN THE EARLY YEARS

3.2.1 The Emergence of the Permanent Establishment Concept

The concept of permanent establishment was developed in the German States, particularly Prussia, in the second half of the nineteenth century. Originally, the expression "*Betriebsstätte*"[444] was not used as a tax concept. A similar term, "*stehendes Gewerbe,*"[445] was instead adopted for municipal regulations to prevent double taxation among the different Prussian municipalities in the middle of the century. It seems reasonable to assume that—at that point in time—this expression required permanence and location within an area, such as a town, rather than physical location in one specific place there.[446]

The concept of permanent establishment was later adopted in German tax statutes in 1885, and in 1891, the term was eventually codified in Prussian legislation. At any rate, the major development was the enactment of the German Double Taxation Act of 1909, which aimed at preventing double taxation among German States. In this piece of legislation, the core elements of the basic concept, as it is known today, i.e., the existence of the place of business, the location of this place at a specific geographical spot, and the permanence of the business, were all included in the definition of permanent establishment.[447,448]

444. This term may be translated into English as "*permanent establishment.*" To this effect, *see* Arvid A. Skaar, *Permanent Establishment—Erosion of a Tax Treaty Principle* (Deventer/Boston: Kluwer Law and Taxation Publishers, 1991) p. 72.

445. This term may be translated into English as "*a trade with a fixed place of business.*" To this effect, *see* Arvid A. Skaar, *Permanent Establishment—Erosion of a Tax Treaty Principle,* p. 72.

446. *See* Arvid A. Skaar, *Permanent Establishment—Erosion of a Tax Treaty Principle,* pp. 72-73 and Federico Otegui Pita, "Article 5—The Concept of Permanent Establishment" in: Thomas Ecker/Gernot Ressler (eds.) *History of Tax Treaties* (Vienna: Linde, 2011) p. 237.

447. *See* Arvid A. Skaar, *Permanent Establishment—Erosion of a Tax Treaty Principle,* pp. 73-75 and Federico Otegui Pita in: Thomas Ecker/Gernot Ressler (eds.) *History of Tax Treaties,* p. 237.

448. The concept, although not the term, was also used in Swiss inter-cantonal case law from 1875 (referring to a branch within the meaning of private or commercial law) and 1892 (referring to a fixed place of business). To this effect, *see* John F. Avery Jones, Luc De Broe/Maarten J. Ellis/Kees van Raad/Jean-Pierre Le Gall/Sanford H. Goldberg/Jürgen Killius/Guglielmo Maisto/Toshio Miyatake/Henri Torrione/Richard J. Vann/David A. Ward/Bertil Wiman, "The Origins of Concepts and Expressions Used in the OECD Model and Their Adoption by States," *Bulletin for International Taxation* (2006) p. 234.

In the context of DTAs, the term permanent establishment was first used in the DTA between the Austro-Hungarian Empire and Prussia, which was signed on June 21, 1899. Pursuant to this DTA, business profits made by a permanent establishment were to be taxed in the country in which the permanent establishment was located.[449] In particular, Art. 2, of this DTA stipulated that the term permanent establishment included "*branch establishments, factories, depots, offices, places where purchases and sales are effected and other business facilities by which the owner, partner, manager, or other permanent representative carries on his business activities.*"[450] This provision—which leans on Prussian domestic law—may be regarded as a first attempt to define the concept of permanent establishment by other means than a mere list of example.[451] In doing so, this definition however only contemplates the permanent establishment as a fixed place of business. Therefore, only a physical agency permanent establishment—where the agent was placed on equal footing with the entrepreneur himself, his co-partner or his proxy[452]—was conceivable.

Other DTAs with similar definitions of a permanent establishment were concluded in the following years—particularly among the Central European countries—until the outbreak of World War I.[453] Hence, although not used by all countries, it appears that the concept of a (physical) permanent establishment was well known in the DTA practice at that point in history.[454]

3.2.2 The Period Between the World Wars

The issue of double taxation led the ICC to request the newly founded League of Nations to take measures to prevent such a problem.[455] In answer to this, the League of Nations decided to establish a theoretical basis for the principles of international tax jurisdiction.[456] This resulted in a report (the Economist Report)[457] in which a group of experts (the Group of Economists) focused on the economic consequences of double

449. *See* Arvid A. Skaar, *Permanent Establishment—Erosion of a Tax Treaty Principle*, p. 75 and Federico Otegui Pita in: Thomas Ecker/Gernot Ressler (eds.) *History of Tax Treaties*, p. 237.
450. To this effect, *see* translation made by Professor Peter Rohn, Director of the University of Washington Treaty Research Centre in Robert L. Williams, *Fundamentals of Permanent Establishments* (The Hague: Kluwer Law International, 2014) p. 3.
451. *See* Arvid A. Skaar, *Permanent Establishment—Erosion of a Tax Treaty Principle*, p. 76.
452. *See* Ekkehart Reimer, "Article 5.—Permanent Establishment" in: Ekkehart Reimer/Alexander Rust (eds.) *Klaus Vogel on Double Taxation Convention—4th edition* (Alphen aan den Rijn: Kluwer Law International, 2015) p. 383.
453. A number of DTAs were also concluded within the Austro-Hungarian Empire and between German States and Swiss Cantons, in particular Swiss cities, such as Basel and Zurich. To this effect, *see* Arvid A. Skaar, *Permanent Establishment—Erosion of a Tax Treaty Principle*, p. 76.
454. *See* Arvid A. Skaar, *Permanent Establishment—Erosion of a Tax Treaty Principle*, p. 76.
455. *See* Arvid A. Skaar, *Permanent Establishment—Erosion of a Tax Treaty Principle*, pp. 77-78.
456. *See* Arvid A. Skaar, *Permanent Establishment—Erosion of a Tax Treaty Principle*, p. 78.
457. League of Nations Economic and Financial Commissions, Professors Bruins, Einaudi, Seligman and Sir Josiah Stamp, "*Report on Double Taxation Submitted to the Financial Committee,*" Document E.F.S.73. F.19, Geneva (April 3, 1923).

taxation and developed principles on the allocation of taxing rights.[458] In concluding that residence taxation should be the preferred method for taxing cross-border income, the Group of Economists recommended that the source country should exempt all non-residents from tax imposed on income drawn from sources within its borders.[459] During the same period, the League of Nations appointed a group of administrative tax officials (the Committee of Technical Experts) to develop a more equitable system for the allocation of income between countries and to prevent double taxation and tax evasion.[460] The Committee of Technical Experts came up with a report (the Report of the Technical Experts)[461] which supported the approach that residence taxation should be the preferred method for allocating taxing rights.[462] However, it found that source taxation could be accepted for the imposition of impersonal taxes. More precisely, the Committee of Technical Experts recommended that source taxation should be applied to: (*i*) immovable property, (*ii*) agricultural undertakings, and (*iii*) industrial and commercial establishments.[463]

As for the latter, the Report of the Technical Experts clarified that "*[i]f the enterprise has its head office in one of the States and in another has a branch, an agency, an establishment, a stable commercial or industrial organisation, or a permanent representative, each one of the contracting States shall tax that portion of the net income produced in its own territory.*"[464] In such a way, the Committee of Technical Experts recognized a right of the source country to tax income made by a foreign enterprise within its borders.[465,466]

458. For a comprehensive analysis of the Economist Report, *see* Michael Kobetsky, *International Taxation of Permanent Establishments: Principles and Policy*, pp. 112 et seq. and Sunita Jogarajan, "Stamp, Seligman and the Drafting of the 1923 Experts' Report on Double Taxation," *World Tax Journal* (2013).
459. *See* Arvid A. Skaar, *Permanent Establishment—Erosion of a Tax Treaty Principle*, p. 80 and Michael Kobetsky, *International Taxation of Permanent Establishments: Principles and Policy*, p. 114.
460. *See* Arvid A. Skaar, *Permanent Establishment—Erosion of a Tax Treaty Principle*, p. 81 and Michael Kobetsky, *International Taxation of Permanent Establishments: Principles and Policy*, p. 117.
461. League of Nations: Technical Experts to the Economic and Financial Committee, "*Double Taxation and Tax Evasion, Report and Resolutions Submitted by the Technical Experts to the Financial Committee of the League of Nations*," Document F.212, Geneva (February 1925).
462. For a comprehensive analysis of the Report of the Technical Experts, *see* Michael Kobetsky, *International Taxation of Permanent Establishments: Principles and Policy*, pp. 117 et seq. and Sunita Jogarajan, *Double Taxation and the League of Nations* (Cambridge: Cambridge University Press, 2018) pp. 22 et seq.
463. *See* Michael Kobetsky, *International Taxation of Permanent Establishments: Principles and Policy*, p. 119.
464. *See* League of Nations: Technical Experts to the Economic and Financial Committee, "*Double Taxation and Tax Evasion, Report and Resolutions Submitted by the Technical Experts to the Financial Committee of the League of Nations*," Document F.212, p. 31.
465. *See* Michael Kobetsky, *International Taxation of Permanent Establishments: Principles and Policy*, p. 119.
466. The Report of the Technical Experts considered "*profits realised through an insurance agent representing in the same locality more than one company*," thereby contemplating a permanent establishment constituted by an insurance agent. To this effect, *see* League of Nations: Technical Experts to the Economic and Financial Committee, "*Double Taxation and Tax Evasion, Report and Resolutions Submitted by the Technical Experts to the Financial Committee of the League of Nations*," Document F.212, p. 31.

Following the Report of the Technical Experts, the League of Nations established a Committee on Double Taxation and Tax Evasion (the Committee of Fiscal Experts. In April 1927, the Committee of Fiscal Experts delivered a report (the 1927 Report),[467,468] where it was formally recognized that a source country was entitled to tax profits derived by non-resident persons through a permanent establishment situated therein. In doing so, it was stipulated that "*[t]he real centres of management, affiliated companies, branches, factories, agencies, warehouses, offices, depots, shall be regarded as permanent establishments. The fact that an undertaking has business dealings with a foreign country through a bonafide agent of independent status (broker, commission agent, etc.), shall not be held to mean that the undertaking in question has a permanent establishment in that country.*"[469,470]

Thereafter, the League of Nations set up a General Meeting of Government Experts on Double Taxation and Tax Evasion (the General Meeting) to continue the work of the Committee of Fiscal Experts. The General Meeting came up with a report (the 1928 Report),[471] in which the definition of permanent establishment was substantially the same as that adopted in the 1927 Report.[472]

The recommendations of General Meeting also led to the establishment of the League of Nations Fiscal Committee, which produced a number of reports to summarize the work performed to solve the problem of double taxation,[473] namely the 1929 Report,[474] the 1930 Report[475] and the 1931 Report.[476] Such documents continued to use the definition of permanent establishment adopted by the General Meeting in the 1928

467. League of Nations: Committee of Technical Experts on Double Taxation and Tax Evasion, "*Double Taxation and Tax Evasion, Report presented by the Committee of Technical Experts on Double Taxation and Tax Evasion,*" Document C. 216. M. 85, London (April 12, 1927).

468. For a comprehensive analysis of the 1927 Report, *see* Sunita Jogarajan, *Double Taxation and the League of Nations*, pp. 98 et seq.

469. *See* League of Nations: Committee of Technical Experts on Double Taxation and Tax Evasion, "*Double Taxation and Tax Evasion, Report presented by the Committee of Technical Experts on Double Taxation and Tax Evasion,*" Document C. 216. *M. 85*, p. 11.

470. It seems probable that the agency permanent establishment provisions contained in the 1927 Report were strongly influenced by UK legislation that had been passed in 1925. To this effect, *see* John F. Avery Jones/Jürgen Lüdicke, "The Origins of Article 5(5) and 5(6) of the OECD Model," *World Tax Journal* (2014) p. 227 and John F. Avery Jones/David A. Ward, "Agents as Permanent Establishments under the OECD Model Tax Conventions," *European Taxation* (1993) pp. 163-164.

471. League of Nations Fiscal Committee, "*Double Taxation and Tax Evasion: Report Presented by the General Meeting of Government Experts on Double Taxation and Tax Evasion,*" Document C.562.M.178.1928.II, Geneva (October 31, 1928).

472. For a comprehensive analysis of the 1928 Report, *see* Michael Kobetsky, *International Taxation of Permanent Establishments: Principles and Policy*, pp. 123 et seq. and Sunita Jogarajan, *Double Taxation and the League of Nations*, pp. 182 et seq.

473. For a comprehensive analysis of such work, *see* Michael Kobetsky, *International Taxation of Permanent Establishments: Principles and Policy*, pp. 128 et seq.

474. League of Nations Fiscal Committee, "*Report to the Council on the Work of the First Session of the Committee,*" Document C516.M.175.1929.II, Geneva (October 17-26, 1929).

475. League of Nations Fiscal Committee, "*Report to the Council on the Work of the Second Session of the Committee,*" Document C.340.M.140.1930.II, Geneva (May 22-31, 1930).

476. League of Nations Fiscal Committee, "*Report to the Council on the Work of the Third Session of the Committee,*" Document C.415.M.171.1931.II.A, Geneva (May 29—June 6, 1931).

Report. Also, next to this, they attempted to redefine an "*autonomous agent.*"[477] In a nutshell, on the basis of the 1929 Report and the 1930 Report, the following categories of agents were deemed to constitute an agency permanent establishment: (*i*) the binding agent,[478] (*ii*) the employee agent, and (*iii*) the stock holding agent.[479,480] However, in the 1931 Report, the common law system had reasserted its influence and the original provision relating to agents of an independent status contained in the 1927 Report and in the 1928 Report was eventually reinstated.[481]

In 1933, the League of Nations Fiscal Committee published a new report (the 1933 Report),[482,483] which contained a new definition of permanent establishment integrating the definition enshrined in the 1927 Report and in the 1928 Report with the outcome of the discussion on the "*autonomous agent.*"[484] In particular, it was stipulated that "*[t]he fact that an enterprise with its fiscal domicile in one of the contracting States has business dealings in another contracting State through an agent of genuinely independent status (broker, commission agent, etc.) shall not be held to mean that it has a permanent establishment in the latter State.*"[485,486] This provision

477. *See* Hans Pijl, "Agency Permanent Establishments: in the name of and the Relationship between Article 5(5) and (6)—Part 1," *Bulletin for International Taxation,* (2013) p. 18.
478. Under a strong civil law influence, two exceptions to the fundamental principle have been dedicated to the broker and the commission agent to clarify that such intermediaries did not constitute binding agents. For further details, *see* Hans Pijl, *Bulletin for International Taxation,* (2013) pp. 20-21, John F. Avery Jones/Jürgen Lüdicke, *World Tax Journal,* (2014) pp. 228-229 and John F. Avery Jones/David A. Ward, *European Taxation,* (1993) pp. 164-165. Also, the rule concerning the "*bonafide agent of independent status (broker, commission agent, etc.)*" was removed since it was concluded that brokers and commission agents did not generally bind other persons and—as a result—they did not fulfill the criteria to constitute an agency permanent establishment by their very nature. *See* Hans Pijl, *Bulletin for International Taxation,* (2013) p. 21.
479. *See* Hans Pijl, *Bulletin for International Taxation,* (2013) p. 21 and Nadine Oberbauer, "The Dependent Agent PE and the Exception for Auxiliary and Preparatory Activities under Article 5(4) of the OECD Model Convention" in: Michael Lang/Pasquale Pistone/Josef Schuch/Claus Staringer/Alfred Storck (eds.) *Dependent Agents as Permanent Establishments* (Vienna: Linde, 2014) p. 219.
480. It was clearly stated that "*[t]here are cases, however, in which the presence of an agent of an enterprise may connote (...) the existence of a permanent establishment, although the enterprise undoubtedly has no fixed depot; this is particularly the case with insurance companies and certain buying agencies.*" *See* League of Nations Fiscal Committee, "*Report to the Council on the Work of the First Session of the Committee,*" Document C516.M175.1929.II, p. 3 and League of Nations Fiscal Committee, "*Report to the Council on the Work of the Second Session of the Committee,*" Document C.340.M.140.1930.II, p. 4. Hence, even though this was a consideration aimed at dismissing the adoption of a general principle in favor of a list of indices which constitute a presumption for the existence of a permanent establishment, it appears as if the League of Nations Fiscal Committee acknowledged that an insurance agent may represent an agency permanent establishment (notably, under points *i*) or *ii*) above).
481. *See* John F. Avery Jones/David A. Ward, *European Taxation,* (1993) pp. 164-165.
482. League of Nations Fiscal Committee, "*Report to the Council on the Fourth Session of the Committee,*" Document C.399.M.204.1933.II.A (Geneva (June 15-26, 1933).
483. For a general overview of the 1933 Report, *see* Michael Kobetsky, *International Taxation of Permanent Establishments: Principles and Policy,* pp. 136 et seq.
484. *See* Hans Pijl, *Bulletin for International Taxation,* (2013) p. 22.
485. *See* League of Nations Fiscal Committee, "*Report to the Council on the Fourth Session of the Committee,*" Document C.399.M.204.1933.II.A, p. 6.
486. It is unclear what determined independence, but—according to Pijl—it may be assumed that this was still the "*absolute independence, both from the legal and economic point of view,*" as

related to the agent of an independent status deriving from the 1927 Report and the 1928 Report (and reintroduced in the 1931 Report) was then followed by a positive specification with a list of cases where a permanent establishment was deemed to exist patterned after the 1929 Report and the 1930 Report.[487]

In 1935, the League of Nations Fiscal Committee published a new report (the 1935 Report),[488,489] which contained the same permanent establishment definition as the 1933 Report, save for an important difference concerning the positive specification. In particular, in the second sentence of the positive specification, the wording "*a permanent establishment shall therefore deemed to exist*" was replaced with the wording "*a permanent establishment shall for instance be deemed to exist,*" thereby widening the scope of the agency permanent establishment and making it less well determined.[490,491]

Before World War II, the League of Nations Fiscal Committee published additional reports, i.e., the 1936 Report,[492] the 1937 Report,[493] the 1938 Report[494] and the 1939 Report.[495] However, no significant developments with respect to the permanent establishment have been reflected therein.[496]

After a meeting of a subcommittee which took place in the Hague in April 1940, the work was carried on at two regional tax conferences held in Mexico City in June 1940 and July 1943 and resulted in a new model (the Mexico Model).[497] After the end

previously specified with respect to formula "*bonafide agent of independent status.*" *See* Hans Pijl, *Bulletin for International Taxation,* (2013) p. 23.

487. *See* League of Nations Fiscal Committee, "*Report to the Council on the Fourth Session of the Committee,*" Document C.399.M.204.1933.II.A, p. 6.
488. League of Nations Fiscal Committee, "*Report to the Council on the Fifth Session of the Committee,*" Document C.252.M.124.1935.II.A, Geneva (June 12-17, 1935).
489. For a general overview of the 1933 Report, *see* Michael Kobetsky, *International Taxation of Permanent Establishments: Principles and Policy,* pp. 137 et seq.
490. *See* Hans Pijl, *Bulletin for International Taxation,* (2013) p. 23.
491. In the 1935 Report, a special provision concerning the allocation of income of insurance enterprises was included. Even so, no relevant change was considered for the purposes of the permanent establishment definition in the insurance business. To this effect, *see* League of Nations Fiscal Committee, "*Report to the Council on the Fifth Session of the Committee,*" Document C.252.M.124.1935.II.A, p. 8.
492. League of Nations Fiscal Committee, "*Work of the Fiscal Committee during Its Sixth Session,*" Document C.450.M.266.1936.II.A, Geneva (October 15-21, 1936).
493. League of Nations Fiscal Committee, "*Report to the Council on the Seventh Session of the Committee,*" Document C.490.M.331.1937.II.A, Geneva (October 11-16, 1937).
494. League of Nations Fiscal Committee, "*Report to the Council on the Work of the Eight Session of the Committee,*" Document C.384.M.229.1938.II.A, Geneva (October 17-20, 1938).
495. League of Nations Fiscal Committee, "*Report to the Council on the Work of the Ninth Session of the Committee,*" Document C.181.M.110.1939.II.A, Geneva (June 12-21, 1939).
496. For a general overview of such documents, *see* Michael Kobetsky, *International Taxation of Permanent Establishments: Principles and Policy,* pp. 138 et seq.
497. League of Nations Fiscal Committee, "*Model Bilateral Conventions for the Prevention of International Double Taxation and Fiscal Evasion, Second Regional Tax Conference, Mexico D.F., July 1943,*" Document C.2.M.2.1945.II.A, Geneva (1945).

of World War II, from 20 to 26 March 1946, the League of Nations Fiscal Committee held its 10th session in London, which led to the publication of another model (the London Model).[498] Thereafter, in November 1946, the Secretariat produced a commentary on both the Mexico Model and the London Model was published.[499] Although international taxing jurisdiction over business profits was substantially different in the two documents,[500] the definition of permanent establishment was the same in both. Such a definition, contained in Art. V of the Protocol to the Mexico Model and the London Model,[501] strongly resembled the definition of permanent establishment enshrined in the 1933 Report and in the 1935 Report.[502,503] As to the agency provisions, Art. V, para. 3, contained the negative rule, i.e., no permanent establishment was deemed to exist in the presence of "*an agent of genuinely independent status (broker, commission agent, etc.)*,"[504] whereas Art. V, para. 4, contained the positive rule, i.e., an enterprise was deemed to have a permanent establishment if the conditions referred to under Art. V, para. 4 were fulfilled.[505,506]

3.2.3 The Aftermath of World War II

After World War II, the task of establishing model treaties provisions was took up by the OEEC. More to the point, the OEEC Fiscal Committee decided to study five subjects through Working Parties. Among others, Working Party No. 1 was the working party

498. League of Nations Fiscal Committee, "*Report on the Work of the Tenth Session of the Committee*," Document C.37.M.37.1946.II.A, Geneva (March 20-26, 1946).
499. League of Nations Fiscal Committee, "*London and Mexico Model Tax Conventions Commentary and Text*," Document C.88.M.88.1946.II.A, Geneva (November 1946).
500. For a comparison of the Mexico Model and the London Model with respect to the taxation of business profits, *see* Arvid A. Skaar, *Permanent Establishment—Erosion of a Tax Treaty Principle*, pp. 89-91 and Michael Kobetsky, *International Taxation of Permanent Establishments: Principles and Policy*, pp. 143-145.
501. *See* League of Nations Fiscal Committee, "*London and Mexico Model Tax Conventions Commentary and Text*," Document C.88.M.88.1946.II.A, pp. 74-77.
502. *See* Hans Pijl, *Bulletin for International Taxation*, (2013) p. 24.
503. As in the 1935 Report, a special provision concerning the allocation of income of insurance enterprises was included. However, no relevant change was considered for the purposes of the permanent establishment definition. To this effect, *see* League of Nations Fiscal Committee, "*London and Mexico Model Tax Conventions Commentary and Text*," Document C.88.M.88.1946.II.A, pp. 82-83.
504. For a comprehensive overview of the meaning of independent agents under the Mexico Model and the London Model, *see* Sidney I. Roberts, "The Agency Element of Permanent Establishment: The OECD Commentaries from the Civil Law View (Part One)," *Intertax* (1993) pp. 411 et seq.
505. *See* Hans Pijl, *Bulletin for International Taxation*, (2013) p. 25.
506. It should be noted that the unofficial commentary suggested that an agent who had the power to make contracts binding the principal was not independent. However, this neither fitted into the historical development of the permanent establishment provisions before 1946, nor into the text (and the internal system) of the Mexico Model and the London Model, nor into the system later adopted in the 1963 OECD Draft. *See* Hans Pijl, *Bulletin for International Taxation*, (2013) p. 25 and John F. Avery Jones/David A. Ward, *European Taxation*, (1993) p. 166.

on permanent establishments and was made up of representatives from Germany and the UK.[507,508]

On September 17, 1956, the OEEC Fiscal Committee submitted the Report of the Working Party No. 1 (the 1956 Report).[509] As for the agency permanent establishment, the 1956 Report deviated from the text used in the Mexico Model and London Model and took the DTAs concluded in the previous decade into account. Specifically, under para. 4 of the permanent establishment definition, the 1956 Report limited the categories of dependent agents who could be deemed to constitute permanent establishments, namely: (*i*) agents that hold and habitually exercise a general authority to negotiate and to enter into contracts and (*ii*) the stock holding agent.[510,511] This limitation was coupled with the introduction of a carve-out for agents of an independent status in the very same positive specification and further clarified in the negative rule, which was shifted to para. 5 of the definition. In doing so, the concepts of "*bonafide*" and "*genuinely*" adopted in previous reports have been reshaped into the more precise and concrete "*acting in the ordinary course of their business as such.*"[512,513] Also, the wording "*etc.*" has been replaced with "*any other agent of a generally independent status.*"[514,515]

---

507. *See* Hans Pijl, "Agency Permanent Establishments: in the name of and the Relationship between Article 5(5) and (6)—Part 2," *Bulletin for International Taxation* (2013) p. 62 and Nadine Oberbauer in: Michael Lang/Pasquale Pistone/Josef Schuch/Claus Staringer/Alfred Storck (eds.) *Dependent Agents as Permanent Establishments*, pp. 220-221.
508. Working Party No. 7 was appointed to consider the allocation of profits to permanent establishments. In doing so, Working Party No. 7 contemplated a specific rule for insurance enterprises, i.e., an apportionment of total income by reference to premium received from policyholders in each of the countries concerned. At any rate, no relevant point was considered for the purposes of the permanent establishment definition. To this effect, *see*—among others—Working Party No. 7 of the OEEC Fiscal Committee, "*Revised report on the allocation of profits to permanent establishments and associated enterprises,*" Document FC/WP7(60)1, Paris (January 18, 1960).
509. OEEC Fiscal Committee, "*Report of Working Party No. 1 on the concept of permanent establishment,*" Document FC/WP1(56)1, Paris (September 17, 1956).
510. *See* OEEC Fiscal Committee, "*Report of Working Party No. 1 on the concept of permanent establishment,*" Document FC/WP1(56)1, p. 4.
511. Under the second sentence of para. 4 of the definition, an employee was considered to give rise to a permanent establishment in the case he satisfied the same conditions. To this effect, *see* OEEC Fiscal Committee, "*Report of Working Party No. 1 on the concept of permanent establishment,*" Document FC/WP1(56)1, pp. 4 and 11.
512. *See* OEEC Fiscal Committee, "*Report of Working Party No. 1 on the concept of permanent establishment,*" Document FC/WP1(56)1, p. 4.
513. At any rate, according to Pijl, the concept of independence continued to imply both economic and legal independence. To this effect, *see* Hans Pijl, *Bulletin for International Taxation*, (2013) p. 67.
514. *See* OEEC Fiscal Committee, "*Report of Working Party No. 1 on the concept of permanent establishment,*" Document FC/WP1(56)1, p. 4. A similar wording was first considered in the commentary on the Mexico Model and the London Model. To this effect, *see* League of Nations Fiscal Committee, "*London and Mexico Model Tax Conventions Commentary and Text,*" Document C.88.M.88.1946.II.A, pp. 16-17.
515. In the 1956 Report, the commentary also suggested that the examples of independent agents could be supplemented, as this might be necessitated by national legislation. *See* OEEC Fiscal Committee, "*Report of Working Party No. 1 on the concept of permanent establishment,*" Document FC/WP1(56)1, p. 12. However, this sentence was eventually eliminated in later

In the following months, some amendments to the 1956 Report have been discussed during additional sessions of the OEEC Fiscal Committee. Some of them have been included in a few revised reports.[516] Among others, in the revised report of January 5, 1957,[517] the agent and the employee have been drawn together in the first sentence of para. 4 and the second sentence of the very same paragraph has been deleted correspondingly.[518] In the revised report of August 29, 1957,[519] the stock holding agent provision has been deleted and—as a consequence—only the agent with an authority[520] to negotiate or[521] to enter into contracts on behalf of the enterprise remained.[522,523] In the Final Report of November 12, 1957,[524] the wording "*to negotiate contracts*" was deleted and the commentary was changed accordingly.[525] Such a document was further discussed and published again on January 31, 1958,[526] with a reservation in respect of Belgium and Luxembourg regarding the stock holding agent.[527,528]

In the draft report of the OEEC Fiscal Committee of February 13, 1958,[529] no significant changes have been made. By contrast, in the revised version of such a draft report of April 19, 1958,[530] the word "*territories*" has been changed into "*Contracting States,*" the language "*on behalf of the enterprise*" in the second part of para. 4 has been changed into "*in the name of the enterprise*" and the commentary was amended

---

reports, probably because the wording "*any other agent of a generally independent status*" was considered to be sufficient. *See* Hans Pijl, *Bulletin for International Taxation,* (2013) pp. 66-67.

516. For a comprehensive overview of such sessions and reports, *see* Hans Pijl, *Bulletin for International Taxation,* (2013) pp. 67 et seq.
517. Working Party No. 1 of the OEEC Fiscal Committee, "*Report on the concept of permanent establishment,*" Document FC/WP1(57)1, Paris (January 5, 1957).
518. *See* Working Party No. 1 of the OEEC Fiscal Committee, "*Report on the concept of permanent establishment,*" Document FC/WP1(57)1, p. 5.
519. Working Party No. 1 of the OEEC Fiscal Committee, "*Report on the concept of permanent establishment,*" Document FC/WP1(57)2, Paris (August 29, 1957).
520. The Revised Report of August 29, 1957 changed "*general authority*" into "*authority.*"
521. The Revised Report of August 29, 1957 changed "*and*" into "*or.*"
522. *See* Working Party No. 1 of the OEEC Fiscal Committee, "*Report on the concept of permanent establishment,*" Document FC/WP1(57)2, p. 5.
523. For a comprehensive overview of this change, *see* John F. Avery Jones/Jürgen Lüdicke, *World Tax Journal,* (2014) pp. 222-223 and John F. Avery Jones, "The Origins of Articles 5(5) and 5(6) of the Model" in: Michael Lang/Pasquale Pistone/Josef Schuch/Claus Staringer/Alfred Storck (eds.) *Dependent Agents as Permanent Establishments* (Vienna: Linde, 2014) pp. 14-15.
524. Working Party No. 1 of the OEEC Fiscal Committee, "*Final Report on the concept of permanent establishment,*" Document FC/WP1(57)3, Paris (November 12, 1957).
525. *See* Working Party No. 1 of the OEEC Fiscal Committee, "*Final Report on the concept of permanent establishment,*" Document FC/WP1(57)3, pp. 5 and 12-13.
526. OEEC Fiscal Committee, "*Concept of permanent establishment,*" Document FC(58)1, Paris (January 31, 1958).
527. *See* OEEC Fiscal Committee, "*Concept of permanent establishment,*" Document FC(58)1, p. 1.
528. The reservation put forward by Belgium and Luxembourg on the stock holding agent has been withdrawn in following sessions. To this effect, *see* Hans Pijl, *Bulletin for International Taxation,* (2013) pp. 71-72.
529. OEEC Fiscal Committee, "*Draft Report by the Fiscal Committee on its activities,*" Document FC(58)2, Paris (February 13, 1958).
530. OEEC Fiscal Committee, "*Draft Report by the Fiscal Committee on its activities,*" Document FC(58)2(1st Revision), Part I, Paris (April 19, 1958). In the online version, the relevant pages on the definition of permanent establishment are missing.

correspondingly.[531,532] In the Report of the OEEC Fiscal Committee of May 28, 1958,[533] some minor changes were additionally made. Finally, on July 11, 1958, the OEEC Council adopted Recommendation C(58)118(Final),[534] which contained the permanent establishment provision as set out in the Report of the OEEC Fiscal Committee of May 28, 1958.[535,536]

3.3 THE CONCEPT OF PERMANENT ESTABLISHMENT IN THE OECD MODEL

3.3.1 Historical Overview

The work on a draft convention was resumed in the early sixties. When doing so, after the foundation of the OECD—which superseded the OEEC—pursuant to a proposal put forward by the Belgian delegation,[537] a last sentence was added to para. 21 of the commentary on Art. 5 of the draft convention to the effect that "*the special problems which can arise in the case of insurance companies dealing by means of intermediaries or variously qualified representatives shall be further studied.*"[538]

Shortly after the adoption of the 1963 OECD Draft, a number of topics regarding the permanent establishment definition were opened up for discussion again.[539] Among others, the Belgian delegation made a concrete proposal in order to determine whether an insurance agent has an authority to conclude contracts in the name of the enterprise as follows: "*[h]owever, an insurance enterprise of a Contracting State shall be deemed to have a permanent establishment in the other State if, either through a representative who is a person to whom this paragraph applies or through an agent of an independent status who has and habitually exercises an authority to conclude contracts*

531. OEEC Fiscal Committee, "*Draft Report by the Fiscal Committee on its activities,*" Document FC(58)2(1st Revision), Part II, Paris (April 19, 1958).
532. No documents explain the second change. For a comprehensive overview of such a change, *see* Hans Pijl, *Bulletin for International Taxation,* (2013) pp. 72-75, John F. Avery Jones/Jürgen Lüdicke, *World Tax Journal,* (2014) pp. 220-222, John F. Avery Jones in: Michael Lang/Pasquale Pistone/Josef Schuch/Claus Staringer/Alfred Storck (eds.) *Dependent Agents as Permanent Establishments*, pp. 12-14.
533. OEEC Fiscal Committee, "*Report by the Fiscal Committee on its activities,*" Document C(58)118, Part I, Paris (May 28, 1958).
534. Recommendation of the Council concerning the elimination of double taxation, C(58)118(Final) (July 15, 1958).
535. *See* Recommendation of the Council concerning the elimination of double taxation, C(58)118(Final), pp. 5-6.
536. *See* Hans Pijl, *Bulletin for International Taxation,* (2013) pp. 71-72.
537. *See* OECD Fiscal Committee, "*Minutes of the 10th Session held at the Chateau de la Muette, Paris, on Tuesday 14th, Wednesday 15th, Thursday 16th and Friday 17th May, 1963,*" Document FC/M(63)4, Paris (June 24, 1963), p. 4.
538. *See* OECD Fiscal Committee, "*Corrigendum and addendum to the English text of the Commentaries,*" Document TFD/FC/161, Paris (June 24, 1963), p. 2.
539. *See* OECD Fiscal Committee, "*Consolidated list of outstanding points concerning the OECD draft convention on income and capital,*" Document TFD/FC/218, Paris (July 21, 1967), pp. 12 et seq.

in its name, it receives premiums in the territory of that other State or insures risks situated in that territory."[540]

In the light of the above, Working Party No. 1 was instructed to continue its work on the permanent establishment definition.[541] In the preliminary report of August 17, 1970,[542] Working Party No. 1 studied all aspects of the permanent establishment definition. In doing so, Working Party No. 1 addressed the issue of an independent agent who has an authority to regularly conclude contracts in the name of another enterprise leaning toward to the conclusion that such an independent agent was not to be regarded a permanent establishment.[543,544] In addition, Working Party No. 1 addressed the issue of the insurance agent clause acknowledging that the language suggested by the Belgian delegation appeared to treat a fully independent insurance representative as a permanent establishment by virtue of the fact that "*the insurance representative who, to outward appearances, acts as an independent agent may be regarded as a PE to the extent that he actually is dependent on an insurance enterprise both legally and economically. Representatives who not only conclude insurance contracts but also collect premiums are normally subject to strict supervision by the insurance company so that, in this respect, they cannot be regarded as economically independent. However, such dependence would not only result from the fact that the company itself insures risks in the State in which the representative operates.*"[545] Having said that, however, Working Party No. 1 concluded that the question of including such a provision should be resolved during the bilateral negotiations.[546]

After the organizational change from the OECD Fiscal Committee to the OECD CFA, the preliminary report of August 17, 1970 was discussed in four meetings.[547] In the third meeting—occurred from January 11 to 14, 1972—the agency permanent establishment provisions have been discussed. The minutes of such a meeting show conflicting opinions both with respect to the independent agent provision and the insurance agent clause.[548] With respect to the latter, Working Party No. 1 decided that

540. *See* OECD Fiscal Committee, "*Consolidated list of outstanding points concerning the OECD draft convention*," Document TFD/FC/218, pp. 17-18.
541. *See* Hans Pijl, *Bulletin for International Taxation*, (2013) p. 79.
542. Working Party No. 1 of the OECD Fiscal Committee, "*Preliminary report on the questions in connection with the definition in article 5 of the term permanent establishment*," Document FC/WP1(70)1, Paris (August 17, 1970).
543. *See* Working Party No. 1 of the OECD Fiscal Committee, "*Preliminary report on the questions in connection with the definition in article 5 of the term permanent establishment*," Document FC/WP1(70)1, paras. 56-58.
544. For a comprehensive analysis of this reasoning, *see* Hans Pijl, *Bulletin for International Taxation*, (2013) pp. 80-81 and John F. Avery Jones/Jürgen Lüdicke, *World Tax Journal*, (2014) pp. 237-238.
545. *See* Working Party No. 1 of the OECD Fiscal Committee, "*Preliminary report on the questions in connection with the definition in article 5 of the term permanent establishment*," Document FC/WP1(70)1, para. 60.
546. *See* Working Party No. 1 of the OECD Fiscal Committee, "*Preliminary report on the questions in connection with the definition in article 5 of the term permanent establishment*," Document FC/WP1(70)1, para. 60.
547. *See* Hans Pijl, *Bulletin for International Taxation*, (2013) p. 81.
548. As for the insurance agent clause, the French delegation stated that the clause which France often inserted in its DTAs, and from which the idea in the Belgian proposal was derived, was less restrictive than the latter in that this expressly covered the case of independent agents. The

it would be for the negotiating parties to decide whether such a special clause should be inserted.[549]

In the second report dated May 18, 1973,[550] on the one hand, Working Party No. 1—which had become Working Group No. 1—confirmed the approach taken on the independent agent in the previous report.[551] On the other hand, Working Group No. 1 revised the language of the insurance agent clause acknowledging that insurance companies could "*do large-scale business in one of the States without being taxed in that State on their profits arising from such business. In order to obviate this possibility, various Conventions concluded by Member States include a provision which stipulates that insurance companies of one State are deemed to have a PE in the other State if they collect premiums in that other State through an agent—other than an agent who already constitutes a PE by virtue of paragraph 4—or insure risks situated in that territory through such agent.*"[552] With this in mind, Working Group No. 1 considered that the decision to include such a provision will depend on the factual and legal situation prevailing in the countries concerned and thus it would not seem advisable to insert a provision along these lines in the model treaties.[553] Pursuant to additional discussions on the second report, on September 7, 1973, a revised commentary on Art. 5 of the draft convention was presented.[554] However, such a document did not touch upon the agency permanent establishment. In the revised report of August 30, 1974,[555] the auxiliary activity exception at the end of Art. 5, para. 4, was extended to encompass the

Austrian delegation shared the views of the French delegation, stating that through the operation of the exemption method the activities in question could not be taxed anywhere, since Austria lost its right to tax. On the contrary, the Portuguese, Spanish, Swedish and Turkish delegations agreed with the Belgian proposal. To this effect, *see* Working Party No. 1 of the OECD CFA, "*Summary of discussions at the third meeting of working party no. 1 on double taxation,*" Document DAF/CFA/WP1/72/3, Paris (February 14, 1972), p. 3.

549. *See* Working Party No. 1 of the OECD CFA, "*Summary of discussions at the third meeting of working party no. 1 on double taxation,*" Document DAF/CFA/WP1/72/3, pp. 2-3.
550. Working Party No. 1 of the OECD CFA, "*Second report by working group no. 1 on potential amendments to article 5 and to the commentary thereon,*" Document DAF/CFA/2697, Paris (May 18, 1973).
551. Such a report contained a sentence in para. 21a stating that the conclusion of any binding contract on the principal or with economic consequences for the principal would fall outside the ordinary course of the business. However, such a sentence—which did not fit into the model—was removed before the 1977 OECD Model came to life. To this effect, *see* Hans Pijl, *Bulletin for International Taxation*, (2013) pp. 81-83 and John F. Avery Jones/Jürgen Lüdicke, *World Tax Journal*, (2014) pp. 238-239.
552. *See* Working Party No. 1 of the OECD CFA, "*Second report by working group no. 1 on potential amendments to article 5 and to the commentary thereon,*" Document DAF/CFA/2697, pp. 27-28.
553. *See* Working Party No. 1 of the OECD CFA, "*Second report by working group no. 1 on potential amendments to article 5 and to the commentary thereon,*" Document DAF/CFA/2697, p. 28.
554. Steering Group of Working Party No. 1 of the OECD CFA, "*Revised commentary on article 5 of the OECD draft convention,*" Document DAF/CFA/73.1, Paris (September 7, 1973).
555. Working Party No. 1 of the OECD CFA, "*Revised report on article 5,*" Document CFA/WP1(74)6, Paris (August 30, 1974).

collection of information.[556] Conversely, no change was proposed to the insurance agent clause.[557]

Following some meetings of Working Party No. 1,[558] a third report was presented on October 13, 1975.[559] In such a report, substantial changes were made to Art. 5 and the related commentary. Among others, building and construction sites were moved to a separate para. 3 and—thus—the provisions on the agency permanent establishment shifted to paras. 5 and 6. Also, in what became para. 5, the *incipit* was changed to clarify that it is not the agent which is a permanent establishment but rather the enterprise that is deemed to have a permanent establishment,[560] the agency permanent establishment was extended to encompass any activities carried out by the agent[561] and the exceptions at the end of the paragraph were largely revised.[562] In what became para. 6, the language "*[a]n enterprise shall not be deemed to have a permanent establishment in the other Contracting State*" was changed into "*[a]n enterprise shall be deemed not to have a permanent establishment in a Contracting State.*"[563,564] In the commentary on Art. 5, pursuant to a suggestion put forward by the delegate for Japan,[565] the first sentence of the insurance agent clause was shortened and—as a result—such a provision assumed its current structure.[566]

556. *See* Working Party No. 1 of the OECD CFA, "*Revised report on article 5,*" Document CFA/WP1(74)6, p. 4.
557. *See* Working Party No. 1 of the OECD CFA, "*Revised report on article 5,*" Document CFA/WP1(74)6, p. 29.
558. For an overview of the main issues related to the definition of an agency permanent establishment discussed during such meetings, *see* Hans Pijl, *Bulletin for International Taxation*, (2013) p. 82.
559. Working Party No. 1 of the OECD CFA, "*Third report on article 5,*" Document CFA/WP1(75)6, Paris (October 13, 1975).
560. To this effect, *see* Working Party No. 1 of the OECD CFA, "*Third report on article 5,*" Document CFA/WP1(75)6, p. 20.
561. The provision contained in para. 14 of the commentary on Art. 5 of the revised report of August 30, 1974 has been reflected—with a few amendments—in para. 31 of the commentary on Art. 5 in the third report of October 13, 1975. In this respect, it should however be noted that this amendment was not consistent with the insertion of the final sentence of para. 33 of the commentary on Art. 5 contained in the third report of October 13, 1975 (and confirmed in later versions of the commentary), which dealt with a commission agent going beyond the ordinary course of business and—thus—deemed to constitute a permanent establishment in respect of a specific activity. To this effect, *see* Sidney I. Roberts, *Intertax*, (1993) pp. 419-420 and John F. Avery Jones/Jürgen Lüdicke, *World Tax Journal*, (2014) p. 240.
562. *See* Working Party No. 1 of the OECD CFA, "*Third report on article 5,*" Document CFA/WP1(75)6, p. 3.
563. *See* Working Party No. 1 of the OECD CFA, "*Third report on article 5,*" Document CFA/WP1(75)6, p. 3.
564. However, it is worth noting that the previous language was eventually reinstated in the 1977 OECD Model.
565. The delegate for Japan thought there was little justification in developing at length the single case of agencies of insurance companies. *See* Working Party No. 1 of the OECD CFA, "*Summary of the discussion at the 16th meeting* of *Working Party n° 1 on double taxation,*" Document DAF/CFA/WP1/75.11, Paris (July 21, 1975), p. 3.
566. *See* Working Party No. 1 of the OECD CFA, "*Third report on article 5,*" Document CFA/WP1(75)6, pp. 23-24.

Further to additional meetings of Working Party No. 1,[567] revised texts of Art. 5 and of its commentaries have been submitted for information on April 7, 1976.[568] In such a document, the independent agent provision assumed the structure in place before the BEPS Project.[569] In the related commentary, additional clarification has been introduced in paras. 29 and 33, bullet points a) and b).[570] A few months later, a revised commentary was submitted to Working Party No. 1 for adoption on November 5, 1976.[571] In such a document, the clarification previously reported in para. 33, bullet points a) and b), assumed the status of separate paragraphs, namely paras. 35 and 36.[572] Thereafter, a full report was submitted to the OECD CFA for adoption.[573] In such a report, in Art. 5, para. 5, the language "*if a person*" has been changed into "*where a person,*" so that such a provision assumed the structure in place before the BEPS Project.[574]

In the following update, which occurred in 1992, it is worth noting that—following a decision delivered by the UK Commissioner[575]—the UK added an observation in para. 45 of the 1992 OECD Model Commentary on Art. 5 so as to clarify that: "*[t]he United Kingdom considers that an agent who is not an agent of independent status within paragraph 6 of this Article and who has the characteristics described in paragraphs 32 and 33 above will represent a permanent establishment of an enterprise if he has the authority to conclude contracts on behalf of the enterprise whether in his own name or that of the enterprise.*"[576] In the next update, pursuant to a proposal put forward by the UK delegate, such language was later inserted as the eighth sentence into para. 32 of the 1994 OECD Model Commentary on Art. 5 as a general clarification and the above UK observation was withdrawn accordingly.[577]

567. *See* Working Party No. 1 of the OECD CFA, "*Summary of discussions concerning the eighteenth meeting of Working Party no. 1 on double taxation,*" Document DAF/CFA/WP1/76.1, Paris (January 9, 1976), and Working Party No. 1 of the OECD CFA, "*Resume des debats de la dix-neuvieme reunion du Groupe de Travail n° 1 sur la double imposition,*" Document DAF/CFA/WP1/76.3, Paris (March 4, 1976).
568. Working Party No. 1 of the OECD CFA, "*Revised texts of Article 5 and of the commentary thereon,*" Document CFA/WP1(76)6, Paris (April 7, 1976).
569. *See* Working Party No. 1 of the OECD CFA, "*Revised texts of Article 5 and of the commentary thereon,*" Document CFA/WP1(76)6, p. 2.
570. *See* Working Party No. 1 of the OECD CFA, "*Revised texts of Article 5 and of the commentary thereon,*" Document CFA/WP1(76)6, pp. 20-23.
571. Working Party No. 1 of the OECD CFA, "*Revised commentary on the 1963 draft convention,*" Document DAF/CFA/WP1/76.19, Paris (November 5, 1976).
572. *See* Working Party No. 1 of the OECD CFA, "*Revised commentary on the 1963 draft convention,*" Document DAF/CFA/WP1/76.19, p. 25.
573. OECD CFA, "*Report on the revision of the 1963 Draft Convention for the avoidance of double taxation,*" Document CFA(76)7, Part I, Paris (December 2, 1976), Part II, Paris (November 22, 1976), Corrigendum to Part II, Paris (December 20, 1976), Part III, Paris (December 21, 1976), Part IV, Paris (December 30, 1976).
574. *See* OECD CFA, "*Report on the revision of the 1963 Draft Convention for the avoidance of double taxation,*" Document CFA(76)7, Part II, Paris (November 22, 1976), p. 16.
575. *See* Hans Pijl, *Bulletin for International Taxation*, (2013) pp. 83-84 and John F. Avery Jones/David A. Ward, *European Taxation*, (1993) p. 161.
576. *See* 1992 OECD Model Commentary on Art. 5, para. 45.
577. For a more detailed analysis of this insertion, *see* Hans Pijl, *Bulletin for International Taxation*, (2013) p. 84.

Although a number of issues regarding the agency permanent establishment (among others, the insurance agent clause) have been extensively discussed within Working Party No. 1 in late nineties,[578] the commentary on such a concept has not been changed until 2003.[579] In that update, it was primarily clarified that agents acting for the foreign enterprise do not need either to be a resident of the source State or to have a place of business therein.[580] Next, the second change concerned the effective power to bind the principal. More precisely, the eighth sentence of para. 32 of the 1994 OECD Model Commentary on Art. 5 was shifted to para. 32.1 of the 2003 OECD Model Commentary on Art. 5 and was supplemented by: (*i*) a statement saying that "*[l]ack of active involvement by an enterprise in transactions may be indicative of a grant of authority to an agent*" and (*ii*) an illustrative example of an agent that solicits and receives (but does not formalize) orders.[581] Third, another change addressed the interpretation of the expression "*habitually exercises (...) an authority to conclude contracts.*"[582] At last, a few changes have been introduced in paras. 38-38.8 to clarify the elements that may be useful in assessing the independence of the agent and the ordinary course of its business. As to the former, according to such changes, besides the entrepreneurial risks borne by the agent,[583] reference should also be made to the control exercised by the principal over the activities of the agent[584] and the number of principals.[585] Instead, with respect to the ordinary course of business, while confirming that one should assess whether the activities performed by the agent belong to the economic sphere of the principal,[586] the OECD also clarified that a comparison should be made against the activities customarily performed by independent agents within a certain trade.[587]

In the 2005 OECD Model Commentary, the OECD clarified that the mere fact that a person participates in meetings for the negotiation of contracts is not enough—in itself—to conclude that the person has exercised an authority to conclude contracts in the name of a foreign enterprise.[588]

578. *See—inter alia*—Working Party No. 1 of the OECD CFA, "*Issues arising under article 5 (permanent establishment) of the model tax convention,*" Document DAFFE/CFA/WP1/WD(95)13/REV2, Paris (October 2, 1995), Working Party No. 1 of the OECD CFA, "*Issues arising under article 5 (permanent establishment) of the model tax convention,*" Document DAFFE/CFA/WP1/WD(95)13/REV3, Paris (September 13, 1996), Working Party No. 1 of the OECD CFA, "*Issues arising under article 5 (permanent establishment) of the model tax convention,*" Document DAFFE/CFA/WP1/WD(95)13/REV6, Paris (December 22, 1997).
579. For a detailed description of such changes, *see* Alessandro Caridi, "Proposed Changes to the OECD Commentary on Article 5: Part II—The Constructive PE Notion, the Negative List and the Agency PE Notion," *European Taxation* (2003) pp. 42 et seq. and Hans Pijl, "The Concept of Permanent Establishment and the Proposed Changes to the OECD Commentary with Special Reference to Dutch Case Law," *Bulletin for International Taxation* (2002) pp. 560-562.
580. *See* 2003 OECD Model Commentary on Art. 5, para. 32.
581. *See* 2003 OECD Model Commentary on Art. 5, para. 32.1.
582. *See* 2003 OECD Model Commentary on Art. 5, para. 33.1.
583. *See* 2003 OECD Model Commentary on Art. 5, para. 38.
584. *See* 2003 OECD Model Commentary on Art. 5, paras. 38.1-38.5.
585. *See* 2003 OECD Model Commentary on Art. 5, para. 38.6.
586. *See* 2003 OECD Model Commentary on Art. 5, para. 38.7.
587. *See* 2003 OECD Model Commentary on Art. 5, para. 38.8.
588. *See* 2005 OECD Model Commentary on Art. 5, para. 33.

Between 2011 and 2012, the OECD released two public discussion drafts dealing with questions related to the permanent establishment definition.[589] In doing so, the OECD identified six questions concerning the agent permanent establishment provisions, one of which being specifically related to the insurance agent clause. In general, the proposed solutions to answer such questions went in the direction of either not restricting the interpretation of the requirements by including some examples in the 2010 OECD Model Commentary or not providing any immediate solutions in view of further work, whereas—with respect to the specific insurance agent clause—it was agreed that no changes should be made to the 2010 OECD Model Commentary. Even so, the analysis of such questions shed some light on a number of issues that has been further scrutinized in the context of the BEPS Project.[590]

As a matter of fact, the OECD took up the work on the permanent establishment definition in the context of Action 7 of the BEPS Project. With specific respect to the dependent agent permanent establishment provisions, in October 2014, the OECD released a discussion draft for public comments with four different alternatives providing possibilities to amend the current wording of the OECD Model and the OECD Model Commentary.[591,592] Thereafter, in May 2015, the OECD released a revised draft for further public comments choosing Option B as the preferred option[593,594] and, in

589. OECD, "*Interpretation and Application of Article 5 (Permanent Establishment) of the OECD Model Tax Convention*," Paris (October 12, 2011) and OECD, "*OECD Model Tax Convention: Revised Proposals Concerning the Interpretation and Application of Article 5 (Permanent Establishment)*," Paris (October 19, 2012). For further comments on such documents, *see*—among others—Oliver R. Hoor, "Comments on the OECD Discussion Draft on the Meaning of 'Permanent Establishment'," *Tax Notes International* (2012) pp. 207-214, Diego Avolio/Paolo Ruggiero, "Le proposte di modifica al Commentario OCSE sulla stabile organizzazione," *Corriere Tributario* (2012) pp. 1112 et seq., Richard Collier, "BEPS Action Plan, Action 7: Preventing the Artificial Avoidance of PE Status," *British Tax Review* (2013) pp. 640-641 and Alessandro Dragonetti/Valerio Piacentini/Anna Sfondrini, *Manuale di fiscalità internazionale* (Milano: IPSOA, 2014) pp. 1024 et seq.

590. To this effect, *see* Alfred Storck/Raffaele Petruzzi, "Permanent Establishments: Proposals Related to the Agency Permanent Establishments—Article 5(5) and (6) of the OECD Model Convention" in: Michael Lang/Pasquale Pistone/Alexander Rust/Josef Schuch/Claus Staringer (eds.) *Base Erosion and Profit Shifting (BEPS)* (Vienna: Linde, 2016) pp. 91-94.

591. *See* OECD, "*Public Discussion Draft—BEPS Action 7: Preventing the Artificial Avoidance of PE Status*," Paris (October 31, 2014).

592. For further comments on the proposed solutions, *see also* Heinz-Klaus Kroppen, "Neues zur Betriebsstätte unter Berücksichtigung der Vorschläge der OECD vom 31.10.2014 und vom 15.5.2015" in: Jürgen Lüdicke/Rudolf Mellinghoff/Thomas Rödder (eds.) *Nationale und internationale Unternehmensbesteuerung in der Rechtsordnung: Festschrift für Dietmar Gosch zum Ausscheiden aus dem Richteramt* (Munich: Beck, 2016) pp. 223-227, Alfred Storck/Raffaele Petruzzi in: Michael Lang/Pasquale Pistone/Alexander Rust/Josef Schuch/Claus Staringer (eds.) *Base Erosion and Profit Shifting (BEPS)*, pp. 96-99 and Patrick Held, *BEPS Aktionspunkt 7: Die Verhinderung der künstlichen Vermeidung einer Betriebsstätte* (Hamburg: Interdisziplinäres Zentrum für Internationales Finanz- und Steuerwesen (IIFS), 2017) pp. 6 et seq.

593. *See* OECD, "*Revised discussion draft—BEPS Action 7: Preventing the Artificial Avoidance of PE Status*," Paris (May 15, 2015).

594. For further comments on the revised draft, *see also* Alfred Storck/Raffaele Petruzzi in: Michael Lang/Pasquale Pistone/Alexander Rust/Josef Schuch/Claus Staringer (eds.) *Base Erosion and Profit Shifting (BEPS)*, pp. 99-100 and Patrick Held, *BEPS Aktionspunkt 7: Die Verhinderung der künstlichen Vermeidung einer Betriebsstätte*, pp. 12 et seq.

October 2015, a final report with a number of proposed amendments, which have been eventually introduced in the current version of the OECD Model and the related OECD Model Commentary in November 2017.[595]

3.3.2 Elements of the Current Provision

3.3.2.1 Wording of the Provision

In its current form, Art. 5, para. 5, of the OECD Model reads as follows:

> Notwithstanding the provisions of paragraphs 1 and 2 but subject to the provisions of paragraph 6, where a person is acting in a Contracting State on behalf of an enterprise and, in doing so, habitually concludes contracts, or habitually plays the principal role leading to the conclusion of contracts that are routinely concluded without material modification by the enterprise, and these contracts are:
>
> (a) in the name of the enterprise; or
> (b) for the transfer of the ownership of, or for the granting of the right to use, property owned by that enterprise or that the enterprise has the right to use; or
> (c) for the provision of services by that enterprise.
>
> that enterprise shall be deemed to have a permanent establishment in that State in respect of any activities which that person undertakes for the enterprise, unless the activities of such person are limited to those mentioned in paragraph 4 which, if exercised through a fixed place of business (other than a fixed place of business to which paragraph 4.1 would apply), would not make this fixed place of business a permanent establishment under the provisions of that paragraph.

On the other hand, Art. 5, para. 6, of the OECD Model stipulates that:

> Paragraph 5 shall not apply where the person acting in a Contracting State on behalf of an enterprise of the other Contracting State carries on business in the first-mentioned State as an independent agent and acts for the enterprise in the ordinary course of that business. Where, however, a person acts exclusively or almost exclusively on behalf of one or more enterprises to which it is closely related, that person shall not be considered to be an independent agent within the meaning of this paragraph with respect to any such enterprise.

3.3.2.2 Rationale of the Provision

The *incipit* of Art. 5, para. 5, of the OECD Model makes it clear that this is a rule that deems a permanent establishment to exist with respect to activities of a foreign enterprise that would not otherwise be attributed to a permanent establishment in the source country as defined under the basic rule. Indeed, as clearly explained in para. 100 of the OECD Model Commentary on Art. 5, such a rule is an alternative to the basic permanent establishment rule contained in Art. 5, para. 1, of the OECD Model

595. The amendments introduced in the context of Action 7 of the BEPS Project have been incorporated in Arts. 12-15 of the MLI. The implementation of such MLI provisions in some selected countries will be analyzed in Chapter 5 below.

and—therefore—if a permanent establishment already exists under the basic rule, the agency permanent establishment rule becomes irrelevant.[596,597]

In a report of 2002 concerning a number of issues with respect to permanent establishments,[598] the OECD argued—on the one hand—that the rationale behind such a provision is to prevent foreign enterprises from escaping source taxation by operating through local agents rather than directly through a fixed place of business. According to such a view, the agency permanent establishment concept may be seen as "*manipulation proof*" clause (according to Vann, even as an anti-avoidance rule)[599,600] to the extent that it prevents situations in which taxpayers might not use a fixed place of business in the source country only for the purpose of not being subject to taxation therein.[601] On the other hand, the OECD also stated that "*paragraph 5 is intended to extend the scope of Article 5 so as to give the source country the right to tax foreign enterprises whenever they participate in the economic life of the source country so as to come within the jurisdiction of that State's taxing rights (...).*"[602] As a consequence, in such a way, the permanent establishment concept may be regarded as a means of achieving—from a tax perspective—the same result in two different situations, namely the presence or not of a fixed place of business.[603] Nevertheless, it is fair to say that there are conflicting opinions on the validity of this latter justification. Most notably, according to Vann,[604] the latter economic justification should be excluded by a paradox. Indeed, pursuant to Art. 5, para. 5, of the OECD Model, a permanent establishment would be deemed to exist where contracts are concluded through an

596. *See* Jacques Sasseville/Arvid A. Skaar in: IFA (ed.) *Is there a permanent establishment?*, pp. 49-50.
597. For an analysis of a basic permanent establishment combined with an agency permanent establishment, *see* Arthur Pleijsier, *The agency permanent establishment: de vaste vertegenwoordiger: proefschrift* (Maastricht: Universitaire Pers Maastricht, 2000) pp. 175-176 and Arthur Pleijsier, "The Agency Permanent Establishment: The Current Definition—Part One," *Intertax* (2001) p. 170.
598. *See* OECD, "*Issues arising under Article 5 (Permanent Establishment) of the Model Tax Convention,*" Paris (November 7, 2002), para. 103.
599. *See* Richard Vann, "Travellers, Tax Policy and Agency Permanent Establishments," *British Tax Review* (2010) p. 540.
600. It is interesting to note that the agency permanent establishment concept has been used as an anti-abuse tool in two recent Russian cases (No. A40-108465/2015 and No. A40-138879/2014). However, in doing so, such a concept was combined with the much broader doctrine of piercing the corporate veil, basically ignoring the criteria applicable to the OECD concept of dependent agent. As a result, such cases seem to contain inherent flaws related to a misunderstanding of the dependent agent concept. For further comments on such cases, *see* Irina Dmitrieva, "Tax Treaty Disputes in Russia" in: Eduardo Baistrocchi (ed.) *A Global Analysis of Tax Treaty Disputes* (Cambridge: Cambridge University Press, 2017) pp. 952-954.
601. To this effect, *see* Raffaele Petruzzi, "The Dependent Agent Permanent Establishment as an Extension of the Permanent Establishment Concept of Article 5(1) of the OECD Model Convention" in: Michael Lang/Pasquale Pistone/Josef Schuch/Claus Staringer/Alfred Storck (eds.) *Dependent Agents as Permanent Establishments* (Vienna: Linde, 2014) p. 36.
602. *See* OECD, "*Issues arising under Article 5 (Permanent Establishment) of the Model Tax Convention,*" para. 101.
603. *See* Raffaele Petruzzi in: Michael Lang/Pasquale Pistone/Josef Schuch/Claus Staringer/Alfred Storck (eds.) *Dependent Agents as Permanent Establishments*, p. 37. In a similar vein, *see* Arvid A. Skaar, *Permanent Establishment—Erosion of a Tax Treaty Principle*, p. 463.
604. *See* Richard Vann, *British Tax Review,* (2010) p. 549.

agent, but not in the case where contracts are concluded directly by the principal itself in the other country. Consequently, according to such a view, the same market penetration might lead to difference results.[605] At any rate, according to Petruzzi,[606] this paradox—which was indeed recognized by the OECD[607] and highlighted by Sasseville and Skaar[608]—should not necessarily lead to the conclusion that the latter economic justification of the agency permanent establishment provision is not valid.

3.3.2.3 The Dependent Agent Provision

3.3.2.3.1 The "Person"

To begin with, the first condition for the existence of a dependent agent permanent establishment is that a "*person*" is acting in a contracting State on behalf of a foreign enterprise. The fact that the OECD makes use of the term "*person*" *in lieu of* the term "*agent*" first suggests that a principal/agent relationship within the meaning of domestic law is not necessary to create a dependent agent permanent establishment.[609,610]

With this in mind, the OECD Model provides for a broad meaning of the term "*person*," which includes individuals, companies and any other body of persons.[611] Therefore, besides individuals, this definition also encompasses commercial and non-profit entities with members (such as joint-stock companies, public or private limited liability companies, proprietary companies, associations, societies, membership corporations) as well as corporate entities without members (such as foundations

605. *See* Raffaele Petruzzi in: Michael Lang/Pasquale Pistone/Josef Schuch/Claus Staringer/Alfred Storck (eds.) *Dependent Agents as Permanent Establishments*, p. 37.
606. *See* Raffaele Petruzzi in: Michael Lang/Pasquale Pistone/Josef Schuch/Claus Staringer/Alfred Storck (eds.) *Dependent Agents as Permanent Establishments*, p. 37.
607. *See* OECD, "*Issues arising under Article 5 (Permanent Establishment) of the Model Tax Convention*," para. 100.
608. *See* Jacques Sasseville/Arvid A. Skaar in: IFA (ed.) *Is there a permanent establishment?*, p. 50.
609. In a similar vein, *see* David Feuerstein, "The Agency Permanent Establishment" in: Michael Lang/Florian Brugger/Patrick Plansky (eds.) *Permanent Establishments in International and EU Tax Law* (Vienna: Linde, 2011) p. 110, Francisco A. Garcia Prats, *El establecimiento permanente: análisis jurídico-tributario internacional de la imposición societaria* (Madrid: Tecnos, 1996) p. 187 and Richard Collier/Sanjay Tolia/Prashant Bohra, "The Agency PE Conundrum," *Tax Management Transfer Pricing Report* (2007) p. 504.
610. Interestingly, while the provision under analysis is generally referred to as "*dependent agent permanent establishment*" or "*agency permanent establishment*," the reference to the terms "*agent*" or "*agency*" ought to be intended in a broad commercial sense of "*intermediary.*" *See* Francisco A. Garcia Prats, *El establecimiento permanente: análisis jurídico-tributario internacional de la imposición societaria*, p. 184, Arvid A. Skaar, *Permanent Establishment—Erosion of a Tax Treaty Principle*, p. 463, John F. Avery Jones/David A. Ward, *European Taxation*, (1993) p. 155 and John F. Avery Jones/Jürgen Lüdicke, *World Tax Journal*, (2014) p. 204.
611. *See* Art. 3, para. 1, let. (a), of the OECD Model.

or trusts).[612] Likewise, partnerships are usually persons under Art. 3 of the OECD Model and may therefore constitute a dependent agent permanent establishment.[613]

In this respect, it is also worth noting that, pursuant to the amendments introduced in the 2003 OECD Model Commentary, such a person does not need to be resident of, nor have a place of business in, the State in which he acts for the enterprise.[614] According to Feuerstein, it is also irrelevant whether the person is liable to tax (either limited or unlimited) in that country.[615]

3.3.2.3.2 The "Activity"

The person needs to carry on an "*activity*" in the other contracting State.[616] It follows that a business activity should be exercised in such other State. According to the author, this presupposes some degree of physical presence in the other contracting State.[617] As a result, in the case that the person carries on business activities solely through electronic means in another State,[618] a dependent agent permanent establishment should not arise.[619,620]

Although it is not specified whether the activity is restricted to certain types of business activities (and thus any business activity would—in principle—be covered by such a provision), it is generally acknowledged that the activities of the agent and the

---

612. To this effect, *see* para. 2 of the OECD Model Commentary on Art. 3, Ekkehart Reimer in: Ekkehart Reimer/Alexander Rust (eds.) *Klaus Vogel on Double Taxation Convention—4th edition*, p. 385 and Arthur Pleijsier, *Intertax*, (2001) p. 168.
613. For further details, *see* Ekkehart Reimer in: Ekkehart Reimer/Alexander Rust (eds.) *Klaus Vogel on Double Taxation Convention—4th edition*, p. 386.
614. *See* para. 83 of the OECD Model Commentary on Art. 5.
615. *See* David Feuerstein in: Michael Lang/Florian Brugger/Patrick Plansky (eds.) *Permanent Establishments in International and EU Tax Law*, p. 110.
616. *See* Ekkehart Reimer in: Ekkehart Reimer/Alexander Rust (eds.) *Klaus Vogel on Double Taxation Convention—4th edition*, p. 387.
617. In a similar vein, *see* Farkas Barsony, "The Agency Permanent Establishment" in: Michael Lang/Hans Jörgen Aigner/Mario Züger (eds.) *Permanent Establishments in International Tax Law*, (Vienna: Linde, 2003) p. 137 and David Feuerstein in: Michael Lang/Florian Brugger/Patrick Plansky (eds.) *Permanent Establishments in International and EU Tax Law*, p. 116.
618. The application of the permanent establishment definition in the context of electronic commerce activities will be further dealt with in Chapter 4 when discussing insurance business models.
619. In a similar vein, *see* David Feuerstein in: Michael Lang/Florian Brugger/Patrick Plansky (eds.) *Permanent Establishments in International and EU Tax Law*, p. 116, Detlev J. Piltz, "When is There an Agency Permanent Establishment?," *Bulletin for International Fiscal Documentation* (2004) p. 200 and Detlev J. Piltz, "Wann liegt eine DBA-Vertreter-Betriebsstätte vor?," *Internationales Steuerrecht* (2004) p. 185.
620. The author does not entirely agree with the reasoning put forward by Pistone and Ruiz Jiménez to argue that the physical presence does not play a relevant role. *See* Pasquale Pistone/César Alejandro Ruiz Jiménez, "Habitual Exercise of Authority to Conclude Contracts under Article 5(5) of the OECD Model Convention" in: Michael Lang/Pasquale Pistone/Josef Schuch/Claus Staringer/Alfred Storck (eds.) *Dependent Agents as Permanent Establishments* (Vienna: Linde, 2014) pp. 152-154. In fact, in their example of contracts negotiated through electronic means, the agent is present (even for a short period of time) in the source country to conclude such contracts.

principal should be interrelated to a certain extent with each other.[621] To this effect, the OECD Model Commentary clarifies that "*[t]he contracts referred to in paragraph 5 must cover contracts relating to operations which constitute the business proper of the enterprise.*"[622] For instance, it may be argued that, where an enterprise engages an agent in another country to advertise goods and services in the local media and such an agent concludes advertising contracts in the name of the foreign enterprise, such an agent would not constitute a dependent agent permanent establishment, provided that the enterprise itself is not engaged in the advertising business.[623]

Furthermore, the OECD Model Commentary also clarifies that "*[i]t would be irrelevant, for instance, if the person concluded employment contracts for the enterprise to assist that person's activity for the enterprise or if the person concluded, in the name of the enterprise, similar contracts relating to internal operations only.*"[624] It follows that a person that only performs internal operations cannot constitute an agency permanent establishment.[625]

In addition, where the person only exercises activities of a preparatory or auxiliary character dealt with under Art. 5, para. 4, of the OECD Model, such a person does not qualify as an agent under Art. 5, para. 5, of the OECD Model to the extent that the latter provision applies only to the activities that constitute the business proper of an enterprise.[626,627] For instance, this includes the delivery agent, the purchasing agent, the information collecting agent (such as a newspaper bureau).[628] Also, a marketing agent who concludes contracts necessary for his marketing activities would not implicate for the marketing agent to fall within the scope of Art. 5, para. 5, of the OECD Model.[629] On the contrary, insofar as after-sale organization may perform an essential

621. *See* Alfred Storck/Sabine Schmidjell-Dommes, "Acting on Behalf of an Enterprise under Article 5(5) of the OECD Model Convention" in: Michael Lang/Pasquale Pistone/Josef Schuch/Claus Staringer/Alfred Storck (eds.) *Dependent Agents as Permanent Establishments* (Vienna: Linde, 2014) pp. 51-52.
622. *See* para. 97 of the OECD Model Commentary on Art. 5.
623. *See* Arthur Pleijsier, *The agency permanent establishment: de vaste vertegenwoordiger: proefschrift*, pp. 172-173 and Arthur Pleijsier, *Intertax*, (2001) p. 172.
624. *See* para. 97 of the OECD Model Commentary on Art. 5.
625. For a more detailed analysis, *see* Alfred Storck/Sabine Schmidjell-Dommes in: Michael Lang/Pasquale Pistone/Josef Schuch/Claus Staringer/Alfred Storck (eds.) *Dependent Agents as Permanent Establishments*, pp. 47-49.
626. *See* para. 85 of the OECD Model Commentary on Art. 5.
627. It is irrelevant to look at the activities that the agent could theoretically carry on in the light of his mandate to the extent that the last part of Art. 5, para. 5, of the OECD Model excludes from the scope of the dependent agent provision the agent whose activities are de facto limited to those listed under Art. 5, para. 4, of the OECD Model. To this effect, *see* Marco Cerrato, "La definizione di stabile organizzazione nelle convenzioni per evitare le doppie imposizioni" in: Claudio Sacchetto/Lauro Alemanno (eds.) *Materiali di Diritto Tributario Internazionale* (Milano: IPSOA, 2002), pp. 135-136 and Klaus Vogel, *Klaus Vogel on Double Taxation Convention*, p. 334.
628. For a number of illustrative examples, *see* Nadine Oberbauer in: Michael Lang/Pasquale Pistone/Josef Schuch/Claus Staringer/Alfred Storck (eds.) *Dependent Agents as Permanent Establishments*, pp. 227-230 and Christian Schoppe/Neeraj Popat, "Lagerung, Einkauf und Austellung als Betriebsstätten ab 2017," *Betriebs-Berater* (2016) pp. 1115 et seq.
629. According to Pleijsier, a marketing agent whose primary activities fall under Art. 5, para. 4, of the OECD Model, but also concludes contracts in the name and on behalf of his principal can only be deemed to constitute a dependent agent permanent establishment in the case where: (*i*)

part of the services of an enterprise,[630] an agent performing after-sale activities cannot on this basis be exempted from a dependent agent status.[631]

In the light of the above, in the context of the insurance business, a dependent agent permanent establishment might arise in the case that the activities of the person in the source country are related to insurance contracts entered into with third parties. According to the author, this covers insurance contracts and the placement of outward reinsurance for insurance companies as well as reinsurance contracts and the placement of outward retrocession for reinsurance companies, respectively.

An interesting question arises in the event that an agent is involved in a mix of activities, e.g., activities that qualify under Art. 5, para. 5, of the OECD Model and activities that do not qualify as such. In a Dutch case,[632] a Dutch insurance agent acted on behalf of a UK property insurance company in two different ways, i.e., as a legal representative and as an authorized agent. In the Netherlands, acting as a legal representative was not considered to be an activity giving rise to a dependent agent permanent establishment, whereas acting as an authorized agent did fall within the scope of permanent establishment provisions. In that respect, the Dutch tax authorities claimed that the overall activities of the Dutch insurance agent were to be divided accordingly. This would have led to a partial taxation of the activities carried out on behalf of the UK insurance company. Nevertheless, the Dutch Supreme Court ruled that the OECD Model and the OECD Model Commentary did not provide a basis for the result that an agent who is acting on the whole as an independent agent could be regarded partially as a dependent agent.[633,634]

In the author's view, this reasoning grounded on a comprehensive assessment does not seem to be convincing to the extent that it may well be that different activities are carried on in a different fashion, even between the very same parties (for instance, by reason of dissimilar terms and conditions). This view appears to be confirmed by para. 99 of the OECD Model Commentary, which provides that, where a dependent agent permanent establishment is deemed to exist, all activities carried out by the intermediary on behalf of the foreign enterprise will be attributed to such a dependent agent permanent establishment.[635] In setting a sort of threshold,[636] this paragraph

the conclusion of contracts constitutes the biggest part of his overall activities, and (*ii*) the contracts concluded relate to operations which constitute the business proper of the principal. *See* Arthur Pleijsier, *The agency permanent establishment: de vaste vertegenwoordiger: proefschrift*, pp. 180-181 and Arthur Pleijsier, *Intertax*, (2001) pp. 176-177.

630. *See* para. 63 of the OECD Model Commentary on Art. 5.

631. *See* Arthur Pleijsier, *The agency permanent establishment: de vaste vertegenwoordiger: proefschrift*, p. 177 and Arthur Pleijsier, *Intertax*, (2001) p. 173.

632. *See* HR (*Hoge Raad*) June 28, 1995, No. 29.435, which dealt with Art. 5, para. 5, of the DTA between the Netherlands and the United Kingdom concluded on November 7, 1980.

633. *See* Arthur Pleijsier, *The agency permanent establishment: de vaste vertegenwoordiger: proefschrift*, pp. 173-175 and Arthur Pleijsier, *Intertax*, (2001) p. 173.

634. The independent agent provision will be dealt with in s. 3.3.2.4 below.

635. For instance, this leads to the result that activities considered under Art. 5, para. 4, of the OECD Model will also be attributed to the permanent establishment. This approach has been applied in the *Roche* case. For further comments on such a case, *see* s. 3.3.2.3.6 below.

636. *See* Arthur Pleijsier, *The agency permanent establishment: de vaste vertegenwoordiger: proefschrift*, p. 178 and Arthur Pleijsier, *Intertax*, (2001) p. 173.

seems to acknowledge that the agent can perform multiple activities under different terms, some of which might trigger Art. 5, para. 5, of the OECD Model to the effect that all the others are to be included in the dependent agent permanent establishment.[637]

3.3.2.3.3 *"On Behalf Of"*

The person also needs to carry on the above activities *"on behalf of"* the foreign enterprise to fulfill the criteria to constitute a permanent establishment. Therefore, it is required that the person involves the foreign enterprise to a particular extent in business activities in the source State.[638] This presupposes a relationship between two separate parties, namely the person in the source country and the foreign enterprise.[639]

In the light of the foregoing, in the event that an entrepreneur acts as his own agent, the existence of a dependent agent permanent establishment is to be excluded.[640,641] On the other hand, the amendments introduced in the context of Action 7 of the BEPS Project clarified that employees of a company,[642] partners of a

637. This reasoning has been confirmed in a recent Dutch case, whereby a Dutch financial, legal and tax specialist was deemed to be a dependent agent permanent establishment in the Netherlands in connection with certain specific activities. Interestingly enough, in such a case, the Advocate-General to the Dutch Supreme Court concluded that the judgment of the lower tier tribunal was to be intended as a clarification that the concept of permanent representative and the concept of independent representative are mutually exclusive. Hence, where a person is acting as an independent representative, it is excluded that such a person also acts as a permanent representative at the same time. On the contrary, it cannot be excluded that a person acts as an independent representative for some of his activities and as permanent representative in respect of other activities. Unfortunately, the Dutch Supreme Court did no go further to provide a clarification as to whether all (other) actions carried out by the Dutch representative for the foreign enterprise had to be attributed to the dependent agent permanent establishment. *See* HR (*Hoge Raad*) April 14, 2017, No. 15/02203.
638. *See* para. 86 of the OECD Model Commentary on Art. 5.
639. *See* Arthur Pleijsier, *The agency permanent establishment: de vaste vertegenwoordiger: proefschrift*, pp. 165-166 and Arthur Pleijsier, *Intertax*, (2001) p. 169.
640. *See* Jacques Sasseville/Arvid A. Skaar in: IFA (ed.) *Is there a permanent establishment?*, p. 50, Arthur Pleijsier, *The agency permanent establishment: de vaste vertegenwoordiger: proefschrift*, p. 164, Arthur Pleijsier, *Intertax*, (2001) p. 169, Farkas Barsony in: Michael Lang/Hans Jörgen Aigner/Mario Züger (eds.) *Permanent Establishments in International Tax Law*, p. 138, Ekkehart Reimer, "Permanent Establishment in the OECD Model Tax Convention" in: Ekkehart Reimer/Stephan Schmid/Marianne Orell (eds.) *Permanent Establishments: A Domestic Taxation, Bilateral Tax Treaty and OECD Perspective* (Alphen aan den Rijn: Kluwer Law International, 2016) Part 2[D] p. 104 and Ekkehart Reimer in: Ekkehart Reimer/Alexander Rust (eds.) *Klaus Vogel on Double Taxation Convention—4th edition*, p. 386.
641. It is worth noting that Pleijsier and Barsony touched upon a US private letter ruling concluding that an entrepreneur could constitute a dependent agent permanent establishment. Even so, according to Pleijsier, the ruling seemed to be prompted from a view to tax the profits of a foreign entrepreneur at any price. To this effect, *see* Arthur Pleijsier, *The agency permanent establishment: de vaste vertegenwoordiger: proefschrift*, pp. 164-166 and Arthur Pleijsier, *Intertax*, (2001) pp. 168-169. On the other hand, Barsony argues that such a ruling is difficult to reconcile with the OECD Model Convention to the extent that the agency permanent establishment concept is based upon the legal concept agency, which presupposes that an agent acts instead of the principal. To this effect, *see* Farkas Barsony in: Michael Lang/Hans Jörgen Aigner/Mario Züger (eds.) *Permanent Establishments in International Tax Law*, pp. 138-139.
642. Employees may be regarded as the most common form of dependent agents under Art. 5, para. 5, of the OECD Model. To this effect, *see* Ekkehart Reimer in: Ekkehart Reimer/Stephan

partnership and directors of a company may qualify as agents under Art. 5, para. 5, of the OECD Model.[643,644]

According to Storck and Schmidjell-Dommes, Art. 5, para. 5, of the French version of the OECD Model—which necessitates that *"une personne agit (...) pour le compte d'une entreprise"*—suggests that a person cannot act for another enterprise only from a legal perspective, but also from an economic standpoint.[645] Under this line of reasoning, which—according to Storck and Schmidjell-Dommes—may be extended to the English or German version of the OECD Model, a potential dependent agent that concludes contracts in his/her own name, but for the account of another enterprise, could be covered by the wording *"on behalf of."*[646]

According to the author, this reasoning has found confirmation in the amendments introduced in the context of Action 7 of the BEPS Project, whereby the OECD clarified that the foreign enterprise must be directly or indirectly affected by the actions of the person in the source country for the present criterion to be fulfilled.[647] In particular, the term *"indirectly"* seems to indicate that the question as to whether the agent acts *"on behalf of"* a foreign enterprise should not be addressed in a strict legal sense. Therefore, it is essential to determine for whom and to what extent the agent is actually acting. To make things more complicated, it may well be that the agent is acting *"on behalf of"* a certain principal in some instances, while also acting *"on behalf*

Schmid/Marianne Orell (eds.) *Permanent Establishments: A Domestic Taxation, Bilateral Tax Treaty and OECD Perspective,* Part 2[D] p. 104, Ekkehart Reimer in: Ekkehart Reimer/Alexander Rust (eds.) *Klaus Vogel on Double Taxation Convention—4th edition,* p. 386 and Alfred Storck/Sabine Schmidjell-Dommes in: Michael Lang/Pasquale Pistone/Josef Schuch/Claus Staringer/Alfred Storck (eds.) *Dependent Agents as Permanent Establishments,* p. 51.

643. *See* para. 86 of the OECD Model Commentary on Art. 5. This clarification overrides the argument put forward by Feuerstein according to which, since directors of a company and partners of a partnership do not represent the enterprise but act as the enterprise itself, they cannot constitute a dependent agent permanent establishment. *See* David Feuerstein in: Michael Lang/Florian Brugger/Patrick Plansky (eds.) *Permanent Establishments in International and EU Tax Law,* pp. 110-111.

644. In this respect, Reimer argues that bodies of a company may also qualify as dependent agent permanent establishments. *See* Ekkehart Reimer in: Ekkehart Reimer/Alexander Rust (eds.) *Klaus Vogel on Double Taxation Convention—4th edition,* pp. 386-387 and Ekkehart Reimer in: Ekkehart Reimer/Stephan Schmid/Marianne Orell (eds.) *Permanent Establishments: A Domestic Taxation, Bilateral Tax Treaty and OECD Perspective,* Part 2[D] p. 104 and footnotes cited therein.

645. According to Pijl, the change from the term *"on behalf of"* into the term *"in the name of"* in the second part of the agency permanent establishment provision, which occurred—as discussed above—in the draft report of April 19, 1958, appears to have been done without any considerations of a material versus a formal nature. To this effect, *see* Hans Pijl, *Bulletin for International Taxation,* (2013) p. 73. Moving from this, Storck and Schmidjell-Dommes derive that the term *"on behalf of"* may be used in a much broader sense as a link to the business activities of the principal, with the term *"in the name of"* to be understood as creating a legally and/or economically binding effect. To this effect, *see* Alfred Storck/Sabine Schmidjell-Dommes in: Michael Lang/Pasquale Pistone/Josef Schuch/Claus Staringer/Alfred Storck (eds.) *Dependent Agents as Permanent Establishments,* p. 50.

646. *See* Alfred Storck/Sabine Schmidjell-Dommes in: Michael Lang/Pasquale Pistone/Josef Schuch/Claus Staringer/Alfred Storck (eds.) *Dependent Agents as Permanent Establishments,* p. 54.

647. *See* para. 86 of the OECD Model Commentary on Art. 5.

of" another principal in some others. Therefore, the specific circumstances of each and every occurrence should be carefully considered.

According to Storck and Schmidjell-Dommes, in doing the business of another person, the agent is bound to a certain extent to directives and instructions of the principal. As a result, the boundaries of the independent agent provision could be relevant *a contrariis* to interpret the term "*on behalf of.*"[648] Specifically, an agent may act "*on behalf of*" an enterprise in the case that he follows detailed instructions from the principal as to the conduct of the work and is subject to significant control by the latter with respect to the manner in which the work is carried out. In addition to this, if the agent conducts business "*on behalf of*" the foreign enterprise in a limited risk environment, dependency may be assumed as well. This is for instance the case where the economic risk of the business lies with the principal, the agent receives his remuneration and the principal receives the profit. Another factor to determine dependency is also the (limited) number of principals.[649]

An interesting question might arise where the agent engages a sub-agent to perform certain duties in the source country. In fact, under the assumption that the remaining conditions for a dependent agent permanent establishment to exist are fulfilled, the foreign enterprise might have both an agent and a sub-agent in the source country, which—according to Pleijsier—should be treated as a single permanent establishment.[650,651]

Differently, in a situation where the sub-agent does not fulfill all the criteria set forth under Art. 5, para. 5, of the OECD Model, he/she would not qualify as a dependent agent permanent establishment. Nonetheless, under the OECD Model Commentary,[652] in the event the general agent is considered to constitute a dependent agent permanent establishment, all the acts carried on for the principal will be included in such a permanent establishment. It follows that, according to Pleijsier, the hiring of the sub-agent is an action of the agent on behalf of the principal and—therefore—should be included in the profits of the permanent establishment.[653]

648. For further comments on the independent agent provision, *see* s. 3.3.2.4 below.

649. *See* Alfred Storck/Sabine Schmidjell-Dommes in: Michael Lang/Pasquale Pistone/Josef Schuch/Claus Staringer/Alfred Storck (eds.) *Dependent Agents as Permanent Establishments*, pp. 54-55. With respect to the limited risk environment, *see also* Arthur Pleijsier, *The agency permanent establishment: de vaste vertegenwoordiger: proefschrift*, p. 164, Arthur Pleijsier, *Intertax*, (2001) p. 168 and Farkas Barsony in: Michael Lang/Hans Jörgen Aigner/Mario Züger (eds.) *Permanent Establishments in International Tax Law*, p. 138.

650. *See* Arthur Pleijsier, *The agency permanent establishment: de vaste vertegenwoordiger: proefschrift*, p. 176 and Arthur Pleijsier, *Intertax*, (2001) p. 174.

651. In a similar vein, with respect to the application of Art. 5, para. 5, of the OECD Model to an advisory company which acted as a kind of sub-agent of a partnership, *see* Jacques Sasseville, "Round Table: On the Desirability to Change the OECD Model Convention and its Commentaries" in: Guglielmo Maisto, *The Meaning of "Enterprise," "Business" and "Business Profits" under Tax Treaties and EU Tax Law* (Amsterdam: IBFD, 2011) pp. 611 et seq.

652. *See* para. 99 of the OECD Model Commentary on Art. 5.

653. *See* Arthur Pleijsier, *The agency permanent establishment: de vaste vertegenwoordiger: proefschrift*, p. 176 and Arthur Pleijsier, *Intertax*, (2001) p. 174.

With this in mind, the author is of the opinion that the conclusions drawn in the *Karnak*[654]—where the First Instance Tax Court of Rimini maintained that the presence of sub-agents would trigger a dependent agent permanent establishment of the agent rather than that of the principal—do not appear convincing.[655] In particular, in such a case, a company tax resident of San Marino active in the market of the wholesale trade of paper entered into a contract with a general agent for the promotion and the conclusion of sale contracts in Italy, San Marino, the Vatican and other European countries. In turn, such a general agent engaged a few sub-agents with a view to carrying on such promotional activities in Italy. Although concluding that the principal did not have an Italian permanent establishment both because the tax assessment was illegitimate and the sub-agents did not have the authority to conclude contracts, the Italian Court maintained that—in order to challenge the existence of a permanent establishment—the Italian tax authorities should have demonstrated the fictitious nature of the contracts entered into between the principal and the agent and between the agent and the sub-agents. However, this reasoning does not appear consistent with the factual determination that a sub-agent is ultimately acting on behalf of the principal, so that the tax authorities do not actually need to challenge the contractual arrangements.

3.3.2.3.4 The Traditional Test Regarding the Conclusion of Contracts

The traditional test concerning the conclusion of contracts has been amended in the aftermath of the BEPS Project. For a start, in a way consistent with the introduction of the supplementary test regarding the principal role leading to the conclusion of contracts,[656] the deletion of the term "*authority*" seems to indicate that such a test deals with situations where an agent concludes contracts binding on the principal, regardless of the general or limited scope of authority conferred to the agent.[657] And more than that, this deletion seems to confirm that there should be no difference between an agent that concludes contracts on the basis of a formal agreement—whether within or

654. *See Commissione Tributaria Provinciale di Rimini* March 12, 2008, No. 26. At that point in time, there was no DTA in force between Italy and San Marino. However, in its judgment, the Court made express reference to the OECD wording.

655. In a similar vein, *see* Giovanni Fort, "Attribuzione dei profitti alla stabile organizzazione personale," *Corriere Tributario* (2013) pp. 3045 et seq.

656. Indeed, it would be difficult to argue that a person concluding contracts regardless of authority did not exercise the principal role leading to the conclusion of contracts. To this effect, *see* Peter H. Blessing, "Preventing the Artificial Avoidance of PE Status" in: Robert Danon (ed.) *Base Erosion and Profit Shifting (BEPS)—Impact for European and international tax policy* (Zürich: Schulthess, 2016) p. 377.

657. For a previous discussion concerning the general or limited scope of authority, *see* Katharina Daxkobler, "Authority to Conclude Contracts in the Name of the Enterprise" in: Michael Lang/Pasquale Pistone/Josef Schuch/Claus Staringer/Alfred Storck (eds.) *Dependent Agents as Permanent Establishments* (Vienna: Linde, 2014) pp. 127-129, Arvid A. Skaar, *Permanent Establishment—Erosion of a Tax Treaty Principle*, pp. 476 et seq., Robert L. Williams, *Fundamentals of Permanent Establishments*, pp. 145 et seq., Francisco A. Garcia Prats, *El establecimiento permanente: análisis jurídico-tributario internacional de la imposición societaria*, pp. 200-201 and Farkas Barsony in: Michael Lang/Hans Jörgen Aigner/Mario Züger (eds.) *Permanent Establishments in International Tax Law*, pp. 140-141.

outside the scope of the authority explicitly granted—and an agent that has been vested with an implied authority to conclude contracts.[658]

In addition, the OECD clarified that the wording "*concludes contracts*" is focused on situations where a contract is considered to have been concluded by a person under the relevant contract law.[659] In other words, the revised guidance clarifies that the threshold for such a traditional test to be fulfilled lies on the legal formation of a contract.[660] On the other hand, circumstances where substantive activities are carried on in the source country without triggering the conclusion of contracts should be assessed under the supplementary test introduced in the context of the BEPS Project.[661,662]

In this particular respect, the OECD also clarified that a contract may be concluded without any active negotiation, so that a mere acceptance of an offer by the agent is sufficient to constitute a permanent establishment.[663] It appears as if this clarification is intended to confirm that situations where an agent has no discretion to negotiate the terms of the contracts may give rise to a dependent agent permanent establishment.[664] For instance, this might be the case of standardized contracts set out with predetermined terms and conditions where the agent has no influence on the contents. Consequently, in the case where an agent accepts offers to enter into standardized contracts, such an agent may be deemed to have concluded such contracts.[665] Likewise, the author believes that a dependent agent permanent establishment may also arise in a situation where an agent collects offers to enter into standardized contracts and the principal is bound to accept such offers and/or accepts such offers without a genuine review. To the contrary, a dependent agent permanent establishment should not arise in a scenario where an agent collects offers to enter into such contracts, but a final genuine decision as to the acceptance/rejection of such offers ultimately lies with the foreign principal.[666]

---

658. For a previous discussion concerning the expressed and implied authority, *see* Katharina Daxkobler in: Michael Lang/Pasquale Pistone/Josef Schuch/Claus Staringer/Alfred Storck (eds.) *Dependent Agents as Permanent Establishments*, pp. 129-130, Arvid A. Skaar, *Permanent Establishment—Erosion of a Tax Treaty Principle*, pp. 498 et seq. and Robert L. Williams, *Fundamentals of Permanent Establishments*, pp. 150 et seq.
659. *See* para. 87 of the OECD Model Commentary on Art. 5.
660. In a similar vein, *see* John Henshall/Roy Donegan, "BEPS Action 7: Part II," *Transfer Pricing International Journal* (2015).
661. *See* para. 88 of the OECD Model Commentary on Art. 5.
662. According to the author, the reference to commercial realities in para. 97 of the OECD Model Commentary on Art. 5 clarifies that such a test should be performed on the basis of the applicable facts and circumstances of the specific case.
663. *See* para. 87 of the OECD Model Commentary on Art. 5.
664. *See* Justus Eisenbeiss, "BEPS Action 7: Evaluation the Agency Permanent Establishment," *Intertax* (2016) pp. 487-488.
665. Daxkobler contended that this situation gave rise to a dependent agent permanent establishment also before the clarification at hands. *See* Katharina Daxkobler in: Michael Lang/Pasquale Pistone/Josef Schuch/Claus Staringer/Alfred Storck (eds.) *Dependent Agents as Permanent Establishments*, pp. 125-127.
666. In a similar vein, *see also* Arthur Pleijsier, *Intertax*, (2001) pp. 175-176, Arthur Pleijsier, *The agency permanent establishment: de vaste vertegenwoordiger: proefschrift*, p. 178 and Katharina Daxkobler in: Michael Lang/Pasquale Pistone/Josef Schuch/Claus Staringer/Alfred Storck (eds.) *Dependent Agents as Permanent Establishments*, p. 123.

According to the author, this reasoning may also be extended to the case where the agent is bound to detailed guidelines defined by the principal, but within such narrow guidelines negotiates the contracts up to the point of actual conclusion, which is left to the principal. As a matter of fact, even though the agent is subject to detailed guidelines, the pivotal element lies again with the review of the principal. While a final genuine review should exclude the existence of a dependent agent permanent establishment, a *pro forma* approval is similar to the situation where the agent concludes contracts.

The OECD further clarified that contracts may be deemed to be concluded by the agent even though the contract is signed outside the country of the customer.[667] As a result, Eisenbeiss argues that informal contracts such as oral agreements may be considered sufficient, thereby creating a potential source of controversy.[668]

In addition, it is clarified that a person who negotiates all elements and details of a contract in way binding on the foreign enterprise may be deemed to conclude the contract even though that contract is signed by another person outside the source country.[669] In such a case, it is then immaterial whether the final signature is made by the agent on behalf of the principal or by the principal himself in his home country.[670] Similarly, according to the author, this also holds true if the agent negotiates contracts and the principal signs such contracts without further inquiring into the terms and conditions. On the other hand, a dependent agent permanent establishment should not arise in the case that the principal retains the final genuine decision as to the accept/reject the business deal negotiated by the agent.[671] Furthermore, the mere fact that the agent has attended or even participated in negotiations is not sufficient by itself to maintain that the agent concluded contracts.[672]

With respect to the insurance business, it is worth noting that the formation of insurance contracts is generally governed under domestic contract laws. Different legal traditions—and in the EU, the absence of harmonization[673]—explain the differences

667. *See* para. 87 of the OECD Model Commentary on Art. 5.
668. *See* Justus Eisenbeiss, *Intertax*, (2016) p. 488.
669. *See* para. 87 of the OECD Model Commentary on Art. 5.
670. Correspondingly, the author believes that a situation where the principal negotiates a business deal up to the point of actual conclusion, but leaves the formality of the signing to the agent should not lead to the creation of a dependent agent permanent establishment. In a similar vein, *see* Katharina Daxkobler in: Michael Lang/Pasquale Pistone/Josef Schuch/Claus Staringer/Alfred Storck (eds.) *Dependent Agents as Permanent Establishments*, pp. 125-127.
671. In a similar vein, *see also* Arthur Pleijsier, *Intertax*, (2001) pp. 175-176, Arthur Pleijsier, *The agency permanent establishment: de vaste vertegenwoordiger: proefschrift*, p. 178 and Katharina Daxkobler in: Michael Lang/Pasquale Pistone/Josef Schuch/Claus Staringer/Alfred Storck (eds.) *Dependent Agents as Permanent Establishments*, p. 123.
672. *See* para. 97 of the OECD Model Commentary on Art. 5.
673. The only exception is Directive 2000/31/EC of the European Parliament and of the Council of 8 June 2000 on certain legal aspects of information society services, in particular electronic commerce, in the Internal Market, which requires that EU Member States recognize the validity of contracts concluded by electronic means. *See* Francesco Seatzu, *Insurance in Private International Law: A European Perspective*, p. 238 and Expert Group on European Insurance Contract Law, *Meeting of 15-16 May 2013—Discussion Paper 2: Differences in Insurance Contract Laws and the Existing EU Legal Framework*, available online at web.actuaries.ie, pp. 2 and 20-23.

across countries. Typically, a valid insurance contract requires both an offer and an acceptance. As a general rule, it is considered that the potential customer submits an offer to enter into an insurance contract, which the insurance company is free to accept or not. In the case of acceptance, some jurisdictions hold that the acceptance is not effective until communicated to the customer, while other jurisdictions hold that actual notice to the customer of the acceptance is not required, unless the terms and conditions of the application require otherwise.[674]

In the light of all the foregoing, in the basic case of standardized insurance contracts, it is crucial to ascertain where the acceptance takes place. More specifically, a dependent agent permanent establishment may arise in the event that: (*i*) the agent accepts offers to enter into standardized contracts, (*ii*) the agent collects offers to enter into standardized contracts and the foreign insurance company is bound to accept such offers, or (*iii*) the agent collects offers to enter into standardized contracts and the foreign insurance company accepts such offers without a genuine review.

On the other hand, in the case of insurance contracts subject to negotiation, a dependent agent permanent establishment may arise in the case that: (*i*) the agent negotiates all elements and details of an insurance contract in way binding on the foreign insurance company even though that contract is formally accepted by the insurance company in its home country or (*ii*) the agent negotiates contracts and the foreign insurance company accepts such contracts without further inquiring into the terms and conditions.

On a different note, it is also worth mentioning that insurance is often taken out in the form of collective insurance contracts. For instance, this might be case of an employer taking out life and/or health insurance for his/her employees, a provider taking out property and liability insurance for his/her customers and so forth. This kind of insurance contract—which governs the terms and conditions applicable to all employees/customers[675]—is characterized by the fact that the contract is signed between the insurance company and the employer/provider rather than between the insurance company and the employees/customers. To put it in other words, the policyholder (i.e., the employer/provider) does not correspond with the insured persons and the beneficiaries (i.e., the employees/customers), who can later join the insurance scheme by providing their consent.[676] In such a case, in light of the fact that the consent of employees/customers to join the scheme is binding on the insurance

674. To this effect, *see* EU Commission, "*Final Report of the Commission Expert Group on European Insurance Contract Law*," pp. 37-38 and Paul Bierly, "General Principles of Insurance," in: *Insurance Law: The Basics* (Tigard, Oregon State Bar, 2011) pp. 4 et seq.

675. *See* Antigono Donati/Giovanna Volpe Putzolu, *Manuale di Diritto delle Assicurazioni—Nona Edizione Aggiornata* (Milano: Giuffrè, 2009) p. 232.

676. The customer is not a party to the collective insurance contract. However, the customer is a party to the insurance scheme to the extent that he can join the protection by giving his consent. In fact, in such a case, rights stemming from the insurance contract are conferred on the customer. For further general comments on insurance contracts concluded on behalf of other persons, *see* Marco Rossetti, *Il diritto delle assicurazioni—Volume 1*, pp. 695 et seq, and Jürgen Basedow/John Birds/Malcolm Clarke/Herman Cousy/Helmut Heiss, *Principles of European Insurance Contract Law (PEICL)* (Munich: Sellier. European Law Publishers, 2009) pp. 261 et seq.

company by virtue of the contract concluded with the employer/provider, there are good grounds to maintain that a dependent agent permanent establishment may arise where the agent collects such consents in the source country.

3.3.2.3.5 The Supplementary Test Regarding the Principal Role Leading to the Conclusion of Contracts

The traditional test regarding the conclusion of contracts has been extended by the addition of the phrase "*habitually plays the principal role leading to the conclusion of contracts that are routinely concluded without material modifications by the enterprise.*"[677] This wording takes the matter further than the conclusion of contracts by providing for a supplementary test focusing on substantive activities aimed at addressing situations where the contracts are not formally concluded by the person in the source country but the conclusion is a direct result of his/her activities. Most notably, according to the OECD, such a phrase must be interpreted to cover cases where the person acts as the sales force of the foreign enterprise. The principal role leading to the conclusion of contracts will typically be associated with the actions of the person who convinced a third party to enter into a contract with the enterprise.[678]

The new guidance also makes clear that this supplementary test applies where a person solicits and receives (but does not formally finalize) orders and the foreign enterprise routinely approves such transactions without material changes. On the contrary, as explained in a first example, such a supplementary test does not apply in a scenario where the person in the source country merely promotes and markets goods and services of the foreign enterprise in a way that does not directly result in the conclusion of contracts.[679]

As a result, this supplementary test requires that the person in the source country is engaged in activities that directly lead to the possibility of a contract being formally concluded. Conversely, activities that require additional subsequent efforts for the purposes of concluding a contract should not trigger such a test.[680] Marketing and promotion activities that do not directly result in the conclusion of contracts should then include—among others—advertising campaigns, public relations and the provision of advice/information on goods and services. In fact, the carrying out of such activities alone cannot directly lead to the conclusion of contracts.

On the other hand, activities that can typically trigger the supplementary test include the negotiation of a contract, like a situation where the person in the source country is given a broad autonomy to negotiate all terms and conditions of the contract with local customers.[681] Indeed, it would be relatively unusual to have substantive

677. This wording has been added in the final report on Action 7 of the BEPS Project to supersede a concept of negotiation of the "*material elements of contracts,*" which was largely criticized during the public consultation for leaving ambiguity.
678. *See* para. 88 of the OECD Model Commentary on Art. 5.
679. *See* para. 89 of the OECD Model Commentary on Art. 5.
680. In a similar vein, *see* Gary D. Sprague, "Playing the Principal Role in Creating a Permanent Establishment," *Tax Management International Journal* (2016).
681. Along the same lines, *see* Gary D. Sprague, *Tax Management International Journal*, (2016).

negotiation of a contract in the source country but the activities of the person performing the principal role leading to the conclusion of the contract not in the source country.[682]

Another illustrative example is contemplated to suggest that this supplementary test can be also met by convincing the customer to accept even predetermined conditions with no actual negotiation required.[683] This can typically be the case of standardized contracts, whereby all terms and conditions are set in advance and the person in the source country is engaged in the activity of convincing customers to purchase products and/or services. To the end, relevant factors may include e-mails, telephone calls and facetime with customers and overall relationship building activities.[684]

Everything that lies between such extreme cases should be scrutinized in the light of the factual circumstances. Most importantly, it seems that one should carefully take into consideration the extent to which the agent takes part in the solicitation and/or negotiation of contracts in the source country. For instance, in the case that the agent is engaged in the negotiation of the main terms and conditions of a contract, the supplementary test is likely to be fulfilled. To the contrary, the mere fact that the agent has attended or even participated in negotiations is not sufficient by itself to maintain that the agent played the principal role leading to the conclusion of contracts routinely concluded without material modification by the foreign enterprise.[685]

Moreover, the second example suggests that a comparison of all factors leading to the conclusion of contracts is demanded.[686] Indeed, it may be argued that a determination of the "*principal role*" presupposes a comparison of the contributions toward the conclusion of contracts of the agent against those of the principal. Nevertheless, it can be reasonably anticipated that such a comparison could bring about significant application difficulties to the extent that this exercise is subjective and relies on factual circumstances which could not be easily available in the real world.[687,688]

682. To this effect, *see* Peter H. Blessing in: Robert Danon (ed.) *Base Erosion and Profit Shifting (BEPS)—Impact for European and international tax policy*, p. 378.
683. The author does not share the view of Wagemann and Bendlinger, who deduce from this illustrative example that a mere provision of information regarding the price structure and the contract terms and conditions to customers fulfils this test. To this effect, *see* Thorsten Wagemann, "Verschärfungen des Betriebsstättenbegriffs nach OECD-MA," *Internationales Steuer-und Wirtschaftsrecht* (2016) pp. 15-16, Stefan Bendlinger, "Art. 5" in: Aigner/Georg Kofler/Michael Tumpel (eds.) *DBA—Doppelbesteuerungsabkommen* (Vienna: Linde, 2019) p. 428 and Stefan Bendlinger/Sabine Kanduth-Kristen/Georg Kofler/Florian Rosenberger, *Internationales Steuerrecht* (Vienna: LexisNexis, 2019) p. 659. Indeed, to meet the supplementary test, this provision of information should be accompanied with the activity of convincing customers.
684. *See* para. 90 of the OECD Model Commentary on Art. 5.
685. *See* para. 97 of the OECD Model Commentary on Art. 5.
686. *See* para. 90 of the OECD Model Commentary on Art. 5.
687. *See* Justus Eisenbeiss, *Intertax*, (2016) p. 488 and Richard Collier, "More Guidance Needed on PE Threshold Issues," *Tax Notes International* (2015b) p. 250.
688. Collier believes that such difficulties could have been avoided if it was made clearer that the principal role test was to be assessed by reference to whether the agent is the principal decision-maker in relation to the relevant contractual terms. However, this is not what the test and the related guidance require. Also, this seems to be a route that the OECD is reluctant to pursue. To this effect, *see* Richard Collier, *Tax Notes International*, (2015b) p. 251.

In addition, the new guidance indicates that the contracts do not need to be formally concluded in the source country. Indeed, the test is intended to cover situations where a contract is subject—outside the source country—to review and approval without such a review resulting in a modification of the key aspects.[689] To put it in other words, a dependent agent permanent establishment can arise even though the principal has a right to review and approve the contracts. More specifically, a review which does not result in material modifications to the contracts can still trigger the existence of a dependent agent permanent establishment.[690] In fact, the prevention of source taxation seems made conditional on the principal making material modifications before the contracts are concluded. Although additional guidance is again missing in this respect, it seems reasonable to assume that the word "*material*" refers to the main terms and conditions of the relevant contract.

With regards to the insurance business, the above considerations suggest that a dependent agent permanent establishment might arise in the case that an insurance agent is engaged in the solicitation of insurance contracts in the source country, even though such contracts are subject to review but such a review does not result in a modification of the most significant terms and conditions of the contracts (like the premium and/or the coverage). The fact that such circumstances are covered under the supplementary test also points toward the inclusion of other situations where the insurance agent goes beyond such a solicitation. This is for instance the case where the insurance agent negotiates business deals or collects offers in the source country and such deals/offers are subject to a review by the foreign insurance company, but such a review does not result in a modification of the most significant aspects thereof.

3.3.2.3.6 Contracts in the Name of the Enterprise

With respect to the phrase "*these contracts are (...) in the name of the enterprise,*" the main interpretation issue is to understand whether the enterprise is bound by the contracts concluded through the agent in the source country. In this respect, a first question arises as to whether the element "*in the name of*" must be taken literally or in the sense that it requires the agent to act in a way binding the principal. On the top of this, ever since the introduction of the last sentence in para. 32 of the 1994 OECD Model Commentary on Art. 5,[691] the use of the term binding as an explanation for the element "*in the name of*" has given rise to the question as to whether a legal or economic approach has to be followed for the interpretation of bindingness.

The answer to such questions is mainly affected by the different concepts of agency adopted in civil law and common law systems. Indeed, in both civil law and

689. *See* para. 88 of the OECD Model Commentary on Art. 5.
690. Arguably, contracts that are binding on the foreign principal and contracts that are approved without inquiring into the terms and conditions should already be covered under the traditional test regarding the conclusion of contracts. For further comments, *see* s. 3.3.2.3.4 above.
691. *See* s. 3.3.1 above.

common law countries, the agent acts in the interest of the principal. In other words, in both civil law and common law countries, the result of the activities carried on by the agent ultimately affects the principal. However, the way in which this result is achieved greatly differs depending on the applicable legal framework.[692]

In civil law countries, a distinction is to be made between direct and indirect representation. Direct representation implies that the agent contracts in the name of the principal and binds the principal (but not the agent) to the third party. It follows that there is just one binding agreement vis-à-vis the third party, i.e., the agreement between the principal and the third party. This agreement, entered into by the agent in the name of the principal, produces effects directly in the hands of the principal. In order to produce the effects of direct representation, the agent must inform the third party with whom he/she deals that he/she is acting in the name of his principal.[693,694]

In the context of indirect representation, the agent acts in his/her own name and binds himself/herself (but not the principal). The agent is then bound to transfer to the principal—by means of a separate transaction—the legal rights and obligations deriving from his/her activities as an agent. Indeed, in such a case, the agreement between the agent and the third party does not determine any effects in the hands of the principal.[695,696]

In common law countries, there is no distinction between direct and indirect representation. Indeed, as a general rule, the activities carried on by the agent on behalf of the principal binds the principal vis-à-vis the third party, regardless of the fact that the agent acted in his/her own name or in the name of the principal. In other words, there is only one contract made between the principal (acting through the agent) and

692. *See* Giuseppe Persico, "Agency Permanent Establishment under Article 5 of the OECD Model Convention," *Intertax* (2000) p. 68.

693. *See* John F. Avery Jones/Jürgen Lüdicke, *World Tax Journal*, (2014) p. 206, Jean Schaffner, *How Fixed Is a Permanent Establishment?*, (Alphen aan den Rijn: Kluwer Law International, 2013) p. 223, Belema R. Obuoforibo, "In the Name of Clarity: Defining a Dependent Agent Permanent Establishment" in: Carlos Gutiérrez/Andreas Perdelwitz (eds.) *Taxation of Business Profits in the 21st Century* (Amsterdam: IBFD, 2013) para. 3.2.2.1, Giuseppe Persico, *Intertax*, (2000) p. 68, Arthur Pleijsier, "The Agency Permanent Establishment under Revision?: "Acting in the name of," or "what's in a name?"!," *Intertax* (1997) pp. 248-249 and John F. Avery Jones/David A. Ward, *European Taxation*, (1993) pp. 156-157.

694. An example of a direct representative is the commercial agent, who normally contracts in the name of the principal. *See* John F. Avery Jones/David A. Ward, *European Taxation*, (1993) p. 157.

695. *See* John F. Avery Jones/Jürgen Lüdicke, *World Tax Journal*, (2014) p. 206, Jean Schaffner, *How Fixed Is a Permanent Establishment?*, p. 222, Giuseppe Persico, *Intertax*, (2000) p. 68 and John F. Avery Jones/David A. Ward, *European Taxation*, (1993) pp. 156-157.

696. An example of an indirect representative is the commissionaire agent, who normally contracts in his own name. *See* Arthur Pleijsier, *Intertax*, (1997) p. 248, John F. Avery Jones/David A. Ward, *European Taxation*, (1993) p. 157 and Leopoldo Parada, "Agents vs. Commissionaires: A Comparison in Light of the OECD Model Convention," *Tax Notes International* (2013) pp. 62-63.

the third party. This generally holds true even when the principal is undisclosed, i.e., the third party is not aware of the principal/agent relationship.[697,698]

In the light of the above, it may be argued that the agency permanent establishment concept is broader under civil law, where indirect representation could result in a dependent agent permanent establishment, while in such a case there would be no permanent establishment under common law. In fact, in very general terms, common lawyers are likely to restrict a permanent establishment risk to intermediaries that can bind their principal, whereas civil lawyers are likely to consider a permanent establishment risk whenever the intermediary acts on behalf of his/her principal, irrespective of whether the intermediary can bind his/her principal or not.[699,700]

Against this background, with respect to the question as to whether the element "*in the name of*" must be taken literally or in the sense that it requires the agent to act in a way binding his/her principal, it has been submitted that it is possible for intermediaries who are not literally acting "*in the name of*" the principal to create a dependent agent permanent establishment. As a matter of fact, Avery Jones, Ward and Pijl concluded that the wording "*in the name of*" should not be construed as requiring the agent to literally act "*in the name of*" the foreign principal. Rather, this should be interpreted as requiring the agent to act in such a way to bind the foreign principal.[701] In addition to this, Roberts takes the view that agents that do not literally act "*in the name of*" the principal and do not fall within the scope of the independent agent provision constitute a permanent establishment.[702,703]

This interpretation has been eventually supported in the context of Action 7 of the BEPS Project. Indeed, the OECD clarified in the OECD Model Commentary on Art. 5 that the reference to contracts "*in the name of*" is not restricted to contracts that are

697. *See* John F. Avery Jones/Jürgen Lüdicke, *World Tax Journal*, (2014) p. 206, Jean Schaffner, *How Fixed Is a Permanent Establishment?*, p. 224, Belema R. Obuoforibo in: Carlos Gutiérrez/Andreas Perdelwitz (eds.) *Taxation of Business Profits in the 21st Century*, para. 3.2.2.2, Giuseppe Persico, *Intertax*, (2000) p. 68, John F. Avery Jones/David A. Ward, *European Taxation*, (1993) p. 158 and Leopoldo Parada, *Tax Notes International*, (2013) pp. 60-61.

698. Under common law, the only circumstances where the principal is not bound, apart from those where the agent exceeds his authority, are (*i*) where the contract so provides (which is uncommon), and (*ii*) where the principal is undisclosed but the doctrine of undisclosed principal is not applicable, such as the case where the agent declares that he/she is the owner. To this effect, *see* John F. Avery Jones/Jürgen Lüdicke, *World Tax Journal*, (2014) p. 206 and John F. Avery Jones/David A. Ward, *European Taxation*, (1993) p. 158.

699. To this effect, *see* Jean Schaffner, *How Fixed Is a Permanent Establishment?*, p. 224, Farkas Barsony in: Michael Lang/Hans Jörgen Aigner/Mario Züger (eds.) *Permanent Establishments in International Tax Law*, p. 152, Giuseppe Persico, *Intertax*, (2000) p. 69 and Marco Cerrato in: Claudio Sacchetto/Lauro Alemanno (eds.) *Materiali di Diritto Tributario Internazionale* pp. 134-135.

700. Such different concepts may of course lead to a number of conflict of laws. For an overview of the main problems that may arise in this area, *see* Arthur Pleijsier, *Intertax*, (1997) p. 249 and John F. Avery Jones/David A. Ward, *European Taxation*, (1993) pp. 158-160.

701. *See* John F. Avery Jones/David A. Ward, *European Taxation*, (1993) p. 161 and Hans Pijl, *Bulletin for International Taxation*, (2013) pp. 96-97.

702. *See* Sidney I. Roberts, *Intertax*, (1993) pp. 401 et seq.

703. Differently, Piltz takes the view that the wording "*in the name of*" is to be taken literally. To this effect, *see* Detlev J. Piltz, *Bulletin for International Fiscal Documentation*, (2004) p. 199 and Detlev J. Piltz, *Internationales Steuerrecht*, (2004) pp. 184-185.

literally *"in the name of"* the foreign enterprise.[704] Still, this does not appear to be the end of the road. For instance, according to Henshall and Donegan, it remains to be seen whether a court would agree that there is sufficient lack of clarity in the wording such that the OECD Model Commentary would become admissible as an aid to interpretation.[705]

Second, with respect to the question as to whether a legal or economic approach has to be followed for the interpretation of bindingness, several authors supported the former approach before the BEPS Project came into play. Among others, Feuerstein was of the opinion that the wording *"concluding contracts in the name of the enterprise"* should not be read as *"concluding contracts economically binding on the enterprise."*[706] In a similar vein, according to Avery Jones, Ward and Pijl, an agent not able to conclude contracts legally binding on his/her principal, such as a civil law indirect representative of an independent status who is acting in the ordinary course of his/her business, could not constitute a dependent agent permanent establishment.[707] It was only according to Roberts that civil law indirect representatives could constitute a permanent establishment subject to the condition that the agent was dependent on the principal and/or not act in the ordinary course of business.[708]

The above conclusion has been supported by some case law of Supreme Courts in France, Norway and Italy.[709] More specifically, although in some countries the

704. *See* para. 93 of the OECD Model Commentary on Art. 5.

705. To this effect, *see* John Henshall/Roy Donegan, *Transfer Pricing International Journal*, (2015).

706. *See* David Feuerstein in: Michael Lang/Florian Brugger/Patrick Plansky (eds.) *Permanent Establishments in International and EU Tax Law*, p. 114.

707. *See* John F. Avery Jones/David A. Ward, *European Taxation*, (1993) p. 178, as further analyzed in Giuseppe Persico, *Intertax*, (2000) p. 71 and Hans Pijl, *Bulletin for International Taxation*, (2013) pp. 96-97.

708. To this effect, *see* Sidney I. Roberts, *Intertax*, (1993) pp. 501-502, as further analyzed in Giuseppe Persico, *Intertax*, (2000) p. 73.

709. In this respect, it should be noted that an economic approach was supported in previous Italian cases. For instance, *see Philip Morris* cases, CC (*Corte di Cassazione*) March 7, 2002, Nos. 3367, 3368 and 3369, March 26, 2002 No. 431926, May 25, 2002, Nos. 7682 and 7689, September 22, 2002, No. 10925 and December 6, 2002, No. 17373. For further comments, *see*—among others—Caterina Innamorato, "The Concept of a Permanent Establishment within a Group of Multinational Enterprises," *European Taxation* (2008) pp. 81-84, Linda Favi, "Italy" in: IFA (ed.) *Is there a permanent establishment?*, Cahiers de droit fiscal international, Vol. 94a (The Hague: Sdu Uitgevers, 2009) pp. 406-409, Carlos E. C. M. A. Toro, "Different Methods of Attributing Profits to Agency PE's," *Tax Notes International* (2009) pp. 425-427, Piergiorgio Valente, *Convenzioni internazionali contro le doppie imposizioni* (Milano: IPSOA, 2012) pp. 267-271, Marco Piazza, *Guida alla fiscalità internazionale* (Milano: Il Sole 24 Ore, 2004) pp. 228-229, Alessandro Dragonetti/Valerio Piacentini/Anna Sfondrini, *Manuale di fiscalità internazionale*, pp. 1044 et seq., Stefano Grilli/Paolo Ruggiero, "La stabile organizzazione nella giurisprudenza interna e internazionale" in: Sigfried Mayr/Benedetto Santacroce (eds.) *La stabile organizzazione delle imprese delle imprese industriali e commerciali* (Milano: Ipsoa, 2013) pp. 363 et seq., and Raffaele Russo/Edoardo Pedrazzini/Caterina Innamorato, "*Italy—Permanent Establishments—Topical Analyses*," last reviewed: May 24, 2019, available online at www.ibfd.org, para. 2.1.6.1. A similar approach was followed in Amsterdam Court of Appeal, June 20, 1978, Case 1106/761, BNB 1979/190). *See* Jean-Paul van den Berg, "Netherlands" in: IFA (ed.) *Is there a permanent establishment?*, Cahiers de droit fiscal international, Vol. 94a (The Hague: Sdu Uitgevers, 2009) p. 477. For further comments, *see also* Alfred Storck/Raffaele Petruzzi in: Michael Lang/Pasquale Pistone/Alexander Rust/Josef Schuch/Claus Staringer (eds.) *Base Erosion and Profit Shifting (BEPS)*, pp. 90-91.

administrative guidance suggests that the element *"in the name of"* could refer to situations where the principal is economically bound by the contract,[710] such case law appears to support the view that the wording *"in the name of"* is to be interpreted as *"legally binding."* To the contrary, there have been peculiarities regarding the Spanish interpretation of the dependent agent permanent establishment provision.

In *Zimmer*,[711] the French Supreme Court decided that a French subsidiary of a UK parent company—operating in France as a commissionaire—did not constitute a French permanent establishment of its parent company. In doing so, when considering the dependent agent provision set forth in the DTA between the UK and France,[712] the French Supreme Court concluded that the French commissionaire was not a permanent establishment of the UK parent company to the extent that it had no power to conclude contracts that were legally binding on the UK parent company.[713,714]

In *Dell Norway*,[715] the Supreme Court of Norway also maintained that sales to Norway through a Norwegian affiliate by means of a commissionaire arrangement did

710. *See* Jacques Sasseville/Arvid A. Skaar in: IFA (ed.) *Is there a permanent establishment?*, pp. 51-52.
711. CE (*Conseil d'État*) March 31, 2010, 304715 and 308525. For further comments on the case, *see—inter alia*—Carlos E. C. M. A. Toro, *Tax Notes International*, (2009) pp. 427-429, Brian J. Arnold, "Tax Treaty News," *Bulletin for International Taxation* (2010) p. 354, Pierre-Jean Douvier/Xenia Lordkipanidze, "Zimmer Case: The Issue of the Deemed Existence of a Permanent Establishment Based on Status as a Commissionaire," *International Transfer Pricing Journal* (2010) pp. 266-269, Bruno Gouthière, "Zimmer: "Commissionaire" Agent Is Not a Permanent Establishment," *European Taxation* (2010) pp. 350-358, Belema R. Obuoforibo in: Carlos Gutiérrez/Andreas Perdelwitz (eds.) *Taxation of Business Profits in the 21st Century*, para. 3.4.1, Séverine Baranger/Lars A. Henie/Mónica Sada Garibay/Ignacio Gordillo/Michele Gusmeroli, "The 2012 Leiden Alumni Seminar: Case Law on Treaty Interpretation Re Commissionaire and Agency PEs," *European Taxation* (2013) pp. 175-177, Amar Mehta, *Permanent Establishment in International Taxation* (New Delhi: Taxmann Publications (P.) Ltd, 2012) pp. 408-409, Pierre-Henri Durand/Jean-Florent Mandelbaum, "The 'French Touch': Determining a PE Using The Dependent Agent Criterion," *Tax Notes International* (2011) pp. 669-670, Jean Schaffner, *How Fixed Is a Permanent Establishment?*, pp. 225-227, Tim Wustenberghs/Ethel Puncher, "Zimmer à la Belge: Could a Commissionaire Arrangement Create an Agency Permanent Establishment in Belgium?," *Bulletin for International Taxation* (2011) pp. 237-238, Leopoldo Parada, *Tax Notes International*, (2013) pp. 64-65 and Stefan Bendlinger, *Die Betriebsstätte in der Praxis des internationalen Steuerrechts* (Vienna: LexisNexis, 2016) pp. 238-239.
712. DTA between the UK and France concluded on May 22, 1968.
713. In its judgment, the French Supreme Court disregarded para. 32.1, as introduced in the 1994 OECD Model Commentary on Art. 5. However, it is not clear whether—in doing so—the French Supreme Court followed the interpretation that subsequent changes are not relevant for the interpretation of DTAs concluded beforehand. Therefore, it is not clear whether the Court would have followed this approach if the DTA had been signed after the 1994 OECD Model Commentary came into being. *See* Séverine Baranger/Lars A. Henie/Mónica Sada Garibay/Ignacio Gordillo/Michele Gusmeroli, *European Taxation*, (2013) p. 177.
714. French lower courts recently followed a similar formalistic approach in the *Google* case. *See* TA (*Tribunal Administratif de Paris*) July 12, 2017, 1505178/1-1 and CAA (*Cour Administrative d'Appel de Paris*) April 25, 2019, 17PA03067. For further comments, *see also* Jérôme Monsenego, "Google France as a Dependent Agent PE of Its Irish Sister Company," *Transfer Pricing International* (2018) pp. 47-51 and Annabelle Bailleul-Mirabaud/Céline Pasquier, "Digital Cases Illustrate Narrow French PE Interpretation," *Tax Notes international* (2018) pp. 1023-1025.
715. HR (*Høyesterett*) December 2, 2011, HR-2011-02245-A. For further comments on the case, *see*—among others—Thor Leegaard, "Supreme Court Holds That Commissionaire Structure

not constitute an agency permanent establishment. In its judgment, the Norwegian Supreme Court found that the presence of a dependent agent under Art. 5, para. 5, of the DTA between Norway and Ireland[716] required the principal to be legally bound by the agreements concluded by the commissionaire with third parties. According to the Supreme Court, the literal meaning of the expressions contained in that provision "*clearly indicates*" that the principal must be legally bound by the contracts concluded by the commissionaire with third parties. While acknowledging that the OECD Model Commentary, in principle, is to be given weight, the Supreme Court found that it does not provide any specific guidance in this case. In reaching this conclusion, the Court referred to para. 32.1 of the 2010 OECD Model Commentary on Art. 5 and emphasized that, while the first part of the paragraph was inserted to give guidance on common law agency concepts, the second part of the paragraph discussed the evidence required to establish what is "*legal binding*" for intermediates other than commissionaires.[717]

In *Boston Scientific*,[718] the Italian Supreme Court concluded that an Italian subsidiary of a Dutch parent company was not to be regarded as a dependent agent permanent establishment of the foreign company. In doing so, the Italian Supreme Court rejected the argument put forward by the Italian tax administration that the authority was not to be assessed under a strictly civil law point of view, but under an economic criterion.[719]

In *Roche*,[720] the Spanish Supreme Court confirmed the judgment of the High Court,[721] which considered that the activities carried on by a Spanish subsidiary of a

---

Does Not Amount to a Permanent Establishment," *European Taxation* (2012) pp. 317-321, Belema R. Obuoforibo in: Carlos Gutiérrez/Andreas Perdelwitz (eds.) *Taxation of Business Profits in the 21st Century*, para. 3.4.1, Joachim M. Bjerke/Simen S. Søgaard, "Dell Wins Important Agency Permanent Establishment Case," *International Transfer Pricing Journal* (2012) pp. 176-178, Séverine Baranger/Lars A. Henie/Mónica Sada Garibay/Ignacio Gordillo/Michele Gusmeroli, *European Taxation*, (2013) pp. 177-179, Amar Mehta, *Permanent Establishment in International Taxation*, pp. 409-410, Jean Schaffner, *How Fixed Is a Permanent Establishment?*, p. 244, Leopoldo Parada, *Tax Notes International* (2013) pp. 64-65 and Stefan Bendlinger, *Die Betriebsstätte in der Praxis des internationalen Steuerrechts*, pp. 239 et seq.

716. DTA between Norway and Ireland concluded on November 22, 2000.

717. *See* Séverine Baranger/Lars A. Henie/Mónica Sada Garibay/Ignacio Gordillo/Michele Gusmeroli, *European Taxation*, (2013) p. 178.

718. CC (*Corte di Cassazione*) March 9, 2012, No. 3769. For further comments on the case, *see*—among others—Alessio Persiani, "Some Remarks on the Notion of Permanent Establishment in the Recent Italian Supreme Court Jurisprudence," *Intertax* (2012) pp. 678 et seq., Stefano Grilli/Paolo Ruggiero in: Sigfried Mayr/Benedetto Santacroce (*eds.*) *La stabile organizzazione delle imprese delle imprese industriali e commerciali*, pp. 386 et seq., Belema R. Obuoforibo in: Carlos Gutiérrez/Andreas Perdelwitz (eds.) *Taxation of Business Profits in the 21st Century*, para. 3.4.3 and Séverine Baranger/Lars A. Henie/Mónica Sada Garibay/Ignacio Gordillo/Michele Gusmeroli, *European Taxation*, (2013) pp. 181-182.

719. *See* Séverine Baranger/Lars A. Henie/Mónica Sada Garibay/Ignacio Gordillo/Michele Gusmeroli, *European Taxation*, (2013) p. 182.

720. (TS) *Tribunal Supremo* January 12, 2012, No. 1626/2008. For further comments on the case, *see*—among others—Néstor Carmona Fernández, "The Concept of Permanent Establishment in the Courts: Operating Structures Utilizing Commission Subsidiaries," *Bulletin for International Taxation* (2013), Belema R. Obuoforibo in: Carlos Gutiérrez/Andreas Perdelwitz (eds.) *Taxation of Business Profits in the 21st Century*, para. 3.4.2, Séverine Baranger/Lars A. Henie/Mónica Sada Garibay/Ignacio Gordillo/Michele Gusmeroli, *European Taxation*, (2013) pp. 179-181, Adolfo J. Martín Jiménez, "The Spanish Position on the Concept of a Permanent

Swiss parent company gave rise to a dependent agent permanent establishment of the parent company under Art. 5, para. 4, of the DTA between Spain and Switzerland.[722] More specifically, although the High Court—and the Supreme Court following its decision—ruled in favor of the existence of a dependent agent permanent establishment by reason of the manufacturing activities carried on by the Spanish subsidiary,[723] it should be noted that such a judgment denied the application of the economic approach for the purposes of interpreting the wording *"in the name of."*

It should however be noted that this conclusion has been recently reversed in the *Dell Spain* case.[724] In fact, the Supreme Court confirmed the decision of the Tribunal Economico-Administrativo Central[725] and the High Court[726] that the reference to *"in the name of"* could not be interpreted in a strict legal sense, such as in giving rise to a legal bond between the client and the principal. Most importantly, for the High Court, it was sufficient that a factual obligation existed for the principal to execute the contracts that the agent had signed in its own name, but on behalf of the principal. The origins of this interpretation can be traced back to the position adopted by the Spanish tax administration, according to which it is possible to defend that the factual, and not the legally binding, nature between the client and the principal is sufficient to constitute a dependent agent permanent establishment in Spain. Although considering that there was no need to express an opinion on the existence of a dependent agent permanent establishment in the presence of a fixed place of business, the Supreme Court still confirmed that there was also a dependent agent permanent establishment to the extent that Art. 5, para. 5, of the OECD Model also covers cases of indirect representation where there is no formal legal relationship between the client and the principal.[727,728]

Establishment: Anticipating BEPS, beyond BEPS or Simply a Wrong Interpretation of Article 5 of the OECD Model?," *Bulletin for International Taxation* (2016) pp. 461-462, Francisco Antonio Vaquer Ferrer, "The Concept of 'Permanent Establishment' at the Spanish Courts: Special Reference to the Roche and Dell Cases," *Intertax* (2016) pp. 674-679 and Stefan Bendlinger, *Die Betriebsstätte in der Praxis des internationalen Steuerrechts*, pp. 247 et seq.

721. AN (*Audiencia Nacional*) January 24, 2008, No. 894/2004.
722. DTA between Spain and Switzerland concluded on April 26, 1966.
723. Such a case is beyond the scope of this research.
724. TS (*Tribunal Supremo*) June 20, 2016, No. 1475/2016. For further comments on the judgments of the Spanish Courts, *see*—among others—Adolfo J. Martín Jiménez, *Bulletin for International Taxation*, (2016) pp. 462-467, Francisco Antonio Vaquer Ferrer, *Intertax*, (2016) pp. 679-682, Francisco A. Garcia Prats, "Notas sobre la Sentencia del Tribunal Supremo de 20 de junio de 2016 (Caso DELL)," *Documentos AEDAF, Sección Fiscalidad Internacional y Precios de Transferencia* (2016), available online at http://www.aedaf.es/es, Alexandra Bal, "The Spanish Dell Case—Do We Need Anti-BEPS Measures If the Existing Rules Are Broad Enough?," *European Taxation* (2016) pp. 574-576, Abelardo Delgado Pacheco, "Spanish Supreme Court anticipates the effects of the BEPS Project," *International Tax Review* (2017) and Paolo Piantavigna, "Il caso spagnolo Dell: un'interpretazione dinamica della nozione di stabile organizzazione," *Rivista di Diritto Finanziario e Scienza delle Finanze* (2017) pp. 52 et seq.
725. TEAC (*Tribunal Economico-Administrativo Central*) March 15, 2012, No. 00/2107/2007.
726. AN (*Audiencia Nacional*) June 8, 2015, No. 182/2012.
727. *See* Adolfo J. Martín Jiménez, *Bulletin for International Taxation*, (2016) pp. 465-466 and 473.
728. In that perspective, Hoor and O'Donnell maintained that the decision in the *Dell Spain* case was exceptional. To this effect, *see* Oliver R. Hoor/Keith O'Donnell, "BEPS Action 7: The Attempt to Artificially Create A Taxable Nexus," *Tax Notes International* (2015) p. 933.

While before the BEPS Project the position of the OECD on this point was anything but clear,[729] a broad interpretation of the wording "*in the name of*" seems to have been eventually endorsed after the BEPS Project. Most notably, when the OECD proposed the introduction of a new sentence in para. 32.1 of the 2010 OECD Model Commentary on Art. 5 dealing with common law agents working for an undisclosed principal,[730] the OECD finally withdrew such a proposal since it was submitted that the wording could also be read as supporting the "*economic binding*" line of reasoning.[731] However, in the context of the changes introduced after the BEPS Project, the OECD clarified that the application of paras. a), b) and c) of Art. 5, para. 5, of the OECD Model is not limited to contracts that create rights and obligations that are legally enforceable between the enterprise and the third parties with which such contracts are concluded[732] and a specific wording concerning situations where the enterprise is undisclosed has been finally introduced.[733]

At any rate, in the insurance business, this shift toward the economic bindingness should not have significant implications. Indeed, the formal legal relationship (namely, the insurance contract) remains between the insurance company and the customer to the extent that insurance distributors cannot enter into insurance contracts with customers in their own name and the underlying rights and obligations stemming from such a contract are eventually executed between the very same parties.

3.3.2.3.7 Contracts for the Provision of Property or Services

In the context of Action 7 of the BEPS Project, two additional indents have been inserted in Art. 5, para. 5, of the OECD Model, namely: (*i*) the transfer of the ownership of, or for the granting of the right to use, property owned by the enterprise or that the enterprise has the right to use and (*ii*) the provision of services by the enterprise.[734] In such a way, the dependent agent permanent establishment provision also applies to contracts that create obligations that will effectively be performed by the foreign enterprise rather than by the person that acts on the enterprise's behalf.[735] In other words, the intention of such amendments is to circumvent the issue of who is legally bound by the contract by focusing on the subject of the contracts. As a matter of fact, the emphasis on the contracts establishes an objective economic link between the contract concluded by the intermediary and the foreign enterprise.[736]

729. Nevertheless, in the author's view, a lack of guidance could accommodate a wide range of interpretations.
730. *See* OECD, "*Interpretation and Application of Article 5 (Permanent Establishment) of the OECD Model Tax Convention,*" paras. 107 et seq. and OECD, "*OECD Model Tax Convention: Revised Proposals Concerning the Interpretation and Application of Article 5 (Permanent Establishment),*" paras. 106 et seq.
731. For further comments, *see also* Richard Collier, *British Tax Review*, (2013) pp. 641-642 and Oliver R. Hoor, *Tax Notes International*, (2012) p. 212.
732. *See* para. 91 of the OECD Model Commentary on Art. 5.
733. *See* para. 93 of the OECD Model Commentary on Art. 5.
734. *See* sub-paras. b) and c) of Art. 5, para. 5, of the OECD Model.
735. *See* para. 94 of the OECD Model Commentary on Art. 5.
736. *See* Justus Eisenbeiss, *Intertax*, (2016), p. 487.

Therefore, pursuant to such amendments to Art. 5, para. 5, of the OECD Model, the legal binding nature will no longer be relevant with the effect that, when a person habitually concludes contracts or plays a leading role in the conclusion of contracts and such contracts result in the transfer of the property and/or rights or services provided by a foreign entity, there is a dependent agent permanent establishment. To put it in other terms, what becomes relevant is whether the actions of the person end up with a factual effect on the foreign principal to sell goods or services to the client.[737]

Under the new rules, commissionaire arrangements—whereby a commissionaire concludes a contract in his/her own name for the sale of goods or the provision of services and the principal effectively performs the obligation of that contract—will typically constitute a dependent agent permanent establishment.[738,739] By the same token, similar strategies—such as synthetic commissionaires—are likely to be caught under the new rules. Other structures—such marketing service companies—should also be carefully assessed.[740]

On the contrary, the changes introduced in the context of Action 7 of the BEPS Project are not intended to cover situations where a person acts on his own behalf, like a distributor that sells to customers products previously bought from another enterprise (including an associated enterprise). This also holds true with respect to low-risk distributor structures implemented between related parties.[741] However, this is not a clear-cut comfort to the extent that BEPS concerns related to such structures should be further assessed in the context of Action 9 of the BEPS Project.[742,743]

In the light of the above, it is fair to say that such changes to Art. 5, para. 5, of the OECD Model should not have significant implications for the insurance business to the extent insurance transactions cannot be regarded as commissionaire arrangements and/or similar strategies falling within the scope of such changes.[744] Unlike in the commissionaire arrangement, insurance distributors cannot enter into insurance contracts with customers in their own name. Nor can reinsurance/retrocession transactions be regarded as commissionaire arrangements and/or similar strategies. In fact,

737. To this effect, *see* Adolfo J. Martín Jiménez, *Bulletin for International Taxation*, (2016) p. 468.
738. *See* para. 92 of the OECD Model Commentary on Art. 5.
739. In this respect, it should be noted that the clampdown on commissionaire arrangements was specifically embodied in the BEPS policy statements. *See* OECD, "*Preventing the Artificial Avoidance of Permanent Establishment Status—Action 7: 2015 Final Report*," para. 2. Still, a specific rule deeming a commissionaire to be a dependent agent permanent establishment has not been even considered. To this effect, *see* Alfred Storck/Raffaele Petruzzi in: Michael Lang/Pasquale Pistone/Alexander Rust/Josef Schuch/Claus Staringer (eds.) *Base Erosion and Profit Shifting (BEPS)*, pp. 101-102 and OECD, "*Comments received on public discussion draft—BEPS Action 7: Prevent the artificial avoidance of PE status*," Paris (January 1, 2015), p. 423.
740. *See* Justus Eisenbeiss, *Intertax*, (2016), p. 486.
741. *See* para. 96 of the OECD Model Commentary on Art. 5.
742. *See* OECD, "*Preventing the Artificial Avoidance of Permanent Establishment Status—Action 7: 2015 Final Report*," para. 9, p. 16.
743. The transfer of risks in the context of Action 9 of the BEPS Project is beyond the scope of this research.
744. In a similar vein, Eisenbeiss argues that insurance agents are not considered similar strategies. To this effect, *see* Justus Eisenbeiss, *Intertax*, (2016), p. 486.

such dealings are in principle genuine business transactions, whereby the ceding company maintains its rights and obligations vis-à-vis final customers.

3.3.2.3.8 *"Habitually"*

In order to constitute a dependent agent permanent establishment, the person must "*habitually*" conclude contracts or play the principal role leading to the conclusion of contracts. In other words, similar to the basic permanent establishment rule, the dependent agent permanent establishment provision requires a connecting factor to justify the link with the source country.[745]

On this point, the OECD Model Commentary simply states that the conclusion of contracts by the person or as a direct result of the actions of that person must take place repeatedly (i.e., more than in isolated cases),[746] the presence should be more than merely transitory, while the extent and frequency of activity should be assessed on a case-by-case depending on the nature of the contracts and the business of the principal.[747]

First of all, in the light of such a (limited) guidance, it may be argued that this test presupposes the activity to be actually exercised. Before the changes introduced in the context of the BEPS Project, it has been submitted that the mere intent of the foreign enterprise to grant the intermediary an authority to conclude contracts on a long-term basis could be sufficient evidence for the duration test.[748] However, considering the wording used until the 2014 OECD Model Commentary, this reasoning did not appear fully convincing to the extent that it was required that the intermediary executed the authority to conclude contracts.[749] Interestingly enough, a similar conclusion was also reached in a case law in the field of the insurance business. In particular, in *Eagle Star Vie*, the French Supreme Court maintained that the mere authority granted to a dependent agent was not sufficient to determine that a French insurance company had a permanent establishment in New Caledonia, in circumstances where the agent did not actually exercise that authority.[750] After the changes introduced in the aftermath of the BEPS Project, the omission of the term "*authority*" clearly points toward a factual assessment as to whether the agent actually concludes contracts or plays the principal role leading to the conclusion of contracts, irrespective of a formal authority.[751]

In addition to this, based on the wording laid down in the OECD Model Commentary on Art. 5, the activity in the source country must: (*i*) be frequent and (*ii*)

745. In a similar vein, *see* Ekkehart Reimer in: Ekkehart Reimer/Stephan Schmid/Marianne Orell (eds.) *Permanent Establishments: A Domestic Taxation, Bilateral Tax Treaty and OECD Perspective*, Part 2[D] p. 106.
746. *See* para. 83 of the OECD Model Commentary on Art. 5.
747. *See* para. 98 of the OECD Model Commentary on Art. 5.
748. *See* David Feuerstein in: Michael Lang/Florian Brugger/Patrick Plansky (eds.) *Permanent Establishments in International and EU Tax Law*, p. 116 and footnotes cited therein.
749. *See* para. 33.1 of the 2014 OECD Model Commentary on Art. 5. For further comments on this topic, *see also* Francisco A. Garcia Prats, *El establecimiento permanente: análisis jurídico-tributario internacional de la imposición societaria*, p. 203.
750. CE (*Conseil d'État*) January 6, 2005, 259618.
751. *See* s. 3.3.2.3.4 above.

have a certain degree of permanence to distinguish it from a mere transitory intervention.[752] Even though such a determination should be based on a factual assessment, it is nevertheless possible to identify some common patterns and elements.

With respect to the permanence test, a critical factor is the relationship between the agent and the principal. Most notably, a long-term relationship may indicate a sufficient degree of permanence.[753] Also, the presence of the agent in the source country may be an indicator of permanence. It goes without saying that the longer the period of stay, the higher the risk of creating a dependent agent permanent establishment.[754] Although there is no specific timeframe, Pistone and Ruiz Jiménez argue that the permanence test may be regarded as fulfilled in the case that the agent is present in the host country for more than 12 months.[755] Instead, Ehlermann and Castelon are of the opinion that if an agent is present in the source country for more than 6 months, there is a high risk of triggering a permanent establishment.[756]

In relation to the frequency test, it may be generally argued that the minimum number of repetitions to consider an event as "*frequent*" is two. As a matter of fact, a single event qualifies as "*frequent*" only in exceptional circumstances.[757] In this regard, one of the greatest difficulties in the determination is also the absence of guidelines in terms of timeframe in which the recurrence should be tested.[758] To resolve this issue, Pistone and Ruiz Jiménez suggest that the use of a 12-month period might be a suitable option to consider, but it should be noted that other possible alternatives also exist.[759]

752. Both criteria should be fulfilled to create a dependent agent permanent establishment. To this effect, *see* Pasquale Pistone/César Alejandro Ruiz Jiménez in: Michael Lang/Pasquale Pistone/Josef Schuch/Claus Staringer/Alfred Storck (eds.) *Dependent Agents as Permanent Establishments*, pp. 152-153 and Jean Schaffner, *How Fixed Is a Permanent Establishment?*, p. 232. In a different vein, Arnold believes that the guidance of the OECD Model Commentary is difficult to justify since the habitual exercise test should be rather based on the frequency alone. *See* Brian J. Arnold, "Time Thresholds in Tax Treaties," *Bulletin for International Taxation* (2008) p. 230.

753. *See* Pasquale Pistone/César Alejandro Ruiz Jiménez in: Michael Lang/Pasquale Pistone/Josef Schuch/Claus Staringer/Alfred Storck (eds.) *Dependent Agents as Permanent Establishments*, pp. 151-152.

754. *See* Christian Ehlermann/Marta Castelon, "When Does a Dependent Agent Act Habitually?," *Tax Notes International* (2016) p. 1143 and Christian Ehlermann/Marta Castelon, "Wann handelt ein abhängiger Vertreter „gewöhnlich"?—Eine Betrachtung aus der deutschen und internationalen Steuerrechtsperspektive," *Internationale Steuer-Rundschau* (2016) p. 389.

755. *See* Pasquale Pistone/César Alejandro Ruiz Jiménez in: Michael Lang/Pasquale Pistone/Josef Schuch/Claus Staringer/Alfred Storck (eds.) *Dependent Agents as Permanent Establishments*, p. 152.

756. In this respect, *see* Christian Ehlermann/Marta Castelon, *Tax Notes International*, (2016) p. 1143 and Christian Ehlermann/Marta Castelon, *Internationale Steuer-Rundschau*, (2016) p. 389.

757. *See* Pasquale Pistone/César Alejandro Ruiz Jiménez in: Michael Lang/Pasquale Pistone/Josef Schuch/Claus Staringer/Alfred Storck (eds.) *Dependent Agents as Permanent Establishments*, pp. 147-148 and Farkas Barsony in: Michael Lang/Hans Jörgen Aigner/Mario Züger (eds.) *Permanent Establishments in International Tax Law*, p. 142.

758. *See* Christian Ehlermann/Marta Castelon, *Tax Notes International*, (2016) p. 1143, Christian Ehlermann/Marta Castelon, *Internationale Steuer-Rundschau*, (2016) p. 389 and Brian J. Arnold, *Bulletin for International Taxation*, (2008) p. 230.

759. *See* Pasquale Pistone/César Alejandro Ruiz Jiménez in: Michael Lang/Pasquale Pistone/Josef Schuch/Claus Staringer/Alfred Storck (eds.) *Dependent Agents as Permanent Establishments*, pp. 148-150.

In the context of insurance business, contracts have often a rather small order value but are concluded on a frequent and standardized basis.[760] It follows that, in order to ascertain whether the activity is recurrent, careful consideration should be given to the number of insurance contracts concluded in a given timeframe rather than the volume of such contracts.

3.3.2.4 The Independent Agent Provision

3.3.2.4.1 Relationship with the Dependent Agent Provision

Under Art. 5, para. 6, of the OECD Model, an agent of an independent status does not constitute an agency permanent establishment, provided that such an agent is acting in the ordinary course of its business. At the outset, before going into more details, a preliminary question arises as to whether Art. 5, paras. 5 and 6, of the OECD Model should be interpreted independently or whether they fit together. Prior to the amendments introduced in the context of the BEPS Project, several authors have assessed the interaction between such provisions with different results.[761]

To begin with, Roberts took the view that such provisions should be interpreted as independent rules. Indeed, according to Roberts, from a civil law perspective, such provisions do not fit together. On the one hand, Art. 5, para. 5, of the OECD Model, which integrates the concepts of direct and indirect representation, has a civil law origin and confuses a common law interpreter. On the other hand, Art. 5, para. 6, of the OECD Model, which has instead a common law origin, does not fit as an exception to the dependent agent provision. This is because brokers, commission agents and other independent agent do not generally conclude contracts in the name of the principal and thus, from a civil law perspective, the reference to agents of an independent status under Art. 5, para. 6, of the OECD Model is superfluous.[762]

On the contrary, Avery Jones, Ward and Pijl argued that such provisions should be read together. More to the point, Avery Jones and Ward supported a main rule/exception system by arguing that Art. 5, para. 5, of the OECD Model is the main rule which should apply first and then, as a second step, Art. 5, para. 6, of the OECD Model should apply as an exception.[763,764] In contrast, Pijl supported an integration system, according to which Art. 5, para. 6, of the OECD Model should apply first, so

760. *See* David Feuerstein in: Michael Lang/Florian Brugger/Patrick Plansky (eds.) *Permanent Establishments in International and EU Tax Law*, p. 115.

761. Another theory, elaborated by Kroppen and Huffmeier, does not go into specific detail on the relationship between such provisions. Nevertheless, this theory suggests that, since Art. 5, para. 6, of the OECD Model is not worded to fit perfectly into Art. 5, para. 5, of the OECD Model, any interpretation departing from the text of the provision would be too hazardous. To this effect, *see* Heinz-Klaus Kroppen/Stephan Huffmeier, "The German Commissionaire as a Permanent Establishment Under the OECD Model Treaty," *Intertax* (1996) pp. 133-136, as further analyzed in Giuseppe Persico, *Intertax*, (2000) pp. 77-79.

762. *See* Sidney I. Roberts, *Intertax*, (1993) pp. 500-502.

763. *See* John F. Avery Jones/David A. Ward, *European Taxation*, (1993) pp. 178-179. This main rule/exception approach is also shared by Garcia Prats. *See* Francisco A. Garcia Prats, *El establecimiento permanente: análisis jurídico-tributario internacional de la imposición societaria*, p. 198.

that if such a provision excludes agents from creating a permanent establishment, there is no need to look at Art. 5, para. 5, of the OECD Model. Conversely, in the case where Art. 5, para. 6, of the OECD Model does not exclude an agent from being regarded as a permanent establishment, one should further apply Art. 5, para. 5, of the OECD Model.[765]

According to Fuentes Hernández, a review of the historical development of the relevant provisions suggests that Art. 5, paras. 5 and 6, of the OECD Model should be read together. Therefore, the main rule/exception system of Avery Jones and Ward and the integration system of Pijl seem to provide a correct interpretation. The main difference between such systems lies on the order in which the two provisions are applied. More to the point, while under the main rule/exception system, Art. 5, para. 5, of the OECD Model is applied first and then Art. 5, para. 6, of the OECD Model is applied in the second step, the integration system supports the application of the latter provision in the first instance. Nevertheless, despite such a divergence, both theories come to the same practical implications.[766]

Avery Jones and Lüdicke argued that, even though both provisions have a common law origin,[767] they do not fit together very well for a number of reasons. Nevertheless, the authors tried to reconcile such provisions and concluded that they have worked for a considerable time. More specifically, they contended that, while Art. 5, para. 5, of the OECD Model is fairly useless from a common law point of view and Art. 5, para. 6, of the OECD Model is fairly useless from a civil law point of view, together they managed to give a reasonably similar result under both systems of law.[768]

The conclusion that such provisions should be read together seems to be supported by the amendments introduced in the aftermath of the BEPS Project.[769] Most importantly, the condition that the dependent agent provision is nevertheless "*subject to the provisions of paragraph 6*" seems to confirm that—according to the OECD—such provisions should be analyzed together in any case. In other words, no matter what, when applying the dependent agent provision, one must always check the provisions set forth under Art. 5, para. 6, of the OECD Model.[770]

764. It should be noted that the authors acknowledged that their interpretation contained a conflict between civil law and common law. *See* John F. Avery Jones/David A. Ward, *European Taxation*, (1993) pp. 178-179.
765. *See* Hans Pijl, *Bulletin for International Taxation*, (2013) pp. 85 and 97.
766. *See* Daniel Fuentes Hernández, "Agents of an Independent Character under Article 5(6) of the OECD Model Convention" in: Michael Lang/Pasquale Pistone/Josef Schuch/Claus Staringer/Alfred Storck (eds.) *Dependent Agents as Permanent Establishments* (Vienna: Linde, 2014) p. 170.
767. Avery Jones and Lüdicke eventually concurred with Pijl that such provisions have a common UK origin. *See* John F. Avery Jones/Jürgen Lüdicke, *World Tax Journal*, (2014) p. 240 and Hans Pijl, *Bulletin for International Taxation*, (2013) p. 97.
768. *See* John F. Avery Jones/Jürgen Lüdicke, *World Tax Journal*, (2014) pp. 240-241.
769. According to the author, such amendments also provide a basis in order to solve the conflict between civil law and common law. For further comments, *see* s. 3.3.2.4.2 below.
770. In this respect, Pleijsier is of the opinion that both paragraphs are so connected that they had to be both analyzed in any case also before the BEPS Project. To this effect, *see* Arthur Pleijsier, "The Artificial Avoidance of Permanent Establishment Status: A Reaction to the BEPS Action 7 Final Report," *International Transfer Pricing Journal* (2016) p. 443.

The amendments formulated after the BEPS Project also seem to reveal the intention of the OECD to consider Art. 5, para. 6, of the OECD Model as an exception to Art. 5, para. 5, of the OECD Model. Most notably, this can be clearly seen in the use of the term "*exception*" in paras. 103 and 113 of the OECD Model Commentary on Art. 5.[771]

3.3.2.4.2 Persons Covered

In the past, the reference to a "*broker,*" a "*general commission agent*" and "*any other agent of an independent status*" gave rise to significant interpretation issues. Indeed, such terms created much uncertainty to the extent that no definition was provided for.[772] The reference to brokers and commission agents was rooted in the strong influence of UK legislation in the period between the World Wars.[773] However, in the absence of the law specifying types of agency contracts in common law, there could not be a precise legal definition. These were therefore commercial expressions with a somewhat uncertain meaning. Most probably, such English expressions were meant to provide typical examples of independent agents (even though such agents did bind their principals when contracting) to make clear that transactions made through such agents could not give rise to a dependent agent permanent establishment.[774] On the other hand, such expressions had no connection with the civil law terms of courtier/Handelsmakler and commissionaire/Kommissionär.[775]

In the aftermath of World War II,[776] even though the above expressions probably comprised most independent agents under common law, the wording "*any other agent of an independent status*" was introduced in order to supplement the examples of brokers and commission agents in view of including other agents independent from their principals in the light of the manner in which the agent conducted its business in a broad sense.[777]

After the implementation of the BEPS Project, the new rules introduce a simplification, namely the omission of the terms "*broker, general commission agent or any other agent of an independent status.*"[778] More to the point, the first sentence of Art. 5, para. 6, of the OECD Model now makes a cross-reference to Art. 5, para. 5, of the OECD

771. *See* Jérôme Monsenego, "The Independent Agent Exception and Group Membership," *Intertax* (2018) p. 945.
772. *See* Arthur Pleijsier, *International Transfer Pricing Journal,* (2016) p. 444.
773. *See* s. 3.2.2 above.
774. To this effect, *see* Hans Pijl, *Bulletin for International Taxation,* (2013) p. 18.
775. For further comments on such terms, *see* John F. Avery Jones/Jürgen Lüdicke, *World Tax Journal,* (2014) pp. 218 et seq., John F. Avery Jones/David A. Ward, *European Taxation,* (1993) pp. 167-169, Arthur Pleijsier, *Intertax,* (2001) pp. 179-180 and Arthur Pleijsier, *The agency permanent establishment: de vaste vertegenwoordiger: proefschrift,* pp. 186-188.
776. *See* s. 3.2.3 above.
777. According to Pijl, non-bindingness is not relevant to this end. To this effect, *see* Hans Pijl, *Bulletin for International Taxation,* (2013) pp. 89-90.
778. This simplification was also suggested a number of years ago. To this effect, *see* John F. Avery Jones/David A. Ward, *European Taxation,* (1993) p. 179, Arthur Pleijsier, *Intertax,* (2001) p. 183 and Arthur Pleijsier, *The agency permanent establishment: de vaste vertegenwoordiger: proefschrift,* pp. 196-197.

Model mentioning the person acting in the source country on behalf of a foreign enterprise. It follows that any such person can now invoke Art. 5, para. 6, of the OECD Model with no distinction among different categories of independent agents. Needless to say, this is clearly something that is to be welcomed in view of reducing the uncertainty when applying the independent agent provision.

According to the author, this simplification may also overcome the conflict of laws as to the application of the independent agent provision.[779] Indeed, the cross-reference to Art. 5, para. 5, of the OECD Model seems to suggest that the independent agent provision comes into play when the conditions laid down in Art. 5, para. 5, of the OECD are fulfilled. To the contrary, in the case that the conditions set forth therein are not fulfilled, the independent agent provision is not relevant. In such a way, Art. 5, para. 6, of the OECD Model can no longer be regarded as redundant and/or useless.

3.3.2.4.3 The Independence Test

The guidance concerning the independence test contained in the OECD Model Commentary on Art. 5 has been considerably reshuffled following the BEPS Project. As a matter of fact, prior to the BEPS Project, it was clearly stated that the agent had to be independent from the foreign enterprise, both legally and economically.[780,781] In order to assess such conditions, a number of factors had to be carefully considered.[782] The guidance set out in para. 37 of the 2014 OECD Model Commentary on Art. 5 has now been deleted in favor of a clarification of what is not an independent agent.[783]

The bulk of the previous guidance on the legal independence test has been retained. Nonetheless, it appears that this test now boils down to operational independence.[784] Most notably, the independence of the agent should now be determined with reference to "*the obligations which this person has vis-à-vis the enterprise.*" To this end, the detail of instructions, the comprehensive control and the allocation of the entrepreneurial risk between the agent and the foreign enterprise should be regarded as the relevant criteria for the purposes of determining independence.[785] In this respect, the

779. *See* s. 3.3.2.4.1 above.
780. *See* para. 37 of the 2014 OECD Model Commentary on Art. 5.
781. This twofold dimension of independence dated back to the work of the League of Nations. For further comments, *see* s. 3.2.2 above.
782. *See* paras. 38-38.8 of the 2014 OECD Model Commentary on Art. 5. For a previous discussion concerning the legal and economic independence, *see* Daniel Fuentes Hernández, in: Michael Lang/Pasquale Pistone/Josef Schuch/Claus Staringer/Alfred Storck (eds.) *Dependent Agents as Permanent Establishments*, pp. 174 et seq., David Feuerstein in: Michael Lang/Florian Brugger/Patrick Plansky (eds.) *Permanent Establishments in International and EU Tax Law*, pp. 117 et seq., Jean Schaffner, *How Fixed Is a Permanent Establishment?*, pp. 238-239, Robert L. Williams, *Fundamentals of Permanent Establishments*, pp. 137 et seq., Francisco A. Garcia Prats, *El establecimiento permanente: análisis jurídico-tributario internacional de la imposición societaria*, pp. 195-197, Farkas Barsony in: Michael Lang/Hans Jörgen Aigner/Mario Züger (eds.) *Permanent Establishments in International Tax Law*, pp. 153 et seq. and Jérôme Monsenego, *Intertax* (2018) pp. 946-951.
783. *See* para. 103 of the OECD Model Commentary on Art. 5.
784. *See* Richard Collier, "Revised BEPS PE Proposals: Indeterminate Agents, Principals, and Principles," *Tax Notes International* (2015a) p. 64.
785. *See* para. 104 of the OECD Model Commentary on Art. 5.

OECD also retained the previous illustrative guidance concerning the control over the activities of the agent,[786] the freedom for the agent to conduct his business,[787] and whether the agent seeks approval from the principal in order to conduct his business.[788] By way of contrast, the control exercised by the parent company over a subsidiary is not relevant for the test.[789,790]

On the other hand, the economic independence test has been removed and only partially reintroduced in paras. 109 and 110 of the OECD Model Commentary on Art. 5.[791] Moving from this, Collier takes the view that, while under the previous guidance one had to look at the position of the agent as a legal entity, the removal of the economic independence test now seems to shift the focus from an entity perspective to a focus directed at the conduct and functions of the individuals conducting agency activities.[792]

In conclusion, it appears as if the amendments have changed the long-standing tests of legal and economic independence into a test of operational independence of the agent[793] with the effect that a previously already vague concept becomes even less clear.[794,795]

3.3.2.4.4 *The Supplementary Independence Test Regarding Related Parties*

The amendments introduced in the context of the BEPS Project have provided for a supplementary independence test with respect to related parties. More to the point, the last sentence of Art. 5, para. 6, of the OECD Model now automatically excludes a person

786. *See* para. 106 of the OECD Model Commentary on Art. 5.
787. *See* para. 107 of the OECD Model Commentary on Art. 5.
788. *See* para. 108 of the OECD Model Commentary on Art. 5.
789. *See* para. 105 of the OECD Model Commentary on Art. 5.
790. This is consistent with Art. 5, para. 7, of the OECD Model. In fact, pursuant to this provision, a controlling interest does not in itself result in a subsidiary being a permanent establishment of the parent company. The same reasoning also applies to the controlling company as well as to any company forming part of a multinational group. *See* paras. 115-118 of the OECD Model Commentary on Art. 5. For further comments, *see*—among others—Ekkehart Reimer in: Ekkehart Reimer/Alexander Rust (eds.) *Klaus Vogel on Double Taxation Convention—4th edition*, pp. 393-395, Alessandro Dragonetti/Valerio Piacentini/Anna Sfondrini, *Manuale di fiscalità internazionale*, pp. 1012-1016 and Luis Eduardo Schoueri/Oliver-Christoph Günther, "The Subsidiary as a Permanent Establishment," *Bulletin for International Taxation* (2010) pp. 69 et seq. In this respect, it should however be noted that, in the *Philip Morris* cases, the Italian Supreme Court found that an Italian company was to be regarded as a permanent establishment of more than one foreign companies pertaining to the same group. Such cases led the Italian representatives to introduce an observation (which is now embodied in para. 181 of the OECD Model Commentary on Art. 5) providing that its jurisprudence is not to be ignored in the interpretation of cases falling in paras. 116-118 of the OECD Model Commentary on Art. 5.
791. *See* Justus Eisenbeiss, *Intertax*, (2016) p. 489.
792. *See* Richard Collier, *Tax Notes International*, (2015a) p. 64.
793. *See* OECD, "*Comments received on revised discussion draft—BEPS Action 7: Prevent the artificial avoidance of PE status*," Paris (June 15, 2015), pp. 127 and 256.
794. To this effect, *see* Richard Collier, *Tax Notes International*, (2015a) p. 64, *see* Richard Collier, *Tax Notes International*, (2015b) pp. 251-252 and Justus Eisenbeiss, *Intertax*, (2016) p. 489.
795. However, the author does not share the view of Garbarino, who argues that in practice the independence requirement is now conflated with the ordinary course of business in a single condition. For further comments on this assertion, *see* Carlo Garbarino, "Permanent Establishments and BEPS Action 7: Perspectives in Evolution," *Intertax* (2019) pp. 378 and 381.

that is acting "*exclusively or almost exclusively on behalf of one or more enterprises to which it is closely related*" from being regarded as an independent agent.

To this end, the OECD has introduced the concept of "*closely related enterprises.*"[796,797] Specifically, enterprises are considered "*closely related*" in the case that "*one has control of the other or both are under the control of the same persons or enterprises. In any case, a person shall be considered to be closely related to an enterprise if one possesses directly or indirectly more than 50 per cent of the beneficial interest in the other (...) or (...) more than 50 per cent of the beneficial interest (...) in the person and the enterprise.*"[798] In this respect, the OECD has specified that such a concept is to be distinguished from the notion of "*associated enterprises,*" which is used in Art. 9 of the OECD Model.[799] With this in mind, at a first glance, the notion of "*closely related enterprises*" could look narrower than that of "*associated enterprises.*" However, differences and similarities between such notions have not been clearly explained in the OECD Model Commentary.[800]

Alongside, the OECD has indicated that the wording "*almost exclusively*" should be held to mean that, where the activities of the person on behalf of enterprises to which he/she is not closely related do not represent a significant part of its business, such a person will not qualify as an independent agent. As an illustrative example, the OECD has explained that, where an agent concludes for enterprises to which he/she is not closely related represent less than 10% of all the sales that he/she concludes as an agent acting for other enterprises, that agent should be regarded as acting exclusively or almost exclusively on behalf of closely related enterprises.[801] However, this example only provides limited guidance. Among others, as noted by Monsenego,[802] the reference to sales concluded by the agent[803] and the fact that the door is left open for parameters other than sales could create more confusion than clarity.

To conclude, the last sentence of Art. 5, para. 6, of the OECD Model introduces an assumption of dependency on the basis of the relationship between the agent and the

796. It should be noted that the first discussion draft proposed that an agent could not qualify as an independent agent in the case that such an agent is working exclusively or almost exclusively for "*one enterprise*" or "*associated enterprises,*" with the latter term being borrowed from Art. 9 of the OECD Model. *See* OECD, "*Public Discussion Draft—BEPS Action 7: Preventing the Artificial Avoidance of PE Status,*" pp. 12-14. During the consultation process, the term "*associated enterprises*" has been later replaced with "*connected enterprises*" and finally with "*closely related enterprises,*" whereas the OECD moved to accept the view that an agent working exclusively or almost exclusively for an unrelated party may nonetheless be independent. For further comments on such changes, *see also* Richard Collier, *Tax Notes International*, (2015a) p. 63 and Jérôme Monsenego, *Intertax* (2018) pp. 954-955.

797. According to Kraft and Weiß, this concept has been taken from Art. 22 of the US Model. To this effect, *see* Gerhard Kraft/Maximilian Weiß, "Vertreterbetriebsstätte: Die geplante Reform des abkommensrechtlichen Begriffs der Vertreterbetriebsstätte und ihre Auswirkungen auf die Kommissionärsstrukturen international tätiger Konzerne," *Internationale Steuer-Rundschau* (2016) p. 35.

798. *See* Art. 5, para. 8, of the OECD Model.

799. *See* para. 119 of the OECD Model Commentary on Art. 5.

800. In a similar vein, *see also* Jérôme Monsenego, *Intertax* (2018) p. 955.

801. *See* para. 112 of the OECD Model Commentary on Art. 5.

802. *See* Jérôme Monsenego, *Intertax* (2018) pp. 952-953.

803. Indeed, the agent would rather act as an intermediary between the seller and the customer.

foreign enterprise.[804] Though not overtly stated by the OECD, Collier believes that the rationale behind such an assumption presumably derives from the high level of suspicion regarding multinational groups.[805] However, while—in practice—such an assumption is not unreasonable[806] and supported by an historical analysis of the independent agent provision,[807] it may be regarded as a discrimination against related parties which seems hard to justify in principle[808] and goes beyond the (narrow) goal of preventing the artificial avoidance of the permanent establishment status.[809]

3.3.2.4.5 The Ordinary Course of Business Test

Pursuant to Art. 5, para. 6, of the OECD Model, the person in the source country should also act for the foreign enterprise in the ordinary course of its business as an independent agent. As already pointed out above,[810] this wording is rooted in the period of the League of Nations and was arguably inspired by the UK legislation in force at that time.[811] Since then, the concepts of "*bonafide*" and "*genuinely*" adopted in previous reports have been reshaped a number of times to arrive at the wording we know today.[812]

Most notably, in light of the changes introduced in the OECD Model Commentary on Art. 5 after the BEPS Project, the only business activities to be considered as part of this analysis are those related to the role of the person as an agent. For instance, where such a person acts both as an agent and a distributor, no account should be taken of the activities carried on as a distributor.[813] In such a way, in line with the removal of the economic independence test,[814] the OECD seems to confirm a shift of focus from an entity perspective to a focus on the activities conducted on an agency basis.[815]

The OECD then went further by clarifying that intermediation activities which, "*in line with the common practice in a particular business sector,*" are sometimes carried on as an agent and sometimes on the enterprise's own account may be regarded

804. Most importantly, the OECD has changed its position regarding the legal dependence. To this effect, *see* Jérôme Monsenego, *Intertax* (2018) p. 955.
805. *See* Richard Collier, *Tax Notes International*, (2015a) p. 63. In a similar vein, *see also* Jérôme Monsenego, *Intertax* (2018) p. 958.
806. To this effect, *see* Justus Eisenbeiss, *Intertax*, (2016) p. 493.
807. *See* Arthur Pleijsier, "The Agency Permanent Establishment in BEPS Action 7: Treaty Abuse or Business Abuse," *Intertax* (2015) pp. 153-154.
808. *See*—among others—OECD, "*Comments received on revised discussion draft—BEPS Action 7: Prevent the artificial avoidance of PE status,*" p. 256. In a similar vein, *see also* Richard Collier, *Tax Notes International*, (2015a) p. 64, Diego Avolio/Benedetto Santacroce, "La stabile organizzazione e l''Action 7' dell'OCSE: la figura del commissionario," *Corriere Tributario* (2015) pp. 831 et seq., Lorenzo Bellavite/Paolo Sella, "La stabile organizzazione personale dopo il Beps: ancora incertezze sulla definizione di 'agente'," *La Circolare Tributaria* (2016) p. 35 and Diego Avolio/Benedetto Santacroce, "Stabile organizzazione e final report dell'OCSE: cosa cambia per i modelli distributivi delle imprese," *Il Fisco* (2016) pp. 958 *et seq.*
809. To this effect, *see* Justus Eisenbeiss, *Intertax*, (2016) p. 493.
810. *See* s. 3.2.2 above.
811. *See* Hans Pijl, *Bulletin for International Taxation*, (2013) pp. 17-18.
812. *See* ss. 3.2.3 and 3.3.1 above.
813. *See* para. 110 of the OECD Model Commentary on Art. 5.
814. *See* s. 3.3.2.4.3 above.
815. In a similar vein, *see also* Richard Collier, *Tax Notes International*, (2015a) p. 64.

as activities that are part of the ordinary course of activity carried on as an agent, provided that such activities are in substance indistinguishable from each other.[816]

Hence, despite the removal of para. 38.8 of the 2014 OECD Model Commentary on Art. 5,[817] the new wording seems to confirm that a comparison with other activities of the very same person should be excluded. Instead, in line with similar conclusions drawn before the BEPS Project,[818] it appears reasonable to test the activities carried on by the person as an agent against the activities that would be expected of an agent operating in the same industry. This view is also supported by the specific reference to the "*the common practice in a particular business sector*" in the last sentence of para. 110 of the OECD Model Commentary on Art. 5, which clearly points toward a comparison with the usual practice of a given industry rather than an assessment of the ordinary course of business at the level of the agent.

In the past, a similar conclusion has been reached in a case law in the field of the insurance business. More to the point, in a Dutch case,[819] the Supreme Court ruled that a Dutch insurance broker of a US insurance company performed duties which a regular insurance broker did not perform. The US insurance company appointed an insurance broker to sell insurance contracts to airline passengers at a Dutch airport. Under the agreement between the parties, the US company delivered standard contracts to the broker. The latter was authorized to issue the contracts, but the premiums were to be paid back to the US company net of a percentage as commission. No negotiation could take place between the broker and the customers to the extent that the role of the broker was only to explain the difference between the only two contracts that could be sold. Also, the broker had to follow a strict and detailed manual governing how he could sell the contracts. Against this background, the Dutch Supreme Court maintained that the principal had granted considerable authority to the broker to the extent that he was allowed to sign the contracts, as well as to authorize other travel agents to sell insurance contracts. In the light of this, the Dutch Supreme Court ruled that this was not in line with the regular way in which a Dutch insurance broker operates. As a consequence, it may be concluded that the activities of the independent agent must be compared to activities regularly performed by fellow agents active in the same kind of

816. *See* para. 110 of the OECD Model Commentary on Art. 5.
817. According to the author, para. 38.8 of the 2014 OECD Model Commentary on Art. 5 was clearer in that respect to the extent that it provided for a straightforward exclusion of a comparison with other business activities carried out by the agent. In a similar vein, *see* Claus Staringer/Felipe Vallada, "Acting in the ordinary course of business under Article 5(6) of the OECD Model Convention" in: Michael Lang/Pasquale Pistone/Josef Schuch/Claus Staringer/Alfred Storck (eds.) *Dependent Agents as Permanent Establishments* (Vienna: Linde, 2014) p. 192 and OECD, "*Issues arising under Article 5 (Permanent Establishment) of the Model Tax Convention,*" para. 134.
818. *See* Claus Staringer/Felipe Vallada in: Michael Lang/Pasquale Pistone/Josef Schuch/Claus Staringer/Alfred Storck (eds.) *Dependent Agents as Permanent Establishments* (Vienna: Linde, 2014) pp. 194-195 and David Feuerstein in: Michael Lang/Florian Brugger/Patrick Plansky (eds.) *Permanent Establishments in International and EU Tax Law*, pp. 122-123.
819. *See* HR (*Hoge Raad*) January 13, 1971, No. 16.445, which dealt with Art. II, para. 1, let. (i), of the DTA between the Netherlands and the United States concluded on April 29, 1948.

business. For instance, shipbrokers must be compared to shipbrokers while insurance agents must be compared to insurance agents.[820,821]

The deletion of para. 38.8 of the 2014 OECD Model Commentary on Art. 5 also implies that no other complementary tests can be used to establish proper parameters. Although this deletion is to be welcomed for the sake of clarity in the case of comparable business sectors, it might give rise to some uncertainty if comparable data and information are not available (for instance, in the case of new industries). In such a latter case, in the absence of specific guidance, the author believes that an analysis of the prospective development in the specific industry under scrutiny is required to assess what would be the reasonable role of an independent agent working within it.[822]

3.3.2.5 The Special Clause for Insurance Agents

3.3.2.5.1 Rationale of the Clause

Unlike the UN Model,[823] there is no insurance agent provision directly referred to in the OECD Model itself. Rather, the description of a special clause for insurance agents is addressed in para. 114 of the OECD Model Commentary on Art. 5. The fact that a specific provision has not been included in the treaty model itself does not mean that issues related to the insurance industry have not been discussed at all. In fact, as outlined in the previous sections,[824] the OECD has extensively studied the issue of large-scale insurance activities carried out in a country through agents without being taxed in such a country. Following such discussions, the OECD introduced in the OECD Model Commentary on Art. 5 a description of a special clause for insurance agents adopted in some DTAs which is clearly intended to go beyond the dependent agent permanent establishment provision.[825] In other words, this special clause has the effect of creating a permanent establishment even though the agent does not fulfill all substantive conditions set forth under Art. 5, para. 5, of the OECD Model. Indeed, insofar as an agent collects premiums or insures risks located in the source country, a permanent establishment is deemed to arise, irrespective of whether such an agent is of a dependent or independent status.[826]

820. *See* Claus Staringer/Felipe Vallada in: Michael Lang/Pasquale Pistone/Josef Schuch/Claus Staringer/Alfred Storck (eds.) *Dependent Agents as Permanent Establishments*, pp. 201-202, Arthur Pleijsier, *Intertax*, (2001) p. 182 and Amar Mehta, *Permanent Establishment in International Taxation*, pp. 386-387.
821. For other cases concerning the independence of insurance intermediaries, *see* ss. 3.4.2.3 and 3.5.2.3 below.
822. In a similar vein, *see* Claus Staringer/Felipe Vallada in: Michael Lang/Pasquale Pistone/Josef Schuch/Claus Staringer/Alfred Storck (eds.) *Dependent Agents as Permanent Establishments*, p. 204.
823. *See* s. 3.4.2.3 below.
824. *See* particularly s. 3.3.1 above.
825. To this effect, *see* Jacques Sasseville/Arvid A. Skaar in: IFA (ed.) *Is there a permanent establishment?*, p. 58.
826. It is also important to note that, as opposed to Art. 5, para. 6, of the UN Model, para. 114 of the OECD Model Commentary on Art. 5 does not provide for a carve-out of reinsurance activities, either.

According to the historical documentation available, in view of the special conditions pertaining to the insurance business, the Belgian delegation suggested such a special clause as a clarification to determine whether the representative has or has not an authority to conclude contracts in the name of the enterprise in the context of the dependent agent provision.[827] Nonetheless, this justification does not appear to be convincing to the extent that the proposed wording did not specifically address the authority to conclude contracts in the name of the enterprise. Rather, this wording seems to be an attempt to rule out the application of the independent agent provision to insurance representatives in the light of the peculiar features of the insurance business to prevent foreign insurance enterprises from escaping source taxation by operating through such representatives.[828] To put it differently, the adoption of such criteria appears to be an alternative approach to a straight exclusion of insurance agents from the scope of Art. 5, para. 6, of the OECD Model.[829] More specifically, this appears an exclusion from the ordinary course of business test originated in the Belgian DTA policy,[830] which is aimed at bringing back within the scope of the permanent establishment provision insurance representatives—who are in principle independent—in the case that the foreign insurance company collects premiums or insures risks in the country where the representative operates. Consequently, according to the author, such a special clause may be regarded as a downright exclusion from the ordinary course of business test that is enshrined in Art. 5, para. 6, of the OECD Model.[831]

This reasoning appears to be supported by the following historical development of this special clause. Indeed, in the context of the discussion preceding the approval of the 1977 OECD Model, the description of such a special clause has been shifted to para. 38 of the 1977 OECD Model Commentary on Art. 5 (which is now para. 114 of the OECD Model Commentary on Art. 5), which specifically concerned Art. 5, para. 6, of the 1977 OECD Model, and a carve-out for dependent agents who already constitute an agency permanent establishment has been introduced with the effect that such a special clause is not relevant for agents caught under Art. 5, para. 5, of the OECD Model.[832]

The historical analysis also demonstrated conflicting opinions with respect to the inclusion of the special clause in a DTA.[833] As a result, the decision as to whether or not such a wording should be included in a DTA has been left to bilateral negotiations depending on the factual and legal situation prevailing in the countries concerned.[834]

827. *See* OECD Fiscal Committee, "*Consolidated list of outstanding points concerning the OECD draft convention*," Document TFD/FC/218, p. 17.
828. In a similar vein, *see* Working Party No. 1 of the OECD Fiscal Committee, "*Preliminary report on the questions in connection with the definition in article 5 of the term permanent establishment*," Document FC/WP1(70)1, para. 59.
829. This view is shared by Avery Jones and Ward when commenting the Belgian DTA policy. To this effect, *see* John F. Avery Jones/David A. Ward, *European Taxation*, (1993) pp. 170-171.
830. For further comments on the Belgian DTA policy in this respect, *see also* s. 5.3.2 below.
831. This conclusion does not appear to be affected by the amendments introduced in the context of the BEPS Project to the extent that such amendments do not materially affect the special clause for insurance agents.
832. *See* s. 3.3.1 above.
833. *See* s. 3.3.1 above.
834. *See* para. 114 of the OECD Model Convention on Art. 5.

As acknowledged in the case law, the OECD decided against such a special clause in the OECD Model for what Vann described as reciprocal reasons, i.e., an attitude that "*we'd collect the same amount from them as they collect from our people.*"[835] True, this mostly reflects the view of developed countries dealing with one another, while it becomes problematic in treaties between developed and developing countries. Though, nothing precludes countries—at whatever stage of development—from inserting such an insurance clause. In the light of this, it is settled case law that the lack of an insurance clause in a DTA suggests that the countries concerned recognize that considerable activity of an insurance business can take place without finding that there is a permanent establishment.[836]

At last, it is worth noting that Action 7 of the BEPS Project also specifically addressed the question as to whether an insurance agent provision patterned after Art. 5, para. 6, of the UN Model was to be introduced in the OECD Model itself. Particularly, it was pointed out that the insurance business raises difficult issues with respect to the question of where profits that represent the remuneration of risk should be eventually taxed. In light of this, in the context of Action 7 of the BEPS Project, in the first discussion draft for public comments, the OECD proposed two alternative approaches to be adopted in order to deal with BEPS concerns related to the artificial avoidance of the permanent establishment threshold in relation to the insurance business, i.e., Option M, according to which a specific insurance agent provision was to be included in the OECD Model itself, or Option N, according to which no specific clause for insurance enterprises was to be added to Art. 5 of the OECD Model, so that the issue of insurance enterprises was to be dealt with through the more general changes proposed to Art. 5, paras. 5 and 6 of the 2014 OECD Model.[837]

Based on the comments received over the course of the public consultation, it was concluded that Option N was the better approach, which means that BEPS concerns related to circumstances where a large network of exclusive agents is used to sell insurance for foreign insurance companies were to be addressed through the more general changes formulated to Art. 5, paras. 5 and 6, of the 2014 OECD Model.[838]

Accordingly, with specific respect to the insurance business, the amendments introduced in the context of the BEPS Project are limited to an acknowledgement that the changes made to Art. 5, paras. 5 and 6, of the OECD Model address some of the concerns that the special clause discussed in para. 114 of the OECD Model Commentary on Art. 5 is intended to address.[839]

835. *See* TTC (Tax Court of Canada) May 16, 2008, *American Income Life Insurance Company v. The Queen*, 2008 TCC 306, para. 85. *See* s. 3.5.2.3 for further details on the case.

836. *See* US Tax Court May 2, 1995, *Taisei Fire and Marine Insurance Co., Ltd. et al. v. Commissioner of Internal Revenue*, 104 T.C. 558, TCC (Tax Court of Canada) May 16, 2008, *American Income Life Insurance Company v. The Queen*, 2008 TCC 306, para. 86, and TCC (Tax Court of Canada) May 16, 2008, *Knights of Columbus v. The Queen*, 2008 TCC 307, paras. 83-85. *See* s. 3.5.2.3 for further details on the cases.

837. *See* OECD, "*Public Discussion Draft—BEPS Action 7: Preventing the Artificial Avoidance of PE Status*," pp. 23-25.

838. *See* OECD, "*Revised discussion draft—BEPS Action 7: Preventing the Artificial Avoidance of PE Status*," pp. 36-37.

839. *See* para. 114 of the OECD Model Commentary on Art. 5.

3.3.2.5.2 *Elements of the Special Clause*

To begin with, the first condition to trigger the special clause for insurance agents is that an insurance company carries on its insurance business in a country other than that of establishment. The specific reference to insurance companies should not be held to mean that this clause is only intended for insurance companies. Instead, the author believes that this term should also cover reinsurance companies and retrocession companies, whose business is essentially the same as that of insurance companies.[840] This view is also supported by the fact that—unlike the UN Model[841]—no specific carve-out for any such companies is addressed in para. 114 of the OECD Model Commentary on Art. 5. To the contrary, this special clause should not become applicable to other companies pertaining to a larger insurance group (for instance, holding companies, service companies, regional offices and so forth) to the extent that such entities are not specifically engaged in the business of insurance.

Such an insurance company should carry on its insurance business in the other country in a way that does not otherwise give rise to a permanent establishment. To put it in other words, such an insurance company should have neither a fixed place of business in the other country within the meaning of Art. 5, para. 1, of the OECD Model, nor a personal connection therein within the meaning of Art. 5, para. 5, of the OECD Model. Indeed, in the event that any of such provisions is fulfilled, it takes priority over the special clause and—thus—the latter clause becomes irrelevant.

The insurance company should nevertheless avail itself of an agent established in the other country. According to the author, account taken of the rationale of the special clause, the reference to the term "*agent*" should not be restricted to the legal concept of an agent within the meaning of domestic law. Instead, it should be intended in a broader commercial sense of any person qualifying under Art. 3 of the OECD Model that carries on the activity of insurance, reinsurance and/or retrocession distribution in favor of a foreign insurance company. More specifically, considering the above-mentioned priority rule, the special clause seems targeted at: (*i*) any such of insurance, reinsurance and/or retrocession distributor that does not fulfill neither the traditional test regarding the conclusion of contracts nor the supplementary test regarding the principal rule leading to the conclusion of contracts within the meaning of Art. 5, para. 5, of the OECD Model and (*ii*) any such of insurance, reinsurance and/or retrocession distributor that does so, but is to be regarded as an agent of an independent status acting in the ordinary course of its business within the meaning of Art. 5, para. 6, of the OECD Model.

The prerequisite that the agent should be "*established*" in the source country does not necessarily require the agent be resident therein. Nonetheless, this seems to indicate that such an agent must be physically present therein with a certain degree of permanence to justify an appropriate taxable link with the source country. This is clearly a determination that should be based on a factual assessment. In the author's view, it is at any rate reasonable to say that, as with the permanence test for the

840. For further comments, *see also* s. 2.2.2.4 above.
841. *See* s. 3.4.2.3 below.

purposes of the habitual test,[842] this requirement can be deemed as met in the case that the agent is present in the source country for more than six months in any given year.

The use of the preposition "*through*" seems to indicate that a relation between the activities of the agent and the business of the foreign insurance company is required to trigger the special rule for insurance agents. More to the point, according to the author, such a relation can be described as a functional integration of the activities carried on by the agent into the business of the foreign insurance company. To put it in other words, the activities of the agent should serve (at least, partially) the business of the foreign insurance company in the source country.

The activities that trigger the special clause for insurance agents are: (*i*) the collection of premiums, or (*ii*) the insurance of risks. On the one hand, the collection of premiums is a rather specific activity that concerns the administration of insurance contracts, i.e., the collection of money to be paid by the insured person. Hence, this criterion should be construed as met in the case that the payment takes place in and/or from the source country.

On the other hand, the insurance of risks appears to have a broad meaning that should be intended to cover multiple activities. Indeed, according to the author, this criterion covers not only activities falling within the scope of Art. 5, para. 5, of the OECD Model,[843] but also circumstances under which offers collected and/or terms and conditions negotiated in the source country are subject to a final genuine review of the insurance company, even where such a review results in material modifications. In addition, the insurance of risks seems to cover other activities preceding the conclusion of contracts (for instance, the coordination of experts for the valuation of items to be insured),[844] the assistance in the administration of such contracts (for instance, the fulfillment)[845] and the assistance in the performance of such contracts,[846] most notably in the event of a claim (for instance, the coordination of lawyers and/or adjusters). As a result, if any of such activities is related to risks situated in the source country, the criterion under analysis can be regarded as met. To the contrary, this criterion should not cover marketing and promotion activities concerning one or more insurance products since such activities do not directly result in the conclusion of an insurance contract and—thus—to the insurance of risks. Also, as long as the special clause appears to be targeted at insurance (sales) agents pursuing the activity of insurance distribution, it is fair to say that this criterion should not cover activities related to outward reinsurance and/or retrocession from the view of the ceding company. In fact, under such circumstances, it should rather be assessed whether the agent could trigger the special clause from the view of the company that takes on inward reinsurance/retrocession.

842. *See* s. 3.3.2.3.8 above.
843. *See* ss. 3.3.2.2.4 and 3.3.2.2.5 above.
844. In a similar vein, *see* Arvid A. Skaar, *Permanent Establishment—Erosion of a Tax Treaty Principle*, p. 535.
845. The fulfillment can be regarded as the preparation and delivery of the insurance policies.
846. In a similar vein, *see* Roberto Baggio/Ermanno Basso, "La stabile organizzazione delle imprese di assicurazione (con particolare riguardo alla convenzione italo-francese del 1958)," *Rivista di Diritto Tributario* (1996) pp. 1098 et seq.

The use of the conjunction *"or"* clearly suggests that the above criteria may be construed as alternatives. Nevertheless, there is no hint of help to clarify which of such criteria should take priority over the other one. Arguably, there is no conflict in the case that the collection of premiums takes place in the same country where the risks are located. However, the place where the risks are located is not always the place where the premiums are collected. As a matter of fact, the insured risks may be located in a given country, while the insurance premiums may be collected in another country. In such a case, both countries may be considered the source of income of the insurance company and double taxation might occur. In seeking an answer to this issue, when discussing the insurance agent provision contained in the UN Model, Skaar explained that—on the one hand—one could argue that the place where the risks are located should have preference over the place where the premiums are collected to the extent that this would eliminate the possibility of relocating the tax basis. On the other hand, one could also argue that the collection of premiums refers to one specific part of the business of the insurance agent, whereas the insurance of risks applies to a variety of functions. As such, the collection of premiums should be regarded as the *lex specialis* which should have primacy over the insurance of risks. However, one could also argue that neither State should have primacy over the other. Under this latter line of reasoning, two different permanent establishments would be deemed to exist simultaneously with the only remaining issue being the attribution of profits to such permanent establishments.[847] In the author's opinion, a review of the historical development of the special clause for insurance agents—whereby such two criteria seem to have equal standing—and the lack of any case law specifically addressing this issue lean toward the latter interpretation.

3.4 THE CONCEPT OF PERMANENT ESTABLISHMENT IN THE UN MODEL

3.4.1 Historical Overview

In mid-1960s, the UN began to take an increased interest in the problem of double taxation as a result of the steady increase of developing UN Member States and as part of its action aimed at promoting the flow of foreign investments to developing countries.[848] In 1968, the UN Secretary-General set up the UN Ad Hoc Group of Experts on Tax Treaties between Developed and Developing Countries, composed of tax

847. *See* Arvid A. Skaar, *Permanent Establishment—Erosion of a Tax Treaty Principle*, pp. 535-536 and Josef Schuch/Eline Huisman, "The Dependent Agent PE under Article 5(5), (6) and (7) of the UN Model Convention" in: Michael Lang/Pasquale Pistone/Josef Schuch/Claus Staringer/Alfred Storck (eds.) *Dependent Agents as Permanent Establishments* (Vienna: Linde, 2014) pp. 279-280.

848. *See* Radhakishan Rawal/Sanjay Kumar, "*UN—Commentary on the Permanent Establishment Concept under the UN Model Tax Convention*," last reviewed: February 1, 2019, available online at www.ibfd.org, para. 1.1 and David Orzechowski, "The Relevance of the Commentaries on the OECD and UN Models for the Interpretation of the UN Model" in: Michael Lang/Pasquale Pistone/Alexander Rust/Josef Schuch/Claus Staringer (eds.) *The UN Model Convention and Its Relevance for the Global Tax Treaty Network* (Amsterdam: IBFD, 2017) para. 1.2.2.

officials and tax experts both from developed and developing countries, appointed on their personal capacity.[849]

The above working group elaborated guidelines for the negotiation of DTAs between developed and developing countries (which have been eventually released in the 1979 UN Manual). Furthermore, in 1978, such a working group received the mandate from the UN Secretary-General to initiate the drafting of a specific model treaty, which was eventually published as the 1980 UN Model a couple of years later.[850]

In the 1990s, the working group—meanwhile renamed as the Ad Hoc Group of Experts on International Cooperation in Tax Matters[851]—recognized that significant changes had taken place in the international economic, financial and fiscal environment. Such changes, along with the appearance of new issues in the international tax arena and the increasingly frequent updates of the OECD Model, led to the establishment of a focus group for the revision of the previous work. This effort eventually resulted in the publication of the 2001 UN Model and the 2003 UN Manual.[852]

In the following years, the UN ECOSOC decided to rename (and upgrade) the working group as the UN Committee of Experts,[853] which assumed its current structure.[854] Immediately after this change, the UN Committee of Experts started working toward a revision of the previous work. This work—which brought together experts in the field of international taxation from government, business and academia[855]—resulted in the 2011 UN Model. Over the recent years, the UN Committee of Experts has committed to an ongoing process of review.[856] This has resulted in the 2016 UN Manual[857] and eventually in the 2017 update of the UN Model, which has addressed some of the issues related to BEPS Project.

849. *See* UN Model, Introduction, p. v.
850. The 1980 UN Model was based to a large extent on the 1977 OECD Model. To this effect, *see* Bast Kosters, "The United Nations Model Tax Convention and Its Recent Developments," *Asia-Pacific Tax Bulletin* (2004) p. 4 and Michael Lennard, "The Purpose and Current Status of the United Nations Tax Work," *Asia-Pacific Tax Bulletin* (2008) p. 24.
851. *See* UN ECOSOC resolution 1980/13 of April 28, 1980.
852. *See* UN Model, Introduction, p. v.
853. *See* UN ECOSOC resolution 2004/69 of November 11, 2004.
854. For additional details on the composition and mandate of the UN Committee of Experts, *see* UN Model, Introduction, pp. v-vi, Michael Lennard, *Asia-Pacific Tax Bulletin*, (2008) pp. 24-25 and Armando Lara Yaffar/Michael Lennard, "An Introduction to the Updated UN Model (2011)," *Bulletin for International Taxation* (2012a) p. 591.
855. To this effect, *see—inter alia—*the note prepared by the Secretariat of the UN Committee of Experts, "*Ad hoc expert group meeting on the 2011 update of the United Nations Model Tax Convention,*" Document E/C.18/2011/3 and the 2016 UN Manual, Introduction, pp. v-viii.
856. To this effect, *see* UN Model, Introduction, p. viii, and Armando Lara Yaffar/Michael Lennard, "The Future of the UN Model," *Bulletin for International Taxation* (2012b) p. 624.
857. The UN Committee of Experts has recently agreed upon the update of the 2016 UN Manual. *See* UN Committee of Experts, "*Report on the eighteenth session,*" Document E/2019/45/Add.1-E/C.18/2019/3 (April 23-26, 2019) p. 13. For the revised text, *see* UN Committee of Experts, "*Revised Manual for the Negotiation of Bilateral Tax Treaties between Developed and Developing Countries,*" Document E/C.18/2019/CRP.5.

3.4.2 Overview of the Current Provision

3.4.2.1 Introduction

While drafting the UN Model, it has been decided to use the OECD Model as the main reference text to take advantage of the accumulated technical expertise embodied therein, and also for the practical reason that the OECD Model was also being used by OECD Member States in the negotiation of DTAs with developing countries.[858]

Nevertheless, while the OECD Model is very much based on the residence principle, the UN Model represents a compromise between the source principle and the residence principle.[859,860] As a matter of fact, the UN Model recognizes the benefits of granting an attractive investment climate, but the source countries will often expect that they may tax the profits from such investments to finance infrastructure to encourage other investments, schools, hospitals and other programs for a sustainable development.[861]

As a result, it can be said that under the UN Model there are more situations that can lead to a permanent establishment than under the OECD Model.[862] Among others, the primary differences vis-à-vis the OECD Model are the following:[863] (*i*) a shorter term and a wider scope for a building or construction sites to constitute a permanent establishment,[864] (*ii*) a service permanent establishment clause,[865] (*iii*) a retention of a

858. *See* Radhakishan Rawal/Sanjay Kumar, "*UN—Commentary on the Permanent Establishment Concept under the UN Model Tax Convention,*" para. 1.2.
859. *See* UN Model, Introduction, p. vi, Michael Lennard, *Asia-Pacific Tax Bulletin,* (2008) p. 25 and Radhakishan Rawal/Sanjay Kumar, "*UN—Commentary on the Permanent Establishment Concept under the UN Model Tax Convention,*" para. 1.2.
860. In this respect, it should also be noted that the UN Model is not intended to be binding and is not to be construed as a formal recommendation of the UN. Rather, the UN Model is intended to facilitate the negotiation, interpretation and practical application of DTAs based upon its provisions. To this effect, *see* UN Model, Introduction, p. vii. In particular, the UN Model Commentary has a very important role to play in explaining and giving guidance on how to interpret the UN Model, especially where the wording is different from the wording of the OECD Model or where the UN Committee of Experts is unable to concur in the interpretation given in the OECD Model Commentary. To this effect, *see* Radhakishan Rawal/Sanjay Kumar, "*UN—Commentary on the Permanent Establishment Concept under the UN Model Tax Convention,*" para. 1.2.
861. *See* Michael Lennard, *Asia-Pacific Tax Bulletin,* (2008) p. 25.
862. To this effect, *see* Bast Kosters, *Asia-Pacific Tax Bulletin,* (2004) p. 5 and Adolfo J. Martin Jiménez, "Chapter VII—Preventing avoidance of permanent establishment status" in: Alexander Trepelkov/Harry Tonino/Dominika Halka (eds.) *United Nations Handbook on Selected Issues in Protecting the Tax Base of Developing Countries—Second Edition* (New York: United Nations, 2017) p. 434.
863. For further general comments on such differences, *see also* Adolfo J. Martin Jiménez in: Alexander Trepelkov/Harry Tonino/Dominika Halka (eds.) *United Nations Handbook on Selected Issues in Protecting the Tax Base of Developing Countries—Second Edition,* pp. 429 et seq.
864. *See* Art. 5, para. 3, let. (*a*), of the UN Model.
865. *See* Art. 5, para. 3, let. (*b*), of the UN Model. Although the OECD Model does not contain such a clause, the 2008 OECD Model Commentary has incorporated service permanent establishment clauses for the contracting parties to discuss. *See* paras. 132-169 of the OECD Model Commentary on Art. 5. For further comments, *see also* Brian J. Arnold, "The Taxation of Income from Services under Tax Treaties: Cleaning Up the Mess," *Bulletin for International Taxation* (2011) pp. 59 et seq., Sriram P. Govind, "The International Tax Treatment of

specific provision on independent personal services,[866] (*iv*) a lack of the term "*delivery*" in the list of preparatory and auxiliary activities,[867] (*v*) a stock-holding agent provision[868] and a specific insurance agent provision.[869]

3.4.2.2 The Dependent Agent Provision

With specific respect to the definition of dependent agent permanent establishment,[870] it may be argued that Art. 5, para. 5, let. (*a*), of the UN Model follows the substance of Art. 5, para. 5, of the OECD. In its earliest version, this provision represented an amalgamation of the ideas contained in the 1977 OECD Model and previous studies conducted by the League of Nations.[871] In the following years, this provision remained essentially the same until the 2017 update of the UN Model, when the UN Committee of Experts decided to modify such a provision in line with the recommendations made in the context of Action 7 of the BEPS Project.

As a result, Art. 5, para. 5, let. (*a*), of the UN Model stipulates that a person that habitually concludes contracts in the name of the foreign enterprise, for the transfer of ownership or the granting of the right to use property of that enterprise or for the provision of services by that enterprise or—alternatively—plays the principal role leading to the conclusion of such contracts creates a sufficient association with the source country for a dependent agent permanent establishment to exist, unless the activities of such a person are limited to those mentioned under Art. 5, para. 4, of the UN Model which, if exercised through a fixed place of business, would not constitute a permanent establishment.[872] The slightly different fashion in which the provision is ordered vis-à-vis Art. 5, para. 5, of the OECD Model does not appear to have significant implications on the application of the provision.

For the most part, the UN Model Commentary quotes the corresponding OECD Model Commentary. In doing so, the UN Model Commentary generally approves the

---

Cross-Border Services," *Bulletin for International Taxation* (2011), Wim Wijnen/Jan de Goede/Andrea Alessi, "The Treatment of Services in Tax Treaties," *Bulletin for International Taxation* (2012) pp. 27-38, Raffaele Petruzzi/Viktoria Wöhrer in: Michael Lang/Pasquale Pistone/Alexander Rust/Josef Schuch/Claus Staringer (eds.) *The UN Model Convention and Its Relevance for the Global Tax Treaty Network*, para. 2.2.2.4.2 and Fernando Souza de Man, *Taxation of Services in Treaties between Developed and Developing Countries—A Proposal for New Guidelines* (Amsterdam: IBFD, 2017) para. 3.3.1.3.

866. *See* Art. 14 of the UN Model. For further comments on this provision, *see also* Brian J. Arnold, *Bulletin for International Taxation*, (2011) pp. 59 et seq., Josef Schuch/Eline Huisman in: Michael Lang/Pasquale Pistone/Josef Schuch/Claus Staringer/Alfred Storck (eds.) *Dependent Agents as Permanent Establishments*, pp. 288-290 and Wim Wijnen/Jan de Goede/Andrea Alessi, *Bulletin for International Taxation*, (2012) pp. 27-38.
867. *See* Art. 5, para. 4, of the UN Model.
868. *See* Art. 5, para. 5, let. (*b*), of the UN Model.
869. *See* Art. 5, para. 6, of the UN Model.
870. As already outlined in ss. 1.5 and 3.1 above, the focus of this research is on the agency permanent establishment provisions and thus other deviations from the OECD Model are beyond the scope of this chapter.
871. *See* Fernando Souza de Man, *Taxation of Services in Treaties between Developed and Developing Countries—A Proposal for New Guidelines*, para. 4.1.1.1.
872. *See* para. 22.2 of the UN Model Commentary on Art. 5.

corresponding OECD Model Commentary, unless it makes its disagreement clear.[873] Therefore, it seems that the UN has endorsed the work of the OECD regarding the dependent agent permanent establishment in the context of the BEPS Project, save for a minority view in respect of the supplementary test regarding the principal role leading to the conclusion of contracts. More specifically, a proposition has been added with reference to contracts "*that are routinely concluded without material modifications by the enterprise.*"[874] In particular, while the note of UN Committee of Experts regarding the case of the supplementary test being fulfilled in respect of some contracts does not seem to add much to the interpretation of the provision, it is interesting to note that the UN Committee of Experts seems to support countries wishing to omit the above wording in an attempt to preserve greater sovereignty for the source country. In such a case, the supplementary test would be met even where the principal makes material modifications before the contracts are concluded.

On a different note, Art. 5, para. 5, let. (*b*), of the UN Model represents a complete deviation from the OECD Model[875] stating that a person who does not have an authority to conclude contracts in the name of the enterprise, but instead habitually maintains a stock of goods or merchandise, will be deemed to constitute a permanent establishment.[876]

3.4.2.3 The Insurance Agent Provision

As portrayed above,[877] another major deviation from the OECD Model is the inclusion of the insurance agent provision under Art. 5, para. 6, of the UN Model to deal with specific features of the insurance business. This is a provision that was extracted from the OECD's store of draft proposals.[878] In fact, the OECD discussed the introduction of a specific provision dealing with the situation of insurance companies when drafting the 1963 OECD Draft and the 1977 OECD Model.[879] However, the OECD eventually concluded that there was no need to introduce such a specific provision.

The UN took a different view. The main concern of developing countries was that insurance companies could achieve considerable profits in a country without a fixed place of business and/or a dependent agent. When discussing the introduction of such

873. *See* Armando Lara Yaffar/Michael Lennard, *Bulletin for International Taxation*, (2012a) p. 592 and David Orzechowski in: Michael Lang/Pasquale Pistone/Alexander Rust/Josef Schuch/Claus Staringer (eds.) *The UN Model Convention and Its Relevance for the Global Tax Treaty Network*, para. 1.5.1.
874. *See* para. 24 of the UN Model Commentary on Art. 5. For an overview of the discussion, *see also* UN Committee of Experts, "*Report on the twelfth and thirteenth sessions*," Document E/2017/45-E/C.18/2017/7 (October 11-14, 2016 and December 5-8, 2016) p. 20.
875. As pointed out in s. 3.2.3 above, in the OECD Model, the stock-holding agent has been deleted after World War II.
876. For an overview of this provision, *see* Josef Schuch/Eline Huisman in: Michael Lang/Pasquale Pistone/Josef Schuch/Claus Staringer/Alfred Storck (eds.) *Dependent Agents as Permanent Establishments*, pp. 274-276.
877. *See* s. 3.4.2.1 above.
878. *See* Fernando Souza de Man, *Taxation of Services in Treaties between Developed and Developing Countries—A Proposal for New Guidelines*, para. 4.1.1.1.
879. *See* s. 3.3.1. above.

a provision, UN Member States also took diverging positions as to the status of insurance agents. In the end, a compromise was struck between source countries and residence countries. Hence, in the 1980 UN Model, it was agreed to include the insurance agent provision with a carve-out for independent agents.[880]

In the following years, this provision remained essentially the same until the 2017 update of the UN Model. In the sessions preceding such an update, the UN Committee of Experts extensively discussed the removal of the reinsurance exception and an alternative solution to allow source taxation of insurance premiums in the absence of a permanent establishment.[881] However, no agreement has been found among the members,[882] so that the insurance agent provision remained fundamentally unchanged, the only amendment being that the carve-out for independent agents has been moved to the *incipit* of the provision. However, this amendment does not appear to have significant implications on the application of the provision.

According to its current formulation, Art. 5, para. 6, of the UN Model stipulates that "*an insurance enterprise of a Contracting State shall, except in regard to reinsurance, be deemed to have a permanent establishment in the other Contracting State if it collects premiums in the territory of that other State or insures risks situated therein through a person.*"

As a result, this provision is in principle triggered when a foreign insurance company collects premiums[883] or insures risks situated in the source country through a person.[884] The term "*person*" has a broad meaning as referred to under Art. 3, para. 1, let. (a), of the UN Model. Among others, this term includes employees, representatives, companies and so forth. Such a person needs to be present in the source country. In fact, the source taxation is based on the assumption that the person through whom the insurance premium is collected or the risk is insured is present in the country where the risk is located.[885] To put it in other words, this assumption should be held to mean that such a person "*becomes active*" in the source country in the sense that he/she is

880. *See* UN, *Tax treaties between developed and developing countries: Second Report* (New York: UN, 1970) pp. 10-11 and Fernando Souza de Man, *Taxation of Services in Treaties between Developed and Developing Countries—A Proposal for New Guidelines*, para. 4.1.1.1.

881. *See* UN Committee of Experts, "*Report on the twelfth and thirteenth sessions,*" Document E/2017/45-E/C.18/2017/7, p. 12, UN Committee of Experts, "*Proposed Base Erosion and Profit-Shifting Related Changes to the United Nations Model Double Taxation Convention between Developed and Developing Countries,*" Document E/C.18/2017/CRP.7 (March 30, 2017) pp. 36-37 and UN Committee of Experts, "*Report on the fourteenth session,*" Document E/2017/45-E/C.18/2017/7 (April 3-6, 2017) p. 20. For further comments, also Brian J. Arnold, "The UN Committee of Experts and the UN Model: Recent Developments," *Bulletin for International Taxation* (2017) p. 135.

882. Since no agreement has been found, issues related to the application of the permanent establishment with respect to insurance activities, including the treatment of reinsurance, are still on the table of the UN Committee of Experts. *See* UN Committee of Experts, "*Report on the sixteenth session,*" Document E/2018/45/Add.1-E/C.18/2018/7 (May 14-18, 2018) p. 19.

883. According to the previous versions of the UN pattern, the place where the premiums are collected should be intended as the place where the premiums are being paid. To this effect, *see* the 1980 UN Model Commentary on Art. 5 and the 2001 UN Model Commentary on Art. 5.

884. For further details on the conflict between the collection of premiums and the insurance of risks, *see* s. 3.3.2.5 above.

885. To this effect, *see* the 1980 UN Model Commentary on Art. 5, the 2001 UN Model Commentary on Art. 5 and Michael Lennard, *Asia-Pacific Tax Bulletin*, (2009) p. 7.

present therein with a view to concluding insurance transactions or collecting the related insurance premium.[886] Conversely, it is not necessary for him/her to be or to have been a resident of that country.[887]

With this in mind, it is quite surprising that—when providing guidance in respect of the new provision regarding fees for technical services[888]—the UN takes for granted the existence of a permanent establishment pursuant to Art. 5, para. 6, of the UN Model without a proper assessment as to whether all the above conditions are met. True, the examples deal with an insurance company that is engaged in business in both the residence country and the source country. Nevertheless, there is no hint about the presence of a person in the source country through which the insurance company collects premiums or insures risks therein. According to the author, this seems due to a lack of coordination in a section of the UN Model Commentary that does not deal with the application of the insurance agent provision. However, this divergence should be solved in future updates to prevent a misunderstanding regarding the scope of the insurance provision under analysis.

It is also worth noting that Art. 5, para. 6, of the UN Model does not contain a carve-out for dependent agents who already constitute a dependent agent permanent establishment under Art. 5, para. 5, of the UN Model. However, para. 27 of the UN Model Commentary on Art. 5 specifically quotes para. 39 of the 2014 OECD Model Commentary on Art. 5,[889] which contains a reference to the carve-out for dependent agents who already constitute an agency permanent establishment under Art. 5, para. 5, of the OECD Model. For this reason, it may be concluded that the insurance agent provision is aimed at targeting agents who do not already constitute a permanent establishment under Art. 5, para. 5, let. (*a*), of the UN Model.

On the other hand, the *incipit* of Art. 5, para. 6, of the UN Model contains a precise carve-out for independent agents. In this respect, it is interesting to note that some UN member countries among developing countries expressed the view that taxation of insurance profits in the country where the premiums were being paid was desirable and should take place irrespective of the status of the agent. Such countries saw their wish to extend the provision to cases where an insurance company was represented by an independent agent supported by the nature of the insurance business, in which independent rather than dependent agents are used. The fact that the insured risks are situated in the country claiming taxing rights was another

886. *See* Martin Blesgen, "Permanent Establishments of Insurance Companies" in: Michael Lang/Hans Jörgen Aigner/Mario Züger (eds.) *Permanent Establishments in International Tax Law* (Vienna: Linde, 2003) p. 190 and Klaus Vogel, *Klaus Vogel on Double Taxation Convention*, p. 335.
887. *See* Klaus Vogel, *Klaus Vogel on Double Taxation Convention*, p. 335.
888. *See* paras. 92-93 of the UN Model Commentary on Art. 12A.
889. The UN Model Commentary on Art. 5 adopts quotes from the 2014 OECD Model Commentary and its 2017 update. This has resulted in minor formal changes made to para. 114 of the OECD Model Commentary on Art. 5 not being included in the UN Model Commentary on Art. 5. The contemplated renumbering does not seem to take such mismatches into consideration. *See* UN Committee of Experts, "*Update of the UN Model Double Taxation Convention between Developed and Developing Countries—Permanent Establishment*," Document E/C.18/2019/CRP.8.

argument asserted for an extension of the provision. Moreover, developing countries argued that it was relatively easy for persons represent insurance companies as agents of an independent status. On the contrary, other countries opposed this extension to independent agents to the extent that they saw no apparent reason to differentiate between the insurance business and other activities as, for instance, the sale of tangible commodities. It would, furthermore, be difficult to ascertain the total amount of business done in the case that the activity was handled through the work of several independent agents within the same country. Consequently, considering that no consensus could be reached between developing and developed countries, it was eventually decided to leave the case of representation through independent agents to bilateral negotiations.[890]

Therefore, the current wording of Art. 5, para. 6, of the UN Model provides for the constitution of a permanent establishment through a dependent insurance agent who collects premiums or insures risks, while—under para. 29 of the UN Model Commentary on Art. 5—the question how to treat independent insurance agents is left to bilateral negotiations. The provisions at stake do not however identify criteria that may be used for the purposes of ascertaining the status of an insurance agent. Rather, in order to determine the status of such an agent, reference must be made to the general elements contained in Art. 5, para. 7, of the UN Model. As a result, the decisive point would therefore be whether an agent of an independent status is operating within the course of his/her ordinary agency business. This means that an otherwise independent agent will be deemed to be a dependent agent in the event he/she acts outside the ordinary course of the agency business. Also, an otherwise independent agent who acts exclusively or almost exclusively on behalf of one or more closely related enterprises will not be considered an agent of an independent status.[891]

With specific respect to the former point, it may be argued that case law has shown an international tendency to consider an insurance agent as acting independently and within the ordinary course of its business.[892] In particular, although a couple of old cases which dealt with DTAs stipulated before the model treaties under analysis came into being have been resolved with the recognition of a permanent establishment,[893] recent case law has been resolved in favor of the taxpayer.[894] For

890. *See* para. 29 of the UN Model Commentary on Art. 5 and Josef Schuch/Eline Huisman in: Michael Lang/Pasquale Pistone/Josef Schuch/Claus Staringer/Alfred Storck (eds.) *Dependent Agents as Permanent Establishments*, p. 278.
891. For further comments, *see* s. 3.4.2.3 below.
892. *See* Martin Blesgen in: Michael Lang/Hans Jörgen Aigner/Mario Züger (eds.) *Permanent Establishments in International Tax Law*, p. 192.
893. The first case, Marine Insurance Agent (HR (*Hoge Raad*) May 17, 1961, No. 14.458), dealt with Art. 5, para. 5, of the DTA between the Netherlands and the United Kingdom concluded on October 15, 1948. In particular, in this case, the Dutch Supreme Court maintained that, for the existence of a dependent agent permanent establishment, it was sufficient that the agent was authorized to conclude contracts with the customers in respect of at least some categories of marine insurance contracts. In other words, the fact that the foreign principal had granted only a limited authority to the agent could not exclude the existence of a dependent agent permanent establishment. For further comments, *see* Amar Mehta, *Permanent Establishment in International Taxation*, pp. 385-386. The second case, Air Insurance Agent (HR (*Hoge Raad*) January

instance, in a German case,[895] the Federal Supreme Court concluded that an independent insurance agent still acts within the ordinary course of its business even where he has a far-reaching authority to collect premiums, to underwrite insurance contracts, to litigate or to authorize other agents.[896] This line of reasoning has also been upheld in a Dutch case,[897] whereby the Dutch Supreme Court ruled that an agent who is acting on the whole as an independent agent could not be regarded partially as a dependent agent.[898] A positive result for the taxpayer has also been reached in *Taisei*,[899] whereby the US Tax Court pointed out that an insurance agent is independent and operating within the ordinary course of its business, provided that he is acting for several insurance companies and that he bears the entrepreneurial risks.[900] More recently, in *American Income Life*, the Tax Court of Canada also found evidence that supported the conclusion that insurance agents were of an independent status and as a result no dependent agent permanent establishment was deemed to exist.[901]

Therefore, in the light of the foregoing, it may be concluded that—under the UN Model—insurance companies can obviate source taxation where they do not have a fixed place of business therein and conduct their business with independent agents who are acting in the ordinary course of the agency business to the extent that no permanent establishment fiction for independent insurance agents has been introduced in the UN Model. As such, with respect to DTAs patterned after the UN Model,[902] it may be reasonably concluded that developing countries do not seem to have

13, 1971, No. 16.445), which dealt with Art. II, para. 1, let. (i), of the DTA between the Netherlands and the United States concluded on April 29, 1948 has already been commented in s. 3.3.2.4.5 above.

894. *See* Peter G. A. van der Hoeven, "Tax Implications on the Third Non-life and Life Directive for EU Based Insurers doing Business in Other Member States," *Intertax* (1995) p. 438.

895. *See* BFH (*Bundesfinanzhof*) April 30, 1975, I R 152/73, which dealt with Art. 2, para. 1(2)(d), of the DTA between Germany and the Netherlands concluded on June 16, 1959.

896. *See* Martin Blesgen in: Michael Lang/Hans Jörgen Aigner/Mario Züger (eds.) *Permanent Establishments in International Tax Law*, p. 192, John F. Avery Jones/David A. Ward, *European Taxation*, (1993) pp. 170 and Arvid A. Skaar, *Permanent Establishment—Erosion of a Tax Treaty Principle*, p. 510.

897. *See* HR (*Hoge Raad*) June 28, 1995, No. 29.435, which dealt with Art. 5, para. 5, of the DTA between the Netherlands and the United Kingdom concluded on November 7, 1980.

898. For further comments on this case, *see* s. 3.3.2.3.2 above.

899. *See* US Tax Court May 2, 1995, *Taisei Fire and Marine Insurance Co., Ltd. et al. v. Commissioner of Internal Revenue*, 104 T.C., which dealt with Art. 9, paras. 4 and 5, of the DTA between the United States and Japan concluded on March 8, 1971. *See* s. 3.5.2 below for further details on the case.

900. *See* Martin Blesgen in: Michael Lang/Hans Jörgen Aigner/Mario Züger (eds.) *Permanent Establishments in International Tax Law*, p. 192 and Roberto Baggio/Ermanno Basso, *Rivista di Diritto Tributario*, (1996) pp. 1098 et seq.

901. *See* TCC (Tax Court of Canada) May 16, 2008, *American Income Life Insurance Company v. The Queen*, 2008 TCC 306, which dealt with Art. V of the DTA between the United States and Canada concluded on September 26, 1980. *See* s. 3.5.2 below for further details on the case.

902. It is important to note that some DTAs contain a specific clause preserving the application of domestic law regarding the taxation of profits from insurance business. Some DTAs also allow for the taxation of insurance profits, irrespective of whether the insurance enterprise carries on its activities in the source State through a permanent establishment through which the same result is achieved. To this effect, *see* Wim Wijnen/Jan De Goede, "The UN Model in Practice 1997-2013," *Bulletin for International Taxation* (2014) p. 124. For some examples, *see also* ch. 5 below.

successfully addressed the issue of taxing profits of insurance companies in the very many circumstances under which such companies operate through agents and/or other persons that—prima facie—fall within the scope of Art. 5, paras. 5 and 6, of the UN Model.[903,904]

In addition, Art. 5, para. 6, of the UN Model also contains a carve-out for reinsurance, where the risk has been transferred from one insurance company to another one, presumably because in such a case the link has been seen as too economically remote to the source country.[905] Clearly, this appears to be a simplifying assumption which is not supported with an economic understanding of the insurance business to the extent that reinsurance is the insurance of the risk borne by the insurer and—thus—there is no economic rationale for distinguishing between insurance and reinsurance.[906] A lack of a uniform understanding in respect of reinsurance also seems to arise from the latest discussion regarding the proposal to delete the reinsurance exception in the UN Model.[907] Nevertheless, besides the fact that this is questionable under an economic perspective, reinsurance has been specifically excluded and no permanent establishment is deemed to arise in the context of the reinsurance business.[908] This has been also acknowledged in a recent Indian case law,[909] whereby—in concluding that the taxpayer did not have a permanent establishment in India—the Income Tax Appellate Tribunal of Mumbai acknowledged the fact that Art. 5, para. 4, of the DTA between India and Switzerland specifically excluded reinsurance activities from the definition of permanent establishment.

3.4.2.4 The Independent Agent Provision

By reason of the specific insurance agent provision set forth under Art. 5, para. 6, of the UN Model, the independent agent clause is contained in Art. 5, para. 7, of the UN Model. Ever since the 1980 version, the first sentence of such a clause has followed Art. 5, para. 6, of the OECD Model.[910] Accordingly, the application of the independent agent provision under is subject to the dependence test and the ordinary course of business test.[911]

903. In a similar vein, *see* Martin Blesgen in: Michael Lang/Hans Jörgen Aigner/Mario Züger (eds.) *Permanent Establishments in International Tax Law*, p. 192.
904. For an analysis of such circumstances, *see* ch. 4 below.
905. *See* Michael Lennard, *Asia-Pacific Tax Bulletin* (2009) p. 7.
906. For further details, *see* s. 2.2.2.4 above.
907. *See* UN Committee of Experts, "*Report on the fourteenth session*," Document E/2017/45-E/C.18/2017/7, p. 20 and Brian J. Arnold, *Bulletin for International Taxation*, (2017) p. 135.
908. It should be noted that in a few DTAs the scope of the insurance agent provision patterned after the UN Model is extended to reinsurance activities. To this effect, *see* Wim Wijnen/Jan De Goede, *Bulletin for International Taxation*, (2014) p. 124.
909. *See* ITAT (Income Tax Appellate Tribunal) February 13, 2015, No. 1667/Mum/2014, *Swiss Re-insurance Company Ltd. v. DDIT*, which dealt with Art. 5, para. 4, of the DTA between India and Switzerland concluded on November 2, 1994.
910. In the 2017 update, the only difference is the cross-reference to Art. 5, para. 6, of the UN Model.
911. For further comments on such tests in the context of the OECD Model, *see* s. 3.3.2.4 above.

In previous versions, the UN Model deviated from the independent agent provision contained in the OECD Model by adding a second sentence stipulating that a person was not be considered an agent of an independent status in a scenario where the activities of such a person were devoted wholly or almost wholly on behalf of one enterprise and the conditions made or imposed between that enterprise and the agent in their commercial and financial relations were not at arm's length.[912]

The inclusion of the second sentence stemmed from a proposal by members of developing countries to broaden the scope of the permanent establishment definition.[913] Under this proposal, an agent who "*habitually secures orders exclusively or almost exclusively for an enterprise of the other Contracting State or a group of centrally controlled affiliated enterprises*" should be treated as a dependent agent "*for the particular members of the group for whom he is acting at a given time.*"[914] Indeed, it was argued that—in such circumstances—an agent, "*although acting in an independent capacity, acted for only one enterprise and devoted his time and activity wholly or almost wholly to that enterprise, he lost his independent status.*"[915]

The addition of such a single principal test was highly criticized to the extent that this sentence had given rise to anomalous situations. Most notably, concern was raised that in the case the number of principals for which an independent agent was working fell to one, the agent would, without further examination, be treated as dependent.[916] In order to prevent this case, an additional arm's length test was introduced in Art. 5, para. 7, of the 2001 UN Model. As a result, the essential criterion for automatically treating an agent as not being of independent status was the absence of dealing at arm's length. The mere fact that the number of enterprises for which the independent agent acts had fallen to one did not of itself change his status from independent to dependent, though it could serve as an indicator of the absence of the independence of that agent.[917] However, considering that developing countries are generally less familiar with transfer pricing issues, this arm's length test made it even more difficult for them to assert the existence of a dependent agent permanent establishment that would allow source taxation.[918]

In the 2011 UN Model, there were no major developments in respect of this matter. Nevertheless, in the 2017 update, this sentence has been removed to the extent that UN Committee of Experts eventually realized that it made it easier to qualify as an

912. *See* Art. 5, para. 7, of the 2011 UN Model.
913. Such a proposal seems to have originated in common law and was later adopted by the League of Nations (for instance in the 1928 Report and in the 1930 Report), but it had never been picked up by the OECD. To this effect, *see* Josef Schuch/Eline Huisman in: Michael Lang/Pasquale Pistone/Josef Schuch/Claus Staringer/Alfred Storck (eds.) *Dependent Agents as Permanent Establishments*, p. 286, Arvid A. Skaar, *Permanent Establishment—Erosion of a Tax Treaty Principle*, p. 531 and Fernando Souza de Man, *Taxation of Services in Treaties between Developed and Developing Countries—A Proposal for New Guidelines*, para. 4.1.1.1.
914. *See* the 1980 UN Model Commentary on Art. 5.
915. *See* the 1980 UN Model Commentary on Art. 5.
916. *See* para. 30 of the 2001 UN Model Commentary on Art. 5.
917. *See* para. 31 of the 2001 UN Model Commentary on Art. 5.
918. *See* Fernando Souza de Man, *Taxation of Services in Treaties between Developed and Developing Countries—A Proposal for New Guidelines*, para. 4.2.1.1.

independent agent under UN standards than under OECD standards.[919] In place of the previous sentence, the UN Model now provides for a supplementary test regarding related parties that follows the wording of Art. 5, para. 6, of the OECD Model. This novelty has been complemented with the introduction of Art. 5, para. 9, of the UN Model, which provides for a clarification on the concept of "*closely related*" along the lines of Art. 5, para. 8, of the OECD Model.

The UN Model Commentary quotes all the relevant paragraphs of the corresponding OECD Model Commentary, as updated in the aftermath of the BEPS Project. Therefore, it seems that the UN has fully endorsed the work of the OECD regarding the independent agent provision in the context of Action 7 of the BEPS Project.

3.5 THE CONCEPT OF PERMANENT ESTABLISHMENT IN THE US MODEL

3.5.1 Historical Overview

Historically, the US has followed a series of model treaties in negotiating DTAs with other countries.[920,921] Nevertheless, more recently, the US Treasury Department has developed its own specific model treaty as a starting point for negotiating DTAs.[922] In particular, the first version (the 1976 US Model) was published in 1976. Following the publication of the 1977 OECD Model, a revised version (the 1977 US Model) has been released almost exactly a year later. In nearly all respects, such two versions are substantially the same. A few years after, a new proposed version (the 1981 US Model) has been published for comment by the US Treasury Department in mid-1981 and supplemented a few months later by an alternative discussion draft of one particularly sensitive provision,[923] that is the "*limitation on benefits*" provision.[924,925]

919. *See* UN Committee of Experts, "*Report on the twelfth and thirteenth sessions*," Document E/2017/45-E/C.18/2017/7, p. 19. This reasoning has also been included in para. 32 of the UN Model Commentary on Art. 5.
920. Richard L. Doernberg, *International Taxation in a nutshell—9th edition* (St. Paul, MN: West Academic Publishing, 2012) p. 125.
921. For instance, the US seemed to have used the DTA with the UK concluded in 1945 as a model for subsequent DTAs concluded before 1963. To this effect, *see* Juan Angel Becerra, *Interpretation and Application of Tax Treaties in North America—2nd edition* (Amsterdam: IBFD, 2013) para. 6.4. Thereafter, DTAs concluded by the US have been substantially influenced by the 1963 OECD Draft. To this effect, *see* Robert L. Williams, "Permanent Establishments in the United States," *The Tax Lawyer* (1975) pp. 286-287.
922. For further details on the hierarchy of law in the US, *see* Anthony C. Infanti, "The United States" in Guglielmo Maisto (ed.) *Tax Treaties and Domestic Law* (Amsterdam: IBFD, 2006) ch. 13.
923. *See* Marianne Burge/Solomon Packer, "New US Model Income Tax Treaty," *Intertax* (1982) p. 53 and William L. Burke, "Report on Proposed United States Model Income Tax Treaty," *Harvard International Law Journal* (1983) p. 219.
924. *See* Art. 16 of the 1981 US Model, then shifted to Art. 22 of the following US model treaties.
925. For further details, *see* Robert R. Oliva, "The Treasury's Twenty Year Battle with Treaty Shopping: Article 16 of the 1977 United States Model Treaty," *Georgia Journal of International and Comparative Law* (1984) pp. 293 et seq.

A new version (the 1996 US Model) has been released in 1996,[926] accompanied for the first time with the 1996 Technical Explanation.[927,928] Just over 10 years later, a revised version of such documents (the 2006 US Model and the 2006 Technical Explanation) has been released in 2006,[929] while a new version of the model (the US Model)[930] has been published in 2016.[931,932]

3.5.2 Overview of the Current Provision

3.5.2.1 Introduction

Over the years, the US has followed the OECD text, with only a few modifications necessary to incorporate specific US policy concerns.[933,934] However, the latest revisions of the US Model did not give effect to Action 7 of the BEPS Project, the only minor revision being the rule to address cases where the 12-month period for construction or

926. For further details, *see* Walter F. O'Connor, "A Comparative Analysis of the 1981 and 1996 U.S. Model Income Tax Treaties," *International Tax Journal* (1998) pp. 9 et seq.
927. The Technical Explanation serves as an official guide to the US Model. *See* 1996 Technical Explanation, Title and Preamble and 2006 Technical Explanation, Title and Preamble.
928. The US Treasury Department has also consistently issued a technical explanation to modern US DTAs and additional protocols. Such documents reflect the US unilateral understanding of US DTAs, and are stated to be an official guide to the treaty or protocol. They reflect the policies behind the particular treaty provisions, as well as understandings reached with regard to the application and interpretation of the treaty. To this effect, *see* Juan Angel Becerra, *Interpretation and Application of Tax Treaties in North America—2nd edition*, para. 6.4.
929. For further details, *see* Reuven S. Avi-Yonah/Martin B. Tittle, "The New United States Model Income Tax Convention," *Bulletin for International Taxation* (2007) pp. 224-234.
930. As of the date of this dissertation, no technical explanations have been released with respect to the latest version of the US Model.
931. For further details, *see*—among others—Allison Christians/Alexander Ezenagu, "Kill-Switches in the U.S. Model Tax Treaty," *Brooklyn Journal of International Law* (2015), Paul Carman, "Comparison of the Proposed Changes to the OECD and US Model Conventions," *Derivatives & Financial Instruments* (2015) and Diane M. Ring, "*United States—Permanent Establishments—Topical Analyses*," last reviewed: March 22, 2019, available online at www.ibfd.org, para. 2.1.1.2.
932. In this respect, two points should be noted: (*i*) given that the latest version of the US Model has been released recently, it has not yet played a formal role in US negotiations; and (*ii*) since 2011, the ratification of DTAs has been blocked by the efforts of one US senator (although efforts continue to be made to resolve this impasse in the US Senate). To this effect, *see* Diane M. Ring, "*United States—Permanent Establishments—Topical Analyses*," para. 2.1.1.2.
933. *See* Allison Christians/Alexander Ezenagu, *Brooklyn Journal of International Law*, (2015) para. 1 and Diane M. Ring, "*United States—Permanent Establishments—Topical Analyses*," para. 2.1.1.2.
934. In a number of cases, US courts applying treaty terms have relied on the OECD guidance to interpret DTAs signed by the US with language similar to the OECD text. In addition, the US tax authorities have sometimes relied on the OECD guidance in a number of rulings. In the context of the DTA signed between the US and Japan, it has been also contended that changes to OECD documents published after the entry into force of a DTA are relevant. *See* Diane M. Ring, "*United States—Permanent Establishments—Topical Analyses*," para. 2.1.1.2 and Martin B. Tittle, "A Unified Approach to Permanent Establishment by Agent in the U.S.," *Tax Notes International* (2007) p. 599. Nevertheless, following the BEPS Project, it remains to be seen whether this will still be the case.

installation permanent establishment is exceeded.[935] In fact, although representatives of the US Treasury Department have actively participated in the work of the BEPS Project, the US has been more skeptical than other countries.[936] In particular, on the basis of the Preamble to the US Model,[937] it appears that the most significant ongoing concerns with respect to the permanent establishment definition derive from: (*i*) the impact of the work on Art. 7 of the OECD Model and the OECD Model Commentary thereon and (*ii*) the impact of the recommendations on permanent establishment and attribution of profits thereto emerging from the BEPS Project. Most notably, in the US view, changes in the permanent establishment definition should be dependent on understanding what the rules for attribution of profits to such permanent establishments will be. For this reason, the US will most probably refrain from adopting the BEPS recommendations regarding the definition of permanent establishment until the existing attribution questions are resolved.[938]

In the light of the foregoing, Art. 5, paras. 5 and 6, of the US Model are patterned after Art. 5, paras. 5 and 6, of the 2014 OECD Model,[939] as such provisions stood before the amendments introduced in the context of the BEPS Project, and the US Model does not contain an insurance agent provision or any other specific provisions dealing with the insurance business.

3.5.2.2 The Dependent Agent Provision

In accordance with Art. 5, para. 5, of the US Model, it is crucial to assess whether a person is acting on behalf of a foreign enterprise and such a person has, and habitually exercises, an authority to conclude contracts that are binding on that foreign enterprise.[940]

In this respect, it is interesting to note that the 2006 Technical Explanation briefly touched upon the interpretation of the element "*binding on the enterprise.*" In particular, the 2006 Technical Explanation pointed out that the OECD text uses the term "*in the name of the enterprise*" rather than "*binding on the enterprise.*" Nevertheless, it then clarified that "*[t]his difference is intended to be a clarification rather*

935. *See* Jonathan Schwarz, "US Model Treaty 2016: What does it say about the US and BEPS?," *Kluwer International Tax Blog* (2016). In his post, the author also argues that the US has declined to follow the AOA to the attribution of profits reflected in the 2010 OECD Model. However, this conclusion appears to be controversial to the extent that the AOA has been included in the 2006 US Model and retained in the most recent version of the US Model. In fact, Art. 7 of the US Model currently follows the wording of Art. 7 of the OECD Model. Rather, what one may infer is that, as announced by the US Treasury Department in a statement on June 7, 2007, the US would not apply the AOA to most existing US DTAs.
936. *See* Daniel Shaviro, "The U.S. Response to OECD-BEPS and the EU State Aid Cases," *NYU Law & Economics Research Paper Series* (2016) Nos. 16-27 p. 6.
937. *See* US Model, Preamble, last paragraph.
938. *See* Diane M. Ring, "*United States—Permanent Establishments—Topical Analyses,*" paras. 2.1.1.2 and 10.
939. As from the 1996 US Model, in Art. 5, para. 6, the US Model adds the language "*as independent agents*" to the end of the provision.
940. For a general overview of such criteria from a US tax perspective, *see* Joel Nitikam, "The Meaning of 'Permanent Establishment' in the 1981 U.S. Model Income Tax Treaty: Part 2," *The International Tax Journal* (1989) pp. 258-265.

than a substantive difference." As a matter of fact, this element should be intended to encompass persons who have "*sufficient authority to bind the enterprise's participation in the business activity in the State concerned.*"[941] Therefore, the US views Art. 5, para. 5, of the US Model as functionally identical to the corresponding provision of the OECD Model despite the difference in terms.[942]

The person must have the authority to conclude contracts that relate to the business proper of the foreign enterprise. Nevertheless, Art. 5, para. 5, of the US Model excepts from its scope dependent agents of an enterprise who engage only in certain activities enumerated in Art. 5, para. 4, of the US Model. Hence, under Art. 5, para. 5, of the US Model, where a dependent agent of a foreign enterprise who acts on behalf of that enterprise and who has and regularly exercises in the relevant country an authority to conclude contracts in the name of the principal nonetheless restricts its activities in that country to one or more of those listed in Art. 5, para. 4, of the US Model, the dependent agent does not constitute a permanent establishment of the enterprise.[943]

In the context of the domestic law,[944] US Tax Courts have generally ruled that a US trade or business exists in the event that US business activities of a foreign enterprise are considerable, continuous, and regular. In order to determine whether an activity is regular and continuous, the number of transactions materially participated in, but not necessarily completed, in the US is frequently relevant.[945]

By contrast, the issue of whether a US person constitutes a dependent agent permanent establishment of the foreign principal in a treaty situation has arisen only in isolated circumstances.[946] This is particularly the case in the context of the insurance

941. *See* 2006 Technical Explanation on Art. 5, para. 5, of the 2006 US Model, which quoted para. 32 of the 2005 OECD Model Commentary on Art. 5.

942. *See* Doug Holland, "Commissionaire Agency Permanent Establishments," *International Transfer Pricing Journal* (2011) p. 35.

943. *See* Diane M. Ring, "*United States—Permanent Establishments—Topical Analyses,*" para. 2.1.4.2.

944. Although this research is not aimed at addressing the concept of permanent establishment under domestic law, it is worth noting that—in non-treaty situations—a foreign corporation is generally subject to US income tax on its net business income if: (*i*) the foreign corporation is engaged in a US trade or business, and (*ii*) income is effectively connected with the conduct of that trade or business. For further details, *see* Ewing W. Madole, "Agents as Permanent Establishments Under U.S. Income Tax Treaties," *Tax Management International Journal* (1994) pp. 286-288, Martin B. Tittle, *Permanent establishment in the United States* (Lake Mary: Vandeplas Publishing, 2007), pp. 45 et seq., Doug Holland, *International Transfer Pricing Journal,* (2011) pp. 33-35 and Diane M. Ring, "*United States—Permanent Establishments—Topical Analyses,*" para. 2.1.1.1. Specific provisions are laid down with respect to foreign companies engaged in life and non-life insurance business in the US. For further details, *see* Diane M. Ring, "*United States—Permanent Establishments—Topical Analyses,*" para. 8.2.

945. *See*—among others—US Court of Appeals for the Second Circuit July 17, 1940, *Pinchot v. Commissioner of Internal Revenue*, 113 F.2d 718, US Court of Appeals Second Circuit June 4, 1956, *United States of America v. Israel Balanovski et al.*, 236 F.2d 298, US Court of Appeals for the Sixth Circuit August 10, 1960, *Spermacet Whaling Shipping Co. S/A v. Commissioner of Internal Revenue*, 281 F.2d 646, US Supreme Court February 24, 1987, *Commissioner of Internal Revenue v. Robert P. Groetzinger*, 480 U.S. 23.

946. For further comments on a handful of cases, *see* Ewing W. Madole, *Tax Management International Journal*, (1994) pp. 283-286 and Martin B. Tittle, *Tax Notes International*, (2007) pp. 609-612.

industry, where—in the past[947]—such an issue has been dealt with only indirectly or has been expressly avoided.[948]

In the context of DTAs concluded by the US, however, it is worth mentioning that, in an interesting case law dealing with the dependent agent permanent establishment provision contained in the previous DTA concluded between the US and Canada, the Federal Court of Canada maintained that the mere fact that a US insurance company does business, and enters into insurance contracts as an underwriter, with a Canadian corporation does not constitute doing business in Canada.[949] In other words, merely insuring Canadian risks where no solicitation or offers take place in Canada generally does not amount to carrying on business in Canada.[950] In particular, in such a case, which involved a US insurance company licensed to insure in Canada, it was concluded that the major parts of all insurance business activities which in any way affected Canadian lives or Canadian interests, originally took place and were controlled in the US. Minimal activities carried on in Canada, such as listing an address in Ontario as its Canadian head office, maintaining several small Canadian bank accounts, having a Canadian company distribute some of its brochures and appointing Canadian agents with powers of attorney, were effected primarily to comply with Canadian regulatory requirements rather than for business reasons. Hence, the Court found no permanent establishment in Canada.[951]

In a similar vein, in *Knights of Columbus*,[952] which dealt with Art. V, para. 5, of the DTA between the US and Canada concluded on September 26, 1980, the Tax Court of Canada found that neither the general agents nor the field agents exercised any authority to conclude contracts in Canada. More to the point, the Court relied on para. 33 of the 2005 OECD Model Commentary on Art. 5 to maintain that the authority to conclude contracts had to cover contracts relating to operations which constituted the business proper of the foreign enterprise (namely, the insurance business), but in any event found that the contracts were concluded in the US.[953]

947. *See* s. 3.5.2.3 below for a more recent case concerning the distinction between dependent agents and independent agents.
948. *See* Ewing W. Madole, *Tax Management International Journal*, (1994) p. 286.
949. *See* Federal Court Trial Division (FCTD) *Capitol Life Insurance Company v. The Queen*, 84 DTC 6087, aff'd by Federal Court of Appeal (FCA) 86 DTC 6164. A summary of the case is also available on https://taxinterpretations.com.
950. *See* Matias Milet, "*Canada—Permanent Establishments—Topical Analyses*," last reviewed: March 20, 2019, available online at www.ibfd.org, para. 8.2.1.
951. *See* Robert L. Williams, *Fundamentals of Permanent Establishments*, p. 165.
952. *See* TCC (Tax Court of Canada) May 16, 2008, *Knights of Columbus v. The Queen*, 2008 TCC 307.
953. *See* Colin Campbell/Terry McDowell, "Canada" in: IFA (ed.) *Is there a permanent establishment?*, Cahiers de droit fiscal international, Vol. 94a (The Hague: Sdu Uitgevers, 2009) p. 187. For further comments on the case, *see also* Robert A. Kopstein/Jasmine Sidhu, "Be Careful What You Wish For," *Canadian Tax Journal* (2008) pp. 748 et seq., Craig Elliffe, "The Meaning of 'Permanent Establishment' in Article 5 of Double Tax Conventions," *New Zealand Journal of Taxation Law and Policy* (2010) pp. 12 et seq. and Craig Elliffe, "Canadian Tax Court on the Meaning of 'Permanent Establishment' in Treaties," *Journal of International Taxation* (2011) pp. 26 et seq.

3.5.2.3 *The Independent Agent Provision*

Moving to independent agents, under Art. 5, para. 6, of the US Model, a foreign enterprise is not deemed to have a dependent agent permanent establishment in the other country merely because it carries on business in that other country through an independent agent, including a broker or general commission agent, in the event that the agent is acting in the ordinary course of its business as an independent agent.

From this, it may be argued that the critical element here lies on the extent to which an agent is independent in fact. As clarified in the 2006 Technical Explanation,[954] in order to qualify as an agent of an independent status, the agent must be: (*i*) both legally and economically independent of the enterprise and (*ii*) acting in the ordinary course of its business in carrying out activities on behalf of the enterprise.[955]

In the domestic law area,[956] the *InverWorld*[957] is instructive as to the distinction between dependent agents and independent agents. In such a case, a Cayman company fully owned the stock of a US corporation. Pursuant to a contract, the US corporation performed financial services activities for the Cayman company and its clients, such as determining what investments to make within parameters set up by the Cayman company, managing its bank account and generally operating as the alter ego of the Cayman company. The contract recited that the US corporation was to be an independent contractor, not an agent. However, the Cayman company worked solely for the US corporation and had virtually no substance of its own. Against this background, the US Court had no difficulty in determining that the label was not controlling and found that the Cayman company was engaged in business in an office in the US. In reaching its conclusion, the US court relied heavily on the factual circumstances which indicated that the US corporation acted almost exclusively for one principal and received nearly all of its income from the one principal for a sustained five-year period, conducted extensive, continuous, and regular activities through its US corporation, and that the daily business operations of the foreign principal were conducted in and from the US office, with extensive direction and control from the foreign principal.[958,959]

At any rate, the most significant US case law concerning the distinction between dependent agents and independent agents was related to the insurance business. Most

954. *See* 2006 Technical Explanation on Art. 5, para. 6, of the 2006 US Model.
955. For a general overview of such conditions from a US tax perspective, *see* Joel Nitikam, *The International Tax Journal*, (1989) pp. 265-269.
956. In the domestic law area, under Treasury Regulation section 1.864-7, an independent agent is similarly defined as a "*general commission agent, broker, or other agent of an independent status acting in the ordinary course of his business in that capacity.*" However, although stating that the facts and circumstances of the agent's activities as agent must be evaluated, Treasury Regulation section 1.864-7 does not provide for legal and economic independent tests.
957. US Tax Court June 27, 1996, *InverWorld, Inc. et al. v. Commissioner of Internal Revenue*, T.C. Memo 1996-301.
958. *See*—among others—Joan C. Arnold, "United States" in: IFA (ed.) *Is there a permanent establishment?*, Cahiers de droit fiscal international, Vol. 94a (The Hague: Sdu Uitgevers, 2009) p. 683 and Martin B. Tittle, *Tax Notes International*, (2007) pp. 606-607.
959. It should however be noted that the US Tax Court has not provided any guidance explaining the circumstances when a near-exclusive activity could be treated as independent.

notably, in *Taisei Fire & Marine Insurance Co.*,[960,961] the issue was whether four Japanese insurance companies each had an agency permanent establishment in the US by virtue of the relationship with a US agent—Fortress Re—which acted as a reinsurance underwriting manager on their behalf.[962] The US Tax Court observed that the taxpayers had authorized the US agent to conclude contracts on their behalf and the agent had exercised such an authority. As a result, the taxpayers had a dependent agent permanent establishment in the US, unless the agent was to be regarded as "*a broker, general commission agent, or any other agent of an independent status*" within the meaning of Art. 9, para. 5, of the DTA between the US and Japan concluded on March 8, 1971. In particular, the parties did not dispute that the US agent was not a broker, or a general commission agent, but disagreed as to whether such a US agent was an "*agent of an independent status.*" Consequently, the decision depended on the status of the US agent. In order to ascertain whether Fortress Re was to be regarded as an agent of an independent status, the Court held that the latter needed to be both legally and economically independent, and that the analysis was a highly factual inquiry.[963]

With respect to the legal independence,[964] the Court noted that there was no ownership by the four Japanese companies in Fortress Re, they did not share any officers, directors or employees and that the daily business of Fortress Re was totally in the control of the latter. The argument put forward by the US tax authorities was that, insofar as Fortress Re was representing only the four Japanese companies during the year, there was "*near-exclusivity*" and that legal independence instead requires non-exclusivity. In addition, the US tax authorities argued that certain limits were placed by the Japanese companies on the amounts of reinsurance contracts that Fortress Re could acquire and—thus—there was no legal independence. However, the Court reviewed the contracts and determined that such limitations were not meaningful. In addition, the Court declined the assertion that the four Japanese companies were acting in concert, so that there was only one foreign principal, and also rejected the contention that exclusivity would preclude legal independence.[965]

With respect to the economic independence,[966] the main contentions put forward by the US tax authorities concerned the fact that Fortress Re was to receive management fees from the four Japanese companies that were intended to cover its current operating expenses and that Fortress Re also earned contingent commissions on the

960. *See* US Tax Court May 2, 1995, *Taisei Fire and Marine Insurance Co., Ltd. et al. v. Commissioner of Internal Revenue*, 104 T.C.
961. For further details on the proceedings of such a case, *see* John Turro, "When Do Foreign Reinsurance Activities in the United States Constitute a Permanent Establishment?," *Tax Notes International* (1992) pp. 536-539, Ewing W. Madole, *Tax Management International Journal*, (1994) pp. 291-292, and Robert S. Schwartz, "Taisei: U.S. Agent Did Not Create Permanent Establishment," *The Journal of International Taxation* (1995) pp. 292-297.
962. *See* Joan C. Arnold, in: IFA (ed.) *Is there a permanent establishment?*, p. 682.
963. *See* Joan C. Arnold in: IFA (ed.) *Is there a permanent establishment?*, p. 682 and Amar Mehta, *Permanent Establishment in International Taxation*, p. 418.
964. *See* US Tax Court May 2, 1995, *Taisei Fire and Marine Insurance Co., Ltd. et al. v. Commissioner of Internal Revenue*, 104 T.C. 552-555.
965. *See* Joan C. Arnold in: IFA (ed.) *Is there a permanent establishment?*, p. 682.
966. *See* US Tax Court May 2, 1995, *Taisei Fire and Marine Insurance Co., Ltd. et al. v. Commissioner of Internal Revenue*, 104 T.C. 555-556.

basis of the profitability of the reinsurance contracts it underwrote. The US tax authorities argued that, insofar as such fees and commissions were payable by highly creditworthy companies, Fortress Re did not have any entrepreneurial risks. However, the Court maintained that this did not mean that Fortress Re bore no risk. Indeed, Fortress Re had to acquire sufficient business to produce the gross premiums and that the provision of a contingent commission was normal for an underwriting manager. Finally, the Court also noted that the profits realized by Fortress Re was significant and could not be regarded as the kind of sum paid to a subservient company.[967]

In the light of the above, the Court concluded that Fortress Re was both legally and economically independent, thus satisfying the definition of an agent of an independent status under Art. 9, para. 5, of the DTA concluded between the US and Japan.[968,969] On the top of this, the Court also noted that the resolution of the issue of the existence of an agent of independent status in the insurance context turns, at least in part, upon the presence of the specific insurance agent provision in the DTA. In the case at issue, given the absence of any such provision, the conclusion was consistent with the approach adopted in the 1963 OECD Draft, whereby an independent insurance agent does not give rise to an agency permanent establishment.[970]

A few years later, in an opposite situation, in *American Income Life*,[971] which dealt with Art. V, para. 7, of the DTA between the US and Canada concluded on September 26, 1980, the Tax Court of Canada found that a US insurance company did not operate through agents who habitually exercise in Canada an authority to conclude contracts in its name and, even in the case that the agents did have such an authority,[972] such agents were agents of an independent status. In this respect, although the Court had found that general and field agents were independent contractors carrying on their own business, this was not sufficient to find that they were agents of an independent status.[973] In its judgment, the Court relied both on the 2005 OECD Model Commentary and the previous decision of the US Tax Court in *Taisei Fire & Marine Insurance Co.* to argue that—in order to be an agent of an independent

967. *See* Joan C. Arnold in: IFA (ed.) *Is there a permanent establishment?*, p. 682.
968. *See* US Tax Court May 2, 1995, *Taisei Fire and Marine Insurance Co., Ltd. et al. v. Commissioner of Internal Revenue*, 104 T.C. 556.
969. It is worth noting that it was not disputed by the US tax authorities that the agent had acted in the ordinary course of its business.
970. *See* US Tax Court May 2, 1995, *Taisei Fire and Marine Insurance Co., Ltd. et al. v. Commissioner of Internal Revenue*, 104 T.C. 558.
971. *See* TCC (Tax Court of Canada) May 16, 2008, *American Income Life Insurance Company v. The Queen*, 2008 TCC 306.
972. Accordingly, such insurance agents could not give rise to a dependent agent permanent establishment. Hence, as pointed out by De Broe and Van Bortel, the reasoning regarding the legal and economic independence of the insurance agents and the ordinary course of business test was no longer relevant. *See* Luc De Broe/Denis Van Bortel, "Grensoverschrijdende activiteiten van verzekeringsondernemingen d.m.v. agenten en de verdeling van heffingsbevoegdheid onder debbelbelastingverdragen" in: Caroline Van Schoubroeck/Wouter Devroe/Koen Geens/Jules Stuick (eds.) *Over Grenzen—Liber amicorum Herman Cousy* (Antwerpen—Cambridge: Intersentia, 2011) p. 948.
973. *See* TCC (Tax Court of Canada) May 16, 2008, *American Income Life Insurance Company v. The Queen*, 2008 TCC 306, para. 72.

status—the agent must be: (*i*) independent both legally and economically[974] and (*ii*) acting in the ordinary course of his or her business.[975]

Specifically, with regard to the legal independence, the Court relied on the following factors:[976]

- the intention of the agents not to be legally dependent;
- the lack of control by the foreign enterprise on how the agents carried on their business;
- the lack of ownership interest in the business of the agents;
- the fact that the enterprise held no capital assets in Canada;
- the fact that the enterprise did not reimburse the agents for the costs of assets;
- the fact that the employees of the agents were the responsibility of the agents; and
- the fact that the agents were not involved in making final decisions on coverage or claims.

Moving to the economic independence, the Court instead looked at the following factors:[977]

- The income of the agents was based on commission, had no minimum or maximum levels and therefore was dependent on their own abilities and efforts.
- The agents could solicit business from any person they chose.
- For the most part, the agents were not required to act exclusively for the enterprise.
- The agents bore all of the economic risk.
- The exclusive dealings of the agents with the enterprise were not determinative.

974. *See* Colin Campbell/Terry McDowell in: IFA (ed.) *Is there a permanent establishment?*, pp. 187-188.

975. The Court did not go into much detail on the ordinary course of business test. In fact, it simply stated that the agents were carrying on their own business. *See* TCC (Tax Court of Canada) May 16, 2008, *American Income Life Insurance Company v. The Queen*, 2008 TCC 306, para. 70. According to De Broe and Van Bortel, this reasoning is questionable since the requirement that the representative should act in the normal course of its business is a condition that must be tested separately. To this effect, *see* Luc De Broe/Denis Van Bortel in: Caroline Van Schoubroeck/Wouter Devroe/Koen Geens/Jules Stuick (eds.) *Over Grenzen—Liber amicorum Herman Cousy*, p. 948.

976. *See* TCC (Tax Court of Canada) May 16, 2008, *American Income Life Insurance Company v. The Queen*, 2008 TCC 306, para. 76, Colin Campbell/Terry McDowell in: IFA (ed.) *Is there a permanent establishment?*, p. 188, Robert A. Kopstein/Jasmine Sidhu, *Canadian Tax Journal* (2008) p. 750 and Luc De Broe/Denis Van Bortel in: Caroline Van Schoubroeck/Wouter Devroe/Koen Geens/Jules Stuick (eds.) *Over Grenzen—Liber amicorum Herman Cousy*, pp. 944-945.

977. *See* TCC (Tax Court of Canada) May 16, 2008, *American Income Life Insurance Company v. The Queen*, 2008 TCC 306, para. 77, Colin Campbell/Terry McDowell in: IFA (ed.) *Is there a permanent establishment?*, p. 188, Robert A. Kopstein/Jasmine Sidhu, *Canadian Tax Journal* (2008) p. 750 and Luc De Broe/Denis Van Bortel in: Caroline Van Schoubroeck/Wouter Devroe/Koen Geens/Jules Stuick (eds.) *Over Grenzen—Liber amicorum Herman Cousy*, p. 945.

- The supply of products to the agents by the enterprise was not in itself sufficient to create economic independence to the extent that the profit depended primarily on the efforts of the agents.

At last, as with *Taisei Fire & Marine Insurance Co.*, the Court concluded that the lack of the insurance agent provision does suggest that the US and Canada do recognize considerable activity of an insurance business can take place without finding there is a permanent establishment.[978]

3.6 FINAL CONSIDERATIONS

The concept of permanent establishment has been used in DTAs for almost 150 years now to address the fundamental questions as to whether and under which circumstances the source country should be entitled to tax profits that non-resident enterprises derive from their business activities therein. In fact, over the years, the concept of permanent establishment has been recognized as a legal convention for source taxation in the earliest DTAs and—subsequently—in model treaties.[979]

Considering an economic environment in which all business activities required a physical presence, this concept has been developed in terms of a threshold grounded on a rather high degree of physical presence in the source country, either through a fixed place of business or a dependent agent acting on behalf of the non-resident enterprise habitually exercising an authority to conclude contracts in the name of such an enterprise.[980]

For a long time, the concept of permanent establishment has been construed in a narrow legal sense to the advantage of resident countries—represented in the OECD—that could reap higher tax revenue in the absence of a permanent establishment in the source country. As a result, the scope of the permanent establishment definition has been consolidated over time and its language remained essentially the same until recently.

In more recent years, however, its scope has been put into question in the context of a changing business environment, most notably with the development of new technologies allowing the conduct of substantive business activities without a physical presence in the source country. In this changing context, the OECD struggled to keep the permanent establishment provision up-to-date with several amendments.[981] This resulted in a steady lowering of the original threshold for source taxation.

The BEPS Project has renewed the debate regarding the source threshold in an attempt to prevent the use of tax avoidance strategies aimed at circumventing the

978. *See* TCC (Tax Court of Canada) May 16, 2008, *American Income Life Insurance Company v. The Queen*, 2008 TCC 306, para. 86.
979. For further comments, *see* Eva Escribano López, "An Opportunistic, and yet Appropriate, Revision of the Source Threshold for the Twenty-First Century Tax Treaties," *Intertax* (2015) p. 8.
980. *See* Eva Escribano López, *Intertax*, (2015) pp. 8-9.
981. *See*—for instance—the incorporation of paras. 42.1-42.10 of the 2003 OECD Model Commentary on Art. 5 dealing with the e-commerce.

application of the permanent establishment provision.[982] In pursuing such a goal, the work of the OECD in the context of Action 7 of the BEPS Project led to dramatic changes to the dependent agent permanent establishment, which have considerably widened the scope of the original provision.

In doing so, the OECD has clearly moved away from the original concept toward an economic approach (also referred to as a "*substance-over-form approach*").[983] More to the point, in respect of the dependent agent permanent establishment, this is particularly evident if one looks at the introduction of the supplementary test regarding the principal role leading to the conclusion of contracts, the amendments to the interpretation of the wording "*in the name of*" and the inclusion of contracts that are concluded for the provision of property and services. The same also holds true in relation to the supplementary independence test regarding related parties.

Such amendments have been made in the light of the paradigm that profits should be taxed in countries where economic activities take place and where value is created.[984] Yet, the author concurs with the view that the concept of value creation is quite vague,[985,986] so is its implementation in the context under scrutiny. While, on the one hand, the above amendments will most probably result in more dependent agent permanent establishments than ever before, on the other hand such changes will also give rise to uncertainty that could result in more litigations between taxpayers and tax administrations and eventually treaty-related disputes between tax administrations themselves.[987]

---

982. *See* OECD, "*Preventing the Artificial Avoidance of Permanent Establishment Status—Action 7: 2015 Final Report*," pp. 13-14.
983. *See* Vishesh Dhuldhoya, "The Future of the Permanent Establishment Concept," *Bulletin for International Taxation* (2018) para. 3.2.2. In a similar vein, *see also* Lars Rehfeld, "Vertreter- und Logistikbetriebsstätten post BEPS 7," *Internationales Steuer- und Wirtschaftsrecht* (2017) p. 211.
984. The paradigm of taxing profits where value is created is at the core of the BEPS Project. To this effect, *see* OECD, "*Explanatory Statement: OECD/G20 Base Erosion and Profit Shifting Project*" (Paris: OECD, 2015) p. 5.
985. *See* Patricia Hofmann/Nadine Riedel, "Comment on J. Becker & J. Englisch, 'Taxing Where Value Is Created: What's 'User Involvement' Got to Do with It?," *Intertax* (2019) p. 173, Mindy Herzfeld, "The Case Against BEPS: Lessons for Tax Coordination," *Florida Tax Review* (2017) pp. 1 et seq., Susan C. Morse, "Value Creation: A Standard in Search of a Process," *Bulletin for International Taxation* (2018) pp. 196 et seq. and Johanna Hey, "'Taxation Where Value is Created' and the OECD/G20 Base Erosion and Profit Shifting Initiative," *Bulletin for International Taxation* (2018) pp. 203 et seq. For further comments in respect of this concept, *see also* Jonathan Schwarz, "Value Creation: Old wine in new bottles or new wine in old bottles," *Kluwer International Tax Blog* (2018), Werner Haslehner, "Taxing where value is created in a post-BEPS (digitalized) world?," *Kluwer International Tax Blog* (2018) and Richard Collier/John Vella, *World Tax Journal*, (2019) para. 2.3.
986. According to Becker and Englisch, this concept can be reconciled with traditional international tax fairness standards. To this effect, *see* Johannes Becker/Joachim Englisch, "Taxing Where Value Is Created: What's 'User Involvement' Got to Do with It?," *Intertax* (2019) p. 165.
987. In a similar vein, *see*—among others—Adolfo J. Martin Jiménez, "Preventing the Artificial Avoidance of PE Status," *UN Papers on Selected Topics in Protecting the Tax Base of Developing Countries* (2014) p. 4, Adolfo J. Martin Jiménez in: Alexander Trepelkov/Harry Tonino/Dominika Halka (eds.) *United Nations Handbook on Selected Issues in Protecting the Tax Base of Developing Countries—Second Edition*, p. 366, Omar Moerer/Benchi Klaver, "The AOA, PE status and BEPS, some reassurance in a time of change?," *BNA Tax Management Transfer Pricing Report* (2015), Kevin Cunningham, "The Post-BEPS World of Permanent

Most importantly, the author is concerned about the supplementary test that was added to the dependent agent provision. In fact, the assessment as to whether the person in the source country plays the "*principal role*" leading to the conclusion of contracts is clearly subjective in nature. To make it even worse, it is unrealistic to believe that the limited guidance provided in the OECD Model Commentary on Art. 5 can be of help in addressing all practical issues that might arise when applying such a test.

In the author's view, to achieve its purported goal, the concept of permanent establishment should be sufficiently clear and objective. The application of such a concept in concrete cases should be based on a common interpretation of all the relevant factual circumstances by the taxpayers and the tax administrations of the countries involved. A subjective test—like the assessment of the "*principal role*" leading to the conclusion of contracts—could bring along an inconsistent application, especially in complex industries—like insurance—that do not seem to be clear enough for tax administrations. Any such inconsistent application could in turn hinder cross-border trade and investments.

By the same token, the amendments to the independent test also seem to be lacking clarity on the precise requirements for what it is now to be regarded as an independent agent. Most of all, given that the BEPS concerns were mainly associated to situations where the agent was closely related to the foreign enterprise on behalf of which he/she was acting,[988] the rationale behind the removal of the economic independence test and the shift toward the operational independence of the agent is anything but clear.

Therefore, the author shares the view that the amendments to Art. 5, paras. 5 and 6, of the OECD Model go far beyond the policy concerns underlying the BEPS Project.[989] As a matter of fact, the outcome of Action 7 of the BEPS Project is a concept of permanent establishment that is very much broad in scope and—arguably—blurrier than what it historically was. In addition, a threshold which is too low could turn out to be rather ineffective. Indeed, under the newly formulated rules, all contracts from which the foreign enterprise could derive some economic benefit could give rise to a dependent agent permanent establishment. All this complemented with the fact that

---

Establishment," *Tax Notes International* (2016) p. 510, Susann van der Ham/Daniel Retzer, "BEPS Aktion Nr. 7 zu Betriebsstätten und die Auswirkungen auf die Betriebsstättengewinnabgrenzung," *Internationales Steuerrecht* (2016) p. 758, Stefan Bendlinger, "Die „neue" Vertreterbetriebsstätte," *Internationales Steuerrecht* (2016) p. 914, Alexander Hemmelrath/Elke Wilcox, "Chapter 8: AOA, BEPS, E-Commerce—"Permanent Establishment" in Flux" in: Heike Jochum/Peter Essers/Michael Lang/Norbert Winkeljohann/Bertil Wiman (eds.) *Practical Problems in European and International Tax Law* (Amsterdam: IBFD, 2016) para. 8.3.5, Julie Bellemare, "Evolution of the Permanent Establishment Concept," *Canadian Tax Journal* (2017) pp. 745-746 and Eva Frehner, "Die Betriebsstätte vor und nach BEPS—Definition, Gewinnaufteilung und Umsetzung," *Expert Focus* (2018) p. 733.

988. *See* OECD, "*Preventing the Artificial Avoidance of Permanent Establishment Status—Action 7: 2015 Final Report*," p. 15.

989. In a similar fashion, *see* Maria Cecilia Villareal Regalado, "Treaty Abuse and Permanent Establishments: Proposed Changes to Article 5(5) and 5(6) of the OECD MC" in: Daniel W. Blum/Markus Seiler (eds.) *Preventing Treaty Abuse* (Vienna: Linde, 2016) pp. 417-418.

there will be presumably little or no additional income to be taxed in the source country.

The UN recognized the importance of the OECD work in the context of the BEPS Project (most notably, Action 1 and Action 7 of the BEPS Project), particularly in relation to its implications on taxing rights of source countries. In fact, among others, UN Committee of Experts also created a specific subcommittee to monitor the issues related to the BEPS Project and communicate on such issues with officials in developing countries.[990]

Most importantly, as noted by Martin Jiménez,[991] although the allocation of taxing rights between source countries and residence countries was not among the goals of the BEPS Project,[992] it is undeniable that Action 7 of the BEPS Project has also shed some light on such a debate. Indeed, a new balance between source countries and residence countries can be struck as an indirect consequence of the changes to the permanent establishment standards to the extent that a lower threshold guarantees an increase of source taxation.[993] For this reason, considering that the UN is generally inclined to concede source countries more taxation rights vis-à-vis the OECD Model,[994] it is no surprise that the UN endorsed the work of the OECD in the context of Action 7 of the BEPS Project and implemented the changes to Art. 5 of the OECD Model into the 2017 update of the UN Model.

In addition to this, the BEPS Project contained several anti-avoidance measures designed to tackle international tax avoidance schemes that were of significant interest to developing countries.[995] As a result, another potential reason that developing

990. For further comments on the work of the UN on issues addressed in the context of the BEPS Project, *see*—among others—Michael Lennard, "Update on the United Nations Tax Committee Developments," *Asia-Pacific Tax Bulletin* (2014) p. 22, Carmel Peters, "Developing Countries" Reactions to the G20/OECD Action Plan on Base Erosion and Profit Shifting', *Bulletin for International Taxation* (2015) pp. 375-376 and Michael Lennard, "Base Erosion and Profit Shifting and Developing Country Tax Administrations," *Intertax* (2016) pp. 740-745.

991. *See* Adolfo Martin Jiménez, *UN Papers on Selected Topics in Protecting the Tax Base of Developing Countries*, (2014) pp. 8-9. The same author has slightly revisited his argument in a following paper. To this effect, *see* Adolfo J. Martin Jiménez in: Alexander Trepelkov/Harry Tonino/Dominika Halka (eds.) *United Nations Handbook on Selected Issues in Protecting the Tax Base of Developing Countries—Second Edition*, pp. 374-375.

992. As noted by Collier and Riedel, at inception, there was however some indication that the BEPS Project might also deal with fundamental international tax principles, such as the balance between source and residence taxation. To this effect, *see* Richard Collier/Nadine Riedel, "The OECD/G20 Base Erosion and Profit Shifting Initiative and Developing Countries," *Bulletin for International Taxation* (2018) para. 3 and OECD, "*Addressing Base Erosion and Profit Shifting*" (OECD Publishing 2013), p. 50.

993. In a similar vein, *see also* Fernando Souza de Man, *Taxation of Services in Treaties between Developed and Developing Countries—A Proposal for New Guidelines*, para. 4.5, Eric M. Zolt, "A Better Deal Post-BEPS" in: Brian J. Arnold (ed.) *Tax Treaties After the BEPS Project—A Tribute to Jacques Sasseville* (Toronto: Canadian Tax Foundation, 2018) p. 382 and Eric M. Zolt, "Tax treaties and developing countries," *Oxford University Centre for Business Taxation: Working paper series* (2018) pp. 37-38.

994. *See* s. 3.4.2.1 above.

995. To this effect, *see* Richard Collier/Nadine Riedel, *Bulletin for International Taxation*, (2018) para. 3.

countries might have had was to secure access to administrative capacity building measures for administering complex anti-avoidance provisions.[996]

Despite the above, as highlighted by Martin Jiménez,[997] it is not yet clear whether the tax administrations of developing countries will easily apply the newly introduced provisions and, in the case where they find a permanent establishment as now defined after Action 7 of the BEPS Project, they will really know how to attribute profits to it. True, there are various options that might be considered for assisting their position.[998] However, it should be ascertained whether such options can be effectively implemented.

On the other hand, the US Model did not give effect to Action 7 of the BEPS Project, the only minor change being the rule to address circumstances under which the 12-month period for construction or installation projects is exceeded.[999] In particular, it appears that—in the US—the most significant concerns derived from: *(i)* the impact of the work on Art. 7 of the OECD Model and the OECD Model Commentary thereon and *(ii)* the impact of the recommendations on permanent establishment and attribution of profits thereto emerging from the BEPS Project. Most notably, in the US view, changes in the permanent establishment definition should be conditional on understanding the rules for attribution of profits to such permanent establishments.[1000] Now that the OECD has published additional guidance on the attribution of profits to permanent establishments,[1001] it remains to be seen whether the US will adopt the BEPS recommendations or not. In the latter case, however, the author believes that the US could be more inclined to incorporate in their model the exceptions to the permanent establishment status for preparatory and auxiliary activities rather than the amendments regarding the dependent agent permanent establishment, that are more of a concern for European civil law countries.

The above shift toward an economic approach contributes to creating a mismatch vis-à-vis the definition of establishment for insurance regulatory purposes. This is particularly the case in the EU, where a key condition for a person to fall within the scope of the right of establishment is that he/she can commit the foreign insurance

996. To this effect, *see* Richard Collier/Nadine Riedel, *Bulletin for International Taxation*, (2018) para. 5.1.

997. *See* Adolfo J. Martin Jiménez in: Alexander Trepelkov/Harry Tonino/Dominika Halka (eds.) *United Nations Handbook on Selected Issues in Protecting the Tax Base of Developing Countries—Second Edition*, pp. 375-376 and 428.

998. *See* Richard Collier/Nadine Riedel, *Bulletin for International Taxation*, (2018) paras. 5.2, 5.3 and 5.4.

999. *See* Jonathan Schwarz, "US Model Treaty 2016: What does it say about the US and BEPS?," *Kluwer International Tax Blog* (2016). In his post, the author also argues that the US has declined to follow the AOA to the attribution of profits reflected in the 2010 OECD Model. However, this conclusion appears to be controversial to the extent that the AOA has been included in the 2006 US Model and retained in the most recent version of the US Model. In fact, Art. 7 of the US Model currently follows the wording of Art. 7 of the OECD Model. Rather, what one may infer is that, as announced by the US Treasury Department in a statement on June 7, 2007, the US would not apply the AOA to most existing US DTAs.

1000. *See* Diane M. Ring, "*United States—Permanent Establishments—Topical Analyses*," para. 2.1.1.2.

1001. *See* OECD, "*Additional Guidance on the Attribution of Profits to Permanent Establishments—BEPS Action 7.*"

company. In the author's view, this commitment was broadly in line with the conclusion of insurance contracts (legally) binding on the foreign insurance company. Hence, it is fair to say that the definition of a dependent agent permanent establishment for tax purposes before the 2017 update of the OECD Model was essentially similar to the corresponding definition adopted for regulatory purposes. Actually, one may argue that the latter was even broader than the previous definition for tax purposes to the extent that the commitment can also derive from activities other than the conclusion of insurance contracts, e.g., the acceptance and the settlement of claims. Now that the application of Art. 5, para. 5, of the OECD Model is no longer limited to the conclusion of insurance contracts, but also includes all the circumstances where the person "*plays the principal role leading to the conclusion of contracts that are routinely concluded without material modifications*" by the foreign insurance company, the definition for tax purposes is clearly much broader than the definition adopted for regulatory purposes.

In the same spirit, the amendments to the independent agent provision (most notably, the introduction of the supplementary independence test regarding related parties) exacerbate the above misalignment by using exclusivity or near-exclusivity as being an irrebutable presumption rather than a factor for determining the independent status of a person in the source country with the effect of bringing more persons within the definition of dependent agent permanent establishment for tax purposes.

The amendments introduced in the context of the BEPS Project do not appear to match consistently to the insurance value chain, either. As a matter of fact, such amendments are intended to catch additional activities leading to the conclusion of contracts, including primarily sales and marketing activities. Nevertheless, sales and marketing is only one of the functions in the insurance value chain. Certainly, the persons engaged in such activities do not undertake KERT functions, as envisaged in the 2010 OECD Report, Part IV.[1002] As a result, it may be argued that the above amendments are likely to increase the number of dependent agent permanent establishments with little or no additional income attributable thereto.[1003]

Instead, the work on the BEPS Project left fundamentally unchanged the wording for the special clause regarding insurance agents under para. 114 of the OECD Model Commentary on Art. 5. While the final decision not to include any such clause in Art. 5 of the OECD Model itself is to be welcomed, it is nevertheless to be noted that the inclusion of this clause in the OECD Model Commentary is not to be supported, either.

To begin with, the special clause for insurance agents looks like an attempt to deny the application of the independent agent provision to insurance representatives which is not grounded on a juridical reasoning. As a matter of fact, this exclusion seems to be deriving from policy considerations with a view to restoring source taxation. Nevertheless, this exclusion is not supported with a proper legal analysis as to the

1002. *See* s. 2.2.3 above.
1003. In a similar vein, *see also* Rick Mitchell/Kevin A. Bell, "More Permanent Establishments Expected Under OECD Draft," *BNA Tax Management Transfer Pricing Report* (2016) and Isabel Gottlieb, "New Taxation Threshold 'No Golden Goose' for Countries," *BNA Tax Management Transfer Pricing Report* (2018).

reasons why insurance agents are denied *a priori* from being regarded as agents of an independent status operating in the ordinary course of their agency business vis-à-vis agents engaged in other industries. On the top of this, this exclusion seems to clash with the tendency in the case law to consider an insurance agent as acting independently and within the ordinary course of his/her agency business.

In addition, the special clause for insurance agents gives rise to some interpretative issues. Most importantly, the term "*agent*" is not defined under Art. 3, para. 1, of the OECD Model. In the author's view, this term should be intended to have a broad meaning not limited to the legal concept of agent under domestic law. Nonetheless, the use of this expression and the lack of guidance thereon could result in uncertainty as to the application of this clause, like that experienced in the past with the previous formulation of the independent agent provision.[1004] This issue has instead been overcome under the UN Model to the extent that the insurance agent provision makes use of the term "*person,*" which is defined under Art. 3, para. 1, of the UN Model.

The collection of premiums alone is also far from being considered as a minimum acceptable threshold for a permanent establishment to exist. The connection with the source country is indeed far too weak in comparison with minimum thresholds required to trigger a permanent establishment in other industries. In such a case, the agent is likely to represent a mere point of contact that provides customers with payment details, particularly in more recent times when the collection of premiums mainly occurs through bank transfers and/or other electronic means of payment. On the top of this, the collection of premiums is also a criterion that can be easily circumvented. It is indeed fairly simple to relocate taxing rights from a country to another by merely making the payment in/from other countries.

On the other hand, the reference to the insurance of risks appears to be general language which may be very broad in scope. As a matter of fact, this reference seems to cover a wide range of activities related to risks situated in the source country, even though the agent does neither assume nor manage such risks. Once again, in this respect, the agent is likely to represent a mere point of contact to assist customers in activities preceding the conclusion of contracts, administrative activities and/or activities related to the performance of the contracts. For instance, this may well be the case of an agent that coordinates lawyers and/or adjusters in the event of a claim. However, here too, the level of activity seems too low for the insurance of risks to be a justifiable threshold for source taxation.

It is also worth noting that many jurisdictions levy insurance premium taxes, along with other parafiscal charges and levies on premiums, which are generally applied depending on where the underlying risk is situated and not where the insurance company is established. Therefore, jurisdictions wishing to tax insurance companies on a risk basis could do so through insurance premium taxes, which are generally easier to administer. In the case that such jurisdictions additionally believe that they have a legitimate claim to tax profits of insurance companies if a risk situated in their territories is insured through a local agent, the reverse is also true. In fact, a risk

1004. *See* s. 3.3.2.4.2 above.

cannot be insured, unless it is properly assumed and managed. As a result, countries where underwriting and risk management functions are performed could also legitimately claim a part of the insurance premium taxes.[1005] Nonetheless, the author believes that the result would be unnecessarily too complicated.

Moreover, the special clause for insurance agents creates a clear-cut mismatch between the definition of permanent establishment for tax purposes and the definition of establishment for regulatory purposes. Arguably, such a clause gives rise to a considerable increase in the number of permanent establishments for tax purposes as opposed to the number of establishments for regulatory purposes. This is particularly the case if the place where the risk is located is different from the place the premium is collected. This in turn leads to a dramatic increase of additional compliance requirements related to the presence of a permanent establishment for tax purposes, such as the maintenance of separate accounting and tax records, the filing of tax returns, and so forth. According to the author, this is a disproportionate and inappropriate compliance burden for insurance companies vis-à-vis other industries which employ agents in countries other than that of establishment. What is more, such compliance requirements will be typically associated with little or no additional income to be taxed in the source country to the extent that agents operating therein are not involved in KERT functions. Not to mention that such requirements might be difficult to enforce for the tax administrations.

The special clause for insurance agents is also not in line with the insurance value chain. As a matter of fact, the special clause for insurance agents is likely to catch activities that are mainly related to sales and marketing, contract and claims management and/or other support functions, none of which can be regarded as a KERT function in the insurance business. Indeed, the KERT function is the assumption of insurance risks, which pertains to the underwriting function.[1006] Accordingly, the KERT function lies with the entity that accepts and manages risks (namely, the insurance company and not the agent). Conversely, the activities of the agent in the source country are instead to be rewarded with a proper arm's length remuneration. Therefore, it seems rather inconsistent to ascribe a permanent establishment in a country where only the above activities are performed.

In the UN Model, the insurance agent provision contains a specific carve-out for independent agents to the extent that no consensus was found among UN countries.[1007] This carve-out marks a crucial difference vis-à-vis the special clause for insurance agents enshrined in para. 114 of the OECD Model Commentary on Art. 5, which is arguably aimed at denying the application of the independence agent provision for

1005. For a similar reasoning in respect of the link between income taxes and value added taxes, *see* Eric C.C.M. Kemmeren, "Should the Taxation of the Digital Economy Really Be Different?," *EC Tax Review* (2018) p. 73. In this respect, when proposing a "*refundable withholding approach*" for electronic commerce transactions, Pinto argued that allocating origin-based value added taxes to a production country would be acceptable. To this effect, *see* Dale Pinto, *E-Commerce and Source-Based Income Taxation* (Amsterdam: IBFD, 2003) p. 228 and Dale Pinto, "The Need to Reconceptualize the Permanent Establishment Threshold," *Bulletin for International Taxation* (2006) p. 279.

1006. *See* s. 2.2.3 above.

1007. *See* s. 3.4.2.3 above.

insurance agents. In doing so, given the general tendency in the international case law to consider an insurance agent as acting independently and within the ordinary course of his/her agency business, the compromise underlying Art. 5, para. 6, of the UN Model does not seem to effectively address the concerns of developing countries as to the taxation of insurance companies at source.

Art. 5, para. 6, of the UN Model is not effective in respect of reinsurance, either. The carve-out for reinsurance contained therein is not economically justified since reinsurance basically consists on the insurance of the risks of other insurance companies.[1008] Accordingly, the author does not see a sound reason to encourage foreign reinsurance companies over foreign insurance companies to participate in local markets. If a given jurisdiction wishes to support its local market, it can more easily do so by letting in both types of entities. For instance, this is the case of the EU, where there is no distinction between insurance and reinsurance neither in the Solvency II Directive nor in the recent Insurance Distribution Directive.[1009]

In the light of the foregoing, the wording for a special clause regarding insurance agents enshrined in para. 114 of the OECD Model Commentary on Art. 5 and the insurance agent provision contained in Art. 5, para. 6, of the UN Model do not represent appropriate thresholds for taxing insurance companies in source countries.

1008. *See* s. 2.2.4 above.
1009. Directive (EU) 2016/97 of the European Parliament and of the Council of 20 January 2016 on insurance distribution.

CHAPTER 4
Analysis of the Insurance Business Models

Chapter 4 seeks to investigate the most common business models adopted by multinational insurance companies to assess whether the peculiar features of such models may give rise to the existence of a dependent agent permanent establishment in a foreign country. More to the point, based on the analytical framework regarding the concept of dependent agent permanent establishment depicted in the preceding chapter, the purpose of this chapter is to carefully scrutinize the most common business models implemented in the insurance industry, with a specific focus on marketing, promotion and distribution of insurance products in foreign jurisdictions without establishing a fixed place of business therein, with a view to ascertaining the existence of a dependent agent permanent establishment in such foreign jurisdictions. More precisely, the business models that are dealt with in this chapter are the following: direct online business carried on through a website, business performed through price aggregator websites and other online business like third-party websites, mobile applications or virtual platforms, other distance selling operations (e.g., with the use of mail, e-mail, (tele)fax, telephone and/or a combination thereof), business through insurance brokers, insurance agents, bancassurance arrangements, multinational programs, and the Lloyd's market operations.

4.1 BACKGROUND OF THE ANALYSIS

In past years, the insurance industry used to be traditionally characterized by a number of specific features vis-à-vis other sectors of the economy (including also sectors which may be—in principle—similar such as the banking and financial sectors). Among others, the (traditional) insurance business has been characterized by the following elements:[1010]

1010. *See* Riccardo Varaldo/Giuseppe Turchetti, *L'E-commerce—le nuove frontiere nella distribuzione assicurativa* (Milano: Franco Angeli, 2000) pp. 19-20, Antonio Coviello, *L'utilizzo delle tecnologie avanzate nel settore assicurativo: l'e-insurance*, (Torino: Giappichelli, 2009) p. 225 and Fabrizio Santoboni, "L'intermediazione assicurativa: profili normative e gestionali" in: Fabrizio Santoboni (ed.) *Manuale di gestione assicurativa* (Padova: CEDAM, 2012) p. 296.

- a low level of competition on the market;
- well-defined operators with specific and separate areas of operations;
- a few distribution channels (the traditional distribution channels were not more than two or three);
- the adoption of a single distribution channel or at least the prevalence of a distribution channel over the others. In this context, the management of the relationship with the customer was left to an insurance intermediary to the effect that the main relationship in the context of the insurance business was that between the intermediary and the customer rather than that between the insurance company and the customer.

However, over the last two decades, the functioning of the insurance markets has been deeply transformed by some significant changes, most notably the globalization of the economy—which may be regarded as a dynamic and multidimensional process of economic integration whereby national resources become more and more internationally mobile while national economies become increasingly interdependent[1011]—and the disruptive innovations in the information and communication technologies.[1012]

On the top of this, over the recent years, the insurance business has also experienced: (*i*) significant changes to the regulatory environment, particularly in the EU Member States,[1013] (*ii*) a rapid evolution of the customer buying behavior, which is now more and more sensitive to issues of a financial and insurance nature, (*iii*) a (r)evolution in the structure of the supply side of the market, which is now characterized by the presence of brand-new operators, (*iv*) the marketing of new products, for instance new life insurance products, which are now characterized by elements of a financial nature, (*v*) a radical change in the relationship management with the final customer, which is no longer intended as a sale of insurance products, but rather as a solution to a problem expressed by the customer, and (*vi*) an introduction of new distribution channels and/or a different use of existing distribution channels.[1014]

In the light of such changes, the (modern) insurance business is now characterized by the following elements:[1015]

- a higher level of competition on the market;
- higher acquisition expenses;
- an increased degree of customer mobility stemming from a higher customer awareness and a broader range of insurance products; and

1011. *See* OECD, "*OECD Handbook on Economic Globalization Indicators*," available online at www.oecd.org, p. 11.
1012. *See* Antonio Coviello, *L'utilizzo delle tecnologie avanzate nel settore assicurativo: l'e-insurance*, pp. 6-8.
1013. *See* s. 2.1 above.
1014. *See* Riccardo Varaldo/Giuseppe Turchetti, *L'E-commerce—le nuove frontiere nella distribuzione assicurativa*, p. 20. Giuseppe Giudici, *I canali della distribuzione assicurativa* (Milano: Franco Angeli, 2003) pp. 37 and 38 and Fabrizio Santoboni in: Fabrizio Santoboni (ed.) *Manuale di gestione assicurativa*, p. 296.
1015. *See* Riccardo Varaldo/Giuseppe Turchetti, *L'E-commerce—le nuove frontiere nella distribuzione assicurativa*, pp. 22-23.

- an increased degree of insurance intermediary mobility.

In the context of such a rapidly evolving environment, the present chapter is intended to describe the most common business models adopted by large insurance companies when investing abroad, with a particular focus on the specific features of such models that may give rise to the existence of a dependent agent permanent establishment in a foreign country.

In order to properly examine such business models, it should be borne in mind that the process of internationalization in the context of the insurance business is mainly driven by a number of specific features which may be found in the insurance business. In fact, such distinctive features may have a significant influence on the decision of an insurance company to extend its operations at international level.[1016]

At the outset, from a technical standpoint, the position of an insurance company is closely related to the size and characteristics of the risk portfolio. In fact, the number, the independence, the nature and the size of risks assumed by an insurance company may affect the relative uncertainty of its portfolio. In other terms, such elements may affect the mismatch between the claim probability estimated upfront (which has a significant influence on the determination of the insurance premium) and the actual frequency of claims. As such, the geographical expansion may partially mitigate random variables strictly connected to the geographical localization of the risks.[1017]

Besides such technical needs, the international expansion of large insurance companies is also driven by business environmental factors. *In primis*, the globalization and the consequent dramatic increase in the international trade have played a key role over the recent years. Other environmental factors also include the role of the country of residence on the international stage, the demand side of the market in the country of residence, the regulatory environment in the country of residence.[1018]

On the top of this, internal factors which exist within the context of an organization (for instance, the business history, the size of the company, the features of the business, the value system, the mission and the objectives of the company) may also significantly affect the business strategy, and perhaps most importantly the approach adopted by the insurance company in terms of geographical expansion.[1019]

It follows that the reasons for an insurance company to expand its activities on foreign markets may be countless, so are the business and operating models adopted for such an expansion.[1020] As a matter of fact, as in any other business sector, the international expansion in the context of the insurance industry may concern a range

1016. *See* Ornella Moro, *L'internazionalizzazione delle imprese di assicurazione* (Milano: Egea, 1990) p. 397.
1017. For further comments on technical factors, *see* Ornella Moro, *L'internazionalizzazione delle imprese di assicurazione*, pp. 397 et seq.
1018. For further comments on business environmental factors, *see* Ornella Moro, *L'internazionalizzazione delle imprese di assicurazione*, pp. 401 et seq.
1019. For further comments on such factors, *see* Ornella Moro, *L'internazionalizzazione delle imprese di assicurazione*, pp. 408 et seq.
1020. For further comments, *see* Ornella Moro, *L'internazionalizzazione delle imprese di assicurazione*, pp. 419 et seq.

of activities, specific operational functions, specific internal processes and/or a mix thereof.

Clearly, this chapter does not pretend to offer a general comprehensive analysis of all business and operating models that may be adopted by an insurance company when carrying on its business abroad and—thus—cover all circumstances where an insurance company may have a permanent establishment in a foreign country. Rather, based on the analytical framework regarding the concept of dependent agent permanent establishment depicted in the preceding section, the purpose of this chapter is to carefully assess some business models implemented in the insurance industry, with a specific focus on marketing, promotion and distribution of insurance products in foreign jurisdictions without establishing a fixed place of business therein.[1021]

More precisely, the business models which will be dealt with in the next sections will be the following:

- direct online business;
- price aggregator websites;
- other online models;
- other distance selling means;
- insurance brokers;
- insurance agents;
- bancassurance;
- multinational business; and
- the Lloyd's market.

Each of the following sections will be dedicated to a specific business model. More precisely, each section will provide at the outset a general overview of the relevant business model, along with an outline of the fact pattern considered for the analysis. From this, the second part of each section will critically assess the circumstances under which the relevant business model may give rise to the existence of a dependent agent permanent establishment under the OECD Model and the UN Model.

1021. In this respect, although it is beyond the scope of this research, it is important to note that the distribution of insurance products is generally subject to regulatory requirements in order to provide fair and clear information about insurance products and therefore improve consumer protection. For instance, in the EU, the regulatory framework has been established by means of EU Directives aimed at providing minimum harmonization rules in order to govern information that should be given to consumers, impose certain conduct of business and transparency rules for insurance distributors, clarify rules for their cross-border business and addresses the supervision and sanctioning of insurance distributors in the case they breach the provisions contained therein. For further comments on the existing EU regulatory framework regarding the distribution of insurance products and after-sale activities, *see*—among others—Pierpaolo Marano/Ioannis Rokas/Peter Kochenburger, *The "Dematerialized" Insurance—Distance Selling and Cyber Risks from an International Perspective* (Cham: Springer International Publishing AG, 2016) pp. 4 et seq.

4.2 DIRECT ONLINE BUSINESS

4.2.1 General Overview

4.2.1.1 Introduction

At the outset, it is worth noting that the Internet may be defined as a "global computer network providing a variety of information and communication facilities, consisting of interconnected networks using standardized communication protocols,"[1022] referred to as the TCP/IP protocols. The Internet—which has no central computer or any physical location—uses routers that determine the best route available at the time to transfer data toward its final destination. In principle, the Internet should be distinguished from the World Wide Web (or simply the Web), which may instead be defined as "an information system on the Internet which allows documents to be connected to other documents by hypertext links, enabling the user to search for information by moving from one document to another."[1023] To put it in other terms, the Web is a subsystem of the Internet, which combines text, images, video, audio and hypertext that allow users to access other related documents on the Web by clicking on links displayed in a particular document. Accessing the Web requires a browser program, which is a software application aimed at reading information accessed from the Web and presenting it to the user in a standard format. A company can collect Web documents (usually referred to as a website), which are generally stored on central computers called servers.[1024,1025]

Although—at the very beginning—the insurance industry appeared to be lagging in the rapid evolution of financial services over the Internet,[1026] it may be argued that the trend has now changed. *In primis*, insurance companies and insurance intermediaries have started exploring ways to develop new business opportunities in the online space environment.[1027] As such, the Internet has become an attractive medium through which insurance companies and insurance intermediaries can optimize their ways of

1022. To this effect, *see* the Oxford English Dictionary, available online at https://en.oxforddictionaries.com/definition/internet.

1023. To this effect, *see* the Oxford English Dictionary, available online at https://en.oxforddictionaries.com/definition/world_wide_web.

1024. *See* US Treasury Department, "*Selected Tax Policy Implications of Global Electronic Commerce*," (November 21, 1996) p. 7.

1025. Web servers and browsers communicate using the HTTP, a special protocol created to transfer hypertext documents over the Web. *See* US Treasury Department, *Selected Tax Policy Implications of Global Electronic Commerce*, p. 7.

1026. To this effect, Gergana Rakovska, "E-Commerce Business Models for Insurance: Application to U.S. and European Markets," *Centre for Risk Management and Insurance Research—Georgia State University* (2001) p. 2, Michael Theil, "Insurance On The Internet: A Different View," *International Business & Economics Research Journal* (2002) pp. 45 et seq. and Aftab Alam/Mairaj Salim/Hassan Shah, "The Potential of E-Commerce in the Insurance Industry: The Road Ahead," *Global Journal of Enterprise Information System* (2009) p. 38.

1027. It is worth noting that, besides new business opportunities, the Internet has also brought about a number of administration and operational benefits for insurance companies. *See*—among others—Giuseppe Giudici, *I canali della distribuzione assicurativa*, pp. 162 et seq. and 182 and Antonio Coviello, *L'utilizzo delle tecnologie avanzate nel settore assicurativo: l'e-insurance*, pp. 227 et seq. However, this additional analysis is beyond the scope of this research.

doing business.[1028,1029] Most notably, as potential customers continue to integrate the use of the Internet in their daily lives, the use of this new technology may help insurance companies and insurance intermediaries to get in touch with potential customers and to distribute insurance products.[1030]

Additionally, along with the penetration of the Internet, there has been a gradual change in customer preferences with respect to the purchase of insurance protection. Such a change has been both behavioral and attitudinal in nature, and is more relevant among young customers. Currently, most of the customer activities are focused toward interacting, communicating and transacting with insurance companies. Such a change provides tremendous growth opportunities for insurance companies to generate sales through online business as customer penetration increases and as more insurance-related services are provided via the Internet.[1031]

4.2.1.2 Common Variations

In the context of this evolving business environment,[1032] insurance companies have responded differently. In particular, a number of insurance companies simply look at the Internet as a tool to market and promote their products. In order to do so, insurance companies generally make available—through their websites,[1033] mobile-specific applications and/or their accounts on social media platforms—institutional information concerning their organization, along with documents and information related to their activities and their products (for instance, presentations, information packages and so forth).[1034] In such a case, the above materials are made available exclusively for the purpose of providing information, so that none of such materials can be intended as an advice, solicitation and/or offer aimed at the sale of insurance products.[1035] As a result, the prospect can make use of the above materials to gather general company information, preliminary product information and make a comparison for personal investment

1028. To this effect, *see* Diana Cerini, *Prodotti e servizi assicurativi—Distribuzione e intermediazione* (Milano: Giuffrè, 2003) p. 90 and Capgemini, "*Trends in Insurance Channels,*" available online at www.capgemini.com, p. 3.
1029. The Internet itself does not represent a new player in the insurance market but rather a new medium for existing players. To this effect, *see* Diana Cerini, *Prodotti e servizi assicurativi—Distribuzione e intermediazione*, p. 90.
1030. *See* Diana Cerini, *Prodotti e servizi assicurativi—Distribuzione e intermediazione*, p. 91 and Capgemini, "*Trends in Insurance Channels,*" p. 3.
1031. *See* Capgemini, "*Trends in Insurance Channels,*" pp. 7-8.
1032. For further comments on the regulatory regime applicable to Internet sales, *see* Pierpaolo Marano/Ioannis Rokas/Peter Kochenburger, *The "Dematerialized" Insurance—Distance Selling and Cyber Risks from an International Perspective*, pp. 44 et seq. and 155 et seq. As for Italy, *see also* Claudia Bortolani, "I canali alternativi di distribuzione dei prodotti assicurativi" in: Marco Prosperetti/Alessandro Colavolpe (eds.) *I gestori del risparmio non bancari e i canali di distribuzione* (Milano: Ipsoa, 2012) pp. 456 et seq.
1033. As a general rule, the websites are now designed to adapt to all devices: the mobile, the tablet or the personal computer.
1034. *See* Fabrizio Santoboni in: Fabrizio Santoboni (ed.) *Manuale di gestione assicurativa*, p. 319, Diana Cerini, *Prodotti e servizi assicurativi—Distribuzione e intermediazione*, p. 92, and Giuseppe Giudici, *I canali della distribuzione assicurativa*, p. 166.
1035. As a general rule, such materials cannot be used in any other way without a prior written permission of the insurance companies.

decision-making purposes, but he/she cannot finalize the purchase of insurance products online.[1036]

The Internet may also grant insurance companies an opportunity to collect data and information regarding Internet users and—thus—on the demand side of the market.[1037] Such a collection can be an active or passive data collection. In respect of the latter, while the user is surfing a website, data can be collected even without his/her explicit registration to the service or without his/her active role. For example, insurance companies can collect IP addresses, cookies and other session identifiers, Internet tags, and other surfing data.[1038] On the other hand, the active data collection presupposes an interaction with Internet users and their willingness to share information on their insurance needs and preferences.[1039] For instance, this can be done through online questionnaires, website registrations, online forums and so forth. Alternatively, insurance companies may also purchase data and information on consumer needs and preferences from price aggregator websites[1040] or other external sources.[1041]

Differently, insurance companies can also solicit direct sales of insurance products online. As a general rule, such direct online sales are currently available for very simple products, which do not require specific advice and/or negotiation. This is for instance the case of basic non-life products, such as motor insurance, travel insurance and home insurance, where prospects can easily select among different product options, generally available at predetermined terms and conditions.

To this end, depending on the specific case, the interaction with the customer on the website of the insurance company may be limited to activities immediately preceding the conclusion of insurance contracts (for instance, the provision of premium quotations, the exchange of information and/or communication between parties and so forth) or can go as far as the actual conclusion of insurance contracts online.[1042]

In the former case, the customer is generally redirected to an insurance intermediary to finalize the purchase. Alternatively, the customer can be provided with the

1036. Often, the website also provides contact details for further phone, mail or e-mail enquiries. However, such other distance selling means will be dealt with more specifically in s. 4.5 below.
1037. In this respect, it is important to note that data and information processing for commercial purposes is generally subject to strict privacy laws and regulations.
1038. To this effect, *see* for instance the Generali Group policy, available at www.generali.com.
1039. *See* Diana Cerini, *Prodotti e servizi assicurativi—Distribuzione e intermediazione*, p. 92.
1040. *See* s. 4.3.1 below.
1041. In this respect, it should be noted that much of the data in the future will be unstructured, so that insurance companies will require the capability to capture data at points of interaction with customer and will need an organization that is skilled at promoting innovation to apply big data, and eager to do so. To this effect, *see* Bain & Company Inc., "*Global Digital Insurance Benchmarking Report 2015—Pathways to success in a digital world,*" available online at www.bain.com, p. 5. For further comments on the concept of big data, *see also* Swiss Re, "*Digital distribution in insurance: a quiet revolution,*" Sigma No. 2/2014, available online at www.swissre.com, pp. 24-25, Bernardo Nicoletti, *Digital Insurance—Business Innovation in the Post-Crisis Era* (Basingstoke: Palgrave Macmillan UK, 2016) pp. 143 et seq. and Michael Naylor, *Insurance Transformed—Technological Disruption* (Cham: Springer International Publishing AG, 2017) pp. 69 et seq.
1042. *See* Diana Cerini, *Prodotti e servizi assicurativi—Distribuzione e intermediazione*, p. 92.

relevant contact details to finalize the purchase through a call center and/or other distance selling means.[1043] In the second case, while the process of buying online insurance varies across insurance companies,[1044] it typically requires the customer to create an online registration account on the website of the relevant insurance company with a user identification code and a password that will provide access to online services. With such codes, the customer can log on to the website of the insurance company, search for insurance products among different options,[1045] select the suitable insurance product by filling out a specific form, obtain a premium quotation from the insurance company,[1046] submit his/her offer through a "*point and click*" interface and proceed with the payment of the insurance premium through a variety of methods (generally including bank transfers or credit cards).

In this respect, it should be noted that—even where there is no actual negotiation between the parties—customers may usually select among different product options (such as the maximum coverage, the deductible and so forth) through the website of the insurance company. As a consequence, under such circumstances, it may be inferred that it is still the customer to select the insurance product and—therefore—submit an offer to the relevant insurance company, which is free to accept it or not.[1047] That being so, in the context of the online business, the insurance contract may be generally regarded as concluded when the electronic impulse generated by the completion of the purchasing process (i.e., the acceptance of the offer submitted by the customer) is available on the server that hosts the website of the insurance company. On the other hand, in the event that the conclusion of the insurance contract requires the insurance company to communicate the acceptance of the offer made by the customer when submitting the application form to the insurance company, the insurance contract may be deemed to be concluded when the electronic impulse generated by the server that hosts the website of the insurance company (which contains the signal of acceptance) is received by the provider that has allowed the customer to access the Internet.[1048]

The place of conclusion has also given rise to debate. Among different theories, it has been submitted that, in the case where the conclusion of the insurance contract requires the insurance company to communicate the acceptance of the offer, the place of conclusion of the insurance contract should be intended as the place where the signal of acceptance is received by the customer, unless there is an agreement to the

---

1043. Such other distance selling means will be dealt with more specifically in s. 4.5 below.

1044. Italian regulations require insurance companies to disclose the procedural steps to conclude insurance contracts online. To this effect, *see* Art. 14 of ISVAP regulation No. 34 of March 19, 2010.

1045. Insurance companies may also provide helpline and live chat options to resolve pre-buying queries.

1046. Insurance companies may also grant specific discounts on premiums when insurance contracts are concluded online.

1047. The materials contained in the website may instead be regarded as an invitation to treat. *See* Marco Rossetti, *Il diritto delle assicurazioni—Volume 1*, p. 908 and Luca De Muri, "Gli aspetti legali e contrattuali del commercio elettronico," *Le guide—Il Fisco—Commercio Elettronico* (2014) pp. 19-21.

1048. *See* Marco Rossetti, *Il diritto delle assicurazioni—Volume 1*, pp. 907-911 and footnotes cited therein.

contrary. This generally corresponds to the place where the customer normally has access to the Internet, which should be regarded as his/her habitual abode or domicile.[1049]

A strictly connected issue is relating to the form of the insurance contract since the substantive requirements in this respect vary considerably across countries.[1050] Among others, if local regulations require the insurance company to provide contractual documents in written form after the conclusion of the contract, this requirement can be fulfilled by: (*i*) providing the customer with a policy in paper form after the conclusion of the contract or (*ii*) providing the customer with a policy in electronic form signed digitally, where admissible under applicable regulations.[1051]

Lastly, the Internet may enable insurance companies to offer a wide range of online administrative services, such as post-sales insurance services, through an online personal account accessible with all devices. As a matter of fact, customers are increasingly using the Internet to access printable insurance identification cards and policy forms as well as to initiate claims procedures. In some cases, the Internet may also be used to modify coverage terms, update personal information, update information about property covered by insurance contracts, change payment information and, for unit-linked policies in the life sector, modify asset allocation.[1052]

4.2.1.3 Fact Pattern

For the purposes of this analysis,[1053] it is assumed that foreign insurance companies directly market, promote and distribute insurance products through the Internet in the source country.[1054] The analysis is primarily based on the insurance business carried on through a website[1055] accessible on a personal computer, a smartphone or a tablet via a standard or mobile browser application, which may be installed locally or available on cloud. Nevertheless, according to the author, comments related to such a business may be reasonably extended to cases where an insurance company has developed its own specific mobile applications or its own accounts on social media

1049. *See* Marco Rossetti, *Il diritto delle assicurazioni—Volume 1*, pp. 911-913 and footnotes cited therein.
1050. *See* EU Commission, "*Final Report of the Commission Expert Group on European Insurance Contract Law*" (2014) p. 38.
1051. *See* Marco Rossetti, *Il diritto delle assicurazioni—Volume 1*, pp. 913-915.
1052. *See* Diana Cerini, *Prodotti e servizi assicurativi—Distribuzione e intermediazione*, pp. 92-93 and Swiss Re, "*Digital distribution in insurance: a quiet revolution*," Sigma No. 2/2014, p. 16.
1053. This analysis is intended to deal with the use of the Internet by insurance companies to directly distribute insurance products. The use of the Internet by insurance intermediaries and other entrepreneurs in the context of indirect schemes will be instead dealt with in the following sections.
1054. The notion of "*source country*" is used to describe the country where the existence of a dependent agent permanent establishment is tested. In doing so, it is assumed that the source country coincides with the "*market country*," with the latter being the country where the customers are located. The same assumption remains valid in the following sections.
1055. The analysis is applicable to both the situation where the Internet website is hosted on traditional servers (either dedicated servers or shared servers) and the situation where the Internet website is hosted on cloud servers.

platforms, which are essentially (mobile-based or Web-based) software applications designed to grant access to similar online contents on smartphones and tablets.

4.2.2 Permanent Establishment Implications

4.2.2.1 Analysis under the OECD Model

4.2.2.1.1 The Standard Version

At the outset, it should be recalled that the OECD addressed the application of the permanent establishment concept in the electronic commerce (or simply the e-commerce)[1056] during the Internet boom when it proposed some changes to the 2000 OECD Model Commentary on Art. 5 to update the interpretation of that provision,[1057] which have been integrated in paras. 42.1-42.10 of the 2003 OECD Model Commentary on Art. 5.[1058]

Similar issues have been discussed again in the context of the BEPS Project, when the OECD recognized that the digitalization and some of the resulting business models present specific challenges.[1059] Most notably, business models based on modern communication systems generate opportunities to operate in other countries and earn substantial revenues therein without giving rise to a permanent establishment.[1060] The

1056. It is worth noting that the concept of e-commerce only covers the buying and selling of products over electronic systems. To this effect, *see*—among others—Noah Gaoua, "Taxation of the Digital Economy: French Reflections," *European Taxation* (2014) p. 11.

1057. *See* OECD, "*Clarification on the application of the permanent establishment definition in e-commerce: changes to the commentary on the model tax convention on article 5*," Paris (December 22, 2000).

1058. For further comments on such amendments, *see—inter alia*—Prafula Fernandez/Gitte Heij/Jeff Pope, "Tax Policy and Electronic Commerce," *Bulletin for International Taxation* (2002) pp. 30 et seq., Marco Piazza, *Guida alla fiscalità internazionale*, pp. 244 et seq., Piergiorgio Valente, *Convenzioni internazionali contro le doppie imposizioni*, pp. 295 et seq., Alessandro Dragonetti/Valerio Piacentini/Anna Sfondrini, *Manuale di fiscalità internazionale*, pp. 1019 et seq., Manoj Kumar Singh, "Taxing E-Commerce on the Basis of Permanent Establishment: Critical Evaluation," *Intertax* (2014) pp. 328 et seq. and OECD, "*Addressing the Tax Challenges of the Digital Economy—Action 1: 2015 Final Report*," Annex A, Prior work on the digital economy, (OECD Publishing October 5, 2015), pp. 151 et seq.

1059. For further comments, *see*—among others—OECD, "*Addressing the Tax Challenges of the Digital Economy—Action 1: 2015 Final Report*," Chapter 7—Broader direct tax challenges raised by the digital economy and the options to address them, pp. 97-106, European Parliament, *Tax Challenges in the Digital Economy* (2016) pp. 16 et seq., Yariv Brauner, "BEPS: An Interim Evaluation," *World Tax Journal* (2014) pp. 14-17, Björn Westberg, "Taxation of the Digital Economy—An EU Perspective," *European Taxation* (2014) pp. 541 et seq., Pierre Collin/Nicolas Colin, *Report to the Minister for the Economy and Finance, the Minister for Industrial Recovery, the Minister Delegate for the Budget and the Minister Delegate for Small and Medium-Sized Enterprises, Innovation and the Digital Economy* (2013) available online at http://www.economie.gouv.fr p. 61 and Luigi Quaratino, "New Provisions Regarding the Taxation of the Digital Economy," *European Taxation* (2014) pp. 215-216.

1060. To this effect, *see—inter alia*—OECD, "*Addressing the Tax Challenges of the Digital Economy—Action 1: 2015 Final Report*," Chapter 5—Identifying opportunities for BEPS in the digital economy, pp. 77 et seq., European Parliament, *Tax Challenges in the Digital Economy*, pp. 23 et seq., Peter Hongler/Pasquale Pistone, "IBFD Blueprints for a New PE Nexus to Tax Business Income in the Era of the Digital Economy," *IBFD White Paper* (2015) pp. 9-10, Daniel W. Blum, "Permanent Establishments and Action 1 on the Digital Economy of the OECD Base

OECD considered some specific options to address such challenges: (*i*) a new nexus based on a significant economic presence, (*ii*) a withholding tax on digital transactions, and (*iii*) an equalization levy.[1061] However, none of such options has been eventually recommended insomuch as other measures developed in the context of the BEPS Project were expected to address BEPS issues exacerbated by the digitalization.[1062] At any rate, the OECD stated that countries could introduce any of them in their domestic laws as additional safeguards against BEPS, provided that they respect existing treaty obligations, or include them in their DTAs.[1063,1064]

In the aftermath of the BEPS Project, the G20 mandated the OECD to deliver an interim report on the implications of the digitalization by April 2018 and a final report in 2020. In March 2018, the OECD published the interim report,[1065] which provided an

---

Erosion and Profit Shifting Initiative—The Nexus Criterion Redefined?," *Bulletin for International Taxation* (2015) pp. 315 et seq., Walter Hellerstein, "Jurisdiction to Tax in the Digital Economy: Permanent and Other Establishments," *Bulletin for International Taxation* (2014) p. 346, Tatiana Falcao/Bob Michel, "Assessing the Tax Challenges of the Digital Economy: An Eye-Opening Case Study," *Intertax* (2014) pp. 317 et seq., and Noah Gaoua, *European Taxation*, (2014) pp. 10-12.

1061. *See* OECD, "*Addressing the Tax Challenges of the Digital Economy—Action 1: 2015 Final Report*," Chapter 7—Broader direct tax challenges raised by the digital economy and the options to address them, pp. 106 et seq. For further comments on such options, *see also* Reuven S. Avi-Yonah/Oz Halabi, "A Model Treaty for the Age of BEPS," *University of Michigan—Law & Economics Research Paper Series* (2014) p. 15, Peter Hongler/Pasquale Pistone, *IBFD White Paper*, (2015) pp. 15 et seq., Andrés Báez Moreno/Yariv Brauner, "Withholding Taxes in the Service of BEPS Action 1: Address the Tax Challenges of the Digital Economy," *IBFD White Paper* (2015) pp. 6 et seq., Sayan Basak, "Equalization Levy: A New Perspective of E-Commerce Taxation," *Intertax* (2016) pp. 846-848, Marcel Olbert/Christoph Spengel, "International Taxation in the Digital Economy: Challenge Accepted?," *World Tax Journal* (2017) pp. 14-21, Georg Kofler/Gunter Mayr/Christhop Schlager, "Taxation of the Digital Economy: "Quick Fixes" or Long-Term Solutions," *European Taxation* (2017) pp. 528-530, Yariv Brauner/Pasquale Pistone, "Adapting Current International Taxation to New Business Models: Two Proposals for the European Union," *Bulletin for International Taxation* (2017) pp. 682-687, Stjepan Gadžo, *Nexus Requirements for Taxation of Non-Residents' Business Income: A Normative Evaluation in the Context of the Global Economy*, paras. 7.3.2 and 7.3.3 and Heinz-Klaus Kroppen/Susann van der Ham, "Die digitale Betriebsstätte: wertschöpfungsgerechte Besteuerung im Zeitalter der Digitalisierung," *Internationales Steuer- und Wirtschaftsrecht* (2018) pp. 339-340.

1062. *See* OECD, "*Addressing the Tax Challenges of the Digital Economy—Action 1: 2015 Final Report*," Chapter 6—Tackling BEPS in the digital economy, pp. 85 et seq. For further comments, *see also* Marcel Olbert/Christoph Spengel, *World Tax Journal*, (2017) pp. 12-14.

1063. OECD, "*Addressing the Tax Challenges of the Digital Economy—Action 1: 2015 Final Report*," Chapter 7—Broader direct tax challenges raised by the digital economy and the options to address them, para. 383.

1064. For further comments on some initiatives at domestic level, *see* Oana Popa, "Taxation of the Digital Economy in Selected Countries—Early Echoes of BEPS and EU Initiatives," *European Taxation* (2016) pp. 38 et seq., Sayan Basak, *Intertax*, pp. 848-852, Marco Allena, "The Web Tax and Taxation of the Sharing Economy: Challenges for Italy," *European Taxation* (2017) pp. 304 et seq., Simone Zucchetti/Armando Tardini/Oreste Lanfranchi, "The Italian "Web Tax": The New Administrative Procedure for Multinational Enterprises to Disclose Hidden Permanent Establishments in Italy," *International Transfer Pricing Journal* (2017) pp. 390 et seq. and Yasin Uslu, "An Analysis of 'Google Taxes' in the Context of Action 7 of the OECD/G20 Base Erosion and Profit Shifting Initiative," *Tax Notes International* (2018) pp. 140 et seq.

1065. *See* OECD, "*Tax Challenges Arising from Digitalisation—Interim Report 2018*," Paris (March 16, 2018).

analysis of the main features that can be generally found in certain highly digitalized business models and the value creation in the digitalized age. In doing so, the OECD emphasized the need to work toward a consensus-based solution by 2020, but did not eventually make any specific recommendations to countries.[1066]

Following the interim report, the OECD intensified its work outlining two pillars that could form the basis for consensus. Most importantly, the first pillar aims at addressing the broader challenges of the digitalized economy by focusing on the allocation of taxing rights. In that respect, the OECD put forward three proposals entailing that businesses would allocate more profits to market countries, regardless of the extent of their physical presence—i.e.: (*i*) the user participation proposal, (*ii*) marketing intangibles proposal, and (*iii*) the significant economic presence proposal.[1067] In order to reach a consensus-based solution, the OECD established a program of work considering some design features, including the design of a new nexus rule.[1068] This ongoing work could clearly lead to significant amendments to the permanent establishment definition, allied with changes to Arts. 7 and 9 of the OECD Model. Nevertheless, pending the outcome of such work, this analysis is based on the 2017 update of the OECD Model.

Against this background, a distinction needs to be made between a website and a server. More to the point, the OECD recognized that an Internet website is a combination of software and electronic data which does not in itself constitute tangible property, whereas the server on which the website is stored and through which such a website is accessible is a piece of equipment having a physical location.[1069] This distinction is important since the enterprise that operates the server may be different from the enterprise that carries on business through the website (in the case at hands, the insurance company). In fact, it is common for the website through which an enterprise carries on its business to be hosted on the server of an ISP.[1070] This is of paramount importance also for an assessment of the dependent agent provision. Indeed, the question arises as to whether Art. 5, para. 5, of the OECD Model may apply to deem: (*i*) the website, (*ii*) the server, (*iii*) the ISP operating the server or (*iv*) other persons maintaining the website to constitute dependent agent permanent establishments of foreign insurance companies whose products are sold through the website in other countries.

1066. *See* OECD, "*Tax Challenges Arising from Digitalisation—Interim Report 2018*," para. 514.
1067. *See* OECD, "*Addressing the Tax Challenges of the Digitalisation of the Economy—Policy Note*," Paris (January 23, 2019) and OECD, "*Public Consultation Document—Addressing the tax challenges of the digitalisation of the economy*," Paris (February 13, 2019). For further comments on such proposals, *see also* Pasquale Pistone/João Félix Pinto Nogueira/Betty Andrade, "The 2019 OECD Proposals for addressing the tax challenges of the digitalization of the economy: an assessment," *IBFD International Tax Studies* (2019) paras. 2, 3 and 4, Randy Buchanan/Carol Tello/Ben Jones/Amanda Cooper/Robert Christoffel/Hyowon Lee/Kunal Nathwani, "OECD Consults on Taxing the Digitalized Economy," *Tax Management Transfer Pricing Report* (2019) and Stef van Weeghel, "Digitalization in a Broader Tax Perspective," *Intertax* (2019) pp. 532-533.
1068. OECD, "*Programme of Work to Develop a Consensus Solution to the Tax Challenges Arising from the Digitalisation of the Economy*," Paris (May 31, 2019).
1069. *See* para. 123 of the OECD Model Commentary on Art. 5.
1070. *See* para. 124 of the OECD Model Commentary on Art. 5.

As for the website, it is worth noting that in the past the issue of software agents has been often discussed.[1071] Among others, it has been proposed to include software agents in the notion of dependent agent permanent establishment.[1072] In addition, it has also been submitted that software agents have the ability to negotiate, conclude and even digitally sign a contract.[1073] Doernberg and Hinnekens have even considered that the mere presence of the software agent on a customer's computer might permit a country to exercise its tax authority.[1074] Nevertheless, such reasonings do not appear to be convincing. As a matter of fact, it should be recalled that a software agent is not a legal person and has no legal capacity.[1075] This conclusion has also been endorsed by the OECD, which clarified that—since the website through which an enterprise carries on its business is not itself a *"person"* as defined under Art. 3 of the OECD Model—Art. 5, para. 5, of the OECD Model cannot apply to deem a permanent establishment to exist by virtue of the website being an agent of the enterprise for purposes of that paragraph.[1076,1077]

Besides the issues related to the term *"person,"* it is important to note that all that such an agent can do is to follow a program made in advance by a human being. Also, any adaptation in its behavior is dependent on instructions given by a person. The real decision-maker is the person behind the program governing the software agent, while the rest is an automatic process. The capability of a human being acting as an agent to contract is in sharp contrast to the programmed behavior of a software agent. Therefore, after all, it appears to be too far-reaching to extend the capacity of human agents under Art. 5, para. 5, of the OECD Model to software agents.[1078]

Likewise, a server is merely a machine normally owned by one person (i.e., the ISP) and used by another person (i.e., the website owner) in exchange for a certain agreed consideration. Consequently, the server cannot be considered as a *"person"*

1071. A software agent has been defined as a program that can be activated by an Internet user simply by clicking on an icon displayed on the website of an enterprise. To this effect, *see* Arthur Pleijsier, "The Agency Permanent Establishment, Practical Applications—Part Two," *Intertax* (2001) p. 228 and Arthur Pleijsier, *The agency permanent establishment: de vaste vertegenwoordiger: proefschrift*, pp. 220-221. This term has been defined to describe programs that act on behalf of people. To this effect, *see* Richard L. Doernberg/Luc Hinnekens, *Electronic Commerce and International Taxation* (The Hague: Kluwer Law International, 1999) p. 89.
1072. *See* Barrett Schaefer, "International Taxation of Electronic Commerce Income: A Proposal to Utilize Software Agents for Source-Based Taxation," *Santa Clara High Technology Law Journal* (2000) pp. 130 et seq.
1073. *See* Björn Westberg, *Cross-Border Taxation of E-Commerce* (Amsterdam: IBFD, 2002) para. 5.4.7.7 and Richard L. Doernberg/Luc Hinnekens/Walter Hellerstein/Li Jinyan, *Electronic Commerce and Multijurisdictional Taxation* (The Hague: Kluwer Law International, 2001) pp. 53-54 and 172-173.
1074. *See* Björn Westberg, *Cross-Border Taxation of E-Commerce,* para. 5.4.7.7 and Richard L. Doernberg/Luc Hinnekens, *Electronic Commerce and International Taxation*, p. 112.
1075. *See* Björn Westberg, *Cross-Border Taxation of E-Commerce,* para. 5.4.7.7 and footnotes cited therein.
1076. *See* para. 131 of the OECD Model Commentary on Art. 5.
1077. The same conclusion has been upheld in respect of mobile applications during the 2016 IFA Congress in Madrid. *See* Hermann Peyerl, "Kann eine „App" eine Betriebsstätte begründen?," *Steuer und Wirtschaft International* (2017) pp. 248-249.
1078. *See* Björn Westberg, *Cross-Border Taxation of E-Commerce,* para. 5.4.7.7.

under Art. 3 of the OECD Model, so that no dependent agent permanent establishment can arise.[1079]

In contrast, an ISP owning and operating a server on which the website is stored may in principle be regarded as a "*person*" under Art. 3 of the OECD Model acting on behalf of an insurance company pursuant to a web housing agreement. Nevertheless, ISPs are usually companies that provide e-mail, web-hosting, or other online storage services to a variety of customers wishing to carry on their business on the Web. In particular, they generally ensure the functioning of such equipment without creating and installing software on the website.[1080] As a consequence, it cannot be said that ISPs conclude insurance contracts or play the principal role leading to the conclusion of insurance contracts binding on foreign insurance companies. On the top of this, ISPs are generally independent from foreign insurance companies, as evidenced by the fact that they typically host websites of many different enterprises. Therefore, it may be concluded that an ISP owning and operating a server on which the website is stored does not generally constitute a dependent agent permanent establishment of foreign insurance companies.[1081]

Hence, under the current rules, it remains to be assessed whether insurance companies have employed persons in the source country to create and maintain a website and/or outsourced such activities to an external webmaster in the source country.[1082] True, in most of the cases, a foreign insurance company can maintain the website and interact with customers remotely without maintaining a presence in the source country. Therefore, under the current version of Art. 5, para. 5, of the OECD Model, no permanent establishment implications come into being. Nonetheless, in the case that the foreign enterprise engages employees and/or webmasters in the source country, concerns can arise. Indeed, it may be argued that such employees and/or webmasters act "*on behalf of*" the foreign insurance company based on the relevant employment contract and the outsourcing contract, respectively.

As a result, one should carefully look at the activities that such persons carry on therein. According to the author, a dependent agent permanent establishment may arise in the event that such employees and/or webmasters in the source country are entrusted with the creation, development and/or maintenance of a website offering a

1079. *See* Arvid A. Skaar, "Erosion of the Concept of Permanent Establishment: Electronic Commerce," *Intertax* (2000) pp. 192-193.

1080. *See* Manoj Kumar Singh, *Intertax*, (2014) pp. 330-331, Gurram Ramachandra Rao, "*India: Concept of Permanent Establishment and Electronic Commerce,*" April 2003, available online at http://www.mondaq.com, and Irmantas Rotomskis/Tomas Girdenis, "Internet Service Provider and the Dependent Agent," *KSI Transactions on Knowledge Society* (2014) pp. 59-60.

1081. To this effect, *see* para. 131 of the OECD Model Commentary on Art. 5. For further comments, *see also* Arvid A. Skaar, *Intertax*, (2000) p. 193, Arthur Pleijsier, *Intertax*, (2001) pp. 227-228, Arthur Pleijsier, *The agency permanent establishment: de vaste vertegenwoordiger: proefschrift*, pp. 218-219 and Michele Aprile/Michele Lenotti, "Aspetti tributari della vendita on-line di prodotti assicurativi: la libertà di prestazione di servizi ed il concetto di stabile organizzazione," *CERAP—Università Bocconi, Working Paper n. 24* (2002) p. 22 and Manoj Kumar Singh, *Intertax*, (2014) p. 330.

1082. From a regulatory perspective, insurance companies are generally accountable for their activities.

complete online sales functionality.[1083] Most notably, a basis may exist for arguing that, in light of the rules governing the formation of online insurance contracts,[1084] the presence of employees and/or webmasters in the source country that create, develop and/or maintain interactive, but pre-programmed, decision software that instruct the server to generate the electronic impulse containing the signal of acceptance and/or transmit the electronic impulse containing the signal of acceptance to a customer having his/her habitual abode or domicile in the source country can fulfill the traditional test regarding the conclusion of contracts. Indeed, even though no active negotiation takes place between the parties,[1085] the acceptance of the offer through a program created, developed and/or maintained by employees and/or webmasters in the source country leads to the conclusion of a valid insurance contract binding on the foreign insurance company.

In addition to this, a dependent agent permanent establishment might arise even though the interaction with a prospect is limited to activities preceding the conclusion of insurance contracts. Indeed, in the case of employees and/or webmasters situated in the source country that create, develop and/or maintain a website that offers an interaction going beyond marketing and information purposes—such as a website that provides binding quotations, so that a foreign insurance company is bound to the terms and conditions reported therein—it can be argued that the employees and/or webmasters are collecting offers to enter into standardized contracts and the foreign insurance company is bound to accept such offers in a later stage, regardless of the fact that the contract is formally concluded through an insurance intermediary or a call center.

Also, in the light of the changes introduced in the context of the BEPS Project, other circumstances where the website offers an interaction going beyond marketing and information purposes should be carefully assessed. As a matter of fact, although the potential customer is typically redirected to an insurance intermediary or a call center in order to formally conclude the insurance contract, the activities of the employees and/or webmasters in the source country might fulfill the supplementary test regarding the principal role leading to the conclusion of contracts.

Under such circumstances, assuming that potential customers can regularly access any of the above websites around the clock, the habitual exercise test is likely to be fulfilled to the effect that a dependent agent permanent establishment may in principle arise, with the only remaining issues being the assessment of whether such employees and/or webmasters can be regarded as agents of an independent status.

1083. In this respect, it is worth noting that—in the *Dell Spain* case—the Tribunal Economico-Administrativo Central claimed that qualified personnel working in the website for the Spanish market gave rise to a fixed place of business in Spain. However, the High Court and the Supreme Court have been more cautious and did not take a clear stand on the issue as to whether the staff working in the website for the Spanish market gave rise to a permanent establishment in Spain. For further comments, *see* Adolfo J. Martín Jiménez, *Bulletin for International Taxation*, (2016) pp. 463 and 465 and Francisco Antonio Vaquer Ferrer, *Intertax*, (2016) p. 681.

1084. *See* ss. 3.3.2.2.4 and 4.2.1.2 above.

1085. The OECD has clarified that a contract can be concluded without any active negotiation. To this effect, *see* para. 87 of the OECD Model Commentary on Art. 5. For further comments, *see also* s. 3.3.2.3.4 above.

In this regard, it is fair to say that—depending on the applicable factual circumstances—webmasters situated in the source country that create, develop and/or maintain websites for a number of non-related principals with respect to any one of whom they are not dependent could fulfill the substantive requirements set forth under Art. 5, para. 6, of the OECD Model. On the other hand, this reasoning cannot clearly be extended to employees of foreign insurance companies. Hence, under the circumstances depicted above, employees of foreign insurance companies situated in the source country that create, develop and/or maintain any such website are likely to give rise to a dependent agent permanent establishment therein.

To the contrary, a dependent agent permanent establishment should not arise if the employees and/or webmasters in the source country are engaged for the creation, development and/or maintenance of a website which merely aims at marketing products, supplying product and other information do not generally give rise to a dependent agent permanent establishment. As a matter of fact, such employees and/or webmasters do not fulfill neither the traditional test regarding the conclusion of contracts nor the supplementary test regarding the principal role leading to the conclusion of contracts.[1086] By the same token, employees and/or webmasters engaged in the source country for the creation, development and/or maintenance of a website only aimed at gathering data and information do not meet the above tests. Similarly, employees and/or webmasters merely engaged in the preliminary setup of a website do not fulfill neither of the above tests.

4.2.2.1.2 The Special Clause for Insurance Agents

In the event that a DTA contains a special clause for insurance agents along the lines of para. 114 of the OECD Model Commentary on Art. 5, it should be ascertained whether (*i*) the ISP operating the server or (*ii*) other persons, such as employees and/or webmasters, that do not otherwise give rise to a dependent agent permanent establishment under the standard version of the OECD Model could be caught under this clause.[1087]

According to the author, although the term "*agent*" ought to be intended in a broad commercial sense,[1088] ISPs that merely provide e-mail, web-hosting or other online storage services cannot be regarded as insurance distributors operating in favor of foreign insurance companies for the purposes of the special clause. As a result, such providers cannot give rise to a permanent establishment in the source country.

On the other hand, employees and/or webmasters situated in the source country that create, develop and maintain a website could fall within the scope of this clause.

1086. To this effect, *see* Valentina Perrone/Gabriele Sepio, "Stabile organizzazione, "vendita a distanza" e commercio elettronico," *Dialoghi Tributari* (2013) pp. 666 et seq., Valentina Perrone/Raffaello Lupi, "Economia digitale tra stabile organizzazione occulta e pubblicità "on line"," *Dialoghi Tributari* (2014) pp. 324 et seq. and Michele Aprile/Michele Lenotti, *CERAP—Università Bocconi,* Working Paper n. 24, (2002) p. 20.

1087. The website and the server are disregarded to the extent that they cannot be regarded as persons. For further comments, *see* s. 4.2.2.2.1 above.

1088. *See* s. 3.3.2.5.2 above.

This might be the case of employees that create, develop and/or maintain websites which do not offer a complete online sales functionality, but still provide customers with a platform for online administrative and/or performance services, including the payment of insurance premiums and the management of claims. By the same token, the special clause for insurance agents is also likely to catch webmasters that create, develop and/or maintain websites which offer a complete online sales functionality and/or websites that do not offer such a complete functionality, but nevertheless provide customers with binding quotations, administrative services and/or services otherwise going beyond marketing and information purposes, irrespective of whether such webmasters can be regarded as agents of an independent status acting in the ordinary course of their business.

To the contrary, as long as the website is only intended to provide general company information, preliminary product information or otherwise gather data and information regarding Internet users, it may be argued that the activities carried on by the insurance company through the website do not directly result in the collection of premiums or the insurance of risks in the source country. In fact, in such a case, the website does not permit to conclude insurance contracts, and thus no actual collection of premiums or insurance of risks takes place through the website.

4.2.2.2 Analysis under the UN Model

The tax issues connected with the e-commerce were discussed at the Tenth Meeting of the Ad Hoc Group of Experts on International Cooperation in Tax Matters held in Geneva on September 10-14, 2001.[1089] It was recommended to undertake a study of the tax issues involved (among others, whether the concept of a permanent establishment needed to be changed to take account of the changes in the economic environment that have occurred since it was first adopted as a principle of taxation).[1090]

As a result, the Eleventh Meeting of the Ad Hoc Group of Experts on International Cooperation in Tax Matters was instructed to develop guidelines for legislation promoting direct and indirect tax requirements based on the strengthening of the tax base to prevent preferential treatment of any specific use of electronic commerce, as well as on principles of transparency, certainty, effectiveness, efficiency and nondiscrimination. However, the Eleventh Meeting held in Geneva on December 15-19, 2003 failed to make progress in the area of electronic commerce.[1091]

Despite the above, following the OECD work in the context of the e-commerce, paras. 42.1-42.10 of the 2003 OECD Model Commentary on Art. 5 have been quoted in para. 36 of the 2011 UN Model Commentary on Art. 5. Save for a renumbering, the quotation remained essentially the same in the 2017 update of the UN Model.[1092]

1089. *See* Ghislain T. J. Joseph, "Electronic Commerce and the United Nations Model Double Taxation Convention," *Intertax* (2004) p. 388.
1090. *See* UN Department of Social Affairs, "*Report of the Ad Hoc Group of Experts on International Cooperation in Tax Matters on the Work of its Tenth Meeting,*" Part One, (June 21, 2002) p. 15.
1091. *See* Ghislain T. J. Joseph, *Intertax,* (2004) p. 388.
1092. Paragraphs 42.1-42.10 of the 2003 OECD Model Commentary on Art. 5 have been renumbered in paras. 122-131 of the OECD Model Commentary on Art. 5.

Consequently, it may be argued that the UN Model Commentary has approved the corresponding OECD Model Commentary, save for a carve-out with respect to the distinction between a contract with an ISP and one with a place of business at the disposal of the enterprise under para. 37 of the UN Model Commentary on Art. 5.

More recently, moving from the OECD/G20 work, the UN Committee of Experts has also constituted a subcommittee to discuss the tax challenges of the digitalization of the economy, particularly issues of relevance for developing countries.[1093] At any rate, pending the outcome of such discussions, the present analysis is based on the 2017 update of the UN Model.

In light of the foregoing, comments related to the current version of the OECD Model[1094] may be in principle extended to the UN Model. However, the UN Model also contains an insurance agent provision to the effect that a permanent establishment may be deemed to arise where a foreign insurance company collects premiums or insures risks through a "*person*" in the source country. In this respect, it should be noted that neither a website nor a server constitutes a "*person*" under Art. 3, para. 1, of the UN Model. Therefore, the question arises as to whether (*i*) ISPs owning and operating the server on which the website is hosted or (*ii*) other persons creating, developing and/or maintaining the website may give rise to a permanent establishment in the source country. In seeking answer to such a question, one should take into consideration that an ISP, an employee of the foreign company and an external webmaster are all to be regarded as persons under the UN Model.

Under Art. 5, para. 5, let. (*a*), of the UN Model, a dependent agent permanent establishment may in principle arise in the case where employees and/or webmasters in the source country are entrusted with the creation, development and/or maintenance of a website offering a complete online sales functionality. This also holds true in the case where such employees and/or webmasters create, develop and/or maintain a website that provides binding quotations to customers, whereas circumstances under which such a website offers an interaction going beyond marketing and information purposes should be assessed on a case-by-case basis to ascertain whether the supplementary test regarding the principal role leading to the conclusion of contracts is fulfilled or not.

In addition to this, the insurance agent provision can also catch employees and/or webmasters in the source country that are involved in the creation, development and/or maintenance of websites that do not offer a complete online sales functionality, but still provide customers with a platform for administrative and/or performance services, such as the collection of insurance premiums and the management of claims. Under such circumstances, the insurance agent provision is also likely to catch ISPs in the source country that own and operate the servers on which such websites are hosted. In fact, insofar as they provide and maintain the equipment, ISPs may be regarded as persons through which premiums are collected and/or risks are insured within the meaning of the insurance agent provision.

1093. For further comments, *see* UN Committee of Experts, "*Tax Issues related to the Digitalization of the Economy: Report*," Document E/C.18/2019/CRP.12 (April 5, 2019).

1094. *See* s. 4.2.2.1.1 above.

Nevertheless, it remains to be ascertained whether any of the above persons may be regarded as agents of an independent status acting in the ordinary course of their business. In general, this should be the case of ISPs owning and operating the server on which the website is hosted and external webmasters creating, developing and/or maintaining a website in the source country. Conversely, this cannot be the case of employees. For this reason, under the circumstances depicted above, an employee situated in the source country that creates, develops and/or maintains any such website is likely to give rise to a permanent establishment therein.

Conversely, a permanent establishment should not arise if the employees and/or webmasters in the source country are engaged for the creation, development and/or maintenance of a website which merely aims at marketing products, supplying product and other information or otherwise gathering data and information regarding Internet users.

4.3 PRICE AGGREGATOR WEBSITES

4.3.1 General Overview

4.3.1.1 Introduction

At the outset, it is fair to say that there is no generally agreed definition of price aggregator websites (otherwise also referred to as price comparison websites, shopping comparison websites or price engine websites). Nonetheless, EIOPA has broadly defined such websites as "*interfaces, the objective of which is to display to Internet users a number of insurance offers, and compare their prices and/or what is covered.*"[1095]

To put it in other words, a price aggregator website is—in its basic form—a list of prices and features for specific products, sourced from different providers.[1096] More to the point, price aggregator websites—which are mostly run by insurance intermediaries[1097,1098]—enable users to specify their requirements and then be presented with prices and information from a selection of insurance companies.[1099] In

1095. *See* EIOPA, "*Report of Good Practices on Comparison Websites,*" Document EIOPA-CCPFI-13/100, Frankfurt (2014) p. 6.
1096. *See* Claudia Wood, "Compare and Contrast: How the UK comparison website market is serving financial consumers," *Resolution Foundation* (2007) p. 10.
1097. Some price aggregator websites are managed by public authorities or consumers' associations.
1098. For further comments on the regulatory regime applicable to price aggregator websites, *see* Pierpaolo Marano/Ioannis Rokas/Peter Kochenburger, *The "Dematerialized" Insurance—Distance Selling and Cyber Risks from an International Perspective*, pp. 18-19 and 70 et seq. In this respect, a number of concerns may raise where a firm "*white labels*" (i.e., uses in its own business) a price aggregator tool provided by a third party website. For further comments on such concerns, *see* Financial Services Authority, *Guidance on the selling of general insurance policies through price comparison websites*, London (2011) pp. 5-6.
1099. In contrast, value comparison websites help customers to choose an insurance contract on the basis of the value *in lieu of* the price. In general, such websites list insurance quotations on the basis of factors that determine how well quotations could meet the needs of the customers (e.g., perils covered) rather than on the mere pricing. To this effect, *see* Deloitte, "*Insurance disrupted: General insurance in a connected world,*" available online at www.deloitte.com, p. 11.

general, such websites will present their results in the form of a table which, on the basis of the information provided by the user, offers a comparison of the relevant products.[1100] Such a table will generally list products vertically and present a range of product information horizontally in separate columns, usually starting with the details of the provider and ending with an "*action*" column, either enabling the consumer to apply for the product, enquire about it, or to see more details.[1101] Typically, more information is available through clicking on the relevant parts of the table and clicking on an "*Apply*" button which will generally take the user to the website of the provider. Depending on the website, other information may also be available (such as product guides and news about the industry). In addition, there has been an emphasis on building community aspects to such sites, with developments such as message boards and ratings of products by the users.[1102]

As for insurance companies (particularly, smaller players), the aggregator represents an innovative opportunity to reach customers. Indeed, with limited marketing budgets and increased competition, smaller insurance companies are finding it hard to attract customers to their own online portals. The aggregators will have marketing strength to compete with and exceed even the dominating insurance companies in the market, and importantly also with the ability to develop and deliver a different and more innovative marketing message than what an insurance company can.[1103]

Price aggregator websites are typically suitable for simple insurance products, like motor insurance, travel insurance, and home insurance. Specifically, motor vehicle insurance is the cash cow product for two reasons. First, the pricing essentially depends on the characteristics of the car and the experience of the driver, which makes it suitable for simple online comparisons. Second, contracts traditionally run for one year and thus are recurrent in nature.[1104]

Over the recent years, price aggregators have enjoyed a boom, as the use of personal computers has grown, people have become more familiar with shopping online and "*shopping around*" has become more common.[1105] In the UK, customers have embraced the use of aggregators to buy insurance, particularly car insurance. In fact, in 2009, aggregator purchases accounted for more than half of total private car insurance sales in the UK, and for 36% of home insurance sales. Today, UK aggregators have attained an even more larger share of the private car insurance market, accounting for an estimated 60% to 70% of new business premiums.[1106] In other countries, aggregators are enjoying rapid growth as well. In France, for example, aggregators have

1100. Des Laffey, "Value Configurations in E-Commerce: Evidence from Comparison Websites," *ECIS, 2008 Proceedings: Paper 36* (2008) p. 3.
1101. *See* Claudia Wood, *Resolution Foundation*, (2007) p. 10.
1102. Des Laffey, *ECIS, 2008 Proceedings: Paper 36*, (2008) p. 3.
1103. To this effect, *see* Kasko Norway AS, "*Are aggregators a threat to all insurance companies?,*" available online at https://kasko.no, p. 4.
1104. *See* University of St. Gallen, "*The Current InsurTech Landscape: Business Models and Disruptive Potential,*" available online at www.ivw.unisg.ch, pp. 48-49.
1105. *See* Claudia Wood, *Resolution Foundation*, (2007) p. 11.
1106. *See* Accenture, "*Coming to Terms with Insurance Aggregators: Global lessons for carriers,*" available online at www.accenture.com, p. 1 and Europe Economics, "*Distribution Channels in Insurance,*" available online at https://www.europe-economics.com, pp. 42-44.

grown at an average rate of 18% per year over the last five years. In Spain and Italy, although they have low penetration, they have anyway achieved the highest growth rates in Europe in the recent years. The aggregators are also growing in other countries like in Japan, in India and in the US.[1107] The different extent of penetration in the markets mainly depends upon several factors. Among others, such factors include customer habits and culture in the market concerned, marketing expenditures by insurance companies, the participation of insurance companies in the services provided by the aggregators, the digital sophistication of insurance companies and aggregators, and distribution cost pressures.[1108]

4.3.1.2 Functioning

Given the different market conditions, there is a wide range of price aggregator websites in the market.[1109] Nevertheless, all of them have some common features in the process leading to the comparison and the purchase of insurance protection. Indeed, while surfing on the Web, the user can access the price aggregator website and fill out an insurance risk profiling form.[1110] Such a form—where the user is required to complete a questionnaire or select suggestions from a list of assumptions—is usually quite detailed and substantially homogenous among different comparison websites.[1111,1112] This form is aimed at collecting the relevant information which is needed by insurance companies to subsequently provide the risk quotation.[1113]

1107. *See* Accenture, "*Coming to Terms with Insurance Aggregators: Global lessons for carriers,*" p. 4 and Europe Economics, "*Distribution Channels in Insurance,*" pp. 44-46.
1108. For further details, *see* Accenture, "*Coming to Terms with Insurance Aggregators: Global lessons for carriers,*" pp. 4-5.
1109. For a categorization of such websites, *see* EIOPA, "*Report of Good Practices on Comparison Websites,*" Document EIOPA-CCPFI-13/100, pp. 9-11.
1110. It is worth noting that inbound clicks can come either directly to the site or through other websites (such as a search engine). The sources of inbound clicks need to be identified for performance monitoring and also because some of them incur payment (e.g., Google's paid search results are charged per click). *See* Des Laffey, *ECIS, 2008 Proceedings: Paper 36* (2008) pp. 7-8.
1111. The risk profiling forms available on the websites of insurance companies sometimes envisage a greater detail to allow increased customization, which may in certain cases produce a risk quotation partially deviating from that provided by price aggregator websites. To this effect, *see* IVASS, "*Investigation into comparison websites in the Italian insurance market,*" available online at www.ivass.it, p. 9.
1112. In general, the data entry part of the process is considered straightforward. *See* Financial Conduct Authority, "*Price comparison website: Consumer market research,*" London (2014) p. 9.
1113. *See* IVASS, "*Investigation into comparison websites in the Italian insurance market,*" pp. 9 and 11.

The submission of the risk profiling form generates a flow of information between the price aggregator website and a number of contracted insurance companies.[1114,1115] This is generally done through a Web service platform connecting the price aggregator website and such insurance companies which allows data exchange in real time. The information entered in the risk profiling form is forwarded to insurance companies, which—in turn—provide a quotation for an insurance contract through predetermined formats.[1116]

Once the quotations of insurance companies have been acquired, the comparison process envisages the publication of a ranking of those received within a certain timing,[1117] in ascending price order and generally distinguished by the logo of the relevant insurance company, but sometimes also identified in a manner not referring to a specific insurance company.[1118,1119] The timing limit is generally set by the aggregators based on the maximum waiting time which is considered acceptable for potential customers to the extent that, beyond a certain waiting time, the rate of withdrawal of

1114. Partnership agreements with contracted insurance companies generally define the scope of the website, consisting in the presentation of the products insurance companies intend to propose for comparison, and regulate the remuneration methods, broken down by type of insurance contract, and varying according to the insurance company concerned. To this effect, IVASS, "*Investigation into comparison websites in the Italian insurance market,*" p. 12. In this respect, it should also be noted that EIOPA recommended a proper disclosure of insurance companies with whom a comparison website has a commercial, contractual or ownership relationship. *See* EIOPA, "*Report of Good Practices on Comparison Websites,*" Document EIOPA-CCPFI-13/100, pp. 13-14.

1115. Some price aggregator websites also publish quotations of insurance companies with which no partnership agreements are in place by a using a computer software technique (referred to as Web scraping or Web spidering) which allows to "*hack*" online estimation systems of insurance companies and to obtain their offers by simulating the access by fictitious users. This is generally aimed at extending the comparison so as to include additional insurance products in order to widen—as much as possible—the market coverage of the service offered and—thus—increasing their appeal among users vis-à-vis other competitors. To this effect, *see* IVASS, "*Investigation into comparison websites in the Italian insurance market,*" p. 10.

1116. *See* IVASS, "*Investigation into comparison websites in the Italian insurance market,*" pp. 10-11.

1117. It is important to note that the ranking may concern only the basic insurance coverage or also add-on products and features which provide potential customers with additional cover options not incorporated within the standard contract. Usually, the potential customer has the option of selecting between the standard contract and such add-ons. Nonetheless, practical evidence has proven that—even where the potential customer selects the basic insurance coverage only—the output contains heterogeneous insurance products, some of which are consistent with the selection, while others also contain non-requested cover options. To this effect, *see* IVASS, "*Investigation into comparison websites in the Italian insurance market,*" p. 10 and Financial Conduct Authority, "*Price comparison website: Consumer market research,*" pp. 9-10. In this respect, it should also be noted that EIOPA recommended a clear disclosure of ranking criteria and product features. *See* EIOPA, "*Report of Good Practices on Comparison Websites,*" Document EIOPA-CCPFI-13/100, pp. 14-15.

1118. *See* IVASS, "*Investigation into comparison websites in the Italian insurance market,*" pp. 10-11.

1119. In order to display the quotations in the output according to the profile set by the potential customer, a creation of interfaced technical systems may be authorized between the price aggregator engine and the Web systems of insurance companies concerned. To this effect, IVASS, "*Investigation into comparison websites in the Italian insurance market,*" p. 12.

potential customers increases. As such, tight timing rewards insurance companies with advanced technological infrastructures capable of providing timely quotations.[1120]

When evaluating the ranking, the potential customer may save the quotations by choosing one of them. At any rate, even in the absence of a selection, price aggregator websites generally send an e-mail to the potential customer with saved quotations or at least the most convenient ones, so that the potential customer may proceed with the purchase at a later time.[1121] In fact, depending on the applicable laws and regulations, the quotations obtained through the price aggregator website can be binding for a certain period of time or until a new pricing is issued by the relevant insurance company.[1122] However, in order to entice potential customers, insurance companies can also offer discounted quotations if the payment is made within stringent deadlines and/or with specific methods (e.g., credit card or PayPal).[1123]

After choosing the most suitable product, in the case of traditional insurance companies, customers are invited to the closest agency for the conclusion of the insurance contract.[1124] However, more often, in the case of insurance companies carrying out online business, customers are generally redirected to the website of the relevant insurance company where the insurance contract may be finalized through an online payment.[1125] More sophisticated price aggregator websites instead offer the Web user the possibility to directly close a contract at the end of the process.[1126]

4.3.1.3 Remuneration

Most price aggregators do not charge consumers directly but generate revenues through other means. In fact, the remuneration model of price aggregator websites is generally based on charges applied to contracted insurance companies. Such charges may take different formats. First, contracted insurance companies may be charged a fixed subscription fee for the right to be listed on the price aggregator website. Second, price aggregator websites may apply click-through fees, whereby insurance companies are charged based on clicks, actions and/or transactions being successfully executed.[1127]

1120. *See* IVASS, "*Investigation into comparison websites in the Italian insurance market*," pp. 10-11.

1121. It should be noted that few customers feel sufficiently confident to go ahead and make a purchase decision during the research session. *See* Financial Conduct Authority, "*Price comparison website: Consumer market research*," p. 13.

1122. In this respect, EIOPA recommended the publication of up-to-date information and a disclosure of the latest update before the search for products is initiated. *See* EIOPA, "*Report of Good Practices on Comparison Websites*," Document EIOPA-CCPFI-13/100, p. 16.

1123. *See* IVASS, "*Investigation into comparison websites in the Italian insurance market*," pp. 10-11.

1124. In some instances, the potential customer may also be re-directed to the website of an insurance agent.

1125. *See* IVASS, "*Investigation into comparison websites in the Italian insurance market*," pp. 10-11.

1126. *See*—among others—EIOPA, "*Report of Good Practices on Comparison Websites*," Document EIOPA-CCPFI-13/100, p. 10.

1127. *See* Europe Economics, "*Distribution Channels in Insurance*," p. 40.

Usually, price aggregator websites also charge commissions to contracted insurance companies upon renewal of insurance contracts. In general, such commissions—which are intended to remunerate the commitment of price aggregator websites not to make direct marketing, i.e., not to require policyholders close to contractual maturity to make a new price comparison—are lower than that applied at the time of the original purchase.[1128]

Lastly, price aggregator websites may also leverage on their ability to attract visitors and charge fees on other companies wishing to place advertising bans on the website. Alternatively, they may also be used as a gateway to other non-insurance websites (for which a link is provided) in exchange for fees or sell information gathered on consumer preferences to insurance companies or other interested parties.[1129]

4.3.1.4 Fact Pattern

The present analysis takes into consideration foreign insurance companies that conclude partnership agreements with owners of price aggregator websites to list their products on such websites for the purposes of marketing, promoting and distributing such products in the source country. In doing so, it is also assumed that the website owners are established in the source country.

4.3.2 Permanent Establishment Implications

4.3.2.1 Analysis under the OECD Model

4.3.2.1.1 The Standard Version

In the business model under analysis, the critical issue is whether Art. 5, para. 5, of the OECD Model may apply to deem the website owner who operates the price aggregator website to constitute a dependent agent permanent establishment of foreign insurance companies whose contracts are ranked on the price aggregator website.[1130]

The website owner running the price aggregator website—who is generally an insurance intermediary—may be regarded as a "*person*" pursuant to Art. 3 of the OECD Model. Moreover, the activities carried on in the source country (namely, sales and distribution of insurance products) are interrelated to operations that constitute the business proper of an insurance company which may exceed preparatory or auxiliary activities dealt with under Art. 5, para. 4, of the OECD Model. In carrying on such activities, the website owner is generally subject to the terms and conditions agreed upon in the partnership agreements and follows marketing strategies frequently

1128. *See* IVASS, "*Investigation into comparison websites in the Italian insurance market,*" p. 12.
1129. *See* Europe Economics, "*Distribution Channels in Insurance,*" p. 40.
1130. The price aggregator website and the server hosting the price aggregator website are disregarded to the extent that they cannot be regarded as persons under Art. 3 of the OECD Model. The ISP operating the server on which the price aggregator website is hosted is disregarded to the extent that it does not fulfill neither the traditional test regarding the conclusion of contracts nor the supplementary test regarding the principal role leading to the conclusion of contracts. For further comments, *see* s. 4.2.2.2.1 above.

discussed with insurance companies in regular meetings.[1131] Therefore, under such circumstances, one cannot exclude that a website owner may be acting *"on behalf of"* foreign insurance companies.[1132] As a consequence, in order to assess whether a dependent agent permanent establishment may be deemed to exist, it is crucial to consider whether an owner of a price aggregator website concludes contracts binding on foreign insurance companies or plays the principal role leading to the conclusion of contracts that are routinely concluded without material modifications by foreign insurance companies.

The answer to such a question mainly depends on the functioning of the price aggregator website. In this perspective, it should be borne in mind that potential customers are generally required to submit a pre-purchasing questionnaire to be completed in order to filter sales according to products which suit the answers given. Therefore, such mapping questions are a key part of ensuring potential customers be able to make an informed decision on which product is best suited for their needs.[1133] On the basis of this, the price aggregator website collects and lists a number of (binding or non-binding) quotations with a comparison of the terms and conditions of different insurance products and the potential customer has the possibility to select a certain number of insurance products in light of their pricing and features, which are generally established by contracted insurance companies.

Insofar as the potential customer is presented with non-binding quotations and subsequently redirected to an insurance agent or to the relevant insurance company for the purposes of enabling the potential customer to purchase an insurance product,[1134] it may be argued that the website owner does not fulfill neither the traditional test regarding the conclusion of contracts nor the supplementary test regarding the principal role leading to the conclusion of contracts. In fact, on the one hand, as long as the insurance company has the power, and does exercise that power, to change the terms and conditions of the quotation or reject the quotation in a later stage, the foreign insurance company retains the power to conclude contracts. On the other hand, assuming that the activities carried on in the source country are limited to the marketing and promotion of insurance products, the supplementary test is not fulfilled.

Conversely, in the event that the potential customer is presented with binding quotations, so that foreign insurance companies are bound to the terms and conditions reported therein, it can be argued that the website owner is collecting offers to enter

1131. The degree of detail and control as to the conduct of the business in the source country clearly depends on the bargaining power of each party in the negotiation.

1132. To the contrary, due to the lack of any written or verbal agreement, it may be argued that a website owner is not acting *"on behalf of"* foreign insurance companies in the case of a recourse to the Web scraping technique.

1133. The mapping of the question set is signed off by insurance companies. However, on a few occasions, the mapping has been changed by price aggregators. To this effect, *see* ABI, "*The ABI's response to the FCA's review of Price Comparison Websites—March 2014*," available online at https://www.abi.org.uk, p. 3.

1134. Circumstances where an insurance agent may give rise to a dependent agent permanent establishment will be addressed in the s. 4.7 below. Circumstances where direct online business may give rise to a dependent agent permanent establishment have already been addressed in s. 4.2 above.

into standardized contracts and foreign insurance companies are bound to accept such offers in a later stage, regardless of the fact that the contract is formally concluded through an insurance agent or directly with the relevant insurance company itself. As a result, in such a case, the traditional test regarding the conclusion of contracts is fulfilled.

Also, in the event that a potential customer is able to directly conclude an insurance contract through a "*point and click*" interface on the price aggregator website at the end of the comparison process,[1135] it may be argued that the owner of such a website is accepting an offer to enter into a standardized contract through interactive, but pre-programmed, decision software that instructs the server on which the price aggregator website is hosted to generate the electronic impulse containing the signal of acceptance. As a consequence, it is fair to say that, in such a case, the traditional test regarding the conclusion of contracts is also fulfilled.

Additional permanent establishment concerns may also arise in the case of sophisticated price comparison websites, which offer additional services, such as the acquisition of precontractual information on behalf of the contracted insurance companies, specific customer pre- or after-sale assistance services and so forth. In such a case, even though the traditional test regarding the conclusion of contracts is not fulfilled, the question as to whether such activities go beyond mere marketing and promotional activities in such a way as to trigger the supplementary test regarding the principal role leading to the conclusion of such contracts should be assessed on a case-by-case basis in light of the applicable factual circumstances.

In the above situations, assuming that potential customers can regularly access price aggregator websites, the habitual exercise test is likely to be fulfilled to the effect that a dependent agent permanent establishment may in principle arise. Nevertheless, it is important to note that—as a general rule—website owners constitute agents of an independent status, as also evidenced by the fact that a price aggregator website provides information on insurance products offered by a variety of insurance companies. This conclusion could also hold true in a situation where a website owner running price aggregator websites is funded by one or more foreign insurance companies[1136] so long as the website owner remains independent from the funding insurance companies and acts in the ordinary course of its business.[1137] In such a peculiar case, however, it should be recalled that the changes introduced in the aftermath of the BEPS Project

1135. For further comments on the online conclusion of insurance contracts, *see* s. 4.2.2.2.1 above.

1136. This should be intended as the situation where insurance companies provide funds or participate in the capital of website owners in a way other than the payment of fees and commissions in consideration for services. This is for instance the case of some UK and US price aggregator websites. To this effect, *see* Europe Economics, "*Distribution Channels in Insurance,*" p. 41 and Accenture, "*Coming to Terms with Insurance Aggregators: Global lessons for carriers,*" p. 8.

1137. For instance, some factors to be considered in determining the status of such a website owner may be related to the market coverage in the price comparison or a difference in treatment between insurance products, such as an advice to pick up specific insurance products or the granting of special discounts on specific insurance products to the users of a price aggregator website. For further details on such critical issues for potential customers, *see* IVASS, "*Investigation into comparison websites in the Italian insurance market,*" pp. 13 et seq.

now provide for a supplementary test regarding related parties, thereby restricting the application of the independent agent provision.[1138] Therefore, a careful assessment should be carried out on a case-by-case basis in light of the applicable factual circumstances.

4.3.2.1.2 *The Special Clause for Insurance Agents*

Should a DTA contain a special clause for insurance agents along the lines of para. 114 of the OECD Model Commentary on Art. 5, it should be ascertained whether the website owner that does not otherwise give rise to a dependent agent permanent establishment under the standard version of the OECD Model could be caught under this clause.[1139]

In particular, the special clause for insurance agents is likely to catch owners of websites that provide an interface through which a potential customer is able to directly conclude an insurance contract at the end of the comparison process and/or websites that do not offer such an interface, but nevertheless provide customers with binding quotations, administrative services, and/or services otherwise going beyond marketing and information purposes, irrespective of whether such website owners can be regarded as agents of an independent status acting in the ordinary course of their business.

Differently, as long as—after the publication of a ranking with an overview of the pricing and the main features of insurance contracts on the price aggregator website—the potential customer is generally required to contact an insurance agent or the relevant insurance company for the purposes of submitting an offer to enter into an insurance contract as well as for the administration and/or the performance of such contracts, there are good grounds to argue that the outcome of the research on the price aggregator website does not directly result in itself in the collection of premiums and/or the insurance of risks in the source country. In fact, at this stage, there is no insurance contract in place and—therefore—no actual collection of premiums and/or insurance of risks takes place at this point of the purchasing process.

4.3.2.2 ***Analysis under the UN Model***

Within the framework of the UN Model, it should be ascertained whether (*i*) the website owner or (*ii*) the ISP owning and operating the server on which the price aggregator website is hosted may give rise to a permanent establishment in the source country.[1140]

1138. *See* s. 3.3.2.4.4 above.

1139. The price aggregator website and the server are disregarded to the extent that they cannot be regarded as persons under Art. 3 of the OECD Model. For further comments, *see* s. 4.2.2.2.1 above. The ISP operating the server is disregarded to the extent that it cannot be regarded as an agent for the purposes of the special clause. For further comments, *see* s. 4.2.2.2.2 above.

1140. The price aggregator website and the server are disregarded to the extent that they cannot be regarded as persons under Art. 3 of the UN Model.

Under Art. 5, para. 5, let. (*a*), of the UN Model, the website owner may in principle give rise to a dependent agent permanent establishment in the case that the customer can directly conclude an insurance contract on the price aggregator website at the end of the comparison process. This is also the case where the customer is presented with binding quotations, whereas cases in which the price aggregator website offers pre- or after-sale services going beyond marketing and information purposes should be assessed on a case-by-case basis to ascertain whether the supplementary test regarding the principal role leading to the conclusion of contracts is fulfilled.

In addition to this, the website owner is likely to fall within the scope of the insurance agent provision in the case that the price aggregator website provides customers with administrative services, including the collection of insurance premiums. Under the same circumstances, the insurance agent provision is also likely to catch ISPs in the source country that own and operate the server on which the price aggregator website is hosted. In fact, insofar as they provide and maintain the equipment, ISPs may be regarded as persons through which premiums are collected and/or risks are insured within the meaning of the insurance agent provision.

Nevertheless, foreign insurance companies can obviate source taxation in the case that the ISP operating the server on which the website is hosted and/or the website owner running the price aggregator website can be regarded as independent agents acting in the ordinary course of their business insomuch as no permanent establishment fiction for independent persons has been introduced in the UN Model. As already outlined above,[1141] this should generally be the case even where such website owners are funded by foreign insurance companies, provided that the supplementary independence test regarding related parties is not triggered.

4.4 OTHER ONLINE MODELS

4.4.1 General Overview

4.4.1.1 Introduction

The following sections are intended to provide a brief overview of a few additional business models developed in order to market, promote and distribute insurance products online.[1142]

4.4.1.2 Ancillary Insurance Coverage

While making online purchases, customers often seek ancillary insurance coverage. For instance, insurance coverage can be bought while booking flight tickets and/or holidays through the websites and/or mobile applications of the relevant service providers (such as online travel operators). In fact, besides their core services, such

1141. *See* s. 4.3.2.1.1 above.

1142. New business model patterns not centered about the distribution of insurance products are beyond the scope of this research.

providers generally offer a number of other ancillary services, including insurance coverage. In general, ancillaries come in two flavors: unbundled, which refers to add-ons that were previously included in a core product offering (such as baggage and in-flight meals for airlines), and incremental or travel-related products, such as ground transportation, tours, activities and travel insurance products.[1143]

As a general rule, in order to offer such insurance coverage, online service providers stipulate with selected insurance companies:[1144] (*i*) a collective insurance contract and (*ii*) a distribution agreement governing the distribution of the relevant insurance products and the collection of the premiums from the customers in consideration for a commission. Moving from this framework, online service providers grant the end users wishing to take out insurance the opportunity to select the relevant insurance products through a *"point and click"* interface during the checkout process at the online point of sale. On the basis of this, the end users will be entitled to the insurance coverage specified in the terms and conditions of the collective insurance contract in consideration for the payment of a premium to the insurance company and a commission to the online service provider at the end of the online purchasing process.

4.4.1.3 Sharing Economy Platforms

The sharing economy is based on the concept that customers may have access to, rather than ownership of, tangible and intangible assets.[1145] On the basis of this concept, some companies have developed digital platforms (for instance, transportation network platforms like Uber or Bla Bla Car and holiday rental platforms like Airbnb) in order to connect demand and supply of share capacity dynamically in real-time much easier than ever before.[1146]

Besides hosting services in order to connect end users, such online connecting platforms also offer a number of other connected services. For instance, such online connecting platforms can include review or ratings facilities, payment facilities, insurance, identity verification or even provide the underlying service that is being offered to the users.[1147] In particular, over the recent years, the rise of the sharing economy has paved the way for the creation of new types of insurance products. For instance, those who sell services in such online marketplaces could need liability cover

1143. *See* Oliver Wyman, "The Ancillaries Challenge in Online Travel Booking," *Transport & Logistics* (2016) p. 1.
1144. This is for instance the case of Europ Assistance and Allianz Global Assistance, which specialize in travel insurance products.
1145. The term *"collaborative economy"* is often used interchangeably.
1146. For further comments with respect to tax policy issues of the sharing economy, *see* European Economic and Social Committee, *"Taxation of the collaborative economy—analysis of possible tax policies faced with the growth of the collaborative economy,"* ECO/434—EESC—2017.
1147. To this effect, *see* EU Commission, *"A European agenda for the collaborative economy,"* COM(2016) 356 final, p. 8. For further comments on this topic, *see also* Tamara Gasparri, "Nuove regole per la sharing economy," *Il Fisco* (2016) pp. 4123 et seq., Giorgio Beretta, "The European Agenda for the Collaborative Economy and Taxation," *European Taxation* (2016) pp. 400 et seq. and Giorgio Beretta, "The Taxation of the 'Sharing Economy'," *Bulletin for International Taxation* (2016).

for buyers. On the other hand, service-users might like to be covered in the case of negligence rather than having to go through possibly cumbersome redress processes or the expense and aggravation of a legal action. Therefore, companies operating such online connecting platforms often partner with insurance companies to provide insurance coverage to their customers.[1148]

In order to do so, such companies generally stipulate cumulative insurance contracts with selected insurance companies for the benefit of the end users that grant the latter entitlement to the insurance coverage specified in the terms and conditions of the cumulative contracts.[1149] In such a case, in contrast to the ancillary insurance coverage referred to in the previous section,[1150] the end users are generally not required to specifically select the insurance coverage when transacting online. As a matter of fact, the insurance coverage is a built-in feature of the underlying service that is being offered to the end users, so that the latter are intrinsically covered by the cumulative insurance contracts stipulated between the companies operating the online connecting platforms and the insurance companies with no additional charge or premium payment to the relevant insurance company.[1151]

4.4.1.4 Cross-Selling of Insurance

Some start-up companies also focus on cross-selling opportunities. Among others,[1152] Simplesurance designs, develops and provides cross-selling software solutions for e-commerce that integrate into the checkout process of online shops and allow customers to purchase insurance products.[1153] In order to do so, the user is generally redirected to the Simplesurance website, where insurance can be bought by going through a number of steps. In particular, the user is required to select an insurance product to place into the shopping cart. After doing so, the user will automatically get to the order summary page. Here, the user can once more view the selected insurance contract and all the necessary references to the terms and conditions. If the user wishes to take out the selected insurance, he/she is required to choose the preferred payment method. On the order summary page, the user is required to click on the payment button and will be forwarded to the payment process. At that point, by clicking on the button "*Place order now,*" he/she is sending through the offer. After successful payment, the user will get to the order confirmation page, where he/she will be shown

1148. *See* Deloitte, "*Insurance disrupted: General insurance in a connected world,*" p. 11.
1149. This is for instance the case of Bla Bla Car, which stipulated a cumulative insurance contract with Axa, and Airbnb, which stipulated cumulative insurance contracts with syndicates in the Lloyd's market and Zurich.
1150. *See* s. 4.4.1.4 above.
1151. As a general rule, such insurance covers coexist with homeowners insurance or car insurance contracts stipulated by the users.
1152. Other insurance cross-selling start-ups include Picsure, Kasko, Virado and Pablow. To this effect, *see* University of St. Gallen, "*The Current InsurTech Landscape: Business Models and Disruptive Potential,*" p. 50.
1153. Simplesurance has concluded an investment and distribution agreement with Allianz Group.

the product information as well as the terms, conditions and information regarding the right of withdrawal.[1154]

4.4.1.5 *Peer-to-Peer Insurance*

A number of start-up companies are making use of social media platforms for the purposes of creating new business models and new ways for consumers to purchase insurance. For instance, social media platforms facilitate peer-to-peer insurance schemes where insurance customers may form online groups to share risk. In a broker model,[1155] the first part of the process is generally similar to that of a price aggregator website, with the end user that can conclude a contract with one of the contracted insurance companies through a "*point and click*" interface on the peer-to-peer platform.[1156] Once the insurance contract has been concluded, the customer can—through the functionalities offered on the peer-to-peer platform—create a group with other customers who bought the same type of insurance.[1157] When the group has reached a minimum size, the group will be constituted and each member will begin to share their own risk with the other members. Once a group has been created, members of such a group pay a portion of their premium into a mutual pool, whereas the balance of their premium is paid to the contracted insurance companies. If no claims are submitted, members of the group can get (partially) refunded at the end of the period of insurance. On the contrary, in the case that claims occur, the refund decreases for each member of the group. Most notably, small claims are settled with the money available in the pool, whereas—in the case of bigger claims—the relevant insurance company covers any amount that exceeds the threshold covered with the mutual pool.[1158]

More recently, the insurance model has also arisen. The insurance model is similar to the broker model except that as the peer-to-peer provider is the actual insurance company. This is for instance the case of Lemonade in the US, which is essentially a digital insurance company. However, in contrast to traditional insurance companies, its business model is based on charity donations and a fee-based revenue mechanism.[1159] In particular, after the customer purchases Lemonade insurance, Lemonade takes a 20% fee out of customer payments for the expenses of running the insurance business, liaises with reinsurance companies to cover major risks and

---

1154. *See* Simplesurance, "*What We Do,*" available online at https://www.simplesurance.com.
1155. In such a model, adopted for instance by Friendsurance in Germany, Inspeer in France and Darwinsurance in Italy, the peer-to-peer provider generally charges brokerage commissions to insurance companies and administration fees to group members.
1156. Such schemes are distinct from group insurance where individuals collectively purchase insurance. *See* Swiss Re, "*Digital distribution in insurance: a quiet revolution,*" Sigma No. 2/2014, p. 10.
1157. Alternatively, customers can join already existing groups.
1158. *See* Accenture, "*The Digital Insurer: Unleashing the Potential of Social Media in Insurance,*" available online at www.accenture.com, p. 7, Deloitte, "*Insurance disrupted: General insurance in a connected world,*" p. 9 and Swiss Re, "*Digital distribution in insurance: a quiet revolution,*" Sigma No. 2/2014, p. 10.
1159. *See* University of St. Gallen, "*The Current InsurTech Landscape: Business Models and Disruptive Potential,*" p. 51.

returns unclaimed remainders as a giveback to charity projects chosen by the customers.[1160]

Other start-ups make use of social media platforms to target underserved insurance markets. In such a case, a so-called social broker identifies customer segments with poorly served insurance needs based on their activity on social media and other online behavior, groups customers with similar needs and negotiates insurance on behalf of groups. In particular, once groups have been created, a social broker negotiates with selected insurance companies to obtain deals for its customers in consideration for a commission to be paid by insurance companies as sales are made.[1161] For instance, Bought by Many in the UK is a social broker which manages a website that can be used to join a group of people, with similar insurance needs, to obtain discounted premiums and/or improved policy terms from selected insurance companies. On the other hand, Bought by Many does not assist in the administration and performance of insurance contracts and does not perform any obligations under any insurance contract. In fact, the insurance contract—and all communications and correspondence leading up to it and during the period of insurance—is entirely between customers and the relevant insurance company.[1162]

4.4.1.6 On-Demand Insurance

Instead of protecting everything at any time, on-demand insurance products can allow customers to cover specific risks at particular moments. In this segment, a number of start-up companies have recently created specific websites and/or mobile applications through which customers can switch their coverage on and off.[1163] Among others, Trov,[1164] Sure[1165] and Slice[1166] have developed software to allow customers to purchase products of selected insurance companies and submit insurance claims,[1167] either through their websites and/or their specific mobile applications.[1168] In order to do so, the user is generally required to create a personal account and provide his/her personal information. When the user has created an account and is logged in, he/she can obtain quotations for short-term insurance in accordance with the details he/she previously filled out, submit his/her offer through a "*point and click*" interface and proceed with

1160. *See* Lemonade, "*About Lemonade,*" available online at https://www.lemonade.com.
1161. *See* Accenture, "*The Digital Insurer: Unleashing the Potential of Social Media in Insurance,*" p. 7 and Deloitte, "*Insurance disrupted: General insurance in a connected world,*" p. 10.
1162. *See* Bought by Many, "*Terms of Website Use,*" available online at https://boughtbymany.com.
1163. *See* University of St. Gallen, "*The Current InsurTech Landscape: Business Models and Disruptive Potential,*" p. 52.
1164. Trov distributes insurance products for electronic items such as mobile phones, tables, laptops, cameras and so forth.
1165. Sure started with distributing micro-duration life insurance coverage during air travel, but now provides a much broader range of insurance products.
1166. Slice distributes homeshare insurance products to hosts using homeshare platforms like Airbnb, HomeAway, OneFineStay.
1167. Trov has concluded a distribution agreement with Axa Group, whereas Sure and Slice have in place distribution agreements with multiple insurance companies.
1168. Further companies offering on-demand insurance services are AppSichern, Cuvva and Metromile. *See* University of St. Gallen, "*The Current InsurTech Landscape: Business Models and Disruptive Potential,*" p. 52.

the payment of the insurance premium. After a successful payment, the user will be displayed all the relevant terms and conditions of the insurance contract. Such information will also be accessible through the personal account in a later stage. The personal account can also be used to submit a claim occurred during the period of insurance.

4.4.1.7 Fact Pattern

The scenario for the present analysis contemplates that foreign insurance companies market, promote and distribute insurance products through the above websites, mobile applications or virtual platforms in the source country, it being understood that the owners of such websites, applications or platforms are established in the source country.

4.4.2 Permanent Establishment Implications

4.4.2.1 Analysis under the OECD Model

4.4.2.1.1 The Standard Version

In the context of the business models depicted in the previous section, the question arises as to whether the owners of the above websites, applications or platforms may be deemed to constitute a dependent agent permanent establishment of foreign insurance companies.[1169]

The answer to such a question essentially depends on the specific business model concerned.[1170] To begin with, online service providers that manage websites offering ancillary insurance coverage as well as the owners of websites and/or mobile applications offering cross-selling opportunities and on-demand insurance may be regarded as persons according to Art. 3 of the OECD Model. The intermediation activities carried out in the source country relate to the operations constituting the business proper of an insurance company which can go beyond activities of a preparatory or auxiliary nature. In carrying on such activities, the above operators generally act "*on behalf of*" foreign insurance companies in compliance with the applicable distribution agreements. Consequently, it should be evaluated whether such intermediaries conclude contracts binding on foreign insurance companies or play the principal role leading to the conclusion of contracts that are routinely concluded without material modifications by foreign insurance companies.

In respect of websites offering ancillary insurance coverage, it should be noted that, when purchasing the underlying service, the end user can usually select the most

1169. The websites, applications and platforms as well as the servers hosting such websites, applications and platforms are disregarded to the extent that they cannot be regarded as persons under Art. 3 of the OECD Model. The ISP operating the servers on which such websites, applications and platforms are hosted is disregarded to the extent that it does not fulfill neither the traditional test regarding the conclusion of contracts nor the supplementary test regarding the principal role leading to the conclusion of contracts. For further comments, *see* s. 4.2.2.2.1 above.
1170. The business models under scrutiny have been outlined in ss. 4.4.1.2-4.4.1.6 above.

suitable insurance coverage through a "*point and click*" interface on the website of the online service provider. In such a case, once the purchasing process is finalized, the terms and conditions of the collective insurance contract stipulated between the online service provider and the contracted insurance company will apply to the end user as insured person and beneficiary. Given that the consent of the end user to opt for the ancillary insurance coverage is binding on the insurance company by virtue of the collective insurance contract concluded with the online service provider, there are good grounds to maintain that the traditional test regarding the conclusion of contracts is fulfilled.

Similarly, in the case of websites and/or mobile applications offering cross-selling opportunities and on-demand insurance, considering that the end user is generally able to directly conclude an insurance contract through a "*point and click*" interface on the relevant website and/or mobile application at the end of the purchasing process,[1171] it may be argued that the owner of such a website and/or mobile application is accepting an offer to enter into a standardized contract through interactive, but pre-programmed, decision software that instructs the relevant server to generate the electronic impulse containing the signal of acceptance. As a result, it is fair to say that the traditional test regarding the conclusion of binding contracts is also fulfilled.

Assuming that potential customers can regularly access such websites and/or mobile applications, the habitual exercise test is likely to be fulfilled to the effect that a dependent agent permanent establishment may in principle arise. Nonetheless, it is should be noted that the online service providers offering ancillary insurance coverage are generally commercial partners with no relation to the insurance companies. Hence, they typically constitute agents of an independent status, so that, insofar as they act in the ordinary course of their business, no dependent agent permanent establishment should arise in the source country. On a different note, owners of websites and/or mobile applications offering cross-selling opportunities and on-demand insurance are start-up companies, whose independence should be carefully assessed on a case-by-case basis. In fact, different contracting powers between start-ups and insurance companies could lead to unbalanced distribution agreements which might turn out in the start-ups being subject to detailed instructions and/or comprehensive control. On the top of this, in order to support their business development, partnered insurance companies may also hold a stake in the capital of such start-ups, so that the supplementary test regarding related parties could also be failed.

All the peer-to-peer operators are generally persons for the purposes of the OECD Model that can perform activities connected with operations constituting the business proper of an insurance company which may go beyond preparatory and auxiliary activities. Nevertheless, the mechanics of the operating model can affect the remaining elements to be considered when assessing the existence of a dependent agent permanent establishment.

1171. For further comments on the online conclusion of insurance contracts, *see* s. 4.2.2.2.1 above.

In the broker model, the creation of a group among peers presupposes a preliminary conclusion of an insurance contract. As such, customers are normally required to conclude an insurance contract with selected insurance companies in the first stage of the operating model. To this end, the owners of such peer-to-peer platforms conclude partnership agreements with a range of insurance companies which delineate the scope of their intermediation activities. For this reason, as with the owners of price aggregator websites,[1172] the owners of such peer-to-peer platforms are usually subject to the terms and conditions agreed upon in the partnership agreements and—thus—it cannot be denied that such peer-to-peer operators may be acting *"on behalf of"* foreign insurance companies. Also, the insurance contract is generally concluded through the virtual platform owned and managed by the peer-to-peer operator. As a result, like the owners of the websites and/or mobile applications dealt with above, the owners of such peer-to-peer platforms can—in principle—give rise to a dependent agent permanent establishment, provided that the habitual exercise test is also satisfied. Still, it should be determined whether, based on the applicable circumstances, such intermediaries that can be deemed as independent from insurance companies. Should this be the case, under the assumption that the owner of a specific platform acts in the ordinary course of its business, no dependent agent permanent establishment should arise in the source country.

The business framework is different in the insurance model. In such a case, as already pointed out above,[1173] the owner of the peer-to-peer platform is in fact the insurance company itself. It follows that the insurance contract is generally concluded through the peer-to-peer platform between the owner of such a platform and the customer. That being so, under the assumption that the owner of the peer-to-peer platform is established in the source country, no additional permanent establishment implications should arise.[1174]

In the social broker model, customers are instead required to join a group of peers with similar insurance needs or otherwise propose creating a new group of peers on the virtual platform. Once a group has been created, the social broker liaises with selected insurance companies to obtain discounted premiums and/or improved policy terms. It follows that the role of the social broker is to group customers with similar needs and negotiate—on behalf of them—discounts and/or improved terms with selected insurance companies by leveraging on the combined purchasing power. Moving from this, customers are generally redirected to the websites of the relevant insurance companies, where they can obtain quotations based on the terms and conditions negotiated by the social broker on their behalf and finalize the purchase of the most suitable insurance

1172. *See* s. 4.3.2.1.1 above.
1173. *See* s. 4.4.1.5 above.
1174. It should be noted that, in the case where the owner of the peer-to-peer platform is established in another country, such a business model would be comparable to a situation of an insurance company which manages a website offering a complete online sales functionality. Accordingly, as already pointed out in s. 4.2.2.2.1 above, a dependent agent permanent establishment may arise if the owner of the peer-to-peer platform avails of employees maintaining the platform in the source country.

product.[1175] In the light of the foregoing, it is fair to say that the social broker represents the interests of the customers. Hence, a social broker does not act on behalf of insurance companies to the effect that no dependent agent permanent establishment should arise.[1176]

The contractual framework is slightly different in the context of the sharing economy schemes. More to the point, companies owning and managing sharing economy platforms usually stipulate cumulative insurance contracts with insurance companies for the benefit of their final users (who are ultimately the insured persons and the beneficiaries). In doing so, as already outlined above,[1177] they offer the insurance coverage as a built-in feature of the underlying core service that is being provided to the final users. Accordingly, even though the subjective requirement and the criterion concerning the nature of the activities performed in the source country are generally fulfilled, such companies do not act as intermediaries on behalf of foreign insurance companies with a view to distribute insurance products to their users through virtual platforms in consideration for a commission. Rather, it is fair to say that they represent the interests of their final users to the effect that no dependent agent permanent establishment should arise.

4.4.2.1.2 The Special Clause for Insurance Agents

With respect to DTAs that contain a special clause for insurance agents patterned after para. 114 of the OECD Model Commentary on Art. 5, it should be ascertained whether any owners of websites, applications and/or platforms that do not otherwise give rise to a dependent agent permanent establishment under the standard version of the OECD Model could fall within the scope of this special clause.[1178]

This can be the case of online service providers that manage websites offering ancillary insurance coverage as well as owners of websites and/or mobile applications offering cross-selling opportunities and on-demand insurance which in principle fulfill the conditions set forth under Art. 5, para. 5, of the OECD Model, but are nevertheless covered under the independent agent provision. As a matter of fact, for the purposes of the special clause, such providers/owners can be clearly regarded as insurance distributors through which foreign insurance companies can collect premiums and/or—at the very least—insure risks in the source country. As a result, such providers/owners can give rise to a permanent establishment, regardless of whether they are or not independent from the relevant insurance company.

1175. Circumstances where direct online business may give rise to a dependent agent permanent establishment have already been addressed in s. 4.2 above.

1176. Circumstances where insurance brokers may give rise to a dependent agent permanent establishment will be addressed in the s. 4.6 below.

1177. *See* s. 4.4.1.3 above.

1178. The websites, applications and platforms as well as the servers hosting such websites, applications and platforms are disregarded to the extent that they cannot be regarded as persons under Art. 3 of the OECD Model. For further comments, *see* s. 4.2.2.2.1 above. The ISP operating the server on which such websites, applications and platforms are hosted is disregarded to the extent that it cannot be regarded as an agent for the purposes of the special clause. For further comments, *see* s. 4.2.2.2.2 above.

In the context of peer-to-peer schemes, the existence of a permanent establishment mainly depends on the specific pattern adopted. In the case of the broker model, the owner of the peer-to-peer platform is likely to fulfill the conditions laid down in the special clause for insurance agents, irrespective of whether it is or not independent. On the other hand, where the owner of the peer-to-peer platform is the insurance company itself, no additional permanent establishment implications should arise.[1179] At last, in the social broker model, the question arises as to whether the owner of the platform may be regarded as an agent of foreign insurance companies for the purposes of the special clause. According to the author, considering that, once a group has been created, the end user is generally redirected to the relevant insurance companies for all the following steps of the purchasing and performance process, it is fair to say that a social broker normally represents the interests of the end users and does not act as an agent of the foreign insurance companies, unless it is engaged in activities related to the administration and performance and insurance contracts (e.g., the collection of premiums, the fulfillment and so forth). As a result, owners of platforms adopting the social broker model not engaged in such activities do not generally give rise to permanent establishment concerns in the source country under the special rule for insurance agents.

In a similar vein, companies owning and managing sharing economy platforms do not operate as insurance distributors on behalf of insurance companies for the purposes of the special clause for insurance agents. As a consequence, the above companies cannot be regarded as agents of foreign insurance companies to the effect that they do not give rise to permanent establishments under the special rule.

4.4.2.2 *Analysis under the UN Model*

In the context of the UN Model, it should be ascertained whether (*i*) the owners of the websites, applications or platforms or (*ii*) the ISPs owning and operating the servers on which such websites, applications or platforms are hosted may give rise to a permanent establishment in the source country.[1180]

Under Art. 5, para. 5, let. (*a*), of the UN Model, a dependent agent permanent establishment may in principle arise with respect to owners of websites offering ancillary insurance coverage. The same also remains true with respect to owners of websites and/or mobile applications offering cross-selling opportunities and on-demand insurance. By the same token, owners of peer-to-peer platforms adopting the broker model can also give rise to a dependent agent permanent establishment.

Owners of peer-to-peer platforms adopting the social broker model and companies owning and managing sharing economy platforms qualify as persons for the purposes of the insurance agent provision, but do not generally perform activities that trigger such a provision. Also, where the owner of the peer-to-peer platform is the

1179. See s. 4.2.2.2 above.

1180. The websites, applications and platforms as well as the servers hosting such websites, applications and platforms are disregarded to the extent that they cannot be regarded as persons under Art. 3 of the UN Model.

insurance company itself, no additional permanent establishment implications should arise.[1181] On the other hand, the insurance agent provision is likely to catch ISPs in the source country that own and operate servers on which such websites, applications or platforms are hosted in the case where the website, the application or the platform provides customers with administrative services, including the fulfillment and/or the collection of insurance premiums. Indeed, insofar as they provide and maintain the equipment, ISPs may be regarded as persons through which premiums are collected and/or risks are insured within the meaning of the insurance agent provision.

At any rate, foreign insurance companies can still obviate source taxation in the event that the owners of the websites, applications or platforms and the ISPs owning and operating the servers on which such websites, applications or platforms are hosted can be regarded as independent agents acting in the ordinary course of their business. In general, this carve-out is applicable to ISPs and owners of websites offering ancillary insurance coverage. Differently, the application of this carve-out to owners of websites and/or mobile applications offering cross-selling opportunities, on-demand insurance and peer-to-peer platforms adopting the broker model should be carefully assessed on the basis of the applicable factual circumstances, also considering the supplementary independence test regarding related parties.

4.5 OTHER DISTANCE SELLING MEANS

4.5.1 General Overview

4.5.1.1 Introduction

Distance sales are sales where the parties are not physically present negotiating at the same place but, instead, communicate, negotiate, and reach an agreement through some technical telecommunication means. To put it in other terms, a distance contract may be basically defined as one where the supplier uses one or more means of distance communication up to and including the time at which the contract is concluded.[1182] In addition to the Internet,[1183] such distance selling means also include mail, e-mail, (tele)fax, telephone and/or a combination thereof. With this in mind, the following sections are intended to provide a brief overview of a few other distance selling means—particularly the telephone, the mail and e-mail—used to distribute insurance products.[1184]

1181. *See* s. 4.2.2.2 above.

1182. To this effect, *see* Pierpaolo Marano/Ioannis Rokas/Peter Kochenburger, *The "Dematerialized" Insurance—Distance Selling and Cyber Risks from an International Perspective*, p. 155.

1183. The direct business over the Internet has already been dealt with in s. 4.2 above.

1184. This section is intended to deal with the use of distance selling means by insurance companies to directly distribute insurance products without the involvement of intermediaries. The use of distance selling means by insurance intermediaries in the context of indirect schemes will be instead dealt with in the following sections.

4.5.1.2 The Telephone

The telephone has become a powerful means for the achievement of a range of purposes in the field of retail financial services. At its simplest, it can act as a means of prospecting for potential new customers. At its complex, it can provide a fully functional service. In between these two extremes sits the use of the telephone as a highly successful means of product distribution,[1185] especially for simple insurance products, such as motor insurance products.[1186,1187]

Telephone-based distribution is often managed through call centers (also referred to as contact centers), which may be defined as organizational units whose task is to enable a service-oriented dialogue with customers and interested callers through modern information technologies.[1188] The purpose of the call center is in fact to provide end-to-end service without having to connect the customer to other units within the insurance company.[1189] On the one hand, the call center may be employed to answer calls (so-called incoming or inbound calls). In such a case, the prospective customer makes the call, usually in response to an advertisement giving a toll-free telephone number. On the other hand, the call center may be used to make calls (so-called outgoing or outbound calls). Such outgoing calls may simply be the return of a previous incoming call or may be a proactive pursuit to contact prospects by initiating the telephone contact (also referred to as cold calling).[1190]

The tasks performed through a call center range from general consulting and guidance on insurance needs to the receipt of applications and claims. In its basic form, the call center can provide prospects with general product information. More often, however, call center operators guide prospects in the selection of the most suitable insurance product for a subsequent conclusion of a contract through other means.[1191] In more sophisticated call centers, operators can also accept offers to enter into standardized insurance contracts at the end of the telephone conversation, subject to notification duties to be fulfilled with this form of contractual commitment which

1185. *See* Christine Ennew/Nigel Waite, *Financial Services Marketing: An International Guide to Principles and Practice—Second Edition* (Abingdon: Routledge, 2013) p. 353.

1186. *See* Fabrizio Santoboni in: Fabrizio Santoboni (ed.) *Manuale di gestione assicurativa*, p. 318, Luigi Farenga, *Diritto delle Assicurazioni Private*, p. 89 and Luigi Farenga, *Manuale di Diritto delle Assicurazioni Private* (Torino: Giappichelli, 2016) p. 139.

1187. Research has shown that approximately 9% of customers used the telephone to purchase or renew insurance in recent years and anticipated that such percentage will remain buoyant in the near future. To this effect, *see* Capgemini, "*World Insurance Report 2016*," available online at www.capgemini.com, p. 15.

1188. A number of insurance groups has also established dedicated to telephone-based distribution. *See* Fabrizio Santoboni in: Fabrizio Santoboni (ed.) *Manuale di gestione assicurativa*, pp. 318-319. This is for instance the case of Genertel, Genertellife, Direct Line, Genialloyd.

1189. *See* Matthias Graumann/Hans-Jürgen Arnold/Nicole Beltjes, "Call Centers: A Case Study on the Interplay Between Organization and Information Technology," *The Geneva Papers on Risk and Insurance* (2003) pp. 111-112.

1190. *See* Christine Ennew/Nigel Waite, *Financial Services Marketing: An International Guide to Principles and Practice—Second Edition*, p. 353 and Geoff Lancaster/Lester Massingham, *Essential of Marketing Management* (Abingdon: Routledge, 2010) p. 340.

1191. *See* s. 4.5.1.4 below for a combination with other distance selling means.

mainly vary according to the applicable regulatory provisions.[1192] In line with the rules governing the formation of an insurance contract,[1193] the conclusion of a contract on the phone requires a valid exchange of an offer put forward by the caller and an acceptance by the call center operator. It follows that a preliminary discussion on the terms and conditions of the contract cannot be construed as a conclusion of a valid contract. For instance, a lawful insurance contract is not concluded in the case that the caller has simply asked for product information and/or guidance. By the same token, a lawful insurance contract is not concluded in the event that the telephone call is followed by a subsequent exchange of correspondence to provide the prospect with a written application form and additional information regarding the applicable terms and conditions of the contract in such a way so as to consider the previous phone contact as a preliminary discussion.[1194,1195]

In the case of contracts concluded over the phone, the caller has direct and immediate knowledge about the acceptance over the telephone wire and/or network. This implies that, where the conclusion of the insurance contract requires the insurance company to communicate the acceptance, the place of conclusion should be regarded as the place where the caller is at the time he/she makes/receives the call.[1196]

Once a valid insurance contract has been concluded, the operators of more sophisticated call centers can also be involved in subsequent activities, like the administration of a contract (for instance, the preparation and delivery of the insurance policy to the customer) and the performance of a contract (such as the receipt and management of claims).

4.5.1.3 Direct Mail or E-Mail

Another direct distribution method is the direct mail.[1197] Typically, this involves mailing a letter of introduction, marketing materials and information sheets which mainly vary according to the applicable regulatory provisions,[1198] along with a blank application form, to customers with whom the insurance company has an already existing relationship.[1199] This is often followed up by a reminder letter, post card or

1192. For further comments on the regulatory regime applicable to distance sales, *see* Pierpaolo Marano/Ioannis Rokas/Peter Kochenburger, *The "Dematerialized" Insurance—Distance Selling and Cyber Risks from an International Perspective*, pp. 44 et seq. and 155 et seq. As for Italy, *see also* Claudia Bortolani in: Marco Prosperetti/Alessandro Colavolpe (eds.) *I gestori del risparmio non bancari e i canali di distribuzione*, pp. 456 et seq.
1193. The formation of distance contracts follows general rules governing insurance contracts. For further comments, *see* s. 3.3.2.3.4 above.
1194. *See* Marco Rossetti, *Il diritto delle assicurazioni—Volume 1*, p. 917 and footnotes cited therein.
1195. *See* s. 4.5.1.4 below for a combination with other distance selling means.
1196. *See* Marco Rossetti, *Il diritto delle assicurazioni—Volume 1*, pp. 916-917 and footnotes cited therein.
1197. Typically, this method is suitable for simple insurance products, like motor vehicle insurance.
1198. Depending on the applicable laws and regulations, the quotations reported therein could be binding or non-binding.
1199. In the context of this distribution method, a major driver for success is targeting and segmentation. In fact, it can be very expensive to simply send the offer to all existing customers of the insurance company. For further comments on the market segmentation, *see*

simply a replication of the mail pack a few weeks later. In its basic form,[1200] the customer can return the written application form in a prepaid envelope generally provided in the mail pack previously sent. In doing so, the customer is filing with the relevant insurance company an offer to enter into a standardized insurance contract. In the case that such an offer is accepted, the insurance company will send the policy to the home address of the customer. It follows that, where the conclusion of the insurance contract requires the insurance company to communicate the acceptance to the customer, the place of conclusion should be regarded as the home address of the customer.[1201]

A slight variation on the direct mail method is the use of the e-mail correspondence. In such a case, the above documents are sent in electronic form to the e-mail address of the customers. In its basic form,[1202] after filling in the application form with his/her personal details, the customer can file an offer to conclude an insurance contract by responding to the previous e-mail correspondence. In the case that the offer is accepted, the insurance company will send the policy to the e-mail address of the customer. In such a case, where the conclusion of the insurance contract requires the insurance company to communicate the acceptance to the customer, it has been submitted that the acceptance should be regarded as received by the customer when the e-mail containing the message of acceptance is available on the server of his/her e-mail service provider.[1203]

4.5.1.4 Other Variations

Insurance companies can combine a direct mail/e-mail with a following outbound call. In such a case, the documents sent via mail/e-mail are generally simpler and anticipate that a call center operator will later make a call. In particular, after allowing enough time for the customer to go through the documents, an outbound call is made in order to discuss the above documents in more details. Although the type of outbound call varies, in most cases a valid insurance contract can be concluded over the phone on the spot through the acceptance of an offer submitted by the customer at the end of the call.[1204]

On the other hand, a preliminary telephone contact can be combined with other means of distance selling. Among others, the telephone call may be followed up with

---

Festus Epetimehin, "Market Segmentation as a Strategy for Goal Attainment in the Insurance Industry," *SSRN Electronic Journal* (2011) pp. 4 et seq.

1200. *See* s. 4.5.1.4 below for a combination with other distance selling means.
1201. *See* Marco Rossetti, *Il diritto delle assicurazioni—Volume 1*, p. 916.
1202. *See* s. 4.5.1.4 below for a combination with other distance selling means.
1203. The different view that the acceptance should be regarded as received by the customer when downloaded does not appear to be convincing to the extent that (*i*) it makes the communication subject to the behavior of the customer and (*ii*) it could lead to opportunities for *mala fide* behavior by the customer in order not to conclude the contract. To this effect, *see* Marco Rossetti, *Il diritto delle assicurazioni—Volume 1*, p. 916 and Federico Azzarri, "La conclusione di contratti telematici nel diritto privato europeo," *I Contratti* (2010) pp. 301 et seq.
1204. *See* Institute of Actuaries of Australia, "*Are direct channels helping life insurers and customers to address underinsurance?*," available at https://actuaries.asn.au, p. 5.

a subsequent mail/e-mail to provide the prospect with additional information regarding the applicable terms and conditions, together with an application form. Upon receipt of such documents, the customer can fill in the application form with his/her personal details and return it via mail/e-mail with a view to filing his/her offer to enter into an insurance contract with the relevant insurance company.

The telephone and direct mail/e-mail correspondence may also be used in combination with other channels. For instance, such means can be used in combination with marketing campaigns on magazines, newspapers and other media like radio and television. In such a case, marketing campaigns are aimed at enticing prospects to contact the relevant insurance company through a call center and/or a direct mail/e-mail correspondence. On the other hand, after an initial contact through the telephone and/or a direct mail/e-mail correspondence, potential customers can also be redirected to the website of the insurance company and/or to insurance representatives for the application process.[1205,1206]

4.5.1.5 Fact Pattern

For the purposes of analyzing the present business model(s), it is supposed that foreign insurance companies market, promote and distribute insurance products through distance selling means (e.g., mail, e-mail, (tele)fax, telephone and/or a combination thereof) in the source country. This analysis is focused on the source country to the effect that the assessment of whether the means under scrutiny could give rise to a permanent establishment in a third country is beyond its scope.

4.5.2 Permanent Establishment Implications

4.5.2.1 Analysis under the OECD Model

4.5.2.1.1 The Standard Version

First of all, it is important to note that—in the source country—the issue of a dependent agent permanent establishment can only arise in respect of cases where insurance contracts are concluded as a consequence of sales and distribution activities carried on through a person therein. In fact, in order to fulfill the requirements to have a dependent agent permanent establishment, there must be a person carrying on business activities in the source country.[1207] As a result, distance sales activities carried out by means of a collection of insurance offers through the telephone, the fax, the mail, the e-mail and the like from abroad cannot be regarded as activities giving rise to

1205. *See* Institute of Actuaries of Australia, "*Are direct channels helping life insurers and customers to address underinsurance?*," pp. 5-6.
1206. Circumstances where direct online business may give rise to a permanent establishment have already been addressed in s. 4.2 above, whereas circumstances where insurance representatives may give rise to a permanent establishment will be addressed in s. 4.7 below.
1207. *See* s. 3.3.2.3.2 above.

a dependent agent permanent establishment in the source country.[1208,1209] Indeed, even though such distance sales activities result in the conclusion of insurance contracts, the only relevant connection with the source country is the local service provider (i.e., the telephone company, the postal courier, the ISP running the e-mail server and the e-mail service provider, as the case may be). In general, such service providers merely supply their postal/(tele)communication services (i.e., the use of a telephone line, the receipt and dispatch of letters, the use of the e-mail server and the receipt and dispatch of e-mails, as the case may be) and most certainly do neither meet the traditional test regarding the conclusion of contracts nor the supplementary test regarding the principal role leading to the conclusion of contracts.[1210] On the top of this, such service providers are generally independent from foreign insurance companies.[1211]

Against this backdrop, it is crucial to ascertain whether foreign insurance companies have engaged employees in the source country in order to manage a call center and/or a mail/e-mail service center or otherwise outsourced such activities to local service providers.[1212] Indeed, an employee and/or a service provider may be clearly regarded as a "*person*" pursuant to Art. 3 of the OECD Model. Furthermore, in such a case, the activities carried on in the source country on behalf of foreign insurance companies (namely, sales and distribution of insurance products) relate to operations which constitute the business proper of an insurance company which may exceed the activities referred to under Art. 5, para. 4, of the OECD Model. Accordingly, it should be assessed whether such persons can fulfill the traditional test regarding the conclusion of binding contracts and/or the supplementary test regarding the principal role leading to the conclusion of such contracts.

To begin with, a dependent agent permanent establishment may arise where employees and/or local service providers sitting in a call center in the source country can accept offers to enter into standardized insurance contracts at the end of the

1208. In a similar vein, *see* Valentina Perrone/Gabriele Sepio, *Dialoghi Tributari*, (2013) pp. 666 et seq.

1209. Interestingly enough, in *Dell Spain*, a part of the Spanish market was serviced through a call center of Dell Ireland located in France, the service in respect of which was provided by the French subsidiary of Dell. For further comments, *see* Adolfo J. Martín Jiménez, *Bulletin for International Taxation*, (2016) pp. 462-643 and Francisco Antonio Vaquer Ferrer, *Intertax*, (2016) p. 680. However, given the confusion of activities between the companies involved, the related dispute mainly concerned the attribution of profits to the Spanish permanent establishment of Dell Ireland. In fact, there was a high degree of confusion in the activities of Dell Ireland, Dell Spain and Dell France, so that sales derived in Spain by Dell France have been included in the tax base of the Spanish permanent establishment of Dell Ireland. In the light of this, according to the author, no specific suggestions may be derived with respect to the existence of a dependent agent permanent establishment in the case of distance sales through a call center established in a country other than the source country.

1210. In a similar vein, *see* Arthur Pleijsier, *Intertax*, (2001) p. 227 and Arthur Pleijsier, *The agency permanent establishment: de vaste vertegenwoordiger: proefschrift*, pp. 217-218.

1211. For further comments on ISPs operating a server on which a website is hosted, *see also* s. 4.2.2.2.1 above.

1212. From a regulatory perspective, insurance companies are generally accountable for their activities.

telephone conversation. By the same token, a dependent agent permanent establishment can also arise in the case that employees and/or local service providers sitting in a mail/e-mail service center in the source country can accept offers to enter into standardized insurance contracts submitted through application forms sent via mail/e-mail.[1213,1214] In fact, in such cases, the test regarding the conclusion of binding contracts is clearly fulfilled.

Similarly, according to the author, the traditional test regarding the conclusion of binding contracts could also be fulfilled in the event that employees and/or local service providers operating in a mail/e-mail service center in the source country collect offers to enter into standardized insurance contracts submitted through application forms with terms and conditions that are binding on the foreign insurance company or otherwise not subject to a following genuine review of the foreign insurance company.

In addition, in the case that such employees and/or local service providers collect offers to enter into standardized insurance contracts submitted through application forms with terms and conditions that, although subject to a following review, are not materially modified by the foreign insurance company, there are good grounds to maintain that the supplementary test regarding the principal role leading to the conclusion of contracts is fulfilled. Furthermore, this supplementary test could also be fulfilled where call center operators provide specific guidance to prospective customers in the selection of the most suitable insurance product in view of a subsequent formal conclusion of the insurance contract through other means.

Should any of the above tests be met, assuming that the activities carried out through the call center and/or the mail/e-mail service center also fulfill the habitual exercise test for a dependent agent permanent establishment to exist, it remains to be assessed whether the call center and/or mail/e-mail service center operators may be regarded as agents of an independent status operating in the ordinary course of their business. Clearly, this cannot be the case of internal call center or mail/e-mail service center operators, who are generally employed either by the foreign insurance company or by a dedicated local subsidiary thereof and thus are subject to control and detailed instructions. Therefore, in such a case, the foreign insurance company is likely to have

1213. This also applies to the combination of a direct mail/email with a following outbound call aimed at concluding the insurance contract over the phone and the combination of an outbound call followed by a mail/e-mail correspondence through which the customer files his/her application form.

1214. In this respect, it is interesting to note that Danish domestic law provides for a specific departure from Art. 5 of the OECD Model to the effect that distance selling by an agent that concludes contracts which are binding on a non-resident person does not create a permanent establishment, provided that the agent is not an employee of the principal. This deviation was adopted in the light of the difficult in interpreting Art. 5 of the OECD Model and in order to promote Denmark as a location for international call centers. Such a rule does not however impact the Danish interpretation of DTAs. To this effect, *see* Niels E. Jensen, "Denmark Permanent Establishment and Fiscal Representatives," *Tax Planning International* (1997) pp. 20-21 and Jens Wittendorff, "Agency Permanent Establishments and the Zimmer Case," *International Transfer Pricing Journal* (2010) pp. 361-362.

a dependent agent permanent establishment in the source country. Conversely, the independence of external call center or mail/e-mail service operators should be assessed on a case-by-case basis in the light of the applicable factual circumstances.

Differently, it may be argued that activities carried out in the source country only for marketing and information purposes should not give rise to permanent establishment concerns. This is for instance the case of employees and/or local service providers running a call center or a mail/e-mail service center in the source country whose activities are limited to the provision of general product information to potential customers.[1215] In addition, this also holds true in the case where the provision of general product information through the telephone and direct mail/e-mail correspondence is combined with marketing campaigns on magazines, newspapers and other media like radio and television. For example, no dependent agent permanent establishment arises in the case that foreign insurance companies engage a local service provider to distribute marketing materials in the source country.[1216] As a matter of fact, in such a case, the local service provider does not fulfill neither the traditional test regarding the conclusion of contracts nor the supplementary test regarding the principal role leading to the conclusion of contracts. And more than that, such a service provider is generally independent from foreign insurance companies.[1217]

4.5.2.1.2 The Special Clause for Insurance Agents

In a situation where the relevant DTA contains a special clause for insurance agents along the lines of para. 114 of the OECD Model Commentary on Art. 5, it is to be ascertained whether any call center and/or a mail/e-mail service center operators in the source country that do not otherwise create a dependent agent permanent establishment under the standard version of the OECD Model could be caught under this clause.

According to the author, this can be the case of local service providers sitting in a call center and/or a mail/e-mail service center that in principle fulfill the conditions set forth under Art. 5, para. 5, of the OECD Model, but are nevertheless covered under the independent agent provision. Indeed, such operators can be clearly regarded as

1215. In a similar vein, *see* Matthias Geurts, "Server as a permanent establishment?," *Intertax* (2000) pp. 174-175.
1216. To this effect, *see* Valentina Perrone/Gabriele Sepio, *Dialoghi Tributari,* (2013) pp. 666 et seq.
1217. In this respect, it is worth noting that Perrone is of the opinion that permanent establishment concerns may arise in the case where the local service provider is not an independent person or where such marketing activities are carried out through a local subsidiary under the control of the foreign company. To this effect, *see* Valentina Perrone/Gabriele Sepio, *Dialoghi Tributari,* (2013) pp. 666 et seq. Nevertheless, according to the author, in the case of mere marketing activities, the existence of a dependent agent permanent establishment should be excluded having regard to the fact that local service providers do not fulfill neither the traditional test regarding the conclusion of contracts nor the supplementary test regarding the principal role leading to the conclusion of contracts rather than to their independence from foreign entities. Clearly, in the case that such local service providers carry on activities that go beyond mere marketing activities, the question as to whether such examples may give rise to dependent agent permanent establishments should be assessed on a case-by-case basis in the light of the applicable factual circumstances.

insurance distributors through which foreign insurance companies insure risks in the source country. Hence, any such local service providers can give rise to a permanent establishment, irrespective of whether they are or not independent from the relevant insurance company.

A permanent establishment can also arise in the event that the requirements of the dependent agent provision are not satisfied. Most notably, the special clause for insurance agents can be triggered in the case of employees and/or local service providers that collect offers in the source country subject to a final genuine review of the insurance company, even where such a review results in material modifications.

In addition, the special clause for insurance agents could also cover situations where a call center and/or a mail/e-mail service center operator in the source country is involved in activities related to the administration and the performance of insurance contracts, including the preparation and delivery of insurance policies as well as the receipt and management of claims. As a matter of fact, such activities are likely to trigger the criterion regarding the insurance of risks in the source country, so that a permanent establishment is deemed to arise, regardless of whether the operator is or not independent from the relevant insurance company.

On the other hand, the special clause for insurance agents should not be triggered insofar as a call center and/or the mail/e-mail service center in the source country is only involved in mere marketing and promotional activities, such as the provision of general product information alone and/or in combination with marketing campaigns on magazines, newspapers and other media like radio and television. In fact, in such circumstances, the activities of the employees and/or the local service providers do not directly result in the actual collection of insurance premiums or insurance of risks in the source country.

4.5.2.2 Analysis under the UN Model

Like the OECD Model, under the UN Model, it should be ascertained whether foreign insurance companies have engaged employees and/or local service providers in order to run a call center and/or a mail/e-mail service center in the source country.[1218]

1218. In this respect, it should be noted that call centers and/or mail/e-mail service centers may also be established in a (third) country other than the source country and that of establishment. Should this be the case, a permanent establishment may accordingly arise in such a third country. An interesting case was touched upon in the Indian Circular Letter No. 1/2004, where the Indian tax authorities dealt with the attribution of profits to Indian permanent establishments. The Indian tax authorities tried to clarify different rules for such attribution of profits distinguishing between core and incidental services. Interestingly enough, as an example of Indian permanent establishments performing incidental services, the Indian tax authorities mentioned a (potentially triangular) case of a foreign insurance company insuring risks in countries other than India that appoints or sets up a call center in India to attend to calls from customers outside India regarding acquisition of new insurance contracts or revision of existing contracts, to disseminate relevant information and accept insurance offers from the customers, while actual policy issuance as well as collection of premium is done outside India by the foreign insurance company. At any rate, Circular Letter No. 1/2004 was subject to widespread criticism in respect of the failure to set parameters to decide the nature of activities (i.e., core or incidental activities) and thus was soon withdrawn with Circular

Should this be the case, under Art. 5, para. 5, let. (*a*), of the UN Model, a dependent agent permanent establishment can in principle arise if such employees and/or local service providers can accept offers to enter into standardized insurance contracts submitted during a phone call and/or through application forms sent via mail/e-mail. The same also holds true in the case where employees and/or local service providers sitting in a mail/e-mail service center collect offers to enter into standardized insurance contracts that are: (*i*) binding on the foreign insurance company, (*ii*) not subject to a following genuine review, or (*iii*) even where such offers are subject to review, the latter review does not result in material modifications. Moreover, call center operators may give rise to a dependent agent permanent establishment if they provide specific guidance to prospects in the selection of the most suitable product in view of a subsequent formal conclusion of the contract through other means.

On the top of this, the insurance agent provision can also cover residual circumstances under which the employees and/or local service providers collect offers to enter into standardized insurance contracts, albeit such offers are subject to review and such a review results in material modifications. Furthermore, the insurance agent provision is also likely to catch employees and/or local service providers that are involved in activities related to the administration and the performance of insurance contracts.

In all the above cases, it should however be recalled that foreign insurance companies may still prevent source taxation in the case that the call center or mail/e-mail service center operators may be regarded as independent agents acting in the ordinary course of their business. To this end, the independence of external call center or mail/e-mail service center operators should be assessed on a case-by-case basis in the light of the applicable factual circumstances. Differently, employees running internal call centers or mail/e-mail service centers cannot be regarded as independent from the foreign insurance company. Hence, in such a case, the latter company is likely to have a permanent establishment in the source country.

At last, it may be argued that activities carried on for mere promotional and advertising purposes should not give rise to permanent establishment issues. In fact, in such a case, employees and/or external providers engaged to perform such activities either from abroad or in the source country do not generally fulfill the conditions laid down in Art. 5, para. 5, let. (*a*), of the UN Model. In addition, under such circumstances, no actual collection of premiums or insurance of risks takes place in the source country through such persons to the effect that the insurance agent provision enshrined under Art. 5, para. 6, of the UN Model is not triggered.

Letter No. 5/2004. For further comments, *see* Vasudha J. Mehta, "*CBDT's BPO Circular—Creating Confusion?*," accessible online at http://www.algindia.com/publication/article1400.pdf.

4.6 INSURANCE BROKERS

4.6.1 General Overview

4.6.1.1 Introduction

Insurance brokers[1219] are insurance intermediaries that find their origin in the English insurance market.[1220,1221] An insurance broker may be regarded as "*an individual or business firm, with some degree of independence from the insurer, which stands between the buyer and the seller of insurance.*"[1222] Typically, insurance brokers represent the interests of the policyholders in the choice of insurance products by providing them with information and advice in respect of their insurance needs.[1223,1224]

1219. Among the largest insurance brokers worldwide are Marsh & McLennan, Aon and Willis Tower Watson.

1220. For further comments on the historical development of insurance brokerage activities in the English market, *see* Emanuela Giacobbe, *Brokeraggio e tipo contrattuale* (Milano: Giuffrè, 2001) pp. 18 et seq. and Stanley D. Chapman, "A History of Insurance Broking" in: Roderick Clews (ed.) *A Textbook of Insurance Broking* (Cambridge: Woodhead-Faulkner, 1980) pp. 1 et seq.

1221. In Italy, in Middle Ages, some insurance intermediaries ("*sensali*" or "*mezzani di sicurtà*") played a role similar to that of a broker. However, over the following centuries, such persons left the way for insurance companies with large networks of insurance agents. *See* Emanuela Giacobbe, *Brokeraggio e tipo contrattuale*, pp. 5 et seq., Luigi Cicchitti, *Il broker di assicurazione e di riassicurazione—Diritti e doveri—Quid facti, quid iuris* (Milano: Giuffrè, 2005) pp. 1-3 and Ettore Pedicini, *Il broker di assicurazioni* (Milano: Giuffrè, 1998) pp. 9-13. Modern insurance brokers first appeared in Italy in the 1970s as a development of multi-firm agents working for different insurance companies. *See*—among others—Luciano Casali, *L'agente e il broker di assicurazione* (Milano: Giuffrè, 1993) pp. 429 et seq., Giuseppe Giudici, *I canali della distribuzione assicurativa*, pp. 56-57 and Emanuela Giacobbe, *Brokeraggio e tipo contrattuale*, pp. 107 et seq. Similar insurance intermediaries also emerged in other European countries (for instance, the "*courtier d'assurances*" in France, the "*courtier*" in Belgium and the "*Versicherungsmakler*" in Germany). *See—inter alia*—Emanuela Giacobbe, *Brokeraggio e tipo contrattuale*, pp. 49 et seq., Jacques Deschamps, *L'Agent Général d'Assurances* (Paris: Litec Droit, 1975) p. 16 and Wilhelm Lührs, *A. Atermann (vorm. J. A. Castendyk) Assekuranz-Makler, 1837—1962* (Bremen: Self-publishing, 1962), pp. 29 et seq.

1222. To this effect, *see* Peter Maas, "How insurance brokers create value: a functional approach," *University of St. Gallen—Working Papers on Risk Management and Insurance* (2006) p. 4 and J. David Cummins/Neil A. Doherty, "The Economics of Insurance Intermediaries," *Wharton School, University of Pennsylvania* (2005), available online at http://www.insurancejournal.com/downloads/WhartonStudy_2005.05.20.pdf, pp. 5-6.

1223. For this reason, the term "*insurance broker*" describes someone who is normally the agent of the customer. To this effect, *see*—among others—Alan Teale, "Insurance Brokers and the Law of Agency" in: Roderick Clews (ed.) *A Textbook of Insurance Broking* (Cambridge: Woodhead-Faulkner, 1980) p. 21 and National Insurance Brokers Association of Australia (NIBA), "*Australia in the Asian Century—Country Strategies,*" available online at https://www.niba.com.au/resource/130531_Australia_in_the_Asian_Century_Submission.pdf, p. 2. In this respect, *see also* World Federation of Insurance Intermediaries (WFII), "*The Role of Insurance Intermediaries,*" available online at https://www.ciab.com/uploadedfiles/resources/roleofinsint.pdf, p. 3, Vincenzo Ferrari, *Nuovi profili di diritto delle assicurazioni—Il fatto assicurativo* (Milano: Giuffrè, 2003) p. 74, Filippo Romeo, "Il broker di assicurazione" in: Guido Alpa (ed.) *Le Assicurazioni private* (Torino: Utet Giuridica, 2006) p. 450, Ernesto Pucci, "L'attività di intermediazione assicurativa e riassicurativa e gli intermediari" in: Marco Prosperetti/Alessandro Colavolpe (eds.) *I gestori del risparmio non bancari e i canali di distribuzione* (Milano: Ipsoa, 2012) pp. 402-403, Giuseppe Giudici, *I canali della distribuzione assicurativa*, pp. 56-57, Marco Rossetti, *Il diritto delle assicurazioni—Volume 1*, p. 603 and Fabrizio Santoboni in: Fabrizio Santoboni (ed.) *Manuale di gestione assicurativa*, p. 305.

Hence, insurance brokers may be generally described as "*intermediaries who bring the parties together and match particular needs of policyholders with the products of insurers.*"[1225,1226]

There are distinctions among brokers depending upon the lines of insurance they intermediate, i.e., all lines of insurance, property and casualty or life/health coverage.[1227] There are also distinctions between "*retail brokers,*" i.e., brokers who deal directly with personal and/or commercial insurance buyers, and "*wholesale brokers,*" i.e., brokers that serve as intermediaries between retail brokers and certain specialized markets. For instance, wholesale brokers play an important role in placing business in the surplus lines market and in the London market, with Lloyd's and other London market insurance companies. In addition, "*reinsurance brokers*" play an important intermediation role between primary (retail) insurance companies, who sell insurance to individual and business customers, and reinsurance companies.[1228] In turn, reinsurance brokers may also be involved in the retrocession of risks by reinsurance companies.[1229]

4.6.1.2 Functions and Activities

The activities carried on in favor of customers are generally governed under a brokerage agreement.[1230] In particular, pursuant to this

1224. For further comments on the role of insurance brokers, *see*—among others—Peter Maas, *University of St. Gallen—Working Papers on Risk Management and Insurance,* (2006) pp. 5-6 and references cited therein, J. David Cummins/Neil A. Doherty, *Wharton School, University of Pennsylvania,* (2005) p. 5, Daniel F. Spulberg, *Market Microstructure: Intermediaries and the Theory of the Firm* (Cambridge: Cambridge University Press, 1999) pp. 329-332, Franklin Allen/Anthony M. Santomero, "The theory of financial intermediation," *Journal of Banking & Finance* (1998) pp. 1480-1482 and Franklin Allen/Anthony M. Santomero, "What do financial intermediaries do?," *Journal of Banking & Finance* (2001) p. 289.
1225. *See* Peter Maas, *University of St. Gallen—Working Papers on Risk Management and Insurance,* (2006) p. 5 and J. David Cummins/Neil A. Doherty, *Wharton School, University of Pennsylvania,* (2005) p. 6.
1226. As a result, the customer generally remains the policyholder in all its insurance contracts, with all the associated rights and responsibilities. As an exception to this, a broker might also be a party of a collective insurance contract stipulated with an insurance company in favor of its customers.
1227. *See* WFII, *The Role of Insurance Intermediaries*, p. 3.
1228. For further comments in relation to reinsurance brokers, *see* J. David Cummins/Neil A. Doherty, *Wharton School, University of Pennsylvania,* (2005) p. 6, Luigi Cicchitti, *Il broker di assicurazione e di riassicurazione—Diritti e doveri—Quid facti, quid iuris*, pp. 255-257, Roberto Moro Visconti, "L'attività di brokeraggio riassicurativo," *Impresa Commerciale Industriale* (2001) pp. 1520 et seq. and Andreas Schwepcke, *Reinsurance: Principles and State of the Art—A Guidebook for Home Learners—2nd Edition*, pp. 92 et seq.
1229. *See* WFII, *The Role of Insurance Intermediaries*, p. 3.
1230. In Italy, account taken of the wide range of services rendered to customers, a question is frequently discussed among scholars as to whether an insurance broker is to be regarded as a mediator, a professional rendering intellectual services or a provider of mixed services. For further comments, *see*—among others—Emanuela Giacobbe, *Brokeraggio e tipo contrattuale*, pp. 187 et seq., Luciano Gioberti, *Manuale del broker di assicurazione* (Milano: Irsa, 1998) pp. 23 et seq., Ettore Pedicini, *Il broker di assicurazioni*, pp. 59 et seq., Ernesto Pucci in: Marco Prosperetti/Alessandro Colavolpe (eds.) *I gestori del risparmio non bancari e i canali di distribuzione*, pp. 403-404, Diana Cerini, *Prodotti e servizi assicurativi—Distribuzione e*

agreement,[1231] insurance brokers traditionally provide their customers with a wide range of services which span the entire insurance purchasing process:[1232]

- risk and insurance analysis;
- assistance in predicting, managing and reducing risks;
- for larger corporations, assistance and advice on alternative risk transfer options, including captive insurance and other arrangements;
- assistance with selecting and arranging appropriate, tailor-made insurance contracts and packages;
- assistance in contacting and selecting insurance companies;
- assistance in negotiating premiums, terms and conditions of insurance contracts; and
- assistance in interpreting, arranging and completing contractual documentation.

Besides the support provided to customers during the purchasing process, brokers typically provide additional assistance with respect to the administration and performance of insurance contracts, both to customers and insurance companies. This includes the collection of premiums from customers, the delivery of insurance policies, the handling and resolution of claims. While the assistance in favor of customers generally fall within the scope of the brokerage agreements, the relationship between the insurance broker and the insurance company is normally regulated under a "*TOBA*," whose purpose is to set out the terms of business between the broker and the insurance company in order to regulate their dealings in respect of the insurance business introduced through the broker.[1233]

---

intermediazione, pp. 16-20, Filippo Romeo in: Guido Alpa (ed.) *Le Assicurazioni private*, pp. 443-542, Fabrizio Santoboni in: Fabrizio Santoboni (ed.) *Manuale di gestione assicurativa*, pp. 306-307 and Andrea Oriani, "Il contratto di brokeraggio assicurativo: qualificazione giuridica e risvolti applicative," *I contratti* (2010) pp. 265 et seq. In this context, the latest case law appears to lean toward a mixed nature of brokerage activities. To this effect, *see* Marco Rossetti, *Il diritto delle assicurazioni—Volume 1*, pp. 604-605.

1231. The contractual obligations can also be supplemented with legal duties based on applicable laws and regulations. For additional comments on duties imposed on Italian insurance brokers, *see* Marco Rossetti, *Il diritto delle assicurazioni—Volume 1*, pp. 609 et seq. and Antigono Donati/Giovanna Volpe Putzolu, *Manuale di Diritto delle Assicurazioni—Ottava Edizione Aggiornata*, pp. 104-105. For additional comments on duties imposed on US insurance brokers, *see* Douglas R. Richmond, "Insurance Agent and Broker Liability," *Tort Trial & Insurance Practice Law Journal* (2004) pp. 10 et seq.

1232. To this effect, *see* NIBA, *Australia in the Asian Century—Country Strategies*, p. 2, EY, "*Vision 2025: brokers driving customer-centric growth*," available online at www.ey.com, p. 56, Filippo Romeo in: Guido Alpa (ed.) *Le Assicurazioni private*, p. 450 and Ettore Pedicini, *Il broker di assicurazioni*, pp. 73-75.

1233. For further comments, *see*—among others—Luciano Casali, *L'agente e il broker di assicurazione*, pp. 436-437, Antigono Donati/Giovanna Volpe Putzolu, *Manuale di Diritto delle Assicurazioni—Ottava Edizione Aggiornata*, pp. 100-101, Filippo Romeo in: Guido Alpa (ed.) *Le Assicurazioni private*, pp. 453-455 and Ettore Pedicini, *Il broker di assicurazioni*, pp. 90-92.

Under the terms of such an agreement, the insurance broker is typically authorized to collect premiums from customers and pay such premiums (net of commissions)[1234] to the insurance company. Under the TOBA, the broker and the insurance company may also stipulate provisions with respect to roles and responsibilities regarding administrative activities, the handling and resolution of claims, and so forth. Hence, for such limited purposes, the insurance broker can also act as an agent of the insurance company.[1235]

Furthermore, over the recent years, fundamental changes in the market environment worldwide have also pushed brokers to provide additional services to both customers and insurance companies in the context of specific consulting engagements. In fact, insurance brokers can now be regarded as a valuable source of tailor-made consulting services for both customers and insurance companies.[1236]

On the one hand, insurance brokers have started providing additional consulting services to customers in the area of risk placement (such as price discovery, application processing and servicing), end-to-end risk management (such as identification, quantification and evaluation of risks, business continuity management, crisis management consulting, enterprise risk management, fraud risk services, provision of alternative risk transfer solutions and claims audit), advisory services (such as capital advisory and modeling, loss control advisory, claims consulting, benefits and HR consulting, administration of insurance captives, security and information management advisory) and other customized administrative services (such as data analytics solutions, technical accounting, benefits administration and claims administration settlements).[1237]

On the other hand, insurance brokers have also started leveraging on their technical expertise and market knowledge to provide additional support to insurance companies. Among others, this additional support includes integrated underwriting solutions (particularly, for standardized insurance products), catastrophe modeling, actuarial consulting, reserve risk analysis, valuation and data analytics solutions.[1238]

1234. For further comments regarding the commissions, *see* s. 4.6.1.3 below.

1235. Indeed, in such cases insurance brokers end up being agents of insurance companies. *See* NIBA, *Australia in the Asian Century—Country Strategies*, p. 2. As a result, in certain cases, an insurance broker can be a dual agent both for the insurance company and the customer, so that a case-specific factual determination is needed when attempting to classify intermediaries. To this effect, *see* Douglas R. Richmond, *Tort Trial & Insurance Practice Law Journal*, (2004) pp. 7-9.

1236. *See* EY, "*Vision 2025: brokers driving customer-centric growth*," pp. 56-57, Peter Maas, *University of St. Gallen—Working Papers on Risk Management and Insurance*, (2006) pp. 11-13 and PwC, "*Broking 2020: Leading from the front in a new era of risk*," available online at www.pwc.com, pp. *i-iii*.

1237. *See* EY, "*Vision 2025: brokers driving customer-centric growth*," p. 57, Peter Maas, *University of St. Gallen—Working Papers on Risk Management and Insurance*, (2006) p. 15 and PwC, "*Broking 2020: Leading from the front in a new era of risk*," p. *iii*.

1238. *See* EY, "*Vision 2025: brokers driving customer-centric growth*," p. 57.

4.6.1.3 *Remuneration*

Insurance brokers are typically remunerated with a fixed percentage of the premium paid on insurance contracts.[1239,1240] Such a fixed percentage may vary significantly by line of business.[1241] Business lines that are more complicated to underwrite, such as lines which are more information-intensive and more complex in terms of coverages and services required, tend to have higher commission percentages.[1242] Premium-based commissions are normally paid by insurance companies to insurance brokers upon the conclusion of insurance contracts stemming from intermediation activities carried out by them.[1243] However, insurance companies frequently incorporate such commissions in the insurance premiums charged to customers, so that the economic burden ultimately lies on customers.[1244] Plus, insurance brokers may also be eligible to receive contingent commissions, which are based on various performance criteria,[1245] such as the profitability of the business placed with an insurance company, persistency (i.e., the extent to which contracts are renewed with the insurance company), and/or the volume of business placed.[1246]

Moreover, many insurance brokers receive fee income from customers, commonly where a significant part of the risk management and risk transfer arranged takes place through alternative risk transfer techniques. Also, as already pointed out above,

1239. Such commissions are frequently labeled as premium-based commissions or direct commissions.
1240. More rarely, insurance brokers are remunerated with a fixed commission, regardless of the amount of the premium.
1241. In this respect, it should be noted that, as opposed to retail brokers, wholesale brokers and reinsurance brokers normally engage with other professional players in the insurance sector (namely, insurance and reinsurance companies). Hence, in such business segments, it is more difficult to articulate a general remuneration policy to the effect that fees and commissions are often negotiated on a transaction-by-transaction basis.
1242. *See* J. David Cummins/Neil A. Doherty, *Wharton School, University of Pennsylvania,* (2005) p. 14.
1243. The commissions are generally regulated under the TOBA stipulated between the insurance company and the insurance broker.
1244. It follows that insurance brokers are remunerated through premium-based commissions in the case that insurance companies and customers decide to enter into insurance contracts. In general, insurance brokers do not intervene in such a decision, so that their remuneration is subject to a decision made by contracting parties. For further comments, *see* Emanuela Giacobbe, *Brokeraggio e tipo contrattuale,* pp. 454 et seq., Luigi Cicchitti, *Il broker di assicurazione e di riassicurazione—Diritti e doveri—Quid facti, quid iuris,* pp. 11 et seq. and Ettore Pedicini, *Il broker di assicurazioni,* pp. 115-118.
1245. In this respect, it should be noted that, following some cases of collusion between insurance companies and insurance brokers, a number of countries has implemented a ban on any insurance company-paid commissions. However, according to some authors, any regulatory action geared toward a ban of commission payments to brokers is likely to be ineffective or even worse might unintentionally lead to adverse consequences. *See* Uwe Focht/Andreas Richter/Jörg Schiller, "Intermediation and (Mis-)Matching in Insurance Markets–Who Should Pay the Insurance Broker?," *The Journal of Risk and Insurance* (2013) pp. 345-346.
1246. On the top of this, in recognition of extra-performance, intermediaries may also receive non-cash compensation (such as travel and vacation awards) from insurance companies. *See* J. David Cummins/Neil A. Doherty, *Wharton School, University of Pennsylvania,* (2005) p. 16.

insurance brokers often provide additional services,[1247] such as risk modeling, risk management consulting, loss mitigation and claims management, which cannot be readily remunerated through a commission-based compensation. Hence, in such cases, insurance brokers and customers usually negotiate specific fees to compensate services rendered.[1248]

On the top of this, insurance brokers may also receive additional fees and commissions from insurance companies.[1249] In general, such fees and commissions are intended to compensate insurance brokers for additional consulting services rendered to insurance companies separately from their traditional insurance brokerage activities, such as advice on the development of their internal systems and processes.

4.6.1.4 Fact Pattern

The factual background for the present analysis is rather straightforward since it contemplates that foreign insurance companies make business in the source country through insurance brokers. In view of this, it is also assumed that the insurance brokers are established in the source country.

4.6.2 Permanent Establishment Implications

4.6.2.1 Analysis under the OECD Model

4.6.2.1.1 The Standard Version

An insurance broker—either an individual or a company—can be clearly regarded as a "*person*" under Art. 3 of the OECD Model. In addition to this, the activities carried on in the source country (namely, the intermediation in the context of insurance transactions) are undoubtedly connected with the operations that constitute the core business of an insurance company which may go beyond activities of a preparatory or auxiliary character described in Art. 5, para. 4, of the OECD Model.

Nonetheless, it is fair to say that traditional insurance brokers are intermediaries that usually represent the interests of customers providing them with a wide range of services for the purposes of taking out insurance pursuant to a brokerage agreement. In fact, over the course of the purchasing process, a traditional insurance broker does not generally act on behalf of foreign insurance companies, so that no dependent agent

1247. Such fee income tends to be most common among large brokers. Most medium to small brokers receive their compensation primarily through premium-based commissions. *See* J. David Cummins/Neil A. Doherty, *Wharton School, University of Pennsylvania*, (2005) p. 15.

1248. *See* J. David Cummins/Neil A. Doherty, *Wharton School, University of Pennsylvania*, (2005) p. 15.

1249. For some example of such additional forms of compensation, *see* for instance Aon Plc, "*Client Engagement and Compensation Guide (2014)*," available online at http://www.aon.com/attachments/risk-services/Aon-Client-Engagement-Guide.pdf, p. 5 and Wills Group Holdings, "*How We Get Paid (2014)*," available online at http://www.willis.com/documents/publications/General_Publications/How_We_Get_Paid.pdf, pp. 2-4.

permanent establishment arises in the source country.[1250] A similar conclusion can be also drawn in situations where more sophisticated brokers provide additional tailored services to customers pursuant to specific consulting agreements.[1251]

To some extent, it is also true that an insurance broker can act as an agent of the insurance company under a TOBA. At any rate, the activities carried out by a traditional broker on behalf of foreign insurance companies are generally very narrow in scope and concern obligations to be executed after the conclusion of insurance contracts (most importantly, the administration and the performance of insurance contracts). As a result, the author believes that such activities do not trigger neither the traditional test regarding the conclusion of contracts nor the supplementary test regarding the principal role leading to the conclusion of contracts. Accordingly, it may be concluded that a traditional insurance broker does not give rise to a dependent agent permanent establishment of a foreign insurance company.

The same also stands valid in the case where a broker provide additional support services to insurance companies governed under a specific consulting agreement.[1252] In fact, under such circumstances, the insurance broker may be regarded as a provider of customized services that supports the insurance company with a view to improving its internal systems and processes. As a result, this additional support does not trigger neither the traditional test regarding the conclusion of contracts nor the supplementary test regarding the principal role leading to the conclusion of contracts.

Conversely, permanent establishment concerns may arise if insurance brokers exceed the above brokerage and/or support activities. Among others, this could happen when insurance companies delegate underwriting authority to retail brokers (e.g., with respect to standardized insurance products). If this is the case, such retail brokers end up being agents of the insurance companies that can accept offers to enter into standardized contracts. As a result, under such circumstances, the traditional test regarding the conclusion of contracts is most likely fulfilled. If any such a broker has this delegated authority, and this authority is not limited to specific circumstances, the habitual exercise test is most probably met, so that all the relevant conditions for a dependent agent permanent establishment to exist under are likely to be fulfilled.

Should this be the case, it remains to be assessed whether an insurance broker may still be covered under the independent agent provision contained in Art. 5, para. 6, of the OECD Model. In this regard, it should be recalled that the activities of the specific broker under analysis ought to be tested against the activities of other insurance brokers.[1253] That being so, even where the relevant broker is independent from the foreign insurance company, it cannot be said that such a broker is acting in the ordinary course of its business. In fact, insofar as a traditional insurance broker does

1250. This also holds true in the case that a broker stipulates a collective insurance contract in favor of its customers. In fact, insomuch as such a broker represents the interests of its customers, this deviation does not change this reasoning.

1251. For some examples of additional consulting services provided to customers, *see* s. 4.6.1.2 above.

1252. For some examples of additional consulting services provided to insurance companies, *see* s. 4.6.1.2 above.

1253. For further comments, *see* s. 3.3.2.4.5 above.

not conclude contracts binding on foreign insurance companies, an insurance broker that does so is not acting in the ordinary course of its business. It follows that such an insurance broker cannot be covered under the independent agent provision to the effect that a dependent agent permanent establishment arises in the source country.

4.6.2.1.2 The Special Clause for Insurance Agents

A traditional insurance broker that does not otherwise create a dependent agent permanent establishment under the standard version of the OECD Model could fall within the scope of the special clause for insurance agents in the case that it is to be regarded as an agent through which a foreign insurance company collects premiums or insures risks in the source country.

This is typically the situation of a traditional insurance broker that represents the interests of customers during the purchasing process, but is authorized to collect premiums from customers and pay such premiums to the insurance company pursuant to specific terms of business stipulated with the insurance company. As a matter of fact, for such purposes, the broker can be regarded as an agent of the insurance company fulfilling the criterion regarding the collection of premiums. In a similar vein, this can also be the case of a broker that is involved in activities like the delivery of insurance policies to customers, claims handling and other activities related to the performance of contracts. Indeed, in such a case, the broker can be regarded as an agent of the insurance company fulfilling the criterion regarding the insurance of risks in the source country. As a result, under such circumstances, the broker can give rise to a permanent establishment of the relevant insurance company, irrespective of whether it is or not independent from such an insurance company.

On the contrary, a traditional broker that is not involved in the above activities for the benefit of an insurance company does not trigger the special clause for insurance agents since it cannot be regarded as an agent of the insurance company for any purpose whatsoever. By the same token, no permanent establishment arises in the circumstances where such a broker provides support to the insurance company in terms of consulting and/or process management applications. Indeed, under such circumstances, the broker does not act as an insurance distributor in favor of the foreign insurance company for the purposes of the special clause.

4.6.2.2 Analysis under the UN Model

Under the UN Model, it is fair to say that traditional insurance brokers in the source country do not generally give rise to a dependent agent permanent establishment. More to the point, even if such brokers could be regarded as acting on behalf of foreign insurance companies for certain activities, such activities are generally very limited in scope, so that neither the traditional test regarding the conclusion of contracts nor the supplementary test regarding the principal role leading to the conclusion of contracts should be triggered.

Traditional insurance brokers involved in activities related to the administration and the performance of insurance contracts (e.g., insurance brokers that collect premiums and/or deliver insurance policies) could in principle be caught under the insurance agent provision to the extent that such brokers may be regarded as persons fulfilling the test regarding the collection of premiums and/or the test regarding the insurance of risks, except where such activities are related to reinsurance contracts. Nevertheless, even under such circumstances, traditional insurance brokers can generally invoke the carve-out envisaged for independent agents, provided that all the relevant tests laid down in Art. 5, para. 7, of the UN Model are satisfied.

By way of contrast, the situation of insurance brokers in the source country that provide additional services to foreign insurance companies should be assessed more carefully in the light of the applicable factual circumstances. In this respect, it may be argued that additional support activities in terms of consulting and process management applications should not give rise to a permanent establishment since the conditions foreseen in Art. 5, para. 5, let. (*a*), of the UN Model are not satisfied. Differently, it may well be that additional activities exceeding traditional brokerage activities—such as the exercise of delegated underwriting authority in respect of standardized insurance contracts—could trigger the traditional test regarding the conclusion of contracts and/or the supplementary test regarding the principal role leading to the conclusion of contracts. Even where this is not the case, such additional activities are nevertheless likely to trigger the test regarding the insurance of risks laid down in Art. 5, para. 6, of the UN Model, save where such additional activities are related to reinsurance contracts.[1254] Should any of such tests be triggered, a dependent agent permanent establishment is very likely to arise in the source country, account taken that the independent agent provision enshrined in Art. 5, para. 7, of the UN Model is generally not applicable to the extent that the ordinary course of business test is most probably failed.

4.7 INSURANCE AGENTS

4.7.1 General Overview

4.7.1.1 Introduction

Insurance agents may be generally regarded as intermediaries that represent the interests of insurance companies in the development of insurance business and the management of the client portfolio in a specific area.[1255,1256] Despite this general

1254. As a result, reinsurance brokers involved in such additional activities should not give rise to a dependent agent permanent establishment under the UN Model.

1255. *See* Marco Rossetti, *Il diritto delle assicurazioni—Volume 1*, p. 532, Carlo Belluzzi, *Agenti brokers e altri ausiliari di assicurazione* (Milano: Sicurtà Libri, 1976) p. 18, Luciano Casali, *L'agente e il broker di assicurazione*, p. 16 and Jacques Deschamps, *L'Agent Général d'Assurances*, pp. 20-22.

1256. This section is focused on insurance agents representing insurance companies vis-à-vis final customers to the extent that insurance agents are generally not used in reinsurance transactions. To this effect, *see*—among others—Andreas Schwepcke, *Reinsurance: Principles and State of the Art—A Guidebook for Home Learners—2nd Edition*, p. 92.

definition, it should however be noted that the term "*agent*" is often used inconsistently even within the insurance industry, in part because of regulatory differences among countries.[1257]

For the present purposes, in an attempt to provide a rational classification of insurance agents, one should at first distinguish between external representatives and internal representatives. As a matter of fact, the former are self-employed professionals or businesses acting on behalf of insurance companies by virtue of agency agreements,[1258] while the latter are salaried insurance company employees authorized by the insurance company employing them to represent it in dealings with third parties in insurance matters on the basis of a (general or specific) power of attorney.[1259,1260] Most importantly, employee sales representatives are licensed insurance agents who sell products of the insurance company employing them through branch networks.[1261]

When speaking of external representatives, it is common to distinguish single-firm agents from multi-firm agents.[1262] On the one hand, a single-firm agent is an intermediary working primarily or exclusively for a single insurance company, who is identified and treated as an agent of the insurance company he represents.[1263] Single-firm agents are not employees of a particular insurance company, but have a contractual obligation to distribute the products of a single insurance company to the public.[1264] On the other hand, a multi-firm agent is instead an intermediary that stipulated agreements to distribute products of a (fixed) selection of insurance companies.[1265]

Insurance agents may also be distinguished based on the insurance products they sell. For instance, some agents specialize in health insurance. Other agents sell mostly health, life and disability policies (all of which arise from the same sector of the

1257. *See* Mark A. Hall, "The Role of Independent Agents in the Success of Health Insurance Market Reforms," *The Milbank Quarterly* (2000) p. 24.
1258. *See* Fabrizio Santoboni in: Fabrizio Santoboni (ed.) *Manuale di gestione assicurativa*, p. 299 and Ernesto Pucci in: Marco Prosperetti/Alessandro Colavolpe (eds.) *I gestori del risparmio non bancari e i canali di distribuzione*, pp. 398-399.
1259. *See* Douglas R. Richmond, *Tort Trial & Insurance Practice Law Journal*, (2004) p. 3.
1260. In Italy, such internal representatives are referred to as "*agenti in economia*." To this effect, *see* Marco Rossetti, *Il diritto delle assicurazioni—Volume 1*, pp. 538-540, Fabrizio Santoboni in: Fabrizio Santoboni (ed.) *Manuale di gestione assicurativa*, p. 299, Antigono Donati/Giovanna Volpe Putzolu, *Manuale di Diritto delle Assicurazioni—Ottava Edizione Aggiornata*, p. 94, Luciano Casali, *L'agente e il broker di assicurazione*, pp. 76-79, Consuelo Cinquanta, *Assicurazioni—Chi può distribuirle* (Genova: Casalini, 2001) p. 14 and Luciano Gioberti, *Manuale dell'agente di assicurazione* (Milano: Irsa, 1995) p. 26.
1261. Employees sales representatives are used in some Asian countries, including China and Korea. To this effect, *see* James I. Hilliard/Laureen Regan/Sharon Tennyson, "Insurance Distribution" in: Georges Dionne (ed.) *Handbook of Insurance* (New York: Springer Science + Business Media New York, 2013) p. 691.
1262. Single-firm agents are also described as exclusive agents or captive agents, while multi-firm agents are also described as non-exclusive agents or independent agents. However, the latter should not be confused with insurance brokers.
1263. *See* Douglas R. Richmond, *Tort Trial & Insurance Practice Law Journal*, (2004) p. 3.
1264. This channel is more common in Europe and in the US. To this effect, *see* James I. Hilliard/Laureen Regan/Sharon Tennyson in: Georges Dionne (ed.) *Handbook of Insurance*, p. 691.
1265. *See* James I. Hilliard/Laureen Regan/Sharon Tennyson in: Georges Dionne (ed.) *Handbook of Insurance*, p. 691.

industry). Others also offer property, casualty or liability insurance, either to individual or businesses.[1266]

In addition, insurance agents may be classified according to the scope of their authority. In doing so, it should be recalled that the authority conferred to insurance agents is normally governed under: (*i*) the applicable domestic law and (*ii*) the agreement concluded with the insurance company. Among others, a general agent is an insurance agent who is granted with nearly unlimited authority to act on behalf of the insurance company he/she represents. In particular, the general agent can accept offers to enter into standardized insurance contracts, agree upon terms and conditions of insurance contracts, amend terms and conditions of existing contracts, renew contracts that are due to expire, collect premiums and so forth. On the contrary, a special agent is an insurance agent whose authority to bind an insurance company is expressly limited. For instance, a soliciting agent is a type of agent normally authorized to solicit insurance, to collect offers to enter into standardized insurance contracts, to deliver policies to customers and to collect the related premiums. On the other hand, a soliciting agent generally cannot accept insurance offers, nor negotiate terms and conditions of insurance contracts.[1267,1268]

Insurance agents may also engage sub-agents to better perform specific duties or to better manage relationships with specific customers, for instance with customers residing in peripheral areas. In general, such sub-agents do not report to the insurance company directly, but rather to the relevant agent based on a sub-agency agreement. As a result, the sub-agents may be regarded as agents of the agents.[1269,1270]

Differently, insurance agents ought to be distinguished from other insurance salespersons, like insurance consultants and/or canvassers. True, the specific name, status and functions of such intermediaries diverge very much depending on the applicable domestic law and contractual arrangements. Nevertheless, it is fair to say that such intermediaries are usually engaged to market and promote insurance

1266. *See* Mark A. Hall, *The Milbank Quarterly*, (2000) p. 24.

1267. To this effect, *see* Douglas R. Richmond, *Tort Trial & Insurance Practice Law Journal*, (2004) pp. 3-4, Marco Rossetti, *Il diritto delle assicurazioni—Volume 1*, pp. 556 et seq., Antigono Donati/Giovanna Volpe Putzolu, *Manuale di Diritto delle Assicurazioni—Ottava Edizione Aggiornata*, p. 98, Luciano Casali, *L'agente e il broker di assicurazione*, pp. 131 et seq., Filippo Romeo in: Guido Alpa (ed.) *Le Assicurazioni private*, pp. 416-418 and Claudio Cacciamani, *L'agente di assicurazioni* (Milano: Egea, 2005) pp. 41-42.

1268. Cinquanta argued that the authority to conclude insurance contracts is a peculiar feature of insurance agents since other distribution channels do not grant the chance to do so. *See* Consuelo Cinquanta, *Assicurazioni—Chi può distribuirle*, p. 15. Nevertheless, this reasoning does not appear to be convincing. As a matter of fact, as outlined in the other sections of this chapter, distribution channels other than insurance agents also allow the conclusion of insurance contracts.

1269. *See* Carlo Belluzzi, *Agenti brokers e altri ausiliari di assicurazione*, pp. 24-25, Fabrizio Santoboni in: Fabrizio Santoboni (ed.) *Manuale di gestione assicurativa*, pp. 304-305 and Ernesto Pucci in: Marco Prosperetti/Alessandro Colavolpe (eds.) *I gestori del risparmio non bancari e i canali di distribuzione*, pp. 401-402.

1270. Sub-agents should be distinguished from co-agents, who are instead agents engaged jointly by an insurance company. To this effect, *see* Antigono Donati/Giovanna Volpe Putzolu, *Manuale di Diritto delle Assicurazioni—Ottava Edizione Aggiornata*, pp. 98-99 and Fabrizio Santoboni in: Fabrizio Santoboni (ed.) *Manuale di gestione assicurativa*, pp. 304-305.

products by visiting potential customers and/or referring potential business opportunities.[1271] As opposed to insurance agents, their activities are generally occasional or—to say the least—they lack the stability of agency activities. Such intermediaries may be engaged to work either on a full-time basis or on a part-time basis along with other non-insurance related activities. Also, such intermediaries may be engaged directly by the insurance company[1272] or by an insurance agent.[1273]

The agent channel is a traditional distribution system, both in life and non-life insurance. In fact, in the context of property-liability insurance, professional agents dominate in Germany, Italy, Portugal, Poland and Turkey in Europe, and in Taiwan and Malaysia in Asia. In the US, multi-firm agents have the largest market share overall in most commercial lines, while single-firm agents hold the largest market share in personal lines.[1274] Distribution via professional agent is the dominant form of life insurance sales as well. In most countries, including the US, Canada, Germany and Japan, most of life insurance agents are either employees or single-firm agents who sell the products of only one insurance company.[1275] However, in the near future, the increasing use of digital channels among younger generations is expected to come largely at the expense of the traditional agent channel, so that the market share of this distribution system is expected to decrease.[1276]

4.7.1.2 *Functions and Activities*

In order to comply with their duties of business development and client portfolio management, external representatives and employee sales representatives dealt with in the previous section are (legally and/or contractually) required to perform a number of activities for the account of their principals/employers (i.e., the insurance companies).[1277] Although their activities are strictly connected to each other, they can be

1271. Insurance consultants may also be engaged by insurance customers in the need of specific advice in the context of insurance. *See* Fabrizio Santoboni in: Fabrizio Santoboni (ed.) *Manuale di gestione assicurativa*, p. 321.
1272. In Italy, a specific section of the single register of insurance and reinsurance intermediaries (RUI) is dedicated to direct canvassers (in Italian, "*produttori diretti*"), who are directly engaged by an insurance company to work on a part-time basis vis-à-vis their principal business activities, carrying on insurance intermediation in the context of life, accident and health insurance on behalf and under the full responsibility of a single insurance company without time or result obligations. For further comments on direct canvassers, *see* Marco Rossetti, *Il diritto delle assicurazioni—Volume 1*, pp. 613 et seq. and Antigono Donati/Giovanna Volpe Putzolu, *Manuale di Diritto delle Assicurazioni—Ottava Edizione Aggiornata*, p. 101.
1273. For further comments and examples, *see* Carlo Belluzzi, *Agenti broker e altri ausiliari di assicurazione*, pp. 25-27, Luciano Casali, *L'agente e il broker di assicurazione*, pp. 79 et seq., Luciano Gioberti, *Manuale dell'agente di assicurazione*, pp. 24-25 and Jacques Deschamps, *L'Agent Général d'Assurances*, pp. 106 et seq.
1274. *See* James I. Hilliard/Laureen Regan/Sharon Tennyson in: Georges Dionne (ed.) *Handbook of Insurance*, pp. 692-694.
1275. *See* James I. Hilliard/Laureen Regan/Sharon Tennyson in: Georges Dionne (ed.) *Handbook of Insurance*, pp. 694-699.
1276. *See* Capgemini, "*World Insurance Report 2016*," pp. 14-15.
1277. The range of activities mainly depends upon the specific terms and conditions applicable between the parties rather than upon the classes of representatives. In the present section,

generally broken down into two main clusters, namely sales activities and administrative activities.[1278]

The first cluster includes a number of activities (directly or indirectly) intended to develop the business of the insurance company. This primarily includes the collection of insurance offers from customers.[1279] It goes without saying that, in the case where the insurance agent has been authorized to conclude contracts, the insurance agent can accept such insurance offers. To the contrary, in the case that the insurance agent is not authorized to do so, the insurance agent is required to transmit such offers to the insurance company for review and acceptance. However, it should be noted that sales activities are not limited to a mere collection of insurance offers. Rather, the agent is required to proactively approach potential customers, convince them to purchase insurance and customize insurance quotations in an attempt to foster sales of insurance products or otherwise establish business relationships.[1280]

In addition to the above core duties, the first cluster also includes the following activities:[1281]

- provision of full insurance coverage to existing customers, both on a personal and family level, as well as for economic activities and personal properties;
- assessments aimed at ensuring that insurance coverage is always adjusted to actual risk exposure; if need be, promptly updates of insured value, maximum coverage and contractual documentation in line with changes in risk elements;
- planning of actual sales activities based on the market analysis to identify potential customers to approach;
- identification of targets to be achieved in liaison with their staff, sub-agents and canvassers;
- technical and commercial support in favor of the internal and/or external sales organization;[1282]
- research and selection of new staff, along with the provision of professional training; and
- monitoring of results achieved.

On the other hand, administrative activities embrace both the relationship with the insurance company and the management of the local agency (such as relationships with their staff, sub-agents and canvassers, relationships with third parties, costs and expenses of the agency). Among others, administrative activities delegated to insurance agents may include contract management and claims management activities,

reference is generally made to insurance agents, but similar considerations can be also extended to sub-agents and employee sales representatives.

1278. *See* Carlo Belluzzi, *Agenti broker e altri ausiliari di assicurazione*, p. 22.

1279. The collection of insurance offers can be also coupled with a preceding negotiation of the relevant terms and conditions.

1280. To this effect, *see* Luciano Casali, *L'agente e il broker di assicurazione*, pp. 37-38 and Marco Rossetti, *Il diritto delle assicurazioni—Volume 1*, pp. 549-550 and footnotes cited therein.

1281. *See* Carlo Belluzzi, *Agenti broker e altri ausiliari di assicurazione*, pp. 22-23.

1282. For further comments on the organization of insurance agencies, *see* Claudio Cacciamani, *L'agente di assicurazioni*, pp. 267 et seq.

such as the collection of claims requests, the claims assessment, the transmission of claims files to the insurance company and to insurance adjusters.[1283] In addition to this, administrative activities also include the following:[1284]

- registration and control of insurance contracts;
- registration of receipts and control of premiums cashed in;
- accounting for the relationships with customers;
- accounting for the relationships with staff;
- accounting for the relationships with sub-agents and canvassers; and
- general accounting and financial management control.

In carrying on the above activities, insurance agents are required to comply with a number of additional duties set forth under the applicable law and/or the agency agreement concluded with the insurance company. For instance, a single-firm agent is required not to accept any assignment from other insurance companies. Also, when carrying out their activities, insurance agents are generally required to protect the interests of the insurance company. In the case where insurance agents fail to comply with their duties and the insurance company is damaged as a result of such failures, insurance agents may obviously be liable for their breaches.[1285]

As a final note, it should be recalled that insurance agents do not have contractual ties with customers. Still, in the performance of their activities, insurance agents also have some duties vis-à-vis prospects governed under applicable law. Most notably, insurance agents are generally required to act with care, skill and diligence. Second, insurance agents are usually compelled to properly inform potential customers about available product options and provide them with a proper set of precontractual documents to duly disclose applicable terms and conditions.[1286] In addition to this, insurance agents may also provide various additional services to customers. For instance, they can assist customers by delivering proof of insurance, changing or updating coverage, answering specific questions about coverage or filing claims requests.[1287]

1283. *See* Carlo Belluzzi, *Agenti broker e altri ausiliari di assicurazione*, p. 23.
1284. *See* Carlo Belluzzi, *Agenti broker e altri ausiliari di assicurazione*, p. 24.
1285. For additional comments on duties imposed on Italian insurance agents, *see* Marco Rossetti, *Il diritto delle assicurazioni—Volume 1*, pp. 549-550. For additional comments on duties imposed on US insurance agents, *see* Douglas R. Richmond, *Tort Trial & Insurance Practice Law Journal*, (2004) pp. 45 et seq.
1286. *See* Marco Rossetti, *Il diritto delle assicurazioni—Volume 1*, p. 550, Antigono Donati/Giovanna Volpe Putzolu, *Manuale di Diritto delle Assicurazioni—Ottava Edizione Aggiornata*, pp. 104-105. For additional comments on duties imposed on US insurance agents, *see also* Douglas R. Richmond, *Tort Trial & Insurance Practice Law Journal*, (2004) pp. 10 et seq.
1287. *See* Daniel Schwarcz/Peter Siegelmann, "Insurance Agents in the 21st Century: The Problem of Biased Advice," in Daniel Schwarcz/Peter Siegelmann (eds.) *Research Handbook in the Law & Economics of Insurance* (Cheltenham, Northampton: Edwar Elgar Publishing, 2015) pp. 36 et seq.

4.7.1.3 Remuneration

External representatives are most commonly compensated through commissions based on premium revenues.[1288] Commissions rates are normally governed under the agency agreement concluded with the insurance company.[1289] Such commission rates normally vary significantly depending upon insurance products and services provided, owing principally to the variation in costs and expenses borne by agents in their activities. In fact, the greater the need for customization of an insurance contract or for the representative to supplement the services of the insurance company, the higher the commission rate.[1290] Besides commission revenue, the agency agreement with the insurance company may also provide for other forms of compensation. This is for instance the case of profit-contingent fees, allowances, contributions and other reimbursements.[1291]

In general, compensation systems tend to differ according to the class of insurance representatives.[1292] As a matter of fact, commission rates for multi-firm agents are generally higher than those for single-firm agents.[1293] In addition to this, there is also some evidence that multi-firm agents are more likely to receive profit-contingent fees than single-firm agents.[1294] Instead, employee sales representatives tend to be compensated with salary and bonus schemes rather than commissions.[1295]

1288. *See* James I. Hilliard/Laureen Regan/Sharon Tennyson in: Georges Dionne (ed.) *Handbook of Insurance*, p. 710.
1289. In Italy, the compensation is a core element of the agency agreement, so that an agency engagement for free is not possible. *See* Marco Rossetti, *Il diritto delle assicurazioni—Volume 1*, p. 551.
1290. *See* Jeffrey Wilder, "Competing for the Effort of a Common Agent: Contingency Fees in Commercial Insurance," *US Department of Justice Antitrust Division Economic Analysis Group Working Paper No. EAG03-4* (2003) p. 4.
1291. *See* Marco Rossetti, *Il diritto delle assicurazioni—Volume 1*, p. 555.
1292. Different compensation systems for different classes of insurance agents often reflect diverging interests and incentive issues in the context of the principal-agent relationship. For further comments on such economic issues, *see* James I. Hilliard/Laureen Regan/Sharon Tennyson in: Georges Dionne (ed.) *Handbook of Insurance*, pp. 711 et seq. and Peter Zweifel/Roland Eisen, *Insurance Economics* (Berlin, Heidelberg: Springer-Verlag Berlin Heidelberg, 2012) p. 171.
1293. In the case of multi-firm agents, new contracts and renewal contracts often receive the same commission rate. Instead, in the case of single-firm agents, commission rates for renewal contracts tend to be lower than those for new business. *See* James I. Hilliard/Laureen Regan/Sharon Tennyson in: Georges Dionne (ed.) *Handbook of Insurance*, p. 705.
1294. However, other forms of compensation, including additional fixed compensation and/or participation in retirement plans, may be available to single-firm agents. *See* James I. Hilliard/Laureen Regan/Sharon Tennyson in: Georges Dionne (ed.) *Handbook of Insurance*, pp. 705 and 711.
1295. *See* James I. Hilliard/Laureen Regan/Sharon Tennyson in: Georges Dionne (ed.) *Handbook of Insurance*, pp. 705 and 711.

4.7.1.4 *Fact Pattern*

The factual background for this analysis is pretty much in line with that analyzed in section 4.6 above. Nevertheless, instead of making business through insurance brokers, the present scenario envisages that foreign insurance companies engage insurance agents. To this end, it is assumed that the insurance agents are established in the source country.

4.7.2 Permanent Establishment Implications

4.7.2.1 *Analysis under the OECD Model*

4.7.2.1.1 *The Standard Version*

In the first place, it is fair to say that the same considerations regarding the subjective requirement and the nature of the activities performed in the source country described above with respect to insurance brokers[1296] remain valid for insurance agents, *mutatis mutandis*. Still, in contrast to insurance brokers, insurance agents generally represent the interests of insurance companies in their dealings with customers. As a result, it may be argued that insurance agents act "*on behalf of*" foreign insurance companies. Nevertheless, there are many different types of insurance agents, who may be categorized by virtue of different criteria.[1297] Hence, the analysis of permanent establishment implications can be multifaceted. For the purposes of the present analysis, it is crucial to ascertain the scope of their activities. In particular, most important is assessing whether—in the context of his/her sales activities[1298]—the insurance agent concludes insurance contracts binding on the foreign insurance company or plays the principal role leading to the conclusion of such contracts.

To begin with, general insurance agents—who are granted a nearly unlimited authority to act on behalf of insurance companies—may indeed give rise to permanent establishment concerns. In fact, among a wide range of activities, such agents may accept offers to enter into standardized insurance contracts, collect insurance offers to enter into standardized insurance contracts binding on foreign insurance companies or otherwise subject to acceptance without a genuine review, negotiate terms and conditions of insurance contracts with potential customers in a way binding on foreign insurance companies or otherwise subject to acceptance without a genuine review, amend terms and conditions of existing contracts and renew contracts that are due to expire. This is for instance the case of the "*agente in gestione libera*" in Italy,[1299] the

1296. *See* s. 4.6.2.1 above.
1297. *See* s. 4.7.1.1 above.
1298. Administrative activities alone may be instead regarded as auxiliary activities under Art. 5, para. 4, of the OECD Model.
1299. Such agents are governed under Arts. 1742-1753 of the Italian Civil Code, the Legislative Decree no. 209 of September 7, 2005 and related implementing regulations issued by IVASS.

"*agent général d'assurance*" in France[1300] and the "*Versicherungsvertreter*" in Germany.[1301,1302] Accordingly, such types of insurance agents generally fulfill the traditional test regarding the conclusion of contracts binding on foreign insurance companies. Considering that such a general authority to represent the insurance company is normally characterized by a certain degree of stability,[1303] the habitual exercise test is generally met. Consequently, it can be said that all conditions set forth under Art. 5, para. 5, of the OECD Model for a dependent agent permanent establishment to exist are most likely fulfilled.[1304]

The same conclusion can be drawn in respect of a general insurance agent that collects from customers their consents to be covered under collective insurance contracts stipulated at predetermined conditions agreed with the insurance company. In fact, in such a case, the insurance company is generally bound by the consents collected through the agency channel.[1305] Therefore, under the assumption that the habitual exercise test is also fulfilled, the insurance company may—in principle—have a dependent agent permanent establishment in the source country.

Special insurance agents can also give rise to a dependent agent permanent establishment. This is for instance the case of the soliciting agent. True, this is a type of special agent that generally cannot accept offers to enter into standardized insurance contracts, nor negotiate terms and conditions of insurance contracts. Nevertheless, in the event that this agent collects offers to enter into standardized insurance contracts and such offers are later accepted without a genuine review by the foreign insurance company, the traditional test regarding the conclusion of contracts could anyway be fulfilled. And more than that, even though such offers are subject to review, where such a review does not result in material modifications, the supplementary test regarding the principal role leading to the conclusion of contracts could be satisfied. On the top of this, insofar as such an agent is generally involved in the solicitation of insurance in the source country, he/she could fulfill the supplementary test, albeit not engaged in the collection of offers.

Other cases of special agents with limited authority should also be assessed on a case-by-case basis having regard to the applicable factual circumstances, with a careful comparison of the contributions toward the conclusion of contracts. For instance, special agents that identify and proactively approach potential customers with a view to convincing them to purchase standardized insurance products could fulfill the supplementary test regarding the principal role leading to the conclusion of contracts,

1300. The "*agent général d'assurance*" is regarded as a "*mandataire*" subject to Art. 1984 of the French Civil Code.
1301. *See* Art. 92, para. 1, of the "*Handelsgesetzbuch.*"
1302. This could also be the case of a managing general agent (MGA), which is a specialized type of insurance intermediary that could be vested with a binding authority from insurance companies.
1303. This is a peculiar feature of insurance agents vis-à-vis other insurance salespersons. For further comments, *see* s. 4.7.1 above.
1304. *See* Sebastian Mailei/Jeremy Brown, "Permanent establishment issues arising from global insurance distribution models," *International Tax Review—Financial Services Industry Guide* (2015) p. 39.
1305. For further comments, *see* s. 3.3.2.3.4 above.

even where the collection of offers takes place through other means. The same also holds true in the case of special agents that persuade already existing customers to purchase a more comprehensive insurance coverage and/or adjust the risk exposure through updates to the existing contracts.

A dependent agent permanent establishment can also arise in the case of a team of internal sales representatives employed to meet potential clients, develop local relationships and negotiate the terms of the contracts locally.[1306] In fact, even where such individuals cannot formally conclude contracts (for instance, because the acceptance is retained in the hands of senior executives based in the country of establishment),[1307] the traditional test regarding the conclusion of contracts could be fulfilled should such individuals negotiate all elements and details of the contract with customers in a way binding on the insurance company. Likewise, the traditional test regarding the conclusion of contracts could also be met if the terms and conditions negotiated by internal sales representatives are subject to a formal acceptance with no genuine review. Furthermore, even though the terms and conditions negotiated by internal sales representatives are subject to review, where such a review does not result in material modifications, the supplementary test regarding the principal role leading to the conclusion of contracts could be fulfilled. On the top of this, insofar as such representatives are generally involved in the solicitation of insurance when meeting potential clients in the source country, they could anyway fulfill the supplementary test, irrespective of whether the terms and conditions of the contracts have been effectively discussed or not.

In the light of the foregoing, it remains to be assessed whether the above agents/representatives may be regarded as agents of an independent status operating in the ordinary course of their business. In this respect, the distinction between internal and external representatives plays a major role. In general, it can be said that the independence status cannot be claimed with respect to internal representatives to the extent that such individuals are usually salaried employees that—as such—are subject to detailed instructions and control of the insurance company. As a result, the above employee sales representatives that are involved in the solicitation of insurance and/or the negotiation of terms and conditions of insurance contracts in the source country will most likely constitute a permanent establishment.

With respect to external representatives, the above assessment will depend on the facts and circumstances of the case at hands. Among others, specific consideration should be given to the degree of control that the principal exerts over the agent.[1308] Therefore, in circumstances where the insurance agent is subject to very detailed instructions and control of the foreign insurance company, the agent would not be regarded as independent. Conversely, the reliance on special skills or knowledge of the

1306. This same reasoning can also be applied to a mobile team of representatives that travel frequently to various jurisdictions.

1307. *See* Sebastian Mailei/Jeremy Brown, *International Tax Review—Financial Services Industry Guide*, (2015) p. 38.

1308. For further comments, *see* s. 3.3.2.4.3 above.

agent (e.g., the knowledge of the local insurance market or the knowledge of certain insurance business lines) is an indication of independence.[1309]

In addition to this, an important factor to consider is the allocation of entrepreneurial risks between the principal and the agent. Hence, it is imperative that the insurance agent can support its own risks.[1310] Another factor to ascertain the independence of an insurance agent is the number of insurance companies represented by such an agent. As a result, multi-firm agents selling products of several insurance companies are more likely to fulfill the condition of independence as to opposed to single-firm agents working primarily or exclusively for a single insurance company. However, according to the OECD, this factor is not in itself determinative.[1311]

Besides the independence status, it should also be assessed whether the insurance agent is acting in the ordinary course of its agency business.[1312] The question as to whether the activities of the agent are within the framework of regular business activities of insurance agents depends on what is to be regarded as customary in the context of the individual case.[1313] Hence, in seeking answer to this question, one should carefully look at the factual circumstances, such as the local insurance market, the nature of the insurance business lines concerned, the applicable law, regulations, and so forth. In fact, on the basis of such circumstances, the power granted to a general insurance agent varies significantly. For example, in a German case concerning the transport insurance business in Bremen, the Federal Supreme Court concluded that an insurance agent still acted within the ordinary course of its business even if he had a far reaching authority to conclude contracts, collect premiums, to litigate or to authorize other agents.[1314] Similarly, in a Dutch case concerning property insurance business, the Dutch Supreme Court found that an insurance agent allowed to conclude contracts, determine the amount of premiums and settle claims was still to be regarded as an independent agent.[1315]

When considering the independent status of an agent, it should be also recalled that changes introduced in the aftermath of the BEPS Project have negative implications for intra-group agent structures whereby an agent in the source country does not act for third party insurance companies or otherwise does so marginally.[1316] In fact, in such circumstances, the last sentence of Art. 5, para. 6, of the OECD Model clearly provides for a non-rebuttable presumption that such an agent cannot be considered as independent.

1309. *See* Sebastian Mailei/Jeremy Brown, *International Tax Review—Financial Services Industry Guide*, (2015) p. 39.

1310. Mailei and Brown argued that this seems to be the determinative test applied by tax authorities in practice. To this effect, *see* Sebastian Mailei/Jeremy Brown, *International Tax Review—Financial Services Industry Guide*, (2015) p. 39.

1311. *See* para. 109 of the OECD Model Commentary on Art. 5.

1312. *See* para. 110 of the OECD Model Commentary on Art. 5.

1313. For further comments, *see also* s. 3.3.2.4.5 above.

1314. *See* BFH (*Bundesfinanzhof*) April 30, 1975, I R 152/73. For further comments on such a case, *see also* s. 3.4.2.3 above.

1315. *See* HR (*Hoge Raad*) June 28, 1995, No. 29.435. For further comments on such a case, *see also* s. 3.4.2.3 above.

1316. *See* Sebastian Mailei/Jeremy Brown, *International Tax Review—Financial Services Industry Guide*, (2015) p. 39.

Differently, it may be argued that marketing and promotion activities that do not directly result in the conclusion of contracts do not give rise to a permanent establishment. In fact, a marketing agent and/or representative merely involved in advertising campaigns does not fulfill neither the traditional test regarding the conclusion of contracts nor the supplementary test regarding the principal role leading to the conclusion of contracts. Also, even if any such agent/representative concludes advertising contracts, this kind of contracts do not relate to operations that constitute the core business of an insurance company, so that such an agent/representative does not constitute a dependent agent permanent establishment.[1317]

The above assessment on the existence of a permanent establishment should also be extended to sub-agents. For instance, in the case where a general insurance agent engages a sub-agent to perform certain duties he himself should perform pursuant to the contract entered into between himself and the insurance company, it could be determined that the foreign insurance company has both an agent and a sub-agent in the source country.[1318] In fact, in the case that a sub-agent concludes insurance contracts, such a sub-agent is ultimately acting on behalf of the insurance company, although—in principle—he is acting on behalf of the general agent, who in turn has been authorized to act on behalf of the insurance company. To the contrary, if a sub-agent does not fulfill neither the traditional test regarding the conclusion of contracts nor the supplementary test regarding the principal role leading to the conclusion of contracts, he/she would not qualify as a dependent agent permanent establishment. However, under the assumption that the general agent is considered to constitute a dependent agent permanent establishment, all the acts carried on for the insurance company (included the hiring of the sub-agent) will be assigned to such a permanent establishment.[1319]

Lastly, a similar factual assessment should also be carried on with respect to other insurance salespersons, e.g., insurance consultants and/or canvassers. As already outlined above,[1320] the status and the functions of such intermediaries can vary significantly based on applicable law and contractual arrangements, so that a thorough analysis should be carried out on a case-by-case basis. Nonetheless, in general, it is fair to say that, even where such intermediaries fulfill either the traditional test regarding the conclusion of contracts or the supplementary test regarding the principal role leading to the conclusion of contracts, their activities lack the stability of agency relationships. Hence, the condition of the habitual exercise set forth under Art. 5, para. 5, of the OECD Model does not appear to be fulfilled to the effect that it is unlikely that a dependent agent permanent establishment arise in such cases.

1317. For further comments, *see also* s. 3.3.2.3.2 above.
1318. In such a case, the agents should be treated as a single permanent establishment. For further comments, *see* s. 3.3.2.3.3 above.
1319. For further comments, *see* s. 3.3.2.3.3 above.
1320. *See* s. 4.7.1.1. above.

4.7.2.1.2 *The Special Clause for Insurance Agents*

Insurance agents that do not otherwise create a dependent agent permanent establishment under the standard version of the OECD Model could fall within the scope of the special clause for insurance agents in the case that such intermediaries can be regarded as agents through which a foreign insurance company collects premiums or insures risks in the source country.

This special clause has a very broad scope of application which might concern all agents and sub-agents engaged in the source country, irrespective of whether such agents are independent or not. *In primis*, this special clause catches all (general and special) insurance agents and sub-agents that fulfill the conditions set forth under the dependent agent provision, but are nevertheless covered under Art. 5, para. 6, of the OECD Model. Indeed, since the criterion related to the insurance of risks in the source country should be intended to cover activities falling within the scope of Art. 5, para. 5, of the OECD Model,[1321] this criterion can be regarded as met to the effect that a permanent establishment arises in the source country. Second, the special clause can catch (special) agents and sub-agents that do not fulfill the conditions of the dependent agent provision due to their limited scope of activities. In fact, the special clause covers a wider range of activities than that of the dependent agent provision. More to the point, should their limited engagement concern activities that fulfill the criteria regarding the insurance of risks (e.g., the collection of offers in the source country, even though such offers are subject to a genuine review that results in material modifications, the valuation of items prior to the conclusion of contracts, the administration of insurance contracts and/or the performance of insurance contracts) or the collection of premiums from customers, a permanent establishment arises in the source country.

A similar reasoning also applies to internal representatives other than employee sales representatives that already constitute a dependent agent permanent establishment under Art. 5, para. 5, of the OECD Model. As a matter of fact, according to the special clause, where a foreign insurance company employs a person involved in the distribution of insurance products in the source country, it should be assessed whether any such employee takes part in activities that fulfill the criteria regarding the insurance of risks or the collection of premiums from customers. Should this be the case, a permanent establishment arises in the source country.

Careful attention should finally be paid to other insurance salespersons involved in the distribution of insurance products. Indeed, in contrast to the dependent agent provision, the special clause for insurance agents does not provide for the habitual exercise test. And more than that, the special clause covers a wider range of activities than that of the dependent agent provision. Hence, although the activities carried out by such intermediaries generally lack the stability of agency relationships, in the case where their activities fall within the scope of the special clause, such intermediaries can give rise to a permanent establishment in the source country.

1321. *See* s. 3.3.2.5.2 above.

4.7.2.2 Analysis under the UN Model

At the outset, it is fair to say that insurance intermediaries having a very broad authority to act on behalf of foreign insurance companies—such as general insurance agents—usually fall within the scope of the dependent agent permanent establishment provision. As a matter of fact, such intermediaries generally fulfill all the conditions set forth under Art. 5, para. 5, let. (*a*), of the UN Model to the effect that a dependent agent permanent establishment is likely to exist in such circumstances.

The situation of special insurance agents and sub-agents should be assessed more carefully in the light of the applicable factual circumstances. In fact, although their authority is generally more limited vis-à-vis general insurance agents, their activities could anyway result in either the traditional test regarding the conclusion of contracts or the supplementary test regarding the principal role leading to the conclusion of contracts being fulfilled. A similar factual assessment should also be carried on in the case where the foreign insurance company employs internal sales representatives in the source country. Should any of the two above tests be satisfied—and under the assumption that the habitual exercise test is also met—the foreign insurance company has a dependent agent permanent establishment in the source country.

On the other hand, other insurance salespersons (like insurance consultants and/or canvassers) do not generally fulfill the habitual exercise test to the extent that their activities usually lack the stability of agency relationships. As a result, in such cases, no dependent agent permanent establishment should in principle arise in the source country by application of Art. 5, para. 5, let. (*a*), of the UN Model.

At any rate, it is worth noting that all such insurance agents, sub-agents, internal sales representatives and other insurance salespersons other than those who already fall within the scope of Art. 5, para. 5, let. (*a*), of the UN Model are generally caught under the insurance agent provision contained in Art. 5, para. 6, of the UN Model. As a matter of fact, the insurance agent provision covers a broader range of activities vis-à-vis the dependent agent provision and does not envisage any habitual exercise test.[1322] It follows that, considering that the above persons are usually involved in a wide range of sales and administrative activities, it appears that all such (internal and external) representatives might be deemed to collect premiums and/or insure risks in the source country to the effect that a permanent establishment is likely to exist.

Nonetheless, it should be recalled that foreign insurance companies can still obviate source taxation in the case that the above intermediaries and/or internal representatives can be regarded as independent agents acting in the ordinary course of their business.[1323] To this end, a careful assessment should be carried out on the basis of factual applicable circumstances. In general, it can be reasonably argued that such an independence status cannot be claimed with respect to internal representatives—such as employee sales representatives—to the extent that such individuals are usually salaried employees subject to detailed instructions and control

1322. *See* Arvid A. Skaar, *Permanent Establishment—Erosion of a Tax Treaty Principle*, p. 435.
1323. Article 5, para. 6, of the UN Model also contains a carve-out for reinsurance. Nevertheless, insurance agents are not generally engaged in reinsurance transactions.

of the insurance company. Therefore, it is most likely that such internal representatives constitute a permanent establishment in the source country.

Differently, with respect to external representatives, although the above assessment should be carried out on a case-by-case basis, it is fair to say that the analysis of international case law has shown a general tendency to consider insurance intermediaries as acting independently and within the ordinary course of their business.[1324] Should this tendency be confirmed in the light of the specific factual circumstances, a foreign insurance company can successfully obviate source taxation.

4.8 BANCASSURANCE

4.8.1 General Overview

4.8.1.1 Introduction

The first appearance of the term "*bancassurance*" was in France,[1325] where cooperation between banks and insurance companies started earlier than in other countries.[1326] This word was coined to indicate the simple distribution of insurance products through bank branches, while now it is used to describe all kinds of relationships between banks and insurance companies.[1327,1328]

The bancassurance phenomenon can be defined in different ways.[1329] For instance, it has been defined as "*the provision of and selling of banking and insurance products by the same organisation under the same roof.*"[1330] Differently, it has also been depicted as "*the process of using a bank's customer relationships to sell life and non-life insurance products and it is emerging as a natural pathway for the effective development of insurance.*"[1331] More broadly, it has also been described as "*a strategy adopted by*

1324. *See* s. 4.7.2.2.1 above.

1325. The bancassurance phenomenon finds its (recent) origin in the 1980s in the major European countries (*in primis*, in France). To this effect, *see* Antonio Coviello, *L'utilizzo delle tecnologie avanzate nel settore assicurativo: l'e-insurance*, pp. 91-92 and Covadonga Diaz Llavona, "Banks In The Insurance Distribution Business—Controversial Issues of the Spanish Regulation And Reference To The Corresponding Provisions In The German Legal System," *Munich Risk and Insurance Center—Working Paper 12* (2012) pp. 3-5.

1326. In Italy, bancassurance started to gain market shares in the early 1990s. *See* Antonio Coviello, *L'utilizzo delle tecnologie avanzate nel settore assicurativo: l'e-insurance*, pp. 92-93 and Claudia Bortolani in: Marco Prosperetti/Alessandro Colavolpe (eds.) *I gestori del risparmio non bancari e i canali di distribuzione*, p. 429.

1327. *See* Ornella Ricci, "The Development of Bancassurance in Europe" in: Franco Fiordelisi/Ornella Ricci (eds.) *Bancassurance in Europe—Past, Present and Future* (London: Palgrave Macmillan, 2012) p. 5.

1328. In Italy, Poste Italiane SpA is also authorized to distribute insurance products like a bank. To this effect, *see* Marco Rossetti, *Il diritto delle assicurazioni—Volume 1*, pp. 620-624.

1329. *See* Nadege Genetaya/Philip Molyneux, *Bancassurance* (London: Palgrave Macmillan, 1998) p. 4 and Ivana Clemente, *Bancassicurazione—L'evoluzione del rischio nei contratti "para-assicurativi"* (Roma: Aracne, 2006) p. 33.

1330. *See* W. Elkington, "Bancassurance," *Chartered Building Societies Institutions Journal* (1993) p. 2.

1331. *See* Serap O. Gonulal, Nick Goulder/Rodney R. Lester, "Bancassurance—A Valuable Tool for Developing Insurance in Emerging Markets," *World Bank Policy Research Working Paper* (2012) p. 2.

banks or insurance companies aiming to operate the financial market in a more or less integrated manner."[1332] At any rate, it is fair to say that bancassurance is ultimately aimed at cross-selling insurance products to bank customers.[1333,1334]

Originally, bancassurers focused on life insurance products (with investment products such as unit-linked policies, index-linked policies and payment protection products like credit insurance and overdraft insurance)[1335] because of their high saving content, along with their similarities and complementaries with asset management activities. More recently, bancassurers have also approached the non-life business with some standardized products (such as car insurance, home insurance and travel insurance), sometimes in cooperation with reinsurance companies. In the future, it is likely that bancassurers will expand their product range, strengthening the offer of insurance contracts and thus moving away from traditional banking activities.[1336]

4.8.1.2 Organizational Models

Bancassurance developed in the latest decades, giving birth to a wide range of organizational models, according to the relationship existing between banks and insurance companies involved.[1337,1338] The choice of the specific organizational model depends on several drivers, ranging from external market conditions to the level of integration desired.[1339]

1332. *See* Swiss Re, "*Bancassurance,*" Sigma No. 2/1992, p. 4.
1333. *See* Ornella Ricci in: Franco Fiordelisi/Ornella Ricci (eds.) *Bancassurance in Europe—Past, Present and Future*, p. 5.
1334. It is important to distinguish bancassurance from different concepts, such as "*assurbanking*" or "*assurfinance,*" which is the provision of financial/banking products through insurance companies, and "*all-finance*" or "*all-finanz,*" which is the bundling of different products (including insurance products) to offer integrated and customized financial solutions to customers (generally through financial conglomerates). *See* Ornella Ricci in: Franco Fiordelisi/Ornella Ricci (eds.) *Bancassurance in Europe—Past, Present and Future*, pp. 5-6, Claudia Bortolani in: Marco Prosperetti/Alessandro Colavolpe (eds.) *I gestori del risparmio non bancari e i canali di distribuzione*, p. 430, Isabella Falautano/Emanuele Marsiglia, "Integrated Distribution of Insurance and Financial Services and Value Creation: Challenges Ahead," *The Geneva Papers on Risk and Insurance* (2003) p. 486 and Gilles Benoist, "Bancassurance: The New Challenges," *The Geneva Papers on Risk and Insurance* (2002) pp. 299-300. Such concepts are beyond the scope of this research.
1335. Such latter products may be structured as collective insurance contracts concluded between the insurance company and the bank on account of its customers. The bank customers can later join the insurance protection giving their consent.
1336. *See* Maria Grazia Starita, "Bancassurance Products" in: Franco Fiordelisi/Ornella Ricci (eds.) *Bancassurance in Europe—Past, Present and Future* (London: Palgrave Macmillan, 2012) pp. 26-27, Claudia Bortolani in: Marco Prosperetti/Alessandro Colavolpe (eds.) *I gestori del risparmio non bancari e i canali di distribuzione*, pp. 432-433 and Munich Re, "*Bancassurance in Practice,*" available online at www.munichre.com, pp. 9-14.
1337. *See* Massimo Caratelli, "The Bancassurance Market in Europe" in: Franco Fiordelisi/Ornella Ricci (eds.) *Bancassurance in Europe—Past, Present and Future* (London: Palgrave Macmillan, 2012) p. 71.
1338. This section is aimed at providing a classification of organizational models on the basis of legal criteria. In practice, however, a wide range of organizational models exists and other classifications can be made.
1339. For further comments, *see* Massimo Caratelli in: Franco Fiordelisi/Ornella Ricci (eds.) *Bancassurance in Europe—Past, Present and Future*, p. 71, Swiss Re, "*Bancassurance:*

The traditional (and simplest) model is the distribution alliance,[1340] whereby an insurance company distributes its products through banking channels based on a distribution agreement.[1341,1342] Such an agreement may take the form of a non-exclusive distribution agreement, whereby the bank sells products of the associated insurance company along with products of other companies. To the contrary, in the case of an exclusive distribution agreement, the credit institution can only sell products of the associated insurance company.[1343] Alternatively, the parties can also conclude a limited distribution agreement, whereby the insurance company provides one or more products / types of products exclusively for the associated credit institution. In such a

---

emerging trends, opportunities and challenges," Sigma No. 5/2007, available online at www.swissre.com, p. 5, Emilia Clipici/Catalina Bolovan, "Bancassurance: Main Insurance Distribution and Sale Channel in Europe," *Scientific Bulletin—Economic Sciences—University of Piteşti* (2012) p. 56, Isabella Falautano/Emanuele Marsiglia, *The Geneva Papers on Risk and Insurance,* (2003) p. 487 and Antonio Coviello, *L'utilizzo delle tecnologie avanzate nel settore assicurativo: l'e-insurance,* p. 107.

1340. The distribution alliance may also be coupled with a cross-shareholding. In such a case, the model is often referred to as strategic alliance. *See* Massimo Caratelli in: Franco Fiordelisi/Ornella Ricci (eds.) *Bancassurance in Europe—Past, Present and Future,* p. 71, Antonio Coviello, *L'utilizzo delle tecnologie avanzate nel settore assicurativo: l'e-insurance,* p. 104, Mark Teunissen, "Bancassurance: Tapping into the Banking Strength," *The Geneva Papers on Risk and Insurance* (2008) p. 409, Alan Leach, *New Initiatives in European Bancassurance* (London: Financial Times, 1996) p. 25, Isabella Falautano/Emanuele Marsiglia, *The Geneva Papers on Risk and Insurance,* (2003) p. 487, Ivana Clemente, *Bancassicurazione—L'evoluzione del rischio nei contratti "para-assicurativi,"* p. 40, Franco Fiordelisi/Ornella Ricci, "Efficiency in the life insurance industry: what are the efficiency gains from Bancassurance?," *EMFI WPs 2* (2010) p. 5 and Luigi Selleri, *Strategie e marketing dell'impresa di assicurazione* (Milano: EDUCatt, 2009) p. 114. This is for instance the case of the strategic alliance between Generali Group and Deutsche Vermögensberatung Aktiengesellschaft (DVAG) in Germany. In fact, Generali Deutschland AG currently owns 40 % of the shares in DVAG, which is the biggest autonomous sales organization for financial services in Germany. For further details on this alliance, *see also* Massimo Caratelli in: Franco Fiordelisi/Ornella Ricci (eds.) *Bancassurance in Europe—Past, Present and Future,* pp. 74-77.

1341. *See* Massimo Caratelli in: Franco Fiordelisi/Ornella Ricci (eds.) *Bancassurance in Europe—Past, Present and Future,* p. 71, Antonio Coviello, *L'utilizzo delle tecnologie avanzate nel settore assicurativo: l'e-insurance,* p. 104, Tobias C. Hoschka, *Bancassurance in Europe* (London: St. Martin's Press, 1994), pp. 78-79, Sergio Pugliese, *Bancassicurazione—La scelta dei prodotti e dei canali* (Roma: Bancaria Editrice, 1994) p. 31, Paolo Molesini, "Il canale bancario per la distribuzione di prodotti assicurativi: Modelli operativi" in: Enrico Granata/Alessandro Nigro/Sergio De Angeli/Paolo Molesini/Giuseppe Godano/Luigi Desiderio (eds.) *Banca e assicurazione: aspetti giuridici ed economici* (Roma: Bancaria Editrice, 1997) p. 48, Gilles Benoist, *The Geneva Papers on Risk and Insurance,* (2002) p. 301, Mark Teunissen, *The Geneva Papers on Risk and Insurance,* (2008) p. 409, Alan Leach, *New Initiatives in European Bancassurance,* p. 25, Isabella Falautano/Emanuele Marsiglia, *The Geneva Papers on Risk and Insurance,* (2003) p. 487, Ivana Clemente, *Bancassicurazione—L'evoluzione del rischio nei contratti "para-assicurativi,"* p. 40, Franco Fiordelisi/Ornella Ricci, *EMFI WPs 2,* (2010) p. 5 and Luigi Selleri, *Strategie e marketing dell'impresa di assicurazione,* p. 114. The distribution agreement might also be reciprocal to the effect that a bank may attempt to distribute its own bank products through the sales network of an insurance company. To this effect, *see* Tobias C. Hoschka, *Bancassurance in Europe,* pp. 78-79.

1342. It is worth noting that insurance companies may also conclude distribution agreements with other business operators (such as supermarket and petrol station owners). However, such agreements are beyond the scope of this research.

1343. Such an agreement may provide for an upfront payment for access to an exclusive distribution network.

latter case, both sides may have different contracts with different partners for products not subject to limited distribution agreements.[1344] Pursuant to such agreements, in consideration for its intermediation activities, the bank is usually remunerated by means of a selling commission to be paid by the insurance company, which may be in turn offset by entry and management fees on-charged to policyholders.[1345]

Another bancassurance model is that of a cooperation between banks and insurance companies realized through a (corporate) joint venture.[1346] A joint venture may be defined as a legally independent entity which is owned by two or more parent companies which exercise a controlling interest over it. In the context of bancassurance, a joint venture is usually between a bank and an insurance company which set up a jointly owned insurance subsidiary[1347] distributing its products to bank customers.[1348] Unlike a distribution alliance, this is an organizational form which constitutes a separate legal entity with a management team having clear responsibilities.[1349] Pursuant to a distribution agreement, such an entity usually distributes its products only through the network of its banking parent company, which is

1344. *See* Emilia Clipici/Catalina Bolovan, *Scientific Bulletin—Economic Sciences—University of Piteşti*, (2012) p. 56.
1345. *See* Massimo Caratelli in: Franco Fiordelisi/Ornella Ricci (eds.) *Bancassurance in Europe—Past, Present and Future*, p. 71, Tobias C. Hoschka, *Bancassurance in Europe*, p. 79 and Mark Teunissen, *The Geneva Papers on Risk and Insurance*, (2008) p. 409.
1346. *See* Massimo Caratelli in: Franco Fiordelisi/Ornella Ricci (eds.) *Bancassurance in Europe—Past, Present and Future*, p. 77, Emilia Clipici/Catalina Bolovan, *Scientific Bulletin—Economic Sciences—University of Piteşti*, (2012) p. 56, Mark Teunissen, *The Geneva Papers on Risk and Insurance*, (2008) p. 409, Paolo Molesini in: Enrico Granata/Alessandro Nigro/Sergio De Angeli/Paolo Molesini/Giuseppe Godano/Luigi Desiderio (eds.) *Banca e assicurazione: aspetti giuridici ed economici*, pp. 47-48, Isabella Falautano/Emanuele Marsiglia, *The Geneva Papers on Risk and Insurance*, (2003) p. 487, Antonio Coviello, *L'utilizzo delle tecnologie avanzate nel settore assicurativo: l'e-insurance*, pp. 104-105, Gilles Benoist, *The Geneva Papers on Risk and Insurance*, (2002) p. 301, Alan Leach, *New Initiatives in European Bancassurance*, p. 25, Ivana Clemente, *Bancassicurazione—L'evoluzione del rischio nei contratti "para-assicurativi,"* p. 40 and Franco Fiordelisi/Ornella Ricci, *EMFI WPs 2*, (2010) p. 5.
1347. Equity contributions in bancassurance joint ventures can vary considerably. In fact, shareholdings could be more or less balanced or there might be a controlling shareholder. *See* Massimo Caratelli in: Franco Fiordelisi/Ornella Ricci (eds.) *Bancassurance in Europe—Past, Present and Future*, p. 77, Emilia Clipici/Catalina Bolovan, *Scientific Bulletin—Economic Sciences—University of Piteşti*, (2012) p. 56, Antonio Coviello, *L'utilizzo delle tecnologie avanzate nel settore assicurativo: l'e-insurance*, pp. 105, Mark Teunissen, *The Geneva Papers on Risk and Insurance*, (2008) p. 409, Paolo Molesini in: Enrico Granata/Alessandro Nigro/Sergio De Angeli/Paolo Molesini/Giuseppe Godano/Luigi Desiderio (eds.) *Banca e assicurazione: aspetti giuridici ed economici*, p. 48 and Luigi Selleri, *Strategie e marketing dell'impresa di assicurazione*, pp. 115-117.
1348. In addition, the relationship between the bank and the insurance company is sometimes reinforced by a strategic cross-shareholding. *See* Massimo Caratelli in: Franco Fiordelisi/Ornella Ricci (eds.) *Bancassurance in Europe—Past, Present and Future*, p. 77 and Mark Teunissen, *The Geneva Papers on Risk and Insurance*, (2008) p. 410.
1349. *See* Tobias C. Hoschka, *Bancassurance in Europe*, p. 89.

remunerated by selling commissions, and sometimes by the entry and management fees charged to policyholders.[1350,1351]

The highest degree of integration is reached in the case where banking and insurance activities are under the same ownership. In such a case, a common holding company owns both a bank and an insurance company giving rise to a financial conglomerate.[1352] This integration can be achieved through different means.[1353] For instance, this can be done through a merger between a bank and an insurance company.[1354] Alternatively, such an integration can be achieved through an acquisition of a bank by an insurance company[1355] or vice versa. Lastly, while a banking group can establish an insurance subsidiary,[1356] an insurance group can also create a banking subsidiary.[1357] In such highly integrated models, in addition to a distribution through agreements stipulated with the affiliated banking network, insurance contracts can also be sold through agreements with external insurance distributors.[1358]

4.8.1.3 Distribution Approach

The diversity of bancassurance may also be seen in the variety of distribution approaches that can be used and reflected in the distribution agreement signed between the parties.[1359,1360] Typically, the sort of distribution approach is strictly

1350. *See* Massimo Caratelli in: Franco Fiordelisi/Ornella Ricci (eds.) *Bancassurance in Europe—Past, Present and Future*, p. 77 and Mark Teunissen, *The Geneva Papers on Risk and Insurance*, (2008) pp. 409-410.
1351. For instance, the joint venture model has been adopted by Barclays and CNP Assurances in Spain and Portugal. For further details on this case, *see also* Massimo Caratelli in: Franco Fiordelisi/Ornella Ricci (eds.) *Bancassurance in Europe—Past, Present and Future*, pp. 77-78.
1352. *See* Mark Teunissen, *The Geneva Papers on Risk and Insurance*, (2008) p. 410 and Franco Fiordelisi/Ornella Ricci, *EMFI WPs 2*, (2010) p. 5.
1353. *See* Emilia Clipici/Catalina Bolovan, *Scientific Bulletin—Economic Sciences—University of Pitești*, (2012) p. 56, Antonio Coviello, *L'utilizzo delle tecnologie avanzate nel settore assicurativo: l'e-insurance*, p. 105, Tobias C. Hoschka, *Bancassurance in Europe*, p. 100, Alan Leach, *New Initiatives in European Bancassurance*, p. 25, Ivana Clemente, *Bancassicurazione—L'evoluzione del rischio nei contratti "para-assicurativi,"* p. 40, Sergio Pugliese, *Bancassicurazione—La scelta dei prodotti e dei canali*, p. 31, Isabella Falautano/Emanuele Marsiglia, *The Geneva Papers on Risk and Insurance*, (2003) p. 487, Gilles Benoist, *The Geneva Papers on Risk and Insurance*, (2002) p. 302 and Luigi Selleri, *Strategie e marketing dell'impresa di assicurazione*, pp. 117-118.
1354. This has been for instance the case of the merger between NMB Postbank Groep and Nationale Nederlanden which gave birth to the ING Group.
1355. This has been for instance the case of the acquisition by Allianz of Dresdner Bank later sold and merged with Commerzbank.
1356. This is for instance the case of Sogécap, which is a life insurance company owned by Société Générale. For further details on this company, *see also* Massimo Caratelli in: Franco Fiordelisi/Ornella Ricci (eds.) *Bancassurance in Europe—Past, Present and Future*, pp. 79-82.
1357. This is for instance the case of Banca Generali, which is a bank under the control of Generali Group.
1358. This is particularly the case where the insurance is an indirect subsidiary of the top holding company. *See* Massimo Caratelli in: Franco Fiordelisi/Ornella Ricci (eds.) *Bancassurance in Europe—Past, Present and Future*, p. 78.
1359. *See* Alan Leach, *New Initiatives in European Bancassurance*, p. 25.
1360. The bancassurance agreement between the bank and the insurance company may also provide for a multi-channel distribution structure in an attempt to offer customers multiple options for access. To this effect, *see* Munich Re, *"Bancassurance in Practice,"* pp. 17-18.

related to the complexity of insurance products sold through the bancassurance arrangement in an attempt to match different insurance products with distribution channels for which they are most suited.[1361,1362]

To begin with, very simple products can be distributed through direct response and/or Internet platforms.[1363] Under the direct response approach, banks may be able to reach out to potential insurance customers that do not frequently visit their bank branch. Remarkably, the bank can make its customers aware about insurance product features through mailing, e-mailing or telephone contacts. In such a case, the customer can submit insurance offers directly by responding to such contacts.[1364] More recently, banks are also using the Internet to distribute simple insurance products. In its basic form, banks provide static product information on their customer portals. Often Internet sales are also integrated with a call center for answering questions and/or submitting offers. Alternatively, banks can also allow their customers to make an appointment request for a personal consultation in a bank branch. In addition to this, the Internet platform of certain banks also contains a link to the website of the insurance partner where the customer can submit insurance offers.[1365]

Simple insurance products may also be sold through salaried bank staff that received training in insurance selling techniques and product requirements.[1366] In such a case, the bank employees generally play an active role in marketing activities. As a matter of fact, they are usually required to generate insurance business with appropriate marketing actions by leveraging on information and knowledge at the disposal of the bank. In doing so, based on the distribution agreement between the bank and the insurance company, their activities may be limited to administrative activities (such as the preparation, collection and review of contractual documents, the collection of insurance premiums and so forth) or can go as far as to the acceptance of insurance offers from the customers. This approach is however not always effective to the extent that the time bank employees can devote to insurance sales is limited, e.g., due to the limited opening hours of the bank branch and to the need to perform other banking duties. A further restriction on the effectiveness of bank employees is that they have a

1361. *See* Munich Re, "*Bancassurance in Practice,*" p. 15, Alan Leach, *New Initiatives in European Bancassurance,* p. 26 and Sergio Paci, *La distribuzione dei servizi assicurativi tramite le aziende di credito* (Milano: EGEA, 1993) pp. 18-19.
1362. Instead, the distribution approach is not directly related to the organizational model depicted in the previous section.
1363. *See* Munich Re, "*Bancassurance in Practice,*" p. 17 and Alan Leach, *New Initiatives in European Bancassurance*, p. 26.
1364. *See* Munich Re, "*Bancassurance in Practice,*" pp. 16-17.
1365. *See* Andreas Grahl, "Online-Banking und Bancassurance" in: Marcel Seidel/Axel Liebetrau (eds.) *Banking & Innovation 2015: Ideen und Erfolgskonzepte von Experten für die Praxis* (Wiesbaden: Springer Gabler, 2015) pp. 188-189.
1366. Such training is normally regulated in the distribution agreement between the bank and the insurance company.

limited target market, i.e., those customers who visit the relevant bank branch during the opening hours.[1367]

Alternatively, the bancassurance arrangement between the bank and the insurance company may provide for a referral scheme. In such a case, pursuant to a referral agreement, the bank undertakes to refer potential customers to the insurance company in consideration for a referral commission. Hence, under such circumstances, sales and marketing activities are carried out by the insurance company. More to the point, such sales and marketing activities can be done through employee sales representatives and/or insurance agents.[1368,1369] To this end, the sales force of the insurance company may be allowed to serve bank customers inside the branch and/or may also visit/receive bank customers outside the branch opening hours in other premises.[1370]

At last, for complex insurance products, the bank employees may also refer potential customers to external advisers specialized in the insurance business (for instance, insurance specialists working for brokerage companies,[1371] financial advisors[1372] and/or brokers),[1373] again in consideration for a referral commission.[1374] The advantage of such arrangements is the availability of dedicated specialists needed for complex insurance matters and—in the case of insurance brokers—the opportunity for

1367. For further comments, *see* Munich Re, "*Bancassurance in Practice,*" pp. 16-17, Alan Leach, *New Initiatives in European Bancassurance*, p. 26, Tobias C. Hoschka, *Bancassurance in Europe*, pp. 125-127 and Sergio Paci, *La distribuzione dei servizi assicurativi tramite le aziende di credito*, pp. 19-20.

1368. In such a latter case, the insurance company is usually required to remunerate both the bank for the referral and the insurance agent for intermediation activities.

1369. For further comments on such insurance representatives, *see* s. 4.7 above.

1370. For further comments, *see* Munich Re, "*Bancassurance in Practice,*" pp. 15-17, Alan Leach, *New Initiatives in European Bancassurance*, p. 26, Tobias C. Hoschka, *Bancassurance in Europe*, pp. 125-127 and Sergio Paci, *La distribuzione dei servizi assicurativi tramite le aziende di credito*, pp. 20-22.

1371. In Italy, brokerage companies ("*società di intermediazione mobiliare*") are joint-stock companies engaged in securities brokerage. For further comments, *see* Marco Rossetti, *Il diritto delle assicurazioni—Volume 1*, pp. 620-624.

1372. In Italy, a financial advisor ("*promotore finanziario*") is a person normally engaged by banks, investment companies and management companies for the off-premise promotion and placement of financial instruments and investment services. The financial advisor can be a salaried employee or an external representative. In any case, he/she can work only for a single employer or principal. A financial advisor can also be engaged directly by an insurance company (in such a case, he can be regarded as an agent of the insurance company) or by an insurance customer (in such a case, he can be regarded as an insurance broker). To this effect, *see* Fabrizio Santoboni in: Fabrizio Santoboni (ed.) *Manuale di gestione assicurativa*, pp. 320-321 and Ernesto Pucci in: Marco Prosperetti/Alessandro Colavolpe (eds.) *I gestori del risparmio non bancari e i canali di distribuzione*, pp. 407-409.

1373. Insurance companies do not favor the broker channel in bancassurance to the extent that it is difficult to forecast how much business the insurance company will receive from the broker. *See* Munich Re, "*Bancassurance in Practice,*" p. 15. For further comments on insurance brokers, *see also* s. 4.6 above.

1374. In such cases, the insurance company is usually required to remunerate both the bank for the referral and the external advisers for intermediation activities.

bank clients to receive offers not only from one insurance company but from a variety of insurance companies.[1375]

4.8.1.4 *Fact Pattern*

The present analysis is built upon the assumption that foreign insurance companies conclude distribution agreements with banking partners to market, promote and distribute insurance products in the source country. This analysis is primarily focused on the distribution approach adopted to implement the bancassurance structure. Nonetheless, the organizational model is considered when relevant for the analysis. In doing so, it is also assumed that the bank employees[1376] and the external advisers are established in the source country.

4.8.2 Permanent Establishment Implications

4.8.2.1 *Analysis under the OECD Model*

4.8.2.1.1 *The Standard Version*

A bank is clearly a "*person*" in the sense of Art. 3 of the OECD Model that can perform activities connected with operations constituting the business proper of an insurance company which may go beyond activities dealt with under Art. 5, para. 4, of the OECD Model. Furthermore, pursuant to the distribution agreements, banks generally act "*on behalf of*" foreign insurance companies. Therefore, it is decisive to assess whether banks can conclude insurance contracts binding on foreign insurance companies or play the principal role leading to the conclusion of such contracts. This assessment is closely entrenched with the kind of distribution approach implemented in the context of the relevant bancassurance arrangement.[1377]

For a start, in the case of simple insurance contracts distributed over the bank counter and/or through distance selling means, it should be ascertained which is the scope of activities carried out by the bank staff. Among others, in the case that the bank employees at the counter can accept offers to enter into standardized insurance contracts, the traditional test regarding the conclusion of contracts is satisfied. The same also applies if the bank staff sitting in a call center can accept offers to enter into standardized contracts at the end of a telephone conversation. By the same token, the traditional test is also fulfilled in the case that bank employees sitting in a mail/e-mail service center can accept offers to enter into standardized insurance contracts submitted through application forms sent via mail/e-mail.

1375. For further comments, *see* Munich Re, "*Bancassurance in Practice*," pp. 16-17, Alan Leach, *New Initiatives in European Bancassurance*, p. 26, Tobias C. Hoschka, *Bancassurance in Europe*, pp. 125-127 and Sergio Paci, *La distribuzione dei servizi assicurativi tramite le aziende di credito*, pp. 20-22.
1376. For the purposes of the present analysis, it is assumed that bank employees represent the bank.
1377. The most common distribution approaches have been outlined in s. 4.8.1.3 above.

This should also hold true in the case where bank employees at the bank counter or sitting in a mail/e-mail service center collect from bank customers offers to enter into standardized insurance contracts binding on foreign insurance companies or otherwise subject to a mere formal acceptance of the insurance company. Likewise, should the same bank staff collect from bank customers their consents to be covered under collective insurance contracts at predetermined terms and conditions stipulated between the bank and the insurance company, it may be argued that the insurance company is bound by the consents collected through the banking channel, so that the traditional test regarding the conclusion of contracts is fulfilled.

Furthermore, where the above bank employees collect offers to enter into standardized contracts subject to a review of the foreign insurance company, but such a review does not result in material modifications, the supplementary test regarding the principal role leading to the conclusion of contracts could be fulfilled. Also, if bank employees are involved in the solicitation of insurance in the source country by enticing and convincing customers to purchase insurance, the bank could fulfill the supplementary test, even though its staff is not engaged in the collection of offers.

Therefore, in the above circumstances, under the assumption that the habitual exercise test is also fulfilled, the bank can give rise to a dependent agent permanent establishment. As a result, it remains to be assessed whether the bank may be regarded as an independent agent operating in the ordinary course of its business. This is primarily interwoven with the relationship between the bank and the insurance company, which is generally reflected in one of the organizational models depicted in the previous section.[1378]

To begin with, in the distribution alliance model, the distribution agreement is generally signed between third parties. Market standard agreements usually provide for a careful allocation of rights and obligations between contracting parties based on a mutual cooperation aimed at optimizing business processes with a view to distribute insurance products. It follows that, as a general rule, the distribution agreement does not assign to the insurance company a significant control over the business of the bank, which freely relies on its own network to distribute insurance products. Therefore, if the bank actually complies with the obligations set forth under a market standard agreement, carries on the functions specified therein, bears the related business risks and is remunerated accordingly, it is fair to say that the bank can be generally regarded as independent from the insurance company.[1379]

Instead, in the case of joint ventures and financial conglomerates, the distribution agreement is often concluded between related parties. In principle, under the assumption that the distribution agreement is concluded along the lines of a market standard

1378. More specifically, *see* s. 4.8.1.2 above.

1379. According to the author, this conclusion still holds true in the case of exclusive distribution agreements. In fact, although the exclusivity encompasses the prohibition to conclude distribution agreements concerning insurance products with other insurance companies in the same territory, a bank is generally free to conclude (and does conclude) additional distribution agreements regarding other financial products, such as bonds, investment fund units, pension fund units and so forth. It follows that a bank usually does not represent a single principal but rather multiple principals, none of which is predominant over the others.

agreement and such an agreement is actually complied with to the effect that the bank is not subject to comprehensive control of the insurance company,[1380] it could be maintained that the bank is still independent from the insurance company. However, it should be recalled that the supplementary independence test regarding related parties introduced in the aftermath of the BEPS Project could in principle prevent a bank from being regarded as independent in the case that such a bank act exclusively or almost exclusively on behalf of one or more insurance companies to which it is closely related. True, it is unlikely that bancassurance activities represent a large part of a bank's business. Nonetheless, in such intra-group situations, the independence of the bank vis-à-vis the insurance company should be carefully assessed in each specific case.[1381] Instead, in the peculiar case where the bank and insurance activities are integrated in a single legal entity, it can be reasonably argued that employees of such an entity operating in the source country cannot be regarded as independent from the head office to the extent that such employees are usually subject to detailed instructions and control of the head office.

With respect to the ordinary course of business test, it is worth noting that, under the applicable regulatory framework,[1382] besides traditional banking activities,[1383] banks are also authorized to provide their customers with additional financial services. Among others, such additional services also encompass insurance intermediation. For instance, in the context of the EU provisions governing the distribution of insurance products, the role of bancassurance operators has been specifically acknowledged in the Insurance Mediation Directive[1384] and more recently in the Insurance Distribution Directive. As a consequence, insofar as the distribution of insurance products in the context of bancassurance arrangements may be regarded as part of customary banking activities authorized under the applicable the regulatory framework,[1385] there are good grounds to conclude that the distribution of insurance products falls within the ordinary course of the banking business.

On the other hand, no dependent agent permanent establishment should arise in the case that the involvement of the bank employees at the bank counter or sitting in a mail/e-mail service center is limited to administrative activities, like the preparation, the collection and the review of contractual documentation and/or the collection of insurance premiums. Indeed, in such cases, neither the traditional test regarding the

1380. Although the application of transfer pricing rules is beyond the scope of this research, it should be noted that this is also crucial to comply with domestic and treaty rules governing transactions between related parties.
1381. This case is similar to that of internal representatives. For further comments, *see* s. 4.7.2.2.1 above.
1382. Although the regulation of banks is beyond the scope of this research, it is worth noting that the activities of banks are strictly regulated under international, EU and national legislation.
1383. Traditional banking activities include the acceptance of deposits and money lending. For instance, in Italy, such banking activities are defined under Art. 10 of the Legislative Decree No. 385/1993.
1384. Directive 2002/92/EC of the European Parliament and of the Council of 9 December 2002 on insurance mediation.
1385. As such, banks are generally required to be registered in a specific register of insurance intermediaries.

conclusion of contracts nor the supplementary test regarding the principal role leading to the conclusion of contracts may be regarded as fulfilled.

Furthermore, it may be argued that a mere marketing and promotion of insurance products through the banking network—at the counter and/or through distance selling means[1386]—should not give rise to a dependent agent permanent establishment. Indeed, in such cases, pursuant to the distribution agreement, the insurance company generally undertakes to prepare and deliver advertising materials (as well as announcements and model forms of contract) regarding insurance products in scope of the arrangement, cooperate with the bank in designing promotional campaigns targeted to potential bank customers and assist the bank in creating and implementing appropriate training programs for the bank staff in insurance matters. On the other hand, the activities of the bank are generally limited to marketing and promotional activities, including the provision of information about the possibility for its customers to be covered under insurance protection, the distribution of the above marketing and promotional materials in a manner agreed between the parties and the delivery of the relevant policy information and documentation.

In a similar vein, no dependent agent permanent establishment should arise in the case that the bank is involved in other administrative activities, such as the preparation of reports regarding its customers, the collection of documents regarding its customers, the collection of insurance premiums from its customers to be subsequently transferred to the insurance company and/or the delivery of the insurance policies to its customers. As a matter of fact, in such cases, the bank does not fulfill neither the traditional test regarding the conclusion of contracts nor the supplementary test regarding the principal role leading to the conclusion of contracts.

Likewise, when the bancassurance arrangement envisages a referral scheme, whereby the bank refers prospects to the insurance company and/or other external advisers specialized in the insurance business, the bank does not create a dependent agent permanent establishment to the extent that it does not fulfill neither of the above tests. Nevertheless, a further assessment will be required for the purposes of addressing the question as to whether this referral scheme might lead to the creation of a dependent agent permanent establishment with respect to the activities carried out in the source country by other persons. In fact, while the reference can be made to employee sales representatives and/or insurance agents,[1387] it is to be ascertained whether other external advisers can give rise to permanent establishment concerns.

Any such external adviser can be regarded as a "*person*" in the sense of Art. 3 of the OECD Model carrying on intermediation activities interrelated to operations which constitute the business proper of an insurance company which may go beyond the activities laid down in Art. 5, para. 4, of the OECD Model. Nevertheless, such advisers are intermediaries that are usually engaged by banks with a view to provide specific advice to bank customers. Accordingly, such advisers do not generally act on behalf of

1386. In the case that the potential customer is re-directed from the platform of the bank to the website of the insurance company, *see* s. 4.2.2 above.

1387. Circumstances where such insurance representatives may give rise to permanent establishment have already been addressed in s. 4.7 above.

foreign insurance companies, so that no dependent agent permanent establishment arises in the source country. On a different note, advisers engaged directly by bank customers can be regarded as agents of the customers and thus assimilated to insurance brokers,[1388] whereas advisers engaged directly by insurance companies can be assimilated to insurance agents.[1389]

4.8.2.1.2 The Special Clause for Insurance Agents

Banks that do not otherwise create a dependent agent permanent establishment under the standard version of the OECD Model could fall within the scope of the special clause for insurance agents in the case that such banks are regarded as agents through which a foreign insurance company collects premiums or insures risks in the source country.

This can be the case of banks that fulfill the requirements laid down in Art. 5, para. 5, of the OECD Model, but are nevertheless covered under the independent agent provision. Indeed, in such a case, the criterion related to the insurance of risks can be regarded as met to the effect that a permanent establishment arises in the source country, regardless of whether the bank is independent or not from the insurance company.

Furthermore, the special clause can catch banks that do not fulfill the conditions of the dependent agent provision. As a matter of fact, the criterion regarding the insurance of risks in the source country also covers situations where banks collect offers to enter into standardized contracts subject to a genuine review of the insurance company, even though such a review results in material modifications. In addition, the special clause can also cover circumstances where bank employees are involved in administrative activities, like the preparation, the collection and the review of contractual documentation and/or the collection of insurance premiums. In fact, while the preparation, the collection and the review of contractual documentation can be covered under the criterion regarding the insurance of risks, the collection of premiums triggers by definition the special clause for insurance agents.

On the other hand, the author is of the opinion that the bank does not give rise to a permanent establishment in the case where the involvement of its employees is limited to marketing and promotion activities, such as the provision of general information regarding products of its insurance partner(s) over the counter, through its website and/or through mailing, e-mailing or telephone correspondence. As a matter of fact, it may be argued that the activities of the bank do not directly result in the actual collection of premiums or insurance of risks takes place in the source country.

The same also holds true in the case where the bank refers potential customers to insurance companies and/or external advisers. However, in such a case, it should be ascertained whether this referral scheme might lead to the creation of a permanent establishment with respect to the activities carried out in the source country by other

1388. Circumstances where such insurance brokers may give rise to a permanent establishment have already been addressed in s. 4.6 above.

1389. Circumstances where such insurance agents may give rise to a permanent establishment have already been addressed in s. 4.7 above.

agents. In particular, should the bank refer prospects to employee sales representatives and/or insurance agents, it is to be ascertained whether such individuals trigger the relevant criteria for the special clause to apply.[1390] Differently, in the case that the bank refers potential customers to external advisers, it may be argued that no permanent establishment should arise. In fact, such advisers are intermediaries that are usually engaged by banks with a view to provide specific advice to bank customers. As a result, such advisers cannot be regarded as agents of the insurance company for the purposes of the special clause.

4.8.2.2 *Analysis under the UN Model*

In general, it may be argued that—under Art. 5, para. 5, let. (*a*), of the UN Model—a bank can fulfill the traditional test regarding the conclusion of contracts in the event that its employees: (*i*) accept insurance offers from bank customers, (*ii*) collect insurance offers and such offers are binding on the foreign insurance company or otherwise only subject to a mere formal acceptance of the insurance company or (*iii*) collect from bank customers their consents to be covered under collective insurance contracts. In addition to this, a bank can fulfill the supplementary test regarding the principal role leading to the conclusion of contracts if its employees: (*i*) collect insurance offers, such offers are subject to review of the insurance company, but such a review does not result in material modifications or (*ii*) solicit insurance business. It follows that, under such circumstances, assuming that the remaining conditions set out in the paragraph under analysis are satisfied, a dependent agent permanent establishment may arise in the source country.

On the top of this, additional situations where bank employees are involved in the collection of insurance offers can be caught under the insurance agent provision, e.g., in the case where such offers are subject to review of the insurance company and such a review results in material modifications. This is also the case where bank employees are involved in administrative activities related to contracts (such as the preparation, collection and review of insurance contracts and/or the collection of premiums from bank customers). Indeed, in such cases, the bank can arguably fulfill the conditions of the collection of premiums and/or insurance of risks in the source country to the effect that a permanent establishment is likely to arise.[1391]

In spite of the above, one should assess whether the bank may be covered under the independence agent provision contained in Art. 5, para. 7, of the UN Model. Although this assessment should be carried out on a case-by-case basis account taken of the applicable circumstances, in general, it can reasonably be upheld that the independence and ordinary course of business tests are likely to be met in the case that the distribution agreement is concluded between third parties. On the other hand, in the context of joint ventures and financial conglomerates, the above tests necessarily

1390. Circumstances where such insurance representatives may give rise to a permanent establishment have already been addressed in s. 4.7 above.

1391. The carve-out for reinsurance contained in Art. 5, para. 6, of the UN Model is not discussed herein to the extent that bancassurance generally involves direct insurance business only.

presuppose a more careful assessment of the applicable circumstances, taking also into consideration the supplementary independence test regarding related parties. Finally, in the event that the banking and insurance activities are integrated in a single legal entity, the independence status cannot be claimed with respect to internal staff due to the fact that such staff is generally subject to detailed instructions and control of the head office.

Lastly, it is worth noting that, in the case where the bancassurance arrangement is based on a referral scheme, the bank does not generally give rise to a permanent establishment. However, in such a case, it should be ascertained whether such a referral scheme can lead to the creation of a permanent establishment with respect to the activities carried out in the source country by other persons. If the reference is made to employee sales representatives and/or insurance agents, it may be argued that such individuals could fulfill either the dependent agent provision or the insurance agent provision.[1392] Conversely, if the reference is made to external advisers, it is fair to say that such advisers do not generally act on behalf of foreign insurance companies, so that the conditions laid down in Art. 5, para. 5, let. (*a*), of the UN Model are not met. On the other hand, while such external advisers could in principle fall within the scope of the insurance agent provision, they are normally covered under the independent agent provision.

4.9 MULTINATIONAL BUSINESS

4.9.1 General Overview

4.9.1.1 Introduction

With the trend toward globalization, there is greater need for insurance solutions intended to cover risks stemming from international operations.[1393] To this end, a multinational may conclude separate, unrelated insurance contracts in each country where it has exposure. In such a case, the insurance contracts are normally underwritten by local insurance companies licensed in the countries where the multinational group carries on its operations. By contrast, a multinational may rely on a single global insurance contract concluded in its home country to cover itself and its worldwide exposures. Such global contracts are generally issued in the home country of the multinational by an insurance company licensed in that country. Alternatively, a multinational group may also opt for a multinational program (also referred to as a global program or controlled master program), which normally combines multiple local contracts issued in various countries with a global contract issued in the home country of the multinational. The global contract is generally linked to local contracts, often through terms agreed in the global contract, which are aimed at ensuring

1392. Circumstances where such insurance representatives may give rise to a permanent establishment have already been addressed in s. 4.7 above.
1393. *See* Generali, "*Multinational Programs*," available online at www.generali.com, p. 2 and AIG, "*Why Go Multinational with AIG?*," available online at www.aig.com.

homogeneity of coverage throughout the different locations. The global contract may also cover risks in countries where there are no local contracts.[1394]

All major insurance groups now offer multinational programs, mainly for large business customers.[1395] Such programs may cover a wide variety of business lines, ranging from commercial/industrial lines (such as property, casualty, marine, aviation, space, engineering, financial lines and so forth) to health insurance (such as medical benefits, out-patient benefits and other specialist cover options) and employee benefits (such as protection and pension solutions) for large customers with globally mobile people.

The design, implementation and management of such arrangements are clearly complex. And, of course, there is no one single way to structure a multinational program. Nonetheless, for the purposes of the present analysis, the most common operating models will be analyzed in more detail below, mostly in terms of origination. In doing so, as opposed to the previous sections, the focus will be on the structure of the multinational program rather than the role of insurance intermediaries involved.[1396]

4.9.1.2 Program Coordination

Multinational programs are generally coordinated through a central team of specialists, which might sit in a dedicated legal entity[1397] or otherwise represent a business unit of a company with larger operations.[1398] Such a central team is normally dedicated to the multinational program and network management activities to meet the needs of the customers.

Among others, the central team is normally in charge of the product development. In fact, all products offered through the multinational programs are designed, developed and approved centrally. Also, the central team might be asked to weigh up the decision to offer a specific product in a certain jurisdiction. Furthermore, the central team is normally responsible for setting the overall framework of multinational programs.[1399] This framework primarily serves as guidance for affiliates to operate within the terms of underwriting limits, which might be set with reference to premium volumes and/or risk selection.[1400] In this regard, such a framework generally governs:

1394. *See* David Halperin, "*How to Build a Multinational Program,*" available online at www.aig.com, p. 3 and Suresh Krishnan/Sheena Shah/Ronald Williams, "*Structuring Multinational Insurance Programs: Cross-border Challenges to Business Travel & Personal Accident Insurance,*" available online at https://www2.chubb.com, p. 3.
1395. For instance, this is the case of Axa (through Axa Corporate Solutions), Generali (Generali Global Corporate & Commercial, Generali Employee Benefits and Generali Global Health), Allianz (Allianz Global Corporate & Specialty), Zurich and AIG.
1396. Being programs designed for large corporate customers, multinational program arrangements are often originated through insurance brokers. For further comments on insurance brokers, *see* s. 4.6 above.
1397. This is for instance the case of Axa Corporate Solutions.
1398. This is for instance the case of multinational programs established in the Generali Group.
1399. Such a framework generally takes the form of internal guidelines in intra-group situations and/or umbrella agreements in dealings with third parties.
1400. The framework may also govern other activities, such as claims handling.

(*i*) the assumption of direct insurance business (underwritten through producing and/or fronting entities), (*ii*) the flows of reinsurance transferred to producing entities and/or a pooling entity and (*iii*) the retrocession of business to third parties.[1401] Lastly, the central team typically provides support functions to local insurance companies in relation to multinational programs. Among others, the support functions include administration, HR, compliance and legal.

4.9.1.3 Origination Through Producing Entities

Under this operating model, multinational programs are generally established in the headquarter country of multinational customers. Such programs are typically sourced through a local insurance company (which plays the key role of the producing entity) established in the same jurisdiction of the multinational customer headquarter. More specifically, the producing entity is normally in charge of deciding the insurance products to be offered in the relevant jurisdiction, save for specific circumstances where central approval is sought.[1402] In addition to this, the producing entity is typically responsible for business development and relationship management activities with multinational customers established in the relevant jurisdiction. To this end, the producing entity interacts with customers and/or intermediaries with a view to bid for master insurance contracts required by multinational companies established therein.

Once business opportunities have been identified, the producing entity is generally responsible for all underwriting activities (including pricing, risk selection and classification) with a view to conclude a master insurance contract with the relevant multinational customer, provided that the underwriting activities performed fall within the overall framework established by the central team.[1403,1404] The master insurance contract is generally based on predetermined forms prepared centrally and is concluded between the producing entity and the parent company of the multinational group. Such a master contract is intended to cover the customer parent company for its insurable interests in its worldwide exposures and to outline general terms and conditions for insuring potential coverage gaps in underlying local contracts concluded as part of the same multinational program. Usually, master contract premiums are paid by the multinational group parent company to the producing entity. Likewise, claims

1401. While the central team is normally responsible for cascading down the underwriting limits to the local entities, the implementation of such a framework is governed locally.
1402. *See* s. 4.9.1.2 above.
1403. *See* s. 4.9.1.2 above.
1404. When an insurance risk is outside underwriting limits, such a risk is normally referred to the central team, who will further investigate whether the risk should be underwritten or not. Once the central team has reviewed the referred risk, it will generally decide whether (*i*) the risk can be accepted, (*ii*) the risk is to be declined or (*iii*) the risk can be accepted with conditions. Still, from a legal standpoint, although the central team may be required to approve risks that exceed underwriting limits, it is worth noting that the risk still sits with the producing entity.

under such a contract are handled by the producing entity and settled to the multinational customer parent company in its jurisdiction.[1405]

Furthermore, the producing entity is also in charge of liaising with other insurance companies to underwrite local specific contracts. In fact, in other locations where multinational customers have activities and thus require insurance, the risks are typically covered via a local contract through a local (fronting) insurance company (the fronting entity), which cedes such risks back to the producing entity.[1406] In other terms, the fronting entity—licensed in the country where the risk to be insured is located—insures that risk on behalf of the producing entity. Such a risk is then transferred from the fronting entity to the producing entity through a reinsurance agreement (the fronting agreement)[1407] in consideration for a remuneration, which takes the form of a commission (the fronting fee).[1408] Hence, under a fronting arrangement, while the recipient of the insurance will receive a policy from the fronting entity, risks associated with that policy are ultimately borne by the producing entity.[1409]

In multinational programs, fronting arrangements might be used for multiple reasons, as follows:

- The producing entity is not licensed to issue the policy in a specific location, so that the fronting entity facilitates the arrangement via the issuance of a policy compliant with local regulations.[1410]
- The producing entity is unable to meet financial strength measures to issue the policy for a specific risk in a specific location.
- To guarantee the servicing of the insurance contract by dedicated local resources knowledgeable of the local market.

1405. It is worth noting that the central team may also set guidelines for performing claims handling activities. In such a case, similar to the underwriting guidelines, the producing entity is responsible for claims handling activities within limits set in the guidelines, whereas any claim that exceeds such limits generally requires approval from the central team.
1406. In the context of multinational programs, fronting arrangements are mainly established among affiliated companies with a view to create an internal integrated network for multinational customers. However, in certain instances, insurance groups are required to partner with third party insurance companies to provide local solutions to customers with operations in jurisdictions where such insurance groups do not have affiliated companies. Such partnership agreements might also be reciprocal in nature in such a way that each party can provide the same fronting services to the other one in the case any of them does not have a presence in a specific jurisdiction.
1407. Fronting arrangements generally provide for a full transfer of risk to the producing entity through a 100% quota share reinsurance agreement, unless local regulations require a minimum risk to be kept in the country of the fronting entity.
1408. Such a commission is sometimes referred to as overriding commission.
1409. For further comments, *see* John Prescott/Deborah Lambert, "*What's Up Front: A Guide to Fronting Arrangements*," available online at www.captive.com.
1410. It is worth noting that multinational insurance programs may also include self-procured, or independently procured, insurance. This term refers to any contract that is concluded with a non-admitted insurance company, i.e., an insurance company not licensed in the country where the risk is located. For further comments on this practice, *see also* ch. 2 above.

Terms and conditions of fronting and servicing activities are generally governed under a framework agreement stipulated between the producing entity and the fronting entity. As a general rule, the fronting entity is responsible for underwriting the insurance risk in conformity with applicable local legislation to the extent that such a risk falls within the framework set in the underwriting guidelines,[1411] issuing policy documents, collecting premiums, handling and settling claims.[1412] Other services may also be agreed between the parties, such as the provision of local technical expertise, the provision of market information and information about the business practice in respect of the lines of insurance business to be underwritten.[1413,1414]

Once business is underwritten, a reinsurance agreement is then arranged between the fronting entity and the producing entity to transfer such a business. The negotiation and the pricing of reinsurance transactions usually take place between the producing entity and the fronting entity within the general framework set centrally. Such a framework also governs the retrocession of business to third parties, if any.[1415]

4.9.1.4 Origination Through Regional Offices

Under this alternative operating model, the central team coordinates a network of regional offices across the globe.[1416] Under the supervision of the central team, such regional offices are generally responsible for business development and relationship management activities in the geographical area falling under their competence. More specifically, such offices are responsible for sourcing and managing multinational programs with parent companies of multinational customers established in their area.

Once business opportunities have been identified, the regional offices are also in charge of relationship management activities with the network of local insurance companies which is to be engaged with a view to concluding local compliant contracts in jurisdictions where multinational customers falling under their responsibility have business operations, including the jurisdiction of the multinational group parent company.

Like the business originated through producing entities, the business originated through regional offices is generally regulated under a framework agreed with the central team. Such a general framework provides the underwriting rules and limits in respect of multinational programs originated through regional offices. In this regard, the local insurance company is generally responsible for underwriting the insurance risk according to its ultimate discretion, provided that such a risk is in line with the general framework. Differently, any decisions to be made by the local entity that would result in a deviation from and/or an excess of parameters laid down in the general

1411. As already outlined above, when an insurance risk is outside underwriting limits, such a risk is normally referred to the central team.
1412. As already outlined above, the central team may also set guidelines for performing claims handling activities.
1413. A separate remuneration might be agreed for such additional services.
1414. Some of such services may also be outsourced to external service providers.
1415. To this effect, *see also* s. 4.9.1.2 above.
1416. Such offices are generally set up in the main regional hubs in order to work closely with customers and intermediaries.

framework is normally referred to the competent regional office in the first instance and successively to the central team, if need be.

Usually, the local insurance company is also responsible for issuing policy documents,[1417] collecting premiums, handling and settling claims,[1418] while the competent regional office normally acts as the single point of contact for multinational customers to answer questions, coordinate customer services, prepare and deliver policy reports and liaise with the network of local insurance companies. In certain instances, once business is underwritten, local insurance companies may retain such a business related to multinational programs originated through regional office structures. However, very often, such a business is centralized through reinsurance agreements in a pool.[1419]

4.9.1.5 Pooling Arrangements

The administration of multinational programs might be inefficient in the case where the business is retained locally. Hence, insurance groups may opt to pool the multinational business underwritten locally in a single entity through proportional reinsurance agreements.[1420] More precisely, with respect to multinational business originated through producing entities, in consideration for a ceding commission, the producing entities and the fronting entities will reinsure the multinational business with the pooling company, which will operate as a reinsurance hub for such a business. Under this centralized model, the reinsurance flows between the producing entities and the fronting entities will be replaced with reinsurance flows ceded from such entities to the pooling company. By the same token, the pooling company may also reinsure the multinational business originated through regional offices and written by local insurance companies. In such a case, the local insurance companies will operate as fronting companies and will centralize such a multinational business through reinsurance agreements in consideration for a ceding commission.

Pooling arrangements may also be combined with a profit sharing scheme aimed at offering a wider range of insurance solutions to customers. To this end, the pooling company stipulates a multinational pooling agreement with the parent company of the multinational customer, whereby the parties agree that the net profit stemming from the relevant multinational program (if any) is paid back to the customer. To determine such a net profit, a pooling booklet is generally prepared on the basis of the duration of the agreement (mostly, on a calendar year basis). The booklet will consider all premiums and claims pertaining to the pooled insurance contracts. Should the

1417. In certain instances, the competent regional office also takes care of the fulfillment, i.e., preparation and delivery of the insurance policies.

1418. As already outlined above, the central team may also set guidelines for performing claims handling activities. For further comments, *see also* s. 4.1.9.3 above.

1419. For further comments, *see* s. 4.1.9.5 below.

1420. The pooling company can be the parent company of the insurance group or another dedicated group company.

algebraic sum of such items, net of risk protection as well as commission, administration and other expenses, be positive, the pooling company will pay back the balance of the pooling booklet to the multinational parent company.

4.9.1.6 *Retrocession to Captives*

Should the business be pooled centrally, the pooling company is responsible for deciding how much risk should be retroceded to third parties and on what terms.[1421] Among others, a specific form of retrocession is the retrocession to captive companies. In a nutshell, captives are wholly owned insurance/reinsurance subsidiaries of multinational groups not engaged in the insurance business,[1422] which have the primary function to insure/reinsure risks of their parent company and/or their affiliates.[1423]

Captives were very much a product of the volatile insurance markets of the 1970s and 1980s and were originally set up by groups looking for a cost saving method to address their rising insurance costs. For this reason, captives are mainly established in exotic island locations, such as Bermuda and Cayman Islands. In Europe, Channel Islands, Luxembourg and Ireland are the market leaders in this field. Nevertheless, over the past decade, the role of captives has changed dramatically, so that captives are now more generally regarded as dynamic vehicles to facilitate risk financing, rather than just alternative risk transfer and/or self-insurance tools.[1424]

In its most common form, the retrocession to captives normally envisages that the pooling company stipulates a retrocession agreement with the captive of the multinational group. Under the terms and conditions of this agreement, the pooling company transfers the risks to the pooling company in consideration for a service fee.[1425]

4.9.1.7 *Fact Pattern*

The factual background for this analysis involves the presence of multiple entities taking part in integrated networks underlying multinational programs. To this end, it is

1421. For instance, protection can be purchased through aggregate stop loss, excess of loss and/or surplus agreements.
1422. For this reason, captives are also referred to as in-house insurance/reinsurance companies.
1423. For further comments, *see*—among others—OECD, "*Taxing Insurance Companies*," available online at www.oecd.com, pp. 35-36, Arvid A. Skaar, *Taxation Issues Relating to Captive Insurance Companies* (Amsterdam: IBFD, 1998) pp. 8-19, William P. Elliott, "Captive Insurance Arrangements: A Comprehensive Update," *Tax Notes International* (2004) pp. 298-300, William P. Elliott, "A Guide to Captive Insurance Companies (Part 1)," *Journal of International Taxation* (2005) pp. 22 et seq., International Risk Management Institute Inc., "*What Is Captive Insurance?*," available online at www.captive.com and Andreas Schwepcke, *Reinsurance: Principles and State of the Art—A Guidebook for Home Learners—2nd Edition*, pp. 17 et seq.
1424. *See* Jeff Soar/Simon Burtwell/James Smith, "Captives to 2020: Opportunities and Challenges," *Derivatives & Financial Instruments* (2014) p. 253.
1425. Usually, the risk is wholly retroceded via a quota share agreement, unless mutually agreed otherwise, account taken of regulatory requirements. However, the retrocession might also be combined with additional forms of protection, such as protection against catastrophe exposure.

assumed that the entities involved in the operating models under scrutiny are established in different countries. In addition, it is also assumed that such entities carry on their business in their respective countries of establishment with no employees and/or intermediaries abroad. For the purposes of the present analysis, each business connection among such entities will be assessed separately.

4.9.2 Permanent Establishment Implications

4.9.2.1 Analysis under the OECD Model

4.9.2.1.1 The Standard Version

First off, it may be argued that all the entities involved in multinational programs (namely, the central team, the producing entities, the fronting entities, the regional offices, the pooling companies and the retrocession companies) generally fulfill the subjective requirement contained in Art. 5, para. 5, of the OECD Model. Hence, in order to assess the existence of a dependent agent permanent establishment, one should primarily look at the involvement of such entities in the operating models outlined in the previous section.

On this front, as already portrayed in the previous section,[1426] the central team is generally responsible for the coordination of multinational programs. According to the author, this coordination does not result in the central team being a dependent agent permanent establishment of insurance companies participating in the program. Indeed, the central team is—*inter alia*—responsible for product development and support activities. Even where the central team sits in an insurance company, such activities may be regarded as preparatory and auxiliary activities pursuant to Art. 5, para. 4, of the OECD Model. Therefore, the central team cannot give rise to a dependent agent permanent establishment of local insurance companies with respect to such activities. Furthermore, the central team is also in charge of setting the framework of multinational programs by means of general guidance. Although this could go beyond preparatory and auxiliary activities, it may be argued that the central team is not acting "*on behalf of*" local insurance companies.[1427] Nor is the central team in such a way fulfilling the traditional test regarding the conclusion of contracts binding on local insurance companies or the supplementary test regarding the principal role leading to the conclusion of such contracts.

Local insurance companies cannot be regarded as dependent agent permanent establishments of the relevant legal entity in which the central team is sitting, either. True, in the case where the central team is sitting in a foreign insurance company, the local insurance companies are involved in activities which constitute the business proper of such a foreign insurance company. Additionally, local insurance companies take part in multinational programs under a framework established centrally to the effect that such companies might in principle be regarded as carrying out their activities

1426. *See* s. 4.9.1.2 above.
1427. It is rather the network of local insurance companies that acts "*on behalf of*" the central team. *See* below for further comments.

"*on behalf of*" the central team, which is governing the multinational program. Nevertheless, local insurance companies do not conclude—or otherwise play the principal role leading to the conclusion of—contracts binding on the legal entity in which the central team is sitting. In fact, the conclusion of insurance contracts with multinational customers is only binding on local insurance companies to the effect that the substantive requirement of the contracts being "*in the name of*" the foreign insurance company is not fulfilled.

In respect of multinational programs that are originated through producing entities,[1428] it may be argued that the producing entity should not be regarded as a dependent agent permanent establishment of any fronting entity. As a matter of fact, although the producing entity is involved in activities which constitute the business proper of the fronting entities, business development and underwriting activities carried out by the producing entity in its jurisdiction (which is the same jurisdiction of the multinational head office) are not performed "*on behalf of*" the fronting entities.[1429]

To the contrary, fronting entities clearly act "*on behalf of*" the producing entity. In fact, once business opportunities have been identified, fronting entities are specifically instructed by the producing entity to enter into local complaint contracts in countries other than that of the relevant multinational customer parent company to provide coverage in respect of local operations. Nevertheless, it may still be argued that the fronting entities do not conclude contracts binding on the producing entity. Indeed, there are good grounds to maintain that local insurance contracts are not binding on the producing entity as long as the subsequent reinsurance between producing and fronting entities is a sound business transaction subject to a genuine negotiation and approval process.[1430] Also, fronting entities do not solicit insurance business underwritten by the relevant producing entity in such a way as to trigger the supplementary test regarding the principal role leading to the conclusion of contracts binding on the producing entity. Instead, it is the producing entity that originates the business and engages the network of fronting entities to underwrite local business. Therefore, it cannot be said that fronting entities create dependent agent permanent establishments of the relevant producing entity.

Moving to multinational programs that are originated through regional offices,[1431] it should be at first assessed whether such offices may create dependent agent permanent establishments of the legal entity in which the central team is sitting. In this respect, under the assumption that both the central team and regional offices are set up within insurance companies, regional offices can be involved in operations which constitute the core business of the insurance company in which the central team is

1428. *See* s. 4.9.1.3 above.
1429. It is rather the network of fronting entities that acts "*on behalf of*" the producing entity. *See* below for further comments.
1430. Most notably, this is the case where the local management is ultimately responsible for signing all reinsurance arrangements and makes the decision with respect to how much business is reinsured on a facultative basis to third parties and how much business is retained.
1431. *See* s. 4.9.1.4 above.

sitting.[1432] In doing so, such regional offices may exceed activities referred to in Art. 5, para. 4, of the OECD Model (just as business development and relationship management activities) under the supervision of the central team in the geographical area under their competence. Also, regional offices take part in multinational programs under a framework established centrally to the effect that such offices might in principle be regarded as carrying out their activities "*on behalf of*" the central team, which is governing the multinational program. Nonetheless, as a general rule, such regional offices do not fulfill the traditional test regarding the conclusion of contracts binding on the above legal entity. Likewise, such offices do not solicit insurance business later underwritten by the central team in such a way as to trigger the supplementary test. In fact, the central team does not enter into insurance contracts in the context of multinational programs, even where the central team is set up within an insurance company. As a result, the existence of a dependent agent permanent establishment should be excluded.

In a similar vein, it should also be excluded that a regional office can give rise to a dependent agent permanent establishment of local insurance companies taking part in multinational programs. As a matter of fact, although the regional offices are involved in activities which constitute the business proper of the local insurance companies, the regional offices do not act "*on behalf of*" such local insurance companies.[1433]

On the other hand, although local insurance companies might be seen as acting "*on behalf of*" the relevant regional office to the extent that such companies are specifically engaged to conclude local complaint contracts in their respective countries, it is fair to say that the local companies do not conclude contracts binding on the legal entity in which the competent regional office is sitting. Indeed, insurance contracts concluded with local subsidiaries of multinational customers are only binding on local insurance companies themselves, so that the substantive requirement of the contracts being "*in the name of*" the foreign insurance company is not fulfilled. Also, local insurance companies do not solicit insurance business that is subsequently underwritten by regional offices in such a way as to trigger the supplementary test. In fact, regional offices do not conclude insurance contracts in the context of multinational programs, even where such offices are set up within insurance companies. Rather, the competent regional office originates the business and engages the network of local insurance companies to underwrite local business. Therefore, it cannot be said that local insurance companies create dependent agent permanent establishments of the relevant regional office.

1432. It is worth noting that a dependent agent permanent establishment might in principle arise only in the country where such activities are carried out, which is often the country where the competent regional office is set up. As a matter of fact, under Art. 5, para. 5, of the OECD Model, a person needs to carry on activities in a given country to constitute a dependent agent permanent establishment therein. For further comments, *see* s. 3.3.2.3.2 above.

1433. It is rather the network of local insurance companies that acts "*on behalf of*" the regional office. *See* below for further comments.

The above reasoning also holds true in the case of pooling arrangements, whereby the multinational business is pooled centrally.[1434] In general, producing and fronting entities do not act "*on behalf of*" the pooling company, save in the situation where central coordination and pooling activities are integrated in a single entity.[1435] Indeed, in such a latter case, local producing and fronting entities might in principle be seen as carrying out multinational business "*on behalf of*" such a coordinating entity. At any rate, even under such circumstances, it may be argued that local producing and fronting entities do not conclude contracts binding on the legal entity in which the central team is sitting and/or the pooling company. More to the point, under the assumption that the following reinsurance is a sound business transaction subject to a genuine negotiation and approval process, it may be argued that the local insurance contracts are only binding on the producing and/or fronting entities, as the case may be. Hence, the requirement of the contracts being "*in the name of*" the foreign insurance company is not fulfilled. In such a case, there are also good grounds to maintain that local insurance companies (most notably, producing entities) do not solicit business that is eventually underwritten by the coordinating entity in such a way as to trigger the supplementary test regarding the principal role leading to the conclusion of contracts. As a matter of fact, the coordinating entity comes into play only to reinsure business previously underwritten on a local basis. As a consequence, under the same assumption that the following reinsurance is a sound business transaction, it can be reasonably concluded that the local insurance companies should not create dependent agent permanent establishments of the coordinating entity.

On the other hand, it is fair to say that the pooling company does not act "*on behalf of*" producing and/or fronting entities, not even in the situation where central coordination and pooling activities are integrated in a single entity. On the top of this, the pooling company does not fulfill neither the traditional test regarding the conclusion of contracts binding on producing and/or fronting entities nor the supplementary test regarding the principal role leading to the conclusion of such contracts.

Profit sharing arrangements do not alter the above conclusions to the extent that the multinational pooling agreement stipulated between the pooling company and the parent company of the multinational customer for the purposes of sharing the balance of the pool (if positive) does not have significant implications on the relationship existing between the pooling company and the producing and/or fronting companies taking part in the multinational program. In addition to this, the pooling company cannot give rise to a dependent agent permanent establishment of the multinational customer. In fact, the insurance activities of the pooling company are not generally interrelated to the operations of the multinational customer, provided that the multinational customer is not itself engaged in the insurance business.

1434. *See* s. 4.9.1.5 above.

1435. For instance, this might be the case where coordination and pooling activities are concentrated at the level of the parent company of the insurance group to better manage multinational programs.

Similar conclusions may be finally extended to the case where the business is retroceded to third parties, including captive companies.[1436] As a matter of fact, on the one hand, retrocession agreements stipulated between the pooling company and external reinsurance companies do not have significant implications on the relationship existing between the pooling company and the producing and/or fronting companies participating in the multinational program. On the other hand, it is interesting to note that the pooling company is clearly involved in activities which constitute the business proper of retrocession companies, including captive companies. In addition to this, in the case where the business is retroceded to captive companies, the pooling company might be regarded as acting "*on behalf of*" captive companies to the extent that it manages the multinational pooling for the purposes of a following transfer to such captives. Nonetheless, no dependent agent permanent establishment should arise since the pooling company does not fulfill the traditional test regarding the conclusion of contracts binding on captives, provided that the retrocession is a sound business transaction subject to a genuine negotiation and approval process. Similarly, the pooling company does not solicit insurance business that is eventually underwritten by captive companies in such a way as to trigger the supplementary test. And more than that, captive companies can be generally regarded as third parties falling within the scope of the independent agent provision set forth under Art. 5, para. 6, of the OECD Model.[1437,1438]

4.9.2.1.2 The Special Clause for Insurance Agents

In the situation where a DTA contains a special clause for insurance agents along the lines of para. 114 of the OECD Model Commentary on Art. 5, it should be ascertained whether any of the multiple entities involved in multinational programs could be caught under this clause.

In this respect, it should be borne in mind that, even where the central team is set up within an insurance company, the central team does not enter into insurance contracts in the context of multinational programs.[1439] In a similar vein, in the event that multinational programs are originated through regional offices, the regional offices do not enter into insurance contracts in the context of multinational programs, regardless of whether such offices are set up within insurance companies or not. It follows that neither a central team nor a regional office carries on insurance business *stricto sensu* for the purposes of the special clause. As a result, legal entities where a

1436. *See* s. 4.9.1.6 above.

1437. For further comments on situations where captive structures can create permanent establishments in the context of non-insurance multinational groups, *see* Arvid A. Skaar, *Taxation Issues Relating to Captive Insurance Companies*, pp. 4-5 and Jeff Soar/Simon Burtwell/James Smith, *Derivatives & Financial Instruments*, (2014) pp. 256-257.

1438. For some examples of circumstances where agents and/or employees of captives may give rise to a dependent agent permanent establishment in countries other than that of establishment, *see* Oscar Grisales-Racini, "Offshore Captive Insurance Companies," *Tax Notes International* (2016) p. 1112.

1439. Cases where central coordination and pooling activities are integrated in a single entity will be dealt with herein below.

central team and/or a regional office is sitting cannot be regarded as having permanent establishments in countries where multinational programs are offered through local insurance companies.

To the contrary, producing entities are indeed (re)insurance companies that carry on their typical business, i.e., the reinsurance of risks in the context of multinational programs. To this end, producing entities avail themselves of fronting entities in countries where risks are located. More to the point, fronting entities come into play to insure such risks in compliance with local regulations on behalf of producing entities in situations where the latter entities cannot do so in a direct fashion. Therefore, the author takes the view that the fronting entities can ultimately fall within a broad interpretation of insurance distributors for the purposes of the special clause for insurance agents. In doing so, it may be argued that a fronting entity triggers the substantive criterion regarding the insurance of risks since it is involved in activities preceding the conclusion of the reinsurance contracts with the relevant producing entity (in the case at hands, the conclusion of the underlying insurance contract to cover the local operations of the multinational customer). As a result, fronting entities can be regarded as agents of the relevant producing entity through which such risks are reinsured, so that the producing entity may be deemed to have permanent establishments in countries where the fronting companies are established.

For the same reasons, the special clause for insurance agents may also be applicable to pooling companies that conclude reinsurance agreements with producing and/or fronting entities, including where central coordination and pooling activities are integrated in a single entity. In particular, in such cases, the producing and/or fronting entities could be regarded in the same way as insurance distributors through which the pooling company reinsures risks in the source countries. Hence, the pooling company may be deemed to have permanent establishments in the countries where the relevant producing/fronting entities are located.[1440]

Similar conclusions may be finally extended to the case where business is retroceded from the pooling company to a captive company. In fact, in such a case, the producing and/or fronting entities could be regarded in the same way as insurance distributors through which the pooling company and the captive reinsure risks in the source countries.[1441] Hence, it might be argued that both the pooling company and the captive can be deemed to have permanent establishments in countries where relevant producing/fronting entities are located with the only remaining issue being the attribution of profits to such different permanent establishments.

4.9.2.2 *Analysis under the UN Model*

At the outset, it may be argued that multinational programs should not create dependent agent permanent establishments under Art. 5, para. 5, let. (*a*), of the UN

1440. Profit sharing arrangements between pooling companies and multinational customers do not alter such conclusions.

1441. According to the author, the producing and/or fronting entities cannot be regarded as insurance distributors of other retrocession companies.

Model. Admittedly, local fronting and producing entities might be carrying on some activities "*on behalf of*" other entities participating in multinational programs, i.e., the relevant producing entity or pooling entity.[1442] Nevertheless, under the assumption that the subsequent reinsurance and/or retrocession is a sound business transaction subject to a genuine negotiation and approval process, it can be generally concluded that local producing and fronting entities do not conclude contracts binding on the relevant producing entity or pooling entity. Also, local fronting and producing entities do not play the principal role leading to the conclusion of contracts binding on the relevant producing entity or pooling entity.

By the same token, although local fronting and producing entities could be regarded as acting "*on behalf of*" the central team (and the regional offices, in the case where the origination takes place through such offices), local fronting and producing entities do not conclude—or otherwise play the principal role leading to the conclusion of—contracts binding on the legal entities in which the central team and regional offices are sitting. Also, even though regional offices might in principle be regarding as acting "*on behalf of*" the central team, such regional offices do not conclude—or otherwise play the principal role leading to the conclusion of—contracts binding on the legal entities in which the central team is sitting.

In addition to this, one should also assess whether multinational programs can give rise to permanent establishments under Art. 5, para. 6, of the UN Model. To this end, it should be recalled that the insurance agent provision enshrined in the UN Model contains a carve-out for reinsurance. As a result, while legal entities in which the central team and regional offices are sitting cannot be regarded as having permanent establishments in other countries under the insurance agent provision to the extent that such entities do not specifically perform insurance business in the context of multinational programs, producing entities and pooling companies can obviate source taxation under the carve-out for reinsurance,[1443] irrespective of the fact that the other requirements set out in the insurance agent provision are in principle fulfilled.

According to the author, the latter reasoning can be extended to the retrocession to third parties.[1444] It follows that retrocession companies (including captives of multinational customers) should be prevented from being regarded as having permanent establishments in the country of the relevant producing/fronting entity under the insurance agent provision.

1442. In such a latter case, this holds true where the central coordination and pooling activities are integrated in a single entity.

1443. This reasoning also covers situations where central coordination and pooling activities are integrated in a single entity.

1444. For further comments, *see* s. 3.4.2.3 above.

4.10 THE LLOYD'S MARKET

4.10.1 General Overview

4.10.1.1 Introduction

At the outset, it is worth noting that Lloyd's is not an insurance company. It is rather a specialist market in which independent insurance underwriters join together in syndicates to sell insurance under the umbrella of the Lloyd's brand name.[1445] The origins of Lloyd's date back to the seventeenth century, at a time when London's importance as a trade center led to increasing demand for ship and cargo insurance. More precisely, Lloyd's originated in a coffee house belonging to Edward Lloyd, which became recognized as the place to go for marine information and insurance. In the following centuries, business transacted at Lloyd's remained confined to marine insurance. However, in the nineteenth century, non-marine business also began to develop and Lloyd's is now a major market for such a business.[1446,1447]

Today, Lloyd's has become a global specialist insurance and reinsurance market with a significant concentration of underwriting expertise. In fact, every day more than 50 leading insurance companies, over 200 registered Lloyd's brokers and a global network of over 4,000 local coverholders operate in and bring business to the Lloyd's market.[1448]

4.10.1.2 The Governance Structure

The Society of Lloyd's (sometimes also referred to as the "*Corporation of Lloyd's*") has been set up as a statutory corporation incorporated by a private act of Parliament in 1871 (the "*Lloyd's Act 1871*"). The Society of Lloyd's does not itself carry on insurance business, nor is it authorized to do so. Conversely, it provides and regulates—through its governing body (the "*Council of Lloyd's*")[1449]—the marketplace where its members carry on insurance business on their own account.[1450] More to the point, the Society of Lloyd's provides the premises and all the facilities for those transacting business within

1445. *See* HMRC, "*HMRC internal manual—Lloyd's Manual,*" available online at https://www.gov.uk/hmrc-internal-manuals/lloyds-manual/llm1010.
1446. To this effect, *see* Lloyd's, "*Corporate History,*" available online at https://www.lloyds.com/lloyds/about-us/history/corporate-history.
1447. For further comments on the history of Lloyd's, *see also* David Eric Wilson Gibb, *Lloyd's of London—A Study in Individualism* (London, The Corporation of Lloyd's, 1972) pp. 1 et seq., David Eric Wilson Gibb, *Il rischio è il nostro mestiere—Storia dei Lloyd's di Londra* (Cesano Maderno: Golden Book, 1978) pp. 7 et seq., Ian Hay Davison, *Lloyd's—A View of the Room—Change and Disclosure* (London: Weidenfeld and Nicolson, 1987) pp. 11 et seq. and Julian Burling, *Lloyd's: Law and Practice* (Abingdon: Informa Law from Routledge, 2013) pp. 13 et seq.
1448. To this effect, *see* Lloyd's, "*What is Lloyd's?,*" available online at https://www.lloyds.com/lloyds/about-us/what-is-lloyds.
1449. The Council of Lloyd's has been set up with an act of Parliament (the "*Lloyd's Act 1982*"), which has defined the governance structure and rules under which Lloyd's operates. For further comments, *see* Lloyd's, "*Lloyd's Governance Structure,*" available online at https://www.lloyds.com/lloyds/corporate-governance/lloyds-governance-structure.
1450. For further comments on the governance structure, *see* Julian Burling, *Lloyd's: Law and Practice*, pp. 63 et seq., Roderick Clews, "Insurance Brokers at Lloyd's" in: Roderick Clews

its jurisdiction, along with regulatory controls aimed at ensuring the market operates efficiently and retains its reputation as the market of choice for specialist insurance and reinsurance risk.[1451]

4.10.1.3 The Market Structure

4.10.1.3.1 Underwriting

In the Lloyd's market, the business is transacted by underwriting members through syndicates.[1452] Underwriting members may be individuals, bodies corporate (including limited liability partnerships) and Scottish limited partnerships.[1453,1454] Such members provide the capital to support the syndicates' underwriting. Although some hundreds of individual members are still underwriting as sole traders with unlimited liability, most of the capital is now provided by corporate members.[1455]

More specifically, members provide capital backing to the syndicate and assume a share of the insurance liabilities in respect of contracts written by the syndicate in proportion to the amount of their share of (i.e., of capital contributed to) the syndicate.[1456] Each member receives a share of the syndicate's profits proportionate to their share of that syndicate's business, and is responsible for the losses which arise on their share of that business.[1457] Where a member participates in a number of different syndicates, it is the sum of the participations which comprises the member's total underwriting activity.

Each member underwrites insurance business through one or more syndicates. A syndicate itself has no legal personality, is not a partnership (since there is no such agreement among its members) and is not an unincorporated association (since there is no central code of rules). It is merely a venture through which its members

(ed.) *A Textbook of Insurance Broking* (Cambridge: Woodhead-Faulkner, 1980) pp. 36-37 and Ian Hay Davison, *Lloyd's—A View of the Room—Change and Disclosure*, pp. 30 et seq. and 145 et seq.

1451. *See* Roderick Clews in: Roderick Clews (ed.) *A Textbook of Insurance Broking*, pp. 36-37 and Lloyd's, "*The Corporation of Lloyd's*," available online at https://www.lloyds.com/lloyds/about-us/what-is-lloyds/the-corporation-of-lloyds.
1452. Members of Lloyd's, including corporate members, may be referred to as "Names." To this effect, *see* HMRC, "*HMRC internal manual—Lloyd's Manual.*"
1453. To this effect, *see* Lloyd's, "*Membership Byelaw*," available online at https://www.lloyds.com/the-market/operating-at-lloyds/regulation/acts-and-byelaws/lloyds-byelaws, para. 3. Until 1994, only individuals were eligible for membership of Lloyd's. To this effect, *see* Julian Burling, *Lloyd's: Law and Practice*, p. 74.
1454. Corporate members are prohibited by Lloyd's from carrying on any activity other than their underwriting business at Lloyd's and activities directly ancillary thereto. To this effect, *see* Lloyd's, "*Membership Byelaw*," para. 23.
1455. For further comments, *see* Julian Burling, *Lloyd's: Law and Practice*, pp. 1-2 and 73 et seq. and Lloyd's, "*The Lloyd's Market*," available online at https://www.lloyds.com/lloyds/about-us/what-is-lloyds/the-lloyds-market.
1456. The amount of capital required is closely regulated.
1457. The liability of each member is confined to the share of the liability that the member has accepted under contracts underwritten on their behalf. In other words, there is no mutualization of liability within or between syndicates.

underwrite insurance. Some syndicates have a single corporate member,[1458] while others have multiple members, sometimes over a thousand.[1459] The composition of a syndicate is established at the beginning of a calendar year and generally remains unchanged for that calendar year, save for exceptional circumstances. Each syndicate is an annual venture underwriting business for a calendar year (also referred to as "*year of account*"). Traditionally, the accounts for each such year of account remain open for 36 months.[1460] At that point in time, a profit or loss is struck by a payment of a RITC premium, usually to the subsequent year of the same syndicate.[1461] Individual syndicates in the Lloyd's market compete against each other but also co-subscribe larger insurance risks, each syndicate taking a specified percentage or line of the risk.[1462]

Lloyd's syndicates are managed by specialized managing agents, which are generally set up as UK limited companies. More precisely, managing agents are professional underwriting companies set up to manage one or more syndicates employing professional underwriters and other staff for that purpose.[1463] A managing agent may manage one or several syndicates, each of which may have different members.[1464]

The relationship between members and the managing agent of a syndicate is governed under a standard form of managing agent's agreement. In accordance to such an agreement, a managing agent is responsible for—among others—determining the underwriting policy, appointing and supervising the active underwriter,[1465] accepting the underwriting risk and agreeing and settling all claims against the syndicate. Other functions include the negotiation and the management of the syndicate reinsurance, the management of the investment of premiums, the maintenance of accounting records, the calculation of reserves and the employment of underwriting staff. Also, the managing agent maintains the premium trust fund into which all premiums are received and out of which claims and expenses are paid.[1466] In order to do so, the managing agent has a very broad authority. In fact, members are required to delegate absolute discretion to the managing agent as to all aspects of the management of the syndicate, most importantly the power to conduct underwriting activities and to enter

1458. In such a case, they are referred to as "*Spread Syndicates.*"
1459. In such a case, they are referred to as "*Aligned Syndicates.*"
1460. This term stems from traditional ship and cargo insurance.
1461. For further comments on the RITC, *see also* David J. Hindley et al., "The Lloyd's Reinsurance To Close Process," *British Actuarial Journal* (2000) pp. 651 et seq. and HMRC, "*HMRC internal manual—Lloyd's Manual.*"
1462. For further comments, *see* Julian Burling, *Lloyd's: Law and Practice*, pp. 2-3 and 97 et seq.
1463. Managing agents are required to have permission to manage a syndicate both from the Council of Lloyd's and the Prudential Regulation Authority. To this effect, *see* Julian Burling, *Lloyd's: Law and Practice*, p. 2.
1464. For further comments, *see* Julian Burling, *Lloyd's: Law and Practice*, pp. 2-3 and 151 et seq.
1465. The active underwriter is the individual who is sitting at the underwriting box with principal authority to accept insurance and reinsurance risk on behalf of the members of a syndicate. To this effect, *see* Lloyd's, "*Glossary*," available online at https://www.lloyds.com/common/help/glossary.
1466. Premium trust funds are governed under a standard deed. To this effect, *see* Lloyd's, "*Premiums Trust Deeds*," available online at https://www.lloyds.com/the-market/operating-at-lloyds/regulation/lloyds-trust-deeds/premiums-trust-deeds.

into insurance contracts on behalf of the members.[1467] In consideration for said services, each member shall pay a remuneration to the managing agent which comprises: (*i*) an annual fee, (*ii*) a profit commission, and (*iii*) the expenses incurred by the managing agent.[1468]

A corporate member can (and an individual member must) participate in a syndicate through arrangements made by a member's agent.[1469,1470] Services and duties of a member's agent are governed under a standard members' agent's agreement.[1471] Pursuant to such an agreement, a member's agent is—among others—responsible for: (*i*) advising members on which syndicate(s) to participate in, (*ii*) on the level of participation in such syndicates, and (*iii*) liaising with the relevant managing agents. In doing so, the member's agent is authorized to act on behalf of the member to provide the services and comply with the duties set out in the above agreement, including the conclusion of contracts related to activities as a member of syndicates.[1472] In consideration for such services, the member's agent is to be remunerated with fees and a profit commission in respect of each year of account.[1473]

In the case where a member's agent is appointed, the members' agent's agreement is combined with two additional agreements. Most notably, the member's agent and the managing agent of the syndicate(s) in which the member participates conclude an agent's agreement. Pursuant to this agreement, the parties acknowledge that the member's agent will be deemed to appoint the managing agent of the relevant syndicate and establish certain conditions to fulfill their respective obligations.[1474] Also, in such a case, the relationship between the member and the managing agent of the syndicate(s) is governed under a specific managing agent's agreement, which takes into consideration the presence of the member's agent.[1475]

4.10.1.3.2 Intermediation

An important feature of the Lloyd's market is that business generally comes to syndicates through professional insurance intermediaries.[1476] In this respect, a distinction can be made between the "*open market business,*" transacted with managing agents of syndicates in the underwriting room at Lloyd's premises in London (or at the

1467. To this effect, *see* Lloyd's, "*Managing Agent's Agreement,*" available online at https://www.lloyds.com/the-market/tools-and-resources/resources/lloyds-standard-agency-agreements, pp. 9-10.
1468. To this effect, *see* Lloyd's, "*Managing Agent's Agreement,*" pp. 20-21 and 42-47.
1469. Corporate members may appoint an adviser instead. To this effect, *see* HMRC, "*HMRC internal manual—Lloyd's Manual.*"
1470. Members' agents are generally set up as UK limited companies.
1471. For further comments, *see* Julian Burling, *Lloyd's: Law and Practice*, pp. 2 and 163 et seq.
1472. *See* Lloyd's, "*The Members' Agent's Agreement,*" available online at https://www.lloyds.com/the-market/tools-and-resources/resources/lloyds-standard-agency-agreements, pp. 15-28.
1473. *See* Lloyd's, "*The Members' Agent's Agreement,*" pp. 28-30 and 39-44.
1474. *See* Lloyd's, "*The Members' Agent's Agreement,*" pp. 46-57.
1475. *See* Lloyd's, "*The Members' Agent's Agreement,*" pp. 59 et seq.
1476. In principle, a managing agent can accept business directly from policyholders. To this effect, *see* Lloyd's, "*Underwriting Byelaw,*" available online at https://www.lloyds.com/the-market/operating-at-lloyds/regulation/acts-and-byelaws/lloyds-byelaws, para. 27. However, it is vitally important that managing agents only deal directly with a policyholder where they are

managing agent's office) by Lloyd's brokers and/or other intermediaries acting on behalf of policyholders,[1477] and the "*coverholder business*" underwritten on behalf of the syndicate members pursuant to a binding authority agreement.[1478]

Lloyd's brokers are UK or overseas professional insurance intermediaries that have certain minimum standards and are accredited by Lloyd's to broke insurance business of their customers at Lloyd's.[1479] Lloyd's brokers can place business directly with any Lloyd's managing agent subject to a *TOBA*.[1480]

In the open business market, the business is most often originated directly through a Lloyd's broker. Nevertheless, it is also possible that other insurance brokers obtain business and pass it to a Lloyd's broker, who will then endeavor to place it with a Lloyd's underwriter. In such a latter case, a client seeking insurance will instruct its local insurance broker to obtain the coverage required.[1481] In turn, the local broker may then appoint a Lloyd's broker, directly or through one or more intermediaries, to obtain quotations from Lloyd's underwriters.[1482]

Business is submitted by means of a slip,[1483] which is a standard form document setting out information regarding the risk to be placed.[1484] After preparing the slip, the broker takes the slip around the market and tries to obtain the required coverage on the

satisfied that they have the necessary competencies to handle and process that business. To this effect, *see* Lloyd's, "*Non-Lloyd's Brokers: A Guide for Managing Agents,*" available online at https://www.lloyds.com.

1477. In this respect, it should however be noted that Lloyd's brokers may also act as agents of the underwriting members for some purposes, e.g., placing outward insurance, preparing and delivering insurance policies, receiving premiums from policyholders, instructing lawyers and adjusters on behalf of the syndicate and obtaining reports from them. To this effect, *see* Julian Burling, *Lloyd's: Law and Practice*, p. 179 and Gordon W. Shaw, *The Lloyd's Broker, The Lloyd's Broker* (London: Lloyd's of London Press, 1995) pp. 59 et seq.

1478. *See* Julian Burling, *Lloyd's: Law and Practice*, p. 4.

1479. For further comments, *see* Julian Burling, *Lloyd's: Law and Practice*, pp. 173-175 and Lloyd's, "*About Lloyd's Brokers,*" available online at https://www.lloyds.com/the-market/i-am-a/broker-agent/about-lloyds-brokers.

1480. Each Lloyd's broker that wishes to do business with a managing agent must enter into an agreement with the managing agent which records the general terms and conditions on which business will be conducted between them. To this effect, *see* Lloyd's, "*Glossary.*" For further comments on the TOBA, *see also* Julian Burling, *Lloyd's: Law and Practice*, pp. 175-176.

1481. Under certain conditions, non-Lloyd's brokers can place business directly with the managing agent. To this effect, see Lloyd's, "*Underwriting Byelaw,*" para. 27. For instance, with respect to certain overseas territories, it is a condition that such a broker is registered as an "*open market correspondent.*" To this effect, *see* Julian Burling, *Lloyd's: Law and Practice*, pp. 176-177.

1482. *See* Julian Burling, *Lloyd's: Law and Practice*, p. 5 and Roderick Clews in: Roderick Clews (ed.) *A Textbook of Insurance Broking*, pp. 37-38.

1483. With effect from July 1, 2007, slips used in the Lloyd's market are generally issued in the Market Reform Contract (*MRC*) format, containing all the proposed terms of the insurance. As such, this format is designed to be capable of use as both the placing document and the final contract documentation in order to obviate the past confusion and/or litigation as to the difference between the slip and an offer. To this effect, *see* Julian Burling, *Lloyd's: Law and Practice*, pp. 5 and 185. For further comments on the previous difference between a slip and an offer, *see also* Gordon W. Shaw, *The Lloyd's Broker, The Lloyd's Broker*, pp. 87-88.

1484. The slip may also be supported by other documents, such as contracts, survey reports, correspondence and so forth. To this effect, *see* Roderick Clews in: Roderick Clews (ed.) *A Textbook of Insurance Broking*, p. 38.

best terms possible.[1485] In the event that an underwriter wishes to accept the business, he will signify his acceptance by scratching the slip on behalf of the syndicate[1486] and the insurance contract is then processed electronically.[1487]

On the other hand, coverholder business is underwritten for the syndicate by coverholders with delegated underwriting authority. Coverholders are UK or overseas insurance intermediaries operating outside the underwriting room, both in the UK and overseas.[1488] As opposed to Lloyd's brokers, coverholders may be regarded as agents of the member(s) of a syndicate (and not of the policyholders). As a matter of fact, such intermediaries are authorized by the managing agent to enter into insurance contracts to be underwritten by the member(s) of a syndicate managed by it in accordance with the terms of an agreement, referred to as "*binding authority.*"[1489,1490]

Binding authority agreements are model form agreements—to be concluded between the coverholder and the underwriting members of a syndicate—with standard clauses and other variable details and/or provisions in a schedule. Most importantly, pursuant to such agreements, in consideration for a commission to be agreed between the parties, members of a syndicate authorize the coverholder to bind insurances for their account,[1491] to act as their agent for the purposes of receiving the premium, settling refunds and to receive claims funds prior to onward transmission to the policyholders.[1492]

As a condition for the underwriting delegation, coverholders are required to meet certain standards. In addition, coverholders must be registered as "*approved coverholders*" or "*restricted coverholders*" before managing agents can delegate the underwriting authority to them. More precisely, while an approved coverholder has full discretion to

1485. For further comments, *see also* Gordon W. Shaw, *The Lloyd's Broker, The Lloyd's Broker*, pp. 7-11.

1486. The underwriter is liable as soon as he has initialled the slip for the proportion of the risk accepted. To this effect, *see* Gordon W. Shaw, *The Lloyd's Broker*, pp. 9-11, 87-88 and 90 and Julian Burling, *Lloyd's: Law and Practice*, p. 187.

1487. As with standard insurance contracts, the legal analysis of the contract formation is that the broker, acting as agent of the proposer, offers a line of the insurance which is then accepted by the underwriter on behalf of the syndicate. To this effect, *see* Julian Burling, *Lloyd's: Law and Practice*, p. 5.

1488. Lloyd's brokers may themselves be coverholders. To this effect, *see* Julian Burling, *Lloyd's: Law and Practice*, p. 4.

1489. To this effect, *see* Lloyd's, "*Definitions Byelaw*," available online at https://www.lloyds.com/the-market/operating-at-lloyds/regulation/acts-and-byelaws/lloyds-byelaws. For further comments, *see also* Julian Burling, *Lloyd's: Law and Practice*, pp. 4 and 200 and Lloyd's, "*About Coverholders*," available online at https://www.lloyds.com/the-market/i-am-a/delegated-authority/compliance-and-operations/about-coverholders.

1490. Typically, the binding authority is placed by a Lloyd's broker on behalf of the coverholder, acting as a sponsor of the coverholder and being the normal channel of communication between the coverholder and the relevant managing agent. To this effect, *see* Julian Burling, *Lloyd's: Law and Practice*, pp. 4 and 169.

1491. Slips for binding authorities are required to conform to specific requirements as to the substantive content. For further comments, *see* Julian Burling, *Lloyd's: Law and Practice*, p. 207.

1492. *See* Lloyd's, "*Binding Authority Wordings*," available online at https://www.lloyds.com/the-market/i-am-a/delegated-authority/compliance-and-operations/binding-authority-wordings.

agree risks within certain parameters, on the other hand a restricted coverholder is subject to much more closely limits defined in a "*restricted binding authority.*"[1493]

As a final note, it is worth noting that a distinct category of approved coverholders are "*service company coverholders.*"[1494] In a nutshell, a service company is either a wholly owned subsidiary of the managing agent or a company within the managing agent's group of companies. By reason of their close connection with a single managing agent, service company coverholders are classified separately. In consideration for a commission to be agreed between the parties, service company coverholders are delegated by the relevant managing agent to underwrite insurance on behalf of the managed syndicate on the basis of a standard form "*service company agreement.*"[1495] In addition, pursuant to this agreement,[1496] service company coverholders can: (*i*) issue contract documentation, endorsements or such other documents evidencing coverage, (*ii*) collect and process premiums and return premiums, and (*iii*) if authorized, handle claims and/or settle claims in accordance with the agreement. Unlike other approved coverholders, service companies are also permitted to subdelegate their underwriting authority to other approved coverholders.[1497]

4.10.1.3.3 Fact Pattern

This analysis envisages the presence of multiple players taking part in the Lloyd's market. In this respect, it is important to recall that a syndicate is a mere vehicle through which its members underwrite insurance. In fact, this form of relationship between the members of a syndicate is made solely for the purposes of—and is limited to—the underwriting of insurance business for a specific year of account. The syndicate has no legal personality, is not a partnership and is not an unincorporated association.[1498] Therefore, the conclusion of insurance contracts should be intended as binding on the members of a certain syndicate. This implies that the present analysis is meant to ascertain whether the members under analysis (and not the syndicate itself) have a dependent agent permanent establishment.[1499]

To this end, it is assumed that members are established in the UK.[1500] With this in mind, it should also be noted that managing agents and members' agents are

1493. *See* Julian Burling, *Lloyd's: Law and Practice,* pp. 4 and 203-205 and Lloyd's, "*About Coverholders.*"
1494. In Singapore, business can be underwritten exclusively through a service company coverholder registered with the Monetary Authority of Singapore. To this effect, *see* Lloyd's, "*Underwriting Byelaw,*" para. 27.
1495. *See* Julian Burling, *Lloyd's: Law and Practice,* p. 202.
1496. This agreement is to be concluded between the service company coverholder and underwriting members of a syndicate.
1497. *See* Lloyd's, "*Service Company Underwriting Agreement,*" available online at https://www.lloyds.com/the-market/i-am-a/delegated-authority/compliance-and-operations/about-coverholders.
1498. *See* s. 4.10.1.3.1 above.
1499. The assessment as to whether the Society of Lloyd's has dependent agent permanent establishments in countries other than the UK is beyond the scope of this analysis.
1500. The UK domestic legislation contains specific provisions dealing with the case where a non-resident company is an underwriting member. In fact, in such a case, the member's agent

generally UK limited companies,[1501] so that in principle such agents do not give rise to dependent agent permanent establishments of members in countries other than the UK.[1502] This also holds true in the case of UK intermediaries, such as UK Lloyd's brokers, UK insurance brokers and UK coverholders.[1503] As a result, it is crucial to investigate whether any such intermediaries operating in countries other than the UK can give rise to a dependent agent permanent establishment of UK members. In doing so, specific arrangements concluded between the Corporation of Lloyd's and local tax authorities are disregarded.[1504] In addition to this, the analysis only deals with underwriting members that take the form of a company, which include some of the world's major insurance and reinsurance groups.[1505] Therefore, individual members and members that take the form of a partnership are beyond the scope of this analysis.

4.10.2 Permanent Establishment Implications

4.10.2.1 Analysis under the OECD Model

4.10.2.1.1 The Standard Version

As with insurance brokers[1506] and insurance agents,[1507] all relevant intermediaries involved in the Lloyd's market, like Lloyd's brokers, other insurance brokers that originate business and coverholders, can be regarded as persons under Art. 3 of the OECD Model. Also, the activities carried on in countries other than the UK (namely, the intermediation of insurance transactions) are interrelated to operations that constitute the business proper of an insurance company which may exceed preparatory or auxiliary activities referred to in Art. 5, para. 4, of the OECD Model. Thus, specific attention should be turned to the nature of the business transacted, as seen in the previous section.

Starting with the open market business,[1508] Lloyd's brokers generally represent the interests of policyholders seeking insurance coverage. In fact, Lloyd's brokers

and the managing agent of the relevant syndicate are to be considered as independent agents acting in the ordinary course of their business, provided certain conditions are met. To this effect, *see* sections 1142 and 1151 of the Corporation Tax Act 2010, available online at https://www.legislation.gov.uk/. For further comments, *see also* Liesl Fichardt, "United Kingdom" in: IFA (ed.) *Is there a permanent establishment?*, Cahiers de droit fiscal international, Vol. 94a (The Hague: Sdu Uitgevers, 2009) pp. 661 and 663-664 and Oliver Davidson, "United Kingdom" in IFA (ed.) *Cross-border outsourcing: issues, strategies and solutions*, Cahiers de droit fiscal international, Vol. 99a (The Hague: Sdu Uitgevers, 2014) pp. 770-771. For this reason, for the purposes of this analysis, the case of a non-UK underwriting member is not dealt with.

1501. *See* s. 10.1.3.1 above.
1502. For the purposes of this analysis, it is assumed that such agents are UK established companies with no activities abroad.
1503. For the purposes of this analysis, it is assumed that such intermediaries are based in the UK with no activities abroad.
1504. For instance, the Corporation of Lloyd's has concluded specific tax arrangements with US and French tax authorities.
1505. *See* s. 4.10.1.3.1 above.
1506. *See* s. 4.6.2.1 above.
1507. *See* s. 4.7.2.1 above.
1508. The open market business has been outlined in s. 4.10.1.3.2 above.

negotiate with Lloyd's underwriters the most suitable terms and conditions for policyholders. Hence, it may be argued that Lloyd's brokers do not usually act on behalf of underwriting members.[1509] It follows that such brokers do not generally qualify as dependent agent permanent establishments of underwriting members under Art. 5, para. 5, of the OECD Model.

Still, it should be recalled that Lloyd's brokers may also act on behalf of the underwriting members for some purposes. In this regard, the fact that Lloyd's brokers are involved in the preparation of insurance policies, the collection of premiums and the coordination of lawyers and/or adjusters when dealing with claims should not give rise to a dependent agent permanent establishment. In fact, in such cases, Lloyd's brokers do not fulfill neither the traditional test regarding the conclusion of contracts nor the supplementary test regarding the principal role leading to the conclusion of such contracts. To the contrary, in the case where Lloyd's brokers are involved in the placement of outward reinsurance, one should carefully assess whether such Lloyd's brokers trigger any of the above tests. For instance, this might be the case where a Lloyd's broker has devised a scheme for foreign risks to be covered through a syndicate with a subsequent automatic reinsurance provided by reinsurance companies sought out by the very same broker on behalf of the members. Under such circumstances, should the habitual exercise test also be satisfied, all the relevant conditions for a dependent agent permanent establishment to exist under Art. 5, para. 5, of the OECD Model are likely to be fulfilled.

In such a case, it remains to be assessed whether the relevant Lloyd's broker may be regarded as an independent agent under Art. 5, para. 6, of the OECD Model. In this respect, it may be argued that, besides the independence of the relevant Lloyd's broker from the members, the critical investigation relates to the ordinary course of business test. Any such investigation must proceed from the proposition that a Lloyd's broker is generally the agent of its customer, namely the prospect seeking insurance coverage. As a result, in the event that a Lloyd's broker places outward reinsurance, such a broker turns out to be the agent of the underwriting member *in lieu of* the agent of the client. According to the author, this does not appear in line with the general role of a Lloyd's broker and—therefore—such a broker cannot be regarded as acting in the ordinary course of its business.

A similar reasoning can be extended to cases where business is placed through a non-Lloyd's broker, both in direct placements where the non-Lloyd's broker deals directly with the managing agent and in placements involving a Lloyd's broker as well. In fact, where no Lloyd's broker is involved in the placement of business, the non-Lloyd's broker plays *mutatis mutandis* the same role of a Lloyd's broker as an agent of the prospect.[1510] In a more complex chain of parties—with a non-Lloyd's broker needing to place business at Lloyd's through a Lloyd's broker—it may be argued that the Lloyd's broker is an agent of the non-Lloyd's broker and eventually a sub-agent of the customer. That being so, in principle, such brokers do not generally qualify as

1509. Circumstances where Lloyd's brokers are also coverholders will be dealt with herein below.
1510. For further comments on circumstances where a non-Lloyd's broker can give rise to a permanent establishment outside the Lloyd's market, *see* s. 4.6 above.

dependent agent permanent establishments of an underwriting member under Art. 5, para. 5, of the OECD Model. Nonetheless, in the event that such brokers also act on behalf of the underwriting members in respect of certain instances, it should be assessed whether such brokers fulfill either the traditional test regarding the conclusion of contracts or the supplementary test regarding the principal role leading to the conclusion of such contracts. Should this be the case, it is likely that dependent agent permanent establishments can arise in countries where such brokers place business.

Turning to the coverholder business,[1511] coverholders (including service company coverholders and subdelegated coverholders) may be regarded as agents of the member(s) of a syndicate. In fact, pursuant to a binding authority agreement, coverholders are generally authorized by the managing agent to enter into insurance contracts to be underwritten by the member(s) of a syndicate. For this reason, under the assumption that the habitual exercise test is also satisfied, all the relevant conditions laid down in Art. 5, para. 5, of the OECD Model are in principle fulfilled.[1512]

As a result, the next issue is to assess whether such coverholders may be regarded as independent agents under the revised Art. 5, para. 6, of the OECD Model. In doing so, the independence status cannot be claimed with respect to coverholders belonging to the same group of the relevant member to the extent that such intermediaries are generally subject to detailed instructions and control of the member itself or the common parent company, as the case may be. Accordingly, in such circumstances, underwriting members are most likely to have a dependent agent permanent establishment in respect of business underwritten through such coverholders.

In this respect, it should also be recalled that the revised version of Art. 5, para. 6, of the OECD Model provides for a supplementary independence test regarding related parties, whereby if the coverholder acts exclusively or almost exclusively on behalf of enterprises to which it is closely related it would not qualify as an independent agent. Therefore, where a coverholder writes business exclusively or almost exclusively on behalf of members to which it is closely related, it would not meet the independent agent test under the newly formulated Art. 5, para. 6, of the OECD Model.[1513]

In other circumstances—e.g., where a coverholder is introduced to the managing agent of a syndicate through a local insurance broker—the question as to whether the coverholder can be considered independent will depend on the facts and circumstances of the specific case. Therefore, if it is found that the coverholder is independent and that the coverholder is acting in the ordinary course of its business, the coverholder is an independent agent that does not create a dependent agent permanent establishment. Conversely, in the case that the coverholder is subject to very detailed

1511. The coverholder business has been described in s. 4.10.1.3.2 above.

1512. In a similar vein, *see* Sebastian Mailei/Jeremy Brown, *International Tax Review—Financial Services Industry Guide*, (2015) p. 39.

1513. In a similar vein, *see* Sebastian Mailei/Jeremy Brown, *International Tax Review—Financial Services Industry Guide*, (2015) p. 39.

instructions or control, the implication could be that the coverholder would not normally be regarded as operating in an independent manner.[1514]

Should the local insurance broker be himself/herself a coverholder, even where it is found that the broker is independent from the members, the ordinary course of business test can hardly be satisfied. Hence, it is likely that a dependent agent permanent establishment can arise in the country where this broker/coverholder places business.

4.10.2.1.2 The Special Clause for Insurance Agents

In the open market business, a Lloyd's broker that does not otherwise create a dependent agent permanent establishment under the standard version of the OECD Model could fall within the scope of the special clause in the case that it is to be regarded as an agent through which a member collects premiums or insures risks in the source country.

This is for example the case where Lloyd's brokers are involved in the collection of premiums from customers. In fact, in such a case, the Lloyd's broker can be regarded as an agent of the member fulfilling the criterion regarding the collection of premiums. In a similar vein, this can also be the case of a Lloyd's broker that is involved in activities like the preparation and delivery of insurance policies to customers, and/or the coordination of lawyers and/or adjusters when dealing with claims. Indeed, in such cases, the Lloyd's broker can be regarded as an agent of the member fulfilling the criterion regarding the insurance of risks in the source country.

This also remains true in the case where business is placed through non-Lloyd's brokers, either directly with the managing agent of a syndicate or through a Lloyd's broker. As a matter of fact, as long as such non-Lloyd's brokers carry out any of the above activities on behalf of the underwriting member(s), a permanent establishment is likely to arise in the country where such brokers are located.

In the coverholder business, the special clause catches all coverholders (including service company coverholders and subdelegated coverholders) that fulfill the conditions set forth under the dependent agent provision, but are nevertheless covered under Art. 5, para. 6, of the OECD Model. Indeed, coverholders are generally delegated by the managing agent to enter into insurance contracts on behalf of the underwriting members. Therefore, coverholders can be clearly regarded as agents of the members fulfilling the criterion regarding the insurance of risks in the source country. As a consequence, all the relevant criteria set forth under the special clause for insurance agents are satisfied to the effect that permanent establishments arise in the countries where coverholders are located, regardless of whether coverholders can be regarded as agents of an independent status or not.

1514. In a similar vein, *see* Sebastian Mailei/Jeremy Brown, *International Tax Review—Financial Services Industry Guide*, (2015) p. 39.

4.10.2.2 Analysis under the UN Model

Under the UN Model, it may be argued that—in the context of the open market business—brokers (both Lloyd's brokers and non-Lloyd's brokers) do not generally give rise to a dependent agent permanent establishment, unless such brokers are involved in activities exceeding their traditional role as the interface between underwriters and policyholders and/or external providers, like the placement of outward reinsurance. In fact, in such a latter case, it is likely that all the substantive conditions laid down in Art. 5, para. 5, let. (*a*), of the UN Model are fulfilled. Furthermore, the provision under analysis can lead to the creation of dependent agent permanent establishments in the context of the coverholder business. Indeed, coverholders (including both service company coverholders and subdelegated coverholders) generally fulfill all the relevant conditions set forth under Art. 5, para. 5, let. (*a*), of the UN Model.

On the top of this, the insurance agent provision contained in Art. 5, para. 6, of the UN Model is likely to catch all brokers that are involved in administrative activities like the preparation of insurance policies, the collection of premiums and the coordination of lawyers and/or adjusters on behalf of underwriting members and any remaining coverholders that do not fulfill all the conditions set forth under Art. 5, para. 5, let. (*a*), of the UN Model.

Under the above circumstances, it remains to be assessed whether such intermediaries can be regarded as agents of an independent status acting in the ordinary course of their business under Art. 5, para. 7, of the UN Model. In respect of brokers, besides the assessment of the independent status, the critical issue lies on the ordinary course of business test. In this respect, the author believes that brokers involved in activities which do not go beyond their traditional role (such as the preparation of insurance policies, the collection of premiums, the coordination of lawyers, adjusters and the like) should not be prevented from being regarded as acting in the ordinary course of their business. In respect of coverholders, it should be recalled that a coverholder cannot be considered independent in the case where it acts exclusively or almost exclusively on behalf of members to which it is closely related. In addition, in the peculiar case where an insurance broker is himself/herself a coverholder, it is unlikely the ordinary course of business test to be fulfilled. Instead, in other situations, such an assessment will fundamentally depend on the applicable facts and circumstances of the specific case under analysis.

4.11 FINAL CONSIDERATIONS

The various business models addressed in the previous sections are in principle examples of genuine business models adopted primarily for legitimate commercial reasons with a view to marketing, promoting and distributing insurance products in countries other than that of establishment. The choice of the specific business model(s) to be implemented in concrete circumstances is generally based on commercial, legal and regulatory—rather than tax—constraints in the relevant countries under analysis.

For example, it should be recalled that, in countries like Switzerland, foreign insurance companies cannot transact insurance business in the absence of a local branch or subsidiary, save for a few specific exceptions.[1515] Therefore, under such circumstances, some of the business models depicted in the previous sections cannot be implemented therein. More specifically, unless one of the above exceptions applies, foreign companies without a Swiss license can only have recourse to reinsurance to cover risks in Switzerland. Other jurisdictions instead require foreign insurance and/or reinsurance companies to appoint a local representative for the purposes of fulfilling local administrative and regulatory requirements designed for the protection of insured persons. Hence, structures put into place to comply with the above limitations cannot be generally regarded as artificial arrangements intended to circumvent the existence of a permanent establishment. Also, and perhaps more importantly, the author believes that a concrete assessment regarding the existence of a permanent establishment for tax purposes cannot be separated from a proper understanding of the applicable regulatory framework.

The author believes that abusive situations, like artificial structures intended to circumvent the existence of a permanent establishment, should be better targeted on a separate individual basis through anti-avoidance provisions and/or doctrines, possibly in combination with transfer pricing measures where the conditions are not at arm's length.[1516] This targeted approach would indeed prevent the unintentional penalization of legitimate structures with sound business purposes on a general basis.

For instance, with respect to genuine fronting arrangements, it cannot be contended that the producing entity and/or the pooling company have a dependent agent permanent establishment in countries where fronting entities are situated, unless there has been avoidance. Indeed, this argument would entail disregarding: (*i*) the separate legal validity of the insurance and reinsurance contracts, (*ii*) the separate legal existence of the fronting entity, (*iii*) the relationship between the insured persons and the fronting entity and (*iv*) the relationship between the fronting entity and the producing entity and/or the pooling company. According to the author, such a recharacterization of legal forms could only occur after it has been established that there has been avoidance, so that such legal forms have been abused and/or misused.

In this respect, the work on Action 7 of the BEPS Project—which ended up with tackling arrangements aimed at circumventing the existence of a permanent establishment by means of amendments to the definition of permanent establishment—may

---

1515. *See* s. 2.1.4 above.

1516. In this perspective, intra-group captive insurance arrangements should be carefully scrutinized. *See* Vikram Chand, "Transfer pricing aspects of captive insurance arrangements: Recommendation to the OECD," *IFF Forum für Steuerrecht* (2017) pp. 164 et seq. For this reason, the OECD has issued draft guidance in this respect. *See* OECD, "*Public Discussion Draft—BEPS Actions 8-10: Financial Transactions*," Paris (July 3, 2018). For further comments on this guidance, *see also* Vikram Chand/Karin Otto, "Transfer Pricing: Accurate Delineation of the Captive Insurance Arrangement—Is the OECD Guidance Clear on this Matter?," *Kluwer International Tax Blog* (2018), Stefan Greil, "Der „Discussion Draft on Financial Transactions" der OECD," *Internationales Steuer- und Wirtschaftsrecht* (2018) pp. 555-556 and Piero Bonarelli, "TP: il Discussion Draft BEPS sull'applicazione del principio di libera concorrenza alle transazioni finanziarie," *Fiscalità & Commercio Internazionale* (2018) no. 11 pp. 5 et seq.

eventually be regarded as a double-edged sword. As a matter of fact, the above amendments transpose the uncertainty concerning the application of anti-avoidance measures to the application of the permanent establishment rules. More specifically, this shift increases the uncertainty regarding the concrete application of the relevant conditions (including their application to genuine business models) and—thus—may lead to an inconsistent application of the permanent establishment concept in the real world.

For instance, the concrete application of the supplementary test regarding the principal role leading to the conclusion of contracts in situations where special insurance agents, internal sales representatives and/or bank employees are involved in the solicitation of insurance business in the source country may lead to different results depending upon a subjective assessment of the relevant facts and circumstances. Indeed, the determination as to whether such persons play the "*principal role*" lies on a subjective comparison of the contributions toward the conclusion of contracts of such persons vis-à-vis those of other persons involved in the context of their respective business models, including the foreign insurance company. Such inevitable margins of subjectivity can clearly result in the inconsistent application of the permanent establishment concept in similar circumstances.

The analysis of the insurance business models also further substantiates some considerations already outlined in Chapter 3. Among others, the amendments introduced in the context of the BEPS Project lead to additional situations where the definition of dependent agent permanent establishment is not aligned with the corresponding definition for regulatory purposes. For example, in the EU, online business models may be treated differently for tax and regulatory purposes. In fact, while insurance activities carried on via electronic commerce are generally subject to the EU provisions relating to the freedom to provide services, more and more situations may now give rise to a dependent agent permanent establishment for tax purposes.

Second, the additional situations in which a dependent agent permanent establishment may be deemed to exist following the amendments introduced in the context of the BEPS Project fundamentally concern sales and marketing activities. This is for instance the case of call center operators that guide prospects in the selection of the most suitable insurance product. By the same token, the above amendments also cover agents and internal sales representatives involved in the solicitation of insurance in the source country. Clearly, such persons do not undertake KERT functions, as envisaged in the 2010 OECD Report, Part IV.[1517] As a result, the analysis of the insurance business models corroborates the argument that the above amendments are likely to increase the number of dependent agent permanent establishments with little or no additional income attributable thereto.

The above inconsistencies are even greater in the case where a DTA contains the special clause for insurance agents patterned after para. 114 of the OECD Model Commentary on Art. 5 or the insurance agent provision laid down in Art. 5, para. 6, of the UN Model. As a matter of fact, such measures are very likely to exacerbate

1517. *See* s. 2.2.3 above.

situations in which a permanent establishment may arise in the source country only for tax purposes with little or no additional income attributable thereto.

Furthermore, it should be recalled that such measures have been originally designed to deal with agents and internal sales representatives that did not trigger neither a fixed place of business nor a dependent agent permanent establishment in the source country.[1518] However, the deployment of (internal and/or external) representatives is only one of the options that can be pursued for the purposes of marketing, promoting and distributing insurance products in foreign jurisdictions. Therefore, the application of such measures can lead to unintended results. For instance, oddly enough, such measures may end up with covering brokers—that are generally agents of the customers seeking insurance—for the mere fact that they are involved in the fulfillment and/or the collection of premiums. Likewise, given the broad scope of application, such measures can also cover banks that distribute insurance products in the context of bancassurance arrangements. Potential implications can also concern legitimate fronting arrangements concluded to underwrite insurance business in specific jurisdictions where an insurance company does not have a local presence, as required by global customers.

The author believes that such results are not consistent with the original objectives of the measures under analysis. To be effective, a threshold should be in principle designed with a view to providing tests that can be applied consistently to all insurance business models. To put it in other terms, the threshold should attempt to reach consistent results, irrespective of the specific business model adopted. If this is not the case, the threshold may end up with an inconsistent treatment of insurance companies, which could in turn undermine the effectiveness of the tax system.

In the UN Model, the above inconsistencies are piled on with the carve-out for independent agents and reinsurance, which might eventually alter the adoption of the business models. In fact, in such a case, insurance companies might be inclined to shape their business models in such a way as to prevent the threshold from being reached, albeit no significant change occurs in terms of underlying economic substance. For instance, this might happen when insurance companies are confronted with the choice between external agents and internal sales representatives and—perhaps more evidently—between insurance and reinsurance.

1518. *See* s. 3.3.1 above.

CHAPTER 5

Analysis of the Swiss Double Tax Treaty Policy

Chapter 5 aims at examining the Swiss double tax treaty policy with respect to the definition of dependent agent permanent establishment. To do so, this chapter elaborates on the perspective adopted by Switzerland in the negotiation of the dependent agent provision and in the interpretation of such a provision. On top of this, Chapter 5 also offers detailed considerations regarding the insurance business shedding some light on certain rules negotiated upon request of the contracting partners. Moving from such an examination, this chapter also compares the definition of dependent agent permanent establishment adopted in Swiss double tax treaties with the practice of other countries to assess different approaches assumed when dealing with this specific topic. This assessment covers some selected countries that take a specific stand on the insurance business and—thus—may serve as a significant comparable for the purposes of the present analysis. More precisely, the selected countries are the following: Australia, Belgium, Chile, Germany and Italy.

5.1 BACKGROUND OF THE ANALYSIS

As already delineated in Chapter 1,[1519] this chapter aims at examining the Swiss policy and the definition of dependent agent permanent establishment adopted in DTAs concluded by Switzerland, with a specific focus on the insurance business. The Swiss policy will also be compared with the practice of other countries in order to assess different approaches adopted when dealing with this specific issue. This critical assessment does not pretend to cover all countries in the world. Rather, the analysis is limited to some selected countries (most notably, Australia, Belgium, Chile, Germany and Italy) that take a specific stand on this matter and—thus—serve as significant comparables for the purposes of the present assessment.

1519. *See* s. 1.5 above.

This assessment is principally focused on DTAs. Hence, the definition of dependent agent permanent establishment laid down in the domestic tax laws of the countries under analysis remains outside the scope of this research and will be referred to only where necessary.

5.2 SWISS DOUBLE TAX TREATY POLICY

5.2.1 The Definition of Permanent Establishment

Switzerland has concluded almost one hundred DTAs,[1520] most of which generally follow the OECD pattern.[1521] As a result, although the Swiss domestic tax legislation does not contain a specific provision dealing with an agency permanent establishment,[1522,1523] the Swiss DTA policy regarding the definition of a dependent agent permanent establishment is in most cases based on OECD standards.[1524,1525]

1520. The DTAs are available online on the portal of the Swiss Government at https://www.admin.ch or otherwise at www.ibfd.org.

1521. *See* Stefan Schmid/Marianne Orell, "Switzerland" in: Ekkehart Reimer/Stephan Schmid/Marianne Orell (eds.) *Permanent Establishments: A Domestic Taxation, Bilateral Tax Treaty and OECD Perspective* (Alphen aan den Rijn: Kluwer Law International, 2016) Part 19.03[B] p. 14.

1522. At federal level, the definition of a Swiss permanent establishment of foreign legal entities is contained in Art. 51, para. 2, of the Federal Direct Tax Law of December 14, 1990. The first sentence of this provision states that a permanent establishment is a fixed place of business in which the business of an enterprise is carried on in full or in part. The second sentence provides instead for a list of examples, which includes permanent representatives. Yet, most scholars take the view that this list has an exemplative rather than a constitutive nature, so that a dependent agent permanent establishment with no fixed place of business should be excluded. *See*—among others—Georg Kofler/Christian Schmidt/Madeleine Simonek, "Vertreterbetriebsstätten in Deutschland, Österreich und der Schweiz im Hinblick auf BEPS-Aktionspunkt 7," *Archiv für Schweizerisches Abgaberecht* (2016/2017) pp. 471-472, Peter Athanas, "Die Betriebsstätte bzw die feste Einrichtung" in: Höhn Ernst (ed.) *Handbuch des Internationalen Steuerrechts der Schweiz 2. Auflage* (Bern: Paul Haupt, 1993) p. 211, Andreas H. Keller/Josef Schuch/Sabine Seibold/Wilhem H. Wacker, "Der Betriebstättenbegriff im Steuerrecht Deutschlands, Österreichs und der Schweiz," *Der Schweizer Treuhänder* (1999) pp. 118-119, Jean-Blaise Paschoud, "Art 51," in: Danielle Yersin/Yves Noël (eds.) *Impot fédéral direct—Commentaire de la loi sur loi fédéral direct* (Basel: Helbing Lichtenhahn, 2008) p. 637, Xavier Oberson/Howard R. Hull, *Switzerland in International Tax Law* (Amsterdam: IBFD, 2011) para. 3.1.2.3, Hans U. Meuter, "Besteuerung einer Vertreterbetriebsstätte," *Zürcher Steuerpraxis* (2012) pp. 18-19, Stefan G. Widmer, "Die Betriebsstättebegründung des Principals nach der allgemeinen Betriebsstättedefinition," *IFF Forum für Steuerrecht* (2005) p. 98, Stefan G. Widmer, "Die Vertreterbetriebsstätte im internationalen Steuerrecht der Schweiz," *Archiv für Schweizerisches Abgaberecht* (2003/2004) pp. 100-102, Marc Vogelsang, *Der Begriff der Betriebsstätte im schweizerischen und internationalen Steuerrecht* (Zürich: Schulthess Verlag, 2015) p. 321 and Stefan Oesterhelt/Susanne Schreiber, "Art 51" in: Martin Zweifel/Michael Beusch (eds.) *Bundesgesetz über die direkte Bundessteuer* (Basel: Helbing Lichtenhahn, 2017) p. 1053. A different opinion is instead expressed in Peter Aigner/Beat Jung/Gotthard Steinmann, *Kommentar zum Gesetz über die direkte Bundessteuer* (Zürich: Schulthess, 1995) pp. 178-179, Peter Locher, *Kommentar zum Bundesgesetz über die direkte Bundessteuer* (Basel: Helbing Lichtenhahn, 2001) pp. 117-118, Daniel de Vries Reilingh, "The Concept of Permanent Establishment: A Comparative Analysis of Tax Treaty and Swiss Domestic Tax Law," *Intertax* (2010) p. 579 and Daniel de Vries Reilingh, *Le droit fiscal intercantonal et le droit fiscal international de la Suisse* (Geneva: Schulthess, 2011) pp. 156-158.

Some of the oldest DTAs are patterned after the 1963 OECD Draft, which contained a carve-out for purchasing agents.[1526] Other DTAs are generally patterned after later versions of the OECD text, albeit antecedent to the changes introduced in the context of the BEPS Project.

In general, Switzerland largely follows the continental European perspective in the interpretation of the DTA provisions regarding the dependent agent permanent establishment.[1527] This is so also considering that the Circular Letter No. 8 of the Federal Tax Administration issued on December 18, 2001 regarding the international tax allocation of principal companies—which appeared to be inconsistent with said perspective—will be repealed shortly in time.[1528] In fact, in the context of the Federal Act on Tax Reform and AHV Financing (TRAF),[1529] a few preferential tax regimes (including the principal company regime) will be abolished under the pressure coming

1523. The term permanent establishment is also used but not further defined in the Federal Direct Tax Harmonization Law of December 14, 1990, which is intended to harmonize cantonal and communal tax rules.

1524. *See* Stefan Schmid/Marianne Orell in: Ekkehart Reimer/Stephan Schmid/Marianne Orell (eds.) *Permanent Establishments: A Domestic Taxation, Bilateral Tax Treaty and OECD Perspective*, Part 19.03[B] p. 16, Markus Mühlemann, "*Switzerland—Permanent Establishments—Topical Analyses*," last reviewed: February 1, 2019, available online at www.ibfd.org, para. 2.1.4.2, Georg Kofler/Christian Schmidt/Madeleine Simonek, *Archiv für Schweizerisches Abgaberecht*, (2016/2017) p. 474, René Schreiber/Kersten A. Honold/Roger Jaun, "Art. 5" in: Martin Zweifel/Michael Beusch/René Matteotti (eds.) *Kommentar zum Schweizerischen Steuerrecht—Internationales Steuerrecht* (Basel: Helbing Lichtenhahn Verlag, 2015) p. 445 and Stefan G. Widmer, *Archiv für Schweizerisches Abgaberecht*, (2003/2004) p. 102.

1525. Certain DTAs broaden the scope of the definition of dependent agent permanent establishment with a stock holding agent provision along the lines of Art. 5, para. 5, let. (b), of the UN Model. *See* Markus Mühlemann, "*Switzerland—Permanent Establishments—Topical Analyses*," para. 2.1.4.2 and René Schreiber/Kersten A. Honold/Roger Jaun in: Martin Zweifel/Michael Beusch/René Matteotti (eds.) *Kommentar zum Schweizerischen Steuerrecht—Internationales Steuerrecht*, pp. 445-446. *See* DTAs with India, Indonesia, Ivory Coast, Jamaica, Malaysia, Morocco, Pakistan, Philippines, Sri Lanka, Thailand, Trinidad & Tobago, Tunisia, Ukraine and Vietnam. The DTAs with Australia and India also contain a provision dealing with an agent that manufacturers or processes goods or merchandise belonging to the foreign enterprise.

1526. *See* Georg Kofler/Christian Schmidt/Madeleine Simonek, *Archiv für Schweizerisches Abgaberecht*, (2016/2017) p. 474 and René Schreiber/Kersten A. Honold/Roger Jaun in: Martin Zweifel/Michael Beusch/René Matteotti (eds.) *Kommentar zum Schweizerischen Steuerrecht—Internationales Steuerrecht*, p. 445. *See* DTAs with Austria, Denmark, France, Germany, Ireland, Italy, Portugal and Sweden. This carve-out also remained in the new DTA concluded with Australia.

1527. *See* Georg Kofler/Christian Schmidt/Madeleine Simonek, *Archiv für Schweizerisches Abgaberecht*, (2016/2017) p. 474.

1528. *See* AFC (*Amministrazione Federale delle Contribuzioni*) December 18, 2001, Circular Letter No. 8, sections 1-2.

1529. In German, "*Bundesgesetz über die Steuerreform und die AHV-Finanzierung (STAF)*." This reform was previously referred to as Tax Proposal 17 (TP17). However, on June 7, 2018, the Council of States (the Upper House of the Swiss Parliament) included CHF 2 billion for the old-age and survivor's insurance in the TP17 in the form of socio-political compensation. Hence, the reform is now known as the TRAF. This reform has been approved by the Parliament on September 28, 2018 and by the Swiss voters on May 19, 2019. For further comments, *see also* FC (*Federal Council*), "*Referendum on the Federal Act on Tax Reform and AHV financing (19.05.2019)*," available online at https://www.efd.admin.ch/efd/en/home/dokumentation/legislation/abstimmungen/staf.html.

from various international bodies (*in primis*, the EU).[1530] As a first step, the Swiss Federal Tax Administration has ensured that the federal practice concerning principal companies is no longer applied to new companies from 2019.[1531] Then, with the entry into force of the TRAF at the beginning of 2020, the federal practice for principal companies will be abolished.[1532]

According to the Swiss standpoint, the dependence of an agent should be intended in a broad economic sense. More to the point, dependence can be found not only in a service and/or employment relationship, but also in a similar contractual relationship. The determination of dependence or independence is generally based on the criteria used to distinguish employment vis-à-vis self-employment as well as on the case law of the Swiss Supreme Federal Court regarding the prohibition of inter-cantonal double taxation.[1533,1534]

The authority to conclude contracts is not understood in a strictly civil law sense, either. In principle, Switzerland follows OECD standards before the changes introduced in the context of the BEPS Project, according to which the dependent agent is deemed to have an authority to conclude contracts in the case he/she negotiates all the terms and conditions of the contract, even though the contract is subsequently sent to the foreign head office for signature.[1535,1536] It is also irrelevant the form in which the

1530. For an overview of the measures contained in the reform, *see* Jacques Kistler/René Zulauf, "Switzerland: Swiss Tax Reform Proposal 17: Swiss Federal Council submits dispatch to Swiss Parliament," *International Tax Review* (2018) and Jacques Kistler/René Zulauf, "Switzerland: Swiss corporate tax reform 2017: Swiss Senate approves revised version of the reform," *International Tax Review* (2018).

1531. *See* AFC (*Amministrazione Federale delle Contribuzioni*) November 15, 2018, Press Release, *TRAF—No more new principal companies and Swiss finance branches from 2019*, available online at https://www.admin.ch/gov/en/start/documentation/media-releases.msg-id-72938.html.

1532. *See* AFC (*Amministrazione Federale delle Contribuzioni*) May 24, 2019, Dispatch, *Pratiche federali in materia di società principali e di Swiss Finance Branches a partire dal 1° gennaio 2020*, available online at https://www.estv.admin.ch/estv/it/home/allgemein/steuerinformationen/dienstleistungen/mitteilungen.html.

1533. *See* Georg Kofler/Christian Schmidt/Madeleine Simonek, *Archiv für Schweizerisches Abgaberecht*, (2016/2017) pp. 474-475.

1534. Inter-cantonal double taxation is prohibited under Art. 127 of the Federal Constitution. For further comments on the case law in inter-cantonal matters, *see*—among others—Stefan Schmid/Marianne Orell in: Ekkehart Reimer/Stephan Schmid/Marianne Orell (eds.) *Permanent Establishments: A Domestic Taxation, Bilateral Tax Treaty and OECD Perspective*, Part 19.03[B] p. 12, Stefan G. Widmer, *IFF Forum für Steuerrecht*, (2005) pp. 99-100, Daniel de Vries Reilingh, *Intertax*, (2010) pp. 580 et seq., Daniel de Vries Reilingh, *Le droit fiscal intercantonal et le droit fiscal international de la Suisse*, pp. 160 et seq. and Marc Vogelsang, *Der Begriff der Betriebsstätte im schweizerischen und internationalen Steuerrecht*, pp. 341 et seq.

1535. *See* Georg Kofler/Christian Schmidt/Madeleine Simonek, *Archiv für Schweizerisches Abgaberecht*, (2016/2017) p. 475, René Schreiber/Kersten A. Honold/Roger Jaun in: Martin Zweifel/Michael Beusch/René Matteotti (eds.) *Kommentar zum Schweizerischen Steuerrecht—Internationales Steuerrecht*, p. 438 and Hans U. Meuter, *Zürcher Steuerpraxis*, (2012) p. 11.

1536. Widmer derives from the Circular Letter No. 8 of the Federal Tax Administration of December 18, 2001 that an agent who acts in the name and for the account of the principal involved in all aspects of the negotiation but does not have the authority to sign the contract does not lead to the creation of a permanent establishment. *See* Stefan G. Widmer, "Switzerland" in: IFA (ed.) *Is there a permanent establishment?*, Cahiers de droit fiscal international, Vol. 94a (The

representative has been authorized. In fact, it is the actual behavior vis-à-vis third parties to be decisive. Hence, an apparent and/or implied authority can suffice.[1537]

On the other hand, in respect of the requirement for the agent to conclude contracts "*in the name of*" the foreign enterprise, the question as to whether Switzerland follows the civil law distinction between direct and indirect representation[1538] or is otherwise inclined to more economic considerations is not entirely clear. There are in fact contradictory positions. The Swiss literature basically follows the civil law view and requires that the agent legally binds the foreign enterprise.[1539] However, there are no court rulings in this respect and a solid administrative practice has not been published.[1540] Differently, in a notice dated February 24, 1987 issued to a German insurance brokerage company, the Swiss Federal Tax Administration considered that a mere intermediation was sufficient for the existence of a permanent establishment.[1541] On the top of this, with respect to outbound situations regarding commissionaire structures depicted in the Circular Letter No. 8 dated December 18, 2001, the Swiss Federal Tax Administration also followed an economic perspective anticipating the related issues discussed in the context of the BEPS Project.[1542]

Most notably, the Circular Letter No. 8 of December 18, 2001 described the typical elements of commissionaire arrangements—which were referred to as principal structures—and maintained that distribution companies exercise the function of an (indirect) representative authorized to conclude contracts (commissionaire) and—thus—were to be regarded as dependent agent permanent establishments under OECD standards, even before the implementation of the changes introduced in the context of the BEPS Project. In doing so, the Circular Letter No. 8 highlighted that this qualification of a commissionaire as a dependent agent permanent establishment was in line with OECD standards, which have been embodied in most of the Swiss DTAs. Also, the Circular Letter No. 8 pointed out that the OECD does not exclude subsidiaries

Hague: Sdu Uitgevers, 2009) p. 640. However, this reasoning does not appear to be in line with the language of the letter under analysis.

1537. *See* Georg Kofler/Christian Schmidt/Madeleine Simonek, *Archiv für Schweizerisches Abgaberecht*, (2016/2017) p. 475, Peter Athanas in: Höhn Ernst (ed.) *Handbuch des Internationalen Steuerrechts der Schweiz 2. Auflage*, p. 219, René Schreiber/Kersten A. Honold/Roger Jaun in: Martin Zweifel/Michael Beusch/René Matteotti (eds.) *Kommentar zum Schweizerischen Steuerrecht—Internationales Steuerrecht*, p. 438 and Stefan G. Widmer, *Archiv für Schweizerisches Abgaberecht*, (2003/2004) p. 111.

1538. Under Swiss civil law, the agency is dealt with under Art. 32 of the Federal Act on the Amendment of the Swiss Civil Code of March 30, 1911.

1539. *See* René Schreiber/Kersten A. Honold/Roger Jaun in: Martin Zweifel/Michael Beusch/René Matteotti (eds.) *Kommentar zum Schweizerischen Steuerrecht—Internationales Steuerrecht*, p. 440, Stefan G. Widmer, *Archiv für Schweizerisches Abgaberecht*, (2003/2004) p. 113 and Marc Vogelsang, *Der Begriff der Betriebsstätte im schweizerischen und internationalen Steuerrecht*, pp. 224-228.

1540. *See* Georg Kofler/Christian Schmidt/Madeleine Simonek, *Archiv für Schweizerisches Abgaberecht*, (2016/2017) p. 476.

1541. *See* Kurt Locher/Walter Meier/Rudolf Von Siebenthal/Andreas Kolb, *Doppelbesteuerungsabkommen Schweiz-Deutschland 1971 und 1978* (Therwil: Verlag für Recht und Gesellschaft, 2007) B 5.4 (6).

1542. *See* AFC (*Amministrazione Federale delle Contribuzioni*) December 18, 2001, Circular Letter No. 8, pp. 1-2.

from being treated as permanent establishments.[1543] As a result, subsidiaries of principal companies could be considered as dependent agent permanent establishments under the same conditions as other agents.[1544]

The Swiss literature raised the concern that the Circular Letter No. 8 of December 18, 2001 was not in line with the traditional Swiss view. In particular, according to Widmer, Schreiber, Honold and Jaun, the Circular Letter No. 8 of December 18, 2001 appeared to contradict the civil law viewpoint.[1545,1546] In fact, only where the contractual relationship between the representative and the third party is governed under common law or under exceptional cases of continental European civil law, a Swiss principal may also be legally bound by acting in a foreign name.[1547,1548] However, this view would only be correct in the case that Switzerland always followed—in the interpretation of a dependent agent permanent establishment under a DTA—the interpretation of the other contracting party and adopted an exemption method for the foreign permanent establishment on the basis of the existence of a permanent establishment in the other country, which is actually not the case.[1549] As it has been noted at the beginning of the present section, such inconsistencies will be overcome with the repeal of the Circular Letter No. 8 of December 18, 2001.

Finally, with respect to the habitual exercise test, according to the Swiss doctrine, the authority to conclude contracts must be exercised repeatedly, regularly and permanently.[1550] The assessment as to whether such a test is fulfilled should be

1543. *See* AFC (*Amministrazione Federale delle Contribuzioni*) December 18, 2001, Circular Letter No. 8, pp. 1-2. For further comments, *see also* Stefan G. Widmer in: IFA (ed.) *Is there a permanent establishment?*, Cahiers de droit fiscal international, Vol. 94a, p. 639.

1544. *See* Stefan G. Widmer in: IFA (ed.) *Is there a permanent establishment?*, Cahiers de droit fiscal international, Vol. 94a, p. 640.

1545. *See* Stefan G. Widmer, *Archiv für Schweizerisches Abgaberecht*, (2003/2004) p. 127 and René Schreiber/Kersten A. Honold/Roger Jaun in: Martin Zweifel/Michael Beusch/René Matteotti (eds.) *Kommentar zum Schweizerischen Steuerrecht—Internationales Steuerrecht*, p. 441.

1546. Widmer argued that a change toward more economic considerations in the rules regarding the dependent agent permanent establishment could only be brought about by an amendment to the OECD standards. Stefan G. Widmer, *Archiv für Schweizerisches Abgaberecht*, (2003/2004) p. 127. For further comments regarding prospective changes in the aftermath of the BEPS Project, *see* s. 5.2.3 below.

1547. *See* Georg Kofler/Christian Schmidt/Madeleine Simonek, *Archiv für Schweizerisches Abgaberecht*, (2016/2017) p. 476 and René Schreiber/Kersten A. Honold/Roger Jaun in: Martin Zweifel/Michael Beusch/René Matteotti (eds.) *Kommentar zum Schweizerischen Steuerrecht—Internationales Steuerrecht*, p. 441.

1548. In buy-sell arrangements, not even in common law jurisdictions a legal connection between the principal and the customer results from the actions of the "*agent.*" To this effect, *see* Stefan G. Widmer in: IFA (ed.) *Is there a permanent establishment?*, Cahiers de droit fiscal international, Vol. 94a, p. 640.

1549. *See* Georg Kofler/Christian Schmidt/Madeleine Simonek, *Archiv für Schweizerisches Abgaberecht*, (2016/2017) p. 476.

1550. *See* Georg Kofler/Christian Schmidt/Madeleine Simonek, *Archiv für Schweizerisches Abgaberecht*, (2016/2017) p. 476, Peter Athanas in: Höhn Ernst (ed.) *Handbuch des Internationalen Steuerrechts der Schweiz 2. Auflage*, p. 219 and René Schreiber/Kersten A. Honold/Roger Jaun in: Martin Zweifel/Michael Beusch/René Matteotti (eds.) *Kommentar zum Schweizerischen Steuerrecht—Internationales Steuerrecht*, p. 445.

conducted irrespective of the residence, stay and/or personal identity of the representatives in the respective State.[1551] The concrete scope of the habitual exercise of authority depends on the type of contracts and the respective business activities and thus escapes a concrete frequency test. For instance, an insurance agent will generally conclude contracts more frequently than an agent involved in the construction business.[1552]

5.2.2 Considerations Regarding the Insurance Business

In Switzerland, insurance companies represent a significant economic factor. In the light of the particular nature of their business and regulatory provisions, insurance companies frequently operate through permanent establishments. Nevertheless, there are no specific guidelines for insurance companies concerning the definition of a permanent establishment.[1553]

In Swiss DTAs, the existence of a dependent agent permanent establishment of an insurance company is generally to be ascertained account taken of the above general considerations,[1554] save for a few exceptions. More to the point, certain DTAs contains a special clause for insurance agents patterned after Art. 5, para. 6, of the UN Model. This is the case of a number of DTAs concluded with developing countries (namely, DTAs with Egypt, Ivory Coast, India, Morocco, Mexico, Pakistan, Qatar, Tunisia and Vietnam).[1555] Likewise, DTAs concluded with Indonesia and Thailand encompass a clause along the lines of Art. 5, para. 6, of the UN Model, the only difference being the fact that such DTAs contain the specification "*through an employee or through a representative*" instead of the general reference to a "*person.*"

In such DTAs, the introduction of the special clause for insurance agents generally represents a concession granted to developing countries,[1556] which derives

1551. *See* Georg Kofler/Christian Schmidt/Madeleine Simonek, *Archiv für Schweizerisches Abgaberecht*, (2016/2017) p. 477 and Stefan G. Widmer, *Archiv für Schweizerisches Abgaberecht*, (2003/2004) pp. 108-109.
1552. *See* Georg Kofler/Christian Schmidt/Madeleine Simonek, *Archiv für Schweizerisches Abgaberecht*, (2016/2017) p. 477 and Stefan G. Widmer, *Archiv für Schweizerisches Abgaberecht*, (2003/2004) p. 116.
1553. *See* Stefan Schmid/Marianne Orell in: Ekkehart Reimer/Stephan Schmid/Marianne Orell (eds.) *Permanent Establishments: A Domestic Taxation, Bilateral Tax Treaty and OECD Perspective*, Part 19.03[D] pp. 17-18.
1554. Locher seems to consider that an insurance company of a contracting State may have a permanent establishment in the other contracting State either when it has a fixed place of business or when it operates through a dependent agent that can conclude contracts. To this effect, *see* Peter Locher, *Einführung in das internationale Steuerrecht der Schweiz* (Bern: Stämpfli Verlag AG, 2000) p. 273. However, considering the Swiss domestic tax provisions, this can only be the case of outbound situations. For further comments, *see also* s. 5.2.1 above.
1555. *See* René Schreiber/Kersten A. Honold/Roger Jaun in: Martin Zweifel/Michael Beusch/René Matteotti (eds.) *Kommentar zum Schweizerischen Steuerrecht—Internationales Steuerrecht*, p. 446 and Peter Locher, *Einführung in das internationale Steuerrecht der Schweiz*, p. 273.
1556. For instance, this has been specifically illustrated in the dispatches concerning the DTAs with Mexico and Morocco. To this effect, *see* FC (*Federal Council*) May 12, 1993, *Botschaft über ein Doppelbesteuerungsabkommen mit Marokko*, available online at https://www.estv.admin.ch, and *see* FC (*Federal Council*) October 27, 1993, *Botschaft über ein Doppelbesteuerungsabkommen mit Mexiko*, available online at https://www.estv.admin.ch.

from the adoption of UN standards and/or a specific request of the DTA partner.[1557] Nevertheless, the special clause for insurance agents generally has limited practical application given the local licensing and regulatory requirements.[1558]

Even more strictly, the DTA concluded with France includes a provision stipulating that an insurance company is deemed to have a permanent establishment in the other contracting State in the case that it collects insurance premiums in that State through a representative or if it insures risks arising in the territory of that other State.[1559] In other words, pursuant to this provision, it is in principle sufficient that a Swiss insurance company insures risks arising in France (even without a local insurance representative) to give rise to a permanent establishment therein.

Also, the DTA concluded with Belgium contains a clause providing that an insurance agent that acts on behalf of a foreign insurance company that has, and habitually exercises, an authority to conclude contracts in the name of the insurance company gives rise to a permanent establishment.[1560] Since this clause fundamentally replicates the dependent agent provision contained under Art. 5, para. 5, of the same DTA rendering the independent agent provision ineffective for insurance agents, it seems a clause intended to deny the independence status of an insurance agent vis-à-vis the foreign insurance company.[1561]

In the DTAs concluded with Australia[1562] and New Zealand,[1563] it is stipulated that Art. 7 should not affect any domestic laws regarding the computation of taxable profits from any form of insurance (other than life insurance) and from life insurance, respectively. As a result, although such clauses do not directly affect the definition of permanent establishment, Australia and New Zealand retain the right to tax Swiss insurance companies (on their profits arising from the non-life business and the life business, respectively) according to their domestic laws, irrespective of the DTA provisions.[1564]

1557. This has been specifically illustrated in the dispatch concerning a Protocol to the DTA with India. To this effect, *see* FC (*Federal Council*) September 13, 2000, *Botschaft über ein Protokoll zur Änderung des Doppelbesteuerungsabkommens mit Indien*, available online at https://www.estv.admin.ch.

1558. In this sense, *see* FC (*Federal Council*) October 27, 1993, *Botschaft über ein Doppelbesteuerungsabkommen mit Mexiko*.

1559. *See* Art. 5, para. 5, of the DTA between Switzerland and France concluded on September 9, 1966.

1560. *See* Art. 5, para. 6, of the DTA between Switzerland and Belgium concluded on August 28, 1978.

1561. *See* René Schreiber/Kersten A. Honold/Roger Jaun in: Martin Zweifel/Michael Beusch/René Matteotti (eds.) *Kommentar zum Schweizerischen Steuerrecht—Internationales Steuerrecht*, p. 446 and Peter Locher, *Einführung in das internationale Steuerrecht der Schweiz*, p. 273. For further comments on the Belgian policy, *see also* s. 5.3.2 below.

1562. *See* Art. 5 of the Protocol to the DTA between Switzerland and Australia concluded on July 30, 2013.

1563. *See* Art. 2 of the Protocol to the DTA between Switzerland and New Zealand concluded on June 6, 1980.

1564. *See* Peter Locher, *Einführung in das internationale Steuerrecht der Schweiz*, p. 273. For further comments on the Australian policy, *see also* s. 5.3.1 below.

A similar rule is envisaged in the DTA concluded with Argentina.[1565] However, the scope of such a latter rule is limited to insurance and/or reinsurance covering property situated in the source country or persons who are residents of the source country. Also, in such a case, the tax chargeable in the source country is limited to 2.5 % of the gross premiums.

In all the above DTAs, it seems that Switzerland negotiated specific rules for the insurance business upon request of the contracting partners. Argentina even refused to ratify the previous DTA lacking a provision concerning reinsurance.[1566] Hence, a specific provision was included in an amending protocol and maintained in the DTA currently in force.[1567] It follows that the adoption of specific rules for the insurance business contained in Art. 5, Art. 7 or the Protocol thereto reflect the DTA policy of certain contracting partners. Being the DTA a matter of negotiation, it cannot be scientifically ascertained whether such specific rules have been agreed upon in consideration for other provisions to the benefit of Switzerland. Instead, what can be said is that such rules generally have limited application (at least, with respect to direct insurance) due to local licensing and regulatory requirements.[1568]

5.2.3 Prospective Developments

Switzerland has been actively participating and contributing to the BEPS Project. As a matter of principle, Switzerland also agrees on the need to counter BEPS issues at a multilateral level and that the OECD is the best forum to address such issues. However, in this respect, Switzerland is primarily focusing on implementing BEPS minimum standards,[1569] which do not include Action 7 of the BEPS Project.[1570]

What is more, Switzerland seems rather skeptical regarding the amendments introduced to the dependent agent permanent establishment in the context of Action 7 of the BEPS Project. As a matter of fact, besides the criticism regarding the fact that there are only minimal and/or difficult allocations of profits stemming from the

1565. *See* Art. 7, para. 7, of the DTA between Switzerland and Argentina concluded on March 20, 2014.
1566. DTA between Switzerland and Argentina concluded on April 23, 1997, which has been terminated.
1567. To this effect, *see* FC (*Federal Council*) October 15, 2014, *Botschaft zu einem neuen Doppelbesteuerungsabkommen zwischen der Schweiz und Argentinien*, available online at https://www.estv.admin.ch.
1568. In this sense, *see* FC (*Federal Council*) October 29, 1980, *Botschaft über ein Doppelbesteuerungsabkommen mit Neuseeland*, available online at https://www.estv.admin.ch.
1569. In the BEPS Project four minimum standards have been articulated in Actions 5, 6, 13 and 14. *See* OECD, "*Explanatory Statement: OECD/G20 Base Erosion and Profit Shifting Project*," pp. 14 et seq.
1570. To this effect, *see* FDF (*Federal Department of Finance*) October 5, 2015, Press Release, *New mandatory international OECD standards with regard to corporate taxation, including for Switzerland*, available online at https://www.efd.admin.ch/efd/en/home/dokumentation/nsb-news_list.msg-id-58972.html, Robert Danon/Christoph Schelling, "Switzerland in a Post-BEPS World," *Bulletin for International Taxation* (2015) pp. 197-198, Natassia Burkhalter, "Switzerland" in: IFA (ed.) *Assessing BEPS: origins, standards, and responses*, Cahiers de droit fiscal international, Vol. 102a (The Hague: Sdu Uitgevers, 2017) pp. 745-746 and 755 and Fabian Streule/Marc Dietschi, "Der Steuerstandort Schweiz 2017," *Internationales Steuer- und Wirtschaftsrecht* (2018) pp. 308-309.

extended scope of Art. 5, paras. 5 and 6, of the OECD Model,[1571] Switzerland also takes the view that there should be a strong relationship between the foreign enterprise and the dependent agent and that the dependent agent must conclude contracts in the name of the enterprise to constitute a permanent establishment.[1572]

Moreover, from a Swiss policy perspective, a permanent establishment can only arise if the business of the enterprise is carried on by the entrepreneur and his own personnel. For this reason, the activities of a subcontractor do not result in a permanent establishment of a subcontractor. For the same reason, under the Swiss view, the insurance of local risks cannot result in a permanent establishment if the insurance activities in the local market are wholly undertaken by independent agents.[1573]

On June 7, 2017, Switzerland was among the 68 jurisdictions that signed the MLI during the signing ceremony hosted by the OECD in Paris.[1574] In compliance with Swiss domestic law,[1575] the Swiss Federal Council designated the Federal Department of Finance to conduct a consultation with all relevant stakeholders concerning the ratification of the MLI.[1576] After the conclusion of the consultation process, the Swiss Federal Council adopted a dispatch on the MLI, thereby requesting the Parliament to approve a Federal Decree aimed at ratifying the MLI.[1577] The Federal Decree has been approved by the Parliament on March 22, 2019.[1578] No referendum was called, so that Switzerland deposited its instrument of ratification on August 29, 2019.

At the time of signature, Switzerland submitted a provisional list of 14 DTAs to be amended through the MLI.[1579] Nevertheless, in the final version deposited with the OECD, the number of DTAs has been reduced to 12.[1580] The list is restricted only to those countries that are willing to agree with Switzerland the precise wording on how

1571. *See* Georg Kofler/Christian Schmidt/Madeleine Simonek, *Archiv für Schweizerisches Abgaberecht*, (2016/2017) p. 491.
1572. *See* Christoph Schelling, "Swiss Tax Treaty Policy," *Bulletin for International Taxation* (2015) p. 218 and Raoul Stocker, "Potential Effects of the OECD Base Erosion and Profit Shifting Initiative on Swiss Transfer Pricing Rules and Swiss Companies," *Bulletin for International Taxation* (2015) p. 214.
1573. *See* Christoph Schelling, *Bulletin for International Taxation*, (2015) pp. 218-219.
1574. *See* OECD, "*Signatories and Parties to the Multilateral Convention to Implement Tax Treaty Related Measures to Prevent Base Erosion and Profit Shifting*," available online at www.oecd .org.
1575. *See* Federal Act on the Consultation Procedure of March 18, 2005.
1576. *See* FC (*Federal Council*) December 20, 2017, Press Release, *Federal Council initiates consultation on BEPS convention*, along with the related draft documents, available online at https://www.admin.ch/gov/en/start/documentation/media-releases.msg-id-69304.html.
1577. *See* FC (*Federal Council*) August 22, 2018, Press Release, *Federal Council adopts dispatch on BEPS convention*, along with the dispatch, the Federal Decree and the report containing the results of the consultation process, available online at https://www.efd.admin.ch/efd/en/home/dokumentation/nsb-news_list.msg-id-71891.html.
1578. *See* the update on the BEPS Project as at August 2019, available online at https://www.efd.admin.ch/efd/en/home/themen/steuern/steuern-international/beps/fb-beps.html.
1579. DTAs with Argentina, Chile, Czech Republic, India, Iceland, Italy, Liechtenstein, Lithuania, Luxembourg, Austria, Poland, Portugal, South Africa and Turkey. *See* "*Confédération suisse—Statut de la liste de réserves et des notifications au moment de la signature*," available online at www.oecd.org, pp. 2-5.
1580. While the DTA with Mexico has been added, the DTAs with India, Liechtenstein and Poland have been taken out. *See* "*Réserves et notifications de la Confédération suisse*," available online at www.oecd.org, pp. 1-2.

the provisions of the existing DTAs will be amended through the MLI.[1581] All such 12 jurisdictions have also signed the MLI and correspondingly included their DTAs with Switzerland as DTAs to be amended through the MLI.

In line with its policy of implementing only the BEPS minimum standards, Switzerland expressed reservations on most of the MLI provisions.[1582] Among others, Switzerland has reserved its right not to apply any of the provisions regarding the avoidance of permanent establishment status under Arts. 12-15 of the MLI.[1583] Most notably, already at the time of signature, Switzerland made a full reservation in accordance to Art. 12, para. 4, of the MLI not to include the amendments introduced in Art. 5, paras. 5 and 6, of the OECD Model in its DTAs to be amended through the MLI.[1584] In the final version deposited with the OECD,[1585] the Swiss position regarding this full reservation has been confirmed.[1586] Therefore, in Swiss DTAs currently in force, the permanent establishment threshold will remain unchanged.[1587]

Besides opting out of Art. 12 of the MLI, Switzerland has also made a reservation in para. 213 of the OECD Model Commentary on Art. 5 to reserve the right to use the formulation of the dependent agent provision before the 2017 update of the OECD Model. Hence, it is also unlikely that Switzerland will include the newly formulated Art. 5, paras. 5 and 6, of the OECD Model in its negotiating basis and therefore consider the amendments introduced in the context of Action 7 of the BEPS Project in bilateral

1581. *See* the dispatch attached to FC (*Federal Council*) August 22, 2018, Press Release, *Federal Council adopts dispatch on BEPS convention*. For further comments, *see also* Christoph Suter/Susanne Schreiber, "OECD BEPS—the Swiss Position," *International Tax Review* (2018).

1582. The treaty-related minimum standards identified in the BEPS Project have been reflected in Arts. 6, 7, 16 and 17 of the MLI. For further comments on such measures, *see* Andreas Langer, "The Legal Relevance of the Minimum Standard in the OECD/BEPS Project" in: Michael Lang/Pasquale Pistone/Alexander Rust/Josef Schuch/Claus Staringer (eds.) *The OECD Multilateral Instrument for Tax Treaties* (Alphen aan den Rijn: Wolters Kluwer, 2018) pp. 89 et seq.

1583. Countries can reserve the right to not apply the entire article in the case that it does not contain a minimum standard. For further comments, *see* Benjamin Walker, "Reservations to the Multilateral Instrument" in: Michael Lang/Pasquale Pistone/Alexander Rust/Josef Schuch/Claus Staringer (eds.) *The OECD Multilateral Instrument for Tax Treaties* (Alphen aan den Rijn: Wolters Kluwer, 2018) pp. 173 et seq.

1584. *See* "*Confédération suisse—Statut de la liste de réserves et des notifications au moment de la signature*," p. 9. For further comments, *see also* Nils Harbeke/Noëlle Mathis, "Schweiz: Aktuelles aus der DBA-Politik bei der Umsetzung des MLI," *Internationales Steuerrecht* (2019) p. 39.

1585. *See* "*Réserves et notifications de la Confédération suisse*," p. 4.

1586. Under Art. 28 of the MLI, reservations made at the time of the signature should be generally confirmed upon the deposit of the instrument of ratification. After that, a reservation can be withdrawn or replaced with a more limited reservation, whereas it is not permitted to notify further reservations. For further comments, *see* Alexandra Miladinovic/Alexander Rust, "Options under the Multilateral Instrument" in: Michael Lang/Pasquale Pistone/Alexander Rust/Josef Schuch/Claus Staringer (eds.) *The OECD Multilateral Instrument for Tax Treaties* (Alphen aan den Rijn: Wolters Kluwer, 2018) pp. 160-162.

1587. In this respect, Frehner called attention to the event that contracting countries could take the view that changes introduced in the context of the BEPS Project have interpretative value. *See* Eva Frehner, *Expert Focus*, (2018) p. 733.

DTA negotiations.[1588] This is also what clearly emerges from the analysis of DTAs recently concluded with Pakistan, Kosovo, Zambia and Brazil[1589] and the protocols amending the DTAs with the UK, Ukraine, South Korea, Iran, the Netherlands and Ireland,[1590] which do not contain any of such amendments.

Should Switzerland change its current position and therefore implement the newly formulated Art. 5, paras. 5 and 6, of the OECD Model in its DTAs in the future, an amendment to the current definition of permanent establishment at domestic level should nonetheless be considered to the effect that business activities without a fixed place of business could also result in a permanent establishment in Switzerland.[1591] As a matter of fact, in the event that the domestic tax law is not amended accordingly, situations in which there would be a dependent agent permanent establishment in Switzerland under a DTA, but which could not be eventually covered due to the lack of a domestic legal basis, will arguably increase. This discrepancy would be beneficial for Switzerland only at a first glance. On the one hand, this would be irrelevant in the case of contracting States avoiding double taxation by means of the credit method. On the other hand, it would be effective in the case of contracting States applying the exemption method only to the extent that the exemption remains unconditionally granted, not being associated with a subject-to-tax clause or a switch-over clause. Hence, Switzerland should think carefully about renouncing its taxable basis in such a way.[1592]

5.3 POLICIES OF OTHER COUNTRIES

5.3.1 Australia

Australia has concluded DTAs with almost 50 countries,[1593] which encompass most of Australia's trading partners.[1594] The form and contents of its DTAs are generally

1588. *See* Georg Kofler/Christian Schmidt/Madeleine Simonek, *Archiv für Schweizerisches Abgaberecht*, (2016/2017) p. 491.
1589. *See* DTA between Switzerland and Pakistan concluded on March 21, 2017, DTA between Switzerland and Kosovo concluded on May 26, 2017, DTA between Switzerland and Zambia concluded on August 29, 2017 and DTA between Switzerland and Brazil concluded on May 3, 2018.
1590. *See* Protocol to the DTA between Switzerland and the UK concluded on November 30, 2017, Protocol to the DTA between Switzerland and Ukraine concluded on January 24, 2019, Protocol to the DTA between Switzerland and South Korea concluded on May 17, 2019, Protocol to the DTA between Switzerland and Iran concluded on June 3, 2019, Protocol to the DTA between Switzerland and the Netherlands concluded on June 12, 2019 and Protocol to the DTA between Switzerland and Ireland concluded on June 13, 2019.
1591. *See* Georg Kofler/Christian Schmidt/Madeleine Simonek, *Archiv für Schweizerisches Abgaberecht*, (2016/2017) p. 491 and Raoul Stocker, *Bulletin for International Taxation*, (2015) p. 214.
1592. *See* Georg Kofler/Christian Schmidt/Madeleine Simonek, *Archiv für Schweizerisches Abgaberecht*, (2016/2017) p. 492.
1593. The DTAs are available online on the portal of the Australian Government at https://treasury.gov.au/tax-treaties/income-tax-treaties/ or otherwise at www.ibfd.org.
1594. *See* Peter Collins/Hamish McElwee, "Australia" in: Ekkehart Reimer/Stephan Schmid/Marianne Orell (eds.) *Permanent Establishments: A Domestic Taxation, Bilateral Tax Treaty and OECD Perspective* (Alphen aan den Rijn: Kluwer Law International, 2016) Part 1.02[C] p. 7.

aligned to the OECD Model, subject to some departures which favor source country taxation to a greater extent than would ordinarily be the case under the OECD Model.[1595] Further, the Australian tax authorities have acknowledged that the OECD Model Commentary will often need to be considered in the interpretation of DTAs concluded by Australia.[1596]

This holds true with respect to the definition of a dependent agent permanent establishment. In fact, under Australian DTAs,[1597] such a definition is in most cases based on OECD standards in place at the time of their conclusion. In this respect, it is also interesting to note that Australia has fully supported the BEPS Project, which has influenced the implementation of domestic laws and DTAs concluded by Australia.[1598] At DTA level, as a reaction to the BEPS Project, Australia has started implementing the changes to the permanent establishment definition discussed in the context of Action 7 of the BEPS Project in the new DTAs with Germany[1599] and Israel.[1600]

On June 7, 2017, Australia signed the MLI during the signing ceremony hosted by the OECD in Paris.[1601] Thereafter, Australia ratified the MLI on August 24, 2018[1602] and deposited its instrument of ratification on September 26, 2018. In the final version of its MLI position, Australia submitted a list of 42 DTAs to be amended through the MLI.[1603,1604] In doing so, despite the fact that its initial approach was to adopt Art. 12

1595. *See* Peter Collins/Hamish McElwee in: Ekkehart Reimer/Stephan Schmid/Marianne Orell (eds.) *Permanent Establishments: A Domestic Taxation, Bilateral Tax Treaty and OECD Perspective*, Part 1.03[B] p. 24.

1596. *See* ATO (*Australian Taxation Office*) December 19, 2001, Taxation Ruling TR 2001/13, para. 104.

1597. As opposed to the Australian typical approach in DTAs, under domestic law, there is no express requirement that the relevant agent be dependent. *See* Peter Collins/Hamish McElwee in: Ekkehart Reimer/Stephan Schmid/Marianne Orell (eds.) *Permanent Establishments: A Domestic Taxation, Bilateral Tax Treaty and OECD Perspective*, Part 1.03[D] p. 32.

1598. *See* Peter Collins/Hamish McElwee in: Ekkehart Reimer/Stephan Schmid/Marianne Orell (eds.) *Permanent Establishments: A Domestic Taxation, Bilateral Tax Treaty and OECD Perspective*, Part 1.03[C] p. 30, Andrew Mills/Dale Pinto, "Australia" in: IFA (ed.) *Assessing BEPS: origins, standards, and responses*, Cahiers de droit fiscal international, Vol. 102a (The Hague: Sdu Uitgevers, 2017) pp. 126-129 and John Walker, "Chapter 18: BEPS in Australia" in: Sam Sim/Mei June Soo (eds.) *Asian Voices: BEPS and Beyond* (Amsterdam: IBFD, 2017) paras. 18.4.1 and 18.4.2.

1599. *See* Art. 5 of the DTA between Australia and Germany concluded on November 12, 2015. For further comments, *see also* Ludmilla Maurer/Christian Port/Tom Roth/John Walker, "A Brave New Post-BEPS World: New Double Tax Treaty Between Germany and Australia Implements BEPS Measures," *Intertax* (2017) pp. 314-316, C. John Taylor, "The 2015 Australia-Germany Tax Treaty, BEPS, and the Multilateral Instrument," *Australian Tax Review* (2017) pp. 168 et seq. and Christian Gaßmann/Timo Welling, "Erweiterung des Betriebsstättenbegriffs am Beispiel des jüngst geschlossenen DBA Australien," *Praxis Internationale Steuerberatung* (2017) pp. 170-172. For further comments on the German policy, *see also* s. 5.3.4 below.

1600. *See* Art. 5 of the DTA between Australia and Israel concluded on March 27, 2019.

1601. *See* OECD, "*Signatories and Parties to the Multilateral Convention to Implement Tax Treaty Related Measures to Prevent Base Erosion and Profit Shifting.*"

1602. *See* Act No. 83 of 2018.

1603. *See* "*Australia—Status of List of Reservations and Notifications upon Deposit of the Instrument of Ratification, Acceptance or Approval,*" available online at www.oecd.org, pp. 2-7.

1604. In doing so, Australia removed the DTA with Taiwan, changing the total number of listed agreements from 43 to 42.

of the MLI without reservation,[1605] Australia has reserved its right not to apply the provisions regarding the dependent agent permanent establishment under Art. 12 of the MLI.[1606] This is linked to the fact that Australia will consider adopting the rules contained in Art. 12 of the MLI bilaterally to enable clarification of their application in practice,[1607] as just seen with Germany and Israel.

A well-established departure from the OECD Model is instead related to the insurance business. This deviation does not directly concern the definition of a permanent establishment, but rather Art. 7 of Australian DTAs.[1608] In fact, in line with the reservation put forward in the OECD Model Commentary,[1609] all of Australia's DTAs contain a provision preserving the operation of the domestic legislation relating to taxation of profits from insurance and reinsurance with non-residents,[1610,1611] although in certain cases this provision is only limited to non-life insurance.[1612]

This provision is aimed at preserving the application of the specific domestic regime laid down in Division 15 of Part III of the Income Tax Assessment Act 1936, which sets out the statutory source rules for insurance and reinsurance taken out with non-residents entities in the case where the contract is not made with a principal office or branch of the foreign insurance (or reinsurance) company in Australia.

Such statutory rules can be traced back to section 28B of the Income Tax Assessment Act 1922, which was introduced by means of the Income Tax Assessment Bill 1930. The Explanatory Memorandum to the Income Tax Assessment Bill 1935—the Bill for the Income Tax Assessment Act 1936—stated that section 28B of the Income Tax Assessment Act 1922 "*was originally introduced to tax ex-Australian underwriters*

1605. *See* Australian Government, "*Australia's Adoption of the BEPS Convention (Multilateral Instrument)—Consultation Paper—December 2016*," available online at https://treasury.gov.au/, p. 20 and Melissa Lim, "Australia's initial approach to the OECD Multilateral Instrument," *International Tax Review* (2017).

1606. *See* "*Australia—Status of List of Reservations and Notifications upon Deposit of the Instrument of Ratification, Acceptance or Approval*," p. 22.

1607. *See* The Parliament of the Commonwealth of Australia, "*Treasury Laws Amendment (OECD Multilateral Instrument) Bill 2018—Explanatory Memorandum*," available online at https://parlinfo.aph.gov.au, p. 49 and Australian Government, "*Multilateral Convention to Implement Tax Treaty Related Measures to Prevent Base Erosion and Profit Shifting*," available online at https://treasury.gov.au.

1608. Many New Zealand's DTAs contain a similar deviation from the OECD Model in respect of life insurance. In fact, New Zealand typically excludes life insurance income from the scope of Art. 7 of its DTAs to preserve the application of its domestic legislation. However, the analysis of the New Zealand policy is beyond the scope of the present research.

1609. *See* para. 85 of the OECD Model Commentary on Art. 7.

1610. *See* Michael Butler, "*Australia—Permanent Establishments—Topical Analyses*," last reviewed: April 11, 2019, available online at www.ibfd.org, para. 8.2.

1611. The introduction of such a provision in the business profits article can be traced back to the DTA between Australia and the UK concluded on October 26, 1946, which has been terminated. For further comments on the relevant negotiation, *see* C. John Taylor, "The Negotiation and Drafting of the UK—Australia Double Taxation Treaty of 1946," *British Tax Review* (2009) pp. 201 et seq.

1612. *See*—for instance—Art. 5 of the Protocol to the DTA between Switzerland and Australia concluded on July 30, 2013.

in respect of Australian business undertaken by them in competition with companies established in Australia."[1613]

Pursuant to such statutory rules, in the case that a person (either a resident or a non-resident) enters into an insurance contract with a non-resident insurance company to insure property situated in Australia, or the insured event is one which can happen only in Australia, the premium is deemed to be derived from sources in Australia and is assessable therein.[1614] Similarly, the premium is also deemed to have an Australian source if a resident person has entered into a contract through an agent or representative of the foreign insurance company in Australia that was in any way instrumental in inducing the entry of the insured person into the contract, regardless of where the property is situated or where the insured event may happen.[1615]

In those situations, the non-resident insurance company is deemed to have a taxable income equal to 10% of the gross premiums. Nevertheless, where the actual profit or loss of the non-resident insurance company can be established, such a profit or loss must be assessed through the normal operation of the Income Tax Assessment Act 1936.[1616,1617]

In this respect, on June 6, 2008, the Australian tax authorities released a noteworthy Interpretative Decision, in which they expressed the view that a dependent agent of a non-resident insurance company is not considered to have a principal office or a branch in Australia within the meaning of section 142 of the Income Tax Assessment Act 1936.[1618]

This Interpretative Decision maintained that there was no statutory definition of the principal office or branch and found that the ordinary meaning of such terms to be used was their definitions in the Macquarie Dictionary. Based on such definitions, the

---

1613. *See* Parliament of Australia, "*Explanatory Memorandum showing alterations contained in the bill for an act to consolidate and amend the Income Tax Assessment Act 1922-1934*," available online at https://www.aph.gov.au/, pp. 142-143.
1614. *See* section 142, para. 1, of the Income Tax Assessment Act 1936. For further comments, *see also* Michael Dirkis, "Ripe for Reform: Australia's Domestic Source Rules," *Bulletin for International Taxation* (2007) p. 171, Michael Butler, "*Australia—Permanent Establishments—Topical Analyses*," para. 8.2 and Tom Toryanik, "*Australia—Corporate Taxation—Country Analyses*," last reviewed: May 26, 2019, available online at www.ibfd.org, para. 12.3.2.
1615. *See* section 142, para. 2, of the Income Tax Assessment Act 1936. For further comments, *see also* Michael Dirkis, *Bulletin for International Taxation*, (2007) pp. 171-172, Michael Butler, "*Australia—Permanent Establishments—Topical Analyses*," para. 8.2 and Tom Toryanik, "*Australia—Corporate Taxation—Country Analyses*," para. 12.3.2.
1616. *See* section 143 of the Income Tax Assessment Act 1936. For further comments, *see also* Michael Dirkis, *Bulletin for International Taxation*, (2007) p. 172, Michael Butler, "*Australia—Permanent Establishments—Topical Analyses*," para. 8.2 and Tom Toryanik, "*Australia—Corporate Taxation—Country Analyses*," para. 12.3.2. In this respect, a decision of the Administrative Tax Court held that the liability is determined by reference to the actual profit, whether or not that produces a higher taxable income than the deemed 10%. *See* Michael Butler, "*Australia—Permanent Establishments—Topical Analyses*," para. 8.2.
1617. The legislation also envisages arrangements to encourage compliance, e.g., the deduction of the premium in the hands of the insured person is made subject to arrangements for the payment of the income tax thereon. *See* sections 145 and 146 of the Income Tax Assessment Act 1936.
1618. *See* ATO (*Australian Taxation Office*) June 8, 2008, Interpretative Decision ID 2008/83.

Interpretative Decision concluded that a syndicate of the Lloyd's insurance market in London—in providing underwriting for general insurance in Australia through an Australian company acting as a coverholder on behalf of the underwriting members—did not transact insurance business in Australia through a principal office or branch therein. This is notwithstanding the fact that the Australian coverholder had a binding authority and carried on the function as an agent for the underwriting members.[1619]

Division 15 of Part III of the Income Tax Assessment Act 1936 also applies where a person carrying on the business of insurance in Australia reinsures the whole or part of any risk with a non-resident. In that situation, it is stipulated that, while reinsurance premiums paid to non-residents are not allowed for deduction and recoveries are not assessable in the hands of the resident person, such reinsurance premiums are not assessable in the hands of the non-resident reinsurance company, unless the resident person makes an election to be taxed as an agent for all the non-resident reinsurance companies. In such a latter case, the resident person is required to lodge tax returns and settle taxes due in respect of the premium income, which is an amount equal to 10% of the gross reinsurance premiums.[1620,1621]

The effect of these rules is to create an obligation on insured persons that make payments of premiums to non-resident insurance and reinsurance companies to collect Australian income tax (currently, at 30%) on the taxable income of such non-resident entities, which is deemed to be 10% of the gross premiums (unless the actual profit or loss of a non-resident insurance company can be established), thereby leading to an effective tax of 3% on the gross premiums. In such a way, these statutory source rules have commonality with the withholding tax rules to the extent that a fixed percentage of the gross premiums is deemed to have an Australian source and the expenses incurred in earning the income are not allowed for deduction.[1622]

However, there is some uncertainty whether—in the case that the non-resident insurance and/or reinsurance company carries on business in Australia through a permanent establishment—the effect of such rules is that the Australian tax liability is to be calculated under the above domestic legislation or the business profits article.[1623] This is particularly the case where the non-resident has a dependent agent permanent establishment in Australia which triggers the application of the regime laid down in Division 15 of Part III of the Income Tax Assessment Act 1936 to the extent that the

1619. *See* Tom Toryanik, "Withholding Tax on Non-Resident Insurers Explained," *Asia-Pacific Tax Bulletin* (2008) p. 406.

1620. *See* section 148 of the Income Tax Assessment Act 1936. For further comments, *see also* Michael Dirkis, *Bulletin for International Taxation*, (2007) p. 172, Michael Butler, "*Australia—Permanent Establishments—Topical Analyses*," para. 8.2 and Tom Toryanik, "*Australia—Corporate Taxation—Country Analyses*," para. 12.3.3.

1621. This provision is applicable only to certain classes of life insurance. To this effect, *see* section 148, para. 10, of the Income Tax Assessment Act 1936.

1622. *See* Michael Dirkis, *Bulletin for International Taxation*, (2007) p. 172 and John Walker/Vida Ghazavi, "Nexus for Taxation in Asia: Contemporary Permanent Establishment and Related Issues," *Asia-Pacific Tax Bulletin* (2005) p. 198.

1623. *See* Michael Butler, "*Australia—Permanent Establishments—Topical Analyses*," para. 8.2.

dependent agent is not considered as a principal office or branch. Indeed, in such a case, the two sets of rules eventually overlap.

5.3.2 Belgium

Belgium has concluded DTAs with approximately a hundred countries,[1624] including its most significant trading partners. While most of Belgium's DTAs are patterned after OECD standards, a minority of DTAs are based on UN standards.[1625] Belgium has also drafted its own model, which sets forth the policy principles that the Belgian negotiators generally follow when discussing DTAs with other countries.[1626] The first version of this Belgian model was published in 2007 and followed to a large extent the 2005 OECD Model.[1627] The Belgian model has been subsequently updated in 2010 mostly in line with the amendments introduced in the 2010 OECD Model.[1628] On the top of this, the position of the Belgian tax authorities is also represented in the official administrative commentary on DTAs,[1629] which was last updated in 1996, but still remains a relevant source of interpretation.[1630]

In Belgian DTAs, the definition of a dependent agent permanent establishment typically follows OECD standards in place at the time of their conclusion.[1631] According

1624. The DTAs are available online on the portal of the Belgian Government at https://finances.belgium.be or otherwise at www.ibfd.org.

1625. *See* Maarten Temmerman/Sofie Van de Perre, "Belgium" in: Ekkehart Reimer/Stephan Schmid/Marianne Orell (eds.) *Permanent Establishments: A Domestic Taxation, Bilateral Tax Treaty and OECD Perspective* (Alphen aan den Rijn: Kluwer Law International, 2016) Part 3.02[C] pp. 5-6 and Patrick Cauwenbergh/André Claes, "Belgium" in: IFA (ed.) *Is there a permanent establishment?*, Cahiers de droit fiscal international, Vol. 94a (The Hague: Sdu Uitgevers, 2009) pp. 131-132.

1626. For additional comments, *see* Luc De Broe, "Belgium's Tax Treaty Policy and the Draft Belgian Model Convention," *Bulletin for International Taxation* (2008) pp. 324-325.

1627. *Convention between ... and the Kingdom of Belgium for the Avoidance of Double Taxation and the Prevention of Fiscal Evasion with respect to Taxes on Income and on Capital—June 2007*, available online at www.ibfd.org.

1628. *Convention between ... and the Kingdom of Belgium for the Avoidance of Double Taxation and the Prevention of Fiscal Evasion with respect to Taxes on Income and on Capital—June 2010*, available online on the portal of the Belgian Government at https://finances.belgium.be or otherwise at www.ibfd.org.

1629. FPS (*Federal Public Service*), "*Algemeen commentaar van de overeenkomsten tot het vermijden van dubbele belasting.*"

1630. *See* Maarten Temmerman/Sofie Van de Perre in: Ekkehart Reimer/Stephan Schmid/Marianne Orell (eds.) *Permanent Establishments: A Domestic Taxation, Bilateral Tax Treaty and OECD Perspective*, Part 3.02[A] p. 5, Patrick Cauwenbergh/André Claes in: IFA (ed.) *Is there a permanent establishment?*, Cahiers de droit fiscal international, Vol. 94a, p. 132 and Lieven Denys, "Belgium: The Concept of Permanent Establishment Revised and Other Reflections Beyond," *Bulletin for International Taxation* (2008) p. 441.

1631. Under Belgian domestic law, a dependent agent is deemed to constitute a Belgian establishment of a foreign principal even if such an agent does not have the authority to contract on behalf of the foreign company. *See* Art. 229, para. 2, of the Belgian Income Tax Code 1992 and FPS (*Federal Public Service*), "*Commentaire du code des impôts sur les revenus,*" para. 229/46. Only agents that are considered independent, who deal with customers in their own name and their own risk, will not give rise to a Belgian establishment, provided that they act in the ordinary course of their business. *See* FPS (*Federal Public Service*), "*Commentaire du code des impôts sur les revenus,*" para. 229/48. For further comments, *see also* Maarten Temmerman/Sofie Van de Perre in: Ekkehart Reimer/Stephan Schmid/Marianne Orell (eds.)

to the Belgian tax authorities, only intermediaries that are both legally and economically dependent on the foreign enterprise may give rise to a dependent agent permanent establishment.[1632,1633] The authority does not necessarily need to be of a general nature. In fact, it is sufficient that the agent can bind the company, albeit to a limited extent. This is for instance the case where the agent is bound by conditions and price arrangements set by the company which he/she represents, provided that he/she is authorized to sign the sales contract on behalf of the company. Likewise, this is also the case where the agent negotiates the contract, even if the contract is signed by another person on behalf of the company.[1634] Moreover, it is required that the agent makes use of this authority regularly and repeatedly and not only occasionally.[1635]

Furthermore, the Belgian tax authorities reiterate the (narrow) approach taken at domestic law level that independent agents are only those that deal with customers in their own name, at their own risk and without any intervention of the foreign principal, such as brokers, commissionaires and customs commissionaires. It follows that it is only under such circumstances that agents can invoke the independent agent provision, provided that they act in the ordinary course of their business.[1636,1637]

Also, the Belgian tax authorities specifically address the situation of insurance agents. *In primis*, it is noted that insurance agents fall under the general provisions concerning dependent and independent agents, regardless of whether the DTA contains a specific provision in this regard. As a result, in the case where a (dependent or independent) insurance agent can bind the foreign insurance company (even though he/she only has that capacity in fact, e.g., if he/she has blank policies and delivers them to customers) and he/she regularly acts as such by concluding contracts in the name of and for the account of the insurance company without having to obtain the

Permanent Establishments: A Domestic Taxation, Bilateral Tax Treaty and OECD Perspective, Part 3.03[D] pp. 21-22, Guy Jorion, *Le non-résident ou la société étrangère face à l'impôt belge* (Brussels: Larcier, 2006) pp. 121-123, Lieven Denys, *Bulletin for International Taxation*, (2008) pp. 448-449, Isabel Verlinden/Xavier van Vlem/Bram Markey, "Commissionaire Agency Permanent Establishment Structures and the Impact of the Zimmer Case," *International Transfer Pricing Journal* (2010) p. 348 and Astrid Pieron, *Résidence fiscale et fiscalité belge des non-résidents* (Brussels: Larcier, 2013) pp. 214-215. The definition has been recently amended to incorporate the supplementary independent test regarding related parties. *See* Art. 61 of the Corporate Income Tax Reform Act dated December 25, 2017.

1632. *See* FPS (*Federal Public Service*), "*Algemeen commentaar van de overeenkomsten tot het vermijden van dubbele belasting*," para. 5/401.

1633. Wustenberghs and Puncher believe that this assertion lies on *a contrario* interpretation of the independent agent provision and thus is to be questioned. To this effect, *see* Tim Wustenberghs/Ethel Puncher, *Bulletin for International Taxation* (2011) p. 242.

1634. *See* FPS (*Federal Public Service*), "*Algemeen commentaar van de overeenkomsten tot het vermijden van dubbele belasting*," para. 5/402.

1635. *See* FPS (*Federal Public Service*), "*Algemeen commentaar van de overeenkomsten tot het vermijden van dubbele belasting*," para. 5/403.

1636. *See* FPS (*Federal Public Service*), "*Algemeen commentaar van de overeenkomsten tot het vermijden van dubbele belasting*," para. 5/502.

1637. Cauwenbergh and Claes believe that this approach is too narrow since it excludes intermediaries that conclude contracts in the name and for the account of the foreign principal. To this effect, *see* Patrick Cauwenbergh/André Claes in: IFA (ed.) *Is there a permanent establishment?*, Cahiers de droit fiscal international, Vol. 94a, p. 146. In a similar vein, *see also* Tim Wustenberghs/Ethel Puncher, *Bulletin for International Taxation* (2011) p. 243.

approval of that company for each contract, that agent must be deemed to constitute a permanent establishment of the foreign insurance company. In this respect, the Belgian tax authorities further maintain that the independence of the insurance agent does not affect the assessment regarding the existence of a dependent agent permanent establishment to the extent that—in such a case—the agent will be considered to act outside the ordinary course of his/her business and therefore fall within the scope of the dependent agent provision.[1638] In such a way, the Belgian tax authorities seem to exclude *a priori* the independence of any insurance agent without recourse to the assessment of applicable facts and circumstances.[1639]

The Belgian tax authorities also consider that a Belgian insurance broker, whether an individual or a company, who has been appointed by a foreign insurance company as its authorized representative in Belgium and is competent to accomplish in its name and for its own account operations such as the acceptance, the signature and delivery of insurance contracts can be regarded as a permanent establishment.[1640]

In light of the foregoing, it is no surprise that many Belgium's DTAs contain a specific provision, which either denies the application of the independent agent provision to insurance agents or introduces additional criteria under which an insurance agent can give rise to a permanent establishment.[1641] The first approach has been applied in DTAs concluded with Germany, Luxembourg, Morocco, Norway and Switzerland.[1642,1643] DTAs concluded with Austria, South Korea, Denmark, Finland, Ireland, Israel, the UK, Sweden and Thailand combine the first approach with the introduction of the tests regarding the collection of premiums and the insurance of risks. DTAs concluded with Brazil, Ivory Coast and France adopt only such latter tests with a carve-out for independent agents, whereas DTAs concluded with Chile, the Philippines and Tunisia also have a carve-out for reinsurance along the lines of the

1638. *See* FPS (*Federal Public Service*), "*Algemeen commentaar van de overeenkomsten tot het vermijden van dubbele belasting*," para. 5/505. For further comments, *see also* Patrick Cauwenbergh/André Claes in: IFA (ed.) *Is there a permanent establishment?*, Cahiers de droit fiscal international, Vol. 94a, p. 149 and Guy Jorion, *Le non-résident ou la société étrangère face à l'impôt belge*, p. 167.

1639. This straight exclusion appears to be at the root of the special clause for insurance agents. For further comments, *see* s. 3.3.2.5.1 above.

1640. *See* FPS (*Federal Public Service*), "*Algemeen commentaar van de overeenkomsten tot het vermijden van dubbele belasting*," para. 5/505. For further comments, *see also* Patrick Cauwenbergh/André Claes in: IFA (ed.) *Is there a permanent establishment?*, Cahiers de droit fiscal international, Vol. 94a, p. 149.

1641. *See* FPS (*Federal Public Service*), "*Algemeen commentaar van de overeenkomsten tot het vermijden van dubbele belasting*," para. 5/506. For further comments, *see also* Patrick Cauwenbergh/André Claes in: IFA (ed.) *Is there a permanent establishment?*, Cahiers de droit fiscal international, Vol. 94a, pp. 149-150.

1642. *See* Maarten Temmerman/Sofie Van de Perre in: Ekkehart Reimer/Stephan Schmid/Marianne Orell (eds.) *Permanent Establishments: A Domestic Taxation, Bilateral Tax Treaty and OECD Perspective*, Part 3.03[D] p. 23.

1643. A similar clause was also included in Art. 5, para. 6, of the DTA between Belgium and the US concluded on July 9, 1970, which has been terminated. The DTA between Belgium and the US concluded on November 27, 2006 does not contain any such clause.

special clause for insurance agents contemplated in the UN Model.[1644] Under the DTA concluded with the Netherlands, it is stipulated that the independent agent provision does not apply to an agent who is acting exclusively on behalf of one or, at the most, two insurance enterprises and who has, and habitually exercises, such authority to conclude contracts in the name of this enterprise or these enterprises.[1645]

At last, in the DTAs concluded with Australia[1646] and New Zealand,[1647] it is stipulated that profits of insurance companies (other than life insurance companies, in the DTA with Australia) resident in a contracting State may be taxable in the other contracting State according to the law of that other State. It follows that, although such a clause does not directly affect the definition of permanent establishment, Belgium retains the right to tax profits of insurance companies that are resident in Australia and New Zealand according to its domestic legislation (and vice versa).[1648]

As a member of the OECD, Belgium supported the BEPS Project, along with the implementation of changes to existing DTAs through a coordinated approach, at least in respect of minimum standards.[1649] On June 7, 2017, Belgium signed the MLI during the signing ceremony held in Paris.[1650] Pursuant to the internal legislative procedure, the Federal Parliament approved the law aimed at the ratification of the MLI on March 21, 2019.[1651] Following the approval of all the Regional and Community Parliaments, Belgium deposited its instrument of ratification on June 26, 2019. In doing so, Belgium submitted a list of 99 DTAs to be amended through the MLI.[1652] As opposed to the position submitted at the time of signature,[1653] Belgium decided to waive its reservation

1644. A similar clause was also included in Art. 5, para. 5, of the DTA between Belgium and the Indonesia concluded on November 13, 1973, which has been terminated. The DTA between Belgium and the Indonesia concluded on September 16, 1997 does not contain any such clause.

1645. *See* Art. 5, para. 6, of the DTA between Belgium and the Netherlands concluded on June 5, 2001.

1646. *See* Art. 7, para. 7, of the DTA between Belgium and Australia concluded on October 13, 1977. For further comments on the Australian policy, *see also* s. 5.3.1 above.

1647. *See* Protocol to the DTA between Belgium and the New Zealand concluded on September 15, 1981.

1648. It is interesting to note that, under Belgian domestic tax law, profits realized in Belgium by foreign insurance companies (except for reinsurance) are taxable therein, even in the absence of a permanent establishment. *See* Art. 228, para. 2 (3°) b), of the Belgian Income Tax Code 1992 and FPS (*Federal Public Service*), "*Commentaire du code des impôts sur les revenus,*" paras. 228/25 and 228/26. For further comments, *see also* Maarten Temmerman/Sofie Van de Perre in: Ekkehart Reimer/Stephan Schmid/Marianne Orell (eds.) *Permanent Establishments: A Domestic Taxation, Bilateral Tax Treaty and OECD Perspective*, Part 3.03[D] p. 23 and Astrid Pieron, *Résidence fiscale et fiscalité belge des non-résidents*, p. 223.

1649. *See* Cabinet Ministre des Finances et de la Lutte contre la Fraude Fiscale, "*Plan d'action pour lutter contre la fraude fiscal,*" available online at http://vanovertveldt.belgium.be, p. 60.

1650. *See* OECD, "*Signatories and Parties to the Multilateral Convention to Implement Tax Treaty Related Measures to Prevent Base Erosion and Profit Shifting.*"

1651. Belgian House of Representatives, "*Projet de loi portant assentiment à la Convention multilatérale pour la mise en oeuvre des mesures relatives aux conventions fiscales pour prévenir l'érosion de la base d'imposition et le transfert de bénéfices et à la Note explicative, faites à Paris le 24 novembre 2016,*" available online at www.lachambre.be.

1652. *See* "*Royaume de Belgique—Statut de la liste de réserves et de notifications au moment du dépôt de l'Instrument de ratification,*" available online at www.oecd.org, pp. 1-14.

1653. *See* "*Kingdom of Belgium—Status of List of Reservations and Notifications at the Time of Signature,*" available online at www.oecd.org, p. 33.

and accept the changes to the dependent agent permanent establishment.[1654] This revised position seems more in line with recent measures adopted in domestic law[1655] and with the stance taken in the latest bilateral negotiations, like in the case of the DTA with Japan.[1656]

5.3.3 Chile

Since the year 1998, with the start of a new government policy,[1657] Chile has concluded DTAs with 34 countries.[1658] The DTAs concluded by Chile follow OECD standards to a great extent. Accordingly, in Chilean DTAs, the concept of permanent establishment is generally based on OECD standards with some departures.[1659]

Among the most common deviations from OECD standards, Chilean DTAs typically include an insurance agent provision along the lines of Art. 5, para. 6, of the UN Model.[1660] In this respect, it is worth noting that the Chilean tax authorities issued a ruling in a specific case concerning the application of the DTA between Chile and Canada. More to the point, in this ruling procedure,[1661] the Chilean tax authorities maintained that—according to the special clause for insurance agents laid down in such a DTA[1662]—the employee or representative of the foreign insurance company must either collect premiums and/or insure risks in Chile. Nevertheless, it is not necessary that such employee or representative is a resident of Chile or that he/she has the power to conclude contracts on behalf of the foreign company. In their view, it is in fact sufficient that the employee or representative be present or has been present in the country to conclude the transaction or to collect the premium.[1663]

This ruling seems to be in line with a proper interpretation of the insurance agent provision in respect of the element that the employee or representative does not need to have a power to conclude contracts on behalf of the foreign insurance company. Differently, while correctly stating that the employee or representative does not need to be a resident of Chile, the ruling seems not to carefully consider the condition for him/her to be "*established*" in the source country. Indeed, this condition seems to require the employee or representative be present in the source country with a certain

1654. *See* "*Royaume de Belgique—Statut de la liste de réserves et de notifications au moment du dépôt de l'Instrument de ratification*," pp. 34-38.
1655. *See* Art. 61 of the Corporate Income Tax Reform Act dated December 25, 2017.
1656. *See* Art. 5, paras. 6-8, of the DTA between Belgium and Japan concluded on October 12, 2016.
1657. *See* Ignacio Melo/Juan Pablo Orellana, "Chile" in: IFA (ed.) *Is there a permanent establishment?*, Cahiers de droit fiscal international, Vol. 94a (The Hague: Sdu Uitgevers, 2009) p. 193.
1658. The DTAs are available online on the portal of the Chilean tax authorities at http://www.sii.cl/pagina/jurisprudencia/convenios.htm or otherwise at www.ibfd.org.
1659. *See* Ignacio Melo/Juan Pablo Orellana in: IFA (ed.) *Is there a permanent establishment?*, Cahiers de droit fiscal international, Vol. 94a, p. 193.
1660. This is the case of DTAs with Belgium, Canada, Colombia, Croatia, Czech Republic, Ecuador, Ireland, Malaysia, Mexico, Norway, Paraguay, Perù, Poland, Portugal, Russia, South Africa, Thailand and the UK.
1661. *See* SII (*Servicio de Impuestos Interno*) May 7, 2007, Ruling No. 986.
1662. *See* Art. 5, para. 6, of the DTA between Chile and Canada concluded on January 21, 1998.
1663. For further comments, *see also* Ignacio Melo/Juan Pablo Orellana in: IFA (ed.) *Is there a permanent establishment?*, Cahiers de droit fiscal international, Vol. 94a, p. 209.

degree of permanence, so that a mere presence for the conclusion of the transaction or the collection of the premium does not appear to be sufficient.

Another noteworthy departure from the OECD Model is also included in the DTAs with Argentina, Australia, Austria, China, New Zealand, Paraguay, the US and Uruguay.[1664] In fact, such DTAs contain a special clause—contemplated in Art. 5, Art. 7 or the Protocol thereto—pursuant to which profits of foreign insurance and/or reinsurance companies are taxable in the source country, regardless of whether the foreign insurance and/or reinsurance company carries on its activities in the source State through a permanent establishment therein.[1665] In such a case, the tax chargeable in the source country is generally limited to a certain percentage of the gross insurance and/or reinsurance premiums paid to the non-resident company.[1666]

Thereby, this provision reserves a right for Chile to tax income derived by foreign insurance and/or reinsurance companies, but it limits the exercise of such a taxing right by determining a ceiling, which may not exceed a percentage of the gross premiums that is negotiated from time to time with the relevant DTA partner. As a result, such a provision has the effect of preserving the application of a withholding tax on gross insurance and/or reinsurance premiums that have a Chilean source.

This withholding tax mechanism has its roots in Chilean domestic legislation, which provides that Chilean-source income includes insurance premiums paid to cover risks in Chile. Indeed, as a general rule, insurance premiums paid to non-resident companies covering property permanently located in Chile, merchandise that is in Chile temporarily or for transit purposes, or the life of domiciled or resident persons are subject to a withholding tax at a rate of 22% on the gross amount of the premium or instalment thereof. In the case of reinsurance for such items, the withholding tax is calculated at a rate of 2% on the gross amount of the transferred premium.[1667]

Clearly, in a DTA situation, such a withholding tax can be levied only in the case where Chile retains its taxing rights on such income. It is no surprise that the Chilean tax authorities confirmed this principle in two rulings concerning reinsurance companies resident of the UK, Spain, Ireland, France and Sweden with no permanent

1664. This departure is consistent with the reservations put forward by Chile in para. 96 of the OECD Model Commentary on Art. 7 and para. 75 of the Annex to the OECD Model Commentary concerning the previous version of Art. 7.

1665. The DTA concluded with Argentina specifies that this clause is only applicable with respect to insurance and/or reinsurance covering property situated in the source country or persons who are residents of the source country. To this effect, *see* Art. 7, para. 4, of the DTA between Chile and Argentina concluded on May 15, 2015. Many Argentina's DTAs contain such a clause. However, the analysis of the Argentinian policy is beyond the scope of this research.

1666. Pursuant to Art. 6 of the Protocol to the DTA between Chile and New Zealand concluded on December 10, 2003, income, premiums or profits from any kind of insurance may be taxed in accordance with the domestic laws of the contracting States, so that such a DTA does not limit taxing rights of the contracting States in respect of the insurance business.

1667. *See* Art. 59, No. 3, of Chilean Income Tax Law. For further comments, *see also* Andrés Bustos, "*Chile—Corporate Taxation—Country Analyses*," last reviewed: April 1, 2019, available online at www.ibfd.org, para. 12.6.2.

establishments in Chile.[1668,1669] In fact, the Chilean tax authorities concluded that in the cases under analysis—pursuant to the DTAs between Chile and the above countries, which do not contain the above special clause—no withholding tax had to be levied in Chile.

DTAs which contain such a special clause generally clarify that the withholding tax is only applicable in the case where the foreign company has a permanent establishment in Chile. However, in the DTAs concluded with New Zealand and Paraguay, some uncertainty remains as to whether the Chilean tax liability is to be calculated according to the business profits article or to the withholding tax mechanism. Should the latter approach prevail, the presence of a special clause governing the withholding tax in such DTAs could—oddly enough—lead to a lower Chilean tax liability and therefore turn out to be more beneficial for the foreign company.

As a member of the OECD since 2010, Chile has been actively participating in the BEPS Project. This is particularly the case in respect of the issues related to the permanent establishment status. In fact, a Chilean tax administration officer led the working group on Action 7 of the BEPS Project.[1670] Accordingly, Chile has incorporated most of the measures introduced in the context of the BEPS Project into its negotiation policy and has implemented them in its most recent DTAs.[1671] On June 7, 2017, Chile signed the MLI during the signing ceremony held in Paris.[1672] At present, the MLI is undergoing the domestic legislative procedure for approval.[1673] As with the provisional list submitted at the time of the signature,[1674] Chile is expected to include all its 34 DTAs concluded so far in the list of DTAs to be amended through the MLI.[1675] Along the same lines,[1676] Chile is also intended to confirm the inclusion of the provisions

1668. *See* SII (*Servicio de Impuestos Interno*) May 19, 2009, Ruling No. 1.745 and SII (*Servicio de Impuestos Interno*) May 20, 2009, Ruling No. 1.746.
1669. In Ruling No. 1.745, the Chilean tax authorities held that the appointment of a Chilean representative for the purposes of transacting reinsurance directly—that is, without the intervention of a reinsurance broker—does not give rise to a dependent agent permanent establishment to the extent that this representation is related to judicial and administrative matters. On the other hand, where reinsurance is transacted through a broker, the Chilean tax authorities acknowledged that the independent agent provision can generally prevent source taxation.
1670. *See* César Toledo Concha/Horacio Viana, "Chile" in: IFA (ed.) *Assessing BEPS: origins, standards, and responses*, Cahiers de droit fiscal international, Vol. 102a (The Hague: Sdu Uitgevers, 2017) pp. 215, 222 and 226.
1671. *See* DTA between Chile and China concluded on May 25, 2015, DTA between Chile and Italy concluded on October 23, 2015, DTA between Chile and Japan concluded on January 21, 2016 and DTA between Chile and Uruguay concluded on April 1, 2016.
1672. *See* OECD, "*Signatories and Parties to the Multilateral Convention to Implement Tax Treaty Related Measures to Prevent Base Erosion and Profit Shifting.*"
1673. The Chilean Chamber of Deputies is currently discussing the text of the MLI that was presented through the Presidential Message 25-367 dated April 8, 2019, available online at www.camara.cl.
1674. *See* "*The Republic of Chile—Status of List of Reservations and Notifications at the Time of Signature,*" available online at www.oecd.org, pp. 1-6.
1675. *See* Presidential Message 25-367 dated April 8, 2019, p. 8.
1676. *See* "*The Republic of Chile—Status of List of Reservations and Notifications at the Time of Signature,*" pp. 14-16.

regarding the dependent agent permanent establishment under Art. 12 of the MLI in the DTAs to be amended through the MLI.[1677]

The above position has also been endorsed in a Circular Letter published on December 7, 2017 with instructions regarding the concept of permanent establishment in Chile.[1678] In such a document—the first Circular Letter on the concept of permanent establishment in Chile—the Chilean tax authorities touched upon some of the elements introduced in the context of Action 7 of the BEPS Project paving the way for a broader concept of permanent establishment. Nevertheless, considering that the Chilean domestic legislation does not provide for a definition of permanent establishment,[1679] the lack of a clear legal framework at domestic level could generate uncertainty as to whether a permanent establishment be present under domestic tax law, even where Chile retains its taxing rights pursuant to a DTA.

5.3.4 Germany

Germany has concluded DTAs with more than a hundred countries.[1680] All German DTAs concluded so far are largely based on OECD standards with some deviations.[1681] Accordingly, under German DTAs, the definition of a dependent agent permanent establishment is in most cases based on OECD standards in place at the time of their conclusion, save for a few deviations.[1682] Germany has also drafted its own basis for negotiation on August 22, 2013,[1683] which fundamentally proposes a German translation of Art. 5, paras. 5 and 6, of the 2010 OECD Model.[1684]

Among the main deviations from the OECD Model, some German DTAs contain specific provisions regarding the insurance business. The DTAs concluded with Argentina, France, Ivory Coast and Tunisia encompass a special clause for insurance agents stipulating that a permanent establishment arises in the case that such agents collect premiums or insure risks in the source country, unless such agents have an

1677. *See* Presidential Message 25-367 dated April 8, 2019, pp. 27-28.
1678. SII (*Servicio de Impuestos Interno*) December 7, 2017, Circular Letter No. 57.
1679. Article 58, No. 1, of the Chilean Income Tax Law only provides some examples of what may be considered as a permanent establishment for Chilean tax purposes, namely branches, offices, agents and representatives.
1680. The DTAs are available online on the portal of the BMF (*Bundesministerium der Finanzen*) at https://www.bundesfinanzministerium.de or otherwise at www.ibfd.org.
1681. *See* Georg Kofler/Christian Schmidt/Madeleine Simonek, *Archiv für Schweizerisches Abgaberecht*, (2016/2017) p. 450.
1682. *See* Stephan Schnorberger, "*Germany—Permanent Establishments—Topical Analyses,*" last reviewed: March 30, 2016, available online at www.ibfd.org, para. 2.1.4.1.2 and Patrick Held, *BEPS Aktionspunkt 7: Die Verhinderung der künstlichen Vermeidung einer Betriebsstätte*, p. 1.
1683. BMF (*Bundesministerium der Finanzen*) August 22, 2013, *Abkommen Zwischen der Bundesrepublik Deutschland und ...—zur Vermeidung der Doppelbesteuerung und zur Verhinderung der Steuerverkürzung auf dem Gebiet der Steuern vom Einkommen und vom Vermögen.*
1684. For further comments, *see also* Marisa Lipp, "Germany's Tax Treaty Negotiation Policy," *European Taxation* (2014) p. 313, Christian J. Schmidt, "Germany" in: Guglielmo Maisto (ed.) *Departures from the OECD Model and Commentaries* (Amsterdam: IBFD, 2014), para. 13.2.3.3 and Wilhelm Haarmann, "Die Vertreterbetriebsstätte und die faktische Verpflichtung (Kommissionärsmodell)" in: Christian Kaeser (ed.) *Festgabe zum 75. Geburtstag von Prof. Dr. Dr. h.c. Franz Wassermeyer* (Munich: Beck, 2015) pp. 161 et seq.

independent status. The DTAs concluded with Azerbaijan, Egypt, Indonesia,[1685] Jamaica, Kenya, Mexico, Pakistan, Romania and Uzbekistan contain an insurance agent provision with a carve-out for reinsurance along the lines of Art. 5, para. 6, of the UN Model. The DTA with Belgium includes a provision excluding the independence of an insurance agent that habitually exercises an authority to conclude contracts in the name of a foreign insurance company.[1686] The DTAs concluded with Australia and New Zealand contain a special clause under Art. 7 to preserve the application of domestic law with respect to income from insurance activities.[1687]

The Federal Ministry of Finance has also issued specific guidelines regarding the insurance business. In particular, pursuant to para. 4.2 of the Circular Letter dated December 24, 1999,[1688] it has been clarified that German branches of foreign insurance companies within the meaning of the Insurance Supervisory Act[1689] are to be regarded as permanent establishments. On the contrary, in the case that there is no branch for the purposes of the supervisory legislation, it is stated that the general principles regarding dependent agent permanent establishments are applicable.

Such guidelines do not appear to be based on a sound legal reasoning. As a matter of fact, on the one hand, it should be recalled that the definition of a branch for insurance supervisory purposes does not necessarily correspond to the basic rule of permanent establishments. Therefore, in the absence of a common legal basis, the first part of the reasoning appears to be oversimplified. On the other hand, a factual assessment regarding the existence of a dependent agent permanent establishment cannot be limited to general principles.[1690] True, this can be the case of DTAs patterned after OECD standards. Nevertheless, some German DTAs contain deviations from OECD standards that should be more carefully considered. This is for instance the case of DTAs that include a special clause for insurance agents, which is intended to go beyond the general rules of the agency permanent establishment. Hence, the second part of the reasoning is somewhat surprising, too.[1691]

In respect of the general rules regarding dependent agent permanent establishments, in para. 1.2.2 of the Circular Letter dated December 24, 1999, the German tax administration acknowledged that an agent must have the authority to conclude contracts to constitute an agency permanent establishment.[1692] According to the

1685. The DTA with Indonesia also contains a special provision regarding representatives of foreign trading companies. For further comments, *see also* s. 6.5 below.
1686. For further comments on the Belgian policy, *see also* s. 5.3.2 above.
1687. For further comments on the Australian policy, *see also* s. 5.3.1 above.
1688. BMF (*Bundesministerium der Finanzen*) December 24, 1999, *Grundsätze der Verwaltung für die Prüfung der Aufteilung der Einkünfte bei Betriebsstätten international tätiger Unternehmen (Betriebsstätten-Verwaltungsgrundsätze)*.
1689. In German, "*Gesetz über die Beaufsichtigung der Versicherungsunternehmen.*"
1690. In the Circular Letter dated December 24, 1999, cross-reference is made to the 1992 OECD Model.
1691. In a similar vein, *see also* Jacques Sasseville/Arvid A. Skaar in: IFA (ed.) *Is there a permanent establishment?*, p. 58.
1692. This authority is not required to constitute a permanent representative (*ständiger Vertreter*) under section 13 of the General Tax Code (*Abgabenordnung*). Therefore, the definition of dependent agent permanent establishment at DTA level is generally narrower than that applicable at domestic level. *See* Milva Helling, *Die Vertreterbetriebsstätte im internationalen*

German perspective, this is the case where the foreign company is legally or economically bound by the agent. To this end, the agent does not need to sign the contract. It is indeed sufficient that he/she negotiates all details of the contract for the foreign company.[1693,1694] Circumstances in which the foreign company retains the right to accept the contract itself should instead carefully assessed.[1695]

The authority to conclude contracts must be habitually exercised. From a German perspective, this is an essential element for a dependent agent permanent establishment to exist. In fact, Germany attaches increased importance to the requirement of minimum duration of representation of the foreign company under Art. 5, para. 5, of the OECD Model in the absence of a residence and/or fixed place of business of the agent in the source country.[1696] To this end, a period of six months is generally considered as a guideline.[1697]

Steuerrecht (Hamburg: Kovać, 2009) p. 24, Stephan Schnorberger, "*Germany—Permanent Establishments—Topical Analyses*," para. 2.1.4.4.2, Franz Wassermeyer/Christian Kaeser, "Art. 5" in: Franz Wassermeyer (ed.) *Doppelbesteuerung: Kommentar zu allen deutschen Doppelbesteuerungsabkommen* (Munich: Beck, 2017) pp. 119-120 and Michael Puls, "Begriff der Betriebsstätte" in: Franz Wassermeyer/Ulf Andresen/Xavier Ditz (eds.) *Betriebsstätten-Handbuch: Gewinnermittlung und Besteuerung* (Cologne: Otto Schmidt, 2018) pp. 112-113.

1693. For further comments, *see also* Petra Eckl, "Germany" in: IFA (ed.) *Is there a permanent establishment?*, Cahiers de droit fiscal international, Vol. 94a (The Hague: Sdu Uitgevers, 2009) p. 333, Stephan Schnorberger, "*Germany—Permanent Establishments—Topical Analyses*," para. 2.1.4.4.2, Georg Kofler/Christian Schmidt/Madeleine Simonek, *Archiv für Schweizerisches Abgaberecht*, (2016/2017) p. 457, Maximilian Görl, "Art. 5" in Klaus Vogel/Moris Lehner (eds.) *Doppelbesteuerungsabkommen der Bundesrepublik Deutschland auf dem Gebiet der Steuern vom Einkommen und Vermögen: Kommentar auf der Grundlage der Musterabkommen* (Munich: Beck, 2015) pp. 754-755, Franz Wassermeyer/Christian Kaeser in: Franz Wassermeyer (ed.) *Doppelbesteuerung: Kommentar zu allen deutschen Doppelbesteuerungsabkommen*, pp. 119-120 and Christian Looks/Oliver Heinsen, *Betriebsstättenbesteuerung: Inboundinvestitionen, Outboundinvestitionen, Steuergestaltungen, Branchenbesonderheiten—3rd Edition* (Munich: Beck, 2017) pp. 81-82.

1694. This is specifically clarified in the DTA concluded with Azerbaijan.

1695. For further comments, *see* Stephan Schnorberger, "*Germany—Permanent Establishments—Topical Analyses*," para. 2.1.4.4.2, Georg Kofler/Christian Schmidt/Madeleine Simonek, *Archiv für Schweizerisches Abgaberecht*, (2016/2017) p. 457 and Maximilian Görl in: Klaus Vogel/Moris Lehner (eds.) *Doppelbesteuerungsabkommen der Bundesrepublik Deutschland auf dem Gebiet der Steuern vom Einkommen und Vermögen: Kommentar auf der Grundlage der Musterabkommen*, p. 755.

1696. *See* para. 180 of the OECD Model Commentary on Art. 5.

1697. *See* BFH (*Bundesfinanzhof*) August 3, 2005, I R 87/04, BStBl. II 2006, S. 220. For further comments, *see also* Petra Eckl, "Germany" in: IFA (ed.) *Is there a permanent establishment?*, Cahiers de droit fiscal international, Vol. 94a, p. 333, Milva Helling, *Die Vertreterbetriebsstätte im internationalen Steuerrecht*, pp. 47-48, Stephan Schnorberger, "*Germany—Permanent Establishments—Topical Analyses*," para. 2.1.4.2, Georg Kofler/Christian Schmidt/Madeleine Simonek, *Archiv für Schweizerisches Abgaberecht*, (2016/2017) pp. 458-459, Franz Wassermeyer/Christian Kaeser in: Franz Wassermeyer (ed.) *Doppelbesteuerung: Kommentar zu allen deutschen Doppelbesteuerungsabkommen*, p. 124, Stefan Bendlinger in: Aigner/Georg Kofler/Michael Tumpel (eds.) *DBA—Doppelbesteuerungsabkommen*, p. 425, Stefan Bendlinger/Sabine Kanduth-Kristen/Georg Kofler/Florian Rosenberger, *Internationales Steuerrecht*, p. 657 and Michael Puls in: Franz Wassermeyer/Ulf Andresen/Xavier Ditz (eds.) *Betriebsstätten-Handbuch: Gewinnermittlung und Besteuerung*, pp. 110-111.

With respect to the independent agent provision,[1698] according to the German standpoint, the decisive criterion appears to be the *"personal independence."* As a result, it is crucial to determine whether the agent bears his/her own entrepreneurial risk. In addition, an agent that operates for only one principal is not necessarily to be regarded as dependent, provided that he/she carries out his/her own economic activity.[1699]

Germany has been a strong advocate of the BEPS Project and has been actively taking part in the related work since inception. With respect to Action 7 of the BEPS Project, Germany has been pursuing two goals. On the one hand, Germany—as an industrialized country—has a strong interest in keeping the permanent establishment definition clear and narrow.[1700] On the other hand, Germany perceived that the existing rules were making certain tax planning structures possible. As a result, Germany was interested in striking a balance between the two objectives.[1701] For the time being, it

1698. Under German domestic law, the distinction between a dependent agent vis-à-vis the independent agent is largely irrelevant for the purposes of the permanent representative definition. However, in the absence of a DTA, German tax authorities would also consider the independence of the representative. *See* BMF (*Bundesministerium der Finanzen*), Income Tax Regulations (*Einkommensteuerrichtlinien*), available online at www.einkommensteuer richtlinien.de, para. 49.1. For further comments, *see also* Huili Wang/Maximilian Schrepfer, "Germany" in: Ekkehart Reimer/Stephan Schmid/Marianne Orell (eds.) *Permanent Establishments: A Domestic Taxation, Bilateral Tax Treaty and OECD Perspective* (Alphen aan den Rijn: Kluwer Law International, 2016) Part 8.03[D] pp. 17-18 and footnotes cited therein.

1699. *See* BFH (*Bundesfinanzhof*) September 14, 1994, I R 116/93, BStBl. II 1995, S. 240. For further comments, *see*—among others—Stephan Schnorberger, "*Germany—Permanent Establishments—Topical Analyses*," para. 2.1.4.3, Huili Wang/Maximilian Schrepfer in: Ekkehart Reimer/Stephan Schmid/Marianne Orell (eds.) *Permanent Establishments: A Domestic Taxation, Bilateral Tax Treaty and OECD Perspective*, Part 8.03[D] p. 17, Georg Kofler/Christian Schmidt/Madeleine Simonek, *Archiv für Schweizerisches Abgaberecht*, (2016/2017) pp. 454-455, Milva Helling, *Die Vertreterbetriebsstätte im internationalen Steuerrecht*, pp. 64 et seq., Maximilian Görl in: Klaus Vogel/Moris Lehner (eds.) *Doppelbesteuerungsabkommen der Bundesrepublik Deutschland auf dem Gebiet der Steuern vom Einkommen und Vermögen: Kommentar auf der Grundlage der Musterabkommen*, pp. 765-766, Franz Wassermeyer/Christian Kaeser in: Franz Wassermeyer (ed.) *Doppelbesteuerung: Kommentar zu allen deutschen Doppelbesteuerungsabkommen*, pp. 129-131 and Michael Puls in: Franz Wassermeyer/Ulf Andresen/Xavier Ditz (eds.) *Betriebsstätten-Handbuch: Gewinnermittlung und Besteuerung*, pp. 111-112.

1700. In the German literature, tax rules are already perceived to be robust compared to those of other countries. As a result, one of main concerns seems related to the fact that the BEPS Project could encourage a further tightening of anti-avoidance rules, thereby creating additional compliance burdens for businesses (mainly to the detriment of the German tax revenue). To this effect, *see*—among others—Daniel Fehling/Karoline Kampermann, "Germany" in: IFA (ed.) *Assessing BEPS: origins, standards, and responses*, Cahiers de droit fiscal international, Vol. 102a (The Hague: Sdu Uitgevers, 2017) p. 369, Wolfgang Haas, "Base Erosion and Profit Shifting (BEPS)—Eine steuerpolitische Bewertung," in: Jens Blumenberg/Georg Crezelius/Dietmar Gosch/Matthias Schüppen (eds.) *Festschrift für Wilhelm Haarmann* (Düsseldorf: IDW, 2015) pp. 563 et seq., Thomas Rödder/Reimar Pinkernell, "Zum Seminar F: 20 Thesen zur BEPS-Diskussion," *Internationales Steuerrecht* (2013) p. 623 and Deborah Schanz/Anna Feller, "Wieso Deutschland (fast) keine BEPS-Bekämpfung braucht," *Betriebs-Berater* (2015) pp. 865 et seq.

1701. *See* Daniel Fehling/Karoline Kampermann in: IFA (ed.) *Assessing BEPS: origins, standards, and responses*, Cahiers de droit fiscal international, Vol. 102a, pp. 380-381 and Ole Schmidt-Heß, "Die Verhinderung der künstlichen Vermeidung einer Betriebsstätte—Der OECD-Bericht zu Maßnahme 7 des BEPS-Aktionsplans," *Internationales Steuerrecht* (2016) p. 166.

appears that the more conservative approach has prevailed and the basis for negotiation has still to be revised. Most importantly, Germany does not seem to be in favor of the changes to the independent agent provision.[1702]

Against this background, on June 7, 2017, Germany signed the MLI during the signing ceremony held in Paris.[1703] At time of the signature, Germany submitted a provisional list of 35 DTAs to be amended through the MLI.[1704,1705] Not surprisingly,[1706] when doing so, Germany has reserved its right not to apply the provisions regarding the dependent agent permanent establishment under Art. 12 of the MLI.[1707]

In addition to opting out of Art. 12 of the MLI, Germany has also filed reservations in: (*i*) para. 213 of the OECD Model Commentary on Art. 5 to reserve the right to use the formulation of the dependent agent provision before the 2017 update of the OECD Model and (*ii*) para. 215 of the OECD Model Commentary on Art. 5 to reserve the right to use the formulation of the independent agent provision before the 2017 update of the OECD Model clarifying that it does not agree with the introduction of the supplementary independence test regarding related parties.

The inclusion of amendments addressed in the context of Action 7 of the BEPS Project will be probably left to bilateral negotiations with contracting partners. This has been particularly the case of the DTA concluded with Australia, which incorporated the changes to Art. 5, paras. 5 and 6 of the OECD Model.[1708] The same could also apply in several other DTAs currently undergoing a revision procedure.[1709]

1702. *See* Georg Kofler/Christian Schmidt/Madeleine Simonek, *Archiv für Schweizerisches Abgaberecht*, (2016/2017) p. 488, Dagmar Möller-Gosoge, "Art. 12" in: Florian Haase (ed.) *Multilaterales Instrument* (Heidelberg: Müller, 2018) p. 189, Martin Kreienbaum, "Das Multilaterale Instrument zur Modifikation bilateraler Doppelbesteuerungsabkommen" in: Jürgen Lüdicke (ed.) *Internationale Geschäftstätigkeiten in der Nach-BEPS-Welt* (Cologne: Otto Schmidt, 2018) p. 213, Stefan Bendlinger, "Multilaterales Instrument zur automatischen Anpassung bestehender Doppelbesteuerungsabkommen," *Steuer und Wirtschaft International* (2017) p. 10 and WTS, "*WTS Tax Weekly—No. 27 / 2016*," available online at www.wts.com/de-de/knowledge/tax-weekly, p. 1.

1703. *See* OECD, "*Signatories and Parties to the Multilateral Convention to Implement Tax Treaty Related Measures to Prevent Base Erosion and Profit Shifting.*"

1704. *See* "*Federal Republic of Germany—Status of List of Reservations and Notifications at the Time of Signature*," available online at www.oecd.org, pp. 2-10.

1705. German constitutional procedures also require a double-track implementation. *See* Georg Kofler/Christian Schmidt/Madeleine Simonek, *Archiv für Schweizerisches Abgaberecht*, (2016/2017) p. 489, Florian Haase, "Zukunft des IStR: Hinzurechnungsbesteuerung und Multilaterales Instrument im Fokus," *Internationale Steuer-Rundschau* (2017) p. 357 and Florian Haase, "Einführung" in: Florian Haase (ed.) *Multilaterales Instrument* (Heidelberg: Müller, 2018) pp. 18-19.

1706. The MLI only allows a combined change in both Art. 5, paras. 5 and 6, of the OECD Model. As a result, countries—like Germany—that are not in favor of a specific provision are inclined to opt out of the entire Art. 12 of the MLI.

1707. *See* "*Federal Republic of Germany—Status of List of Reservations and Notifications at the Time of Signature*," p. 24.

1708. *See* Art. 5 of the DTA between Australia and Germany concluded on November 12, 2015. For further comments on this provision and the Australian policy more in general, *see also* s. 5.3.1 above.

1709. For a list of DTAs under revision, *see* BMF (*Bundesministerium der Finanzen*) January 17, 2019, *Stand der Doppelbesteuerungsabkommen und anderer Abkommen im Steuerbereich sowie der Abkommensverhandlungen am 1. Januar 2019*, IV B 2—S 1301/07/10017-10.

5.3.5 Italy

Italy has concluded DTAs with almost a hundred countries.[1710] While DTAs concluded with OECD countries are generally patterned after OECD standards, DTAs concluded with developing countries also contain clauses based on UN standards. More to the point, the definition of dependent agent permanent establishment is generally based on the wording of the 1963 OECD Draft with some deviations.[1711]

As a result, the majority of Italian DTAs contains a wording in the dependent agent provision stipulating that it is the agent to be a permanent establishment of the foreign enterprise rather than the foreign enterprise to have a permanent establishment in the source country. At any rate, this language does not appear to have significant implications on the application of the provision.[1712] Also, based on the wording of the 1963 OECD Draft, many Italian DTAs do not contain the language according to which the foreign enterprise has a permanent establishment in the source country in respect of any activities of the agent. However, this general language does not preclude a factual assessment on a case-by-case basis.[1713] In addition, for the same reason, many Italian DTAs do not carve-out from the dependent agent provision auxiliary and/or preparatory activities, except where the "*activities are limited to the purchase of goods or merchandise for the enterprise.*"[1714,1715]

Some DTAs also contain specific clauses in respect of the insurance business. This is particularly the case of the DTAs concluded with Brazil, Indonesia, Ivory Coast and Mexico, which encompass a special clause for insurance agents.[1716] In doing so,

1710. The DTAs are available online on the portal of the MEF (*Ministero dell'Economia e delle Finanze*) at http://www.finanze.gov.it/ or otherwise at www.ibfd.org.

1711. *See* Fabrizio Acerbis/Francesco Nuzzolo, "Italy" in: Ekkehart Reimer/Stephan Schmid/Marianne Orell (eds.) *Permanent Establishments: A Domestic Taxation, Bilateral Tax Treaty and OECD Perspective* (Alphen aan den Rijn: Kluwer Law International, 2016) Part 11.03[B] p. 12, Marco Piazza, *Guida alla fiscalità internazionale*, p. 254 and Alessandro Dragonetti/Valerio Piacentini/Anna Sfondrini, *Manuale di fiscalità internazionale*, p. 1053.

1712. To this effect, *see* Marco Piazza, *Guida alla fiscalità internazionale*, p. 255 and Alessandro Dragonetti/Valerio Piacentini/Anna Sfondrini, *Manuale di fiscalità internazionale*, p. 1053.

1713. *See* Marco Piazza, *Guida alla fiscalità internazionale*, p. 255.

1714. In the case of auxiliary and/or preparatory activities, the existence of a dependent agent permanent establishment could nevertheless be excluded under Italian domestic legislation. *See also* (*Corte di Cassazione*) February 15, 2008, No. 3889 commented in Paola Sella, "Le modifiche alla Legge di Bilancio 2018 alla definizione di stabile organizzazione," *Fiscalità & Commercio Internationale* (2018) no. 5 pp. 11 et seq.

1715. More recent DTAs, like DTAs with Barbados, Panama and Romania, have been patterned after later versions of OECD standards and do not contain such peculiarities.

1716. A similar clause was included in the previous DTA concluded with France on October 29, 1958 (now terminated). Such a clause has been scrutinized by the Italian Supreme Court in a case concerning the deduction of foreign losses incurred by a French permanent establishment of an Italian insurance company that was put in run-off. *See* CC (*Corte di Cassazione*) March 27, 1996, No. 3585. In its judgment, the Italian Supreme Court held that the residual activities maintained in France for the purposes of managing and performing existing insurance contracts could no longer be considered as constituting a permanent establishment within the meaning of the special clause for insurance agents. Hence, such losses could be attributed to the Italian head office and allowed for deduction accordingly. Nevertheless, this conclusion does not appear to be properly motivated. As a matter of fact, even though the insurance business is put in run-off, some residual activities (e.g., the collection of annual premiums, the settlement of claims and so forth) are still required to be executed and—most probably—the

DTAs with Brazil, Indonesia, Ivory Coast contain a carve-out for independent agents, whereas the DTA with Mexico also contemplates a carve-out for reinsurance along the lines of Art. 5, para. 6, of the UN Model. The DTAs concluded with Australia and New Zealand contain a special clause under Art. 7 to preserve the application of domestic law with respect to income from insurance activities.[1717]

It is also worth noting that, as a reaction to the updates introduced in the 2005 OECD Model Commentary, the Italian representatives at the OECD inserted an observation stipulating that "*Italy wishes to clarify that, with respect to paragraphs 97, 116, 117 and 118, its jurisprudence is not to be ignored in cases falling in the above paragraphs.*"[1718] This observation is aimed at preserving the jurisprudence of the Italian Supreme Court in the *Philip Morris* cases.[1719] Most notably, from the Italian perspective, the participation in negotiations with customers should carefully be considered for the purposes of the traditional test regarding the conclusion of contracts and/or the supplementary test regarding the principal role leading to the conclusion of contracts.[1720] Furthermore, Italy pays specific attention to intra-group control relationships.[1721] For instance, in a multinational group, an Italian company can constitute a multiple permanent establishment of foreign companies that belong to the same group and pursue a common strategy.

A broad interpretation of the permanent establishment concept has been confirmed in more recent case law. For instance, the Italian Supreme Court held that a dependent agent permanent establishment arises where a foreign company entrusts—even de facto, i.e., without a power of attorney—the management of its business operations to another entity, with or without legal personality.[1722] Also, the Regional Tax Court of Lombardy maintained that an Italian company engaged in promotional activities and technical assistance on behalf of its US parent company gave rise to a dependent agent permanent establishment. As a matter of fact, despite not having the power and/or authority to conclude contracts in the name and on behalf of the parent company, the directors of the Italian company were delegated to propose

---

agent is still engaged (at least) in some of such activities. Therefore, in principle, both the tests regarding collection of premiums and the insurance of risks could still be met in such a final stage. For further comments, *see also* Roberto Baggio/Ermanno Basso, *Rivista di Diritto Tributario*, (1996) pp. 1098 et seq.

1717. For further comments on the Australian policy, *see also* s. 5.3.1 above.

1718. *See* para. 181 of the OECD Model Commentary on Art. 5.

1719. *See* CC (*Corte di Cassazione*) March 7, 2002, No. 3367, 3368 and 3369, March 26, 2002 No. 431926, May 25, 2002, No. 7682 and 7689, September 22, 2002, No. 10925 and December 6, 2002, No. 17373. For further comments, *see also* ch. 3 above.

1720. The same position taken in the *Philip Morris* cases has been confirmed in subsequent decisions. *See*—among others—CC (*Corte di Cassazione*) July 28, 2006, No. 17206, CC (*Corte di Cassazione*) April 9, 2010, No. 8488, CC (*Corte di Cassazione*) April 21, 2011, No. 9166 and CC (*Corte di Cassazione*) June 28, 2012, No. 10802.

1721. This has been confirmed in the manual of the Italian tax police for tax audits. *See* GdF (*Guardia di Finanza*) December 4, 2017, Circular Letter No. 1/2018.

1722. *See* CC (*Corte di Cassazione*) May 29, 2012, No. 20678. For further comments, *see also* Diego Avolio, "La stabile organizzazione: profili definitori" in: Sigfried Mayr/Benedetto Santacroce (eds.) *La stabile organizzazione delle imprese delle imprese industriali e commerciali* (Milano: Ipsoa, 2013) p. 51 and Diego Avolio/Benedetto Santacroce, "Per la stabile organizzazione basta l'affidamento degli affari," *Corriere Tributario* (2012) pp. 2258 et seq.

new payment terms, to grant discounts and/or to receive requests for commercial proposals. In such a case, the Italian company could not be regarded neither as legally independent (since it was part of a multinational group of companies) nor economically independent (since there was just one principal).[1723] On a different note, in a very recent case, the Regional Tax Court of Lombardy held that an Italian agent did not create a dependent agent permanent establishment of a UK software company. Besides arguing that the activities carried out by the Italian agent were auxiliary and preparatory in nature, the Court also held that the communication and reporting obligations of the agent were in line with the practice of the business sector and aimed at ensuring the correct execution of the agency relationship, without compromising the discretion of the agent.

The Italian Revenue Agency also took a specific view in respect of the insurance business in a ruling procedure.[1724] More to the point, the case concerned a UK insurance company which decided to restructure its Italian operations for strategic reasons. In fact, following some years in which the UK insurance company operated through a branch under the rules governing the freedom of establishment, it decided to limit its Italian operations to activities performed under the freedom to provide services. In view of such a restructuring, the UK insurance company asked the Italian Revenue Agency to confirm that the insurance activity carried out under the freedom to provide services does not result in corporate and local tax liability in Italy.[1725]

In answer to this request, the Italian Revenue Agency argued that the insurance regulation does not have direct effects on tax matters and therefore it cannot be excluded *a priori* that insurance activities carried out under the freedom to provide services could be exercised in such a way so as to give rise to a permanent establishment tax wise. As a matter of fact, the fashion in which the insurance activities are concretely exercised under the freedom to provide services could be such as to create a permanent establishment in the country where such activities are performed.

In light of the current framework, one can only agree with the reasoning of the Italian Revenue Agency in the sense that the analysis regarding the existence of a permanent establishment is to be carried out on a case-by-case basis, without taking for granted that the conclusions concerning the demarcation between the freedom to provide services and the freedom of establishment for regulatory purposes are relevant for tax purposes, too.[1726] Indeed, under the existing framework, there are gaps and

---

1723. *See* CTR Lombardia (*Commissione Tributaria Regionale Lombardia*) September 12, 2016, No. 4597, commented in Paola Sella, *Fiscalità & Commercio Internationale*, (2018) no. 5 pp. 11 et seq.
1724. *See* AdE (*Agenzia delle Entrate*) November 7, 2006, Ruling No. 124/E.
1725. *See* CTR Lombardia (*Commissione Tributaria Regionale Lombardia*) November 23, 2017, No. 4869. For further comments, *see also* Paola Sella, *Fiscalità & Commercio Internationale*, (2018) no. 5 pp. 11 et seq. and Stefano Guarino, "Quando la presenza di obbligazioni a carico dell'agente non configura una stabile organizzazione?—Il commento," *Corriere Tributario* (2018) pp. 1431 et seq.
1726. In a similar vein, *see also* Alberto Santi, "La stabile organizzazione delle imprese assicurative va individuata con le regole fiscali," *Corriere Tributario* (2006) pp. 3849 et seq., Marco Bargagli/Ciro Cesarano, "Attività assicurativa in regime di libera prestazione di servizi: profili giuridici e fattuali per una stabile organizaazione," *Fiscalità e Commercio Internazionale* (2017) pp. 13 et seq.

overlaps between the two sets of rules, but each set should be carefully assessed separately.

Over the recent years, Italy has invested significant resources to address issues falling within the scope of the BEPS Project, most notably to deal with issues related to the digital economy and the permanent establishment definition.[1727] In line with this commitment, Italy has also included the newly formulated Art. 5, paras. 5 and 6, of the OECD Model its most recent DTAs concluded with Chile, Jamaica and Colombia.[1728]

On June 7, 2017, Italy signed the MLI during the signing ceremony held in Paris.[1729] At the time of the signature, Italy submitted a provisional list with a significant number of DTAs (namely, 84 DTAs) to be amended through the MLI.[1730] Even so, quite surprisingly, Italy has reserved its right not to apply the provisions regarding the dependent agent permanent establishment under Art. 12 of the MLI.[1731] Hence, in principle, existing DTAs should not be affected by such provisions.

A few months later, in the 2018 Budget Law,[1732] Italy went back to its original commitment and thus amended the domestic definition of permanent establishment in line with the changes introduced in the context of Action 7 of the BEPS Project. More to the point, Italy fundamentally aligned Art. 162, paras. 6, 7 and 7-*bis*, of the Income Tax Code with the newly formulated Art. 5, paras. 5, 6 and 8, of the OECD Model, the only significant difference being related to the fact that Italy—in its domestic dependent agent provision—did not refer to the "*principal role*" leading to the conclusion of contracts. In the absence of any clarification from the Italian tax administration, according to the author,[1733] the omission of such an element could result in the domestic definition having a broader scope of application vis-à-vis the OECD Model to

1727. *See* Francesco Bungaro, "Italy" in: IFA (ed.) *Assessing BEPS: origins, standards, and responses*, Cahiers de droit fiscal international, Vol. 102a (The Hague: Sdu Uitgevers, 2017) pp. 429 and 441 et seq.

1728. *See* Art. 5 of the DTA between Italy and Chile concluded on October 23, 2015, Art. 5. Of the DTA between Italy and Jamaica concluded on January 19, 2018 and Art. 5 of the DTA between Italy and Colombia concluded on January 26, 2018.

1729. *See* OECD, "*Signatories and Parties to the Multilateral Convention to Implement Tax Treaty Related Measures to Prevent Base Erosion and Profit Shifting.*"

1730. *See* "*Italy—Status of List of Reservations and Notifications at the Time of Signature,*" available online at www.oecd.org, pp. 2-16.

1731. *See* "*Italy—Status of List of Reservations and Notifications at the Time of Signature,*" p. 32. For further comments on the position of Italy, *see* Bruno Ferroni, "Firmata la Convenzione Multilaterale del progetto BEPS: effetti su migliaia di trattati fiscali in tutto il mondo," *Il Fisco* (2017) pp. 2952 et seq.

1732. Law No. 205 of December 27, 2017.

1733. In supporting the same reasoning, some Italian literature argues that this deviation might stem from *Philip Morris,* where it was held that the participation in negotiations with customers should be carefully considered. In this respect, Mayr and Fort also take the view that, by virtue of the observation reported in para. 181 of the OECD Model Commentary on Art. 5, this reasoning could also be extended in a DTA situation. To this effect, *see* Sigfried Mayr/Giovanni Fort, "La nuova definizione di stabile organizzazione (Art. 162 del TUIR)," *Bollettino Tributario* (2018) p. 505, Fabio Brunelli/Sabrina Tronci, "La nuova definizione di stabile organizzazione personale e la disciplina del transfer pricing nell'ambito dei gruppi," *Bollettino Tributario* (2018) pp. 1219-1220 and Luca Rossi/Sara Flisi, "La stabile organizzazione personale tra significant people functions e risk management functions," *Corriere Tributario* (2019) pp. 81 et seq. Instead, the author does not share the view of Avolio, Corso and Odetto that this can be considered as a mere difference in wording vis-à-vis the OECD

the extent that any activity that directly leads to the conclusion of a contract could trigger the existence of a dependent agent permanent establishment under domestic tax law, with the only caveat being that the foreign enterprise routinely approves the transaction without material modifications.

Leaving aside the above mismatch, the update of the domestic definition is undoubtedly a crucial step toward the implementation of the measures set out in the context of Action 7 of the BEPS Project in a broader domestic set of rules governing permanent establishments, which has been revamped over the latest few years (most importantly, with the enactment of the AOA and the branch exemption regime).[1734]

On a different note, one can clearly spot a lack of coordination between the option submitted by Italy when signing the MLI on the one hand and the choices made by Italy in the latest DTA negotiations and in the amendments to the domestic permanent establishment definition on the other hand.[1735] True, as noted by the literature,[1736] Italy had—*in primis*—to amend its domestic legislation concerning the permanent establishment definition in order to avoid that—to circumvent the more restrictive provisions of the MLI—taxpayers could resort to Art. 169 of the Income Tax Code, according to which more favorable domestic legislation prevails over the provisions of DTAs. Nonetheless, in the present scenario, the newly formulated domestic provisions are essentially ineffective in a DTA situation,[1737] given that more favorable DTA provisions negotiated before the BEPS Project would apply.[1738] Perhaps, the above inconsistency could be due to diverging opinions within the Italian tax administration or simply because of a "*wait-and-see*" approach adopted by the Italian tax administration at the time of the signature. Should this be the case, Italy has the chance to review its position on Art. 12 of the MLI during the ratification process. If not, Italy will need to renegotiate the permanent establishment definition in nearly all its DTAs on a bilateral basis.

Model. *See* Diego Avolio, "La nuova definizione di stabile organizzazione," *Corriere Tributario* (2018) pp. 265 et seq. and Luisa Corso/Gianluca Odetto, "La nuova nozione di stabile organizzazione" in: *Quaderni Eutekne 2017—Le novità della Legge di bilancio 2018 e del DL collegato* (Torino: Eutekne, 2017), pp. 177-178.

1734. In a similar vein, *see* Bruno Ferroni, "Stabile organizzazione: la disciplina nazionale si adegua al BEPS e introduce la 'continuativa presenza economica'," *Il Fisco* (2018) pp. 632 et seq.

1735. According to Mayr and Fort, it remains to be seen whether the Italian tax administration takes the view that the changes to the OECD Model, the OECD Model Commentary and the domestic legislation could have interpretative value. *See* Sigfried Mayr/Giovanni Fort, *Bollettino Tributario*, (2018) p. 503. However, the author shares the view expressed by Assonime, Antonini and Mariella, who have excluded the interpretative nature of the new domestic provisions. *See* Assonime (*Associazione fra le Società Italiane per Azioni*) June 27, 2018, Circular Letter No. 15/2018 and Massimo Antonini/Maria Letizia Mariella, "Stabile Organizzazione: la parola ad Assonime," *Corriere Tributario* (2018) p. 2599.

1736. *See* Bruno Ferroni, *Il Fisco*, (2018) pp. 632 et seq., Carlo Garbarino/Patrizia Occhiuto, "Lo strumento multilaterale per la modifica dei trattati contro le doppie imposizioni," *Fiscalità & Commercio Internationale* (2018) no. 2 pp. 44 et seq., Luisa Corso/Gianluca Odetto in: *Quaderni Eutekne 2017—Le novità della Legge di bilancio 2018 e del DL collegato*, pp. 179-180 and Luca Bosco/Salvatore Sanna, "La nozione di stabile organizzazione nell'imposizione diretta: il BEPS Action 7 e la Raccomandazione 2016/136," *La gestione straordinaria delle imprese* (2016) p. 116.

1737. In a similar vein, *see* Bruno Ferroni, *Il Fisco*, (2018) pp. 632 et seq. and Paola Sella, *Fiscalità & Commercio Internationale*, (2018) no. 5 pp. 11 et seq.

1738. *See* Art. 75 of Presidential Decree No. 600 of September 29, 1973.

5.4 FINAL CONSIDERATIONS

The above sections clearly show that—despite global standards and best practices embodied in model treaties—there is no universal international tax policy, but rather multiple national tax policies which derive from different domestic legal traditions and other diverging domestic perspectives. Still, this does not necessarily mean that such policies cannot be assessed and compared against each other. Therefore, the following section will offer an analysis of the most significant elements observed in view of the normative claims to be addressed in Chapter 6, also considering that the final impact of the MLI on the network of DTAs is still to be determined.

In their DTAs, all countries considered in the analysis maintain their taxing rights on business profits of foreign insurance companies in the presence of a permanent establishment. Instead, at domestic level, while Italy, Germany and Switzerland do not have specific rules for insurance companies, in Australia, Belgium and Chile, profits of foreign insurance companies are taxable even in the absence of a permanent establishment. As a result, such latter countries aim at preserving their taxing rights on such an income with the introduction of specific clauses in their DTAs.

More specifically, save for a few DTAs in which specific rules have been agreed at the request of the other contracting party, Italy, Germany and Switzerland generally follow OECD standards with respect to the existence of a dependent agent permanent establishment. Yet, some differences may also be found among such countries.

Most importantly, Switzerland does not contain a specific provision concerning the dependent agent permanent establishment under domestic law. For this reason, even where a person can be regarded as a dependent agent permanent establishment pursuant to a DTA patterned after OECD standards, under Swiss domestic law, such a person could give rise to a permanent establishment only if he/she carries on business through a fixed place of business attributable to the foreign enterprise.[1739]

This clearly shows that a country which aims at taxing a certain element should carefully consider a coordination between the provisions contained in its DTAs and its domestic tax law rules. In Switzerland, considering that the scope of the domestic legislation regarding the permanent establishment definition is generally narrower than that of the DTAs, no Swiss tax can be levied on a dependent agent without a fixed place of business therein. Such a coordination is also of paramount importance to safeguard a proper functioning of the DTAs, and eventually of the model treaties themselves. In fact, any such lack of coordination can pave the way for avoidance opportunities. For instance, in the case where a dependent agent permanent establishment is present in Switzerland pursuant to a DTA, but he/she is not subject to tax therein due to a lack of a domestic legal basis, the adoption of the exemption method

1739. In Switzerland, there is consensus that a DTA can only limit the rules of Swiss domestic law to subject a certain element to Swiss taxation (the so-called negative effect of DTAs). In fact, a DTA is never a sufficient legal basis to levy a Swiss tax in the absence of Swiss domestic legislation. To this effect, *see*—among others—Xavier Oberson/Howard R. Hull, *Switzerland in International Tax Law—Fourth Revised Edition*, para. 2.4. and Peter Brülisauer, "Switzerland" in: IFA (ed.) *The attribution of profits to permanent establishments*, Cahiers de droit fiscal international, Vol. 91b (The Hague: Sdu Uitgevers, 2006) p. 641.

to eliminate double taxation without a switch-over clause and/or other clauses aimed at tackling abusive practices could eventually lead to a double non-taxation.

Differently, both Germany and Italy contemplate the concept of dependent agent permanent establishment under domestic law. While in Germany the domestic concept is sometimes narrower, but usually wider than the corresponding concept under the DTAs,[1740] in Italy the domestic concept is definitely much broader than that agreed in the DTAs as long as Italy has implemented the amendments discussed in the context of Action 7 of the BEPS Project in its domestic legislation.

In Italy, a broad interpretation of the permanent establishment concept has been settled over time, most notably in intra-group situations. In fact, in such cases, the presence of a permanent establishment hidden in the Italian subsidiary(-ies) of foreign parent companies is frequently challenged by reason of the activities carried out by the directors/employees of the Italian subsidiary(-ies) and their lack for independence from the parent companies.[1741] In Germany, instead, the interpretation of the dependent agent provision seems narrower, whereas the independence of the agent appears to be based on the assessment as to whether the agent carries out his/her own economic activity running the related entrepreneurial risks.

Interestingly, both German and Italian tax administrations have also issued some specific guidance regarding the insurance business. What stands out from such guidance is that the German tax administration opened up for a definition of a fixed place of business coordinated with the definition of a branch pursuant to the German Insurance Supervisory Act. Nonetheless, under the current framework, this coordination seems to be lacking a legal basis. This is also the key takeaway from the guidance of the Italian tax administration. This attempt to coordinate the tax and regulatory definitions will be however resumed in Chapter 6 below.

On the other hand, Australia, Belgium and Chile are used to introducing specific provisions dealing with the insurance business directly in Art. 5 and/or Art. 7 of their DTAs. In particular, Belgium is used to negotiating a provision aimed at denying the application of the independent agent provision to insurance agents in Art. 5 of its DTAs, sometimes also in combination with additional rules dealing with insurance agents. Most probably, this provision derives from the assertion put forward by the Belgium tax authorities that insurance distributors act outside the ordinary course of their business, so that the independent agent provision does not become applicable.[1742] Nevertheless, this exclusion is not supported with a proper legal analysis as to why

1740. *See* Georg Kofler/Christian Schmidt/Madeleine Simonek, *Archiv für Schweizerisches Abgaberecht*, (2016/2017) p. 451 and Franz Wassermeyer/Christian Kaeser in: Franz Wassermeyer (ed.) *Doppelbesteuerung: Kommentar zu allen deutschen Doppelbesteuerungsabkommen*, p. 119.

1741. *See*—among others—Piergiorgio Valente/Luigi Vinciguerra, *Stabile organizzazione occulta—Profili applicativi nelle verifiche* (Milano: IPSOA, 2013) pp. 10 et seq., Omar Salvini, "La nuova definizione di stabile organizzazione nel BEPS," *Rassegna Tributaria* (2016) pp. 67 et seq., Diego Avolio, "Esterovestizione e stabile organizzazione sotto la lente della Guardia di Finanza," *Il Fisco* (2018) pp. 1607 et seq. and Marco Bargagli, "Elementi sintomatici della stabile organizzazione occulta," *Fiscalità & Commercio Internazionale* (2019) pp. 28 et seq.

1742. This assertion also seems to be at the roots of the special clause for insurance agents. For further comments, *see also* s. 3.3.2.5.1 above.

insurance distributors are to be regarded as acting outside the course of their business without having recourse to an assessment of the applicable factual circumstances. This indeed seems an unjustified stretch of the permanent establishment rule aimed at taxing profits of foreign insurance companies. It is also quite odd that Belgium takes this arbitrary view intended to pinpoint the presence of a permanent establishment considering that—under Belgian domestic tax law—profits of foreign insurance companies (except for reinsurance) are taxable therein even in the absence of a permanent establishment. Therefore, Belgium could maintain its taxing rights on such profits through more legally justifiable alternatives, like those adopted by Australia and Chile.

In fact, like Belgium, Australia and Chile also have domestic source rules stipulating that profits of foreign insurance companies are taxable even in the absence of a permanent establishment. In order to preserve such taxing rights in DTA situations, Australia has made a reservation in para. 85 of the OECD Model Commentary on Art. 7 and all its DTAs contain a provision aimed at preserving the operation of the domestic legislation relating to profits of foreign insurance and reinsurance companies. Pursuant to such domestic rules, in the case where non-resident insurance and reinsurance companies derive premiums that are deemed to have an Australian source, an effective tax of 3% is withheld on the gross premiums, unless—in the case of insurance—the actual net profit or loss of the foreign company can be established. The provision contained in Art. 7 of Australian DTAs is designed in such a way that the domestic legislation applies in full, even in a DTA situation. Interestingly, such domestic provisions also envisage arrangements to encourage voluntary compliance that will be touched upon in Chapter 6 below.

Chile has a similar withholding tax mechanism rooted in its domestic legislation, which provides that insurance and reinsurance premiums paid to cover risks in Chile are subject to a 22% and 2% withholding tax rate, respectively. As opposed to Australian DTAs, in general, Chilean DTAs either prevent the application of such a withholding tax or provide for reduced rates, at least with respect to insurance premiums. In such a latter case, however, under Chilean DTAs, the withholding tax eventually levied in Chile is generally higher than that set forth under the Australian domestic tax legislation.

The Australian and Chilean examples[1743] clearly indicate that countries wishing to extend a withholding tax mechanism in respect of insurance premiums existing at domestic level in a DTA situation should contemplate the introduction of a specific provision in their DTAs going beyond the permanent establishment rule.[1744] However, once again, countries wishing to do so should carefully consider a coordination between the provisions contained in their DTAs and their domestic tax law rules.

1743. As already outlined above, this reasoning also applies for Argentina and New Zealand, which adopt similar policies.

1744. This reasoning does not generally work in the opposite situation due to a lack of legal basis at domestic level.

In both countries, there is for instance some uncertainty in respect of the interplay between a tax calculation under the business profits article and the withholding tax mechanism.[1745] In answer to such uncertainty, the author believes that a throwback rule intended to give priority to the application of the general principles set forth under the business profits article should be considered at DTA level.[1746] This would secure that all insurance income attributable to such a permanent establishment in the source country is consistently taxed therein. Clearly, this throwback rule should be carefully drafted to specifically cover income which is "*effectively connected*" with the permanent establishment. This would prevent tax planning strategies aimed at minimizing source taxation depending on the most favorable regime.

It is also interesting to note that Australia and Chile take different stands with respect to the reinsurance business. On the one hand, Australia does not differentiate between insurance and reinsurance in terms of withholding tax rates to the extent that a 3 % effective tax liability applies in both situations, albeit some peculiarities exist in terms of compliance requirements. In contrast, Chile envisages different withholding tax rates for insurance and reinsurance, both at domestic and DTA level. While this difference in treatment could in principle derive from a weaker connection with the source country, this is not economically justified to the extent that reinsurance consists on the insurance of the risks of other insurance companies. What is more, this mismatch could also give rise to tax planning and/or avoidance opportunities. Foreign insurance companies could for example establish fronting arrangements in liaison with local insurance companies *in lieu of* distributing insurance products directly in view of applying the lower withholding tax rate envisaged for reinsurance. As a result, a similar treatment for both insurance and reinsurance is more justifiable and arguably more effective.

The analysis of the behavior in relation to the MLI also offers some interesting insights on DTA policies. *In primis*, the initial goal for the MLI to be a mechanism for amending a significant number of DTAs without bilateral negotiations to implement measures discussed in the context of the BEPS Project does not seem to have been fully accomplished. As a matter of fact, the selection of DTAs to be covered reveals that the MLI will not be far-reaching. In addition, the need to comply with domestic legal procedures in ratifying the MLI seems to be another major challenge that has been underestimated when drafting the MLI.[1747] This is particularly the case of Switzerland and Germany. Indeed, in such countries, the coverage is rather low[1748] and domestic procedures require additional negotiations with contracting partners to implement changes to the existing DTAs. Additional interpretative issues might also arise with

1745. In Australia, this uncertainty is specifically related to the existence of a dependent agent permanent establishment.

1746. This route has been followed in Chilean DTAs concluded with Argentina, Australia, Austria, China, the US and Uruguay.

1747. In this respect, *see also* Johann Hattingh, "The Multilateral Instrument from a Legal Perspective: What May Be the Challenges?," *Bulletin for International Taxation* (2017) pp. 77 et seq. and Heinz Jirousek, "Das MLI—eine Erfolgsgeschichte?," *Steuer und Wirtschaft International* (2018) pp. 525-526.

1748. The coverage rates for Switzerland and Germany are about 15% and 35% of existing DTAs, respectively.

respect to the interaction between the MLI and the DTAs it is purported to amend and/or supplement.[1749]

A mixed and surprising set of results also arise in respect of the provisions regarding the dependent agent permanent establishment under Art. 12 of the MLI. As a matter of fact, such results clearly illustrate a lack of consensus at international level. Overall, only slightly more than half of the signatories have opted in for the changes addressed in Art. 12 of the MLI.[1750] In the sample of countries under analysis, it is only Chile that did so upon signature of the MLI, while Belgium eventually decided to do so later. This is not surprising to the extent that a Chilean administration officer led the work on Action 7 of the BEPS Project, so that it may be argued that changes addressed therein somehow reflected the Chilean view. It was also expected for Switzerland to opt out of the changes to the permanent establishment definition. Changes at DTA level would indeed need to be coordinated with corresponding amendments to the domestic legislation, which does not currently encompass a specific provision dealing with the dependent agent permanent establishment.

What is instead surprising is that fervent champions of the BEPS Project (including Australia, Germany and Italy) opted out.[1751] This does not necessarily mean that such countries are against the amendments to the permanent establishment definition. Among other reasons, according to Hatting,[1752] this behavior could be due to the implementation of unilateral anti-avoidance measures, like those adopted in Australia. In his view, the fact that such anti-avoidance measures only apply to inbound scenarios in turn reveals that tax competitiveness was also a significant consideration in choosing which optional amendments to adopt.

What emerges above all, however, is that, while developing countries are keener on adopting the newly formulated provisions, very many developed countries still need some time to arrive at a final decision in this regard.[1753] Most probably, further analysis is still needed to digest and fully understand the practical application of the above provisions, which may indeed affect the allocation of taxing rights between source and

1749. In this respect, *see*—among others—Michael Lang, "Die Auslegung des multilateralen Instruments," *Steuer und Wirtschaft International* (2017) pp. 11 et seq., Svetlana Wakounig, "Interpretation of Terms Used in the Multilateral Instrument" in: Michael Lang/Pasquale Pistone/Alexander Rust/Josef Schuch/Claus Staringer (eds.) *The OECD Multilateral Instrument for Tax Treaties: Analysis and Effects* (Alphen aan den Rijn: Wolters Kluwer, 2018) pp. 21 et seq., Daniel W. Blum, "The Relationship between the OECD Multilateral Instrument and Covered Tax Agreements: Multilateralism and the Interpretation of the MLI," *Bulletin for International Taxation* (2018) pp. 131 et seq. With respect to synthesized texts, *see also* Alexander Hartley, "Countries disagree on advantages of MLI 'synthesised texts'," *International Tax Review* (2018) and Heinz Jirousek, *Steuer und Wirtschaft International*, (2018) pp. 526-527.

1750. *See* Johann Hattingh, "The Impact of the BEPS Multilateral Instrument on International Tax Policies," *Bulletin for International Taxation* (2018) p. 239.

1751. In a similar vein, *see* Johann Hattingh, *Bulletin for International Taxation*, (2018) p. 239.

1752. *See* Johann Hattingh, *Bulletin for International Taxation*, (2018) pp. 239-240.

1753. Among developed countries, only France, the Netherlands, New Zealand and Uruguay opted in for all the amendments to permanent establishment definition under the MLI. To this effect, *see* Johann Hattingh, *Bulletin for International Taxation*, (2018) p. 240. The final Belgian position on MLI provisions concerning the permanent establishment definition other than Art. 12 of the MLI is not known yet.

residence countries. Such concerns are also accentuated by the uncertainty regarding the outcome of the current discussion about a potential digital permanent establishment.[1754] As a result, it is fair to say that the debate about the permanent establishment definition is not over yet and it is not to be excluded that some changes to the current MLI positions will occur in the future.

A parallel development is also taking place at bilateral level. As a matter of fact, there are countries that have incorporated the newly formulated provisions in their DTAs—before and after the MLI was signed—even though they have opted out of Art. 12 of the MLI. Hence, it appears that countries are more inclined to adopt the measures addressed in the context of Action 7 of the BEPS Project as a negotiation position for new DTAs and/or for the renegotiation of their existing DTAs. This suggests that bilateral negotiations are a better setting to discuss the practical application of the new potentially far-reaching provisions, account taken of the economic environment existing in the relevant contracting parties.

The above takeaway seems to confirm that the impact of the MLI is for now somewhat disappointing. The lack of consensus at international level, coupled with the discretion underlying the MLI provisions other than minimum standards, led to the unsatisfactory result of the MLI being a sort of checklist from which countries can choose DTA provisions to be later negotiated at a bilateral level. True, this can be—at least partially—explained with the very short time frame available for drafting the MLI.[1755] Nevertheless, additional fine-tuning will be needed on the consensus for the multilateralism to play a more prominent role in view of achieving international tax coordination, the next big thing on the table being the digitalization of the economy.[1756]

1754. *See* Johann Hattingh, *Bulletin for International Taxation,* (2018) p. 240. For further comments, *see also* s. 4.2.2.1.1 above.

1755. In the same spirit, *see also* Caroline Silberztein/Benoît Granel/Jean-Baptiste Tristram, "OECD Multilateral Convention to Prevent BEPS: Implementation Guide and Initial Thoughts," *International Transfer Pricing Journal* (2017) p. 330.

1756. *See* s. 4.2.2.1.1 above.

CHAPTER 6

Assessment of the Existing Rules and Reform Proposals

Chapter 6 is devoted to address the research questions represented in Chapter 1 and submit some normative claims in respect of the topics outlined in the previous chapters. More precisely, the research questions addressed in this chapter are the following: (*i*) whether a specific provision for agents in the insurance business should be considered when discussing the scope of Art. 5 of double tax treaties, (*ii*) whether the identification of KERT functions within the framework of a functional and factual analysis performed for the purposes of attributing profits to a permanent establishment under Art. 7 of the OECD Model may potentially affect the currently existing standards for determining the existence of a dependent agent permanent establishment under Art. 5 of the model treaties, and (*iii*) whether the definition of dependent agent permanent establishment enshrined in Art. 5 of the model treaties and the definition of establishment adopted for regulatory purposes should be aligned. Next, based on the answers to the research questions, the final sections of this chapter also take a normative stand by assessing a few alternative approaches to the currently existing measures dealing with insurance agents.

6.1 INTRODUCTION

As delineated in the research outline,[1757] Chapter 6 is devoted to a comprehensive assessment of the existing rules and reform proposals. More precisely, this part of the book is aimed at providing the answers to the research questions put forward at the outset of this book.[1758] Furthermore, based on the answers to the research questions, the final sections of this chapter also evaluate a few alternative approaches to the currently existing measures dealing with the insurance business discussed throughout this book. Nonetheless, before proceeding to such assessments, the author believes

1757. *See* s. 1.5 above.
1758. *See* s. 1.4 above.

that it is useful at the outset to shed some light on the rationale behind the idea of a specific provision for the insurance business.

6.2 A SPECIFIC PROVISION FOR THE INSURANCE BUSINESS

As outlined in Chapter 2,[1759] a major feature of the insurance business is the inversion of the production cycle, according to which the service, i.e., the payment of the claim, takes place after the payment of the premium. For this reason, insurance companies are subject to stringent regulatory constraints, such as solvency capital obligations and obligations to create technical reserves. Equally important, considering their role in the society, insurance companies are subject to regulation requirements aimed at ensuring a fair treatment of policyholders in terms of servicing and pricing.

It follows that insurance is a highly regulated business and much of the organizational structure of insurance groups is eventually driven by what is required by regulators (e.g., how much solvency capital is required and in which jurisdiction, how much risk is retained in a particular jurisdiction) and what allows the most efficient use of the capital within such regulatory constraints (e.g., the incorporation of foreign subsidiaries versus the creation of foreign permanent establishments, the use of reinsurance with internal and/or external parties).[1760] That is to say that the regulatory requirements established under insurance supervisory laws and regulations determine the way insurance companies do business, including the decision as to create a foreign permanent establishment.

For instance, it was submitted that, in the context of the EU single insurance market, insurance companies may opt to operate in other EU Member States relying either on the right of establishment or under the freedom to provide services.[1761] To the contrary, in other countries, like Switzerland, foreign insurance companies cannot operate in the absence of a local branch or subsidiary, save for a few exceptions.[1762]

In light of the above, it may be argued that the implementation of the insurance business models (among others, the business models aimed at marketing, promoting and distributing insurance products in foreign jurisdictions) is a direct result of the applicable regulatory framework.[1763] As a consequence, according to the author, it is fair to say that the insurance business presents specific features that considerably influence the business operations of the insurance companies in such a way as to justify a specific provision concerning insurance in the permanent establishment article.

The idea of elaborating a specific provision concerning the insurance business in Art. 5 of the main model treaties is not new. In fact, the historical overview of the OECD

1759. *See* s. 2.1.1 above.
1760. *See* OECD, "*Comments received on public discussion draft—BEPS Action 7: Prevent the artificial avoidance of PE status*," p. 444.
1761. *See* s. 2.1.2 above.
1762. *See* s. 2.1.4 above.
1763. For further considerations, *see* s. 4.11 above. In a similar vein, *see also* 2010 OECD Report, Part IV, para. 11 and OECD, "*Comments received on public discussion draft—BEPS Action 7: Prevent the artificial avoidance of PE status*," p. 356.

Model[1764] and the UN Model[1765] undoubtedly reflects that insurance was specifically regarded as a business that could deserve a special rule in the permanent establishment article. The introduction of a specific provision for the insurance business was indeed extensively discussed during the development of such two model treaties, albeit the position finally taken was different. True, the author believes that the rules discussed in that context are not appropriate thresholds to achieve a proper allocation of taxing rights in the insurance business.[1766] Nevertheless, such rules admit that the special nature of the insurance business could justify a specific provision (more precisely, a specific threshold) in the permanent establishment article.

The question as to whether a specific provision for the insurance business should be considered came up again in the context of the work undertaken by the OECD on the BEPS Project. On that occasion, most of the written comments and interventions during the public consultation put forward the view that there should be no special rules applicable to insurance, which should be treated like other businesses.[1767] Based on such comments, the OECD concluded that no specific rule tailored for the insurance business was to be added in the OECD Model. Nevertheless, the author believes that this conclusion should be reconsidered to the extent that commentators have been confronted solely with two alternative approaches, namely the introduction of an insurance agent provision along the lines of Art. 5, para. 6, of the UN Model (i.e., Option M) and the reference to more general changes proposed to Art. 5, paras. 5 and 6, of the OECD Model to address BEPS concerns (i.e., Option N).[1768] Hence, according to the author, the outcome of the public consultation should be rather construed as a rejection of the insurance agent provision rather than a rejection of a specific provision for the insurance business.

Additionally, the OECD acknowledged that the insurance industry presents unique challenges to tax authorities when dealing with the attribution of profits to permanent establishments. For this reason, the OECD provided special considerations for the purposes of applying the AOA to permanent establishments of insurance companies.[1769] In doing so, the OECD reiterated that insurance companies may find it useful to operate through permanent establishments in foreign jurisdictions because of regulatory reasons, such as home country regulation and lower solvency capital requirements.[1770] Consequently, the OECD recognized that the specific issues of the insurance business need to be addressed through special guidance. In this specific respect, the special guidance supplements the general principles underlying the AOA, also considering the regulatory conditions that are imposed in the country where the permanent establishment is situated.

1764. *See* s. 3.3.1 above.
1765. *See* s. 3.4.2.3 above.
1766. For further comments, *see* s. 6.2 below.
1767. *See* OECD, "*Revised discussion draft—BEPS Action 7: Preventing the Artificial Avoidance of PE Status*," p. 36.
1768. For further comments, *see also* s. 3.3.2.5.1 above.
1769. For further comments, *see also* s. 2.2.1 above.
1770. To this effect, *see* 2010 OECD Report, Part IV, para. 2.

It is also worth noting that the domestic laws of some countries provide for special rules governing the taxation of non-resident insurance companies. For instance, countries like Australia and Chile have foreseen specific provisions regarding the taxation of foreign insurance companies, irrespective of a threshold requirement.[1771] Such countries then attempt to maintain their broad jurisdiction to tax non-resident insurance companies under domestic laws in Art. 5 and/or Art. 7 of their DTAs, thereby deviating from the corresponding provisions of the most common model treaties.

Furthermore, it should be recalled that the idea of a specific provision for the insurance business does not come in isolation. Indeed, the model treaties and domestic laws contain special rules for other types of business income that are widely accepted. As a matter of fact, the OECD Model and the UN Model distinguish between different types of business profits as well as between business profits and investment income.[1772] For instance, the traditional permanent establishment definition for construction activities set forth under Art. 5, para. 2, of the OECD Model is intended to provide a rule applicable in respect to a specific business. In addition to this, Art. 6 of the OECD Model provides for specific rules regarding income from business involving immovable property. Furthermore, Art. 8 of the OECD Model establishes special rules for income derived from international shipping and air transportation.[1773] By the same token, many countries also distinguish between various categories of business income for domestic tax purposes. Therefore, it may be argued that different rules may be admitted for different types of business.

Along the same line of thinking, even Arnold,[1774] who is a strong supporter of a single threshold applicable to all types of business profits, acknowledges that the OECD Model and the UN Model recognize that different threshold requirements may be used for different types of business. Clearly, as he noted, a different threshold designed for a specific business should be grounded on compelling reasons. Nevertheless, if it is accepted that a specific provision concerning the insurance business in the permanent establishment article is admissible, it should also be conceded that such a specific provision can take the form of a specific threshold requirement. As a result, the author believes that a specific threshold for the insurance business in the permanent establishment article should be admitted in the light of its specific features.

1771. *See* ss. 5.3.1 and 5.3.3 above, respectively.

1772. *See* Brian J. Arnold, "Threshold Requirements for Taxing Business Profits under Tax Treaties" in: Brian J. Arnold/Jacques Sasseville/Eric M. Zolt (eds.) *The Taxation of Business Profits Under Tax Treaties* (Toronto: Canadian Tax Foundation, 2003) p. 64 and Brian J. Arnold, "Threshold Requirements for Taxing Business Profits under Tax Treaties," *Bulletin for International Taxation* (2003) p. 478.

1773. For further comments on the reasons for such special rules, *see* Georg Kofler, "Chapter 7: Article 8 OECD Model: Time for a Change?" in: Guglielmo Maisto (ed.) *Taxation of Shipping and Air Transport in Domestic Law, EU Law and Tax Treaties* (Amsterdam, IBFD, 2017) para. 7.2.

1774. To this effect, *see* Brian J. Arnold in: Brian J. Arnold/Jacques Sasseville/Eric M. Zolt (eds.) *The Taxation of Business Profits Under Tax Treaties*, p. 64 and Brian J. Arnold, *Bulletin for International Taxation* (2003) p. 478.

6.3 APPROPRIATENESS OF THE EXISTING MEASURES DEALING WITH INSURANCE AGENTS

As already outlined in Chapter 1,[1775] one of the aims of this research is to provide a response to the question as to whether a specific provision for agents in the insurance business should be considered when discussing the scope of Art. 5 of a DTA. For the purposes of the present analysis, this question is tackled in the first place to the extent that the answer to such a question provides valuable insights with a view to addressing the other two research questions, along with the normative claims.

The reasoning elaborated in the previous section suggests that a specific provision concerning insurance ought to be considered when discussing the scope of the permanent establishment article. More precisely, it has been submitted that a specific threshold requirement in respect of the insurance business in the permanent establishment article should be admitted in the light of its specific features.[1776]

Nevertheless, the evidence gathered throughout this book suggests that neither the special clause regarding insurance agents enshrined in para. 114 of the OECD Model Commentary on Art. 5 nor the insurance agent provision contained in Art. 5, para. 6, of the UN Model represent appropriate thresholds for taxing foreign insurance companies in source countries. Indeed, such measures are not suitable to achieve a proper allocation of taxing rights in the insurance business.

More to the point, the analysis made in Chapter 3 clearly indicates that such measures are not grounded on a sound juridical reasoning and contain several inherent flaws which undermine their application, interpretation and effectiveness, not counting that such thresholds will be typically associated with little or no additional income to be taxed in the source countries.[1777] Furthermore, as discussed in Chapter 4, another major problem associated with the current measures is related to the fact that the deployment of representatives is just one of the options that can be pursued with a view to marketing, promoting and distributing insurance products in foreign countries. Hence, a specific threshold designed only for insurance agents does not seem to be consistent with the different ways insurance companies do business and may eventually lead to unintended results.[1778] Moreover, the survey of DTA policies addressed in Chapter 5 revealed that there is no consensus regarding the adoption of such measures in DTAs. Also, the variety of treatment identified in such a survey can be a source of uncertainty for both insurance companies and tax administrations.[1779] And more than that, such measures are likely to have limited practical application given the local licensing and regulatory requirements that influence the business operation of insurance companies.[1780]

In the light of the foregoing, it may be concluded that the most common model treaties (along with their related commentaries) currently fail to provide for an

1775. *See* s. 1.4 above.
1776. *See* s. 6.2 above.
1777. *See* s. 3.6 above.
1778. *See* s. 4.11 above.
1779. *See* s. 5.4 above.
1780. *See* s. 6.2 above.

appropriate threshold with a view to taxing insurance companies engaged in the marketing, promotion and distribution of insurance products in countries other than that of establishment.

Yet, the author strongly believes that the right of source countries to tax such insurance companies should at any rate be made conditional on the satisfaction of a threshold. As noted by Arnold,[1781] some sort of threshold requirement for taxing business profits is indeed necessary for the purposes of addressing juridical double taxation. More specifically, in the context of the insurance business, while a threshold provides legal certainty for both insurance companies and tax authorities, this is not always the case for systems based on the absence of a threshold to the extent that the application of multiple source rules might lead to uncertainties. In turn, such uncertainties may have a negative effect on cross-border trade and investments. In addition, despite their alleged simplicity, systems based on a lack of a threshold can generate critical normative issues. For instance, as further illustrated below,[1782] a withholding tax on gross insurance premiums would bring about severe issues from the perspective of equity, efficiency and practicability.

Accordingly, another threshold for taxing insurance companies engaged in the marketing, promotion and distribution of insurance products in countries other than that of establishment should be specifically devised. Clearly, the threshold should comply with the normative requirements to be carefully considered when drafting rules aimed at taxing business income of non-residents in the source country. On the top of this, unlike the current measures, such a threshold should be designed to apply not only with respect to insurance agents but also more generally to all the business models that insurance companies could put into place.[1783]

Considering that the introduction of a new specific threshold requirement for insurance companies is not only admissible, but also desirable, the following sections will address the remaining research questions, also with a view to ascertaining whether a more appropriate threshold requirement may be elaborated moving from the identification of KERT functions and/or the definition of establishment adopted for regulatory purposes.[1784]

1781. In general, *see* Brian J. Arnold in: Brian J. Arnold/Jacques Sasseville/Eric M. Zolt (eds.) *The Taxation of Business Profits Under Tax Treaties*, pp. 77-78, Brian J. Arnold, *Bulletin for International Taxation*, (2003) p. 482 and Brian J. Arnold, *Bulletin for International Taxation*, (2008) p. 219. In a similar vein, *see also* Ekkehart Reimer in: Ekkehart Reimer/Stephan Schmid/Marianne Orell (eds.) *Permanent Establishments: A Domestic Taxation, Bilateral Tax Treaty and OECD Perspective*, Part 1[B] pp. 12-13 and Vishesh Dhuldhoya, *Bulletin for International Taxation*, (2018) para. 3.3.1.

1782. For further comments on the implications deriving from the absence of a threshold, *see also* s. 6.6.2.2 below. For further comments on normative issues specifically related to the withholding tax option, *see* s. 6.6.2.3 below.

1783. *See* s. 4.11 above.

1784. Such approaches have been briefly touched upon during the discussion regarding the amendments to be introduced in the context of Action 7 of the BEPS Project. However, no specific analysis was made in that respect. *See* OECD, "*Comments received on public discussion draft—BEPS Action 7: Prevent the artificial avoidance of PE status,*" p. 458, OECD, "*Revised discussion draft—BEPS Action 7: Preventing the Artificial Avoidance of PE Status,*" pp. 36-37 and OECD, "*Comments received on revised discussion draft—BEPS Action 7: Prevent the artificial avoidance of PE status,*" p. 135.

6.4 RELATIONSHIP BETWEEN THE DEFINITION OF DEPENDENT AGENT PERMANENT ESTABLISHMENT AND THE ATTRIBUTION OF PROFITS THERETO

As already outlined in Chapter 1,[1785] another aim of the present research is to address the question as to whether the identification of KERT functions within the framework of a functional and factual analysis performed in the context of the AOA for the purposes of attributing profits to a permanent establishment under Art. 7 of the OECD Model may potentially affect the currently existing standards for determining the existence of a dependent agent permanent establishment under Art. 5 of the model treaties.

In this respect, it should *in primis* be noted that the concept of KERT function does not currently match to the definition of dependent agent permanent establishment. Indeed, on the one hand, in the context of the insurance business, a KERT function "*is one which requires active decision-making with regard to the assumption and/or management (subsequent to the transfer) of the individual risks and portfolios of risks that have been identified as the most important under the functional and factual analysis.*"[1786] On the other hand, the types of activities that can give rise to a dependent agent permanent establishment are much broader. In addition to this, once a dependent agent permanent establishment is deemed to arise by virtue of certain activities, all the others are to be included in such a permanent establishment.[1787] In the context of the insurance business, the evidence gathered throughout this book indeed suggests that the nature of the functions that can be carried on through a dependent agent permanent establishment on behalf of a foreign insurance company may go far beyond KERT functions ranging from sales and marketing functions to support functions.[1788]

It clearly follows that a dependent agent permanent establishment may arise in the source country, irrespective of whether a KERT function is carried on therein. To put it differently, this means that the performance of KERT functions does not currently determine the existence of a dependent agent permanent establishment, the only consequence being the fact that—in the absence of KERT functions—little profit can be ultimately allocated to such a permanent establishment. In the future, it is reasonable to assume that such situations will eventually increase following the amendments introduced in the context of the BEPS Project. In fact, the evidence found throughout this research clearly shows that the amendments introduced in the latest version of the main model treaties are likely to increase the number of dependent agent permanent establishments, even though the amount of profits attributable to such permanent establishments are likely to be low or zero to the extent that no KERT functions would be carried on in the source country.[1789]

1785. *See* s. 1.4 above.
1786. *See* 2010 OECD Report, Part IV, para. 68. For further comments, *see also* s. 2.2.3 above.
1787. *See* s. 3.3.2.3.2 above.
1788. For further comments on such activities, *see* the insurance business models addressed in Chapter 4.
1789. *See* ss. 3.6 and 4.11.

This apparent discrepancy stems from the very essence of the AOA, which essentially is "*to apply the arm's length principle of article 9 of the OECD Model (...) to the attribution of profits to a PE using the arm's length principle under article 7(2).*"[1790] More to the point, while the AOA deals with the attribution of profits, it does not address the question as to whether a permanent establishment exists, nor is it intended to affect the standards for determining the existence of a permanent establishment. For such latter purposes, reference is instead made to Art. 5 of the OECD Model.[1791]

This assertion has been reiterated when the OECD provided for some specific guidance related to dependent agent permanent establishments, both in the general part of the 2010 OECD Report and in Part IV devoted to the insurance business. In this respect, the OECD indeed specified that the major goal of the AOA is not to examine the issue of whether a dependent agent permanent establishment exists or not, but rather to deal with the consequences of finding that a dependent agent permanent establishment exists in terms of profit attribution.[1792,1793] And more than that, this objective does not seem to have been substantially modified following the amendments introduced in the context of Action 7 of the BEPS Project.[1794]

More broadly, the above assertion is also in line with the relationship between Art. 5 of the OECD Model, which encompasses the permanent establishment definition, and Art. 7 of the OECD Model, which instead incorporates the AOA. Indeed, the assessment as to whether a permanent establishment exists under Art. 5 of the OECD Model precedes the attribution of profits thereto under Art. 7 of the OECD Model. Accordingly, it is only if the requirements set forth under Art. 5 of the OECD Model are fulfilled that the second issue regarding the quantitative allocation of profits thereto comes into consideration under Art. 7 of the OECD Model.[1795]

This direct relationship—according to which Art. 7 of the OECD Model is to be applied following Art. 5 of the OECD Model—is rooted in the historical evolution of such provisions. More specifically, although the topic of the profit attribution to

1790. *See* 2010 OECD Report, Part I, para. 53.

1791. *See* 2010 OECD Report, Part I, para. 6.

1792. *See* 2010 OECD Report, Part I, para. 227 and 2010 OECD Report, Part IV, para. 113. For further comments, *see also* Raffaele Petruzzi/Raphael Holzinger, *World Tax Journal*, (2017) pp. 275 et seq.

1793. In addition to this, it should be noted that the AOA also mitigates cliff effects generated by the application of Art. 5, para. 5, of the OECD Model. *See* 2010 OECD Report, Part I, para. 227. For further comments, *see also* Raffaele Petruzzi/Raphael Holzinger, *World Tax Journal*, (2017) p. 275.

1794. *See* OECD, "*Additional Guidance on the Attribution of Profits to Permanent Establishments, BEPS Action 7*," para. 30.

1795. In this respect, *see* para. 1 of the OECD Model Commentary on Art. 5 and para. 2 of the OECD Model Commentary on Art. 7. For further comments regarding this relationship, *see also* Ekkehart Reimer in: Ekkehart Reimer/Alexander Rust (eds.) *Klaus Vogel on Double Taxation Convention—4th edition*, pp. 334 and 505, Ekkehart Reimer in: Ekkehart Reimer/Stephan Schmid/Marianne Orell (eds.) *Permanent Establishments: A Domestic Taxation, Bilateral Tax Treaty and OECD Perspective*, Part 1[B] p. 13 and Giuseppe Corasaniti/Paolo De' Capitani di Vimercate/Victor Uckmar/Caterina Corrado Oliva, *Diritto tributario internazionale—Manuale—Seconda Edizione*, p. 71. With specific respect to dependent agent permanent establishments, *see* 2010 OECD Report, Part I, para. 228, OECD, "*Additional Guidance on the Attribution of Profits to Permanent Establishments, BEPS Action 7*," para. 31 and Raffaele Petruzzi/Raphael Holzinger, *World Tax Journal*, (2017) p. 294.

permanent establishments was already dealt with in the period between the World Wars,[1796] the separation of the permanent establishment definition from the provision concerning business profits was originally considered during the work of the OEEC in the early sixties[1797] and subsequently embedded in the OECD standards. When doing so, in the 1963 OECD Draft Commentary, the OECD specifically clarified that Art. 7 of the OECD Model *"is in many respects a continuation of, and a corollary to, Article 5 (...)"* of the OECD Model,[1798] thereby acknowledging the direct relationship existing between such two provisions. This language remained the same until the rephrasing adopted in the 2010 OECD Model Commentary on Art. 7, which however has not fundamentally changed such a relationship.

Similarly, the direct relationship does not seem to be influenced in a scenario where Arts. 7 and 9 of the OECD Model overlap. When both Arts. 7 and 9 of the OECD Model are applicable—e.g., in the case that the dependent agent and the foreign company are associated enterprises—the question arises as to which of such provisions should apply first. In this respect, although the OECD explained that the order in which Arts. 7 and 9 of the OECD Model are applied does not impact the amount of profits to be taxed in the source country, provided that the countries take a consistent approach,[1799] the literature does not seem to fully agree with this explanation.[1800] Therefore, different opinions have come up as to the order of application.[1801] Nonetheless, this open discussion regarding the order in which Arts. 7 and 9 of the OECD

1796. In that period, the two provisions were integrated in a single article. For further comments on the historical background, *see* Raffaele Russo, "Report on the historical development of article 7 of the OECD model" in: IFA (ed.) *The attribution of profits to permanent establishments*, Cahiers de droit fiscal international, Vol. 91b (The Hague: Sdu Uitgevers, 2006) pp. 89 et seq., Irene J.J. Burgers, "*OECD—Commentary on Article 7 of the OECD Model*," last reviewed: March 1, 2019, available online at www.ibfd.org, ch. 3, Roberto Bernales in: Carlos Gutiérrez /Andreas Perdelwitz (eds.) *Taxation of Business Profits in the 21st Century—Selected Issues under Tax Treaties*, para. 6.2.1, Louis Nouel, "The New Article 7 of the OECD Model Tax Convention: The End of the Road?," *Bulletin for International Taxation* (2011) pp. 5-6 and Raffaele Petruzzi/Raphael Holzinger, *World Tax Journal*, (2017) pp. 267 et seq.

1797. *See* OEEC Fiscal Committee, "*Draft Report Of The Fiscal Committee To The Council*," Document FC(60)1, Paris (March 14, 1960).

1798. To this effect, *see* para. 1 of the 1963 OECD Draft Commentary on Art. 7.

1799. *See* OECD, "*Additional Guidance on the Attribution of Profits to Permanent Establishments, BEPS Action 7*," para. 35. For further comments, *see also* Sony Kassam, "Order of Applying Two Tax Convention Articles is Trivial: OECD," *BNA Tax Management Transfer Pricing Report* (2018).

1800. It has been submitted that the application of Arts. 7 and 9 of the OECD Model might lead to some different outcomes. To this effect, *see*—among others—Alex M. Parker, "Jenn: OECD Clarifying, Not Rewriting, Allocation Rules on PE," *BNA Tax Management Transfer Pricing Report* (2016), Raffaele Petruzzi/Raphael Holzinger, *World Tax Journal*, (2017) pp. 281-282, Sony Kassam, *BNA Tax Management Transfer Pricing Report* (2018) and Lisa Spinosa/Vikram Chand, "A Long-Term Solution for Taxing Digitalized Business Models: Should the Permanent Establishment Definition Be Modified to Resolve the Issue or Should the Focus Be on a Shared Taxing Rights Mechanism?," *Intertax* (2018) pp. 483-485.

1801. In this respect, Moshammer, Tumpel, Andrus, Collier and Sprague suggest that Art. 9 of the OECD Model should take priority over Art. 7 of the OECD Model. To this effect, *see* Harald Moshammer/Michael Tumpel in: Michael Lang/Pasquale Pistone/Josef Schuch/Claus Staringer/Alfred Storck (eds.) *Dependent Agents as Permanent Establishments*, pp. 237 et seq., Joseph L. Andrus/Richard Collier, "OECD Discussion Draft: additional guidance on the attribution of profits to permanent establishments," *British Tax Review* (2017) pp. 514-515

Model are applied does not seem to affect the direct relationship currently existing between Arts. 5 and 7 of the OECD Model, which fundamentally remains the same, irrespective of whether Art. 7 of the OECD Model is to be applied before, simultaneously or after Art. 9 of the OECD Model.

Any change to this direct relationship between Arts. 5 and 7 of the OECD Model would entail a change of paradigm that does not seem in line with the historical, systematic and teleological interpretation of such provisions. Most importantly, the allegation of a reverse relationship—according to which the application of Art. 7 of the OECD Model would potentially affect the application of Art. 5 of the OECD Model—would be contrary to the fundamental function that Art. 5 of the OECD Model fulfils as a definition article for the purposes of other provisions of the OECD Model, including Art. 7 of the OECD Model, which connects the identification of a permanent establishment to substantive legal consequences.[1802]

Against this background, it can be concluded that the identification of KERT functions within the framework of a functional and factual analysis carried out in the context of the AOA—which is the guiding principle contained in Art. 7 of the OECD Model—cannot be held to have a reverse relationship with Art. 5 of the model treaties in such a way as to potentially affect the currently existing standards for determining the existence of a dependent agent permanent establishment.

In the light of the above analysis, the idea of connecting the identification of KERT functions to the taxable presence of foreign insurance companies in the source country cannot be endorsed as the appropriate solution in order to devise a new threshold requirement specifically designed for the insurance business aimed at solving the problems with the currently existing measures identified throughout this research.

6.5 RELATIONSHIP BETWEEN TAX AND REGULATORY CONCEPTS

As submitted in Chapter 1,[1803] another aim of this research is to examine the correlation between the definition of dependent agent permanent establishment for tax purposes enshrined in Art. 5 of the model treaties and the definition of establishment adopted for regulatory purposes—along with their respective areas of overlapping and divergence—in view of addressing the question of whether such concepts should be eventually aligned.

In this respect, the evidence gathered throughout this book suggest that the definition of establishment adopted for regulatory purposes does not currently match to the definition of dependent agent permanent establishment. Still, at a closer look,

and Gary D. Sprague, *BNA Tax Management Transfer Pricing Report* (2018). On the other hand, Tracana takes the view that the two provisions should be applied simultaneously. To this effect, *see* Dinis Tracana, *Bulletin for International Taxation*, (2017) pp. 225-226 and 231. Stack and Hawes instead complain about a lack of any additional clarity from the OECD on this crucial issue. To this effect, *see* Bob Stack/Jamie Hawes, *BNA Tax Management Transfer Pricing Report* (2018).

1802. For further comments, *see also* Ekkehart Reimer in: Ekkehart Reimer/Alexander Rust (eds.) *Klaus Vogel on Double Taxation Convention—4th edition*, p. 505.

1803. *See* s. 1.4 above.

when one draws parallels between the tax and regulatory definitions, it is fair to say that, in the EU, before the amendments introduced in the aftermath of the BEPS Project, the three conditions for an independent person to fall within the right of establishment[1804] could be correlated with the main elements that gave rise to a dependent agent permanent establishment well enough.

To begin with, the author believes that the first condition regarding the direction and control of the insurance company could be reconciled *a contrario* with the independence test enshrined in the independent agent provision. Indeed, elements like the degree of direction and control exercised by the foreign insurance company on the person in the source country as well as the number of principals represented by such a person therein appeared to be common factors to be carefully considered with a view to determining whether said person could be regarded as dependent or independent from the insurance company. Admittedly, additional considerations regarding the independence of the person in the source country were also referred to in previous OECD guidance, but it is fair to say that the bulk of such assessment appeared to be similar for both tax and regulatory purposes.[1805]

Likewise, notwithstanding the apparent divergences in terms of wording, the second condition regarding the commitment of the insurance company could be reasonably reconciled with the element of the (legal) bindingness contained in the dependent agent provision. Both such notions indeed are to be construed in such a way as to require that the acts and the decisions of the person in the source country vis-à-vis third parties directly create legal obligations between the foreign insurance company and such third parties with no need for a direct intervention coming from the insurance company.[1806]

In a similar vein, the third and last condition regarding the permanent brief to be given to the independent person could be essentially reconciled with the habitual exercise test contained in the dependent agent provision. As a matter of fact, in order to justify a sufficient link with the host country, both such requirements seem to demand that the physical presence of the person therein is more than transitory and its activities are to be exercised more than just temporarily and/or occasionally.

True, despite the above areas of overlapping, some discrepancies between the two definitions already existed before the 2017 changes. Most notably, this was the case of the insurance business carried out through remote means of communication.

1804. *See* s. 2.1.3 above.

1805. Likewise, the absence of the ordinary course of business test in the regulatory definition does not seem to jeopardize the reconciliation between the requirements under analysis. In fact, this is a complementary test that does not change the essence of the independence test, which is rather intended to assess the "*genuinely*" independent status of the person in the source country. For further comments on such a test, *see also* s. 3.3.2.4.5 above.

1806. The commitment stemming from the brief given to the independent person clearly presupposes that such a person is acting "*on behalf and for the account of*" the insurance company. Interestingly, as opposed to the definition for tax purposes, in the regulatory definition, this commitment can also derive from activities other than the conclusion of insurance contracts, like the acceptance and the settlement of claims. Nevertheless, this does not seem to jeopardize the essence of the reconciliation between the concept of commitment and that of bindingness.

Indeed, while the EU Commission clarified that such this form of insurance business is subject to the provisions relating to the freedom to provide services,[1807] the investigation conducted in previous sections[1808] suggests that—though under limited circumstances—a dependent agent permanent establishment could be present in the source country.

In any case, following the 2017 updates of the OECD Model and the UN Model, the shift toward the economic approach underlying Action 7 of the BEPS Project has undoubtedly exacerbated the discrepancies between the two definitions. Most importantly, this shift has been associated with the introduction of the supplementary test regarding the principal role leading to the conclusion of contracts in the dependent agent provision and the supplementary independence test regarding related parties in the independent agent provision. It is abundantly clear that such amendments have widened the scope of the dependent agent permanent establishment definition to the effect that the definition that can be found in the most common model treaties is now much broader than the definition of establishment adopted for regulatory purposes.[1809]

On the other hand, Switzerland—like other non-EU countries—generally requires foreign insurance companies to establish either a local subsidiary organized under domestic laws or a local branch to transact insurance in Switzerland.[1810] With specific respect to the latter option, considering that the term "*branch*" is to be intended as a business establishment,[1811] such a concept might be better reconciled with the definition of a fixed place of business—as set forth under the basic permanent establishment rule—rather than with the definition of a dependent agent permanent establishment. Against this backdrop, it may be concluded that the Swiss insurance regulation does not currently admit foreign insurance companies to operate in Switzerland through a person that can potentially fulfill the substantive requirements to be regarded as a dependent agent permanent establishment under the main model treaties to the effect that the latter concept is generally not applicable to foreign insurance companies wishing to transact insurance in Switzerland.

The mismatches depicted above essentially stem from the fact that—under the existing framework—the tax and regulatory provisions are two legally independent sets of rules with their own purposes and standards to the effect that each of them should be carefully assessed separately. Accordingly, under the current circumstances, even though the requirements to be considered for identifying a dependent agent permanent establishment partially overlap with the corresponding criteria envisaged for regulatory purposes, the determination of whether a foreign insurance company has a dependent agent permanent establishment in the source country is legally independent from the question as to whether the same insurance company can be admitted to transacting insurance therein for regulatory purposes.[1812]

1807. *See* s. 2.1.3 above.
1808. *See* Chapter 4.
1809. For further comments, *see also* ss. 3.6 and 4.11 above.
1810. *See* s. 2.1.4 above.
1811. *See* s. 2.1.4 above.
1812. To this effect, *see also* 2010 OECD Report, Part IV, paras. 64 and 113.

The comparative analysis laid out in Chapter 5 above[1813] revealed that the German Federal Ministry of Finance attempted to draw a parallel between the concept of a branch within the meaning of the local regulatory provisions and the concept of a permanent establishment for tax purposes by means of a Circular Letter dated December 24, 1999.[1814] Nonetheless, although such an attempt is in principle to be welcomed, a proper legal basis seems to be missing to the extent that—at the present time—the definition of a branch for regulatory purposes does not necessarily match to the permanent establishment definition for tax purposes. As already portrayed above,[1815] this criticism seems to have been endorsed by the Italian Revenue Agency when dealing with a tax-ruling request concerning insurance activities carried out under the freedom to provide services in Italy. More specifically, the Italian tax authorities pinpointed that the assessment regarding the existence of a permanent establishment for tax purposes should be carried out on a stand-alone basis, thereby highlighting the legal independence of the two sets of rules. Hence, the fundamental point to be taken away here is that regulatory rules cannot be currently employed to determine whether a dependent agent permanent establishment exists for tax purposes, thereby overcoming the relevant tax provisions. To put it differently, if one wishes to bridge the gap between the two sets of rules, a legal basis needs to be created accordingly.

In any case, as already seen in the context of the analysis carried out in previous sections,[1816] which pointed out that a specific provision—or better a specific threshold—dealing with the insurance business should be admitted, the regulatory requirements set forth under insurance supervisory provisions are incumbent on the way insurance companies do business. It is indeed the local licensing and regulatory framework that ultimately determines whether (and to what extent) insurance activities are admitted in a specific jurisdiction, ahead of any relevant tax considerations.

Accordingly—even under the current circumstances, where the tax and regulatory provisions are two legally independent set of rules—a concrete assessment regarding the existence of a dependent agent permanent establishment for tax purposes should be well entrenched with a preliminary analysis regarding the applicable regulatory framework. In fact, any such assessment cannot be isolated from a proper understanding of the framework in which the relevant insurance company carries out its activities.[1817]

Against this backdrop, the author believes that it is suitable for the tax and regulatory concepts to be ultimately aligned. More specifically, the author believes that—leaving aside the circumstances under which a foreign insurance company has a physical presence in the source country, that would otherwise trigger the basic permanent establishment rule—a taxable presence in the form of a dependent agent permanent establishment should more consistently arise only in the case where the

1813. More precisely, *see* s. 5.3.4 above.
1814. In that case, the concept of a fixed place of business within the meaning of the basic permanent establishment rule.
1815. *See* s. 5.3.5 above.
1816. More specifically, *see* s. 6.1 above.
1817. *See* s. 4.11 above.

foreign insurance company is legally admitted to transacting insurance in the source country through a person that gives rise to a regulatory presence therein.

Insofar as the insurance business is very closely linked to the regulatory framework, this alignment facilitates a more consistent assessment regarding the existence of a dependent agent permanent establishment against the legal and economic environment in which insurance companies operate, most importantly against the activities that can be concretely done in the host country in compliance with regulatory requirements. Any redundant complexity, such as that generated by the currently existing asymmetries, should indeed be kept at an absolute minimum in view of preventing interpretation disputes between taxpayers and tax administrations, which could eventually turn out to be a potential source of double taxation issues.

Considering the findings illustrated above, to achieve a suitable alignment, this necessarily requires the creation of a proper legal basis. More precisely, the author suggests that such an alignment be achieved through a (partial) redefinition of the dependent agent permanent establishment concept enshrined in DTA law with a view to making it correlated to the definition adopted for regulatory purposes. In doing so, any necessary adjustments between the two concepts should be kept at the minimum.

It is true that the concept of permanent establishment has been developed as a legal convention created by international tax law for source taxation.[1818] As a result, throughout the years, such a concept has received little influence from other fields of law. Nevertheless, the author does not envisage any significant legal obstacle that would prevent modifying the boundaries of the permanent establishment concept with elements stemming from the insurance regulatory framework, especially considering that such a concept is also experiencing more dramatic changes inspired by disciplines other than law, most importantly the shift toward an economic approach underlying the BEPS Project. Rather, according to the author, any amendments to the boundaries of the permanent establishment concept intended to make it more consistent with the legal and economic environment in which insurance companies operate is not only suitable, but also desirable.

The above alignment can also prevent peculiar circumstances under which the dependent agent permanent establishment rule is de facto ineffective. This is for instance the case where foreign insurance companies are not admitted to transacting insurance through a person that can potentially fulfill the substantive requirements to be regarded as a dependent agent permanent establishment under the main model treaties, so that such a concept is ultimately not applicable to foreign insurance companies.[1819] If and to the extent that the determination of a dependent agent permanent establishment is properly correlated to the lawful feasibility of doing business as such pursuant to the applicable regulatory provisions, any such inconsistencies are ultimately prevented. In a similar vein, the alignment between tax and regulatory provisions can deal more adequately with circumstances under which local regulatory provisions necessarily prescribe foreign insurance companies to appoint a

1818. To this effect, *see* s. 3.6 above.
1819. As already pointed out throughout this dissertation, this is for instance the case of Switzerland.

legal representative in the source country with a view to fulfilling applicable local compliance requirements (such as legal, tax and accounting requirements) for the purposes of transacting insurance therein.

Additionally, with a view to preventing abusive situations, the alignment between tax and regulatory provisions can be structured in such a way as to apply only to the extent that regulatory provisions are complied with. More to the point, under the applicable regulatory framework, foreign insurance companies can be either admitted or not admitted to transacting insurance through a person in the source country. As a result, if and to the extent that the person in the source country remains within the range of activities he/she is admitted to performing, the tax and regulatory provisions will be applied accordingly. Conversely, in the case that such a person actually goes beyond admitted activities,[1820] leaving aside the associated regulatory sanctions that should be dealt with correspondingly,[1821] the above alignment will be consequently denied. And, on the top of this, it should be also recalled that specific abusive situations, like artificial structures intended to circumvent the existence of a permanent establishment, can be in any case targeted on a separate individual basis through anti-avoidance provisions and/or doctrines.[1822]

To the contrary, the author believes that the admissibility of other practices like the "*self-procurement*" from an unlicensed insurance company should be instead left to regulatory provisions. Indeed, this scheme does not generally involve a foreign insurance company carrying on its business in the source country, but rather a customer seeking insurance protection outside the country where the commitment or risk is situated. Therefore, such a scheme does not seem to give rise to abusive situations (at least, for tax purposes).

It is also interesting to note that the formulation of a specific provision concerning a business subject to regulatory and licensing requirements that overrides the dependent agent provision is not completely new. In fact, the DTA concluded between Germany and Indonesia provides for a specific clause in respect of persons acting as a "*representative of a foreign trading company*" in Indonesia.[1823] While a detailed analysis of this specific case is clearly beyond the scope of this research, it is important here to emphasize that such representatives can give rise to specific permanent establishment concerns in Indonesia,[1824] so that the two countries under analysis agreed to specifically regulate their status in such a way that such representatives do not constitute dependent agent permanent establishments, provided that their activities are confined to the limitations set forth under applicable Indonesian trade laws and regulations. Although this case does not directly concern the insurance business, it

1820. For instance, this might be the case of non-admitted insurance companies.

1821. The prospect of regulatory sanctions could be a factor to consider in ensuring and monitoring compliance for both regulatory and tax purposes. *See* OECD, "*Comments received on public discussion draft—BEPS Action 7: Prevent the artificial avoidance of PE status*," p. 444.

1822. *See also* s. 4.11 above.

1823. *See* Art. 1 of the Protocol to the DTA between Germany and Indonesia concluded on October 30, 1990. For further comments on the German policy, *see also* s. 5.3.4 above.

1824. For further comments, *see* Nazly Siregar/David Dorson, "Taxation of Trade Representative Offices," *Asia-Pacific Tax Bulletin* (2014) pp. 338 et seq.

clearly demonstrates that the alignment between tax and regulatory provisions can be a legally admissible option to deal with a regulated business that would otherwise pose interpretation disputes.

In a similar vein, a new specific provision based on the alignment between tax and regulatory definitions can represent a suitable coordinated solution to better deal with a disputed matter like the allocation of taxing rights in the context of the insurance business, in relation to which no agreement has been found among countries and currently existing measures have proved to be inadequate.[1825] As a matter of fact, research has shown that approximately 30% of DTAs contain a specific provision for insurance activities. And, even among such DTAs, very many deviations have emerged.[1826] All such deviations—associated with the absence of a mutual understanding among countries on such a disputed matter, little guidance and case law available—can evidently result in significant uncertainties and—thus—lead to potential interpretation problems in several circumstances.

And more than that, such a coordinated solution can also refrain countries from introducing unilateral domestic measures aimed at restoring source taxation, albeit the applicable DTA provides otherwise. For instance, as discussed with respect to the taxation of income from services,[1827] such domestic measures might take the form of limitations to the deduction of payments (in the case at hands, payments to foreign insurance companies). Although the concrete application of such domestic provisions in a DTA situation is rather limited,[1828] it is nevertheless expected that a coordinated solution can ultimately discourage countries from designing such measures.

Against the background of the preceding considerations, the following sections will then formulate a normative proposal for a more appropriate threshold requirement specifically designed for the insurance business elaborated moving from the idea of aligning the definition of dependent agent permanent establishment for tax purposes with the definition of establishment adopted for regulatory purposes.

1825. *See* s. 6.2 above.

1826. For further details, *see* Wim Wijnen/Jan De Goede, *Bulletin for International Taxation*, (2014) p. 124.

1827. *See* Brian J. Arnold, "The Taxation of Income from Services," *Papers on Selected Topics in Protecting the Tax Base of Developing Countries*, Draft Paper No. 2—May 2013, available online at www.un.org, p. 50, Jinyan Li, "Protecting the Tax Base in the Digital Economy," *Papers on Selected Topics in Protecting the Tax Base of Developing Countries*, Paper No. 9—June 2014, available online at www.un.org, p. 42 and Andrés Báez Moreno, "The Taxation of Technical Services under the United Nations Model Double Taxation Convention: A Rushed—Yet Appropriate—Proposal for (Developing) Countries?," *World Tax Journal* (2015) para. 3.2.4.2.

1828. This is mainly due to nondiscrimination provisions contained in the main model treaties. *See* Andrés Báez Moreno, *World Tax Journal*, (2015) para. 3.2.4.2. On the top of this, the application of such measures is generally limited to business-to-business transactions.

6.6 ANALYSIS OF REFORM PROPOSALS

6.6.1 Proposal for a New Threshold

6.6.1.1 Introduction

Throughout the initial sections of this chapter, it has been submitted that a specific threshold requirement for the insurance business in the permanent establishment article is admissible and desirable. Nonetheless, the existing measures dealing with insurance agents do not represent appropriate thresholds for taxing insurance companies engaged in the marketing, promotion and distribution of insurance products in countries other than that of establishment. Hence, while addressing the research questions, other alternative approaches have been evaluated with a view to designing a normative proposal. While the idea of connecting the identification of KERT functions to the taxable presence in the source country has been dismissed, it has been found that the alignment between the tax and regulatory concepts is suitable and desirable. Therefore, the following sections are aimed at formulating a policy proposal based on the idea of aligning such two concepts. In such sections, this policy proposal will be referred to as the *"insurance regulatory permanent establishment."*

In doing so, the threshold for taxing insurance companies in the source country would be amended in such a way as to be more consistent with the legal and economic background in which insurance companies concretely operate. However, the threshold would also need to comply with the relevant normative requirements to be carefully considered when drafting rules aimed at taxing business income of non-residents in the source country. As a result, before formulating a normative proposal for a new threshold based on the findings derived from the analysis made in the previous sections, the following sections will focus on the normative considerations.

6.6.1.2 Normative Considerations

6.6.1.2.1 Normative Requirements

At this point of the book, before embarking on a normative assessment of the insurance regulatory permanent establishment, it seems useful to briefly reiterate the fundamental normative requirements to be carefully considered when drafting reform proposals with a view to taxing business income of non-residents in the source country.

First and foremost, the threshold needs to be aligned with general international law principles regarding income tax jurisdiction. Most notably, as already outlined above,[1829] the legal justification for the assignment of tax jurisdiction among countries is generally considered to be the principle of sovereignty. It follows that the requirement of a specific connection between the sovereign spheres of a State and the taxable subject/object is indeed a fundamental element of the international law of income tax jurisdiction.[1830] As a result, the threshold necessarily presupposes a connection between the income and the territorial sphere of State sovereignty.

1829. *See* s. 1.3 above.

1830. *See* Stjepan Gadžo, *Nexus Requirements for Taxation of Non-Residents' Business Income: A*

In addition to this basic requirement, a threshold should also comply with traditional standards of equity,[1831] efficiency and practicability, without granting supremacy to one of such standards alone.[1832] It is clearly beyond the scope of this research to delve into the general normative value of such standards in the context of international tax law. Nevertheless, it is important to shed at least some light on what such normative standards entail in relation to the issue of identifying a specific threshold for taxing business income of non-residents in the source country.

As examined by Gadžo,[1833] from a tax equity perspective, a new proposal should be designed considering that: (*i*) a taxing claim is legitimate in the case that a country provides public benefits to a non-resident taxpayer in respect of the relevant economic activity (i.e., the inter-taxpayer or inter-individual equity perspective)[1834] and (*ii*) the taxation of a non-resident taxpayer is equitable when factors related to the production of income—on the side of supply and/or on the side of demand[1835]—are located in the

Normative Evaluation in the Context of the Global Economy, para. 2.2.6. In a similar vein, *see*—among others—*See* Klaus Vogel, *Klaus Vogel on Double Taxation Convention*, p. 11, Wolfgang Schön, "International Tax Coordination for a Second-Best World (Part I)," *World Tax Journal* (2009) p. 93 and Michael Lang, *Introduction to the Law of Double Taxation Conventions—2nd edition*, p. 27.

1831. According to Debelva, equity—along with equality and justice—falls within the umbrella term of fairness. To this effect, *see* Filip Debelva, "Fairness and International Taxation: Star-Crossed Lovers?," *World Tax Journal* (2018) para. 2.

1832. For further comments regarding such normative standards in the context of the allocation of taxing rights, *see* Wolfgang Schön, *World Tax Journal*, (2009) p. 93. For further comments regarding their use in a tax system, *see* Matthijs Alink/Victor van Kommer, *Handbook on Tax Administration* (Amsterdam: IBFD, 2016) para. 1.7.1, David H. Rosenbloom, "Where's the Pony? Reflections on the Making of International Tax Policy," *Bulletin for International Taxation* (2009) p. 538, Diane M. Ring, "International Tax Relations: Theory and Implications," *Tax Law Review* (2007) pp. 87-90 and Robert L. Palmer, "Toward Unilateral Coherence in Determining Jurisdiction to Tax Income," *Harvard International Law Journal* (1989) pp. 9 et seq.

1833. *See* Stjepan Gadžo, *Nexus Requirements for Taxation of Non-Residents' Business Income: A Normative Evaluation in the Context of the Global Economy*, paras. 5.1.4 and 5.4.

1834. According to Gadžo and de Wilde, both the ability to pay principle and the benefit principle are measurements of inter-individual equity. Nevertheless, while playing a secondary role vis-à-vis the ability to pay principle in a purely domestic setting, the benefit principle has normative value in a cross-border context. To this effect, *see* Stjepan Gadžo, *Nexus Requirements for Taxation of Non-Residents' Business Income: A Normative Evaluation in the Context of the Global Economy*, para. 5.1.2, Maarten F. de Wilde, *Sharing the Pie: Taxing Multinationals in a Global Market* (Amsterdam: IBFD, 2016) para. 2.2.2.2. In a similar vein, *see* Ian Roxan, "Limits to Globalisation: Some Implications for Taxation, Tax Policy, and the Developing World," *LSE Law—Society and Economy Working Papers* (2012) pp. 16-17. On this front, Debelva acknowledges that, although such principles were primarily designed for being applied in a domestic context, their influence on international tax rules cannot be denied. To this effect, *see* Filip Debelva, *World Tax Journal*, (2018) para. 3.1.2. Instead, for a fundamental critique of the usefulness of the benefit principle in the context of international taxation, *see* Wolfgang Schön, *World Tax Journal*, (2009) pp. 75 et seq.

1835. In the past, the preference has been given to the supply approach. To this effect, *see*—among others—Carsten Wendt, *A Common Tax Base for Multinational Enterprises in the European Union* (Wiesbaden: Gabler, 2009) p. 39 and Eva Escribano López, *Intertax*, (2015) p. 8. However, the digitalization of the economy has reopened the debate in favor of a combined supply-and-demand approach. For further comments regarding the proposals under discussion with respect to the digitalization of the economy, *see* s. 4.2.2.1.1 above.

territory of the country (i.e., the inter-nation equity perspective, which is grounded on the doctrine of economic allegiance).[1836]

On the other hand, efficiency requires that the tax system should be as neutral as possible. As such, from a tax efficiency perspective, the issue can be outlined in terms of avoiding frictions—or "*quantum leaps*"[1837]—in recognizing the taxing claim of a country over the business income of a non-resident. To put it in other terms, a threshold signaling a taxable presence in a country should be commensurate with the potential extent of the economic activities carried out therein. As a result, there must be a clear, sizeable difference in the economic substance of the activities that are not taxable in a foreign country—because the threshold has not been met—and other activities, which entail having foreign taxable presence. In such a way, the threshold causes minimal distortions to the decisions of taxpayers.[1838]

Finally, in terms of practicability (also referred to as administrability and/or simplicity), a proposal needs to be sufficiently clear and objective to ensure a consistent interpretation and application by both tax administrations and taxpayers. A clear and objective threshold is also crucial for another aspect of practicability, namely the enforceability, which is particularly important in the context of international taxation. As a matter of fact, while on the one hand taxpayers involved in cross-border activities inevitably face higher tax compliance burden, on the other hand tax authorities are also confronted with parallel challenges in the collection of tax.[1839] Therefore, the threshold should carefully consider the issue of enforceability in that direction.

6.6.1.2.2 Normative Assessment

To start with, it may be argued that a proposal based on the idea of aligning the definition of dependent agent permanent establishment for tax purposes with the definition of establishment adopted for regulatory purposes complies with general international law principles regarding income tax jurisdiction. Indeed, in such a case, there exists a clear and sufficient connection between the territory of the source country and the business income of the insurance company that is generated through the activities of the person that triggers the existence of an establishment for regulatory purposes therein.

Taking this into account, from the inter-taxpayer equity perspective, it should be noted that the existence of an insurance regulatory permanent establishment in the territory of the source country presupposes that the foreign insurance company has a physical presence in that country through a person which is engaged for the purposes of doing business therein. This clearly implies that the foreign insurance company

1836. According to Peters, there is an increasing "blurring" of such equity norms. To this effect, *see* Cees Peters, *On the Legitimacy of International Tax Law* (Amsterdam: IBFD, 2014) para. 4.3.3.
1837. *See* Wolfgang Schön, *World Tax Journal*, (2009) p. 102.
1838. *See* Stjepan Gadžo, *Nexus Requirements for Taxation of Non-Residents' Business Income: A Normative Evaluation in the Context of the Global Economy*, paras. 5.2.2 and 5.4.
1839. *See* Stjepan Gadžo, *Nexus Requirements for Taxation of Non-Residents' Business Income: A Normative Evaluation in the Context of the Global Economy*, paras. 5.3.1 and 5.4.

receives public benefits from the source country, which can relate—*inter alia*—to physical infrastructure (e.g., roads and telecommunications), economic infrastructure (e.g., banking systems), legal infrastructure (e.g., the court systems and regulatory bodies), public safety, national security and skilled workforce.[1840] As a consequence, from the inter-taxpayer equity perspective, the taxing claim of the source country is legitimate to the extent that the foreign insurance company receives public benefits from the source country and is therefore demanded to contribute to the public funds of this country through income taxes.

Second, the insurance regulatory permanent establishment can be also justified from the inter-nation equity perspective. As a matter of fact, the physical presence of a person that carries on insurance business activities in the source country may be clearly regarded as a factor associated with the production of business income therein that justifies the levying of corporate income tax based on the supply approach.

The above conclusions lead to a reverse question with respect to the international allocation of the rights to tax business income, i.e., the question as to whether countries where customers are located could claim taxing rights to the extent that they provide a market to foreign insurance companies, irrespective of any physical presence therein. Indeed, the use of remote means of communication (such as the Internet, the telephone, and so forth)[1841] makes it now possible for insurance companies to derive income from customers located in countries other than that of establishment without the need to establish even a minimal physical presence therein. This is of paramount importance considering that, at least in certain countries (for instance, in the EU),[1842] the underlying business models do not give rise to an establishment for regulatory purposes, so that the insurance regulatory permanent establishment would not be applicable. Also, taken to its extremes, this reasoning could be applied in "*self-procurement*" schemes, where admitted under regulatory laws and regulations.

At a first sight, one might argue that the above reverse question deserves a positive answer. More to the point, from the inter-taxpayer equity perspective, the existence of a market inevitably requires some physical, economic and legal infrastructure.[1843] Hence, along this line of reasoning, foreign insurance companies should

1840. For further comments on such public benefits, *see also* Stjepan Gadžo, *Nexus Requirements for Taxation of Non-Residents' Business Income: A Normative Evaluation in the Context of the Global Economy*, para. 7.1.1.1, Fred B. Brown, "An Equity-Based, Multilateral Approach for Sourcing Income Among Nations," *Florida Tax Review* (2011) p. 608 and Stephen E. Shay/J. Clifton Fleming, Jr./Robert J. Peroni, "What's Source Got to Do with It?: Source Rules and US International Taxation," *Tax Law Review* (2002) p. 90.

1841. *See* ss. 4.2-4.5 above.

1842. *See* s. 2.1.3 above.

1843. To this effect, *see*—among others—Stjepan Gadžo, *Nexus Requirements for Taxation of Non-Residents' Business Income: A Normative Evaluation in the Context of the Global Economy*, para. 7.1.1.1, Fred B. Brown, *Florida Tax Review*, (2011) pp. 609-610, Wolfgang Schön, "Ten Questions about Why and How to Tax the Digitalized Economy," *Bulletin for International Taxation* (2018) p. 285, Michael P. Devereux/John Vella, "Implications of digitalization for international corporate tax reform," *Oxford University Centre for Business Taxation—Working paper series* (2017) p. 18, Peter Hongler/Pasquale Pistone, *IBFD White Paper*, (2015) p. 22, Dale Pinto, "Options to Address the Direct Tax Challenges Raised by the Digital Economy—A Critical Analysis," *Canadian Tax Journal* (2017) pp. 320-321, Dale Pinto, *E-Commerce and Source-Based Income Taxation*, para. 2.2.1 and Dale Pinto, *Bulletin for*

contribute to the financing of such public benefits. Likewise, in principle, the taxing claim could also be justifiable from the inter-nation equity perspective. First, this is related to the fact that the supply of goods and services (including insurance) necessarily requires the customer demand for it. In the second place, it should also be noted that customers can now have a more active role on the supply side and—thus—contribute to the value of goods and services in different ways.[1844]

Nevertheless, at a closer look, there are equally valid arguments against a shift of taxing rights toward countries where customers are located.[1845] For a start, the benefit argument associated with the existence of a market can be extended to all sales of goods and services,[1846] regardless of the business model implemented. Following this line of reasoning, any sort of threshold (particularly, quantitative thresholds) would then be in contrast with the equity standard, thereby leaning toward a taxation of income in countries where customers are located without any threshold requirements (arguably, through the introduction of withholding taxes). However, leaving aside the fact that some of the current proposals aimed at addressing the digitalization of the economy envisage the introduction of quantitative thresholds,[1847] it should also be noted that both the absence of any thresholds[1848] and the introduction of withholding taxes[1849] would cause even more fundamental issues.

Furthermore, while it is true that business models that use remote means of communication clearly require Internet and telecommunication networks, data centers and so forth, it is also fair to say that the (public and/or private) provision of such infrastructure is often subject to a fee payment and/or similar considerations without giving rise to a justification to tax. Also, it may be even argued that the use of such infrastructure requires a lower level of public input vis-à-vis traditional infrastructure.[1850]

International Taxation, (2006) p. 268.

1844. To this effect, *see* Stjepan Gadžo, *Nexus Requirements for Taxation of Non-Residents' Business Income: A Normative Evaluation in the Context of the Global Economy*, para. 7.1.1.1, Maarten F. de Wilde, *Sharing the Pie: Taxing Multinationals in a Global Market*, para. 6.2.2.3, Wolfgang Schön, *World Tax Journal*, (2009) p. 92 and Wolfgang Schön, *Bulletin for International Taxation*, (2018) p. 285.

1845. According to Schön, given that the traditional notion of "*source country*" does not necessarily coincide with that of "*market country*," the proposed extension of the permanent establishment boundaries in market countries is flawed to the extent that the concept of permanent establishment is aimed at empowering source countries vis-à-vis residence countries. To this effect, *see* Wolfgang Schön, *Bulletin for International Taxation*, (2018) p. 288. For further comments on the emergence of market countries in the context of the digital economy, *see also* Georg Kofler/Julia Sinnig, "Equalization Taxes and the EU's 'Digital Services Tax'," *Intertax* (2019) p. 178 and João Félix Pinto Nogueira, "The Compatibility of the EU Digital Services Tax with EU and WTO Law: Requiem Aeternam Donate Nascenti Tributo," *IBFD International Tax Studies* (2019) para. 4.4.2.

1846. *See* Wolfgang Schön, *Bulletin for International Taxation*, (2018) p. 286.

1847. Among the main proposals, *see* Peter Hongler/Pasquale Pistone, *IBFD White Paper*, (2015) pp. 23 et seq. and Reuven S. Avi-Yonah/Oz Halabi, *University of Michigan—Law & Economics Research Paper Series* (2014) p. 15.

1848. For further comments, *see* ss. 6.2 and 6.3 above and s. 6.6.2.2 below.

1849. For further comments, *see* s. 6.6.2.3 below.

1850. *See* Wolfgang Schön, *Bulletin for International Taxation*, (2018) p. 286.

Also, and perhaps more importantly, the demand side of the market is already covered by value added taxes and other similar consumption-oriented taxes.[1851] For its part, insurance—which is generally exempt from and/or not subject to such taxes—is most often subject to insurance premium taxes, along with other parafiscal charges and levies on premiums, which are generally applied depending on where the underlying risk is situated. A question therefore arises as to whether corporate income tax is to be transformed into a sales-based tax on top of already existing taxes and levies.[1852,1853] In seeking answer to such a question, one should *in primis* recall that corporate income tax is a tax on the return on equity capital derived by shareholders.[1854] Therefore, the above transformation would require a special case for a fundamental shift in approach to the taxation of income.[1855] Arguably, this shift is not necessarily in line with the paradigm of the value creation, as introduced in the context of the BEPS Project,[1856] and the existing transfer pricing rules.[1857] Also, this might lead to frictions and inconsistencies with the framework of domestic taxation.[1858] On the top of this, the implementation of this shift to destination-based taxation and its interpretation would realistically be diverse among countries, thereby resulting in an increase in disputes and double taxation cases,[1859] not to consider more general economic effects.[1860]

Furthermore, as noted by Schön,[1861] value added tax and other similar consumption-oriented taxes have clearly emerged as successful tax regimes that cover the demand side of the market. Accordingly, those who plead for taxation of inbound digital services must demonstrate that such taxes do not sufficiently perform their role.

1851. *See* Wolfgang Schön, *Bulletin for International Taxation,* (2018) p. 286 and Luzius U. Cavelti/Christian Jaag/Tobias F. Rohner, "Why Corporate Taxation Should Mean Source Taxation: A Response to the OECD's Actions against Base Erosion and Profit Shifting," *World Tax Journal* (2017) p. 377.
1852. Similarly, *see* Krister Andersson, "Taxation of the Digital Economy," *Intertax* (2017) p. 592.
1853. The lines between the objects of income taxation and those of consumption taxes might become blurred. *See* Georg Kofler/Gunter Mayr/Christhop Schlager, *European Taxation,* (2017) p. 524 and Francisco José Nocete Correa, "The Spanish Digital Services Tax: A Paradigm for the Base Enlargement & Profit Attraction (BEPA) Plan for the Digitalized Economy," *European Taxation* (2019) para. 1.2.
1854. This has been acknowledged by the OECD in the Final Report regarding Action 1 of the BEPS Project. To this effect, *see* OECD, "*Addressing the Tax Challenges of the Digital Economy—Action 1: 2015 Final Report,*" p. 22. Similarly, *see also* Wolfgang Schön, "International Tax Coordination for a Second-Best World (Part III)," *World Tax Journal* (2010) p. 256 and Wolfgang Schön, *Bulletin for International Taxation,* (2018) p. 289.
1855. *See* Wolfgang Schön, *Bulletin for International Taxation,* (2018) p. 286 and OECD, "*Tax Challenges of Digitalisation—Comments received on the Request for Input,*" p. 89.
1856. To this effect, *see* Johannes Becker/Joachim Englisch, *Intertax,* (2019) pp. 163-165, Patricia Hofmann/Nadine Riedel, *Intertax,* (2019) p. 173 and Johannes Becker/Joachim Englisch, "EU Digital Services Tax: A Populist and Flawed Proposal," *International Tax Blog* (2018).
1857. *See* OECD, "*Tax Challenges of Digitalisation—Comments received on the Request for Input,*" p. 89.
1858. *See* Wolfgang Schön, *World Tax Journal,* (2010) p. 257.
1859. *See* Krister Andersson, *Intertax,* (2017) p. 592.
1860. *See* Krister Andersson, "Should We Use Value Creation or Destination as a Basis for Taxing Digital Businesses?—Krister Andersson's Comments on the 2018 Klaus Vogel Lecture Given by Professor Michael Devereux," *Bulletin for International Taxation* (2018) para. 6.
1861. *See* Wolfgang Schön, *Bulletin for International Taxation,* (2018) p. 286 and Wolfgang Schön, *World Tax Journal,* (2009) p. 90.

And more than that, in the case where countries providing a market for goods and services argue that they have a legitimate claim in terms of corporate income tax, the reverse is also true, i.e., countries providing a production market for the same goods and services could also legitimately claim a part of consumption taxes.[1862] In the context of the insurance business, this can be translated into the assertion that a risk cannot be insured, unless it is properly assumed and managed. Therefore, as already illustrated above,[1863] countries where underwriting and risk management functions are performed could also legitimately claim a part of the insurance premium taxes. Nonetheless, the result would be unnecessarily too complicated.

Moving to efficiency, one should consider at the outset that the choices a taxpayer has at its disposal in establishing international business activities include a continuous range of operations, starting from selling goods and services to foreign customers and/or purchasing goods and services from foreign suppliers to a full relocation of all its economic activities in foreign countries.[1864] It clearly follows that the mere existence of any threshold provides a friction when it comes to the extension of international business activities. Any such frictions could distort business decisions of taxpayers (in the case at hands, the choice of the business model aimed at marketing, promoting and distributing insurance products in foreign jurisdictions) and—therefore—should in principle be avoided. Nonetheless, the key point to be ascertained here is whether any such threshold represents a "*quantum leap*" that justifies the allocation of taxing rights to the source country.[1865]

In this respect, it has been submitted that the physical presence of employees and/or intermediaries in the source country is per se not decisive for several reasons, including the fact that the provision of sales and services can now take place through electronic means.[1866] Still, the author believes that this assertion should be reconsidered in the context of the insurance business. In fact, the presence of any such person is a key element that can determine whether a foreign insurance company has an establishment for regulatory purposes in the source country and can—thus—carry on its activities therein in compliance with the related laws and regulations. To put it differently, depending on the country and the applicable regulatory framework, the presence of a person in the source country can determine if and under which rules a foreign insurance company can lawfully operate in such a country.

As a result, although the insurance regulatory permanent establishment provides for a threshold that—as with any threshold[1867]—could interfere with the continuum of business decisions, the author believes that such a threshold identifies a clear and sizeable difference in the activities of insurance companies (i.e., the admission to carry

1862. *See* Eric C.C.M. Kemmeren, *EC Tax Review*, (2018) p. 73. Similarly, *see* Dale Pinto, *E-Commerce and Source-Based Income Taxation*, p. 228 and Dale Pinto, *Bulletin for International Taxation*, (2006) p. 279.
1863. *See* s. 3.6 above.
1864. *See* Wolfgang Schön, *World Tax Journal*, (2009) p. 96.
1865. *See* Wolfgang Schön, *World Tax Journal*, (2009) p. 102.
1866. *See* Wolfgang Schön, *World Tax Journal*, (2009) p. 103 and Stjepan Gadžo, *Nexus Requirements for Taxation of Non-Residents' Business Income: A Normative Evaluation in the Context of the Global Economy*, para. 7.1.1.2.
1867. Gadžo acknowledges that it is extremely hard to envisage norms that do not bring about at

on insurance activities in the source country in compliance with the applicable regulatory regime) that justifies the allocation of taxing rights to the source country. Such a new threshold is undoubtedly less prone to manipulation than the currently existing thresholds. True, this presupposes that the person in the source country remains within the range of activities he/she is admitted to performing. However, as already stated above,[1868] to prevent abusive situations, the new threshold can be structured in such a way so as not to apply in the case where such a person goes beyond activities that are admitted under the applicable regulatory regime.

There is also another argument in favor of the insurance regulatory permanent establishment vis-à-vis existing measures. In fact, existing measures dealing with the insurance business have been designed to apply with respect to insurance agents and their application to other business models could lead to inconsistencies.[1869] To the contrary, the new threshold would be applicable irrespective of the business model implemented by foreign insurance companies, thereby causing fewer distortions of business decisions and—therefore—reducing efficiency losses.

In that respect, one may raise the question as to whether foreign insurance companies that adopt business models based on the use of remote means of communication could obtain a competitive advantage in countries (like EU Member States) where such models do not give rise to an establishment for regulatory purposes. While this issue cannot be ignored, it should nevertheless be noted that a specific tax regime for such business models would also have its significant limitations. First and foremost, this would mean ring-fencing such business models in such a way as to create new, unnecessary distortions of business decisions. Second, very many insurance companies are now relying on a multi-channel strategy (based on both physical presence and remote means of communication) to reach out to customers. Accordingly, specific rules would certainly be required to deal with such mixed situations.[1870] In addition to this, more practical considerations should not be forgotten. In fact, leaving aside inter-nation equity considerations, the absence of a permanent establishment in the source country does not necessarily lead to a competitive advantage in situations where the income is subject to a comparable tax burden in the country of establishment. This might in principle generate issues only with respect to insurance companies established in a low or no-tax jurisdiction, but in practice such situations appear to be limited. For instance, to operate in the EU, insurance companies established in a low or no-tax jurisdiction outside the EU would be generally required to set up a new fixed place of business in the territory of an EU Member State, so that the advantage would be lost.

Besides complying with the standards of equity and efficiency, the insurance regulatory permanent establishment is also clear and objective enough for both

---

least some efficiency losses. *See* Stjepan Gadžo, *Nexus Requirements for Taxation of Non-Residents' Business Income: A Normative Evaluation in the Context of the Global Economy*, para. 7.1.1.2.

1868. *See* s. 6.5 above.
1869. *See* s. 4.11 above.
1870. In more general terms, *see also* Wolfgang Schön, *Bulletin for International Taxation*, (2018) pp. 281-282 and Marcel Olbert/Christoph Spengel, *World Tax Journal*, (2017) p. 16.

insurance companies when structuring their international operations and tax administrations when performing their audit activities. Indeed, under the new proposal, tax administrations and insurance companies are confronted with clear, objective and relatively simple tests to ascertain whether the permanent establishment threshold has been passed (most importantly, the assessment as to whether there is an establishment for regulatory purposes), without the need to duplicate the assessment under the currently existing measures employed in model treaties, which—among other issues—relies on sophisticated and arguably subjective elements.[1871]

The insurance regulatory permanent establishment also brings about significant advantages in terms of enforceability, which is another aspect of administrability. More to the point, the new proposal certainly offers tax administrations the possibility to overcome the inherent deficiencies of readily available information with respect to foreign insurance companies carrying on business in their respective territories. To begin with, tax administrations can leverage on information gathered through reporting obligations set out for the purposes of insurance premium taxes and other levies on premiums. As a matter of fact, such a reporting—already available to tax administrations—generally include information regarding business activities of foreign insurance companies in the relevant country (e.g., information regarding activities carried on under the freedom of establishment and/or the freedom to provide services, the appointment of a local representative, and so forth).

At any rate, the most important advantage of using such a threshold for tax administrations lies on the registration duties set forth under insurance supervisory laws and regulations. More precisely, insurance supervisory authorities are generally required to keep, maintain and update a public register of insurance and reinsurance companies licensed to pursue business in their respective territories, which contains the essential information for the identification of such companies, including non-resident companies. This registration scheme is indeed a powerful tool in the hands of tax administrations to cope with the above information discrepancy that could otherwise jeopardize their ability to effectively recognize foreign insurance and reinsurance companies and assess their tax liabilities accordingly. True, one could argue that such registration requirements are in force already. However, this argument should not be overestimated. As a matter of fact, under the currently existing framework, the value of such evidence is far more limited to the extent that tax and regulatory provisions are currently two legally independent set of rules, so that the applicable regulatory regime is per se not directly relevant for the existence of a dependent agent permanent establishment.

The effectiveness of such registration duties could also be accompanied with a closer cooperation between tax administrations and insurance supervisory authorities. For instance, this cooperation might take the form of additional information exchange between such authorities, joint audits on foreign insurance companies and/or the application of combined sanctions in the case of noncompliance. Undoubtedly, such

1871. To this effect, *see* s. 3.6 above.

forms of coordinated action however deserve additional specific research, along with proper domestic legal instruments and administrative guidelines.[1872]

As a final note, the insurance regulatory permanent establishment does not specifically require a new dedicated enforcement mechanism aimed at the collection of taxes beyond the borders of the source country, if need be.[1873] In fact, in the case where a foreign insurance company is deemed to have a permanent establishment in the source country in accordance with this proposal and the relevant tax administration has assessed its tax liability accordingly, the extra-territorial tax collection can take place pursuant to the already existing legal instruments that govern the international assistance in the recovery of tax claims,[1874] including the DTAs that contain a provision regarding the mutual assistance in the recovery of tax claims patterned after Art. 27 of the OECD Model[1875] or Art. 27 of the UN Model.[1876]

6.6.1.3 Incorporation in Model Treaties

Considering that the introduction of a new specific threshold for insurance companies based on the alignment between the tax and regulatory concepts is suitable, desirable, and compliant with normative requirements to be considered when drafting rules aimed at taxing business income of non-residents in the source country, the next logical step is to weigh up how such a threshold can be incorporated in the most common model treaties.

On this front, the author believes that the insurance regulatory permanent establishment can be incorporated through a new paragraph to Art. 5 of the model treaties. This paragraph would supplement the currently existing concepts, primarily the fixed place of business and the dependent agent permanent establishment, that

1872. *See also* s. 6.6.1.8 below.
1873. This issue generally arises if a non-resident taxpayer has no assets within the source country that may serve to recover the tax claim.
1874. For further comments on such instruments, *see* Philip Baker/Ernst Czakert/Arie van Eijsden/María Amparo Grau Ruiz/Liselott Kana, "International Assistance in the Collection of Taxes," *Bulletin for International Taxation* (2011) pp. 282-283, Annet W. Oguttu, "The Role of International Cooperation in Preventing Tax Evasion: A Critique on 'Assistance in the Collection of Taxes'—A South African Perspective," *Bulletin for International Taxation* (2014) paras. 3-5, Louise Parker, "Mutual Assistance in the Collection of Taxes," *Bulletin for International Taxation* (2017) para. 3. and Ana P. Dourado/Kamilla Zembala, "Article 27.—Assistance in the Collection of Taxes" in: Ekkehart Reimer/Alexander Rust (eds.) *Klaus Vogel on Double Taxation Convention—4th edition* (Alphen aan den Rijn: Kluwer Law International, 2015) pp. 1948-1952.
1875. For further comments on this provision, *see*—among others—Michael Lang, *Introduction to the Law of Double Taxation Conventions—2nd edition*, ch. 16 and Ana P. Dourado/Kamilla Zembala in: Ekkehart Reimer/Alexander Rust (eds.) *Klaus Vogel on Double Taxation Convention—4th edition*, pp. 1952 et seq. For further comments on the historical background, *see also* Francisco A. Garcia Prats, "Mutual Assistance in the Collection of Tax Debts," *Intertax* (2002) pp. 56 et seq.
1876. For further comments on this provision, *see* Pasquale Pistone/Pedro G. L. Schoueri, "Exchange of Information and Mutual Assistance in the Collection of Taxes" in: Michael Lang/Pasquale Pistone/Alexander Rust/Josef Schuch/Claus Staringer (eds.) *The UN Model Convention and Its Relevance for the Global Tax Treaty Network* (Amsterdam: IBFD, 2017) para. 11.3.

would remain as they stand today. This evolutionary approach, specifically focused on the insurance business, seems more in line with the scope and purposes of the present research vis-à-vis a fundamental reform of the permanent establishment concept enshrined in Art. 5 of the model treaties that would otherwise deserve additional research.

More precisely, while in the OECD Model and in the US Model, such a paragraph can be introduced immediately after Art. 5, para. 5, of such model treaties (and thus numbered para. 5.1), in the UN Model, such a paragraph can supersede the insurance agent provision currently contained in Art. 5, para. 6, of the UN Model. To attain its intended objectives,[1877] with respect to insurance companies, such a provision should be carefully designed in such a way as to apply *in lieu of* the dependent agent provision contained in Art. 5, para. 5, of the model treaties.

To this end, a first option could be drafting the new paragraph in such a way as to reproduce the requirements set forth under supervisory laws and regulations. However, this approach would be inevitably defective due to several issues which could arise when it is applied in practice. As a matter of fact, it seems to be hard—if not impossible—to draft a paragraph that fits the countless regulatory schemes existing in the various countries. True, one may argue that such requirements could be open for negotiation between DTA partners to reflect the relevant schemes. Nevertheless, this could be counterproductive to the extent that the regulatory schemes may differ even between the relevant DTA partners and the partner that is in a better negotiating position may try to impose its preference on the other partner. Also, and perhaps more importantly, this approach could pave the way for a myriad of diverging thresholds which could eventually hinder its practicability.

Alternatively, the new paragraph could be structured in such a way as to exclude the existence of a permanent establishment in the case that the activities carried out in the source country do not give rise to an establishment for regulatory purposes. For instance, a similar approach has been adopted for dealing with the specific situation of a "*representative of a foreign trading company*" in the DTA concluded between Germany and Indonesia.[1878] Nonetheless, this approach would entail applying the dependent agent provision in the first instance and subsequently carve-out persons carrying out limited activities as a second step. Hence, it does not seem in line with the intended objective of applying the new paragraph instead of the dependent agent provision contained in Art. 5, para. 5, of the model treaties.

This also holds true in the case that the new paragraph is designed in such a way that, in the absence of a regulatory establishment, a foreign insurance company would not have a taxable presence in the source country, but if such company has a regulatory presence therein, the normal tax rules would apply to determine its taxable status.[1879] Indeed, under such circumstances, the new paragraph would apply like a throwback

1877. *See* s. 6.5 above.

1878. *See* Art. 1 of the Protocol to the DTA between Germany and Indonesia concluded on October 30, 1990. For further comments, *see also* s. 6.5 above.

1879. For a similar proposal, *see* OECD, "*Comments received on public discussion draft—BEPS Action 7: Prevent the artificial avoidance of PE status,*" p. 458.

rule, which would result in the situation of insurance companies having a regulatory presence made ultimately subject to the general rules of Art. 5, paras. 5 and 6, of the model treaties with all the weaknesses thereof.

Instead, the most logical solution is drafting a paragraph stipulating that a foreign insurance company has a permanent establishment in the source country in the case that it carries on its business therein through a person that gives rise to an establishment under the applicable insurance laws and regulations. In such way, the new paragraph indeed applies as a *lex specialis* prevailing over the above general rules, with no throwback thereto. Furthermore, because of its flexible nature, such a paragraph can be more easily applied in practice. In fact, when applying such a paragraph, the cross-reference to the applicable regulatory framework makes it possible to consider the specificities of the regulatory landscape in the relevant countries.

6.6.1.4 The Wording of the Proposal

Considering the findings presented in the previous sections, a new paragraph would have to be incorporated after Art. 5, para. 5, of the most common model treaties. More specifically, in the context of the OECD Model,[1880] the new paragraph could read as follows:[1881]

> Notwithstanding the provisions of paragraph 5, an insurance enterprise of a Contracting State shall be deemed to have a permanent establishment in the other Contracting State only if it carries on its business therein through a person that constitutes an establishment in accordance with the provisions of the applicable insurance laws and regulations, provided that its business is authorized and carried on in compliance with such insurance laws and regulations. However, where the activities carried on in that other State are solely intended to ensure compliance with such insurance laws and regulations, and such activities are limited to those mentioned in paragraph 4 which, if exercised through a fixed place of business (other than a fixed place of business to which paragraph 4.1 would apply), would not make this fixed place of business a permanent establishment under the provisions of that paragraph, the insurance enterprise shall not be deemed to have a permanent establishment in that other State.

This wording would need to be complemented with some changes to the OECD Model Commentary with a view to: (*i*) deleting the current para. 114 of the OECD Model Commentary on Art. 5 outlining the wording for a special clause for insurance agents and (*ii*) providing additional guidance on the wording of the new provision. Furthermore, the new proposal would also require a few amendments to the 2010 OECD Report to transpose the alignment between the tax and regulatory definitions into the guidance dealing with the attribution of profits to permanent establishments. Such amendments will be discussed in more detail in the following sections.

1880. In the present section, in view of discussing the new proposal, reference is primarily made to the OECD Model and the OECD Model Commentary. However, the author believes that the same wording can also be incorporated in the UN Model and the US Model.

1881. As already in s. 6.6.1.3 above, this provision could be for example numbered as Art. 5, para. 5.1, of the OECD Model.

6.6.1.5 Adjustments to Commentaries

To begin with, the incorporation of a new paragraph concerning the insurance regulatory permanent establishment in the OECD Model would necessarily require some corresponding amendments to the OECD Model Commentary. Most importantly, in line with the findings reported earlier in this chapter,[1882] para. 114 of the OECD Model Commentary on Art. 5 outlining the wording for a special clause for insurance agents should be deleted to the extent that this clause does not provide for an appropriate threshold with a view to taxing insurance companies engaged in the marketing, promotion and distribution of insurance products in countries other than that of establishment.

On the other hand, additional guidance on the wording of the new provision would need to be added in the OECD Model Commentary. Most notably, relevant terms would need to be defined and the cross-reference to applicable insurance laws and regulations would need to be further clarified for the purposes of a consistent interpretation among countries. To this end, a specific section dealing with the new provision would need to be incorporated after the section dedicated to Art. 5, para. 5, of the OECD Model[1883] and the relevant paragraphs would need to be numbered accordingly.

Under this section, it would need to be clarified *in primis* that the new paragraph lays down a specific rule for "*insurance enterprises*" that applies notwithstanding the provisions of Art. 5, para. 5, of the OECD Model,[1884] account taken of the specific features of the insurance business. In this respect, the reference to "*insurance enterprises*" should be intended to cover any "*enterprise*" pursuant to Art. 3 of the OECD Model that is engaged in the business of insurance. Nevertheless, the accompanying commentaries would also need to explain that such a reference should not be held to mean that this paragraph is only intended for insurance companies. Instead, this term should also be construed in such a way as to include reinsurance companies and retrocession companies, whose business is essentially the same as that of insurance companies.[1885,1886] Moreover, the accompanying commentaries would also need to clarify that the reference to the term "*person*"—which is defined under Art. 3 of the OECD Model—neutralizes a potential conflict over the nature of the relationship existing between the foreign insurance company and the person carrying on business in the source country,[1887] thereby making sure that this new provision can be consistently applied not only to insurance agents like the current measures dealing

1882. *See* s. 6.3 above.
1883. *See* paras. 82-101 of the OECD Model Commentary on Art. 5.
1884. Conversely, this paragraph would remain subject to the provisions Art. 5, para. 1, of the OECD Model.
1885. For further comments, *see* s. 2.2.2.4 above.
1886. In the following sections, in view of discussing the new proposal, reference will primarily be made insurance companies. However, this reference should be intended to include reinsurance and retrocession companies.
1887. For further comments, *see* s. 3.6 above.

with insurance were originally meant to do,[1888] but also to the other business models that can be adopted by insurance companies.

Furthermore, the accompanying commentaries would also need to clarify that—in relation to the business carried on through the person in the source country—the existence of an insurance regulatory permanent establishment is made subject to the existence of an *"establishment"* under the regulatory framework applicable in such a country,[1889] not being a fixed place of business otherwise falling within the scope of Art. 5, para. 1, of the OECD Model. This cross-reference is intended to restrict the application of the new paragraph in circumstances under which insurance business can be lawfully carried on through such a person. To the contrary, in countries where a foreign insurance company cannot carry on business as such (for instance, in countries that do not grant any authorization, unless the foreign insurance company incorporates a local subsidiary and/or establishes a fixed place of business therein), it would need to be clarified that the assessment regarding the existence of a permanent establishment should be made pursuant to the general provisions laid down in Art. 5 of the OECD Model. Likewise, a similar reasoning can also be applied in the case where: (*i*) the relevant regulatory framework does not contain any definition of *"establishment,"* (*ii*) the relevant regulatory framework does not contain a definition of *"establishment"* covering the specific circumstances of a person carrying on business in that country,[1890] and (*iii*) in the unlikely event that a regulatory framework does not exist at all.

The commentaries would also need to further clarify the reference to authorization and compliance with the above laws and regulations. More to point, the expression *"authorized"* should be held to include insurance companies that have formally received a license and/or the authorization to transact insurance in the source country from the relevant supervisory authorities. To put it differently, this reference should exclude from the application of the insurance regulatory permanent establishment those companies that do not operate under the relevant laws and regulations. Among others, this should lead to the exclusion of non-licensed insurance companies (also referred to as non-admitted insurance companies), insurance companies that are exempted from compliance with the requirement that they obtain a license to do business for any reasons whatsoever, and more in general any other insurance companies not authorized and/or not entitled to carry on insurance business in the source country. On the other hand, the term *"compliance"* should be held to mean that, besides being authorized to conduct business in the source country, insurance companies must also conform to the relevant laws and regulations. As a result, to prevent abusive situations, insurance companies that breach any of the conditions on which the license/authorization is granted should be correspondingly excluded from the application of the insurance regulatory permanent establishment. Accordingly,

1888. For further comments, *see* s. 6.3 above.

1889. This reasoning could be applied not only to a general supervisory framework, but also to special insurance schemes.

1890. Any difference in the terminology adopted should however be reconciled to the extent possible.

with respect to insurance companies that are not authorized to transact insurance in the source country and/or are not (even partially)[1891] compliant with the relevant laws and regulations, it would need to be clarified that the assessment regarding the existence of a permanent establishment should be made pursuant to the general provisions laid down in Art. 5 of the OECD Model.

The commentaries would also need to further elaborate on the second sentence of the new provision, which would provide that—even where all the conditions envisaged under the new paragraph are met—the insurance regulatory permanent establishment should not apply if: (*i*) the activities performed by the person in the source country are merely intended to ensure compliance with applicable laws and regulations and (*ii*) such activities are limited to activities mentioned in Art. 5, para. 4, of the OECD Model which, if exercised through a fixed place of business, would be deemed not to create a permanent establishment. In this respect, it would need to be clarified that this carve-out is rooted in the fact that since, pursuant to the general provisions contained in Art. 5 of the OECD Model, preparatory or auxiliary activities are deemed not to constitute a permanent establishment, a person whose activities are restricted to such purposes should not correspondingly create an insurance regulatory permanent establishment. For instance, where a person in the source country is solely engaged in administrative activities (like the filing of documents with the supervisory authorities) for the purposes of complying with insurance laws and regulations, the new provision should not apply to the extent that such activities can be regarded as preparatory or auxiliary.

Analogous adjustments would need to be made to the UN Model Commentary to delete the current paras. 27-29 of the UN Model Commentary on Art. 5 and provide the above additional guidance on the wording of the insurance regulatory permanent establishment. In the latter respect, a cross-reference could alternatively be made to the relevant paragraphs of the OECD Model Commentary. In addition to this, the above adjustments would also need to be correspondingly reflected in the next update of the 2016 UN Manual, which is due to be issued in 2019.

6.6.1.6 *Adjustments to the Guidance on the Attribution of Profits*

The incorporation of a new paragraph concerning the insurance regulatory permanent establishment in the OECD Model would also require some changes to the 2010 OECD Report, Part IV. While the attribution of profits for the insurance regulatory permanent establishment is beyond the scope of this book,[1892] it is nevertheless worth noting that some amendments need certainly to be made in respect of certain sections dealing with the functional and factual analysis in the first step of the AOA. This is primarily the case of the current paragraphs stipulating that tax and regulatory provisions should be assessed independently.[1893]

1891. For instance, this might be the case of insurance companies not authorized and/or not compliant in respect of a specific line of business.
1892. *See* s. 1.4 above.
1893. For instance, *see* 2010 OECD Report, Part IV, paras. 64 and 113.

It follows that the 2010 OECD Report, Part IV, would need to be carefully reviewed with the aim to reflect the alignment between the tax and regulatory definitions in such a guidance, at least in the first step of the AOA. At any rate, the author believes that such a review could be harnessed to address the subsequent question concerning the second step of the AOA, i.e., the question as to whether a reconciliation can be done with the existing guidance regarding the determination of profits or instead specific rules/guidance should be elaborated in respect of the new provision. By the same token, a similar exercise should also be done in respect of the additional guidance on the attribution of profits to permanent establishments that has been released by the OECD in the aftermath of the BEPS Project,[1894] albeit it is still unclear how this additional guidance fits into the more general framework of the 2010 OECD Report.[1895] When doing so, it might also be envisaged extending the practical approach based on illustrative examples adopted in the latter document to the insurance regulatory permanent establishment. Nonetheless, before going any further, additional research should be conducted in that field.

Specific attention would also need to be paid to the attribution of profits to the insurance regulatory permanent establishment in the context of the UN Model to the extent that Art. 7 of the UN Model does not incorporate the AOA, but rather the limited force of attraction principle.[1896] Indeed, even though the application of such a latter principle might arguably push toward an easier profit attribution,[1897] it is nevertheless worthy of further research outside the scope of this book.

6.6.1.7 *Integration in DTAs*

The most common model treaties and their accompanying commentaries have a remarkable influence on the negotiation of DTAs. In this respect, although the dynamics of the negotiations is clearly beyond the scope of this research, it is fair to say that the insurance regulatory permanent establishment could be incorporated into the currently existing DTAs through an amending protocol. Nevertheless, this may not be a suitable solution to amend DTAs that already contain specific measures dealing with insurance. This is for instance the case of Australian DTAs, which include a deviation from Art. 7 of the model treaties,[1898] and some Chilean DTAs, which encompass a special clause in Art. 5, Art. 7 or the Protocol thereto.[1899] Indeed, under such circumstances, the incorporation of the new provision *in lieu of* the previous measures could be better dealt with through a renegotiation of the DTAs for a more comprehensive revision of the existing measures.

1894. *See* OECD, "*Additional Guidance on the Attribution of Profits to Permanent Establishments—BEPS Action 7.*"
1895. To this effect, *see* Bob Stack/Jamie Hawes, *BNA Tax Management Transfer Pricing Report* (2018).
1896. *See* Art. 7, paras. 1(b) and 1(c), of the UN Model.
1897. To this effect, *see* para. 6 of the UN Model Commentary on Art. 7.
1898. *See* s. 5.3.1 above.
1899. *See* s. 5.3.3 above.

Still, the author is concerned about the fact that separate bilateral negotiations might lead to a myriad of adaptations in practice, particularly in a field like insurance where countries are struggling to find a consensus. Admittedly, countries do not necessarily need to adopt an identical wording to attain the intended objectives of the provision. Nonetheless, the discretion left to treaty partners upon the negotiation of an amending protocol and/or the renegotiation of a DTA might be counterproductive. As a matter of fact, the lack of a consensus (not to consider the proliferation of unilateral measures), together with the diverging regulatory schemes among countries, might jeopardize a consistent adoption and interpretation of the new provision.

As a result, a more desirable alternative would be to incorporate the insurance regulatory permanent establishment in a multilateral treaty like the MLI, which would ensure a better coordination among countries. Indeed, even though for the time being the result of the MLI can be regarded as a little disappointing,[1900] this approach would ensure a more homogeneous adoption of the provision, which in turn could result in a more consistent implementation and interpretation of the same. To this end, an amendment to the MLI might be introduced to provide for a standardized wording of the insurance regulatory permanent establishment that can be integrated in the DTAs of the signatories,[1901] without giving much leeway for countries to adapt the scope and the wording of the provision in their DTAs.

6.6.1.8 Domestic Law Considerations

To be enforceable in a DTA context, the insurance regulatory permanent establishment necessarily requires a corresponding right to tax under the domestic law of the source country. Indeed, DTA provisions can be enforced to the extent that the right to tax set forth under the relevant DTA is also provided under domestic law. To the contrary, absent a domestic legal basis, the source country is unable to exercise its right to tax.

In this respect, it may be argued that, for the proposal to be enforceable, the source country would need to retain—in its domestic law—the right to tax non-residents in accordance with a provision that is drafted along the lines of the dependent agent permanent establishment rule. More to the point, since the new proposal would be designed as a special rule specifically tailored for insurance companies that applies *in lieu of* the dependent agent permanent establishment rule, for the new proposal to be enforceable in a DTA context, a domestic legislation that provides for the right to tax non-residents when carrying on business in the form of a dependent agent permanent establishment in the source country might arguably suffice.

The comparative analysis outlined in Chapter 5 of this book demonstrated that many countries have introduced in their domestic legislation a threshold requirement along the lines of the dependent agent permanent establishment rule to tax business

1900. *See* s. 5.4 above.
1901. For further comments on the amendments to the MLI, *see* Nathalie Bravo, "Future Changes to Covered Tax Agreements and of the Multilateral Convention to Implement Tax Treaty-Related Measures to Prevent BEPS" in: Michael Lang/Pasquale Pistone/Alexander Rust/Josef Schuch/Claus Staringer (eds.) *The OECD Multilateral Instrument for Tax Treaties* (Alphen aan den Rijn: Wolters Kluwer, 2018) pp. 254 et seq.

income of non-residents. However, the example of Switzerland clearly shows that this is not always the case.[1902] It is abundantly clear that, based on their sovereignty, countries retain the right to limit their tax jurisdiction in accordance with their specific policy objectives. Nevertheless, this right does not affect the argument that a corresponding right to tax under domestic law is needed, so that it would be desirable that countries bring into line their domestic legislation with a view to enforcing the proposal and safeguarding a proper functioning of DTAs.

Additional measures might also be adopted to improve the enforcement of the insurance regulatory permanent establishment. Among others, it would be desirable that countries enhance the internal cooperation between tax administrations and insurance supervisory authorities. From a legal perspective, this might for instance be translated into the development of domestic legal instruments and administrative guidance that could regulate a proper link with public registers maintained for regulatory purposes and govern a proper information exchange between such authorities, joint audit procedures and/or the application of combined sanctions.[1903]

6.6.2 An Alternative Proposal: A Withholding Tax on Insurance Premiums

6.6.2.1 Introduction

At the outset, it should be recalled that a withholding tax is not a separate tax,[1904] but rather a collection system.[1905] In its basic form, the payor (the "*withholding agent*") withholds a certain tax portion (commonly described as the "*withholding tax*") from a specific item of income payable to the payee (the "*income recipient*"). The withholding agent then transfers the tax withheld to the relevant tax administration for the account of the income recipient, who receives the income net of tax.[1906]

In many countries, a withholding tax applies to different items of income paid out to non-residents.[1907] First and foremost, this is the case of withholding taxes on passive income (such as interest, dividend and royalty income). Nevertheless, in some jurisdictions, a withholding tax also applies to certain items of business income. Among others, some countries (like Chile)[1908] impose—at domestic law level—a withholding tax on certain insurance premiums paid to foreign insurance companies and aim at preserving the application of such a withholding tax mechanism in a DTA situation, albeit this represents a deviation from the main model treaties.

1902. *See* s. 5.2 above.
1903. *See also* s. 6.6.1.2.2 above.
1904. A withholding tax should not be confused with equalization levies based on the amount of gross premiums paid to foreign insurance companies.
1905. *See* Karin Simader, *Withholding Taxes and the Fundamental Freedoms* (Alphen aan den Rijn: Kluwer Law International, 2013) p. 7 and footnotes cited therein.
1906. *See* Chang Hee Lee/Ji-Hyun Yoon, "General Report" in: IFA (ed.) *Withholding tax in the era of BEPS, CIVs and digital economy*, Cahiers de droit fiscal international, Vol. 103b (The Hague: Sdu Uitgevers, 2018) p. 7.
1907. *See* Chang Hee Lee/Ji-Hyun Yoon in: IFA (ed.) *Withholding tax in the era of BEPS, CIVs and digital economy*, pp. 19-20.
1908. *See* s. 5.3.3 above.

Against this background, considering that a specific provision concerning insurance is admissible,[1909] the following sections will address the question as to whether a potential solution for taxing insurance companies engaged in the marketing, promotion and distribution of insurance products in countries other than that of establishment lies in the introduction of a withholding tax on insurance premiums in the main model treaties. To this end, before going through a normative assessment regarding such a potential solution, the following section will discuss the most important implications related to the absence of a threshold for taxing non-residents.

6.6.2.2 *The Absence of a Threshold*

The absence of a threshold designed for taxing foreign insurance companies could allegedly provide more simplicity vis-à-vis the current framework. More to the point, the deletion of any thresholds implies getting rid of currently existing permanent establishment thresholds and giving up on additional attempts to design more suitable thresholds to deal with the taxation of foreign insurance companies. Indeed, in such a case, all that is needed is a provision allowing the source country to tax business income of foreign insurance companies (like a withholding tax provision) set forth at DTA level,[1910] coupled with a corresponding right to tax under the domestic law of the source country. Under such circumstances, taxation in the source country would not require the fulfillment of any additional requirement whatsoever, so that it seems obvious that the removal of thresholds is a simple solution that could prevent some issues typically associated with thresholds, most importantly the assessment as to whether the threshold is reached or not. Nonetheless, it cannot be ignored that some issues will inevitably remain. For instance, uncertainties might at any rate arise with respect to the determination of the applicable source rules. Also, and perhaps more importantly, as already touched upon above,[1911] tax systems based on the absence of a threshold brings about severe normative issues that will be addressed more specifically when dealing with the normative assessment of the withholding tax option in the following section.

Second, one could argue that, in the absence of a threshold, there is less risk that taxpayers put into place artificial arrangements aimed at avoiding the threshold being reached. Put it simply, as noted by Báez Moreno with respect to the taxation of services,[1912] there is no need to avoid a threshold that does not even exist. Nonetheless, this does not necessarily mean that the removal of thresholds per se does away with all abusive strategies, most notably treaty shopping strategies. Furthermore, a threshold requirement that is carefully designed could significantly reduce the margin for abusive

1909. *See* s. 6.2 above.
1910. For instance, a withholding tax provision could be introduced in Art. 7 of the model treaties. To this effect, *see* Andrés Báez Moreno/Yariv Brauner, *IBFD White Paper* (2015) p. 23. This path has been followed in some Chilean DTAs. For further comments, *see* s. 5.3.3 above.
1911. *See* s. 6.3 above.
1912. *See* Andrés Báez Moreno, *World Tax Journal*, (2015) para. 3.2.1.1.3. In a similar vein, *see also* Monique T. Malan, "New Article 12A of the UN Model Regarding Fees for Technical Services: Ahead of Its Time or a Step Too Far?," *Bulletin for International Taxation* (2019) para. 3.1.2.

situations.[1913] And, more than that, it should be recalled that specific abusive situations, like artificial structures intended to circumvent the existence of a permanent establishment, can be targeted on a separate individual basis through anti-avoidance provisions and/or doctrines.[1914]

Moreover, although the attribution of profits to permanent establishments is beyond the scope of this research,[1915] one may argue that, in the case where the permanent establishment threshold is reached, theoretical and practical application issues might come up in relation to the attribution of profits thereto. With specific respect to the insurance business, as already outlined above,[1916] the introduction of a specific threshold would necessarily require a review of the currently existing guidance to ascertain whether the same can be extended to the newly envisaged provision. As a result, one could instinctively argue that the elimination of permanent establishment thresholds could solve such issues at their roots to the extent that no computational rules are necessary. Nevertheless, while the absence of any such a threshold might result in equally troublesome issues (e.g., the decision as to which withholding tax rate should be applied in the source country), one should also consider that there might be room for solving potential issues related to the attribution of profits not only through the traditional transfer pricing analysis, but also with more pragmatic approaches.[1917] For instance—leaving aside the formulary apportionment system, which would require a fundamental paradigm shift—one alternative option could be to supplement the currently existing guidance with safe harbor rules and formulaic elements, at least to deal with more complicated circumstances.[1918] Nevertheless, such options clearly deserve additional detailed analysis that is outside the scope of the present research.

6.6.2.3 *Normative Assessment*

To begin with the assessment, it is fair to say that—in principle—a withholding tax on insurance premiums could be in line with general international law principles regarding income tax jurisdiction, provided that the envisaged source rules postulate a clear

1913. *See* s. 6.6.1.4 above.
1914. *See* ss. 4.11 and 6.5 above.
1915. *See* s. 1.4 above.
1916. *See* s. 6.6.1.6 above.
1917. Simplified conventions are also being considered in the context of the digitalized economy. For further comments, *see also* s. 4.2.2.1 above.
1918. For further comments on the attempt to reconcile the arm's length principle with formulaic elements, *see*—among others—Brian D. Lepard, "Is the United States Obligated to Drive on the Right?: A Multidisciplinary Inquiry into the Normative Authority of Contemporary International Law Using the Arm's Length Standard as a Case Study," *Duke Journal of Comparative & International Law* (1999) pp. 50 et seq., Eduardo Baistrocchi, "The Transfer Pricing Problem: A Global Proposal for Simplification," *Tax Lawyer* (2006) pp. 955 et seq., Jens Wittendorff, *Transfer Pricing and Arm's Length Principle in International Tax Law* (Alphen aan den Rijn: Kluwer Law International, 2010) pp. 700-701, Reuven S. Avi-Yonah, "Between Formulary Apportionment and the OECD Guidelines: A Proposal for Reconciliation," *World Tax Journal* (2010) pp. 16 et seq., Susan C. Morse, "The Transfer Pricing Regs Need a Good Edit," *Pepperdine Law Review* (2013) and Sol Picciotto, "Problems of Transfer Pricing and Possibilities for Simplification," *Institute of Development Studies—Working Paper 86* (2018), pp. 43-44.

and sufficient link between the business income of the foreign insurance company and the territory of the source country. For example, without any pretensions to being exhaustive, a sufficient connection with the territory of the source country could be deemed to exist in respect of insurance contracts covering risks related to individuals that are resident in the source country, goods and properties that are situated in the source country and/or events that can only take place in the source country.

Despite the above, the withholding tax option brings about serious issues from the equity perspective.[1919] *In primis*, the application of a withholding tax on a gross basis cannot be reconciled with the ability to pay principle.[1920] Indeed, such a principle generally presupposes business income be subject to tax on a net basis, i.e., with a deduction of the expenses incurred for the purposes of the relevant business activities. For example, foreign insurance companies with the same amount of gross premiums that incurred in different amounts of expenses would be subject to the same withholding tax in the source country. It follows that a withholding tax applied on gross insurance premiums contravenes the above principle.[1921]

In seeking a solution to mitigate such an issue, some features of the withholding tax option could be ameliorated. The first pragmatic solution could be the adoption of a low withholding tax rate.[1922] Nonetheless, the author believes that this option could only mitigate the equity issue without solving its very essence. As a matter of fact, the concept of high or low withholding tax rate seems rather arbitrary, so that what is reasonably low fundamentally depends from the perspective adopted.

A second solution could consist in allowing the deduction of expenses incurred for the purposes of the relevant business activities, thereby achieving a net taxation more in line with the equity standard. This alternative solution could be implemented through different technical instruments that should be carefully assessed. A first alternative would be the application of the withholding tax on a certain percentage of the gross premiums,[1923] which is a system comparable to presumptive taxation.[1924] In its basic form, presumptive taxation involves the use of some indirect means to

1919. For a critical view regarding issues of equality among taxpayers deriving from the application of withholding taxes, *see also* Karin Simader, *Withholding Taxes and the Fundamental Freedoms*, p. 32.

1920. Camacho Palma even argues that gross taxation is more detrimental than double taxation. To this effect, *see* Rui Camacho Palma, "The Paradox of Gross Taxation at Source," *Intertax* (2010) p. 640.

1921. For a similar reasoning concerning withholding tax options to address issues deriving from the digitalization of the economy, *see* Stjepan Gadžo, *Nexus Requirements for Taxation of Non-Residents' Business Income: A Normative Evaluation in the Context of the Global Economy*, para. 7.3.3.3.2.

1922. For a similar reasoning concerning the taxation of income from services, *see* Andrés Báez Moreno, *World Tax Journal*, (2015) para. 3.2.1.2.1 and Brian J. Arnold, *Papers on Selected Topics in Protecting the Tax Base of Developing Countries*, pp. 14-15. For a similar reasoning concerning a "*refundable withholding approach*" to address issues deriving from the electronic commerce, *see* Dale Pinto, *E-Commerce and Source-Based Income Taxation*, para. 8.3.4.1 and Dale Pinto, *Bulletin for International Taxation*, (2006) p. 277.

1923. For instance, this alternative is applied in Australia. For further comments, *see also* s. 5.3.1 above.

1924. For a similar reasoning concerning the taxation of income from services, *see* Andrés Báez Moreno, *World Tax Journal*, (2015) para. 3.2.1.2.1, Brian J. Arnold, *Papers on Selected Topics*

ascertain a notional income, which differ from the general rules based on the actual income. The term "*presumptive*" is used to indicate that there is a legal presumption that the income is no less than the amount resulting from application of the indirect method.[1925] In this context, the notional income of the foreign insurance companies would be a percentage of the gross premiums. In such a way, the taxation of a limited part of the actual income would permit some relief for the expenses incurred for the purposes of the relevant business activities.[1926]

Presumptive methods can be rebuttable or non-rebuttable.[1927] Should the percentage of the gross premiums be designed as a non-rebuttable exclusive[1928] presumption, the withholding tax option would provide simplicity and minimal disincentive effects. Even so, such an option would again suffer from a lack of equity to the extent that foreign insurance companies that report different amounts of actual income would be subject to the same withholding tax liability if their gross premium amount is the same.[1929]

On the other hand, a withholding tax system grounded either on a non-rebuttable minimum[1930] presumption or a rebuttable presumption would be more equitable at the expense of the simplicity which is at the core of solutions based on the absence of thresholds (including the withholding tax option). In fact, a non-final withholding tax system would necessarily require two tax bases to be calculated and compared.[1931] In addition to this, such alternatives would require foreign insurance companies to file a tax return for the purposes of disclosing the actual income to be taxed in the source country with a credit (or even a refund in the second option) for the tax withheld.[1932] And more than that, one should also consider that foreign insurance companies might not have any incentive to submit a tax return in the source country in the case where their net tax liability is higher than the amount of withholding tax payable, so that the

---

in Protecting the Tax Base of Developing Countries, p. 14 and Fernando Souza de Man, *Taxation of Services in Treaties between Developed and Developing Countries—A Proposal for New Guidelines*, para. 7.2.

1925. *See* Victor Thuronyi, "Ch. 12—Presumptive Taxation" in: Victor Thuronyi (ed.) *Tax Law Design and Drafting* (Washington: International Monetary Fund, 1996) p. 1 and Richard M. Bird, "Administrative Dimensions of Tax Reform," *Asia-Pacific Tax Bulletin* (2004) p. 142.
1926. As noted by Arnold in respect of the taxation of income from services, this alternative would be more transparent than fixing a low withholding tax rate. To this effect, *see* Brian J. Arnold, *Papers on Selected Topics in Protecting the Tax Base of Developing Countries*, p. 14.
1927. For further comments, *see* Victor Thuronyi in: Victor Thuronyi (ed.) *Tax Law Design and Drafting*, pp. 3-4 and Vito Tanzi/Milka Casanegra de Jantscher, "Presumptive Income Taxation: Administrative, Efficiency and Equity Aspects," *International Monetary Fund—Working Paper 87/54*, available online at https://www.imf.org, p. 9.
1928. An exclusive presumption implies that the tax liability is determined under the presumption alone, even though the general rules might lead to a higher tax liability. *See* Victor Thuronyi in: Victor Thuronyi (ed.) *Tax Law Design and Drafting*, p. 4.
1929. In general, *see* Victor Thuronyi in: Victor Thuronyi (ed.) *Tax Law Design and Drafting*, p. 4.
1930. A minimum presumption implies that the tax liability is no less than that determined under the presumptive rules. To this effect, *see* Victor Thuronyi in: Victor Thuronyi (ed.) *Tax Law Design and Drafting*, p. 4.
1931. To this effect, *see* Victor Thuronyi in: Victor Thuronyi (ed.) *Tax Law Design and Drafting*, p. 4.
1932. For a similar reasoning concerning the taxation of income from services, *see* Andrés Báez Moreno, *World Tax Journal*, (2015) para. 3.2.1.2.1.

withholding tax rate should be set at a sufficiently high level, compared to the effective rates of income tax in the source country.[1933]

This intrinsic complexity would arguably raise concerns from the perspective of practicability.[1934,1935] First and foremost, such options would result in extra compliance burdens for foreign insurance companies that would need to maintain additional records, calculate separate bases and submit tax returns in the source country. On the other side, non-final approaches would also present corresponding concerns for the tax administrations. Besides the fact that clear rules should be established with respect to the selection of deductible expenses, such approaches would indeed require audit activities, for instance in relation to general expenses and/or expenses incurred abroad.[1936]

The application of a withholding tax on insurance premiums cannot be reconciled with the benefit principle, either. In fact, as with all solutions lacking qualitative and/or qualitative thresholds,[1937] the withholding tax option implies that foreign insurance companies are subject to tax in the source country, irrespective of the degree of integration therein. True, for the purposes of transacting insurance in the source country, such companies must have access to the local market and this access can be associated with some public benefits. Nevertheless, the author believes that source taxation should be subject to a threshold that reflects a minimum level of benefits.[1938] This would indeed prevent situations where foreign insurance companies with negligible contacts in the source country (particularly, small and medium-sized companies) are subject to burdensome compliance requirements.

Finally, a withholding tax on insurance premiums can be hardly justified from the inter-nation perspective. The main problem here is that the envisaged source rules might not be aligned with the presence of income-producing factors within the country imposing the withholding tax. For instance, this might be the case a withholding tax applied on insurance premiums related to contracts covering risks regarding goods and properties pertaining to non-residents. Indeed, in such a case, there seems to be no production factor located within that country, neither on the supply side nor on the demand side. Also, as already illustrated above,[1939] the demand side of the market is

1933. *See* Stjepan Gadžo, *Nexus Requirements for Taxation of Non-Residents' Business Income: A Normative Evaluation in the Context of the Global Economy*, para. 7.3.3.3.1.
1934. *See also* s. 6.3 above.
1935. Such issues have been recognized even by Pinto, who is a proponent of a "*refundable withholding approach*" for electronic commerce transactions. To this effect, *see* Dale Pinto, *E-Commerce and Source-Based Income Taxation*, pp. 227-228 and Dale Pinto, *Bulletin for International Taxation*, (2006) p. 278.
1936. For a similar reasoning concerning the taxation of income from services, *see* Andrés Báez Moreno, *World Tax Journal*, (2015) para. 3.2.1.2.1.
1937. *See also* ss. 6.3 and 6.6.2.2 above.
1938. For a similar reasoning concerning withholding tax options to address issues deriving from the digitalization of the economy, *see also* Stjepan Gadžo, *Nexus Requirements for Taxation of Non-Residents' Business Income: A Normative Evaluation in the Context of the Global Economy*, para. 7.3.3.3.2. Instead, in respect of the taxation of income from services, Souza de Man takes a different view. *See* Fernando Souza de Man, *Taxation of Services in Treaties between Developed and Developing Countries—A Proposal for New Guidelines*, para. 7.2.
1939. *See* s. 6.6.1.2.2 above.

frequently subject to insurance premium taxes, along with other parafiscal charges and levies on premiums, which are generally levied depending on where the underlying risk is located. Therefore, the implementation of a withholding tax on premiums would inevitably require a broader review of the allocation of taxing rights among countries. However, this seems unnecessarily too complicated.

Turning to efficiency, one might contend at the outset that the withholding tax option would eliminate the distorting effect of the "*all-or-nothing rule,*" which is typical of permanent establishment thresholds. Riding the wave of this contention, proponents of withholding tax options to address issues deriving from the digitalization of the economy and the taxation of income from services have put forward that a breach of the "*continuity approach,*"[1940] whereby the crossing of the threshold leads from no source taxation to full taxation of income attributable to the permanent establishment, could lead to non-efficient results.[1941] Nonetheless, as already discussed above,[1942] this argument should be reconsidered in the insurance business, where a threshold aligned with regulatory requirements identifies a clear and sizeable difference in the activities of insurance companies.

Furthermore, it is also worth noting that the withholding tax option brings about a trade-off in relation to its application in the context of B2C transactions.[1943] On the one hand, the exclusion of B2C transactions from the scope of the withholding tax option would generate efficiency issues to the extent that foreign insurance companies could transact insurance with private customers free of withholding tax in the source country, thereby obtaining significant competitive advantages vis-à-vis foreign insurance companies engaged in B2B transactions.[1944] On the other hand, the inclusion of B2C transactions in the scope of the withholding tax option would inevitably lead to practical issues to the extent that requiring private customers to withhold and remit the tax withheld to the relevant tax administration would be troublesome. To solve the latter issue, a potential solution could be the imposition of withholding obligations on financial institutions and/or other intermediaries involved in the insurance premium payment process that are suitable to act as withholding agents. Nevertheless, this

1940. According to Schön, the "*continuity approach*" presupposes that the gradual extension of business activities from the domestic arena to another country is associated with an incremental extension of taxability, thereby avoiding arbitrary or sudden "*frictions.*" For further comments regarding the "*all-or-nothing rule*" and the "*continuity approach,*" *see* Wolfgang Schön, *World Tax Journal,* (2009) pp. 99-101.

1941. To this effect, *see* Andrés Báez Moreno/Yariv Brauner, *IBFD White Paper* (2015) p. 18 and Andrés Báez Moreno, *World Tax Journal,* (2015) para. 3.2.1.1.1, respectively.

1942. *See* s. 6.6.1.2.2 above.

1943. For a similar analysis in respect of withholding tax options to address issues deriving from the digitalization of the economy, *see* Stjepan Gadžo, *Nexus Requirements for Taxation of Non-Residents' Business Income: A Normative Evaluation in the Context of the Global Economy,* paras. 7.3.3.3.1 and 7.3.3.3.2. For a similar analysis, but with a different position, *see* Andrés Báez Moreno, *World Tax Journal,* (2015) para. 3.2.1.2.4 in respect of the taxation of income from services, and Andrés Báez Moreno/Yariv Brauner, *IBFD White Paper* (2015) pp. 17-18 in respect of withholding tax options to address issues deriving from the digitalization of the economy.

1944. As noted by Pinto, such competitive advantages have also been exploited in the field of indirect taxes. To this effect, *see* Dale Pinto, *E-Commerce and Source-Based Income Taxation,* pp. 185-186.

alternative is not free from blame since its technical implementation would at any rate bring about additional practicability concerns for the designated withholding agents.[1945]

On the top of this, one should not forget that practicability concerns might also arise in the context of B2B transactions. For instance, the withholding tax option could generate multiple source issues. This might be the case of multinational programs, where several parties could be involved and the underlying risk could arise in different countries. True, a specific source rule could be singled out for the purposes of applying the withholding tax in such circumstances. Also, additional guidance could be provided to anticipate source conflicts. Nevertheless, leaving aside the assessment as to whether the envisaged rule/guidance is appropriate,[1946] this is not the end of the story since circumstances might change during the relevant fiscal year and/or during the lifetime of the relevant insurance contract (particularly, in the case of multi-annual contracts which involve the payment of annual premiums). It follows that business customers taking out insurance would be confronted with new and different practical difficulties in their role as withholding agents, not to mention their obligations to remit the tax withheld at source and to file withholding tax returns with the relevant tax administrations.[1947]

On their side, insurance companies would inevitably incur in additional compliance time and costs. For example, insurance companies might be required to provide the relevant withholding agents with documentary evidence (such as tax residence certificates) for the purposes of applying a DTA withholding tax rate. Additional documentary evidence might also be associated with filing obligations in their respective countries. For instance, in the case where relief against double taxation is provided by means of the credit method, insurance companies would predictably need to obtain sufficient documentary evidence regarding the amounts withheld from the withholding agents to offset such amounts in their tax returns.

Equally important, tax authorities would incur in additional administrative efforts to properly ensure the enforcement of a withholding tax system. In the first place, tax administrations would need to devise appropriate enforcement mechanisms to detect and identify insurance premiums subject to withholding tax. The implementation of such mechanisms pretty much depends on the source rule(s) selected for the application of the withholding tax. Arguably, since the withholding tax option could no longer be associated with physical presence and/or the performance of insurance business activities in the source country, the implementation of such mechanisms could be troublesome. For instance, it could be stipulated that insurance premiums are

1945. The OECD also highlighted that the application of this approach could result in opportunities for tax avoidance strategies in the case where the relevant intermediaries are situated in third-countries. *See* OECD, "*Addressing the Tax Challenges of the Digital Economy—Action 1: 2015 Final Report*," Chapter 7—Broader direct tax challenges raised by the digital economy and the options to address them, para. 297.
1946. This assessment clearly depends upon the specific rule/guidance.
1947. For further comments regarding potential issues and guidelines for withholding agents, *see* Chang Hee Lee/Ji-Hyun Yoon in: IFA (ed.) *Withholding tax in the era of BEPS, CIVs and digital economy*, pp. 25-26.

not allowed for deduction in the hands of business customers, unless they adhere to certain withholding and reporting obligations.[1948] However, while a system in which the deduction is made conditional on effective withholding and reporting would be self-enforcing, it would in turn create additional compliance burdens for business customers. On the top of this, a withholding-based system would naturally require tax administrations to implement specific audit activities to control the correct enforcement of the same (e.g., the application of the correct withholding tax rate, the correct remittance of the tax withheld in due time, the correct filing of the withholding tax returns in due time, and so forth).

The above practicability issues would be exacerbated in the context of the UN Model, which already contains a specific provision dealing with the application of a withholding tax on "*fees for technical services.*"[1949] To this end, the UN makes a conceptual distinction between "*technical*" services and non-technical services. In this respect, the UN has clarified that the ordinary meaning of the term "*technical*" should involve "*the application of specialized knowledge, skill or expertise with respect to a particular art, science, profession or occupation.*"[1950] However, a fundamental issue here is related to the identification of services that do not involve the application of (at least, certain) specialized knowledge, skill or expertise.[1951]

In the UN Model Commentary, there is no conclusive guidance regarding such a conceptual issue. Moreover, the examples contained therein seem rather confusing, to say the least. Indeed, while excluding from the objective scope of the new article the provision of general and/or standardized services, the UN Model Commentary also illustrates that technical services involve "*specialized knowledge, skill and expertise*" on behalf of a "*particular client.*" Most notably, with respect to insurance, the fourth example suggests that an insurance company which provides insurance against a wide variety of risks through standard form insurance contracts is indeed using its "*knowledge, skill and expertise*" to develop insurance products that are sold to its clients, but it is not applying its "*knowledge, skill and expertise*" directly for the benefit of each "*particular client.*"[1952] On the contrary, in the case where the very same insurance company stipulates customized insurance contracts dealing with special risks for some clients in the source country, the insurance premiums may be considered "*fees for*

1948. This mechanism has been adopted in Australia with respect to reinsurance. For further comments, *see* s. 5.3.1 above. For a similar reasoning concerning a withholding tax option to address issues deriving from the digitalization of the economy, *see* Andrés Báez Moreno/Yariv Brauner, *IBFD White Paper* (2015) pp. 15-16. For a similar reasoning concerning income from services, *see* Andrés Báez Moreno, *World Tax Journal,* (2015) para. 2.
1949. *See* Art. 12A of the UN Model.
1950. *See* para. 64 of the UN Model Commentary on Art. 12A.
1951. This issue has been acknowledged even by some supporters of the provision on fees for technical services. For instance, *see* Andrés Báez Moreno, *World Tax Journal,* (2015) para. 3.2.1.2.2, Fernando Souza de Man, *Taxation of Services in Treaties between Developed and Developing Countries—A Proposal for New Guidelines,* para. 7.1.5, Tizhong Liao, "*Taxation of Cross-Border Trade in Service: A Review of the Current International Tax Landscape and the Possible Future Policy Options,*" E/C.18/2013/CRP.16, available online at www.un.org, pp. 26-27, Jan de Goede, "The Treatment of Services in Tax Treaties," *IBFD White Paper* (2013) p. 3.
1952. *See* para. 92 of the UN Model Commentary on Art. 12A.

technical services."[1953] Hence, while on the one hand, the UN seems to acknowledge that insurance presupposes the application of "*specialized knowledge, skill or expertise,*" on the other hand, the withholding tax set forth under Art. 12A of the UN Model is to be applied only where such "*knowledge, skill or expertise*" is used for a "*particular client.*" Nevertheless, this fine line between standardized and customized services seems to be lacking both a legal basis and policy reasons.[1954]

Considering the uncertainties regarding the scope of the new provision and the lack of clear guidance thereon, significant interpretative issues might arise with respect to the technical character of the services. Therefore, while the introduction of the new article could reduce the litigation regarding the classification of payments for technical services as royalties, it could nevertheless increase the litigation regarding the nature of the services provided.[1955] Needless to say, the introduction of a withholding tax on insurance premiums that potentially overlaps with the already existing withholding tax on "*fees for technical services*" would eventually pile on practicability issues for both taxpayers and tax administrations.

What is more, a withholding tax on insurance premiums should also be coordinated with the insurance agent provision set forth under Art. 5, para. 6, of the UN Model. As already portrayed above,[1956] it is hard enough to reconcile the latter provision with the withholding tax on "*fees for technical services*" to the extent that the current guidance is not based on an accurate analysis since—in the fact patterns depicted in the UN Model Commentary[1957]—there is no hint about the presence of the agent in the source country, nor are the collection of premiums and the insurance of risks therein clearly ascertained. If a withholding tax on insurance premiums is introduced on top of the existing measures, such a reconciliation might become even more problematic and thus give rise to additional practicability issues.

Bearing in mind all equity, efficiency and practicability issues outlined in this section, the author strongly believes that the introduction of a provision setting forth a withholding tax on insurance premiums (even combined with mechanisms aimed at tackling some of the above issues) in the main model treaties with a view to taxing insurance companies engaged in the marketing, promotion and distribution of insurance products in countries other than that of establishment does not seem advisable.

1953. *See* para. 93 of the UN Model Commentary on Art. 12A.
1954. Along the same line, *see also* Andrés Báez Moreno, *World Tax Journal*, (2015) para. 3.2.1.2.2 and Dikshit P. Sengupta, "Chapter 21: India: Siemens Ltd—To Be Taxed as Fees for Technical Services Some Human Intervention Is a Must" in: Eric C.C.M. Kemmeren (ed.) *Tax Treaty Case Law around the Globe 2014* (Amsterdam: IBFD, 2014) para. 21.5.
1955. *See* Fernando Souza de Man, *Taxation of Services in Treaties between Developed and Developing Countries—A Proposal for New Guidelines*, para. 7.1.5 and Francisco A. Garcia Prats, "Chapter 14: Impact of the Position of the BRICS on the UN Model Convention in BRICS and the Emergence of International Tax Coordination" in: Yariv Brauner/Pasquale Pistone (eds.) *BRICS and the Emergence of International Tax Coordination* (Amsterdam: IBFD, 2014) para. 14.4.1.
1956. *See* s. 3.4.2.3 above.
1957. *See* para. 93 of the UN Model Commentary on Art. 12A.

CHAPTER 7
Concluding Remarks

Chapter 7 ties up the various elements of this research with the major concluding remarks. More to the point, this concluding chapter is intended to deliver a final wrap-up of the research findings, revisit the overall research aims and provide some remarks on what the answers to the research questions may entail for future academic research and future developments of the concept of permanent establishment.

7.1 OUTCOME OF THE RESEARCH

This book aimed at investigating the concept of permanent establishment in the context of the insurance business in light of its specific features, value chain and business models. More precisely, the research was focused on the specific circumstances under which insurance companies can give rise to a dependent agent permanent establishment when marketing, promoting and distributing their products in foreign jurisdictions without establishing a fixed place of business therein. To this end, the author followed a systematic approach, thereby setting the general framework in which insurance companies operate for the purposes of subsequently assessing the most common business models adopted by insurance companies.

At the outset, Chapter 2 depicted the regulatory landscape and its latest developments in the EU and in Switzerland. In doing so, it has been demonstrated that insurance is a highly regulated business and much of the organizational structure of insurance groups is eventually driven by what is required for regulatory purposes. Among others, such regulatory provisions also influence the decision related to the incorporation of foreign subsidiaries versus the creation of foreign permanent establishments. It was indeed submitted that, in the EU single insurance market, insurance companies may opt to operate in other EU Member States relying either on the right of establishment or under the freedom to provide services.[1958] In this respect, the research

1958. *See* s. 2.1.2 above.

has shown that uncertainties might arise with respect to the demarcation between right of establishment and the freedom to provide services. As a result, the EU Commission issued an Interpretative Communication to clarify the principles underlying such fundamental freedoms, including the circumstances under which an independent person falls within the scope of the right of establishment.[1959] To the contrary, it has been delineated that, in other countries, like Switzerland, foreign insurance companies cannot operate in the absence of a local branch or subsidiary, save for a few exceptions.[1960]

Chapter 2 further explored the insurance value chain, along with the most common functions that may be found in a traditional insurance business, namely product development, sales and marketing, underwriting, risk management, contract and claims management, asset management, and other support functions.[1961] In this respect, it has also been demonstrated that—in the financial sector—the OECD still uses the concept of KERT function in describing the functions relevant for the attribution of both risks and assets in the first step of the AOA. More specifically, the KERT function "*is one which requires active decision-making with regard to the assumption and/or management (subsequent to the transfer) of the individual risks and portfolios of risks that have been identified as the most important under the functional and factual analysis.*"[1962] Moving from this, the research has shown that, in the insurance business, the OECD identified the KERT function in the assumption of insurance risk which is carried out by the underwriting function.[1963]

In Chapter 3, the general framework was completed with the analysis of the dependent agent permanent establishment concept from the early years to the work conducted by the OECD, the UN and the US,[1964] including the latest developments stemming from the BEPS Project. In this latter respect, it has been demonstrated that the OECD moved away from the original concept toward an economic approach, thereby extending the scope of the dependent agent permanent establishment definition. However, the amendments introduced in the context of the BEPS Project (most notably, the supplementary test regarding the principal role leading to the conclusion of contracts, which is subjective in nature) seem to be lacking clarity. Hence, while such amendments will most probably result in more dependent agent permanent establishments, such uncertainties could result in more litigations between taxpayers and tax authorities. All this complemented with the fact that there will be presumably little or no additional income to be taxed in the source country. Unsurprisingly, the UN endorsed the work of the OECD in the context of the BEPS Project and implemented the above changes into the 2017 update of the UN Model. On the other hand, the US did not give effect to Action 7 of the BEPS Project in the 2016 update of the US Model.

Chapter 3 also shed specific light on the existing measures dealing with insurance agents. In that respect, while such measures have been left fundamentally unchanged

1959. *See* s. 2.1.3 above.
1960. *See* s. 2.1.4 above.
1961. *See* ss. 2.2.2.1-2.2.2.7 above.
1962. *See* 2010 OECD Report, Part IV, para. 68.
1963. *See* s. 2.2.3 above.
1964. *See* ss. 3.2-3.5 above.

after the BEPS Project, the research has shown the lack of a sound juridical reasoning and several inherent flaws which undermine their application, interpretation and effectiveness. In addition to this, it has been contended that such thresholds will typically be associated with little or no additional income to be taxed in the source countries.[1965]

Against the general framework outlined in the preceding sections, Chapter 4 explored the most common business models adopted by insurance companies with a view to marketing, promoting and distributing their products in countries other than that of establishment, with a focus on the specific features of such models that may give rise to the existence of a dependent agent permanent establishment.[1966] In doing so, it has been explained that the choice of the business model to be adopted is generally based on genuine commercial, legal and regulatory reasons, rather than tax motives. Hence, abusive situations should be better targeted on a separate individual basis through anti-avoidance provisions and/or doctrines.[1967]

The analysis of the business models also corroborated the argument that the amendments introduced in the context of the BEPS Project bring about uncertainties and inconsistencies. Most notably, it has been argued that such amendments transposed the uncertainties regarding the application of anti-avoidance measures to the application of the permanent establishment concept. In addition to this, the research has also shown that the above changes are not consistent with the insurance regulation and the insurance value chain. Such inconsistencies are even greater in the case where the currently existing measures dealing with insurance agents come into play, particularly in the context of the UN Model. Indeed, such measures have been originally designed to deal with insurance agents and internal sales representative that do not trigger neither a fixed place of business nor a dependent agent permanent establishment in the source country. Accordingly, their application to other insurance business models can lead to unintended results.[1968]

The comparative analysis conducted in Chapter 5 revealed that there is no universal tax policy, but rather multiple national tax policies which derive from different domestic legal traditions and diverging domestic views.[1969] In their DTAs, all countries considered in the analysis maintain their taxing rights on business profits of foreign insurance companies in the presence of a permanent establishment in their territories. Even so, significant variations have been identified at domestic level. Most notably, Italy, Germany and Switzerland do not have specific permanent establishment rules for insurance companies in their domestic legislation. However, the research has shown that Switzerland does not have a specific internal provision concerning the dependent agent permanent establishment, either. Hence, under Swiss domestic law, a person cannot give rise to a permanent establishment, unless he/she carries on business through a fixed place of business attributable to a foreign enterprise. To the

1965. *See* s. 3.6 above.
1966. *See* ss. 4.2-4.10 above.
1967. *See* s. 4.11 above.
1968. *See* s. 4.11 above.
1969. *See* ss. 5.2 and 5.3 above.

contrary, it has been demonstrated that, in Australia, Belgium and Chile, domestic provisions stipulate that profits of foreign insurance companies are taxable even in the absence of a permanent establishment. As a result, such latter countries aim at preserving their taxing rights on such an income with the introduction of specific clauses in their DTAs.[1970]

The research conducted in Chapter 5 has also shown that the impact of the MLI is for now somewhat disappointing. More precisely, it has been asserted that the lack of consensus at international level, along with excessive flexibility underlying the adoption of MLI provisions other than minimum standards (most notably, Art. 12 of the MLI concerning changes to the dependent agent permanent establishment), led for the time being to unsatisfactory results. Therefore, in the future, additional fine-tuning will be needed on the consensus for the multilateralism to play a more prominent role in view of achieving international tax coordination.[1971]

Based on the findings presented in the previous chapters, Chapter 6 provided a comprehensive assessment of the existing rules and reform proposals. In doing so, it has been demonstrated that a specific provision concerning insurance ought to be considered when discussing the scope of the permanent establishment article. More precisely, it has been submitted that a specific threshold requirement in respect of the insurance business in the permanent establishment article should be admitted in the light of its specific features.[1972]

Nevertheless, this research has shown that neither the special clause regarding insurance agents enshrined in para. 114 of the OECD Model Commentary on Art. 5 nor the insurance agent provision contained in Art. 5, para. 6, of the UN Model represent appropriate thresholds. Accordingly, another threshold for taxing insurance companies engaged in the marketing, promotion and distribution of insurance products in countries other than that of establishment would need to be specifically devised.[1973]

It has also been submitted that the identification of KERT functions within the framework of a functional and factual analysis carried out in the context of the AOA cannot be held to have a reverse relationship with Art. 5 of the model treaties in such a way as to potentially affect the currently existing standards for determining the existence of a dependent agent permanent establishment. As a result, the idea of connecting the identification of KERT functions to the taxable presence of foreign insurance companies in the source country does not represent an appropriate solution to devise a new threshold requirement specifically designed for the insurance business.[1974]

On the other hand, the author attempted to demonstrate that the alignment between tax and regulatory concepts is suitable, desirable and in line with normative requirements to be considered when drafting thresholds for taxing business income of non-residents.[1975] For this reason, the author proposed a (partial) redefinition of the

1970. *See* s. 5.4 above.
1971. *See* s. 5.4 above.
1972. *See* s. 6.2 above.
1973. *See* s. 6.3 above.
1974. *See* s. 6.4 above.
1975. *See* s. 6.5 above.

current concept of dependent agent permanent establishment contained in the main model treaties through the introduction of a new paragraph (that has been referred to as "*insurance regulatory permanent establishment*") intended to make it correlated to the definition of establishment adopted for regulatory purposes.[1976]

Finally, the analysis conducted in Chapter 6 has also revealed that a withholding tax on insurance premiums (even in combination with some corrective mechanisms) would bring about significant equity, efficiency and practicability issues. Accordingly, its introduction in the main model treaties does not seem advisable.[1977]

7.2 OPPORTUNITIES FOR FUTURE RESEARCH

The scope of the present research was limited to the concept of permanent establishment in the context of the insurance business. There are clearly additional topics connected to this concept, which have been only briefly touched upon due to time and space constraints. Such topics would deserve specific attention and might be the subject matter of future research.

Most interestingly, additional research could be conducted with respect to the attribution of profits to the insurance regulatory permanent establishment. Indeed, the question as to whether the currently existing OECD guidance could be consistently applied in this context would need to be analyzed more in depth. In a similar vein, additional research could be carried out with respect to the attribution of profits in the context of the UN Model, which does not incorporate the AOA, but rather the limited force of attraction principle. Future research could finally expand the analysis regarding the alignment between tax and regulatory concepts and therefore include other industries in the financial services sector that are subject to equally stringent regulatory constraints, like banking and global trading.

1976. *See* s. 6.6.1 above.
1977. *See* s. 6.6.2 above.

Bibliography

Accenture, *Coming to Terms with Insurance Aggregators: Global lessons for carriers*, available online at www.accenture.com.

Accenture, *The Digital Insurer—Unleashing the Potential of Social Media in Insurance*, available online at www.accenture.com.

Fabrizio Acerbis/Francesco Nuzzolo, "Italy" in: Ekkehart Reimer/Stephan Schmid/Marianne Orell (eds.) *Permanent Establishments: A Domestic Taxation, Bilateral Tax Treaty and OECD Perspective* (Alphen aan den Rijn: Kluwer Law International, 2016).

AIG, *Why Go Multinational with AIG?*, available online at www.aig.com.

Peter Aigner/Beat Jung/Gotthard Steinmann, *Kommentar zum Gesetz über die direkte Bundessteuer* (Zürich: Schulthess, 1995).

Aftab Alam/Mairaj Salim/Hassan Shah, "The Potential of E-Commerce in the Insurance Industry: The Road Ahead," *Global Journal of Enterprise Information System* (2009).

Matthijs Alink/Victor van Kommer, *Handbook on Tax Administration* (Amsterdam: IBFD, 2016).

Franklin Allen/Anthony M. Santomero, "The theory of financial intermediation," *Journal of Banking & Finance* (1998).

Franklin Allen/Anthony M. Santomero, "What do financial intermediaries do?," *Journal of Banking & Finance* (2001).

Marco Allena, "The Web Tax and Taxation of the Sharing Economy: Challenges for Italy," *European Taxation* (2017).

Krister Andersson, "Taxation of the Digital Economy," *Intertax* (2017).

Krister Andersson, "Should We Use Value Creation or Destination as a Basis for Taxing Digital Businesses?—Krister Andersson's Comments on the 2018 Klaus Vogel Lecture Given by Professor Michael Devereux," *Bulletin for International Taxation* (2018).

Joseph L. Andrus/Richard Collier, "OECD Discussion Draft: additional guidance on the attribution of profits to permanent establishments', *British Tax Review* (2017).

Massimo Antonini/Maria Letizia Mariella, "Stabile Organizzazione: la parola ad Assonime," *Corriere Tributario* (2018).

Aon Plc, *Client Engagement and Compensation Guide (2014)*, available online at www.aon.com.

Michele Aprile/Michele Lenotti, "Aspetti tributari della vendita on-line di prodotti assicurativi: la libertà di prestazione di servizi ed il concetto di stabile organizzazione," *CERAP—Università Bocconi, Working Paper n. 24* (2002).

Brian J. Arnold, "Threshold Requirements for Taxing Business Profits under Tax Treaties" in: Brian J. Arnold/Jacques Sasseville/Eric M. Zolt (eds.) *The Taxation of Business Profits Under Tax Treaties* (Toronto: Canadian Tax Foundation, 2003).

Brian J. Arnold, "Threshold Requirements for Taxing Business Profits under Tax Treaties," *Bulletin for International Taxation* (2003).

Brian J. Arnold, "Time Thresholds in Tax Treaties," *Bulletin for International Taxation* (2008).

Brian J. Arnold, "Tax Treaty News," *Bulletin for International Taxation* (2010).

Brian J. Arnold, "The Taxation of Income from Services under Tax Treaties: Cleaning Up the Mess," *Bulletin for International Taxation* (2011).

Brian J. Arnold, "The Taxation of Income from Services," *Papers on Selected Topics in Protecting the Tax Base of Developing Countries, Draft Paper No. 2*, May 2013, available online at www.un.org.

Brian J. Arnold, "The UN Committee of Experts and the UN Model: Recent Developments," *Bulletin for International Taxation* (2017).

Joan C. Arnold, "United States" in: IFA (ed.) *Is there a permanent establishment?*, Cahiers de droit fiscal international, Volume 94a (The Hague: Sdu Uitgevers, 2009).

Assonime (*Associazione fra le Società Italiane per Azioni*) June 27, 2018, Circular Letter No. 15/2018.

Peter Athanas, "Die Betriebsstätte bzw die feste Einrichtung" in: Höhn Ernst (ed.) *Handbuch des Internationalen Steuerrechts der Schweiz 2. Auflage* (Bern: Paul Haupt, 1993).

John F. Avery Jones, "The Origins of Articles 5(5) and 5(6) of the Model" in: Michael Lang/Pasquale Pistone/Josef Schuch/Claus Staringer/Alfred Storck (eds.) *Dependent Agents as Permanent Establishments* (Vienna: Linde, 2014).

John F. Avery Jones/Luc De Broe/Maarten J. Ellis/Kees van Raad/Jean-Pierre Le Gall/Sanford H. Goldberg/Jürgen Killius/Guglielmo Maisto/Toshio Miyatake/Henri Torrione/Richard J. Vann/David A. Ward/Bertil Wiman, "The Origins of Concepts and Expressions Used in the OECD Model and Their Adoption by States," *Bulletin for International Taxation* (2006).

John F. Avery Jones/Jürgen Lüdicke, "The Origins of Article 5(5) and 5(6) of the OECD Model," *World Tax Journal* (2014).

John F. Avery Jones/David A. Ward, "Agents as Permanent Establishments under the OECD Model Tax Conventions," *European Taxation* (1993).

Reuven S. Avi-Yonah, *International Tax as International Law—An Analysis of the International Tax Regime* (Cambridge: Cambridge University Press, 2007).

Reuven S. Avi-Yonah, "Between Formulary Apportionment and the OECD Guidelines: A Proposal for Reconciliation," *World Tax Journal* (2010).

Reuven S. Avi-Yonah/Oz Halabi, "A Model Treaty for the Age of BEPS," *University of Michigan—Law & Economics Research Paper Series* (2014).

Reuven S. Avi-Yonah/Martin B. Tittle, "The New United States Model Income Tax Convention," *Bulletin for International Taxation* (2007).

Diego Avolio, "La stabile organizzazione: profili definitori" in: Sigfried Mayr/Benedetto Santacroce (eds.) *La stabile organizzazione delle imprese delle imprese industriali e commerciali* (Milano: Ipsoa, 2013).

Diego Avolio, "Esterovestizione e stabile organizzazione sotto la lente della Guardia di Finanza," *Il Fisco* (2018).

Diego Avolio, "La nuova definizione di stabile organizzazione," *Corriere Tributario* (2018).

Diego Avolio/Paolo Ruggiero, "Le proposte di modifica al Commentario OCSE sulla stabile organizzazione," *Corriere Tributario* (2012).

Diego Avolio/Benedetto Santacroce, "Per la stabile organizzazione basta l'affidamento degli affari," *Corriere Tributario* (2012).

Diego Avolio/Benedetto Santacroce, "La stabile organizzazione e l''Action 7' dell'OCSE: la figura del commissionario," *Corriere Tributario* (2015).

Diego Avolio/Benedetto Santacroce, "Stabile organizzazione e final report dell'OCSE: cosa cambia per i modelli distributivi delle imprese," *Il Fisco* (2016).

Federico Azzarri, "La conclusione di contratti telematici nel diritto privato europeo," *I Contratti* (2010).

Andrés Báez Moreno, "The Taxation of Technical Services under the United Nations Model Double Taxation Convention: A Rushed—Yet Appropriate—Proposal for (Developing) Countries?," *World Tax Journal* (2015).

Andrés Báez Moreno/Yariv Brauner, "Withholding Taxes in the Service of BEPS Action 1: Address the Tax Challenges of the Digital Economy," *IBFD White Paper* (2015).

Roberto Baggio/Ermanno Basso, "La stabile organizzazione delle imprese di assicurazione (con particolare riguardo alla convenzione italo-francese del 1958)," *Rivista di Diritto Tributario* (1996).

Annabelle Bailleul-Mirabaud/Céline Pasquier, "Digital Cases Illustrate Narrow French PE Interpretation," *Tax Notes International* (2018).

Bain & Company Inc., *Global Digital Insurance Benchmarking Report 2015—Pathways to success in a digital world*, available online at www.bain.com.

Eduardo Baistrocchi, "The Transfer Pricing Problem: A Global Proposal for Simplification," *Tax Lawyer* (2006).

Philip Baker/Ernst Czakert/Arie van Eijsden/María Amparo Grau Ruiz/Liselott Kana, "International Assistance in the Collection of Taxes," *Bulletin for International Taxation* (2011).

Alexandra Bal, "The Spanish Dell Case—Do We Need Anti-BEPS Measures If the Existing Rules Are Broad Enough?," *European Taxation* (2016).

Séverine Baranger/Lars A. Henie/Mónica Sada Garibay/Ignacio Gordillo/Michele Gusmeroli, "The 2012 Leiden Alumni Seminar: Case Law on Treaty Interpretation Re Commissionaire and Agency PEs," *European Taxation* (2013).

Marco Bargagli, "Elementi sintomatici della stabile organizzazione occulta," *Fiscalità & Commercio Internazionale* (2019).

Marco Bargagli/Ciro Cesarano, "Attività assicurativa in regime di libera prestazione di servizi: profili giuridici e fattuali per una stabile organizaazione," *Fiscalità e Commercio Internazionale* (2017).

Farkas Barsony, "The Agency Permanent Establishment" in: Michael Lang/Hans Jörgen Aigner/Mario Züger (eds.) *Permanent Establishments in International Tax Law* (Vienna: Linde, 2003).

Sayan Basak, 'Equalization Levy: A New Perspective of E-Commerce Taxation', *Intertax* (2016).

Jürgen Basedow/John Birds/Malcolm Clarke/Herman Cousy/Helmut Heiss, *Principles of European Insurance Contract Law (PEICL)* (Munich: Sellier. European Law Publishers, 2009).

Juan Angel Becerra, *Interpretation and Application of Tax Treaties in North America*, 2nd edn. (Amsterdam: IBFD, 2013).

Johannes Becker/Joachim Englisch, "EU Digital Services Tax: A Populist and Flawed Proposal," *International Tax Blog* (2018).

Johannes Becker/Joachim Englisch, "Taxing Where Value Is Created: What's 'User Involvement' Got to Do with It?," *Intertax* (2019).

Lorenzo Bellavite/Paolo Sella, "La stabile organizzazione personale dopo il Beps: ancora incertezze sulla definizione di 'agente'," *La Circolare Tributaria* (2016).

Julie Bellemare, "Evolution of the Permanent Establishment Concept," *Canadian Tax Journal* (2017).

Andrea Bellucci, *Le imprese di assicurazione. Profili gestionali, organizzativi e contabili* (Torino: Giappichelli, 2004).

Andrea Bellucci, *Strategia, gestione del rischio e creazione di valore nelle imprese assicurative* (Torino: Giappichelli, 2014).

Carlo Belluzzi, *Agenti brokers e altri ausiliari di assicurazione* (Milano: Sicurtà Libri, 1976).

Stefan Bendlinger, *Die Betriebsstätte in der Praxis des internationalen Steuerrechts* (Vienna: LexisNexis, 2016).

Stefan Bendlinger, "Die „neue" Vertreterbetriebsstätte," *Internationales Steuerrecht* (2016).

Stefan Bendlinger, "Multilaterales Instrument zur automatischen Anpassung bestehender Doppelbesteuerungsabkommen," *Steuer und Wirtschaft International* (2017).

Stefan Bendlinger, "Art. 5" in: Aigner/Georg Kofler/Michael Tumpel (eds.) *DBA—Doppelbesteuerungsabkommen* (Vienna: Linde, 2019).

Stefan Bendlinger/Sabine Kanduth-Kristen/Georg Kofler/Florian Rosenberger, *Internationales Steuerrecht* (Vienna: LexisNexis, 2019).

Gilles Benoist, "Bancassurance: The New Challenges," *The Geneva Papers on Risk and Insurance* (2002).

Giorgio Beretta, "The European Agenda for the Collaborative Economy and Taxation," *European Taxation* (2016).

Giorgio Beretta, "The Taxation of the 'Sharing Economy'," *Bulletin for International Taxation* (2016).

Roberto Bernales, "The Authorized OECD Approach: An Overview" in: Carlos Gutiérrez/Andreas Perdelwitz (eds.) *Taxation of Business Profits in the 21st Century—Selected Issues under Tax Treaties* (Amsterdam: IBFD, 2013).

Paul Bierly, "General Principles of Insurance," in: Oregon State Bar (ed.) *Insurance Law: The Basics* (Tigard: Oregon State Bar, 2011).

Richard M. Bird, "Administrative Dimensions of Tax Reform," *Asia-Pacific Tax Bulletin* (2004) p. 142.

Joachim M. Bjerke/Simen S. Søgaard, "Dell Wins Important Agency Permanent Establishment Case," *International Transfer Pricing Journal* (2012).

Martin Blesgen, "Permanent Establishments of Insurance Companies" in: Michael Lang/Hans Jörgen Aigner/Mario Züger (eds.) *Permanent Establishments in International Tax Law* (Vienna: Linde, 2003).

Peter H. Blessing, "Preventing the Artificial Avoidance of PE Status" in: Robert Danon (ed.) *Base Erosion and Profit Shifting (BEPS)—Impact for European and international tax policy* (Zürich: Schulthess, 2016).

Daniel W. Blum, "Permanent Establishments and Action 1 on the Digital Economy of the OECD Base Erosion and Profit Shifting Initiative—The Nexus Criterion Redefined?," *Bulletin for International Taxation* (2015).

Daniel W. Blum, "The Relationship between the OECD Multilateral Instrument and Covered Tax Agreements: Multilateralism and the Interpretation of the MLI," *Bulletin for International Taxation* (2018).

BNA, "OECD Releases Draft Guidance on Allocating Profits to Insurance Pes, Affiliates," *BNA Tax Management Transfer Pricing Report* (2005).

Piero Bonarelli, "TP: il Discussion Draft BEPS sull'applicazione del principio di libera concorrenza alle transazioni finanziarie," *Fiscalità & Commercio Internazionale* (2018).

Luca Bonfanti, "L'Additional Guidance dell'OCSE per l'attribuzione del reddito alla stabile organizzazione," *Fiscalità & Commercio Internazionale* (2018).

Claudia Bortolani, "I canali alternativi di distribuzione dei prodotti assicurativi" in: Marco Prosperetti/Alessandro Colavolpe (eds.) *I gestori del risparmio non bancari e i canali di distribuzione* (Milano: Ipsoa, 2012).

Luca Bosco/Salvatore Sanna, "La nozione di stabile organizzazione nell'imposizione diretta: il BEPS Action 7 e la Raccomandazione 2016/136," *La gestione straordinaria delle imprese* (2016).

Bought by Many, *Terms of Website Use*, available online at https://boughtbymany.com.

Yariv Brauner, "BEPS: An Interim Evaluation," *World Tax Journal* (2014).

Yariv Brauner/Pasquale Pistone, "Adapting Current International Taxation to New Business Models: Two Proposals for the European Union," *Bulletin for International Taxation* (2017).

Nathalie Bravo, "Future Changes to Covered Tax Agreements and of the Multilateral Convention to Implement Tax Treaty-Related Measures to Prevent BEPS" in: Michael Lang/Pasquale Pistone/Alexander Rust/Josef Schuch/Claus Staringer (eds.) *The OECD Multilateral Instrument for Tax Treaties* (Alphen aan den Rijn: Wolters Kluwer, 2018).

Fred B. Brown, "An Equity-Based, Multilateral Approach for Sourcing Income Among Nations," *Florida Tax Review* (2011).

Vincent Brulhart, *Droit des assurances privées* (Bern: Stämpfli Editions SA, 2008).

Peter Brülisauer, "Switzerland" in: IFA (ed.) *The attribution of profits to permanent establishments*, Cahiers de droit fiscal international, Vol. 91b (The Hague: Sdu Uitgevers, 2006).

Fabio Brunelli/Sabrina Tronci, "La nuova definizione di stabile organizzazione personale e la disciplina del transfer pricing nell'ambito dei gruppi," *Bollettino Tributario* (2018).

Randy Buchanan/Carol Tello/Ben Jones/Amanda Cooper/Robert Christoffel/Hyowon Lee/Kunal Nathwani, "OECD Consults on Taxing the Digitalized Economy," *Tax Management Transfer Pricing Report* (2019).

Francesco Bungaro, "Italy" in: IFA (ed.) *Assessing BEPS: origins, standards, and responses*, Cahiers de droit fiscal international, Vol. 102a (The Hague: Sdu Uitgevers, 2017).

Marianne Burge/Solomon Packer, "New US Model Income Tax Treaty," *Intertax* (1982).

Irene J.J. Burgers, *OECD—Commentary on Article 7 of the OECD Model*, last reviewed: March 1, 2019, available online at www.ibfd.org.

William L. Burke, "Report on Proposed United States Model Income Tax Treaty," *Harvard International Law Journal* (1983).

Natassia Burkhalter, "Switzerland" in: IFA (ed.) *Assessing BEPS: origins, standards, and responses*, Cahiers de droit fiscal international, Vol. 102a (The Hague: Sdu Uitgevers, 2017).

Julian Burling, *Lloyd's: Law and Practice* (Abingdon: Informa Law from Routledge, 2013).

Andrés Bustos, *Chile—Corporate Taxation—Country Analyses*, last reviewed: April 1, 2019, available online at www.ibfd.org.

Michael Butler, *Australia—Permanent Establishments—Topical Analyses*, last reviewed: April 11, 2019, available online at www.ibfd.org.

Claudio Cacciamani, *L'agente di assicurazioni* (Milano: Egea, 2005).

Rui Camacho Palma, "The Paradox of Gross Taxation at Source," *Intertax* (2010).

Colin Campbell/Terry McDowell, 'Canada' in: IFA (ed.) *Is there a permanent establishment?*, Cahiers de droit fiscal international, Vol. 94a (The Hague: Sdu Uitgevers, 2009).

Capgemini, *Trends in Insurance Channels*, available online at www.capgemini.com.

Capgemini, *World Insurance Report 2016*, available online at www.capgemini.com.

Massimo Caratelli, "The Bancassurance Market in Europe" in: Franco Fiordelisi/Ornella Ricci (eds.) *Bancassurance in Europe—Past, Present and Future* (London: Palgrave Macmillan, 2012).

Alessandro Caridi, "Proposed Changes to the OECD Commentary on Article 5: Part II—The Constructive PE Notion, the Negative List and the Agency PE Notion," *European Taxation* (2003).

Paul Carman, "Comparison of the Proposed Changes to the OECD and US Model Conventions," *Derivatives & Financial Instruments* (2015).

Néstor Carmona Fernández, "The Concept of Permanent Establishment in the Courts: Operating Structures Utilizing Commission Subsidiaries," *Bulletin for International Taxation* (2013).

Loredana Carpentieri/Raffaello Lupi/Dario Stevanato, *Il diritto tributario nei rapporti internationali* (Milano: Il Sole 24 Ore, 2003).

Luciano Casali, *L'agente e il broker di assicurazione* (Milano: Giuffrè, 1993).

Patrick Cauwenbergh/André Claes, "Belgium" in: IFA (ed.) *Is there a permanent establishment?*, Cahiers de droit fiscal international, Vol. 94a (The Hague: Sdu Uitgevers, 2009).

Luzius U. Cavelti/Christian Jaag/Tobias F. Rohner, "Why Corporate Taxation Should Mean Source Taxation: A Response to the OECD's Actions against Base Erosion and Profit Shifting," *World Tax Journal* (2017).

Diana Cerini, "Note in tema di esercizio dell'attività assicurativa in regime di libertà di prestazione di servizi e in regime di stabilimento," *Diritto ed Economia dell'Assicurazione* (1999).

Diana Cerini, *Prodotti e servizi assicurativi—Distribuzione e intermediazione* (Milano: Giuffrè, 2003).

Marco Cerrato, "La definizione di stabile organizzazione nelle convenzioni per evitare le doppie imposizioni" in: Claudio Sacchetto/Lauro Alemanno (eds.) *Materiali di Diritto Tributario Internazionale* (Milano: IPSOA, 2002).

Vikram Chand, "Transfer pricing aspects of captive insurance arrangements: Recommendation to the OECD," *IFF Forum für Steuerrecht* (2017).

Vikram Chand/Karin Otto, "Transfer Pricing: Accurate Delineation of the Captive Insurance Arrangement—Is the OECD Guidance Clear on this Matter?," *Kluwer International Tax Blog* (2018).

Chang Hee Lee/Ji-Hyun Yoon, "General Report" in: IFA (ed.) *Withholding tax in the era of BEPS, CIVs and digital economy*, Cahiers de droit fiscal international, Vol. 103b (The Hague: Sdu Uitgevers, 2018).

Stanley D. Chapman, "A History of Insurance Broking" in: Roderick Clews (ed.) *A Textbook of Insurance Broking* (Cambridge: Woodhead-Faulkner, 1980).

Allison Christians/Alexander Ezenagu, "Kill-Switches in the U.S. Model Tax Treaty," *Brooklyn Journal of International Law* (2015).

Luigi Cicchitti, *Il broker di assicurazione e di riassicurazione—Diritti e doveri—Quid facti, quid iuris* (Milano: Giuffrè, 2005).

Consuelo Cinquanta, *Assicurazioni—Chi può distribuirle* (Genova: Casalini, 2001).

Ivana Clemente, *Bancassicurazione—L'evoluzione del rischio nei contratti "para-assicurativi"* (Roma: Aracne, 2006).

Roderick Clews, "Insurance Brokers at Lloyd's" in: Roderick Clews (ed.) *A Textbook of Insurance Broking* (Cambridge: Woodhead-Faulkner, 1980).

Emilia Clipici/Catalina Bolovan, "Bancassurance—Main Insurance Distribution and Sale Channel in Europe," *Scientific Bulletin—Economic Sciences—University of Piteşti* (2012).

Richard Collier, "BEPS Action Plan, Action 7: Preventing the Artificial Avoidance of PE Status," *British Tax Review* (2013).

Richard Collier, "Revised BEPS PE Proposals: Indeterminate Agents, Principals, and Principles," *Tax Notes International* (2015a).

Richard Collier, "More Guidance Needed on PE Threshold Issues," *Tax Notes International* (2015b).

Richard Collier/Nadine Riedel, "The OECD/G20 Base Erosion and Profit Shifting Initiative and Developing Countries," *Bulletin for International Taxation* (2018).

Richard Collier/Sanjay Tolia/Prashant Bohra, "The Agency PE Conundrum," *Tax Management Transfer Pricing Report* (2007).

Richard Collier/John Vella, "Five Core Problems in the Attribution of Profits to Permanent Establishments," *World Tax Journal* (2019).

Peter Collins/Hamish McElwee, "Australia" in: Ekkehart Reimer/Stephan Schmid/Marianne Orell (eds.) *Permanent Establishments: A Domestic Taxation, Bilateral Tax Treaty and OECD Perspective* (Alphen aan den Rijn: Kluwer Law International, 2016).

Giuseppe Corasaniti/Paolo De' Capitani di Vimercate/Victor Uckmar/Caterina Corrado Oliva, *Diritto tributario internazionale—Manuale—Seconda Edizione* (Padova: CEDAM, 2012).

Luisa Corso/Gianluca Odetto, "La nuova nozione di stabile organizzazione" in: *Quaderni Eutekne 2017—Le novità della Legge di bilancio 2018 e del DL collegato* (Torino: Eutekne, 2017).

Antonio Coviello, *L'utilizzo delle tecnologie avanzate nel settore assicurativo: l'e-insurance*, (Torino: Giappichelli, 2009).

Giovanni Cucinotta/Laura Neri, *Le Assicurazioni* (Bologna: Il Mulino, 2005).

J. David Cummins/Neil A. Doherty, "The Economics of Insurance Intermediaries," *Wharton School, University of Pennsylvania* (2005), available online at http://www.insurancejournal.com/downloads/WhartonStudy_2005.05.20.pdf.

Kevin Cunningham, "The Post-BEPS World of Permanent Establishment," *Tax Notes International* (2016).

Robert Danon/Christoph Schelling, "Switzerland in a Post-BEPS World," *Bulletin for International Taxation* (2015).

Oliver Davidson, "United Kingdom" in IFA (ed.) *Cross-border outsourcing—issues, strategies and solutions*, Cahiers de droit fiscal international, Vol. 99a (The Hague: Sdu Uitgevers, 2014).

Ian Hay Davison, *Lloyd's—A View of the Room—Change and Disclosure* (London: Weidenfeld and Nicolson, 1987).

Katharina Daxkobler, "Authority to Conclude Contracts in the Name of the Enterprise" in: Michael Lang/Pasquale Pistone/Josef Schuch/Claus Staringer/Alfred Storck (eds.) *Dependent Agents as Permanent Establishments* (Vienna: Linde, 2014).

Filip Debelva, "Fairness and International Taxation: Star-Crossed Lovers?," *World Tax Journal* (2018).

Luc De Broe, "Belgium's Tax Treaty Policy and the Draft Belgian Model Convention," *Bulletin for International Taxation* (2008).

Luc De Broe/Denis Van Bortel, "Grensoverschrijdende activiteiten van verzekeringsondernemingen d.m.v. agenten en de verdeling van heffingsbevoegdheid onder debbelbelastingverdragen" in: Caroline Van Schoubroeck/Wouter Devroe/Koen Geens/Jules Stuick (eds.) *Over Grenzen—Liber amicorum Herman Cousy* (Antwerpen—Cambridge: Intersentia, 2011).

Jan de Goede, "The Treatment of Services in Tax Treaties," *IBFD White Paper* (2013).

Abelardo Delgado Pacheco, "Spanish Supreme Court anticipates the effects of the BEPS Project," *International Tax Review* (2017).

Deloitte, *Insurance disrupted—General insurance in a connected world*, available online at www.deloitte.com.

Luca De Muri, "Gli aspetti legali e contrattuali del commercio elettronico," *Le guide—Il Fisco—Commercio Elettronico* (2014).

Lieven Denys, "Belgium: The Concept of Permanent Establishment Revised and Other Reflections Beyond," *Bulletin for International Taxation* (2008).

Jacques Deschamps, *L'Agent Général d'Assurances* (Paris: Litec Droit, 1975).

Michael P. Devereux/John Vella, "Implications of digitalization for international corporate tax reform," *Oxford University Centre for Business Taxation—Working paper series* (2017).

Daniel de Vries Reilingh, "The Concept of Permanent Establishment: A Comparative Analysis of Tax Treaty and Swiss Domestic Tax Law," *Intertax* (2010).

Daniel de Vries Reilingh, *Le droit fiscal intercantonal et le droit fiscal international de la Suisse* (Geneva: Schulthess, 2011).

Maarten F. de Wilde, *Sharing the Pie: Taxing Multinationals in a Global Market* (Amsterdam: IBFD, 2016).

Vishesh Dhuldhoya, "The Future of the Permanent Establishment Concept," *Bulletin for International Taxation* (2018).

Covadonga Diaz Llavona, "Banks In The Insurance Distribution Business—Controversial Issues of the Spanish Regulation And Reference To The Corresponding Provisions In The German Legal System," *Munich Risk and Insurance Center—Working Paper 12* (2012).

Antonello Di Mascio, *Le imprese di assicurazione: il nuovo modello di gestione* (Milano: Egea, 2001).

Michael Dirkis, "Ripe for Reform: Australia's Domestic Source Rules," *Bulletin for International Taxation* (2007).

Irina Dmitrieva, "Tax Treaty Disputes in Russia" in: Eduardo Baistrocchi (ed.) *A Global Analysis of Tax Treaty Disputes* (Cambridge: Cambridge University Press, 2017).

Richard L. Doernberg, *International Taxation in a nutshell*, 9th edn. (St. Paul, MN: West Academic Publishing, 2012).

Richard L. Doernberg/Luc Hinnekens, *Electronic Commerce and International Taxation* (The Hague: Kluwer Law International, 1999).

Richard L. Doernberg/Luc Hinnekens/Walter Hellerstein/Li Jinyan, *Electronic Commerce and Multijurisdictional Taxation* (The Hague: Kluwer Law International, 2001).

Anna Dokuchayeva/Berwin Cohen, "The History and Taxation of Offshore Reinsurance Companies," *Tax Management International Journal* (2016).

Antigono Donati, *Trattato del diritto delle assicurazioni private—Volume 1* (Milano: Giuffrè, 1952).

Antigono Donati/Giovanna Volpe Putzolu, *Manuale di Diritto delle Assicurazioni—Ottava Edizione Aggiornata* (Milano: Giuffrè, 2006).

Antigono Donati/Giovanna Volpe Putzolu, *Manuale di Diritto delle Assicurazioni—Nona Edizione Aggiornata* (Milano: Giuffrè, 2009).

António Carlos dos Santos/Cidália Mota Lopes, "Tax Sovereignty, Tax Competition and the Base Erosion and Profit Shifting Concept of Permanent Establishment," *EC Tax Review* (2016).

Ana P. Dourado/Kamilla Zembala, "Article 27.—Assistance in the Collection of Taxes" in: Ekkehart Reimer/Alexander Rust (eds.) *Klaus Vogel on Double Taxation Convention*, 4th edn. (Alphen aan den Rijn: Kluwer Law International, 2015).

Pierre-Jean Douvier/Xenia Lordkipanidze, "Zimmer Case: The Issue of the Deemed Existence of a Permanent Establishment Based on Status as a Commissionaire," *International Transfer Pricing Journal* (2010).

Alessandro Dragonetti/Valerio Piacentini/Anna Sfondrini, *Manuale di fiscalità internazionale* (Milano: IPSOA, 2014).

Pierre-Henri Durand/Jean-Florent Mandelbaum, "The 'French Touch': Determining a PE Using The Dependent Agent Criterion," *Tax Notes International* (2011).

Petra Eckl, "Germany" in: IFA (ed.) *Is there a permanent establishment?*, Cahiers de droit fiscal international, Vol. 94a (The Hague: Sdu Uitgevers, 2009).

Christian Ehlermann/Marta Castelon, "Wann handelt ein abhängiger Vertreter 'gewöhnlich'?—Eine Betrachtung aus der deutschen und internationalen Steuerrechtsperspektive," *Internationale Steuer-Rundschau* (2016).

Christian Ehlermann/Marta Castelon, "When Does a Dependent Agent Act Habitually?," *Tax Notes International* (2016).

Justus Eisenbeiss, "BEPS Action 7: Evaluation the Agency Permanent Establishment," *Intertax* (2016).

W. Elkington, "Bancassurance," *Chartered Building Societies Institutions Journal* (1993).

Craig Elliffe, "The Meaning of 'Permanent Establishment' in Article 5 of Double Tax Conventions," *New Zealand Journal of Taxation Law and Policy* (2010).

Craig Elliffe, "Canadian Tax Court on the Meaning of 'Permanent Establishment' in Treaties," *Journal of International Taxation* (2011).

William P. Elliott, "Captive Insurance Arrangements—A Comprehensive Update," *Tax Notes International* (2004).

William P. Elliott, "A Guide to Captive Insurance Companies (Part 1)," *Journal of International Taxation* (2005).

Christine Ennew/Nigel Waite, *Financial Services Marketing: An International Guide to Principles and Practice*, 2nd edn. (Abingdon: Routledge, 2013).

Festus Epetimehin, "Market Segmentation as a Strategy for Goal Attainment in the Insurance Industry," *SSRN Electronic Journal* (2011).

Eva Escribano López, "An Opportunistic, and yet Appropriate, Revision of the Source Threshold for the Twenty-First Century Tax Treaties," *Intertax* (2015).

Europe Economics, *Distribution Channels in Insurance*, available online at https://www.europe-economics.com.

Expert Group on European Insurance Contract Law, *Meeting of 15-16 May 2013—Discussion Paper 2: Differences in Insurance Contract Laws and the Existing EU Legal Framework*, available online at web.actuaries.ie.

EY, *Global insurance trends analysis 2018*, available online at www.ey.com.

EY, *Vision 2025: brokers driving customer-centric growth*, available online at www.ey.com.

Isabella Falautano/Emanuele Marsiglia, "Integrated Distribution of Insurance and Financial Services and Value Creation: Challenges Ahead," *The Geneva Papers on Risk and Insurance* (2003).

Tatiana Falcao/Bob Michel, "Assessing the Tax Challenges of the Digital Economy: An Eye-Opening Case Study," *Intertax* (2014).

Luigi Farenga, *Diritto delle Assicurazioni Private* (Torino: Giappichelli, 2001).

Luigi Farenga, *Manuale di Diritto delle Assicurazioni Private* (Torino: Giappichelli, 2016).

Charles Farley Trenerry, *The Origin and Early History of Insurance: Including the Contract of Bottomry* (London, The Lawbook Exchange, Ltd., 1926).

Linda Favi, "Italy" in: IFA (ed.) *Is there a permanent establishment?*, Cahiers de droit fiscal international, Vol. 94a (The Hague: Sdu Uitgevers, 2009).

Daniel Fehling/Karoline Kampermann, "Germany" in: IFA (ed.) *Assessing BEPS: origins, standards, and responses*, Cahiers de droit fiscal international, Vol. 102a (The Hague: Sdu Uitgevers, 2017).

Leonardo Felician, *La catena del valore nelle imprese di assicurazione* (Trieste: Edizioni Goliardiche, 2007).

Prafula Fernandez/Gitte Heij/Jeff Pope, "Tax Policy and Electronic Commerce," *Bulletin for International Taxation* (2002).

Vincenzo Ferrari, *Nuovi profili di diritto delle assicurazioni—Il fatto assicurativo* (Milano: Giuffrè, 2003).

Bruno Ferroni, "Firmata la Convenzione Multilaterale del progetto BEPS: effetti su migliaia di trattati fiscali in tutto il mondo," *Il Fisco* (2017).

Bruno Ferroni, "Stabile organizzazione: la disciplina nazionale si adegua al BEPS e introduce la 'continuativa presenza economica'," *Il Fisco* (2018).

David Feuerstein, "The Agency Permanent Establishment" in: Michael Lang/Florian Brugger/Patrick Plansky (eds.) *Permanent Establishments in International and EU Tax Law* (Vienna: Linde, 2011).

Liesl Fichardt, "United Kingdom" in: IFA (ed.) *Is there a permanent establishment?*, Cahiers de droit fiscal international, Vol. 94a (The Hague: Sdu Uitgevers, 2009).

Franco Fiordelisi/Ornella Ricci, "Efficiency in the: Life Insurance Industry: What Are the Efficiency Gains from Bancassurance?," *EMFI WPs 2* (2010).

Alberto Floreani, *Economia delle imprese di assicurazione* (Bologna: Il Mulino, 2011).

Uwe Focht/Andreas Richter/Jörg Schiller, "Intermediation and (Mis-)Matching in Insurance Markets–Who Should Pay the Insurance Broker?," *The Journal of Risk and Insurance* (2013).

Giovanni Fort, "Attribuzione dei profitti alla stabile organizzazione personale," *Corriere Tributario* (2013).

Eva Frehner, "Die Betriebsstätte vor und nach BEPS—Definition, Gewinnaufteilung und Umsetzung," *Expert Focus* (2018).

Marco Frigessi di Rattalma, "La libertà di prestazione assicurativa nel diritto comunitario derivato," *Diritto e Pratica dell'Assicurazione* (1989).

Daniel Fuentes Hernández, "Agents of an Independent Character under Article 5(6) of the OECD Model Convention" in: Michael Lang/Pasquale Pistone/Josef Schuch/Claus Staringer/Alfred Storck (eds.) *Dependent Agents as Permanent Establishments* (Vienna: Linde, 2014).

Fundación Mapfre, *An Introduction to Reinsurance*' Institute of Insurance Science 2013, available online at www.fundacionmapfre.org.

Stjepan Gadžo, *Nexus Requirements for Taxation of Non-Residents' Business Income—A Normative Evaluation in the Context of the Global Economy* (Amsterdam: IBFD, 2018).

Noah Gaoua, "Taxation of the Digital Economy: French Reflections," *European Taxation* (2014).

Carlo Garbarino, "Permanent Establishments and BEPS Action 7: Perspectives in Evolution," *Intertax* (2019).

Carlo Garbarino/Patrizia Occhiuto, "Lo strumento multilaterale per la modifica dei trattati contro le doppie imposizioni," *Fiscalità & Commercio Internationale* (2018).

Francisco A. Garcia Prats, *El establecimiento permanente: análisis jurídico-tributario internacional de la imposición societaria* (Madrid: Tecnos, 1996).

Francisco A. Garcia Prats, "Mutual Assistance in the Collection of Tax Debts," *Intertax* (2002).

Francisco A. Garcia Prats, "Chapter 14: Impact of the Position of the BRICS on the UN Model Convention in BRICS and the Emergence of International Tax Coordination" in: Yariv Brauner/Pasquale Pistone (eds.) *BRICS and the Emergence of International Tax Coordination* (Amsterdam: IBFD, 2014).

Francisco A. Garcia Prats, "Notas sobre la Sentencia del Tribunal Supremo de 20 de junio de 2016 (Caso DELL)," *Documentos AEDAF, Sección Fiscalidad Internacional y Precios de Transferencia* (2016), available online at http://www.aedaf.es/es.

Tamara Gasparri, "Nuove regole per la sharing economy," *Il Fisco* (2016).

Christian Gaßmann/Timo Welling, "Erweiterung des Betriebsstättenbegriffs am Beispiel des jüngst geschlossenen DBA Australien," *Praxis Internationale Steuerberatung* (2017).

Generali, *Multinational Programs*, available online at www.generali.com.

Nadege Genetaya/Philip Molyneux, *Bancassurance* (London: Palgrave Macmillan, 1998).

Matthias Geurts, "Server as a permanent establishment?," *Intertax* (2000).

Emanuela Giacobbe, *Brokeraggio e tipo contrattuale* (Milano: Giuffrè, 2001).

David Eric Wilson Gibb, *Lloyd's of London—A Study in Individualism* (London: The Corporation of Lloyd's, 1972).

David Eric Wilson Gibb, *Il rischio è il nostro mestiere—Storia dei Lloyd's di Londra* (Cesano Maderno: Golden Book, 1978).

Luciano Gioberti, *Manuale dell'agente di assicurazione* (Milano: Irsa, 1995).

Luciano Gioberti, *Manuale del broker di assicurazione* (Milano: Irsa, 1998).

Giuseppe Giudici, *I canali della distribuzione assicurativa* (Milano: Franco Angeli, 2003).

Serap O. Gonulal/Nick Goulder/Rodney R. Lester, "Bancassurance—A Valuable Tool for Developing Insurance in Emerging Markets," *World Bank Policy Research Working Paper* (2012).

Maximilian Görl, "Art. 5" in Klaus Vogel/Moris Lehner (eds.) *Doppelbesteuerungsabkommen der Bundesrepublik Deutschland auf dem Gebiet der Steuern vom Einkommen und Vermögen: Kommentar auf der Grundlage der Musterabkommen* (Munich: Beck, 2015).

Isabel Gottlieb, "New Taxation Threshold 'No Golden Goose' for Countries," *BNA Tax Management Transfer Pricing Report* (2018).

Bruno Gouthière, "Zimmer: "Commissionaire" Agent Is Not a Permanent Establishment," *European Taxation* (2010).

Sriram P. Govind, "The International Tax Treatment of Cross-Border Services," *Bulletin for International Taxation* (2011).

Andreas Grahl, "Online-Banking und Bancassurance" in: Marcel Seidel/Axel Liebetrau (eds.) *Banking & Innovation 2015: Ideen und Erfolgskonzepte von Experten für die Praxis* (Wiesbaden: Springer Gabler, 2015).

Matthias Graumann/Hans-Jürgen Arnold/Nicole Beltjes, "Call Centers: A Case Study on the Interplay Between Organization and Information Technology," *The Geneva Papers on Risk and Insurance* (2003).

Stefan Greil, 'Der "Discussion Draft on Financial Transactions" der OECD', *Internationales Steuer- und Wirtschaftsrecht* (2018).

Stefano Grilli/Paolo Ruggiero, "La stabile organizzazione nella giurisprudenza interna e internazionale" in: Sigfried Mayr/Benedetto Santacroce (eds.) *La stabile organizzazione delle imprese delle imprese industriali e commerciali* (Milano: Ipsoa, 2013).

Oscar Grisales-Racini, "Offshore Captive Insurance Companies," *Tax Notes International* (2016).

Stefano Guarino, "Quando la presenza di obbligazioni a carico dell'agente non configura una stabile organizzazione?—Il commento," *Corriere Tributario* (2018).

Eugene N. Gurenko/Alexander Itigin/Renate Wiechert, *Insurance Risk Transfer and Categorization of Reinsurance Contracts*, The World Bank Finance and Private Sector Development Non-Banking Financial Institutions, December 2012, available online at http://documents.worldbank.org/curated/en/2012/12/17124490/insurance-risk-transfer-categorization-reinsurance-contracts.

Wilhelm Haarmann, "Die Vertreterbetriebsstätte und die faktische Verpflichtung (Kommissionärsmodell)" in: Christian Kaeser (ed.) *Festgabe zum 75. Geburtstag von Prof. Dr. Dr. h.c. Franz Wassermeyer* (Munich: Beck, 2015).

Wolfgang Haas, "Base Erosion and Profit Shifting ('BEPS')—Eine steuerpolitische Bewertung" in: Jens Blumenberg/Georg Crezelius/Dietmar Gosch/Matthias Schüppen (eds.) *Festschrift für Wilhelm Haarmann* (Düsseldorf: IDW, 2015).

Florian Haase, 'Zukunft des IStR: Hinzurechnungsbesteuerung und Multilaterales Instrument im Fokus', *Internationale Steuer-Rundschau* (2017).

Florian Haase, "Einführung" in: Florian Haase (ed.) *Multilaterales Instrument* (Heidelberg: Müller, 2018).

Michael Hafeman, *The Role of the Actuary in Insurance*, Primer series on insurance, Issue 4, May 2009, available online at www.worldbank.org/nbfi.

Mark A. Hall, "The Role of Independent Agents in the Success of Health Insurance Market Reforms," *The Milbank Quarterly* (2000).

David Halperin, *How to Build a Multinational Program*, available online at www.aig.com.

Georges Hamon, *Histoire générale de l'assurance en France et à l'étranger* (Paris: L'Assurance moderne, 1897).

Nils Harbeke/Noëlle Mathis, "Schweiz: Aktuelles aus der DBA-Politik bei der Umsetzung des MLI," *Internationales Steuerrecht* (2019).

Alexander Hartley, "Countries disagree on advantages of MLI 'synthesised texts'," *International Tax Review* (2018).

Werner Haslehner, "Taxing where value is created in a post-BEPS (digitalized) world?," *Kluwer International Tax Blog* (2018).

Johann Hattingh, "The Multilateral Instrument from a Legal Perspective: What May Be the Challenges?," *Bulletin for International Taxation* (2017).

Johann Hattingh, "The Impact of the BEPS Multilateral Instrument on International Tax Policies," *Bulletin for International Taxation* (2018).

Maurizio Hazan/Stefano Taurini, "Assicurazioni Private," *Itinera—Guide Giuridiche Ipsoa* (2015).

Patrick Held, *BEPS Aktionspunkt 7: Die Verhinderung der künstlichen Vermeidung einer Betriebsstätte* (Hamburg: Interdisziplinäres Zentrum für Internationales Finanz- und Steuerwesen (IIFS), 2017).

Walter Hellerstein, "Jurisdiction to Tax in the Digital Economy: Permanent and Other Establishments," *Bulletin for International Taxation* (2014).

Milva Helling, *Die Vertreterbetriebsstätte im internationalen Steuerrecht* (Hamburg: Kovać, 2009).

Joseph Hémard, *Théorie et pratique des assurances terrestres* (Paris: Contant-Laguerre, 1924).

Alexander Hemmelrath/Elke Wilcox, "Chapter 8: AOA, BEPS, E-Commerce—"Permanent Establishment" in Flux" in: Heike Jochum/Peter Essers/Michael Lang/Norbert Winkeljohann/Bertil Wiman (eds.) *Practical Problems in European and International Tax Law* (Amsterdam: IBFD, 2016).

John Henshall/Roy Donegan, "BEPS Action 7: Part II," *Transfer Pricing International Journal* (2015).

Mindy Herzfeld, "The Case Against BEPS: Lessons for Tax Coordination," *Florida Tax Review* (2017).

Johanna Hey, "'Taxation Where Value is Created' and the OECD/G20 Base Erosion and Profit Shifting Initiative," *Bulletin for International Taxation* (2018).

James I. Hilliard/Laureen Regan/Sharon Tennyson, "Insurance Distribution" in: Georges Dionne (ed.) *Handbook of Insurance* (New York: Springer Science + Business Media New York, 2013).

David J. Hindley et al., "The Lloyd's Reinsurance To Close Process," *British Actuarial Journal* (2000).

Patricia Hofmann/Nadine Riedel, "Comment on J. Becker & J. Englisch, 'Taxing Where Value Is Created: What's "User Involvement" Got to Do with It?'," *Intertax* (2019).

Doug Holland, "Commissionaire Agency Permanent Establishments," *International Transfer Pricing Journal* (2011).

Kevin Holmes, *International Tax Policy and Double Tax Treaties*, 2nd Rev. edn. (Amsterdam: IBFD, 2014).

Peter Hongler/Pasquale Pistone, "IBFD Blueprints for a New PE Nexus to Tax Business Income in the Era of the Digital Economy," *IBFD White Paper* (2015).

Oliver R. Hoor, "Comments on the OECD Discussion Draft on the Meaning of 'Permanent Establishment'," *Tax Notes International* (2012).

Oliver R. Hoor/Keith O'Donnell, "BEPS Action 7: The Attempt to Artificially Create A Taxable Nexus," *Tax Notes International* (2015).

Tobias C. Hoschka, *Bancassurance in Europe* (London: St. Martin's Press, 1994).

Erica Howard/Robin Saunders, "The future of Part IV (Insurance of the OECD report on attribution of profits to PEs," *BNA Tax Management Transfer Pricing Report* (2007a).

Erica Howard/Robin Saunders, "Attribution of profits to permanent establishments—insurance update," *BNA Tax Management Transfer Pricing Report* (2007b).

Steef Huibregtse/Louan Verdoner/Igne Valutyte/René Offermanns, "Status of Implementation of the Authorized OECD Approach into Domestic Tax Law and Tax Treaties," *European Taxation* (2015).

Anthony C. Infanti, "The United States" in Guglielmo Maisto (ed.) *Tax Treaties and Domestic Law* (Amsterdam: IBFD, 2006).

Caterina Innamorato, "The Concept of a Permanent Establishment Within a Group of Multinational Enterprises," *European Taxation* (2008).

Institute of Actuaries of Australia, *Are direct channels helping life insurers and customers to address underinsurance?*, available at https://actuaries.asn.au.

International Risk Management Institute Inc., *What Is Captive Insurance?*, available online at www.captive.com.

Niels E. Jensen, "Denmark Permanent Establishment and Fiscal Representatives," *Tax Planning International* (1997).

Heinz Jirousek, "Das MLI—eine Erfolgsgeschichte?," *Steuer und Wirtschaft International* (2018).

Sunita Jogarajan, "Stamp, Seligman and the Drafting of the 1923 Experts' Report on Double Taxation," *World Tax Journal* (2013).

Guy Jorion, *Le non-résident ou la société étrangère face à l'impôt belge* (Brussels: Larcier, 2006).

Ghislain T. J. Joseph, "Electronic Commerce and the United Nations Model Double Taxation Convention," *Intertax* (2004).

Erik Kamphuis, "Significant People Functions and Functional Ownership: The New Motto in Transfer Pricing," *BNA Tax Management Transfer Pricing Report* (2008).

Erik Kamphuis, "Proposed OECD Risk Allocation Examination Process And Its Implications for Transfer Pricing Design," *BNA Tax Management Transfer Pricing Report* (2009).

Kasko Norway AS, *Are aggregators a threat to all insurance companies?*, available online at https://kasko.no.

Sony Kassam, "Order of Applying Two Tax Convention Articles is Trivial: OECD," *BNA Tax Management Transfer Pricing Report* (2018).

Andreas H. Keller/Josef Schuch/Sabine Seibold/Wilhem H. Wacker, "Der Betriebstättenbegriff im Steuerrecht Deutschlands, Österreichs und der Schweiz," *Der Schweizer Treuhänder* (1999).

Eric C.C.M. Kemmeren, "Legal and Economic Principles Support an Origin and Import Neutrality-Based over a Residence and Export Neutrality-Based Tax" in: Michael Lang/Pasquale Pistone/Josef Schuch/Claus Staringer/Alfred Storck/Martin Zagler (eds.) *Tax Treaties: Building Bridges between Law and Economics* (Amsterdam: IBFD, 2010).

Eric C.C.M. Kemmeren, "Should the Taxation of the Digital Economy Really Be Different?," *EC Tax Review* (2018).

Jacques Kistler/René Zulauf, "Switzerland: Swiss Tax Reform Proposal 17: Swiss Federal Council submits dispatch to Swiss Parliament," *International Tax Review* (2018).

Jacques Kistler/René Zulauf, "Switzerland: Swiss corporate tax reform 2017: Swiss Senate approves revised version of the reform," *International Tax Review* (2018).

Robert W. Klein, "The Insurance Industry and Its Regulation: An Overview" in: Martin F. Grace/Robert W. Klein (eds.) *The Future of Insurance Regulation in the United States* (Washington: The Brookings Institution, 2009).

Michael Kobetsky, *International Taxation of Permanent Establishments: Principles and Policy* (Cambridge: Cambridge University Press, 2011).

Georg Kofler, "Chapter 7: Article 8 OECD Model: Time for a Change?" in: Guglielmo Maisto (ed.) *Taxation of Shipping and Air Transport in Domestic Law, EU Law and Tax Treaties* (Amsterdam, IBFD, 2017).

Georg Kofler/Gunter Mayr/Christhop Schlager, "Taxation of the Digital Economy: "Quick Fixes" or Long-Term Solutions," *European Taxation* (2017).

Georg Kofler/Christian Schmidt/Madeleine Simonek, "Vertreterbetriebsstätten in Deutschland, Österreich und der Schweiz im Hinblick auf BEPS-Aktionspunkt 7," *Archiv für Schweizerisches Abgaberecht* (2016/2017).

Georg Kofler/Julia Sinnig, "Equalization Taxes and the EU's 'Digital Services Tax'," *Intertax* (2019).

Robert A. Kopstein/Jasmine Sidhu, "Be Careful What You Wish For," *Canadian Tax Journal* (2008).

Bast Kosters, "The United Nations Model Tax Convention and Its Recent Developments," *Asia-Pacific Tax Bulletin* (2004).

Gerhard Kraft/Maximilian Weiß, "Vertreterbetriebsstätte: Die geplante Reform des abkommensrechtlichen Begriffs der Vertreterbetriebsstätte und ihre Auswirkungen auf die Kommissionärsstrukturen international tätiger Konzerne," *Internationale Steuer-Rundschau* (2016).

Martin Kreienbaum, "Das Multilaterale Instrument zur Modifikation bilateraler Doppelbesteuerungsabkommen" in: Jürgen Lüdicke (ed.) *Internationale Geschäftstätigkeiten in der Nach-BEPS-Welt* (Cologne: Otto Schmidt, 2018).

Suresh Krishnan/Sheena Shah/Ronald Williams, *Structuring Multinational Insurance Programs: Cross-border Challenges to Business Travel & Personal Accident Insurance*, available online at https://www2.chubb.com.

Heinz-Klaus Kroppen, "Neues zur Betriebsstätte unter Berücksichtigung der Vorschläge der OECD vom 31.10.2014 und vom 15.5.2015" in: Jürgen Lüdicke/Rudolf Mellinghoff/Thomas Rödder (eds.) *Nationale und internationale Unternehmensbesteuerung in der Rechtsordnung: Festschrift für Dietmar Gosch zum Ausscheiden aus dem Richteramt* (Munich: Beck, 2016).

Heinz-Klaus Kroppen/Stephan Huffmeier, "The German Commissionaire as a Permanent Establishment Under the OECD Model Treaty," *Intertax* (1996).

Heinz-Klaus Kroppen/Susann van der Ham, "Die digitale Betriebsstätte: wertschöpfungsgerechte Besteuerung im Zeitalter der Digitalisierung," *Internationales Steuer- und Wirtschaftsrecht* (2018).

Des Laffey, "Value Configurations in E-Commerce: Evidence from Comparison Websites," *ECIS, 2008 Proceedings: Paper 36* (2008).

Geoff Lancaster/Lester Massingham, *Essential of Marketing Management* (Abingdon: Routledge, 2010).

Michael Lang, *Introduction to the Law of Double Taxation Conventions*, 2nd edn. (Vienna: Linde, 2013).

Michael Lang, "Die Auslegung des multilateralen Instruments," *Steuer und Wirtschaft International* (2017).

Andreas Langer, "The Legal Relevance of the Minimum Standard in the OECD/BEPS Project" in: Michael Lang/Pasquale Pistone/Alexander Rust/Josef Schuch/Claus Staringer (eds.) *The OECD Multilateral Instrument for Tax Treaties* (Alphen aan den Rijn: Wolters Kluwer, 2018).

Armando Lara Yaffar/Michael Lennard, "An Introduction to the Updated UN Model (2011)," *Bulletin for International Taxation* (2012a).

Armando Lara Yaffar/Michael Lennard, "The Future of the UN Model," *Bulletin for International Taxation* (2012b).

Antonio La Torre, *L' assicurazione nella storia delle idee. La risposta giuridica al bisogno di sicurezza economica: ieri e oggi* (Roma: Giuffrè, 1995).

Antonio La Torre, *Cinquant'anni col diritto—Diritto delle assicurazioni—Volume 2* (Milano: Giuffrè, 2008).

Alan Leach, *New Initiatives in European Bancassurance* (London: Financial Times, 1996).

Thor Leegaard, "Supreme Court Holds That Commissionaire Structure Does Not Amount to a Permanent Establishment," *European Taxation* (2012).

Lemonade, *About Lemonade*, available online at https://www.lemonade.com.

Michael Lennard, "The Purpose and Current Status of the United Nations Tax Work," *Asia-Pacific Tax Bulletin* (2008).

Michael Lennard, "The UN Model Tax Convention as Compared with the OECD Model Tax Convention—Current Points of Difference and Recent Developments," *Asia-Pacific Tax Bulletin* (2009).

Michael Lennard, "Update on the United Nations Tax Work," *Asia-Pacific Tax Bulletin* (2010).

Michael Lennard, "Update of the United Nations Model Tax Convention," *Asia-Pacific Tax Bulletin* (2012).

Michael Lennard, "Update on the United Nations Tax Committee Developments," *Asia-Pacific Tax Bulletin* (2014).

Michael Lennard, "Base Erosion and Profit Shifting and Developing Country Tax Administrations," *Intertax* (2016).

Brian D. Lepard, "Is the United States Obligated to Drive on the Right?: A Multidisciplinary Inquiry into the Normative Authority of Contemporary International Law Using the Arm's Length Standard as a Case Study," *Duke Journal of Comparative & International Law* (1999).

Rodney Lester/Oliver Reichart, *Insurance Governance and Risk Management*, Primer series on insurance, Issue 11, November 2009, available online at www.worldbank.org/nbfi.

Jinyan Li, "Protecting the Tax Base in the Digital Economy," *Papers on Selected Topics in Protecting the Tax Base of Developing Countries*, Paper No. 9—June 2014, available online at www.un.org.

Tizhong Liao, *Taxation of Cross-Border Trade in Service: A Review of the Current International Tax Landscape and the Possible Future Policy Options*, E/C.18/2013/CRP.16, available online at available online at www.un.org.

Melissa Lim, "Australia's initial approach to the OECD Multilateral Instrument," *International Tax Review* (2017).

Marisa Lipp, "Germany's Tax Treaty Negotiation Policy," *European Taxation* (2014).

Lloyd's, *About Coverholders*, available online at https://www.lloyds.com/the-market/i-am-a/delegated-authority/compliance-and-operations/about-coverholders.

Lloyd's, *About Lloyd's Brokers*, available online at https://www.lloyds.com/the-market/i-am-a/broker-agent/about-lloyds-brokers.

Lloyd's, *Binding Authority Wordings*, available online at https://www.lloyds.com/the-market/i-am-a/delegated-authority/compliance-and-operations/binding-authority-wordings.

Lloyd's, *Corporate History*, available online at https://www.lloyds.com/lloyds/about-us/history/corporate-history.

Lloyd's, *Definitions Byelaw*, available online at https://www.lloyds.com/the-market/operating-at-lloyds/regulation/acts-and-byelaws/lloyds-byelaws.

Lloyd's, *Glossary*, available online at https://www.lloyds.com/common/help/glossary.

Lloyd's, *Lloyd's Governance Structure*, available online at https://www.lloyds.com/lloyds/corporate-governance/lloyds-governance-structure.

Lloyd's, *Managing Agent's Agreement*, available online at https://www.lloyds.com/the-market/tools-and-resources/resources/lloyds-standard-agency-agreements.

Lloyd's, *Membership Byelaw*, available online at https://www.lloyds.com/the-market/operating-at-lloyds/regulation/acts-and-byelaws/lloyds-byelaws.

Lloyd's, *Non-Lloyd's Brokers—A Guide for Managing Agents*, available online at https://www.lloyds.com.

Lloyd's, *Premiums Trust Deeds*, available online at https://www.lloyds.com/the-market/operating-at-lloyds/regulation/lloyds-trust-deeds/premiums-trust-deeds.

Lloyd's, *Service Company Underwriting Agreement*, available online at https://www.lloyds.com/the-market/i-am-a/delegated-authority/compliance-and-operations/about-coverholders.

Lloyd's, *The Corporation of Lloyd's*, available online at https://www.lloyds.com/lloyds/about-us/what-is-lloyds/the-corporation-of-lloyds.

Lloyd's, *The Lloyd's Market*, available online at https://www.lloyds.com/lloyds/about-us/what-is-lloyds/the-lloyds-market.

Lloyd's, *The Members' Agent's Agreement*, available online at https://www.lloyds.com/the-market/tools-and-resources/resources/lloyds-standard-agency-agreements.

Lloyd's, *Underwriting Byelaw*, available online at https://www.lloyds.com/the-market/operating-at-lloyds/regulation/acts-and-byelaws/lloyds-byelaws.

Lloyd's, *What is Lloyd's?*, available online at https://www.lloyds.com/lloyds/about-us/what-is-lloyds.

Peter Locher, *Einführung in das internationale Steuerrecht der Schweiz* (Bern: Stämpfli Verlag AG, 2000).

Peter Locher, *Kommentar zum Bundesgesetz über die direkte Bundessteuer* (Basel: Helbing Lichtenhahn, 2001).

Kurt Locher/Walter Meier/Rudolf Von Siebenthal/Andreas Kolb, *Doppelbesteuerungsabkommen Schweiz-Deutschland 1971 und 1978* (Therwil: Verlag für Recht und Gesellschaft, 2007).

Christian Looks/Oliver Heinsen, *Betriebsstättenbesteuerung: Inboundinvestitionen, Outboundinvestitionen, Steuergestaltungen, Branchenbesonderheiten*, 3rd edn. (Munich: Beck, 2017).

Benjamin Lorent, "Risks and Regulation of Insurance Companies. Is Solvency II the Right Answer?," *Centre Emile Bernheim—CEB Working Paper N° 08/007* (2008).

John Lowry/Philip Rawlings/Robert Merkin, *Insurance Law: Doctrines and Principles*, 3rd edn. (Oxford: Hart Publishing, 2011).

Wilhelm Lührs, *A. Atermann (vorm. J. A. Castendyk) Assekuranz-Makler, 1837–1962* (Bremen: Self-Publishing, 1962).

Peter Maas, "How insurance brokers create value—a functional approach," *University of St. Gallen - Working Papers on Risk Management and Insurance* (2006).

Lionel Macedo, *The Role of Underwriter in Insurance*, Primer series on insurance, Issue 8, September 2, 2009, available online at www.worldbank.org/nbfi.

Ewing W. Madole, "Agents as Permanent Establishments under U.S. Income Tax Treaties," *Tax Management International Journal* (1994).

Sebastian Mailei/Jeremy Brown, "Permanent establishment issues arising from global insurance distribution models," *International Tax Review—Financial Services Industry Guide* (2015).

Monique T. Malan, "New Article 12A of the UN Model Regarding Fees for Technical Services: Ahead of Its Time or a Step Too Far?," *Bulletin for International Taxation* (2019).

Pierpaolo Marano/Ioannis Rokas/Peter Kochenburger, *The "Dematerialized" Insurance—Distance Selling and Cyber Risks from an International Perspective* (Cham: Springer International Publishing AG, 2016).

Adolfo J. Martin Jiménez, "Preventing the Artificial Avoidance of PE Status," *UN Papers on Selected Topics in Protecting the Tax Base of Developing Countries* (2014).

Adolfo J. Martín Jiménez, "The Spanish Position on the Concept of a Permanent Establishment: Anticipating BEPS, beyond BEPS or Simply a Wrong Interpretation of Article 5 of the OECD Model?," *Bulletin for International Taxation* (2016).

Adolfo J. Martin Jiménez, "Chapter VII—Preventing avoidance of permanent establishment status" in: Alexander Trepelkov/Harry Tonino/Dominika Halka (eds.) *United Nations Handbook on Selected Issues in Protecting the Tax Base of Developing Countries*, 2nd edn. (New York: United Nations, 2017).

Ludmilla Maurer/Christian Port/Tom Roth/John Walker, "A Brave New Post-BEPS World: New Double Tax Treaty Between Germany and Australia Implements BEPS Measures," *Intertax* (2017).

Sigfried Mayr/Giovanni Fort, "La nuova definizione di stabile organizzazione (Art. 162 del TUIR)," *Bollettino Tributario* (2018).

Andrew McGee, *The Single Market in Insurance: Breaking Down the Barriers* (Dartmouth: Ashgate, 1998).

McKinsey&Company, *Global Insurance Industry Insights: An in-depth perspective—McKinsey Global Insurance Pools—seventh edition, 2018*, available online at www.mckinsey.com.

Amar Mehta, *Permanent Establishment in International Taxation* (New Delhi: Taxmann Publications (P.) Ltd, 2012).

Vasudha J. Mehta, *CBDT's BPO Circular—Creating Confusion?*, accessible online at http://www.algindia.com/publication/article1400.pdf.

Arthur Meier-Hayoz/Peter Forstmoser/Peter Iordanov, *Droit Suisse des sociétés* (Bern: Stämpfli Editions SA, 2015).

Federigo Melis, *Origini e sviluppi delle assicurazioni in Italia (secoli XIV-XVI)* (Roma: Istituto Nazionale delle Assicurazioni, 1975).

Ignacio Melo/Juan Pablo Orellana, "Chile" in: IFA (ed.) *Is there a permanent establishment?*, Cahiers de droit fiscal international, Vol. 94a (The Hague: Sdu Uitgevers, 2009).

Robert Merkin, *Insurance Law: An Introduction* (London: Informa Law from Routledge, 2007).

Robert Merkin/Angus Rodger, *EC Insurance Law* (London: Longman, 1997).

Hans U. Meuter, "Besteuerung einer Vertreterbetriebsstätte," *Zürcher Steuerpraxis* (2012) pp. 18-19,

Alexandra Miladinovic/Alexander Rust, "Options under the Multilateral Instrument" in: Michael Lang/Pasquale Pistone/Alexander Rust/Josef Schuch/Claus Staringer (eds.) *The OECD Multilateral Instrument for Tax Treaties* (Alphen aan den Rijn: Wolters Kluwer, 2018).

Matias Milet, *Canada—Permanent Establishments—Topical Analyses*, last reviewed: March 20, 2019, available online at www.ibfd.org.

Andrew Mills/Dale Pinto, "Australia" in: IFA (ed.) *Assessing BEPS: origins, standards, and responses*, Cahiers de droit fiscal international, Vol. 102a (The Hague: Sdu Uitgevers, 2017).

Rick Mitchell/Kevin A. Bell, "More Permanent Establishments Expected Under OECD Draft," *BNA Tax Management Transfer Pricing Report* (2016).

Omar Moerer/Benchi Klaver, "The AOA, PE status and BEPS, some reassurance in a time of change?," *BNA Tax Management Transfer Pricing Report* (2015).

Paolo Molesini, "Il canale bancario per la distribuzione di prodotti assicurativi: Modelli operativi" in: Enrico Granata/Alessandro Nigro/Sergio De Angeli/Paolo Molesini/Giuseppe Godano/Luigi Desiderio (eds.) *Banca e assicurazione: aspetti giuridici ed economici* (Roma: Bancaria Editrice, 1997).

Dagmar Möller-Gosoge, "Art. 12" in: Florian Haase (ed.) *Multilaterales Instrument* (Heidelberg: Müller, 2018).

Jérôme Monsenego, "The Independent Agent Exception and Group Membership," *Intertax* (2018).

Jérôme Monsenego, "Google France as a Dependent Agent PE of Its Irish Sister Company," *Transfer Pricing International* (2018).

Ornella Moro, *L'internazionalizzazione delle imprese di assicurazione* (Milano: Egea, 1990).

Roberto Moro Visconti, "L'attività di brokeraggio riassicurativo," *Impresa Commerciale Industriale* (2001).

Susan C. Morse, "The Transfer Pricing Regs Need a Good Edit," *Pepperdine Law Review* (2013).

Susan C. Morse, "Value Creation: A Standard in Search of a Process," *Bulletin for International Taxation* (2018).

Molly Moses, "OECD Releases New Draft of Part IV On Insurance in Profit Attribution Report," *BNA Tax Management Transfer Pricing Report* (2007).

Molly Moses, "OECD Told to Broaden KERT Definition, Recognize Reinsurance in Part IV of Report," *BNA Tax Management Transfer Pricing Report* (2007).

Harald Moshammer/Michael Tumpel, "Attribution of Profits to a Dependent Agent PE" in: Michael Lang/Pasquale Pistone/Josef Schuch/Claus Staringer/Alfred Storck (eds.) *Dependent Agents as Permanent Establishments* (Vienna: Linde, 2014).

Markus Mühlemann, *Switzerland—Permanent Establishments—Topical Analyses*, last reviewed: February 1, 2019, available online at www.ibfd.org.

Munich Re, *Bancassurance in Practice*, available online at www.munichre.com.

W. Joseph Murphy/Geoffrey Armstrong, "Transfer Pricing in the context of a PE: the OECD view," *BNA Tax Management Transfer Pricing Report* (2007).

National Insurance Brokers Association of Australia (NIBA), *Australia in the Asian Century—Country strategies*, available online at https://www.niba.com.au/resource/130531_Australia_in_the_Asian_Century_Submission.pdf.

Michael Naylor, *Insurance Transformed—Technological Disruption* (Cham: Springer International Publishing AG, 2017).

John Neighbour/Jennifer Coletta, "Attribution of Profits to Insurance Branches," *The Tax Journal* (2006).

Kristin Nemeth, "European Insurance Law: A Single Insurance Market," *European University Institute—EUI Working Paper LAW No. 2001/4* (2001).

Bernardo Nicoletti, *Digital Insurance—Business Innovation in the Post-Crisis Era* (Basingstoke: Palgrave Macmillan UK, 2016).

Joel Nitikam, "The Meaning of 'Permanent Establishment' in the 1981 U.S. Model Income Tax Treaty: Part 2," *The International Tax Journal* (1989).

Francisco José Nocete Correa, "The Spanish Digital Services Tax: A Paradigm for the Base Enlargement & Profit Attraction (BEPA) Plan for the Digitalized Economy," *European Taxation* (2019).

Louis Nouel, "The New Article 7 of the OECD Model Tax Convention: The End of the Road?," *Bulletin for International Taxation* (2011).

Nadine Oberbauer, "The Dependent Agent PE and the Exception for Auxiliary and Preparatory Activities under Article 5(4) of the OECD Model Convention" in: Michael Lang/Pasquale Pistone/Josef Schuch/Claus Staringer/Alfred Storck (eds.) *Dependent Agents as Permanent Establishments* (Vienna: Linde, 2014).

Xavier Oberson/Howard R. Hull, *Switzerland in International Tax Law* (Amsterdam: IBFD, 2011).

Belema R. Obuoforibo, "In the Name of Clarity: Defining a Dependent Agent Permanent Establishment" in: Carlos Gutiérrez/Andreas Perdelwitz (eds.) *Taxation of Business Profits in the 21st Century* (Amsterdam: IBFD, 2013).

Walter F. O'Connor, "A Comparative Analysis of the 1981 and 1996 U.S. Model Income Tax Treaties," *International Tax Journal* (1998).

Stefan Oesterhelt/Susanne Schreiber, "Art 51" in: Martin Zweifel/Michael Beusch (eds.) *Bundesgesetz über die direkte Bundessteuer* (Basel: Helbing Lichtenhahn, 2017).

Annet W. Oguttu, "The Role of International Cooperation in Preventing Tax Evasion: A Critique on 'Assistance in the Collection of Taxes'—A South African Perspective," *Bulletin for International Taxation* (2014).

Marcel Olbert/Christoph Spengel, "International Taxation in the Digital Economy: Challenge Accepted?," *World Tax Journal* (2017).

Robert R. Oliva, "The Treasury's Twenty Year Battle with Treaty Shopping: Article 16 of the 1977 United States Model Treaty," *Georgia Journal of International and Comparative Law* (1984).

Andrea Oriani, "Il contratto di brokeraggio assicurativo: qualificazione giuridica e risvolti applicativi," *I contratti* (2010).

David Orzechowski, "The Relevance of the Commentaries on the OECD and UN Models for the Interpretation of the UN Model" in: Michael Lang/Pasquale Pistone/Alexander Rust/Josef Schuch/Claus Staringer (eds.) *The UN Model*

Convention and Its Relevance for the Global Tax Treaty Network (Amsterdam: IBFD, 2017).

Federico Otegui Pita, "Article 5—The Concept of Permanent Establishment" in: Thomas Ecker/Gernot Ressler (eds.) *History of Tax Treaties* (Vienna: Linde, 2011).

Oxford English Dictionary, available online at https://en.oxforddictionaries.com.

Sergio Paci, *La distribuzione dei servizi assicurativi tramite le aziende di credito* (Milano: EGEA, 1993).

Robert L. Palmer, "Toward Unilateral Coherence in Determining Jurisdiction to Tax Income," *Harvard International Law Journal* (1989).

Leopoldo Parada, "Agents vs. Commissionnaires: A Comparison in Light of the OECD Model Convention," *Tax Notes International* (2013).

Alex M. Parker, "Jenn: OECD Clarifying, Not Rewriting, Allocation Rules on PE," *BNA Tax Management Transfer Pricing Report* (2016).

Louise Parker, "Mutual Assistance in the Collection of Taxes," *Bulletin for International Taxation* (2017).

Giulio Partesotti/Marco Ricolfi, *La nuova disciplina dell'impresa di assicurazione sulla vita in attuazione della Terza Direttiva* (Padova: CEDAM, 2000).

Jean-Blaise Paschoud, "Art 51," in: Danielle Yersin/Yves Noël (eds.) *Impot fédéral direct—Commentaire de la loi sur loi fédéral direct* (Basel: Helbing Lichtenhahn, 2008).

Ettore Pedicini, *Il broker di assicurazioni* (Milano: Giuffrè, 1998).

Valentina Perrone/Raffaello Lupi, "Economia digitale tra stabile organizzazione occulta e pubblicità "on line"," *Dialoghi Tributari* (2014).

Valentina Perrone/Gabriele Sepio, "Stabile organizzazione, "vendita a distanza" e commercio elettronico," *Dialoghi Tributari* (2013).

Alessio Persiani, "Some Remarks on the Notion of Permanent Establishment in the Recent Italian Supreme Court Jurisprudence," *Intertax* (2012).

Giuseppe Persico, "Agency Permanent Establishment under Article 5 of the OECD Model Convention," *Intertax* (2000).

Carmel Peters, "Developing Countries' Reactions to the G20/OECD Action Plan on Base Erosion and Profit Shifting," *Bulletin for International Taxation* (2015).

Cees Peters, *On the Legitimacy of International Tax Law* (Amsterdam: IBFD, 2014).

Raffaele Petruzzi, "The Dependent Agent Permanent Establishment as an Extension of the Permanent Establishment Concept of Article 5(1) of the OECD Model Convention" in: Michael Lang/Pasquale Pistone/Josef Schuch/Claus Staringer/Alfred Storck (eds.) *Dependent Agents as Permanent Establishments* (Vienna: Linde, 2014).

Raffaele Petruzzi/Raphael Holzinger, "Profit Attribution to Dependent Agent Permanent Establishments in a Post-BEPS Era," *World Tax Journal* (2017).

Raffaele Petruzzi/Viktoria Wöhrer, "Business Profits, Permanent Establishments and Associated Enterprises" in: Michael Lang/Pasquale Pistone/Alexander Rust/Josef Schuch/Claus Staringer (eds.) *The UN Model Convention and Its Relevance for the Global Tax Treaty Network* (Amsterdam: IBFD, 2017).

Hermann Peyerl, "Kann eine „App" eine Betriebsstätte begründen?," *Steuer und Wirtschaft International* (2017).

Paolo Piantavigna, "Il caso spagnolo Dell: un'interpretazione dinamica della nozione di stabile organizzazione," *Rivista di Diritto Finanziario e Scienza delle Finanze* (2017).

Marco Piazza, *Guida alla fiscalità internazionale* (Milano: Il Sole 24 Ore, 2004).

Sol Picciotto, "Problems of Transfer Pricing and Possibilities for Simplification," *Institute of Development Studies—Working Paper 86* (2018).

Astrid Pieron, *Résidence fiscale et fiscalité belge des non-résidents* (Brussels: Larcier, 2013).

Hans Pijl, "The Concept of Permanent Establishment and the Proposed Changes to the OECD Commentary with Special Reference to Dutch Case Law," *Bulletin for International Taxation* (2002).

Hans Pijl, "Agency Permanent Establishments: in the name of and the Relationship between Article 5(5) and (6)—Part 1," *Bulletin for International Taxation* (2013).

Hans Pijl, "Agency Permanent Establishments: in the name of and the Relationship between Article 5(5) and (6)—Part 2," *Bulletin for International Taxation* (2013).

Detlev J. Piltz, "Wann liegt eine DBA-Vertreter-Betriebsstätte vor?," *Internationales Steuerrecht* (2004).

Detlev J. Piltz, "When is There an Agency Permanent Establishment?," *Bulletin for International Fiscal Documentation* (2004).

Dale Pinto, *E-Commerce and Source-Based Income Taxation* (Amsterdam: IBFD, 2003).

Dale Pinto, "The Need to Reconceptualize the Permanent Establishment Threshold," *Bulletin for International Taxation* (2006).

Dale Pinto, "Options to Address the Direct Tax Challenges Raised by the Digital Economy—A Critical Analysis," *Canadian Tax Journal* (2017).

João Félix Pinto Nogueira, "The Compatibility of the EU Digital Services Tax with EU and WTO Law: Requiem Aeternam Donate Nascenti Tributo," *IBFD International Tax Studies* (2019).

Pasquale Pistone/João Félix Pinto Nogueira/Betty Andrade, "The 2019 OECD Proposals for addressing the tax challenges of the digitalization of the economy: an assessment," *IBFD International Tax Studies* (2019).

Pasquale Pistone/César Alejandro Ruiz Jiménez, "Habitual Exercise of Authority to Conclude Contracts under Article 5(5) of the OECD Model Convention" in: Michael Lang/Pasquale Pistone/Josef Schuch/Claus Staringer/Alfred Storck (eds.) *Dependent Agents as Permanent Establishments* (Vienna: Linde, 2014).

Pasquale Pistone/Pedro G. L. Schoueri, "Exchange of Information and Mutual Assistance in the Collection of Taxes" in: Michael Lang/Pasquale Pistone/Alexander Rust/Josef Schuch/Claus Staringer (eds.) *The UN Model Convention and Its Relevance for the Global Tax Treaty Network* (Amsterdam: IBFD, 2017).

Arthur Pleijsier, "The Agency Permanent Establishment Under Revision?: 'Acting in the name of', or 'what's in a name?'!," *Intertax* (1997).

Arthur Pleijsier, *The agency permanent establishment: de vaste vertegenwoordiger: proefschrift* (Maastricht: Universitaire Pers Maastricht, 2000).

Arthur Pleijsier, "The Agency Permanent Establishment: The Current Definition—Part One," *Intertax* (2001).

Arthur Pleijsier, "The Agency Permanent Establishment, Practical Applications—Part Two," *Intertax* (2001).

Arthur Pleijsier, "The Agency Permanent Establishment in BEPS Action 7: Treaty Abuse or Business Abuse," *Intertax* (2015).

Arthur Pleijsier, "The Artificial Avoidance of Permanent Establishment Status: A Reaction to the BEPS Action 7 Final Report," *International Transfer Pricing Journal* (2016).

Oana Popa, "Taxation of the Digital Economy in Selected Countries—Early Echoes of BEPS and EU Initiatives," *European Taxation* (2016).

John Prescott/Deborah Lambert, *What's Up Front: A Guide to Fronting Arrangements*, available online at www.captive.com.

Ernesto Pucci, "L'accesso all'attività assicurativa e riassicurativa" in: Marco Prosperetti/Alessandro Colavolpe (eds.) *Le Assicurazioni* (Milano: Ipsoa, 2012).

Ernesto Pucci, "L'attività di intermediazione assicurativa e riassicurativa e gli intermediari" in: Marco Prosperetti/Alessandro Colavolpe (eds.) *I gestori del risparmio non bancari e i canali di distribuzione* (Milano: Ipsoa, 2012).

Sergio Pugliese, *Bancassicurazione—La scelta dei prodotti e dei canali* (Roma: Bancaria Editrice, 1994).

Michael Puls, "Begriff der Betriebsstätte" in: Franz Wassermeyer/Ulf Andresen/Xavier Ditz (eds.) *Betriebsstätten-Handbuch: Gewinnermittlung und Besteuerung* (Cologne: Otto Schmidt, 2018).

PwC, *Broking 2020: Leading from the front in a new era of risk*, available online at www.pwc.com.

Luigi Quaratino, "New Provisions regarding the Taxation of the Digital Economy," *European Taxation* (2014).

Gergana Rakovska, "E-Commerce Business Models for Insurance: Application to U.S. and European Markets," *Centre for Risk Management and Insurance Research—Georgia State University* (2001).

Gurram Ramachandra Rao, *India: Concept of Permanent Establishment and Electronic Commerce*, April 2003, available online at http://www.mondaq.com.

Radhakishan Rawal/Sanjay Kumar, *UN—Commentary on the Permanent Establishment Concept under the UN Model Tax Convention*, last reviewed: February 1, 2019, available online at www.ibfd.org.

Lars Rehfeld, "Vertreter- und Logistikbetriebsstätten post BEPS 7," *Internationales Steuer- und Wirtschaftsrecht* (2017).

Ekkehart Reimer, "Article 5.—Permanent Establishment" in: Ekkehart Reimer/Alexander Rust (eds.) *Klaus Vogel on Double Taxation Convention*, 4th edn. (Alphen aan den Rijn: Kluwer Law International, 2015).

Ekkehart Reimer, "Permanent Establishment in the OECD Model Tax Convention" in: Ekkehart Reimer/Stephan Schmid/Marianne Orell (eds.) *Permanent Establishments: A Domestic Taxation, Bilateral Tax Treaty and OECD Perspective* (Alphen aan den Rijn: Kluwer Law International, 2016).

William Reynolds Vance, "The Early History of Insurance Law," *Columbia Law Review* (1908).

Ornella Ricci, "The Development of Bancassurance in Europe" in: Franco Fiordelisi/Ornella Ricci (eds.) *Bancassurance in Europe—Past, Present and Future* (London: Palgrave Macmillan, 2012).

Douglas R. Richmond, "Insurance Agent and Broker Liability," *Tort Trial & Insurance Practice Law Journal* (2004).

Diane M. Ring, "International Tax Relations: Theory and Implications," *Tax Law Review* (2007).

Diane M. Ring, *United States—Permanent Establishments—Topical Analyses*, last reviewed: March 22, 2019, available online at www.ibfd.org.

Sidney I. Roberts, "The Agency Element of Permanent Establishment: The OECD Commentaries from the Civil Law View (Part One)," *Intertax* (1993).

Thomas Rödder/Reimar Pinkernell, "Zum Seminar F: 20 Thesen zur BEPS-Diskussion," *Internationales Steuerrecht* (2013).

Julie Rogers-Glabush, *International Tax Glossary*, 7th edn. (Amsterdam: IBFD, 2015).

Filippo Romeo, "Il broker di assicurazione" in: Guido Alpa (ed.) *Le Assicurazioni private* (Torino: Utet Giuridica, 2006).

David H. Rosenbloom, "Where's the Pony? Reflections on the Making of International Tax Policy," *Bulletin for International Taxation* (2009).

Marco Rossetti, *Il diritto delle assicurazioni—Volume 1* (Milano: Cedam, 2011).

Luca Rossi/Sara Flisi, "La stabile organizzazione personale tra significant people functions e risk management functions," *Corriere Tributario* (2019).

Irmantas Rotomskis/Tomas Girdenis, "Internet Service Provider and the Dependent Agent," *KSI transactions on knowledge society* (2014).

Ian Roxan, "Limits to Globalisation: Some Implications for Taxation, Tax Policy, and the Developing World," *LSE Law—Society and Economy Working Papers* (2012).

Raffaele Russo, "Report on the historical development of article 7 of the OECD Model" in: IFA (ed.) *The attribution of profits to permanent establishments*, Cahiers de droit fiscal international, Vol. 91b (The Hague: Sdu Uitgevers, 2006).

Raffaele Russo/Edoardo Pedrazzini/Caterina Innamorato, *Italy—Permanent Establishments—Topical Analyses*, last reviewed: May 24, 2019, available online at www.ibfd.org.

Sachin Sachdeva, "Overriding Tax Treaty Overrides: Proposing a Solution," *European Taxation* (2013).

Omar Salvini, "La nuova definizione di stabile organizzazione nel BEPS," *Rassegna Tributaria* (2016).

Alberto Santi, "La stabile organizzazione delle imprese assicurative va individuata con le regole fiscali," *Corriere Tributario* (2006).

Fabrizio Santoboni, "L'intermediazione assicurativa: profili normative e gestionali" in: Fabrizio Santoboni (ed.) *Manuale di gestione assicurativa* (Padova: CEDAM, 2012).

Jacques Sasseville, "A Tax Treaty Perspective: Special Issues" in: Guglielmo Maisto (ed.) *Tax Treaties and Domestic Law* (Amsterdam: IBFD, 2006).

Jacques Sasseville, "Round Table: On the Desirability to Change the OECD Model Convention and its Commentaries" in: Guglielmo Maisto, *The Meaning of "Enterprise", "Business" and "Business Profits" under Tax Treaties and EU Tax Law* (Amsterdam: IBFD, 2011).

Jacques Sasseville/Arvid A. Skaar, "General Report" in: IFA (ed.) *Is there a permanent establishment?*, Cahiers de droit fiscal international, Vol. 94a (The Hague: Sdu Uitgevers, 2009).

Barrett Schaefer, "International Taxation of Electronic Commerce Income: A Proposal to Utilize Software Agents for Source-Based Taxation," *Santa Clara High Technology Law Journal* (2000).

Jean Schaffner, *How Fixed Is a Permanent Establishment?* (Alphen aan den Rijn: Kluwer Law International, 2013).

Deborah Schanz/Anna Feller, "Wieso Deutschland (fast) keine BEPS-Bekämpfung braucht," *Betriebs-Berater* (2015).

Christoph Schelling, "Swiss Tax Treaty Policy," *Bulletin for International Taxation* (2015).

Stefan Schmid/Marianne Orell, "Switzerland" in: Ekkehart Reimer/Stephan Schmid/Marianne Orell (eds.) *Permanent Establishments: A Domestic Taxation, Bilateral Tax Treaty and OECD Perspective* (Alphen aan den Rijn: Kluwer Law International, 2016).

Christian J. Schmidt, "Germany" in: Guglielmo Maisto (ed.) *Departures from the OECD Model and Commentaries* (Amsterdam: IBFD, 2014).

Ole Schmidt-Heß, "Die Verhinderung der künstlichen Vermeidung einer Betriebsstätte—Der OECD-Bericht zu Maßnahme 7 des BEPS-Aktionsplans," *Internationales Steuerrecht* (2016).

Stephan Schnorberger, *Germany—Permanent Establishments—Topical Analyses*, last reviewed: March 30, 2016, available online at www.ibfd.org.

Wolfgang Schön, "International Tax Coordination for a Second-Best World (Part I)," *World Tax Journal* (2009).

Wolfgang Schön, "International Tax Coordination for a Second-Best World (Part III)," *World Tax Journal* (2010).

Wolfgang Schön, "Ten Questions about Why and How to Tax the Digitalized Economy," *Bulletin for International Taxation* (2018).

Christian Schoppe/Neeraj Popat, "Lagerung, Einkauf und Austellung als Betriebsstätten ab 2017," *Betriebs-Berater* (2016).

Luis Eduardo Schoueri/Oliver-Christoph Günther, "The Subsidiary as a Permanent Establishment," *Bulletin for International Taxation* (2010).

René Schreiber/Kersten A. Honold/Roger Jaun, "Art. 5" in: Martin Zweifel/Michael Beusch/René Matteotti (eds.) *Kommentar zum Schweizerischen Steuerrecht—Internationales Steuerrecht* (Basel: Helbing Lichtenhahn Verlag, 2015).

Josef Schuch/Eline Huisman, "The Dependent Agent PE under Article 5(5), (6) and (7) of the UN Model Convention" in: Michael Lang/Pasquale Pistone/Josef Schuch/Claus Staringer/Alfred Storck (eds.) *Dependent Agents as Permanent Establishments* (Vienna: Linde, 2014).

Daniel Schwarcz/Peter Siegelmann, "Insurance Agents in the 21st Century: The Problem of Biased Advice," in: Daniel Schwarcz/Peter Siegelmann (eds.) *Research Handbook in the Law & Economics of Insurance* (Cheltenham, Northampton: Edwar Elgar Publishing, 2015).

Robert S. Schwartz, "Taisei: U.S. Agent Did Not Create Permanent Establishment," *The Journal of International Taxation* (1995).

Jonathan Schwarz, "US Model Treaty 2016: What does it say about the US and BEPS?," *Kluwer International Tax Blog* (2016).

Jonathan Schwarz, "Value Creation: Old wine in new bottles or new wine in old bottles," *Kluwer International Tax Blog* (2018).

Andreas Schwepcke, *Reinsurance: Principles and State of the Art—A Guidebook for Home Learners*, 2nd edn. (Unterföhring: Swiss Re Germany AG, 2004).

Francesco Seatzu, *Insurance in Private International Law: A European Perspective* (Oxford: Hart Publishing, 2003).

Paola Sella, "Le modifiche alla Legge di Bilancio 2018 alla definizione di stabile organizzazione," *Fiscalità & Commercio Internationale* (2018).

Luigi Selleri, *Economia delle imprese di assicurazioni* (Milano: Giuffrè, 1965).

Luigi Selleri, *Economia e management delle imprese di assicurazione* (Milano: Etas libri, 1991).

Luigi Selleri, *Impresa di assicurazione e strategie di valore* (Milano: Etas libri, 2003).

Luigi Selleri, *Strategie e marketing dell'impresa di assicurazione* (Milano: EDUCatt, 2009).

Dikshit P. Sengupta, "Chapter 21: India: Siemens Ltd—To Be Taxed as Fees for Technical Services Some Human Intervention Is a Must" in: Eric C.C.M. Kemmeren (ed.) *Tax Treaty Case Law around the Globe 2014* (Amsterdam: IBFD, 2014).

Daniel Shaviro, "The U.S. Response to OECD-BEPS and the EU State Aid Cases," *NYU Law & Economics Research Paper Series* (2016).

Gordon W. Shaw, *The Lloyd's Broker, The Lloyd's Broker* (London: Lloyd's of London Press, 1995).

Stephen E. Shay/J. Clifton Fleming Jr./Robert J. Peroni, "What's Source Got to Do with It?: Source Rules and US International Taxation," *Tax Law Review* (2002).

Caroline Silberztein/Benoît Granel/Jean-Baptiste Tristram, "OECD Multilateral Convention to Prevent BEPS: Implementation Guide and Initial Thoughts," *International Transfer Pricing Journal* (2017).

Karin Simader, *Withholding Taxes and the Fundamental Freedoms* (Alphen aan den Rijn: Kluwer Law International, 2013).

Simplesurance, *What We Do*, available online at https://www.simplesurance.com.

Manoj Kumar Singh, "Taxing E-Commerce on the Basis of Permanent Establishment: Critical Evaluation," *Intertax* (2014).

Nazly Siregar/David Dorson, "Taxation of Trade Representative Offices," *Asia-Pacific Tax Bulletin* (2014).

Arvid A. Skaar, *Permanent Establishment—Erosion of a Tax Treaty Principle* (Deventer/Boston: Kluwer Law and Taxation Publishers, 1991).

Arvid A. Skaar, *Taxation Issues Relating to Captive Insurance Companies* (Amsterdam: IBFD, 1998).

Arvid A. Skaar, "Erosion of the Concept of Permanent Establishment: Electronic Commerce," *Intertax* (2000).

Jeff Soar/Simon Burtwell/James Smith, "Captives to 2020: Opportunities and Challenges," *Derivatives & Financial Instruments* (2014).

Fernando Souza de Man, *Taxation of Services in Treaties between Developed and Developing Countries—A Proposal for New Guidelines* (Amsterdam: IBFD, 2017).

Evan M. Spangler, *Swiss Supervisory Laws and Regulations for the Business of Insurance* (Bern: Stämpfli Editions SA, 2010).

Lisa Spinosa/Vikram Chand, "A Long-Term Solution for Taxing Digitalized Business Models: Should the Permanent Establishment Definition Be Modified to Resolve the Issue or Should the Focus Be on a Shared Taxing Rights Mechanism?," *Intertax* (2018).

Gary D. Sprague, "Playing the Principal Role in Creating a Permanent Establishment," *Tax Management International Journal* (2016).

Gary D. Sprague, "Additional Guidance on the Attribution of Profits to Permanent Establishments—A Welcome Development," *BNA Tax Management Transfer Pricing Report* (2018).

Daniel F. Spulberg, *Market Microstructure: Intermediaries and the Theory of the Firm* (Cambridge: Cambridge University Press, 1999).

Bob Stack/Jamie Hawes, "OECD Guidance Doesn't Resolve Fundamental Issue for Attribution of Profits to Permanent Establishments," *BNA Tax Management Transfer Pricing Report* (2018).

Claus Staringer/Felipe Vallada, "Acting in the ordinary course of business under Article 5(6) of the OECD Model Convention" in: Michael Lang/Pasquale Pistone/Josef Schuch/Claus Staringer/Alfred Storck (eds.) *Dependent Agents as Permanent Establishments* (Vienna: Linde, 2014).

Maria Grazia Starita, "Bancassurance Products" in: Franco Fiordelisi/Ornella Ricci (eds.) *Bancassurance in Europe—Past, Present and Future* (London: Palgrave Macmillan, 2012).

Raoul Stocker, "Potential Effects of the OECD Base Erosion and Profit Shifting Initiative on Swiss Transfer Pricing Rules and Swiss Companies," *Bulletin for International Taxation* (2015).

Alfred Storck/Raffaele Petruzzi, "Permanent Establishments: Proposals Related to the Agency Permanent Establishments—Article 5(5) and (6) of the OECD Model Convention" in: Michael Lang/Pasquale Pistone/Alexander Rust/Josef Schuch/Claus Staringer (eds.) *Base Erosion and Profit Shifting (BEPS)* (Vienna: Linde, 2016).

Alfred Storck/Sabine Schmidjell-Dommes, "Acting on Behalf of an Enterprise under Article 5(5) of the OECD Model Convention" in: Michael Lang/Pasquale Pistone/Josef Schuch/Claus Staringer/Alfred Storck (eds.) *Dependent Agents as Permanent Establishments* (Vienna: Linde, 2014).

Fabian Streule/Marc Dietschi, "Der Steuerstandort Schweiz 2017," *Internationales Steuer- und Wirtschaftsrecht* (2018).

Christoph Suter/Susanne Schreiber, "OECD BEPS—the Swiss Position," *International Tax Review* (2018).

Swiss Re, *Bancassurance: emerging trends, opportunities and challenges*, Sigma No. 5/2007, available online at www.swissre.com.

Swiss Re, *Digital distribution in insurance: a quiet revolution*, Sigma No. 2/2014, available online at www.swissre.com.

Vito Tanzi/Milka Casanegra de Jantscher, "Presumptive Income Taxation: Administrative, Efficiency and Equity Aspects," *International Monetary Fund—Working Paper 87/54*, available online at https://www.imf.org.

C. John Taylor, "The Negotiation and Drafting of the UK—Australia Double Taxation Treaty of 1946," *British Tax Review* (2009).

C. John Taylor, "The 2015 Australia-Germany Tax Treaty, BEPS, and the Multilateral Instrument," *Australian Tax Review* (2017).

Alan Teale, "Insurance Brokers and the Law of Agency" in: Roderick Clews (ed.) *A Textbook of Insurance Broking* (Cambridge: Woodhead-Faulkner, 1980).

Maarten Temmerman/Sofie Van de Perre, "Belgium" in: Ekkehart Reimer/Stephan Schmid/Marianne Orell (eds.) *Permanent Establishments: A Domestic Taxation, Bilateral Tax Treaty and OECD Perspective* (Alphen aan den Rijn: Kluwer Law International, 2016).

Mark Teunissen, "Bancassurance: Tapping into the Banking Strength," *The Geneva Papers on Risk and Insurance* (2008).

Michael Theil, "Insurance On The Internet: A Different View," *International Business & Economics Research Journal* (2002).

Victor Thuronyi, "Ch. 12—Presumptive Taxation" in: Victor Thuronyi (ed.) *Tax Law Design and Drafting* (Washington: International Monetary Fund, 1996).

Martin B. Tittle, "A Unified Approach to Permanent Establishment by Agent in the U.S.," *Tax Notes International* (2007).

Martin B. Tittle, *Permanent Establishment in the United States* (Lake Mary: Vandeplas Publishing, 2007).

César Toledo Concha/Horacio Viana, "Chile" in: IFA (ed.) *Assessing BEPS: origins, standards, and responses*, Cahiers de droit fiscal international, Vol. 102a (The Hague: Sdu Uitgevers, 2017).

Carlos E. C. M. A. Toro, "Different Methods of Attributing Profits to Agency PE's," *Tax Notes International* (2009).

Tom Toryanik, "Withholding Tax on Non-Resident Insurers Explained," *Asia-Pacific Tax Bulletin* (2008).

Tom Toryanik, *Australia—Corporate Taxation—Country Analyses*, last reviewed: May 26, 2019, available online at www.ibfd.org.

Dinis Tracana, "The Effect of the OECD/G20 BEPS Initiative on the Attribution of Profits to Permanent Establishments: The Special Case of Agency Permanent Establishments," *Bulletin for International Taxation* (2017).

Mitchell J. Tropin, "OECD PE Draft to Replace KERT Concept with 'Significant People Function' Concept," *BNA Tax Management Transfer Pricing Report* (2006).

Mitchell J. Tropin, "KERT Will Apply to Financial Intermediaries, But Not Other Taxpayers, OECD Official Says," *BNA Tax Management Transfer Pricing Report* (2006).

John Turro, "When Do Foreign Reinsurance Activities in the United States Constitute a Permanent Establishment?," *Tax Notes International* (1992).

University of St. Gallen, *The Current InsurTech Landscape: Business Models and Disruptive Potential*, available online at www.ivw.unisg.ch.

Yasin Uslu, "An Analysis of 'Google Taxes' in the Context of Action 7 of the OECD/G20 Base Erosion and Profit Shifting Initiative," *Tax Notes International* (2018).

Piergiorgio Valente, *Convenzioni internazionali contro le doppie imposizioni* (Milano: IPSOA, 2012).

Piergiorgio Valente/Luigi Vinciguerra, *Stabile organizzazione occulta—Profili applicativi nelle verifiche* (Milano: IPSOA, 2013).

Jean-Paul van den Berg, "Netherlands" in: IFA (ed.) *Is there a permanent establishment?*, Cahiers de droit fiscal international, Vol. 94a (The Hague: Sdu Uitgevers, 2009).

Susann van der Ham/Daniel Retzer, "BEPS Aktion Nr. 7 zu Betriebsstätten und die Auswirkungen auf die Betriebsstättengewinnabgrenzung," *Internationales Steuerrecht* (2016).

Peter G. A. van der Hoeven, "Tax Implications on the Third Non-life and Life Directive for EU Based Insurers doing Business in Other Member States," *Intertax* (1995).

Richard Vann, "Travellers, Tax Policy and Agency Permanent Establishments," *British Tax Review* (2010).

Francisco Antonio Vaquer Ferrer, "The Concept of 'Permanent Establishment' at the Spanish Courts: Special Reference to the Roche and Dell Cases," *Intertax* (2016).

Josine S.A. van Wanrooij, "Comments on the Proposed Article 7 of the OECD Model Convention," *Intertax* (2009).

Stef van Weeghel, "Digitalization in a Broader Tax Perspective," *Intertax* (2019).

Riccardo Varaldo/Giuseppe Turchetti, *L'E-commerce—le nuove frontiere nella distribuzione assicurativa* (Milano: Franco Angeli, 2000).

Emmett J. Vaughan/Therese M. Vaughan, *Fundamentals of Risk and Insurance*, 10th edn. (Hoboken: John Wiley & Sons Inc., 2008).

Isabel Verlinden/Xavier van Vlem/Bram Markey, "Commissionaire Agency Permanent Establishment Structures and the Impact of the Zimmer Case," *International Transfer Pricing Journal* (2010).

Maria Cecilia Villareal Regalado, "Treaty Abuse and Permanent Establishments: Proposed Changes to Articles 5(5) and 5(6) of the OECD MC" in: Daniel W. Blum/Markus Seiler (eds.) *Preventing Treaty Abuse* (Vienna: Linde, 2016).

Klaus Vogel, *Klaus Vogel on Double Taxation Conventions* (London: Kluwer Law International, 1997).

Klaus Vogel, "The Domestic Law Perspective" in: Guglielmo Maisto (ed.) *Tax Treaties and Domestic Law* (Amsterdam: IBFD, 2006).

Klaus Vogel/Alexander Rust, "Introduction" in: Ekkehart Reimer/Alexander Rust (eds.) *Klaus Vogel on Double Taxation Convention*, 4th edn. (Alphen aan den Rijn: Kluwer Law International, 2015).

Marc Vogelsang, *Der Begriff der Betriebsstätte im schweizerischen und internationalen Steuerrecht* (Zürich: Schulthess Verlag, 2015).

Thorsten Wagemann, "Verschärfungen des Betriebsstättenbegriffs nach OECD-MA," *Internationales Steuer- und Wirtschaftsrecht* (2016).

Svetlana Wakounig, "Interpretation of Terms Used in the Multilateral Instrument" in: Michael Lang/Pasquale Pistone/Alexander Rust/Josef Schuch/Claus Staringer (eds.) *The OECD Multilateral Instrument for Tax Treaties: Analysis and Effects* (Alphen aan den Rijn: Wolters Kluwer, 2018).

Benjamin Walker, "Reservations to the Multilateral Instrument" in: Michael Lang/Pasquale Pistone/Alexander Rust/Josef Schuch/Claus Staringer (eds.) *The OECD Multilateral Instrument for Tax Treaties* (Alphen aan den Rijn: Wolters Kluwer, 2018).

John Walker, "Chapter 18: BEPS in Australia" in: Sam Sim/Mei June Soo (eds.) *Asian Voices: BEPS and Beyond* (Amsterdam: IBFD, 2017).

John Walker/Vida Ghazavi, "Nexus for Taxation in Asia: Contemporary Permanent Establishment and Related Issues," *Asia-Pacific Tax Bulletin* (2005).

Huili Wang/Maximilian Schrepfer, "Germany" in: Ekkehart Reimer/Stephan Schmid/Marianne Orell (eds.) *Permanent Establishments: A Domestic Taxation, Bilateral Tax Treaty and OECD Perspective* (Alphen aan den Rijn: Kluwer Law International, 2016).

Franz Wassermeyer/Christian Kaeser, "Art. 5" in: Franz Wassermeyer (ed.) *Doppelbesteuerung: Kommentar zu allen deutschen Doppelbesteuerungsabkommen* (Munich: Beck, 2017).

Carsten Wendt, *A Common Tax Base for Multinational Enterprises in the European Union* (Wiesbaden: Gabler, 2009).

Björn Westberg, *Cross-Border Taxation of E-Commerce* (Amsterdam: IBFD, 2002).

Björn Westberg, "Taxation of the Digital Economy—An EU Perspective," *European Taxation* (2014).

Stefan G. Widmer, "Switzerland" in: IFA (ed.) *Is there a permanent establishment?*, Cahiers de droit fiscal international, Vol. 94a (The Hague: Sdu Uitgevers, 2009).

Stefan G. Widmer, "Die Vertreterbetriebsstätte im internationalen Steuerrecht der Schweiz," *Archiv für Schweizerisches Abgaberecht* (2003/2004).

Stefan G. Widmer, "Die Betriebsstättebegründung des Principals nach der allgemeinen Betriebsstättedefinition," *IFF Forum für Steuerrecht* (2005).

Wim Wijnen/Jan De Goede, "The UN Model in Practice 1997–2013," *Bulletin for International Taxation* (2014).

Wim Wijnen/Jan de Goede/Andrea Alessi, "The Treatment of Services in Tax Treaties," *Bulletin for International Taxation* (2012).

Jeffrey Wilder, "Competing for the Effort of a Common Agent: Contingency Fees in Commercial Insurance," *US Department of Justice Antitrust Division Economic Analysis Group Working Paper No. EAG03-4* (2003).

Robert L. Williams, "Permanent Establishments in the United States," *The Tax Lawyer* (1975).

Robert L. Williams, *Fundamentals of Permanent Establishments* (The Hague: Kluwer Law International, 2014).

Wills Group Holdings, *How We Get Paid (2014)*, available online at www.willis.com.

Alexandra Wintsch, "Attribution of Profits to Permanent Establishments: The 2008 Article 7 versus the 2010 Article 7 of the OECD Model Tax Convention," *International Transfer Pricing Journal* (2017).

Jens Wittendorff, "Agency Permanent Establishments and the Zimmer Case," *International Transfer Pricing Journal* (2010).

Jens Wittendorff, *Transfer Pricing and Arm's Length Principle in International Tax Law* (Alphen aan den Rijn: Kluwer Law International, 2010).

Claudia Wood, "Compare and Contrast: How the UK comparison website market is serving financial consumers," *Resolution Foundation* (2007).

World Federation of Insurance Intermediaries (WFII), *The Role of Insurance Intermediaries*, available online at https://www.ciab.com/uploadedfiles/resources/roleofinsint.pdf.

Tamu N. Wright, "OECD Removes KERT Language From Most of PE Income Allocation Project," *BNA Tax Management Transfer Pricing Report* (2007).

WTS, *WTS Tax Weekly—No. 27 / 2016*, available online at www.wts.com/de-de/knowledge/tax-weekly.

Tim Wustenberghs/Ethel Puncher, "Zimmer à la Belge: Could a Commissionaire Arrangement Create an Agency Permanent Establishment in Belgium?," *Bulletin for International Taxation* (2011).

Oliver Wyman, "The Ancillaries Challenge in Online Travel Booking," *Transport & Logistics* (2016).

Eric M. Zolt, "A Better Deal Post-BEPS" in: Brian J. Arnold (ed.) *Tax Treaties After the BEPS Project—A Tribute to Jacques Sasseville* (Toronto: Canadian Tax Foundation, 2018).

Eric M. Zolt, "Tax treaties and developing countries," *Oxford University Centre for Business Taxation—Working paper series* (2018).

Simone Zucchetti/Armando Tardini/Oreste Lanfranchi, "The Italian "Web Tax": The New Administrative Procedure for Multinational Enterprises to Disclose Hidden Permanent Establishments in Italy," *International Transfer Pricing Journal* (2017).

Zurich Financial Services, *Investment Management—a creator of value in an insurance company,* March 2009, 2nd edn., available online at www.zurich.com.

Peter Zweifel/Roland Eisen, *Insurance Economics* (Berlin, Heidelberg: Springer-Verlag Berlin Heidelberg, 2012).

Index

www.ingramcontent.com/pod-product-compliance
Lightning Source LLC
LaVergne TN
LVHW010653300926
849161LV00005B/1114
9789403532837